217
223

Cover design and frontispiece: Figures and Dog Before the Sun by Joan Miró

(Courtesy of Kunstmuseum of Basel, Switzerland. Photography courtesy of
Colorphoto Hinz, Basel, Switzerland)

ABNORMAL BEHAVIOR AND PERSONALITY

a biosocial learning approach

THEODORE MILLON AND **RENÉE MILLON**

UNIVERSITY OF ILLINOIS

1974 W. B. SAUNDERS COMPANY · Philadelphia · London · Toronto

W. B. Saunders Company: West Washington Square
Philadelphia, PA 19105

12 Dyott Street
London, WC1A 1DB

833 Oxford Street
Toronto, Ontario M8Z 5T9, Canada

Abnormal Behavior and Personality: ISBN   0-7216-6390-7
a biosocial learning approach

Last digit is the print number: 9   8   7   6   5   4   3   2   1

To Rosie and Bill

PREFACE

If at all successful in its educational aims, this book should provide the student with a stimulating body of data and ideas basic to his understanding of abnormal behavior. A few words elaborating the authors' goals may be useful in orienting the student to the text.

Efforts were made to strike a balance between the scholarship of a scientific discipline, on the one hand, and the curiosity that first attracts the student to the subject, on the other. To create a sense of participation and challenge, complex and controversial issues were presented in neither predigested nor oversimplified form. At the same time, an ample number of illustrative case histories were included, and professional jargon was carefully limited.

If we have succeeded in striking the proper balance between scholarship and interest, there is no reason why the text could not serve equally well for both majors and nonmajors alike, furnishing some solid underpinnings for later work among those who wish to make the study of psychology a career, and exposing a rich vein of information for those seeking depth in their liberal arts education.

Toward the end of making the subject meaningful and relevant to the student, and in contrast to most other books on "abnormal psychology," the text devotes two long chapters to what are termed *abnormal personalities in everyday life.* These are not the bizarre varieties of mental disorder that are the stock-in-trade of hospital psychiatry. Rather, they portray those forms of maladaptive behavior that students are likely to encounter in the course of their everyday lives — in their families and among their friends. In addition to making the text more meaningful and relevant, the inclusion of these milder pathologies enables the student to see the continuity between lesser and more severe disorders, and to trace the manner in which serious abnormalities develop.

This book is a substantially revised and abbreviated version of a previous work, *Modern Psychopathology,* written by the first author in the late 1960s. The earlier volume was highly regarded by fellow professionals and was adopted in its first years by over 200 colleges; it will remain in print, since it continues to be used at many universities — but usually in graduate-level courses. Despite its favorable reception, we noted that with each passing year an increasing number of instructors decided that the text was too comprehensive and too innovative a book for undergraduates embarking on their first formal study of abnormal behavior.

To avoid the information overload contained in the earlier text, the revision is significantly shortened. Moreover, each of the 20 chapters is tightly organized to focus on one major topic only, and brief enough to be read comfortably in a single sitting.

We have taken the opportunity of this revision to update the content of the book and to direct attention more sharply to trends that were only beginning to take hold in the late sixties. Many of the new and exicting ideas generated in the community mental health movement have been incorporated. An even more significant change stems from our conviction that behavior abnormality can best be understood within the framework of social learning theory; we have added material and reorganized our presentation accordingly.

It should be noted that the approach of this book differs in several respects from texts written by other "social learning" psychologists. *First,* and in contrast to colleagues who de-emphasize man's physiological tendencies, ours is a *bio*social-learning model, reflecting the belief that people differ significantly in their basic biological equipment. We contend that constitutional differences, such as energy and temperament, are important determinants of both personality and abnormal behavior. Biological tendencies increase the likelihood that certain life events will be experienced as positively or negatively reinforcing, thereby influencing which forms of behavior will ultimately be learned. *Second,* and again in distinction to other social learning theorists, our discussion of abnormality focuses on significant problems of everyday personality functioning and interpersonal behavior, not on obscure or essentially trivial disturbances such as snake phobias or behavioral tics. It is of deep concern to us that "learning" approaches to abnormality have become, in the eyes of both public and profession, synonymous with a variety of neat, therapeutic techniques employed largely in relieving rare or insignificant symptoms.

We believe that the social learning approach can provide the science of psychology with more than a few useful methods for modifying symptomatic behaviors. It is a major intent of ours to demonstrate in the text that social learning theory is the most fruitful tool available for understanding the origins, development and functions of abnormal behavior.

As with the prior volume, the book has benefited immeasurably from the guidance and labors of others. We owe much to many.

In addition to our formal teachers, most notably Gardner Murphy, Kurt Goldstein and Ernst Kris, we have profited greatly from the writings of a host of other clinical scientists. Our debt to those who are still living and active contributors to the field is hereby acknowledged: Albert Bandura, Norman Cameron, Leon Eisenberg, Erik H. Erikson, Hans J. Eysenck, D. O. Hebb, Paul E. Meehl, Lois B. Murphy, B. F. Skinner, Roger J. Williams and Joseph Zubin.

Many former and present colleagues furnished the stimulus of encouragement and intellectual discourse so necessary to spur us on through our work. Among our current associates, we are especially appreciative of the support and inspiration provided by Melvin Sabshin, Gene Borowitz, Hyman Muslin, Ruth Sosis, Robert Meagher, Terry Brown, Carol Millman and Bruce Wilson; a special note of thanks is due Leila Foster, not only for her unstinting efforts on several joint research projects but for her contributions in writing the student guide and the instructor's manual for the text. Luberta Shirley, secretary nonpareil, merits signal praise for her diligence and skill in decoding our inscrutable script. And, once more, it is a distinct pleasure to convey our appreciation to the staff of the W. B. Saunders Company for making the task of authorship as pleasurable as it has been.

Last, but not least, mention should be made of the joint family enterprise that the text represents. Our eldest daughters, Diane and Carrie, served with distinction in various research endeavors; our son, Andy, prepared the indices with sound judgment and high accuracy; and Adrienne, our youngest daughter, drew upon her artistic talents to aid in the selection of chapter illustrations. To round off this cooperative labor of love, we affectionately dedicate the book to our parents—Rosie and Bill.

THEODORE MILLON

RENÉE MILLON

CONTENTS

PART 3   ABNORMALITIES OF MODERATE SEVERITY

CHAPTER 14

PSYCHOPHYSIOLOGIC (PSYCHOSOMATIC) DISORDERS, 311

PART 4   ABNORMALITIES OF MARKED SEVERITY

CHAPTER 15

SCHIZOPHRENIC DISORDERS AND PATTERNS, 329

CHAPTER 16

AFFECTIVE DISORDERS AND PATTERNS, 353

ABNORMAL BEHAVIOR AND PERSONALITY

Edvard Munch—*Anxiety*

1 INTRODUCTION TO ABNORMAL PSYCHOLOGY

INTRODUCTION

Abnormal psychology is probably unique among the sciences in its interest to men in all walks of life. This interest is not new. Throughout written history, man has observed, described and pondered strange behaviors and thoughts within himself. The questions that man has posed about these experiences seem so simple and basic. Why do we seek to please our friends, but have incredible difficulty being congenial with our families? Why do we shift so often between hopeful fantasy and oppressive despair? Why do we dream and suffer terrifying nightmares? Why do we submit to foolish temptations against our better judgment? Questions such as these have puzzled and intrigued man since ancient times. They persist to challenge us today. Despite their apparent simplicity, they raise some of the most complex issues that face psychological and medical science.

What day has gone by in recent years without encountering news or TV reports of suicide, crime, "nervous breakdowns" and sexual perversion? Events such as these are intriguing, no doubt, but they are dramatic and extreme. They give us a distorted view of the full scope of abnormal behavior.

It is the undramatic problems of life, the quiet but persistent anxieties, the repetitive and immobilizing conflicts that hinder millions of Americans day after day that best represent the true subject matter of abnormal psychology. These milder disorders usually are "taken for granted" as part of man's "fate" or "nature": the promising college freshman who cannot settle down to his studies, frittering away his time in wasteful daydreaming and TV watching; the "old maid" high school teacher who is extremely permissive with the young boys in her classes, but easily angered and short-tempered with the girls; the father who cannot tolerate disagreement from his children and flies into a rage when his authority is questioned; the self-conscious college student who can never gather the courage to call a girl for a date; the housewife who constantly complains of fatigue and headaches, for which no organic disorder can be found; the mother who must be engaged in a whirl of social activity to escape her home responsibilities; the successful businessman who cannot relax on his vacation, checking constantly at the office to see if things are all right without him.

Signs of abnormal behavior become more obvious as we shift our focus from these "commonplace" maladjustments to the more moderately severe disorders: the physician who withdraws from a successful practice because he fears that he will harm his patients; the housewife who is unable to sleep in anticipation of someone stealing into her home to murder her family; the college coed who criticizes her friends and tests their loyalty so persistently that they ultimately are alienated from her; the husband who leans upon his wife for every decision and cannot hold a job for more than a few months; the quiet and scholarly choir boy who steals cars; the shy student who exposes himself in the college library; the alcoholic father who physically attacks members of his family and then threatens suicide to relieve his guilt.

Finally, there are markedly abnormal individuals whose disordered state is evident to all: the disheveled woman who walks the streets muttering to herself and cursing at passersby; the unemployed man who "knows" that others are plotting to take his life; the aged grandfather who wanders at night conversing with long dead relatives; the depressed young mother, immobilized by the responsibilities of caring for her newborn son and dreading her impulse to kill him; the socially isolated college student who always seems perplexed, speaks of vague mystical experiences, and shouts at persons unseen by others.

Historically, professionals and public alike considered only the markedly severe disorders to be part of abnormal psychology. They reflected a narrow view that the milder disturbances of personality, which we know today to be the beginnings of more serious disorders, were a measure of moral inferiority or dissipation. Rather than recognizing that milder disturbances were early stages of potentially more severe disorders, they attacked them with ridicule and condemnation. Fortunately, these inhumane views have given way in recent years to more sympathetic and psychologically sound attitudes.

In the following sections of this chapter we will attempt to answer a number of questions that students ask at the beginning of their study of abnormal psychology. With these answers as a foundation, we will be able to proceed in later chapters to more detailed discussions and case histories.

WHAT DO WE MEAN BY ABNORMAL BEHAVIOR?

All people experience discomforting periods in their lives when they fear that they are "falling apart" or having a "nervous breakdown." Such concerns occur primarily when major life events have gone badly: when important relationships have been lost or have "turned sour," or significant aspirations have been hopelessly frustrated or long sought-for wishes are achieved but have proved to be marked disappointments. Beyond these realistic justifications for feeling discouragement and anxiety are events which stem from man's fertile imagination. Thus, in what has been coined the *medical student's disease*, persons who read details about different physical ailments become overly alert and sensitive to ordinary aspects of their own bodily functions and frequently convince themselves that they "must have" this or that fatal illness. Similar fearful fantasies often occur among those who read about mental disturbances; hence, it might be useful for us to begin this section with a brief discussion of what abnormal behavior is not; that is, we will present a number of misconceptions that are believed by large segments of our society.

MISCONCEPTIONS ABOUT ABNORMAL BEHAVIOR

There are four commonly held, but false, beliefs about mental disorders that should be dispelled:

1. *The belief that all forms of abnormal behavior are inherited.* It would be difficult to find a family in which some relative has not experienced one or more periods of serious emotional disorder. As a consequence, the fear that one may be "tainted" genetically is extremely common. The facts are that only a very small percentage of mental disorders are transmitted through heredity and that these tend to be limited largely to severe forms of mental retardation. Although several research scientists are convinced that "dispositions" to specific psychological abnormalities may be genetically based, the evidence for their views are debatable and are not shared by other, equally respected scientists. Where mental disorders do "run in families," the likely cause is the family's unwholesome atmosphere and troubled relationships which serve to "teach" its younger members ineffective and abnormal ways of behaving. What is transmitted, then, is abnormal learnings, not abnormal genes.

2. *The belief that abnormal behavior is always irrational and bizarre.* In ancient times, the mentally disturbed were considered to be "possessed" by demons—to be inhuman, dangerous and frightening. Today, rather sadly, the popular media—newspapers, television and movies—portray patients in a similar manner, depicting them as "far-out crazies," people who stare into space all day, twiddle their thumbs, rant and rave, commit perverse acts, pose as Jesus Christ or Napoleon—that is, exhibit a continuous stream of humorous, frightening or irrational behaviors. Nothing could be further from the truth. With the exception of a small percentage of the very severely disturbed (and even among these such displays are infrequent), the great majority of those experiencing emotional problems exhibit everyday behaviors that would make it difficult to distinguish them in most respects from persons we consider to be perfectly "normal."

3. *The belief that abnormal behavior is disgraceful and shameful.* For the most part, people are fairly open about their physical ailments; in fact, for some persons it is a point of pride to be able to talk about their "operation." Willingness to consult with and talk about experiences with physicians, dentists or lawyers does not extend to emotional problems or to visits with psychologists or psychiatrists. Similarly, most persons are quite sympathetic to those who suffer serious physical impairments, such as crippled children or heart attack victims; these same persons rarely show much empathy or personal concern for equally ill mental patients. If there is any response to the emotionally disturbed that characterizes our public attitudes, as recent research has suggested (National Commission on Community Health Services, 1967), it is that of shame and rejection. Despite efforts on the part of mental health associations, these old and naive views persist, only slightly improved since the turn of the century. Most mental patients wish to rid themselves of their disabling symptoms, but a significant segment of the public persists in the belief that they could get better "if they only used their will-power"; if that was all there was to it, our mental hospitals and clinics would be empty in a week.

Mental disorders call for the same sympathic understanding that is given to those suffering physical disorders. Emotional difficulties are not experiences of which to be ashamed; they are not a stigma arising from an inborn "taint" or from a lack of will-power or perversity. They are a direct consequence of unfortunate life events which the patient wishes, more than you or I, would not occur to him.

4. *The belief that abnormal behaviors are fixed and unmodifiable.* It is still argued by many in the general population that once a person suffers an emotional disorder he is "doomed" for the rest of his life. Some people believe that if a person is hospitalized in a mental institution, he will "never come out"; others, slightly more sophisticated, recognize that patients do leave such institutions, but "can never be trusted," that a shadow has been cast upon them and that it is only common sense to be suspect of them. Certainly, there are some patients, particularly the severely retarded or very aged, who cannot be "cured" and who will probably remain hospitalized for their entire lives. But excepting these two groups, almost 90 per cent of all mental patients who are institutionalized return to their homes, and the great majority of these do so within a three month period.

There is no justification for believing that persons who have been hospitalized or treated psychotherapeutically are "forever doomed" or are deserving of suspicious watching and discrimination. In fact, a substantial proportion grow in response to their experience and function at a psychologically superior level *following* their emotional difficulties. All we need recall in this regard are the many distinguished leaders, such as Caesar, Jefferson, Lincoln and Churchill, who rose to positions of world prominence within years after disabling emotional problems.

CRITERIA OF ABNORMALITY

On what basis do we decide whether or not a person's behavior should be judged to be abnormal? Unfortunately, there is no simple and uniform criterion. Many different grounds for this appraisal have been proposed and it will be useful to present a number of these criteria as a means of noting the complexities and issues involved.

Statistical Criteria. In a sense, "abnormality" is a statistical term, one defined in the dictionary as an event or trait which "deviates from the norm or average." For example, test measures of intelligence distribute themselves into a normal bell-shaped curve. Infrequent scores, which fall at the extremes, deviate statistically from the middle range or norm of the distribution and can, thereby, be considered *ab*normal. If we follow this example, abnormal behaviors would be those which occur infrequently; accordingly, a person would be judged abnormal if his behaviors were unusual, that is, unlike those of most people.

Despite its appeal as an objective and quantifiable gauge of abnormality, the statistical criterion presents a number of problems. To illustrate, there are numerous traits and behaviors which occur infrequently, even rarely, but are seen neither as problems nor as undesirable (e.g., unusually superior intelligence). The statistical criterion also equates mental health with the commonplace and the ordinary, behaviors that tend to signify social conformity. "Being like everyone else" does not indicate mental health; moreover, psychologically imaginative and innovative persons, such as writers and artists, do not lack mental health simply because they often are nonconforming and inventive.

Legal Criteria. The term insanity is essentially a label of legal significance only. Actually, it is applied to three clearly different areas in which judgments of mental health are related to legal matters: *competency, commitment* and *criminal responsibility.*

A legal judgment of *incompetency* is based on whether or not a person was psychologically capable of understanding or carrying out the responsibilities of a legal contract, such as agreeing to marriage, completing a will, purchasing property or initiating a divorce. If a person is judged incompetent, a decision made usually by a judicial court in consultation with a psychiatrist, legal obligations that were previously made can be annulled and future legal transactions may be deemed void. The primary purpose of an incompetency judgment is to prevent a psychologically "unsound" person from being victimized.

Legal *commitment*, a procedure that varies somewhat from state to state, pertains to the criteria and steps involved in mandatory placement in a psychiatric institution. The primary criteria employed are whether the person is judged "dangerous," that is, capable of harming either himself or others; the certified assessment justifying commitment is essentially a medical one and usually requires the concurrence of two physicians (not necessarily psychiatrists). Serious questions have been raised as to motives underlying many legal commitments and the loss of civil rights of those hospitalized as a consequence (Szasz, 1963; Halleck, 1970). Commitment, unless initiated voluntarily for a specified time by the patient, requires that he remain incarcerated until he is medically discharged by the institution.

Decisions of *criminal irresponsibility*, the third area in which legal considerations of mental health are involved, are based on England's *M'Naghton Rule* of 1843 and its American modification, the *New Hampshire Rule* of 1869. In essence, a person is not considered criminally responsible if his act is a *direct* consequence of his particular type of "mental disease." Thus, a psychiatrically diagnosed patient who hears voices which tell him to kill someone would not be criminally responsible for his act; however, were he to sell stolen goods knowingly to fellow patients, an act of "wrongdoing" not clearly an outgrowth of the nature of his psychiatric diagnosis, he would be held responsible.

Given the complexity and nebulous character of most psychological impairments, the lack of hard facts about the patient's mental state at the time of his act, the rather shaky correspondence between fine legal distinctions and psychiatric knowledge, as well as the inappropriateness of applying medical considerations to issues of social ethics and morality, the use of legal criteria for "insanity" would appear to be a poor basis for determining abnormal behavior.

Disease Criteria. The view that abnormal behavior is due to biological causes was first presented by Hippocrates about four centuries B.C. The prime theorist of psychiatric classification at the turn of the century, Emil Kraepelin, likewise argued that mental disorders were physical diseases; numerous contemporary researchers contend that it is merely a matter of time before all psychological problems will be understood in terms of their biological roots. More will be said about this viewpoint in Chapter 5. For the moment, it will suffice to state that with very few exceptions, notably those due to brain damage or infections such as syphilis, a hundred years of intensive research has failed to uncover bodily diseases that are causally involved in psychological abnormalities.

Hence, there is no practical way at present in which the major forms of abnormal behavior can be defined or understood by the use of disease criteria.

Cultural Criteria.   In many ways, cultural and statistical criteria are similar in that both gauge abnormality by comparing behaviors against a norm or standard. However, the cultural criterion *assumes* there is a pattern of behavior that is "acceptable" within a society; behavioral deviations from this social standard are judged abnormal. The major problem associated with this criterion is the presence of different and changing standards within cultural groups. For example, homosexuality has generally been considered abnormal in Western societies. However, in the days of the early Greeks, it was not only sanctioned but was viewed by such leaders as Plato in the following way: "They (homosexuals) act in this way because they have a strong soul, manly courage, and a virile character." Turning to recent times, attitudes toward homosexuality in the United States are divergent: older people tend to see them as dangerous "queers" and perverts, middle-aged persons typically consider them to be "sick," whereas the younger generation approaches homosexuals as interesting and liberated types.

Personal Criteria.   This approach to defining abnormality depends on the person's own subjective appraisal, that is, he uses himself as his standard and examines his current mood and state of comfort. If the person reports an unusual degree of tension, conflict or depression, then he may be spoken of as demonstrating a psychological abnormality.

Although the personal criterion is an important consideration in mental health, used by itself it presents a number of problems. For example, personal unhappiness may be a transitory state, associated with realistic environmental events such as job loss, receiving an unanticipated poor grade or being turned down on a date; temporary reactions of unhappiness such as these seem a feeble basis for any stable or meaningful determination of abnormality. Similarly, since this criterion depends entirely on the correctness with which the person describes his mood, many severely disturbed patients who are not "in touch with reality" would provide wholly inaccurate self-assessments. Also not to be overlooked are those euphorically manic patients who act and say that they are ecstatically happy but, in fact, on every other criterion would be judged to be severely disturbed.

Comment.   It would seem to follow from the preceding sections that no single criterion can provide us with a sure means of defining or gauging all varieties of "abnormality"; yet, when a person's behavior is extremely deviant or severe, almost any of the criteria mentioned would suffice. Part of the difficulty is that there is no sharp line between normality and abnormality, regardless of how the latter is defined. Moreover, people are so complex that certain of their behaviors may be viewed as abnormal while others are not. To add to these complications, environmental circumstances change from time to time; behaviors that are considered healthy in one setting or period may be viewed to be abnormal in another.

It may be useful, in conclusion, to note two criteria other than those presented which may help in characterizing psychological abnormality. First, the psychologically abnormal person displays an *adaptive inflexibility,* that is, he lacks or is incapable of using alternative means for relating to others, for achieving his goals and for coping with difficulties. Second, the primary ways in which he deals with his world *foster vicious circles,* that is, his behaviors, rather than helping him achieve gratification, not only perpetuate and intensify his old problems, but tend to create new ones. More will be said about these two criteria in later chapters.

HOW COMMON IS ABNORMAL BEHAVIOR?

That the incidence of both mild and severe disorders is strikingly high in contemporary society cannot be denied. Perhaps it reflects the strain of life in the twentieth century, or what sociologists have depicted as our *age of anxiety.* Whatever its cause, the inescapable facts are that each year Americans spend more than a hundred million dollars for tranquilizers, tens of billions for liquor and aspirin, and purchase enough books promising successful personal adjustment to fill a good-sized college library.

Famine, epidemics and a majority of the biological ills have been conquered. Americans now have the time to turn to themselves, to their desires for psychological contentment and happiness, for greater social acceptance and for deeper meanings and purposes of existence. Our struggle with the physical environment has been largely won, but a host of new problems has appeared to plague us. Technological innovations have led to industrial automation and to high speed communication and transportation. Not only has the pace of life been heightened, but other societal, economic and religious changes have taken place so rapidly that we can no longer depend upon the traditions and values which gave earlier generations a feeling of stability and regularity. Divorce upsets the pattern of an increasing number of families; the threat of global and atomic war hangs in the balance; racial tension and social resentments have increased. In this rapid whirl of change and ambiguity, an atmosphere of social confusion and psychological instability has arisen to replace the anxieties of starvation, disease and economic insecurity.

No wonder then that the toll of psychological strain, discontent and bewilderment has increased to a point where it accounts for more illness than all other health problems combined. One out of every ten Americans, at the current rate, will spend part of his life in a mental hospital. More than half of all hospital beds in this country are filled with mental patients and, even more startling, is the fact that for every hospitalized patient there are 20 other less severely handicapped Americans who need psychotherapy.

Recent mental hospital surveys report a resident population of roughly one half million patients (*prevalence*); equally impaired noninstitutionalized individuals may be double the hospitalized figure. Hospital admissions each year average about 100,000 (annual *incidence*). These figures, of course, merely scratch the surface of a much deeper and wider problem. Epidemiological research suggests that only 15 to 20 per cent of the general population are entirely free of psychological symptoms; more than 20 to 25 per cent possess psychological impairments sufficient to interfere seriously with ordinary life adjustments. The billions of dollars spent in this country on liquor and tranquilizers attest to the wide prevalence and severity of emotional difficulties.

Prevalence and incidence figures are difficult to establish with any precision; although the arithmetic procedure for gathering data is theoretically simple, there is little uniformity in the definition and assignment of the various diagnostic categories. Moreover, the sources from which these data are obtained tend to be unrepresentative of the population in general; for example, the lower socioeconomic classes of the general population, cared for primarily in state institutional systems, are overrepresented in most hospital-based studies. The criteria used to define the presence and character of specific abnormal patterns are highly unreliable; they differ from one population survey to another, and are subject to changing fashions in diagnosis. Institutional statistics vary considerably; not only are they markedly influenced by differences in the availability of outpatient and preventive facilities but they reflect differing hospital policies governing admission and diagnostic classification. All of these are minor complications when compared to the problem of identifying and classifying noninstitutionalized patients. Not only is diagnostic terminology especially confusing in the less severe abnormalities but research methods are notoriously unreliable and susceptible to the pitfalls of biased population sampling.

Discouraging as these introductory comments may be, we must recognize that current frequency and diagnostic statistics are highly ambiguous at best and misleading at worst. Until steps are taken to obtain greater representativeness in population samples, and greater uniformity in criteria, terminology and methodology, we must view current prevalence and incidence data as both inadequate in scope and unreliable in details.

Fortunately, abnormal psychology is no longer viewed as a remote province of professional study tacked on as a postgraduate specialty for interested physicians. It is a necessary part today not only of the training of psychiatrists, psychologists, teachers and ministers, whose work brings them to serve the needs of the troubled, but is a significant part of the curricula of all colleges. Thirty-five thousand competent clinical psychologists, psychiatrists and psychiatric social workers are trained to deal with these problems with compassion and intelligence. In addition, we are spending over a billion dollars a year for research, treatment and care of the mentally disturbed. We have come to realize, finally, that the problems of abnormal behavior can be combatted by scientific and humane action.

HOW DO WE DETERMINE THE CHARACTER OF ABNORMAL BEHAVIOR?

Place yourself in the role of a practicing psychologist, psychiatrist, social worker, or teacher in the expanding area of paraprofessional psychology or any relevant aspect of the healing profession. Your primary daily activity is working directly with troubled and disturbed people. Your day consists largely of gathering information which will enable you to understand the complex background of each patient's problems and, with this knowledge in hand, to engage in a program of therapy which will relieve their difficulties and give them a fresh approach to life. No matter what therapeutic technique you use, it will be based on an analysis of the patient's present behavior and feelings, the historical sequence and situational context within which these problems arose, and the maladaptive solutions he has adopted to cope with them. Although many of his problems will not be understood fully until therapy is well underway, a thorough clinical study will serve as a useful initial guide in your therapeutic work.

Clinical analysis would be simple if the patient could put into words all we need to know about him. His complaints and self-analyses often are useful, but there are relevant facts which he is unable or unwilling to provide. Deeply ingrained thoughts and behaviors escape his notice because they are so "natural" a part of him. He may lack a means for comparing his thoughts with others and may assume that his feelings and attitudes are typical when in fact they are not. More importantly, he may deny his motives because they are too unbearable to admit to himself or too unacceptable and socially embarrassing. Thus, to preserve his self-esteem and his psychological equilibrium, he may be unable to provide precisely those facts which are most important to our study. Because of these limitations, the clinician must go beyond self-reports; his analysis must rely on a variety of indirect methods which enable him to fill out and verify the patient's statements. Direct observation, documentary sources, family interviews, laboratory measures and psychological tests are among the major techniques he may use to obtain a full and hopefully valid clinical picture.

In traditional fields of medical science, the goal of a thorough clinical analysis is accurate diagnosis, that is, establishing the "disease" which "underlies" the overt clinical symptoms. This diagnostic model is ill-suited to the problems of abnormal behavior, since mental disorders rarely can be ascribed to a single cause or "disease." Of course, certain events may have played a central role in the development of a disorder, but these initial influences interweave with new influences and reactions which then become an essential part of the disorder. A network of secondary factors emerge over time to add fresh momentum to the initial influences and to extend them in ways that are far removed from the original circumstances. Given the complexity of this sequence, any effort to diagnose *the* disease or *the* cause will be futile indeed. To decide what best can be done to remedy the problem then, one must evaluate it in light of the entire configuration of experiences and behaviors which have evolved into the patient's personality and behavior.

But this is an awesome task; the clinician cannot survey every aspect of experience and behavior which may be pertinent to a case. The diversity and complexity of a man's life are infinite, and selections must be made only of those aspects which will provide a maximum return for the clinician's efforts. He must use the guidelines of a theory to concentrate on those features of behavior and experience which have proven helpful to other clinicians. The established tools of the clinical profession also will be used as a means of directing his attention to those processes which are most relevant to his goals. With both theory and tool in hand then, the clinician can narrow his focus from the broad sphere of total human functioning and experience to a more limited sphere of maximum pertinence and usefulness.

OBJECTIVES OF CLINICAL ANALYSIS

The specific objectives of a clinical study will differ in different settings (psychiatric hospitals, out-patient clinics and private practice), but the central objective of all clinical analysis is to gather information which ultimately will be useful in increasing a patient's well-being. The procedures by which this objective can be attained will be rendered orderly and intelligible if they are divided into four steps.

First, the clinician undertakes an examination of the patient's current functioning. This preliminary survey of the problem is based on a variety of symptoms or clinical signs derived from data at each of several levels of observation. For example, overt behaviors are observed during interviews, testing, and on the ward; attitudes and feelings are verbalized to an interviewer, to nurses and to relatives; unconscious conflicts and defensive maneuvers are inferred from a variety of behaviors and test data; biological capacities, dispositions and dysfunctions are assessed in physical examinations and laboratory tests.

Second, an attempt is made to trace the social learning history and current situational environment which led to the patient's problem. Family discord, adolescent difficulties and vocational failures all illustrate some of the many experiences which may have contributed to its development. In this phase of his study, the clinician seeks to identify the complex of events which have shaped the disorder and which currently keep it active. With this knowledge, he can better understand why the patient behaves as he does.

Third, once the elements of social learning and present functioning have been gathered, and the connection between them established, the clinician next organizes his findings into a coherent pattern or syndrome. He attempts in this step to fashion an internally consistent image or working model of the patient in which the dominant features of his personality make-up are highlighted against the background of his present environment and the major developmental influences of his life. The model or syndrome focuses on the long-term aspects of the patient's maladaptive function, and relates them to his current social environment.

Fourth, the relationship between the patient's personality and his present environmental circumstances is appraised in order to make judgments about therapy; the chief purpose of clinical analysis should be intelligent remedial action. Much of the information contained in a thorough clinical study may prove irrelevant and may complicate decisions to be made about treatment. Unless the analysis lends itself to these practical objectives, it becomes an interesting intellectual exercise, at best, and a consumer of valuable time, at worst.

PROBLEMS OF CLINICAL ANALYSIS

Significant errors and biases by even the most experienced practitioners arise in most fields of clinical science. These problems are especially prominent, however, in abnormal psychology. Here, clinicians possess few of the objective and quantitative instruments found in other sciences, and must depend on procedures which are unstandardized, imprecise and highly subjective. Different sources of clinical data (a patient's account of his illness, the observable symptoms he displays and the facts of his past history) frequently lead to contradictory clinical impressions. Conflicting judgments arise also from the tendency of different examiners to ask different questions, emphasize different features of pathology unequally and interpret the information they have gathered in idiosyncratic and biased ways. Thus, not only is there considerable difference in the basic data from which clinical analyses are derived, but this difficulty is compounded by a lack of uniformity in clinical procedures and a low reliability in clinical judgment.

Two factors should be kept in mind. First, there is no evidence to date indicating the superiority of one source or one method for obtaining and interpreting clinical information. Second, there are typical errors and biases which frequently distort the data of clinical analyses.

The precise procedures which produce an excellent clinical study have not been established, but the complications which diminish clinical accuracy are well known. In this section we shall alert the beginning student to some of these problems.

PATIENT AND SITUATIONAL VARIABILITY

Man is a changeable creature; his behaviors, thoughts and feelings shift from moment to moment. Consequently, the symptoms or signs of abnormality observed in one context or at one point in time may not be displayed in another. In part, this variability signifies differences in the stimulating properties of the environment. It reflects complex internal processes, such as memories, subliminal sensation and moods, which combine in innumerable ways to create changing surface impressions and clinical pictures. But, most important, behaviors change as a function of the situation within which the person finds himself.

Basic to all psychological theory and research is the established fact that behavior is influenced by environmental stimulation. Despite his knowledge, clinicians often assume that the data of their clinical analysis were not influenced by the procedures, settings and timing of their evaluation. The assumption is unjustified; there is ample research to show the many subtle ways in which situational and interpersonal factors do influence clinical data (Sarason, 1954; Masling, 1960; Mischel, 1968). The questions asked of the patient, the examiner's personality (friendly or reserved), his status (intern or senior staff) and physical characteristics (age and sex), the setting (outpatient clinic, hospital ward, private consultation or staff meeting), the clinical procedure (testing or interviews) and the time of evaluation (emergency admission, after drugs or following hospital adjustment) illustrate some of the many factors which may influence and distort the character of clinical data.

In addition to these objective situational influences, the clinician must consider the relationship between the patient's motivations, expectations and the context of the evaluation. The behavior and feelings exhibited by a patient will reflect such matters as his attitudes (e.g., fears of a "state hospital" or "psychiatrists") and the conditions which prompted the clinical study (e.g., involuntary commitment or hospital discharge planning).

The student should keep in mind that the patient's behavior, in large measure, is a product of the situation in which he has been observed. The more the student is aware of these potential influences, the more certain he can be that his data are representative and his interpretations of them are accurate.

OBSERVATIONAL BIASES

Abnormal psychologists differ in their clinical judgments because they have different views as to what data should be observed and how these observations should be interpreted. Despite protests that their judgments are objective, clinicians committed to a theoretical viewpoint invariably emphasize data that are consistent with their preferred theory (Pasamanick et al., 1959), whereas characteristics that fit other theoretical biases are overlooked. Furthermore, by probing and asking leading

questions, clinicians often evoke responses that support their expectations. Gill and Brenman describe this process as follows (1948):

If a therapist believes dreams are important in helping a patient, he will show interest in the patient's dreams. Merely asking if the patient has any may result in
including many more dreams in the raw data than are gathered by a therapist
who is not especially interested in dreams. This is on the grossest level. The
subtleties of showing interests in certain kinds of material, often not consciously
detected either by therapist or patient, are manifold. They may include a questioning glance, a shifting of visual focus, a well-timed "um-hum," a scarcely per-
ceptible nod, or even a clearing of the throat.

Clearly, what a clinician "sees" often is a product of what he expects to
see. Other observers may not record the same findings since their perceptions and behaviors have been conditioned by different theoretical
beliefs. It should be obvious then, that the more a clinician looks at and
interprets data from alternate viewpoints, the more comprehensive and
potentially accurate will be his analysis.

SKILL OF THE CLINICIAN

Not all of the many inferences which a clinician makes are valid or useful.
He is limited by the scope of his knowledge, and that knowledge is restricted by the incomplete state of the science. To compensate for these
shortcomings the clinician draws upon an ill-defined "intuitive" sense.
Unfortunately, this intituitive process is an entirely subjective act that
can be neither communicated to others nor examined critically.

Given the obscure nature of this intuitive process, and the differences in
skill even among experienced clinicians, some psychologists have
suggested that the job of interpretation should be taken out of the hands
of the clinician since it can be done more reliably and validly by *actuarial*
methods. In the actuarial approach, interpretation is based on statistically demonstrated correlations between such clinical data as test
scores, biographical information and behavior signs, on the one hand,
and a variety of relevant clinical criteria such as the future course of certain disorders and the response of patients to particular forms of therapy, on the other. For example, instead of sitting down, reflecting and
intuitively deciding what certain test scores may mean, the clinician
simply looks into a statistical "cookbook" and notes the patterns with
which these scores have been shown to correlate. With these cookbooks,
the task of prediction and decision making is greatly simplified, and the
accuracy of interpretations is assured of at least some validity.

The logic for the statistical or actuarial approach, sketched briefly here,
has been convincingly argued by Meehl (1954, 1956 and 1965) and Sarbin (Sarbin, 1943; Sarbin, Taft and Bailey, 1960). Both men recognize
that some clinicians are especially skillful, and acknowledge that the actuarial approach may be of fairly limited utility in its present state, but
they note that where comparisons of the two methods have been made,
the statistical approach is clearly superior.

Despite impressive evidence favoring the statistical method, few actuarial formulas have been devised to handle the varied therapeutic
decisions which clinicians face daily. Furthermore, it is unlikely that all
aspects of clinical judgment can be replaced by a statistical equation.
Nevertheless, advances in actuarial prediction and decision making continue to be made, and the student should utilize the results of this
work whenever feasible.

WHAT ARE THE MAJOR PSYCHOLOGICAL ABNORMALITIES?

Clinical analysis attempts to discover the major factors which have prevented the patient from experiencing personal satisfaction and social adjustment. This is done by carefully reviewing his current clinical picture, noting the situational environment within which he operates, and reconstructing the developmental forces which have contributed to his abnormalities.

RATIONALE OF CLINICAL SYNDROMES

A clinical study which attempted to review all of the elements of a patient's past and present would be an exhausting task indeed. To make the job less difficult, the clinician narrows his attention to certain features of a patient's social history and behavior which may prove significant. This reduction process requires that the clinician make a series of discriminations among the data he observes. He must find a core of factors which capture the essential character of the patient, and which will serve to guide his analysis. Several assumptions are made by the diagnostician in narrowing his clinical focus. He assumes that each patient possesses behaviors and attitudes which are central to his pathology, that these characteristics are found in common among identifiable groups of patients and that prior knowledge regarding the features of these distinctive patient groups, known as *clinical syndromes,* will help him in his clinical responsibilities and functions.

What support is there for these assumptions?

There are both theoretical and empirical justifications for the belief that people display a reasonable degree of consistency over time in their functioning. Careful study of an individual will reveal a congruency among his behaviors. This coherence or unity of psychological functioning is a valid phenomenon; it follows logically from the fact that people possess relatively enduring biological dispositions which give a consistent coloration to their experiences, and that the actual range of their social learning experiences have been highly limited and repetitive. It should not be surprising, therefore, that individuals develop a learned pattern of deeply ingrained behaviors, attitudes and needs. Once several of these dominant or key characteristics are identified, the clinician should have a sound basis for inferring the presence of correlated features of the patient's social learning history and present functioning.

If we accept the assumption that people display a pattern of socially learned characteristics, we are led next to the question of whether certain patients evidence a commonality in the central characteristics they display. The notion of clinical syndromes rests on the assumption that there are a limited number of key characteristics which can be used profitably to distinguish certain groups of patients. The hope is that the assigning of a patient within one of these syndrome groups will clue the clinician to the larger pattern of the patient's difficulty, thereby simplifying his task immeasurably. Thus, once he identifies these key characteristics in a particular patient, he will be able to utilize the knowledge he has learned about other patients in that syndrome, and apply that knowledge to his present patient.

The fact that patients can profitably be categorized into clinical syndromes does not negate the fact that patients, so categorized, display

considerable differences. The philosopher, Grunbaum, illustrates this
thesis in the following (1952):

Every individual is unique by virtue of being a distinctive assemblage of characteristics not precisely duplicated in any other individual. Nevertheless, it is quite
conceivable that the following . . . might hold: if a male child having specifiable
characteristics is subjected to maternal hostility and has a strong paternal attachment at a certain stage of his development, he will develop paranoia during adult
life. If this . . . holds, then children who are subjected to the stipulated conditions
in fact become paranoiacs, however much they may have differed in other
respects in childhood and whatever their other differences may be once they
are already insane.

There should be little concern about the fact that certain "unique" characteristics of each patient will be lost when he is grouped in a category or
syndrome; differences among members of the same syndrome will exist,
of course. The question that must be raised is *not* whether all patients in
a particular syndrome are the same, since no category meets this criterion, but whether placement in a syndrome complicates or simplifies a variety of clinically relevant objectives. Thus, if this grouping of key characteristics simplifies his task by alerting the clinician to features of the
patient's social learning history and present functioning which he has
not yet observed, or if it enables clinicians to communicate effectively
about their patients, or guides their selection of beneficial therapeutic
plans or assists researchers in the design of experiments, then the existence of these categories has served many useful purposes. No single classification schema can serve all of the purposes for which syndrome categories can be formed; all we can ask is that it simplify and, hopefully,
improve certain clinical and research functions.

The next question we must ask is whether such categories or syndromes
exist?

CLASSIFICATION AND LABELING

Once we accept the idea that syndromes may prove useful, the question
arises as to whether the system in current use fulfills as many functions
as possible. If it does not, then we must ask which features should be retained, which features should be added to increase its utility and how the
system can best be reorganized. For purposes of reference and comparison in later chapters, the student might profitably scan at this time Table
1–1, which outlines the clinical categories of the revised "traditional"
diagnostic and statistical manual of the American Psychiatric Association, referred to in the text as the DSM-II.

Numerous shortcomings have been noted in the literature concerning
the DSM-II classification system (Millon, 1969), among which are the following: (1) categories are based on the most dramatic symptom that patients exhibit, rather than less dramatic and more typical "everyday" behaviors, (2) categories are developed on the basis of tradition and
"clinical impression," rather than in line with the findings of modern statistical and social learning research, (3) the classification format does not
possess a coherent theory from which the principal syndromes could be
logically derived and coordinated, (4) syndromes are separated into distinct and unconnected categories, rather than grouped in terms of their
close clinical interrelationships, and (5) the most common form of abnormality, the mild personality patterns that occur in everyday life, are

minimized and, instead, attention focuses on the infrequent, bizarre or very severe forms of abnormality.

There are three additional problems concerning the use of diagnostic syndromes which deserve special emphasis because they raise serious questions about the entire notion of patient classification itself.

Unreliability of Clinical Classification. Reliability in classification is determined by the degree to which different clinicians agree in their categorizing of patients. Research studies have uncovered a number of disappointing findings. Schmidt and Fonda (1956), using a sample of 426 recently hospitalized patients, noted an 85 per cent agreement among psychiatrists when they were asked to separate patients into such broad categories as organic versus non-organic disorders; however, when they attempted to categorize specific patient subtypes, such as among the many varieties of personality and neurotic syndromes, agreement fell well below the 50 per cent level. Equally dismaying, two studies (Mehlman, 1952; Raines and Rohrer, 1955) found that clinicians had "preferred" categories, that is, each tended to classify most of his patients in a limited number of categories to the exclusion of all others. In another investigation (Ward et al., 1962), designed to explore the basis of classification errors, it was found that only 5 per cent of diagnostic disagreements could be attributed to patient variability; however, over 32 per cent resulted from differences among clinicians in the information they sought, the weight they gave to different factors and the interpretations they made of the same information; and most appalling of all, 63 per cent of the errors resulted from ambiguities and inadequacies in the DSM classification system itself.

Circular Explanations. A diagnostic label such as "paranoid" or "schizophrenic" is simply a word, a term used by clinicians to summarize the particular thoughts and behaviors that characterize a patient, and nothing more!

Unfortunately, these descriptive labels often become transformed into "explanations" of the very behaviors they were intended to simply summarize. For example, if the presence of delusional thinking in a patient led a clinician to classify him as "paranoid," it makes no sense, either for the clinician or others, to explain the delusions by saying that the patient thinks that way because he *is* a paranoid. This form of circular reasoning arises when the diagnostician adheres to a "disease model" of emotional disorders; that is, clinicians with this orientation act as if the term "paranoid" represented diseases such as cancer or tuberculosis, rather than being a word that merely summarizes, and does not explain, descriptions of behavior. There is no "disease" or "thing" such as paranoid. Although it may be useful to speak of patients as exhibiting paranoid behavior and thinking, what this means only is that a complex pattern of symptoms has been portrayed with a single word. Use of such descriptive words for purposes of explanation is most unfortunate, and it leads some theorists to argue that all diagnostic labels be eliminated from the vocabulary of abnormal psychology.

Social and Behavior Consequences of Labeling. There are complications associated with labels other than those resulting in circular reasoning. In a recent review (Stuart, 1970), several personal and social consequences of being designated as "mentally ill" were elaborated. Thus, as Rosenthal and Jacobsen (1968) and Sarbin and Mancuso (1970) have noted, classifying a patient in this manner often justifies subjecting him to social

I Mental Retardation

- ☐ 310. Borderline
- ☐ 311. Mild
- ☐ 312. Moderate
- ☐ 313. Severe
- ☐ 314. Profound
- ☐ 315. Unspecified

With each: Following or associated with

- ☐ .0 Infection or intoxication
- ☐ .1 Trauma or physical agent
- ☐ .2 Disorders of metabolism, growth or nutrition
- ☐ .3 Gross brain disease (postnatal)
- ☐ .4 Unknown prenatal influence
- ☐ .5 Chromosomal abnormality
- ☐ .6 Prematurity
- ☐ .7 Major psychiatric disorder
- ☐ .8 Psycho-social (environmental) deprivation
- ☐ .9 Other condition

II Organic Brain Syndromes (OBS)

A Psychoses

Senile and Pre-Senile Dementia

- ☐ 290.0 Senile dementia
- ☐ 290.1 Pre-senile dementia

Alcoholic Psychosis

- ☐ 291.0 Delirium tremens
- ☐ 291.1 Korsakov's psychosis
- ☐ 291.2 Other alcoholic hallucinosis
- ☐ 291.3 Alcohol paranoid state
- ☐ 291.4* Acute alcohol intoxication*
- ☐ 291.5* Alcoholic deterioration*
- ☐ 291.6* Pathological intoxication*
- ☐ 291.9 Other alcoholic psychosis

Psychosis Associated With Intracranial Infection

- ☐ 292.0 General paralysis
- ☐ 292.1 Syphilis of central nervous system
- ☐ 292.2 Epidemic encephalitis
- ☐ 292.3 Other and unspecified encephalitis
- ☐ 292.9 Other intracranial infection

Psychosis Associated With Other Cerebral Condition

- ☐ 293.0 Cerebral arteriosclerosis
- ☐ 293.1 Other cerebrovascular disturbance
- ☐ 293.2 Epilepsy
- ☐ 293.3 Intracranial neoplasm
- ☐ 293.4 Degenerative disease of the CNS
- ☐ 293.5 Brain trauma
- ☐ 293.9 Other cerebral condition

Psychosis Associated With Other Physical Condition

- ☐ 294.0 Endocrine disorder
- ☐ 294.1 Metabolic and nutritional disorder
- ☐ 294.2 Systemic infection
- ☐ 294.3 Drug or poison intoxication (other than alcohol)
- ☐ 294.4 Childbirth
- ☐ 294.8 Other and unspecified physical condition

B Non-Psychotic OBS

- ☐ 309.0 Intracranial infection
- ☐ 309.13* Alcohol* (simple drunkenness)
- ☐ 309.14* Other drug, poison or systemic intoxication*
- ☐ 309.2 Brain trauma
- ☐ 309.3 Circulatory disturbance
- ☐ 309.4 Epilepsy
- ☐ 309.5 Disturbance of metabolism, growth, or nutrition
- ☐ 309.6 Senile or pre-senile brain disease
- ☐ 309.7 Intracranial neoplasm
- ☐ 309.8 Degenerative disease of the CNS
- ☐ 309.9 Other physical condition

III Psychoses Not Attributed To Physical Conditions Listed Previously

Schizophrenia

- ☐ 295.0 Simple
- ☐ 295.1 Hebephrenic
- ☐ 295.2 Catatonic
- ☐ 295.23* Catatonic type, excited*
- ☐ 295.24* Catatonic type, withdrawn*
- ☐ 295.3 Paranoid
- ☐ 295.4 Acute schizophrenic episode
- ☐ 295.5 Latent
- ☐ 295.6 Residual
- ☐ 295.7 Schizo-affective
- ☐ 295.73* Schizo-affective, excited*
- ☐ 295.74* Schizo-affective, depressed*
- ☐ 295.8* Childhood*
- ☐ 295.90* Chronic undifferentiated*
- ☐ 295.99* Other schizophrenia*

Major Affective Disorders

- ☐ 296.0 Involutional melancholia
- ☐ 296.1 Manic-depressive illness, manic
- ☐ 296.2 Manic-depressive illness, depressed
- ☐ 296.3 Manic-depressive illness, circular
- ☐ 296.33* Manic-depressive, circular, manic*
- ☐ 296.34* Manic-depressive, circular, depressed*
- ☐ 296.8 Other major affective disorder

Paranoid States

- ☐ 297.0 Paranoia
- ☐ 297.1 Involutional paranoid state
- ☐ 297.9 Other paranoid state

Other Psychoses

- ☐ 298.0 Psychotic depressive reaction

IV Neuroses

- ☐ 300.0 Anxiety
- ☐ 300.1 Hysterical
- ☐ 300.13* Hysterical, conversion type*
- ☐ 300.14* Hysterical, dissociative type*

TABLE 1-1

CLINICAL CATEGORIES AND NOMEN-CLATURE OF THE REVISED DIAGNOSTIC AND STATISTICAL MANUAL (DSM-II)*
From American Psychiatric Association (1968)

TABLE 1–1

Continued

- ☐ 300.2 Phobic
- ☐ 300.3 Obsessive compulsive
- ☐ 300.4 Depressive
- ☐ 300.5 Neurasthenic
- ☐ 300.6 Depersonalization
- ☐ 300.7 Hypochondriacal
- ☐ 300.8 Other neurosis

V Personality Disorders and Certain Other Non-Psychotic Mental Disorders

Personality Disorders
- ☐ 301.0 Paranoid
- ☐ 301.1 Cyclothymic
- ☐ 301.2 Schizoid
- ☐ 301.3 Explosive
- ☐ 301.4 Obsessive compulsive
- ☐ 301.5 Hysterical
- ☐ 301.6 Asthenic
- ☐ 301.7 Antisocial
- ☐ 301.81* Passive-aggressive*
- ☐ 301.82* Inadequate*
- ☐ 301.89* Other specified types*

Sexual Deviation
- ☐ 302.0 Homosexuality
- ☐ 302.1 Fetishism
- ☐ 302.2 Pedophilia
- ☐ 302.3 Transvestitism
- ☐ 302.4 Exhibitionism
- ☐ 302.5* Voyeurism*
- ☐ 302.6* Sadism*
- ☐ 302.7* Masochism*
- ☐ 302.8 Other sexual deviation

Alcoholism
- ☐ 303.0 Episodic excessive drinking
- ☐ 303.1 Habitual excessive drinking
- ☐ 303.2 Alcohol addiction
- ☐ 303.9 Other alcoholism

Drug Dependence
- ☐ 304.0 Opium, opium alkaloids and their derivatives
- ☐ 304.1 Synthetic analgesics with morphine-like effects
- ☐ 304.2 Barbiturates
- ☐ 304.3 Other hypnotics and sedatives or "tranquilizers"
- ☐ 304.4 Cocaine
- ☐ 304.5 Cannabis sativa (hashish, marihuana)
- ☐ 304.6 Other psycho-stimulants
- ☐ 304.7 Hallucinogens
- ☐ 304.8 Other drug dependence

VI Psychophysiologic Disorders
- ☐ 305.0 Skin
- ☐ 305.1 Musculoskeletal
- ☐ 305.2 Respiratory

- ☐ 305.3 Cardiovascular
- ☐ 305.4 Hemic and lymphatic
- ☐ 305.5 Gastro-intestinal
- ☐ 305.6 Genito-urinary
- ☐ 305.7 Endocrine
- ☐ 305.8 Organ of special sense
- ☐ 305.9 Other type

VII Special Symptoms
- ☐ 306.0 Speech disturbance
- ☐ 306.1 Specific learning disturbance
- ☐ 306.2 Tic
- ☐ 306.3 Other psychomotor disorder
- ☐ 306.4 Disorders of sleep
- ☐ 306.5 Feeding disturbance
- ☐ 306.6 Enuresis
- ☐ 306.7 Encopresis
- ☐ 306.8 Cephalalgia
- ☐ 306.9 Other special symptom

VIII Transient Situational Disturbances
- ☐ 307.0* Adjustment reaction of infancy*
- ☐ 307.1* Adjustment reaction of childhood*
- ☐ 307.2* Adjustment reaction of adolescence*
- ☐ 307.3* Adjustment reaction of adult life*
- ☐ 307.4* Adjustment reaction of late life*

IX Behavior Disorders of Childhood and Adolescence
- ☐ 308.0* Hyperkinetic reaction*
- ☐ 308.1* Withdrawing reaction*
- ☐ 308.2* Overanxious reaction*
- ☐ 308.3* Runaway reaction*
- ☐ 308.4* Unsocialized aggressive reaction*
- ☐ 308.5* Group delinquent reaction*
- ☐ 308.9* Other reaction*

X Conditions Without Manifest Psychiatric Disorder and Non-Specific Conditions
Social Maladjustment Without Manifest Psychiatric Disorder
- ☐ 316.0* Marital maladjustment*
- ☐ 316.1* Social-maladjustment*
- ☐ 316.2* Occupational maladjustment*
- ☐ 316.3* Dyssocial behavior*
- ☐ 316.9* Other social maladjustment*

Non-Specific Conditions
- ☐ 317* Non-specific conditions*

No Mental Disorder
- ☐ 318* No mental disorder*

XI Non-Diagnostic Terms For Administrative Use
- ☐ 319.0* Diagnosis deferred*
- ☐ 319.1* Boarder*
- ☐ 319.2* Experiment only*
- ☐ 319.3* Other*

*Categories added to ICD-8 for use in U.S. only.

isolation, personal humiliation and a host of unpleasant forms of "treat-ment" such as shock therapy and psychosurgery.

Moreover, "mental" labels are not temporary, but remain a "verdict" or "stigma" that becomes attached to the person and from which he often cannot escape for much of his life. The work of Scheff (1973) and Goff-man (1973) relates directly to this point. According to them, the act of labeling leads patients to adopt a role that reflects society's expectations of mental patients. Once designated as "mentally ill," patients not only exhibit behaviors they have previously learned are "typical" of the "men-tally ill" role, but they experience the rewards of "good behavior" only when they are "sick" in the way in which their caretakers expect. Thus, despite the fact that most emotional disorders would, taking their own course, be transitory, the process of labeling has the effect, through role expectations and rewards, of "forcing" patients to maintain their behav-iors, thereby making their difficulties more permanent.

Comment.   The problems of classification and labeling, such as those described above, have been noted by many writers (Ash, 1949; Rotter, 1954; Phillips and Rabinovich, 1958; Zigler and Phillips, 1961; Phillips, 1968). Some critics believe that the present system should be abandoned as troublesome and worthless (Sarbin and Mancuso, 1970); others have suggested major revisions (Millon, 1969), whereas a third group claims that it merely needs refinement. (Lorr, 1966).

The whole notion of categorization has been indicted by some. This con-demnation overlooks the many benefits of an adequate system; it ap-pears as if these critics have overreacted to the shortcomings of syn-drome categories without recognizing any of its advantages.

Indeed, there is reason for dismay, especially when one observes that many clinicians are content merely to label a patient as "fitting" a cate-gory, and leaving matters stand at that. The adherence on the part of other clinicians to ambiguous categories, and their resistance to changes proposed through systematic research, is further reason for dismay. But these legitimate complaints do not justify "throwing out the baby with the bathwater." The notion of categorization and labeling should not be abolished if its products have been misused by some, or if they are only partially successful. One need not champion the features of any specific system of categories in order to recognize the merits of classification it-self. Nor should we expect that any one system will satisfy all the features which might prove useful to the study of abnormal behavior.

A classification system of syndromes, at best, is like a theory in that it serves to simplify the search for relevant characteristics. Thus, as noted earlier, if a system enables the clinician to deduce characteristics of the patient's make-up or development which are not otherwise obtainable, or if they guide him to a particular course of therapy, or alert him to po-tentially serious complications, or any other clinical decision-making process, then the system is well worth using.

WHAT ARE THE MAJOR APPROACHES TO PSYCHOTHERAPY AND BEHAVIOR CHANGE?

Beset with troublesome "mental" difficulties, patients are given a bewil-dering "choice" of psychotherapies that might prove emotionally upset-ting in itself, even to a well-balanced individual. Thus, patients may not only be advised to purchase this tranquilizer rather than that one or told to take vacations or leave their jobs or go to church more often, but if they explore the possibilities of formal psychological therapy, they must choose among numerous "schools" of treatment, each of which is claimed by its adherents to be the most efficient and by its detractors to be both ineffective and unscientific.

Should a patient or his family show a rare degree of "scientific sophistication," they will inquire into the effectiveness of alternative therapeutic approaches. What they will learn is that the "outcome" of different treatment approaches is strikingly similar, and that there is little data available to indicate which method is "best" for the particular difficulty they face. Moreover, they will learn the startling fact that most patients improve *without benefit of psychotherapy* almost as frequently as those who are subjected to prolonged psychological treatment.

This state of affairs is most discouraging. However, the "science" as opposed to the "art" of psychotherapy is relatively new, perhaps no older than one or two decades. Given the confusing picture that prevails among psychological treatment methods, it may be useful to provide a brief outline of the history and development of the major therapeutic procedures in use today; more detailed discussions will be presented in later chapters.

HISTORICAL ORIGINS

Psychotherapy has a long history, although the concept of treatment by psychological methods was first formally proposed in 1803 by Johannes Reil. In this section we will briefly review some of the major approaches to be elaborated in later chapters; for the present we will arrange the history of psychotherapy into several phases or periods.

ANCIENT DEMONOLOGY

Primitive man and ancient civilizations alike viewed the unusual and strange within a magical and mythological frame of reference. Behavior which could not be understood was thought to be controlled by demons and animistic spirits.

Given this explanation of mental disorder, the course of treatment was clear. Demons were to be *exorcised,* or driven from the body. The casting out of evil spirits was attempted initially through prayer, incantation, foul odors and bitter concoctions. In several societies operations called *trephining* were performed by chipping away a circular segment of the skull through which the demons might escape. If, by chance, the disordered behavior was viewed to signify mystical powers, as was epilepsy among the early Greeks, the patient was thought to be possessed by sacred spirits with which the gods had honored him. This favorable view of mental affliction grew in time into a more uniformly sympathetic approach to the ill.

THERAPY IN GREECE AND ROME

"Psychological" treatment was first recorded in the temple practices of early Greeks and Egyptians in the eighth century B.C. In Egyptian

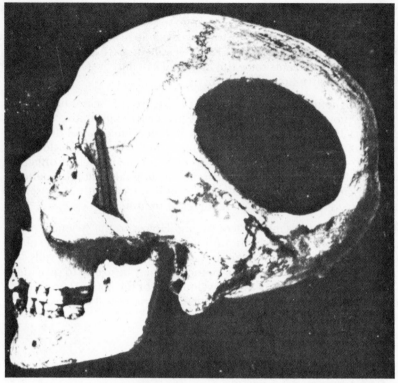

Figure 1-1   Trephined Neolithic Skull. (The Bettmann Archive, Inc.)

"hospices," physician-priests interpreted dreams and suggested solutions both to earthly and heavenly problems. In the Grecian Asclepiad temples, located in regions remote from sources of stress, the sick were provided with rest, given various nourishing herbs, massaged and surrounded with soothing music. During the fifth century B.C., Hippocrates suggested that exercise and physical tranquility should be employed to supplant the more prevalent practices of exorcism and punishment. Asclepiades, a Roman in the first century B.C. devised a variety of measures to relax patients, and openly condemned harsh "therapeutic" methods such as bloodletting and mechanical restraints. The influential practitioner Soranus (120 A.D.) suggested methods to "exercise" the mind by having the patient participate in discussions with philosophers who could aid him in banishing his fears and sorrows. The value of philosophical discussions proposed by Soranus may be viewed as a forerunner of many contemporary psychological therapies.

MEDIEVAL WITCHCRAFT

The enlightened ideas of the early Greeks and Romans were submerged for centuries following the fall of the Roman empire. During the thousand years of the Dark Ages, superstition, demonology and exorcism returned in full force only to be elaborated with greater intensity into sorcery and witchburning. Signs for detecting those possessed of demons became indiscriminate. During epidemics of famine and pestilence, thousands wandered aimlessly until their haggard appearance and confusion justified the fear that they were cursed and possessed of demons. As the terrifying uncertainties of medieval life persisted, fear

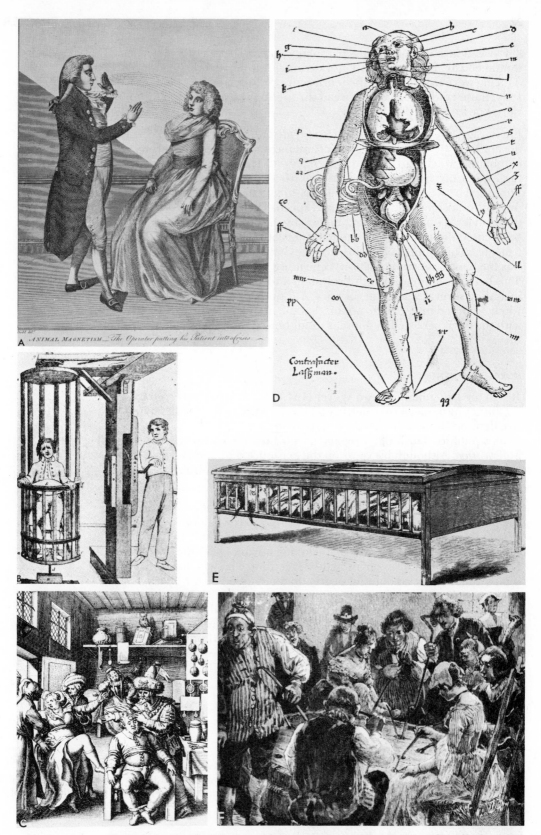

Figure 1–2 Prescientific therapies. A, Animal magnetism. (National Library of Medicine, Bethesda, Maryland.) B, Rotating device. (The Bettmann Archive, Inc.) C, Medieval brain surgery. (The Bettmann Archive, Inc.) D, Bloodletting chart. (Philadelphia Museum of Art.) E, The crib. (The Bettmann Archive, Inc.) F, The baquet. (The Bettmann Archive, Inc.)

led to wild mysticism and mass pathology. Entire societies were swept simultaneously. Epidemic manias of raving, jumping, drinking and wild
dancing were first noted in the tenth century. Referred to as *tarantism* in
Italy, these epidemic manias spread throughout Europe where they
were known as *St. Vitus's Dance.*

Encouraged by the 1484 *Summis Desiderentes Affectibus,* in which Pope Innocent VIII advised the clergy to use all means for detecting and
eliminating witchcraft, Johann Sprenger and Heinrich Kraemer issued
their notorious manual, *Malleus Maleficarum* (The Witches' Hammer).
Published between 1487 and 1489, this "divinely inspired" text set out to
prove the existence of witchcraft and specify the procedures of examination and legal sentence. Given sanction by the church, witch-hunters
persecuted thousands of the mentally ill. With torture recommended as
a means of obtaining confession, the inevitable consequence for most
was the penalty of strangulation, beheading and burning at the stake.
This barbaric epidemic swept Protestant and Catholic countries alike,
including several American colonies. Although the last execution of a
witch occurred in 1782, the notion that the mentally ill were in league
with the devil persisted in popular thought well into the nineteenth century.

MORAL TREATMENT

It is to the Dutchman Johann Weyer (1515–1588), often referred to as
the father of modern psychiatry, that credit must go for the first effective denunciation of demonology. His major work, *De Praestiguo Dae-
monum* published in 1563, provided a vigorous attack upon the *Malleus
Maleficarum.* Although his views on the existence of demons is ambiguous, he stated forthrightly that "witches" were ill and insisted that their
treatment be medical and humane.

The second phase of true psychological treatment, what may be termed
the period of "hospital reformation" and "moral treatment," began following the French Revolution. It was the distinguished physician and
scholar, Philippe Pinel (1754–1826), taking advantage of the French
Revolutionary emphasis on individual freedom, who was most effective
in proving the success of humane treatment. Guided by the belief that
institutionalized patients could be brought from their stage of depravity
by exposure to a physically attractive environment and by contact with
socially kind and moralistically proper hospital personnel, Pinel initiated
an approach to mental hospital care that took hold, although slowly and
gradually. Moral treatment as practiced by responsible and considerate
hospital personnel failed to take root for many years. This occurred for

Figure 1-3 A, Johann Weyer. (The Bettmann Archive, Inc.) B, Philippe Pinel. (National Library of
Medicine, Bethesda, Maryland.)

A   B

several reasons: there was a decline in the nineteenth century of psychiatric "idealism"; innumerable practical difficulties prevented the staffing of institutions with adequately motivated workers; and there was a growth in the early twentieth century of the "disease model," turning the attention of psychiatrists to methods of medical rather than psychological treatment.

HYPNOSIS AND PSYCHOANALYSIS

The practice of psychoanalysis, characterized by treatment techniques that focus on one patient at a time and attempt to uncover the unconscious basis of his problems, may be said to have begun with Mesmer's investigations of "animal magnetism," i.e., hypnotism. Although the concept of magnetic forces was soon dispelled, Mesmer's occult procedures set the stage for a more scientific study of unconscious processes and strengthened the view that "suggestion" can be a potent factor in influencing mental symptoms. Moreover, Mesmer's enormous success with well-to-do "neurotics" in his private salon may be viewed as a precursor of modern day office practice.

Psychoanalysis as we know it today did not begin until the discovery of hypnosis and its relation to hysteria. The early work of Jean Charcot and H. Bernheim was instrumental in leading Sigmund Freud to the thesis that mental illness was essentially a psychological process traceable to the persistence of unconscious memories and conflicts. Psychoanalysis, the first of the systematic and rationally grounded treatment techniques, was designed by Freud to release these unconscious forces and reconstruct the self-defeating defenses that patients employed to deal with them. For many years, well into the midpart of this century, psychotherapy was viewed as synonymous with Freud's psychoanalytic procedure. Although new techniques were conceived, they were for the most part modifications of the Freudian approach.

Subjected to dissenting views, even among its early adherents, the practice of psychoanalysis splintered into numerous subvarieties. Despite these deviations, the focus on unconscious processes and the office practice model with individual patients remained well entrenched as a treatment style.

BIOLOGICAL THERAPIES

The first "scientific" form of biological therapy was Wagner-Jauregg's use of a malarial infection in 1917 to curtail neurosyphilis. Another early form of biotherapy was devised in 1921 by Jacob Klaesi who used drugs to induce prolonged sleep as a form of rest for "irritated" nerve cells.

The modern era of biological therapy began in the 1930's with the almost simultaneous development of insulin coma therapy, convulsion treatment and cerebral surgery. In none of these techniques did their discoverers understand the biophysical processes that accounted for their methods; they either stumbled on them by accident or formulated them on the basis of erroneous notions of their action.

Manfred Sakel's insulin procedure, first described in 1933, rested on the now disproved thesis that psychoses resulted from excessive adrenaline. Lazlo Meduna's contention that epilepsy and schizophrenia were mutually exclusive diseases has shown to be in error; yet it led him to induce convulsions in schizophrenics by a chemical named metrazol. In 1937, Ugo Cerletti induced convulsions by electrical means, a technique popularly known as "electric shock" treatment, but more appropriately termed today as electroconvulsive therapy (ECT). Meduna and Cerletti believed that their techniques were beneficial in cases diagnosed as schizophrenia; their value however, seems limited to depressive disorders.

Surgical incursions into the brain were first attempted in 1890 by G. Burkhardt. This operative approach was discontinued due to medical and public objections, and was not attempted again until Egas Moniz performed the first of his "prefrontal lobotomies" in 1935. Surgical procedures, together with insulin coma and electroconvulsive therapies, continued to be the principal forms of biotherapy until the mid-1950's.

A significant step toward a scientific medical approach to treatment took place with the accidental discovery of two drugs: chlorpromazine and reserpine. Originally intended as means of controlling high blood pressure, these drugs were found in 1952 to have "tranquilizing" effects on emotionally disturbed patients. In the past two decades numerous variations have been developed on the basis of these pharmacological agents, ushering new confidence among those who seek to treat mental "illness" by chemical means.

SELF-ACTUALIZING APPROACHES

Another stage in the development of psychological treatment may be said to have begun with the opening of mental health clinics for the young. This movement led to a new therapeutic goal, "freeing" the patient to develop his full potentials without the constraints of inhibiting social forces.

"Clinics" were common in medicine for many centuries. But it was not until Lightner Witmer opened the first psychoeducational clinic in 1896 at the University of Pennsylvania that the problems of the young became a major focus of psychological treatment. The character and problems of children and adolescents led inevitably to a therapeutic philosophy that differed from those used in the service of hospital psychotics and adult neurotics. The clientele of school and college clinics was composed of moderately well young people who appeared to be suffering from parental, social and educational forces that blocked their efforts to develop natural "growth" potentials. To remedy these difficulties, clinical therapists began to devise techniques which would "free" the patient to be himself, to "actualize" his capacities and to develop a sense of "personal self-regard." Thus, by the early 1950's, the idea of Carl Rogers on "client-centered" therapy and Abraham Maslow on "humanistic-existential" approaches gradually came to the fore as primary methods employed in outpatient clinics and school counseling services. In time, their views took root as a worthy philosophy not only in clinic centers, but in office practice and hospital settings as well.

BEHAVIOR MODIFICATION

Along with the development of "office psychoanalysis" and "self-actualizing therapy," laboratory scientists were gathering a body of research data on the basic processes of learning and behavior change. It was many years, however, before the early work of Ivan P. Pavlov, Edward L. Thorndike and John B. Watson and the later concepts of Clark Hull and

B. F. Skinner began to be translated into principles applicable to therapy. By the mid-1950's, a variety of "behavior modification" techniques, employing procedures such as reinforcement and extinction and avoiding notions such as "unconscious forces" or "actualizing needs," were devised by men such as O. H. Mowrer, J. Wolpe, H. J. Eysenck and A. Bandura. The emergence of these treatment methods, in contrast to other psychological techniques, grew not out of clinical need and observation, but out of systematic laboratory research. Although less than two decades old, behavior techniques quickly rose to the status of one of the major alternatives of psychological therapy.

The behaviorist's approach to therapy specifies first what behaviors are maladaptive and what behaviors should be reinforced to supplant them. Once the desired changes are specified, a program of environmental experiences and reinforcements to shape the new behavior is devised. These reinforcements are given in the form of words, images or direct experience. By creating imaginary or real parallels to situations which previously had evoked maladaptive responses, these responses are extinguished and new, more adaptive ones learned in their stead. Through this "behavior modification," the individual is "cured" of his disorder.

SOCIAL AND COMMUNITY APPROACHES

The most recent stage in this historical progression has been the emergence of what is termed "the third mental health revolution" — namely, the shift in focus away from the individual patient to that of the social environment within which he lives. Using the "public health" model as its foundation, interest here is directed toward preventive approaches, early identification of problems and attempts to restructure community life so as to make it health-promoting.

Stimulated in the 19th century by the work of Dorothea Dix, a Massachusetts school teacher, the "Mental Hygiene Movement" at the turn of this century became the prime moving force for this community approach. Scientific support for their ideas was drawn from the pioneering studies of sociologists and anthropologists, notably E. Durkheim and A. Kroeber. It took many years, however, well into the 1960's, before serious national efforts were made to act on these ideas. Recent psychological theorists such as G. Caplan and J. Kelly have formulated procedures for analyzing social systems and their health-detracting features. Of even greater significance, they have outlined specific methods, such as "consultation" and "crisis intervention," by which both professionals and non-professionals can implement community changes beneficial to mental health. No less important through this period has been the growth of a variety of *sociotherapies*, among them the "hospital milieu" approach, the many varieties of group therapy and the more recent "family treatment" procedures.

As with many of the therapeutic approaches surveyed briefly above, social and community methods will be presented in greater detail in later chapters.

GOALS AND PROCESS OF BEHAVIOR CHANGE

Two elements comprise the character of therapeutic goals. The first deals with *who* selects the goals, the second refers to *what* these goals are.

The problem of who determines the goals of treatment distinguishes what have been termed "directive" and "nondirective" therapies.

In directive approaches, the therapist, by virtue of his professional knowledge and the patient's emotional state, assumes responsibility for choosing the objectives of treatment; the "doctor" diagnoses what is wrong and guides the patient through what he decides is the best course of action.

In nondirective approaches, the patient decides more or less the steps and aims of the therapeutic process; in fact, it is the patient's increasing capacity to choose his life goals that is considered central to the therapeutic experience. Nondirective therapists intrude minimally into the patient's commentaries and reminiscences; at most, he helps the patient clarify his thoughts and feelings.

Therapists may be distinguished also by the goals they emphasize.

Some therapists focus on extinguishing maladaptive behaviors or relieving abnormal emotions; the aim of treatment is to bring the patient back to *his* normal state rather than to spur him to a "better" way of life. If growth should occur, it is expected to follow of its own accord, once the troublesome symptomatology has been eliminated.

Other therapists exert their primary efforts in the direction of developing new, more effective behaviors, considering the reduction of symptomatology to be of less significance than the acquisition of "better" ways of life. As they view it, current symptoms should fade of their own accord once the patient has gained alternative ways of resolving difficulties and achieving fulfillments.

Few therapists are committed firmly to one *or* another of these divergent goals; however, preference for "symptom extinction" versus "constructive response alternatives" may be noted among different therapies.

Of the several dimensions in which therapies are differentiated, none is more crucial to our understanding than the "process" by which they seek to produce beneficial changes. The major distinction here is between *insight-expressive* and *action-suppressive* processes.

Those inclined to the *insight-expressive* approach maintain that improvement is created by new self-understandings and by the ventilation of highly charged but previously unexpressed emotions. To them, overt behaviors are merely surface phenomena that represent deeply rooted attitudes and feelings which must be understood and discharged. The process of therapy, then, consists of methods to uncover and release these attitudes and feelings. With insight and emotional ventilation achieved, it is expected that the patient will be able to confront life's tasks with equanimity, new powers of rational thinking and rapid personality growth.

Therapists inclined to the *action-suppressive* approach devalue the significance of self-understanding and emotional ventilation. They do not believe that insight is the essence of therapy or that emotional ventilation leads to adaptive changes. Self-understanding and emotional catharsis are viewed at best as adjuncts to the ultimate goal of treatment, that is, producing demonstrable alterations in *real life behaviors*. The principal task of therapy, then, is to produce adaptive *actions* or responses.

CONCLUDING COMMENT

It should be noted, before proceeding to later chapters, that no single treatment method works for all problems. Would it not be shocking if a physician prescribed his favorite remedy for all patients, regardless of the disease or difficulty they suffered? Should it not be equally distressing if a psychotherapist did likewise? Obviously, a wide variety of different abnormalities should call for a variety of different therapies.

The primary reason most approaches to therapy often appear to be equally "good or bad" is that they succeed with only a small proportion of the many varieties of abnormality they set out to treat (Eysenck, 1966; Bergin and Garfield, 1971; Bergin and Strupp, 1972). The probability of success in a varied patient population will be increased, it seems to us, if several approaches, rather than one approach, are employed.

As we review the specific theories and therapies chapters, let us keep in mind that no single approach is sufficient to deal with all types of abnormality. Each theoretical school and therapeutic approach carves out a small slice of this vast complex for its special focus. Let us remember that theories are "inventions" created by man to aid him in understanding nature, and are not realities themselves. Theories and the therapies they generate must fit reality, not the other way around.

Given the limited degree of our current knowledge, there can be no justification for employing one therapeutic technique to the exclusion of others; flexibility in approaches are mandatory. Until data exist to enable us to specify the optimal matching of treatment to problem, we must assume an eclectic approach, employing the best for each case and continuing to experiment with alternative methods.

PART 1

APPROACHES TO ABNORMAL BEHAVIOR AND PERSONALITY

Leonard Baskin—*Betrayal*

2

BEHAVIORAL APPROACHES

INTRODUCTION

Behaviorism originated with the view that subjective introspection was "unscientific" and that it should be replaced by the use of objectively observable behaviors. Further, all environmental influences upon behavior were likewise to be defined objectively. If unobservable processes were thought to exist within the individual, they were to be defined strictly in terms of observables which indicate their existence. Bindra states this position strongly in the following (1959):

> . . . conscious and unconscious wishes, desires, frustrations, anxieties and other motivational entities as the determiners of normal and abnormal behavior, have failed to contribute significantly to the problems of causation or psychopathology. . . . Research on the problems of causation, diagnosis and treatment of behavior disorders should concentrate, not on "psychodynamics" or other hypothetical processes, but on observed behavior. Descriptions of subjective states, not being subject to publicly observable or objective reliability checks, should not be considered as statements about crucial psychopathological events. The aim of diagnostic and research procedures should be the measurement of significant aspects of behavior . . . rather than *ad hoc* variables which appear temporarily to be of some practical significance.

Recent behavior theories of psychological abnormality have used concepts developed originally in experimental learning research. Theorists using these concepts lay claim to the virtues of science since their heritage lies with the objective studies of systematic learning research and not with the dubious methods of clinical speculation. That learning concepts are helpful in understanding abnormalities cannot be denied, but behavior theorists take a stronger position. They state that mental disorder is learned behavior that develops according to the same laws as those governing the development of normal behavior. Disturbed behavior differs from normal behavior only in magnitude, frequency and social adaptiveness. Were these behaviors more adaptive, or less frequent and extreme, they would possess no other distinguishing features.

EARLY VIEWPOINTS

BEGINNINGS OF LEARNING THEORY

The origin of modern learning theory may be traced back to the memory studies of Hermann Ebbinghaus and the "law of effect" idea formulated by Edward Lee Thorndike (1874–1949) at the turn of the twentieth century. Thorndike stressed the signal importance of reward and punishment in learning, formulating his concept succinctly in the following statement (1905):

Any act which in a given situation produces satisfaction becomes associated with that situation, so that when the situation recurs the act is more likely than before to recur also. Conversely, any act which in a given situation produces discomfort becomes dissociated from that situation, so that when the situation recurs the act is less likely than before to recur.

Despite the clarity of Thorndike's statement, it remained for the great Russian physiologist, Ivan Petrovitch Pavlov (1849–1936), to demonstrate experimentally that behavior is modified as a function of learning.

Pavlov's discoveries resulted from an unanticipated observation made during studies of digestive reflexes. In the year 1902, while measuring saliva secreted by dogs in response to food, he noticed that dogs salivated either at the sight of the food dish or upon hearing the footsteps of the attendant who brought it in. Pavlov realized that the stimulus of the dish or the footsteps had become, through experience, a substitute or signal for the stimulus of food. When he presented his findings in 1903 before the fourteenth International Congress of Medicine in Madrid, he coined the term *conditioned reflex* (cr) for the learned response and labeled the learned signal as a *conditioned stimulus* (cs). As his work progressed, Pavlov noted that conditional reflexes persisted over long periods. They could be inhibited briefly by various distractions and completely extinguished by repeated failure to follow the signal or conditioned stimulus with the usual reinforcement.

Pavlov came to realize that words could replace physical stimuli as signals for conditioned learning. He divided human thought into two signal-systems, stating (1928):

Sensations, perceptions and direct impressions of the surrounding world are primary signals of reality. Words are secondary signals. They represent themselves as abstractions of reality and permit generalizations. The human brain is composed of the animal brain, the first signaling system, and the purely human part related to speech, the second signaling system.

Pavlov noted that under emotional distress behavior shifts from the symbols of the second-signal system to the bodily expression of the first signal-system. He also used the concept of the second-signal to show how verbal therapy can influence the underlying first-signal system it represents. Thus, words could alter brain processes in the neurotic individual via persuasion and suggestion. Another of Pavlov's important contributions to psychopathology, his studies of experimentally-produced "neuroses" in animals, was prompted directly by his acquaintance with Freud's writings. In this work, agitation and anger are created in previously cooperative animals by presenting them with conflicting or intense stimuli.

Figure 2-1 Founders of learning theory and behaviorism. A, Edward L. Thorndike. B, John B. Watson. (Photographs A and B from Murchison, C. (ed.): A History of Psychology in Autobiography. Vol. III. Worchester, Massachusetts, Clark University Press, 1936. Reprinted by Russell & Russell, Inc., 1961.) C, Ivan P. Pavlov. (National Library of Medicine, Bethesda, Maryland.)

EMERGENCE OF BEHAVIORISM

In 1913 an American psychologist, John Broadus Watson (1878–1958), proposed a point of view called *behaviorism* which was intended as an antidote to the preoccupation with consciousness and introspection among his contemporaries. To him, consciousness was a subjectively private experience; as such, it failed to meet a major tenet of science that data should be objective or publicly verifiable. Watson became acquainted with the conditioned reflex studies of Pavlov in 1915, and saw quickly that this method could be used to circumvent introspective reports and give him the overt and objective data he sought. From that point, and with each succeeding publication, Watson made the conditioned reflex a central concept in behaviorism. He rejected the physiological orientation of Pavlov, however. He had no interest in the inner structure or processes of the organism, stating that concepts defined at the level of behavior were sufficient to account for all learning processes.

THE BRIDGE TO PATHOLOGY AND THERAPY

Not until the early 1920's were efforts made to demonstrate conditioning procedures in the acquisition of pathological behaviors (Watson and Rayner, 1920; Bagby, 1922; Smith and Guthrie, 1922). Soon thereafter, in 1924, behavior principles were first applied to treatment. Two publications of that year signaled the beginning: the research of Mary Cover Jones and the theoretical notions of William Burnham.

Jones (1924) tried two ways of extinguishing a child's fear of white furry animals. The child, a two and a half year old dubbed Little Peter, was seen to exhibit less fear when he observed other children calmly handling a white rat. By introducing several such "fearless' children as models for Peter to observe, Jones was the first to demonstrate the behavior modification technique of "model imitation." In another study with Peter, Jones progressively exposed the child to a formerly feared white rabbit by a series of graduated steps that brought him into closer and closer contact with the animal; in due course, Peter was able to fondle the rabbit calmly. By following a course of progressive "toleration" of what previously was anxiety-producing, Jones' technique was the forerunner of the behavioral procedure termed "desensitization"

Burnham (1924) "translated" psychoanalysis into learning concepts such as stimulus and reinforcement. Similarly, he proposed a number of behavioral modification procedures which anticipated the techniques developed fully in the 1950's.

By the late 1930's, behavior theories and research had taken firm root. Pavlov's early studies of experimentally induced conflict "neuroses" (1927) had stimulated numerous investigators such as Liddell, Gantt and Maier to explore how pathological behaviors can be conditioned. In 1943, Masserman reported the first of a long series of animal studies employing behavioral procedures to overcome experimentally produced pathologies. Several years earlier, Max (1935) paired an electric shock with evocative stimuli as a method to extinguish homosexual thoughts, and Mowrer and Mowrer (1938) utilized a similar procedure to control night time enuresis. It was during the same decade that Dunlap (1932) proposed a habit extinction procedure termed "negative practice," a forerunner of modern behavior conditioning techniques.

Many academic "learning" psychologists were called upon to perform "clinical" psychological services during World War II. Upon their return to academia, several sought to bridge these two fields and provided thereby a fresh momentum to the behavioral movement. It was hoped that learning principles might furnish a firm scientific basis for therapy and at the same time that clinical processes might provide a new source of data to enrich the rather narrow sphere within which learning research had long been confined.

The first of these "integrative" efforts (Shaw, 1946; Shoben, 1948; Dollard and Miller, 1950) limited themselves to translating therapeutic processes into the language of learning theory. Although the writings of Dollard and Miller were especially influential in suggesting a new way of explaining traditional forms of disorder and therapy, they suggested no new conceptions of abnormality and no new techniques as to how therapy might be executed.

MODERN THEORIES

It was not until the 1950's that several theorists began in earnest to question the entire foundation of abnormal psychology by proposing entirely new concepts for understanding the development and modification of mental disorders. Several researchers, trained initially in the tradition of academic and experimental psychology, proposed that the proper application of behavioral and learning principles should lead the field into a totally new formulation of abnormal psychology. As these views took hold in the early 1960's, three theoretical viewpoints emerged as paramount. Although agreeing in their fundamental allegiance to the philosophy of behaviorism and the "laws" of learning, they stressed different features of their common orientation; it is these differences to which our attention will next be directed.

A   B

Figure 2-2   A, John Dollard; B, Neal Miller.

CLASSICAL CONDITIONING THEORIES

The basic theme of Pavlov's research on learning, referred to as classical conditioning, has been proposed as the key to understanding how abnormal responses are acquired, most notably by Joseph Wolpe (1958, 1973) and Hans J. Eysenck (1965, 1973).

Wolpe and Eysenck propose that mental disorders are learned when intense anxiety becomes associated improperly with various environmental conditions. If anxiety is experienced in situations in which no objective threat exists, the individual will acquire a maladaptive fear response. The following quote illustrates the basic classical conditioning model (Eysenck, 1959):

How, then, does modern learning theory look upon neurosis? In the first place, it would claim that neurotic symptoms are learned patterns of behavior which for some reason or other are inadaptive. The paradigm of neurotic symptom formation would be Watson's famous experiment with little Albert, an eleven months old boy who was fond of animals. By a simple process of classical Pavlovian conditioning. Watson created a phobia for white rats in this boy by standing behind him and making a very loud noise by banging on an iron bar with a hammer whenever Albert reached for the animal. The rat was the conditioned stimulus in the experiment, the loud fear-producing noise was the unconditional stimulus. As predicted, the unconditioned response (fear) became conditioned to the C.S. (the rat), and Albert developed a phobia for white rats, and indeed for all furry animals. This latter feature of the conditioning process is of course familiar to all students as the generalization gradient. . . .

The fear of the rat thus conditioned is unadaptive (because white rats are not in fact dangerous) and hence is considered to be a neurotic symptom; a similarly

Figure 2-3 A, Joseph Wolpe; B, Hans J. Eysenck.

A   B

conditioned fear of snakes would be regarded as adaptive; and hence not neurotic. Yet the mechanism of acquisition is identical in both cases. This suggests that chance and environmental hazards are likely to play an important part in the acquisition of neurotic responses. If a rat happens to be present when the child hears a loud noise, a phobia results; when it is a snake that is present, a useful habit is built up!

As can be seen from the preceding, the essential component of abnormal learning is the simple pairing of a previously neutral stimulus (the rat) with the unconditioned stimulus (loud noise) and its associated fear response. Why does this association persist when it is obviously so maladaptive? According to Eysenck, the learned abnormal response fails to extinguish because the person avoids exposure to the conditioned feared stimulus (e.g., the rat, a dentist, airplanes). By not allowing himself an opportunity to acquire new ways of experiencing and feeling about the stimulus, the originally learned response retains its power, essentially unaltered. The task of therapy, or behavior modification, as it is called, is to provide a series of experiences which will break or modify the learned abnormal connection between the unconditioned stimulus and response. These techniques will be elaborated in later sections of this chapter.

INSTRUMENTAL CONDITIONING THEORIES

By far the major figure of that approach to abnormal behavior termed *instrumental* or *operant* conditioning is B. F. Skinner (1956, 1959, 1973). In contrast to classical conditioning theorists, Skinner contends that most forms of learning are acquired *not* by the simple pairing of an unconditioned stimulus with an established response but by producing or activating new responses or strengthening old responses under conditions of *reinforcement.* For example, a child may note, perhaps by chance, that whenever he runs to his room after a fight with his parents, they finally give in to his wishes (i.e., provide him with a positive reinforcement). As he learns over time that this form of behavior consistently produces the desired effect, we may speak of his having acquired an instrumental act, that is, learned to perform certain behaviors as a means of evoking a desired result.

To Skinner, most forms of "abnormality" simply are acquired instrumental behaviors that society deems by its standards to be pathological

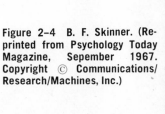

Figure 2–4 B. F. Skinner. (Reprinted from Psychology Today Magazine, Sepember 1967. Copyright © Communications/ Research/Machines, Inc.)

(Skinner, 1973; Ullmann and Krasner, 1965, 1973). One task of therapy is to change the reinforcements a person has achieved when engaging in socially unacceptable behaviors, e.g., not giving in to a child's tantrum and instead rewarding him only when he behaves acceptably. Another task is that of forming new adaptive behaviors in areas that may be deficient through methods of positive reinforcement and shaping, e.g., teaching an overly shy child to relate to others in a step-by-step fashion by providing encouragement and rewards whenever he acts in the desired sociable manner.

Skinner's formulation of abnormality was the first to restrict its concepts entirely to objective behavioral processes, avoiding all reference to internal states such as the unconscious, innate dispositions or conscious thoughts. Hypothetical inner states are discarded and explanations are formulated solely in terms of external sources of stimulation and reinforcement. Environmental reinforcements shape the behavioral repertoire of the individual, and differences between adaptive and maladaptive behaviors can be traced entirely to differences in the reinforcement pattern to which individuals are exposed.

Skinner disavows the necessity for a complex theory, and the simplicity of his formulation reflects his conviction that all behavior — normal or pathological — can be reduced to a few objective principles and concepts. This first "pure" behavior theory has had an impressive beginning in the field of behavior modification therapy; however, further research will be necessary to appraise Skinner's rather simplified formulation of abnormal behavior development.

SOCIAL LEARNING THEORIES

Another variant of the behavioral school is that known generally as the "social learning" approach, most clearly formulated in the work of Julian Rotter (1954, 1966, 1972, 1973) and Albert Bandura (1963, 1968, 1969, 1973).

Rotter, an early follower of Skinner, proposes two concepts as basic to his theory: *behavior potential* and *expectancy*. The first refers to the thesis that behaviors that have most frequently led to positive reinforcements in the past have the greatest potential for occurring again. The second concept is defined as "the probability held by the individual that a partic-

A   B

Figure 2–5   A, Albert Bandura; B, Julian Rotter.

ular reinforcement will occur as a function of a specific behavior on his part". For a particular behavior potential to remain high, the individual must continue to expect that it will lead to positive reinforcement. Katkovsky (1968) outlines Rotter's explanation of the learning of mal-adaptive behavior as follows:

If the behavior is negatively sanctioned by the culture and generally leads to some type of discomfort or punishment, how do we explain the fact that its potential remains high? Should not the individual learn to expect negative consequences rather than rewards for acting in maladjusted ways and therefore become less likely to do so? Apparently this does not happen. The continuation of the behavior indicates that the individual's expectancy for reward for that behavior remains higher than his expectancy for punishment. The problem in understanding maladjusted behavior, then, is to explain why a person subjectively expects to gain some type of satisfaction for a behavior which his culture regards as undesirable and which experience should teach him will lead to negative consequences.

A common, but often overlooked, reason for the existence of maladjusted behavior is that the individual's environment directly encourages it. Sometimes the encouragement is rather blatant, as in the case of a highly dependent and fear-ridden child whose fears are continually reinforced by the fact that his parents respond to them with increased protectiveness, attention, and reluctance to allow him to experience potential dangers. Sometimes the encouragment of malad-justment is very subtle and complex and involves the expectancies, needs, and reactions of important persons in the environment who, without realizing it, are more comfortable if deviant behavior occurs than they would be if it did not occur. Many forms of maladjustment also are positively reinforced by the attention, concern, and special privileges they bring.

In addition to other more traditional notions of how learning occurs, Bandura proposes such concepts as *vicarious conditioning* and *self-reinforcement systems*. The first pertains to the fact that people can learn their pathological attitudes simply by observing the experiences and feelings of others; for example, if a youngster happened to be glancing out the window when he saw a neighborhood dog chasing another child, the observing youngster may learn to fear that dog even though he had no frightening experience with it himself. The second concept refers to the fact that persons reinforce their attitudes and emotions simply by thinking about them. Bandura states this thesis as follows (1968):

Until recently, self-reinforcing behavior has been virtually ignored in psychological theorizing and experimentation, perhaps because of the common preoccupation with animal learning. Unlike human subjects, who continually engage in self-evaluative and self-reinforcing behavior, rats or chimpanzees are disinclined to pat themselves on the back for commendable performances, or to berate themselves for getting lost in cul-de-sacs. By contrast, people typically make self-reinforcement contingent on their performing in ways they have come to value as an index of personal merit. Self-administered positive and negative stimuli may thus serve both as powerful incentives for learning and as effective reinforcers in maintaining behavior in humans.

. . . behavior can become completely controlled by fictional contingencies and fantasied consequences powerful enough to override the influence of the reinforcements available from the social environment.

Bandura and Rotter's use of such behavior learning principles as conditioning and reinforcement has extended the range of these laboratory-derived concepts to include aspects of maladaptive learning that are overlooked by other behavior theorists. However, it should be noted that these principles have been stretched, so to speak, beyond the data of overt behavior to such internal mediating processes as cognitive expectancies, vicarious learnings and self-reinforcing thoughts.

CONCEPTIONS OF THERAPY

As noted earlier, with the exception of a few scattered pioneers, "behavior modification" therapy has risen to the status of a major treatment alternative only in the last fifteen years. There are differences in theory and technique among adherents of this approach, but they share certain important beliefs in common, a few of which will be noted here by way of an introduction.

First, the data emphasized by behaviorists differentiate them from other therapeutic "schools." Behaviorists consider objectively observable actions and events to be the primary subject matter of psychological science: They avoid, where possible, all reference to subjective or unconscious processes which play a central role in other therapies.

Second, behaviorists argue that the procedures of therapy should consist of the systematic application of experimentally derived principles. They avoid "loosely formulated" techniques derived from unverifiable clinical observations which they contend typify other treatment approaches.

Third, behavior therapists subscribe in common to the concepts and methods of learning research. This orientation reflects their desire to adhere to "scientific" principles and their belief that abnormality is learned behavior that is socially maladaptive or deficient. According to this view, whatever has been learned, adaptive or maladaptive, can be "unlearned" by the therapeutic application of the same principles and conditions that led to its initial acquisition.

Fourth, to achieve the goals of treatment, the therapist must first specify both the maladaptive behaviors (overt symptoms) and the environmental conditions (stimuli and reinforcements) that sustain them. Once these have been identified, the therapist can arrange "learning" procedures tailored specifically to the elimination of the maladaptive responses and to the institution of more adaptive ones.

Accordingly, behavior therapists take great care to unburden themselves of all therapeutic activities considered to be peripheral to effective treatment (Kanfer and Phillips, 1970). They make no effort to trace the developmental roots of the patient's problem, considering this historical analysis to be an unnecessary diversion from the task at hand. Similarly, they do not "waste their time" exploring unconscious conflicts or insights since these are considered nonproductive of therapeutic gain. In short, they free themselves of all the time-consuming techniques associated with other treatment procedures, and concentrate exclusively on those basic learning principles which have proved to be scientific.

Behavior therapists arrange their methods in accord with the presenting problem, limiting and focusing their attention to those features only. For example, if the patient complains of a particular fear, procedures are designed to eliminate just that symptom, and therapy is completed when it has been removed.

The planning and procedures of behavior modification typically take the following course.

Explicit Specification of Abnormal Behaviors.   Although patient self-reports are characteristically vague and global, efforts are made to translate these verbal generalities into their precise behavioral correlates. Thus, a general phrase such as "I'm just tense much of the time" is carefully probed until it yields more specific and tangible features such as "chest tightness," "cold, clammy hands," "fear of fainting" and so on.

Explicit Specification of Stimulus Conditions Which Provoke and Reinforce Abnormal Behaviors.   In a similar manner efforts are made to identify precisely the antecedent circumstances that precipitate the disturbed behaviors and the consequent reinforcements that sustain them or cause them to persist.

Explicit Formulation of Treatment Goals and Procedures.   Following these steps the therapist specifies which behaviors and stimulus conditions should and can be altered, and then designs a program of systematic procedures to achieve these well-defined objectives.

In the following sections we will separate behavior therapies on the basis of their primary objectives. The *first* set of approaches, termed "behavior elimination methods," consists of procedures that are limited to, but especially well-suited for, the task of weakening existent pathological responses. The *second* group, labeled "behavior formation techniques," includes procedures that can fulfill several goals; they can be employed not only to eliminate pathological behaviors, but also to strengthen existent adaptive responses and acquire entirely new adaptive ones. Although this two-fold division is not without overlap, it possesses the merit of stressing the utility of methods as instruments for achieving the two primary objectives of behavior modification — the elimination of maladaptive behaviors and the formation or strengthening of adaptive ones.

METHODS OF BEHAVIOR ELIMINATION

The following are the most expedient and direct procedures for eliminating or overcoming maladaptive responses.

DESENSITIZATION

This technique, most fully developed by Joseph Wolpe (1958, 1969), seeks to counteract the discomforting effects of fear-producing stimuli by interposing and associating a relaxation response to these stimuli. Hopefully, by repeated conditioning, the fear response will be replaced by its opposite, relaxation (Bellack, 1973). Not only are the discomforts of fear eliminated thereby, but the patient may now be free to acquire adaptive responses that had previously been blocked.

Wolpe's procedure follows a precise and well-planned sequence.

First, on the basis of interviews and psychological tests, stimulus events that evoke marked emotional discomforts are identified. These events are grouped and ranked into one or more "hierarchies" (a graded list with a common theme ranging from the least to the most disturbing event). It is Wolpe's contention, shared by other behavior therapists, that the typical, vague and inarticulate complaints of patients must and can be differentiated into a set of discriminable responses (e.g., types of fears, fears of varying intensity and so on) to specific stimulus antecedents (e.g., particular scenes, thoughts and memories). On the basis of such discriminations, lists comprising separate classes of fears, differentiated further in terms of intensity, are constructed. Table 2–1 illustrates two fear "hierarchies" devised for a housewife concerned with death and physical illness. The items in each list progress upward from the least to the most distressing.

In the *second* phase of desensitization training, the patient is taught deep muscle relaxation in accord with Jacobson's (1938) progressive body relaxation technique; occasionally, hypnosis or drugs are employed to facilitate a calm state. This period of training proceeds for several sessions until the patient is able to achieve a state of total relaxation rapidly and on his own.

The *third* and central treatment phase consists of pairing the relaxed state with each of the anxiety-producing stimuli on the hierarchy list. This is accomplished by starting with the lowest ranking, that is, the least discomforting item. While the patient feels calm and relaxed, he is asked

TABLE 2–1 TYPICAL DESENSITIZATION HIERARCHIES*	Fear of Death	Fear of Physical Symptoms
	a. Seeing first husband in his coffin	a. Irregular heartbeat
	b. Attending a burial	b. Shooting chest pains
	c. Seeing a burial assemblage from afar	c. Pains in left shoulder and back
	d. Reading an obituary notice of a young person dying of heart attack	d. Pain in top of head
	e. Driving past a cemetery	e. Buzzing in ears
	f. Seeing a funeral	f. Tremor in hands
	g. Passing a funeral home	g. Numbness or pain in fingertips
	h. Reading an obituary notice of an old person	h. Difficulty in breathing after exertion
	i. Being inside a hospital	i. Pain in left hand (old injury)
	j. Seeing a hospital	
	k. Seeing an ambulance	

*From Wolpe (1958)

to imagine a vivid and life-like representation of the stimulus event. Should the patient experience even the slightest degree of anxiety at this time, he signals the therapist who then instructs him to discontinue the image until the relaxed state is regained. When the patient can visualize the stimulus image without experiencing discomfort, the entire sequence of relaxation and imagination is repeated with the next and slightly more disturbing stimulus item from the hierarchy. The procedure continues for as many sessions as necessary until the most distressing stimulus from the list can be visualized calmly.

The logic of Wolpe's procedure is simple and straightforward: relaxation is incompatible with fear; by arranging a properly graded sequence, the previously conditioned association between each stimulus item and the response of fear is eliminated. Wolpe claims with some justification that the relaxed attitude acquired in the consulting room generalizes to real-life situations, that is, the patient is able to face the actual, previously feared environmental event without reacting as he had in the past.

AVERSIVE LEARNING

Whereas desensitization attempts to eliminate responses (e.g., fear) that inhibit desirable behaviors (e.g., facing and solving previously feared situations), aversive learning seeks only to eliminate undesirable responses (e.g., aggressive sexual acts) (Rachman and Teasdale, 1969; Callahan and Leitenberg, 1973). This distinction may be seen more clearly by the fact that desensitization achieves its aims by conditioning an *unpleasant* response (fear) with a pleasant one (relaxation); in contrast, aversive learning conditions a formerly *pleasant* response (drinking or sexual excitement) with an unpleasant one (nausea or pain).

The classic example of aversion therapy is the use of nauseant drugs in the treatment of alcoholism (Lemere and Voegtlin, 1950). In this procedure, the patient first ingests the drug. Then, moments prior to the onset of nausea, he is given a drink of liquor. Since the drink immediately precedes the sickening nausea and vomiting, the patient learns over a number of such sessions to associate drinking with an unpleasant rather than a pleasant experience.

Aversive procedures have been utilized to combat numerous maladaptive habits. For example, male homosexuals have been given a moderately painful shock in conjunction with photographs of nude men; the shock is terminated when a picture of a nude woman replaces that of a man (see Figure 2–6). Hopefully, the patient learns not only to associate feelings of pain with homosexuality, but to view heterosexuality as a comforting alternative (Freund et al., 1973).

IMPLOSIVE THERAPY

This technique is similar to desensitization in that it has as its goal the elimination of inhibitory responses such as fear and anxiety (Barrett, 1969). The procedural steps of these two methods are quite alike also in that the patient's most disturbing thoughts and feelings are identified, and he is asked to imagine them during treatment sessions. In contrast to desensitization, however, the innovator of the implosive technique, Stampfl (London, 1964; Stampfl and Levis, 1967), introduces the *most* anxiety-arousing event immediately, seeking thereby to frighten the patient overwhelmingly rather than to calm and relax him. Stampfl argues

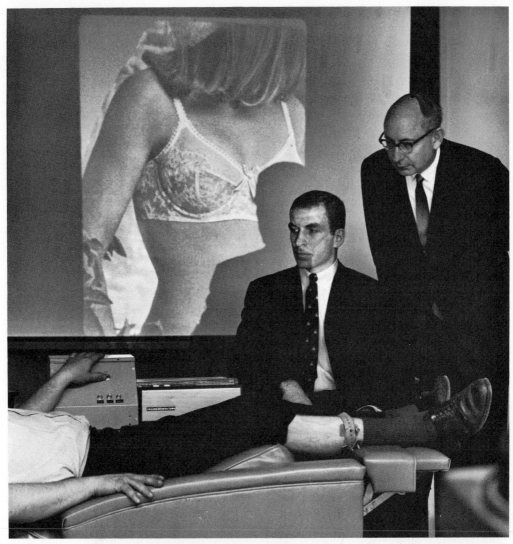

Figure 2–6 Aversive learning. Joseph Wolpe, right, and an associate, administer electric shocks to a homosexual man through an electrode strapped to his calf. When a nude male figure is on the screen, the shocks begin; when a female figure is projected, they cease. The idea is that the homosexual stimulus will be associated with, and eventually inhibited by, the pain. (New York Times Magazine Section, June, 4, 1967, © Bernie Cleff.)

that by flooding the patient's imagination with the very worst of his fears, *in a setting in which no actual harm does occur,* the patient will gradually learn that his fears are unfounded (unreinforced) since nothing really detrimental happens to him. The following outlines a typical sequence in the extinction of a phobia through implosive methods.

A female college student of 19 with a lifelong fear of spiders was introduced to two therapists and given a general idea in her first session of the purpose and procedure of implosive therapy. Returning a few days later for her second session, she was asked to close her eyes and imagine herself in her room alone, suddenly confronted with a spider on her window curtain. Following that, one of the therapists suggested that she visualize seeing several spiders surging rapidly out of a hole in the wall next to the window....

CASE 2–1

Implosive Therapy

Hundreds of them begin to creep over her furniture, around the walls and up the ceiling. She can't escape them—the door is bolted and covered with menacing spiders. One by one, the spiders crawl toward her. The first spider, a particularly large creature, creeps onto her leg—another suddenly lands on her head. Then five, 20, 50, a 100 of them creep all over her—into her eyes, nostrils, up her dress, into her mouth—fat, hairy, monstrous spiders swarming on her body, into her clothes, down her throat, into her vagina, anus, intestines, stomach....

Needless to say, the patient is extremely tense, at her wit's end. Then, suddenly, the patient is "awakened" from her nightmarish vision. The spiders are gone—she's "all right"—nothing, in fact, has happened to her.

Two approaches as contrasting as implosive and desensitization therapy for the same types of problems would be hard to conceive, yet adherents of both methods report substantial success in achieving their common goals.

REINFORCEMENT WITHDRAWAL

Rather than forcing the patient to be flooded and overwhelmed by his disturbing thoughts and feelings as in implosive therapy, the reinforcement withdrawal tactic allows the undesirable behavior to dissipate naturally, simply by failing to provide the reinforcements it previously evoked. In further contrast to implosive therapy, in which the therapist seeks to overcome *inhibiting* responses such as fear, reinforcement withdrawal is most suitable for combating behaviors that *should be inhibited,* such as aggression and compulsive acts. To illustrate, Walton (1960) was able to extinguish a woman's severe habit of scratching her skin by advising her family to refrain from providing sympathy and attention in conjunction with her ailment; withdrawal of these positive reinforcements led to a rapid cessation of the habit. In another study, Williams (1959) achieved the control of bedtime tantrum behavior in a child by advising his parents to pay no attention to him as he cried and raged; by the eighth night, the youngster not only failed to whimper, but even smiled as he quietly went to bed.

METHODS OF BEHAVIOR FORMATION

Until recently, most types of therapy had as their principal goal the elimination of faulty attitudes, feelings and behaviors. It was argued or assumed implicitly that when these symptoms were removed the patient would be "free" to utilize or develop more adaptive habits. Such constructive consequences do follow for many patients, but not all. The notion of "forming" new constructive behaviors by direct procedures is an important departure from more traditional therapeutic methods. Our attention will turn in this section to two behavioral methods employed to achieve the goal of response "formation": *selective positive reinforcement* and *model imitation.* Although acquisition and strengthening of adaptive behaviors are the distinguishing objectives of these procedures, both may be used to eliminate maladaptive responses as well.

SELECTIVE POSITIVE REINFORCEMENT

Changes in behavior must be achieved by manipulating external events, according to this technique. Central to these manipulations are reinforcements, that is, environmental rewards and punishments. By an arrangement of reinforcing consequences, behaviors can be either strengthened or weakened.

The most fully developed schema based on the selective reinforcement model is operant conditioning, a technique devised by B. F. Skinner and his many associates and disciples. Briefly, operant methods provide rewards when the patient exhibits the desired behavior and withhold them when undesired responses occur. Through this selective application of positive reinforcement, present adaptive behaviors are fortified, and through sequences of "successive approximation" and "shaping," new adaptive responses are built into the patient's behavioral repertoire.

The utility of this procedure as a means of restoring social competence and self-reliance among seriously ill patients has been demonstrated in a number of hospital studies. King et al. (1960), for example, reinforced at first simple motor acts in a group of withdrawn "schizophrenics"; gradually, they built these simple responses into more complicated cooperative and communicative behaviors by making the receipt of reinforcement contingent on adequate performance.

Along similar lines, Ayllon and Azrin (1965, 1968) were able to condition self-care and productive work among hospitalized psychotics by making the receipt of desired comforts and privileges contingent on the execution of these behaviors. The investigators noted, as part of their research design, that these same patients quickly abandoned their responsibilities and lapsed into their habitual lethargy and invalidism when these same rewards were made available to them regardless of their performance. Adaptive and productive behaviors were reacquired quickly when special privileges once more were made dependent on self-care and productive performance (see Figure 2–7).

MODEL IMITATION

According to Bandura (1962, 1965, 1969), the primary exponent of behavior modification through imitative modeling, selective positive reinforcement is an exceedingly inefficient method for promoting the acqui-

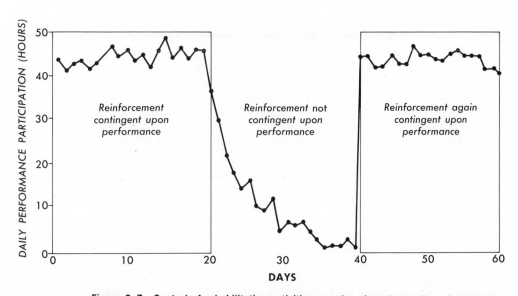

Figure 2–7 Control of rehabilitative activities as a function of selective reinforcement. (After Ayllon, T., and Azrin, N. H.: The measurement and reinforcement of behavior of psychotics. Journal of the Experimental Analysis of Behavior., 8:357–383, 1965. Copyright 1965 by the Society for the Experimental Analysis of Behavior, Inc.

sition of *new* adaptive learnings. Effective though operant procedures may be for strengthening and building upon responses that *already exist* in the patient's behavioral repertoire, they demand extremely ingenious and time-consuming manipulations to generate new response patterns. Contributing to this difficulty is the fact that the patient must perform the desired response or some close approximation of it *before* the therapist can apply the appropriate reinforcement. Where the sought for response is highly complex (e.g., speaking meaningful sentences), the probability is likely to be zero that it will be spontaneously emitted. Approximations of complicated responses may be achieved by an intricate chain of reinforced steps, but this sequence is bound to be both laborious and prolonged. Rather than struggle through this tiresome and at best unreliable procedure, the task of forming *new* responses can be abbreviated and accelerated by arranging conditions in which the patient simply observes and imitates a model performing the desired act. The sheer simplicity of the modeling procedure, Bandura argues, justifies its use in preference to operant methods.

Modeling sequences are designed most often in combination with reinforcement; thus, in a typical procedure, the patient will obtain a reward when he imitates an act performed by a model. To illustrate, Lovaas et al. (1966, 1968) taught "mute" schizophrenic children to talk by rewarding only those vocalizations which duplicated *sounds* articulated first by the therapist. Gradually, rewards were provided only in response to *words* and then to *phrases* modeled by the therapist; ultimately, it was possible to teach the *meaning* of words, as well as a variety of complex communicative skills and social behaviors. Similar effects, generating a wide range of newly acquired responses, have been produced not only with live models, but with models presented through the medium of films (Goldstein et al., 1973). Imitative modeling has also proved efficient and economical in the elimination of inhibitory (fear) and socially undesirable (aggression) responses (Bandura, Grusec and Menlove, 1967; Chittenden, 1942; Kazdin, 1973).

EVALUATION

The techniques of behavior modification have been subjected to more systematic research despite their brief history than all other psychological treatment approaches combined. This reflects, in part, the strong academic-experimental orientation of those who practice behavior therapy; most behaviorists have sought to provide a firm link between the scientific discipline of psychology proper and the applied problems of clinical treatment. Since behavior therapies will continue to be rigorously examined at each stage of their development, it is likely that most of them, once established, will withstand the test of time (Priest, 1972).

Despite the fact that most published studies of behavior therapy represent reports of clinical rather than controlled experimental research, the overall picture that emerges is extremely impressive. More specifically, the effectiveness of methods for eliminating symptom disorders is well documented (Sobell and Sobell, 1973). Similarly, selective reinforcement and imitative modeling techniques have proved suitable for strengthening and forming adaptive social behaviors (Eisler et al., 1973). That these attainments have been achieved rapidly, economically and in the hands of only moderately sophisticated agents (e.g., nurses or attendants) adds further to the value of these methods.

Behavioral approaches have not demonstrated high success with diffuse and pervasive abnormal impairments such as personality patterns, maladaptive coping strategies or "existential crises." Many of these difficult to pinpoint problems appear to resist the sharply focused procedures of behavior therapy. Although advances in treatment methodology may ultimately bring these forms of disturbed functioning within the techniques of behavior therapy, for the present they seem more suitably handled by other treatment approaches.

Paul Delvaux — *The Prisoner*

3 PSYCHOANALYTIC APPROACHES

INTRODUCTION

The position that mental disorders are primarily caused by unconscious conflicts is relatively new, given the long history of abnormal psychology. The patient's chemistry and nervous system function normally, according to this view, but his inner thoughts and feelings are distorted and his behavior is maladaptive. The major theory proposing this position is known as *psychoanalysis*, first formulated by Sigmund Freud (1856–1939).

Psychoanalytic theorists stress the importance of early childhood anxieties since these experiences may dispose the individual to a lifelong pattern of pathological adaptation. Childhood anxieties establish deeply ingrained defensive systems which may lead the individual to react to new situations as if they were duplicates of what occurred in childhood. These anticipatory defenses persist throughout life and result in progressive or chronic disorders.

Psychoanalytic theorists contend that these two determinants of adult behavior, childhood anxieties and defensive maneuvers, are unconscious, that is, cannot be brought to awareness except under unusual conditions. It is the search for these unconscious processes which is the distinguishing feature of their approach. The obscure and elusive phenomena of the unconscious are the data which they uncover and use for their concepts. These data consist first, of repressed childhood anxieties that persist within the individual and attach themselves to ongoing experiences, and second, of unconscious adaptive processes which protect the individual against the resurgence of these anxieties. The *intrapsychic* label often attached to these theorists reflects their common focus on these two elements of the unconscious.

EARLY VIEWPOINTS

DISCOVERY OF UNCONSCIOUS PROCESSES

The origin of the concept of the unconscious—inner thought and feelings beyond immediate awareness—began with the dramatic methods of an Austrian physician, Franz Anton Mesmer (1734–1815). Borrowing Paracelsus' notion of planetary magnetism, Mesmer deduced that illness resulted from an imbalance of universal magnetic fluids. This imbalance, he believed, could be restored either by manipulating magnetic

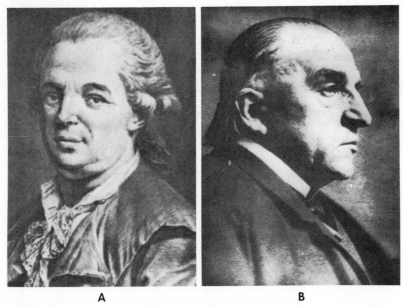

Figure 3-1 A, Franz Anton Mesmer, (Institute for the History of Medicine, Vienna); B, Jean-Martin Charcot (Institute for the History of Medicine, Zurich).

devices or drawing upon invisible magnetic forces from one person to another. Mesmer established a successful therapeutic practice of "animal magnetism" in 1778. Patients grasped iron rods protruding from a *baquet,* a tub containing "magnetic" chemicals, while Mesmer brought fluids into his patients by the wave of his magnetic wand. Despite the naiveté of his theory, Mesmer's patients responded in extraordinary ways, including the "cure" of several "paralyses."

James Braid (1795–1860), an English surgeon, dispelled the notion of magnetic influence and formulated the modern idea that *hypnosis,* the term he coined for Mesmer's method, was a function only of the suggestive power of the physician's gestures and words. In France, A. A. Liebault (1823–1904), a country doctor from Nancy, included hypnosis among the tools of his otherwise conventional practice. He was instrumental in teaching the technique to both Jean Martin Charcot (1825–1893) and Hippolyte-Marie Bernheim (1840–1914).

Charcot began a series of detailed studies of the amazingly diverse and puzzling symptoms of hysteria at the Salpetriére hospital. Because of his neurological orientation, he viewed trances, memory loss and bodily anesthesia as diagnostically difficult cases of nervous system disease. Not until his associates demonstrated that the symptoms of hysteria could be induced by hypnosis did Charcot reconsider his views. Charcot could not forego the biological tradition of his day, however. Thus, he proposed that hysteria was a result of congenital neurological deficiency; hypnosis merely served as a stimulant which revealed this inborn defect.

Bernheim, a psychiatrist in the Nancy Medical School, vigorously disagreed with Charcot. He maintained that hysteria was a state of heightened self-suggestion and that hypnosis was an equivalent state caused by the actions of others. Bernheim advanced the view that hysteria was a purely psychological disorder and coined the term *psychoneurosis* for this and similar symptom patterns.

The study of hysteria was carried on by two distinguished psychiatrists,

Figure 3–2   Charcot demonstrating hypnosis. (The Bettmann Archive, Inc.)

Pierre Janet (1859–1947) and Sigmund Freud. Janet might very well have been considered the most original thinker of psychodynamic psychiatry had he not been overshadowed by the brillant Freud. Both Freud and Janet explored the inner thoughts and feelings of hysteric patients. Janet gradually evolved a theory in which these neuroses were seen to result from an inability to integrate conflicting conscious processes. In his concept of *dissocation*, Janet noted that intolerable thoughts and feelings take on an independent existence within the person and display themselves as amnesia, multiple personality, hysterical fits and paralyses. In this formulation, Janet recognized that different systems of thought could become pathologically separated and lost to consciousness. This observation strengthened the idea that unconscious processes reside within the person. However, Janet's long association with Charcot limited his perspective. Dissociation was viewed to be the result of either a constitutional defect or a temporary but excessive state of fatigue.

DEVELOPMENT OF FREUDIAN PSYCHOANALYSIS

It would not be misleading to say that Sigmund Freud was the most influential psychologist and psychiatrist of the twentieth century. His reinterpretation of the observations first made by Charcot and Bernheim initiated an intellectual revolution. Along with Copernicus, who forced man to accept his peripheral place in the universe, and Darwin, who forced him to accept his nonunique and animalistic origins, Freud forced man to recognize that his rational superiority over other animals was but another of his delusions.

As early as 1880, Joseph Breuer (1842–1925), a well-known Viennese physician, observed that the recall of early traumatic experiences during hypnosis often resulted in therapeutic relief for hysterical patients. Freud first became acquainted with the relationship between hypnosis and hysteria in 1885 and adopted the hypnotic method of Breuer. After an intensive treatment of several cases of hysteria by this technique, Freud and Breuer reported their studies in an article in 1893, and more

Figure 3-3   A, Pierre M. F. Janet. (The Bettmann Archive, Inc.) B, Joseph Breuer.

fully in their epochal book *Studies of Hysteria* published in 1895. They
claimed that painful thoughts and feelings were repressed into an unconscious force which exerted powerful pressures within the patient.
This pressure expressed itself in symptoms which symbolically represented the repressed thoughts and feelings. Intense emotional outbursts
during hypnosis, known as *abreaction*, relieved the unconscious pressure
and, in turn, eliminated the symptom that the pressure had created.

Freud soon found that hypnosis was of limited value. Some patients
could not be hypnotized and symptoms often returned after the hypnotic trance. Freud devised an original technique to meet these problems. The technique, called *free association*, consisted merely of requiring
that the patient speak aloud every thought and feeling, inhibiting
nothing that came to his mind. This method, together with reports of
dreams, provided Freud with all the clinical data he needed to build a
new system of psychology which he named *psychoanalysis*.

As Freud learned to unfold the strategies for self protection and conflict
resolution, such seemingly purposeless behavior as dreams, phobias,
compulsions and even everyday slips of the tongue took on meaning and
clarity. Freud argued that the individual unconsciously adopted extreme
defensive maneuvers to deny, falsify or distort the pain of unfulfilled
strivings and fears.

In his early writings, Freud believed that disorders resulted primarily
from traumatic childhood experience. His later work minimized the importance of trauma and stressed that indulgence or frustration during
any of the crucial early stages of development was the major cause of
disorders. The remnants of these early experiences were deeply imbed-
ded within the unconscious and were not accessible to the modifying influence of changing circumstance. As the pressure of these memories
persisted, the individual anticipated and recreated new experiences similar to those of his childhood. Freud specified different forms of abnormal behavior depending on the intensity and the stage when these difficulties arose first. From this notion he derived such disorders as the
oral and anal characters.

Personality structure was conceived by Freud to consist of three major

Figure 3-4 Sigmund Freud.

components — *id, ego* and *superego* — interacting in dynamic balance (1973).

The *id* represented inborn and unmodifiable instinctual strivings within the individual; these strivings seek expression unmindful of reality. The similarities Freud observed between the instinctual behavior of infants and the expression of adult sexuality led him to speak of infantile strivings as sexual in nature; the sequence through which these early instinctual drives unfolded were termed the *psychosexual stages.* The second component of personality, referred to as the *ego,* represented processes geared to reality adaptations. These processes — judgment, memory, knowledge, anticipation and the unconscious mechanisms of defense — controlled the instinctual drives of the id and directed their expression within the boundaries of practical reality. The third personality structure, the *superego,* consisted of internalized social prohibitions that inhibited instinctual impulses; these took the form of guilt feelings and fears of punishment. Practical compromises between the impulses of the id and the inhibitions of the superego are a primary function of the ego; a failure to reconcile these opposing forces led inevitably to tension and emotional disorder.

Freud's views on therapy followed logically from his theories of personality and its development; replace the unconscious with the conscious, eliminate conflicts generated during the infantile stages of psychosexual development, and overcome imbalances between id and superego by strengthening the resources of the ego. Maladaptive behaviors were eliminated by eliciting memories and developing insights into the past through the techniques of free association and dream analysis; the major goal was the extinction of the patient's disposition to reactivate his childhood difficulties in current life experiences. This was achieved by an analysis of the *transference phenomenon,* that is, the patient's tendency to act toward the therapist with the same attitudes and feelings that he developed in relation to his parents. Through this procedure, the patient became aware of the roots and the persistence of his maladaptive behavior; with these insights, his ego could be reorganized into a more efficient and adaptive pattern.

DEVIATIONS FROM FREUD

Carl Gustav Jung (1875–1961) and Alfred Adler (1870–1937) were among the early and most important disciples to diverge from Freud and to develop theories of their own.

Although chosen by Freud as his heir, Jung could not agree with Freud's emphasis on the "sexual" nature of development, and established his own system of *Analytic Psychology* in 1911. The concept of racial memories, known as the *collective unconscious*, was proposed to suggest that instinctual forces were more than seething animalistic impulses; according to Jung, these forces contained social dispositions as well (1973). These primitive dispositions were often expressed in folklore and mystical beliefs. When no acceptable outlet could be found for them in societal life, they took the form of symptoms such as phobias, delusions and compulsions, Jung's belief in unconscious social dispositions led also to his formulation of two basic personality types, the *extravert* and the *introvert*.

Alfred Adler, founder of the school of *Individual Psychology*, became an outspoken opponent of Freud's views on infantile sexuality at the same time as Jung in 1911. On the basis of his own clinical observations, Adler concluded that superiority and power strivings were more fundamental to pathology than was sexuality. Although many of his patients were not overtly assertive, he observed that their disorder enabled them to dominate others in devious and subtle ways. Phobias, for example, not only excused a patient from disagreeable tasks, but allowed him to control and manipulate others. Adler hypothesized that these strivings for superiority were a consequence of the inevitable and universally experienced weakness and inferiority in early childhood. In this conception, Adler attempted to formulate a universal drive which would serve as an alternative to Freud's universal sexual strivings. According to Adler, basic feelings of inferiority led to persistent compensatory efforts. These were manifested as pathological struggles for power and triumph if the individual experienced unusual deficiencies or weaknesses in childhood. Among healthier personalities, compensation accounted for strivings at self-improvement, and interests in social change and welfare. These compensatory strivings, acquired by all individuals as a reaction to the restrictions imposed by their more powerful parents, led to a general pattern of behavior which Adler called the *style of life*.

Figure 3–5 Early Freudian dissidents. A, Carl G. Jung (National Library of Medicine, Bethesda, Maryland). B, Alfred Adler (The Bettmann Archive, Inc.).

MODERN THEORIES

In the past two or three decades, many revisions have been proposed of Freud's original formulations. These fall into two major groups, the *neo-Freudian social theorists*, led by Karen Horney (1885–1952), Erich Fromm and Harry Stack Sullivan (1892–1949), and the *neo-Freudian ego-theorists*, led by Heinz Hartmann, David Rapaport (1911–1960) and Erik Erikson. Although both groups took issue with Freud's biological orientation, preferring to emphasize social and developmental factors instead, they regarded themselves as renovators rather than deviators from his theories.

NEO-FREUDIAN SOCIAL THEORIES

Horney stressed the fact that the central determinant of pathology is anxiety stemming from the child's feelings of insecurity, isolation and helplessness in a potentially hostile world. Without warmth, encouragement and affection, the child's need for basic security will be adversely affected (1973).

According to Horney, the child attempts, at first, to cope with anxiety by adopting a variety of spontaneous strategies; he may be submissive, hostile, ambitious, avoidant, exploitive, independent or perfectionistic, all at different times. Eventually, one of three basic "character patterns" emerges as dominant: *moving toward people*, as manifested in a search for approval and love, and in compliant and submissive behavior; *moving against people*, as evidenced in struggles for power, and in displays of arrogance, rebellion and hostility; or *moving away from people*, as indicated by social withdrawal or detachment.

Disturbances arise when one of these patterns is adopted to the exclusion of the others. A single dominant character style can resolve anxiety and insecurity only partially; more seriously, an inflexible way of relating to others leads often to a vicious circle that creates anew the very problem the individual sought to prevent. For example, by always putting forth a front of haughty arrogance to avoid rejection, an individual may alienate himself further from others, thereby creating, rather than diminishing, experiences of rejection.

Adherence to a rigid character pattern leads to what Horney calls the *basic conflict*, that is, the individual finds that he cannot relate to others in

Figure 3–6 Karen Horney (National Library of Medicine, Bethesda).

ways that conflict with his ingrained pattern. Since different behaviors are expected of individuals in the course of life's activities, these conflicts are inevitable. For example, a compliant person will experience severe conflict in situations that call for assertion or competition; likewise, an aggressive person will experience marked discomfort when affection and warmth are expressed to him by others.

The basic conflict is avoided by what Horney terms the *idealized self-image*. What this means is that the individual learns to misrepresent his feelings and thoughts by maintaining a fictional image of himself that caricatures his neurotic character pattern. For example, a compliant person will act completely helpless, and an assertive person will exhibit supreme confidence in himself. Unfortunately, as the person struggles to live up to his false image, he drains his energies and deprives himself of potentially satisfying life experiences. And, in time, he becomes alienated from his real feelings, caught in his own web of pretense.

Erich Fromm, a social philosopher and psychologist, was the first of Freud's disciples to concentrate his writings on the role of society in mental disorder. He argued that social conformity forced the individual to relinquish his natural spontaneity and freedom. To Fromm, neurotic behavior is a consequence of insufficient encouragement and warmth from one's parents which could have strengthened the individual against the demands of society. Fromm perceived the goal of therapy to be a bolstering of the individual's capacities for self-responsibility, and not conformist adjustment. Fromm's interest in societal influences led him to modify Freud's psychosexual character types into social character types, such as the "marketing" and "hoarding" characters (1973). Along with similar modifications formulated by Horney, these types depicted contemporary patterns of personality disorder with extraordinary clarity.

Sullivan devised a developmental system based on the role of interpersonal communication, reflecting his belief that the developmental feature which distinguished man from other animals was not his sexual drives but his capacity to communicate with others. Anxiety also plays a central role in Sullivan's theory. However, he did not view anxiety to be a product of instinctual frustration or deprivation, but a direct result of in-

Figure 3–7   Erich Fromm.

terpersonal experiences: they stemmed, first, from relationships with an anxious and malevolent mother and, later, from social ostracism, ridicule or punishment.

To avoid interpersonal threat, children learn which behaviors are rewarded, that is, lead to feelings of security, and which behaviors are punished, that is, lead to anxiety. In time, a complex pattern of self-protective attitudes and behaviors develop, which Sullivan refers to as the *self-system*. This system consists of a variety of measures that produce the rewards of security and avoid the anxieties of insecurity (1973).

Sullivan's concern with the interpersonal aspect of pathology led him to recognize a pathogenic source that had been overlooked by previous theorists: the detrimental effects of normally well-meaning but inconsistent parents. To Sullivan, contradictory or confusing guides for behavior not only produce anxiety, but have the effect of immobilizing the child. Trapped in what has been referred to as a *double-bind*, the child is unable to act in a single and nonconflictful way to others. As a simple illustration, picture the discomfort and indecision experienced by a youngster whose father appears to be in a friendly and jovial mood, but has on numerous previous occasions quickly changed his "tune" and been harshly critical and deprecating; should he extend himself to his father now, hoping to gain the benefits of his cheerful spirits, or should he keep his distance and not chance a repetition of past humiliations?

NEO-FREUDIAN EGO THEORIES

Two major objections to Freud's theories characterize the men to be discussed in this section. First, Freud emphasized a single innate drive within man. These theorists feel that man possesses innate drives other than that of primitive sexuality. Second, Freud believed that man's drives led inevitably to conflict. These men conceived man as possessing innate ego drives which are constructive and which strengthen his adaptation to reality. Thus, the focus has shifted from troublesome sexual and aggressive instincts to an interest in constructive instincts.

To Freud, the ego was conceived as that part of the personality which served to reconcile the drives of the id to reality and to the restrictions of the superego. Ego processes were not inborn but were learned in order to meet the defensive needs of the individual. The neo-Freudian analyst, Heinz Hartmann (1958, 1973), and the psychologist, David Rapaport (1958, 1959), considered this conception of the ego too restrictive.

Figure 3-8   H. S. Sullivan.

Figure 3-9 A, Heinz Hartmann; B, David Rapaport.

In a series of papers published in the 1940's and 1950's, they proposed that the ego possessed inborn capacities which matured independently of the instinctual drives of the id. The *autonomous apparatuses* of the ego, as Hartmann referred to them, were preadapted to handle "average expectable environments." Thus, as the infant matures, a variety of innate capacities progressively unfold, each appearing in time to enable him to deal competently with the tasks and experiences that typically face youngsters of his age (1973).

Rapaport proposed, further, that the maturation of these ego capacities was dependent on a *stimulus nutriment* diet. What he meant by this concept was that these inborn capacities required periodic stimulation in order to develop properly. To Rapaport, social isolation or environmental deprivation led to a decline in the effectiveness of these capacities. For example, if an infant is over-protected by a mother who "does everything for him," he may be deprived of opportunities to exercise his maturing motor skills, and may fail, as a consequence, to develop his inherent physical competencies.

Erik H. Erikson constructed a sequence for the development of the ego which paralleled the stages of psychosexual development formulated by Freud (1950, 1959). Erikson called this developmental sequence the *phases of epigenesis.* As with Hartmann and Rapaport, Erikson believed

Figure 3-10   Erik H. Erikson.

TABLE 3–1
ERIKSON'S EIGHT PHASES OF EPIGENESIS*

Life Phases	Psychosocial Crises	Significant Relations	Psychosocial Modalities and Tasks	Psychosexual Stage (Freudian)
I. Infancy	Trust vs. mistrust	Mother	To get; to give in return	Oral-sensory
II. Early childhood	Autonomy vs. shame and doubt	Parents	To hold (on); to let (go)	Anal-muscular
III. Play age	Initiative vs. guilt	Basic family	To make; to play roles	Genital-locomotor
IV. School age	Industry vs. inferiority	Neighborhood school	To make things; to make them together	Latency
V. Adolescence	Identity vs. identity diffusion	Peer groups and out-groups; models of leadership	To be oneself (or not to be)	Puberty
VI. Young adult	Intimacy and solidarity vs. isolation	Partners in friendship, sex, competition, cooperation	To lose and find oneself in another	Genitality
VII. Adulthood	Generativity vs. self-absorption	Divided labor and shared household	To make be; to care for	
VIII. Mature age	Integrity vs. despair	"Mankind," "my kind"	To be through having been; to face not being	

*Adapted from Erikson, 1959.

that Freud's focus on psychosexuality was too narrowly conceived. He recognized a broader pattern of sensorimotor, cognitive and social capacities in the infant's biological equipment, and proposed the notion of *developmental modes* which represented the unfolding of these genetically endowed capacities. Each of these modes is characterized by a phase specific task to which solutions must be found. Satisfactory solutions prepared the child to progress to the next phase; unsuccessful solutions led to chronic adaptive difficulties.

Eight stages of ego epigenesis were constructed by Erikson; the expressions, interactions and relationships arising during each of these phases of development are presented in Table 3–1. Each phase is associated with a crisis for the individual, a decisive encounter with others which will shape the course of his future development. For example, the oral-sensory stage, or infancy nursing period, determines whether the child will develop trust or mistrust; the struggle over retention and elimination during the anal-muscular stage influences whether the child will emerge with a sense of autonomy or with shame and doubt.

Erikson conceived an innate *mutuality* between the phases of child maturation, on the one hand, and adult phases of development, on the other. He envisioned a mutual regulation, or a *cogwheeling of the life cycles,* such that adult phase specific tasks were innately coordinated to the phase specific needs of the child. For example, infantile helplessness not only elicits a nurturant response from the mother, but fulfills the mother's generative-phase nurturant needs. In all cultures, according to Erikson, the basic timetable of human interaction is determined by this inborn pattern of symbiotic relationships (1973).

CONCEPTIONS OF THERAPY

Despite inevitable differences in emphasis, psychoanalytic therapists share certain beliefs and goals in common that distinguish them from other orientations; two will be noted below.

First, psychoanalytic therapists focus on internal processes that "underlie" overt behavior. Their attention is directed to those inner events that operate at the "unconscious" rather than the conscious level. To them, overt behaviors and conscious reports are merely "surface" expressions of repressed emotions and their associated defensive strategies. "True" change occurs only when the deeply ingrained forces of the unconscious are unearthed and analyzed. The task of therapy, then, is to pierce resistances that cover up these inner elements, bring them into consciousness and rework them into more constructive forms.

Second, psychoanalytic therapists see as their goal the reconstruction of the patient's personality, not the removal of a symptom or the change of attitudes. To extinguish an isolated symptom or to redirect this or that perception, is too limited an aim, one that touches but a mere fraction of a complex pathological system. Wolberg illustrates this philosophy in the following analogy (1967):

A leaky roof can expeditiously be repaired with tar paper and asphalt shingles. This will help not only to keep the rain out, but also ultimately to dry out and to eliminate some of the water damage to the entire house. We have a different set of conditions if we undertake to tear down the structure and to rebuild the dwelling. We will not only have a water-tight roof, but we will have a better house. . . . If our object is merely to keep the rain out of the house, we will do better with the short-term repair focused on the roof, and not bother with the more hazardous, albeit ultimately more substantial reconstruction.

Reconstruction, then, rather than repair is the option chosen by psychoanalytic therapists. They set for themselves the laborious task of rebuilding those functions and structures which comprise the substance of personality, not merely its "facade." As a consequence, most psychoanalytic therapists believe that successful treatment requires the exploration and reworking of the infantile origins of adult abnormalities. This necessitates probing and uncovering the "conflicts" of early instinctual "psychosexual" development and the "neurotic" defenses that the patient has devised to keep them from consciousness. To bring out the reliving of the past, the patient reclines on a couch, faces away from the therapist, becomes immersed in his own reveries and is allowed to wander in his thoughts, undistracted by external promptings. Significant childhood memories and emotions are revived during these "free associations," guided only by the therapist's occasional questions and carefully phrased interpretations; these comments are employed selectively to pierce the patient's defensive resistances to the recall of repressed material.

CLASSICAL PSYCHOANALYSIS

In their joint studies of hysteria, published in 1895, Breuer and Freud concluded that the neurotic symptom represented a repressed painful emotion that had been converted into a symbolic bodily form. They observed that by discharging (abreaction) these repressed emotions during hypnotic sessions, the patient's hysterical symptom frequently and suddenly disappeared. This confirmed, for Freud at least, the notion that hysteria was "bound energy" stemming from a repressed emotion. The technique of its release was referred to as the "cathartic" method.

Freud explored alternative methods by which to achieve the cathartic effect since many of his patients were unreceptive to hypnosis. He soon discovered that comparable results could be obtained simply by having patients consciously recall and ventilate emotions associated with their painful experiences. However, he ran against new complications since many patients seemed unable to bring their memories and feelings into consciousness. To overcome this obstacle, he devised the method of "free association," having the patient relax on a couch and verbalize any thoughts which crossed his mind, no matter how trivial or embarrassing. This procedure circumvented many of the memory blocks that had prevented the recall of significant past events and the discharge of their associated emotions. The following transcript indicates the typical flow of verbalizations in free association; comments noted in parentheses represent unverbalized observations and interpretations by the therapist (Wolberg, 1954).

CASE 3–1

Free Association

Patient So I started walking, and walking, and decided to go behind the museum and walk through Central Park. So I walked and went through a back field and felt very excited and wonderful. I saw a park bench next to a clump of bushes and sat down. There was a rustle behind me and I got frightened. I thought of men concealing themselves in the bushes. I thought of the sex perverts I read about in Central Park. I wondered if there was someone behind me exposing himself. The idea is repulsive, but exciting too. I think of father now and feel excited. I think of an erect penis. This is connected with my father. There is something about this pushing in my mind. I don't know what it is, like on the border of my memory. (pause)

Therapist Mm hmm. (pause) On the border of your memory?

Pt. (The patient breathes rapidly and seems to be under great tension.) As a little girl, I slept with my father. I get a funny feeling. I get a funny feeling over my skin,

Figure 3-11   Classical psychoanalytic procedure.

CASE 3-1
Continued

tingly-like. It's a strange feeling, like a blindness, like not seeing something. My mind blurs and spreads over anything I look at. I've had this feeling off and on since I walked in the park. My mind seems to blank off like I can't think or absorb anything. (This sounds like a manifestation of repression, with inhibition of intellectual functioning, perhaps as a way of coping with the anxiety produced by a return of the repressed.)

Th. The blurring of your mind may be a way of pushing something out you don't want there. (interpreting her symptoms as resistance)

Pt. I just thought of something. When father died, he was nude. I looked at him, but I couldn't see anything, I couldn't think clearly. I was brought up not to be aware of the difference between a man and a woman. I feared my father, and yet I loved him. I slept with him when I was very little, on Saturdays and Sundays. A wonderful sense of warmth and security. There was nothing warmer or more secure. A lot of pleasure. I tingle all over now. It was a wonderful holiday when I was allowed to sleep with father. I can't seem to remember anything now. There's a blur in my mind. I feel tense and afraid.

Th. That blur contaminates your life. You are afraid of something or afraid of remembering something. (focusing on her resistance)

Pt. Yes, yes, but I can't. How can I? How can I?

Th. What comes to your mind?

Freud's search for the past led him next to the discovery of dreams as the "royal road to the unconscious." As he viewed it, repressed fears and desires filtered through the patient's defenses at night, although they took form in various symbolic disguises. By an introspective analysis of his own dreams, Freud was able to present a technique for deciphering the unconscious significance of typical dream symbols. Wolberg (1954) provides the following transcript to demonstrate the character of dream recall, and the insight it often furnishes the patient regarding previously repressed emotions.

CASE 3-2
Dream Recall and Analysis

Patient I dreamt my father was quite ill and I was taking care of him. I don't know what was the matter with him, but he was ill. I guess my sisters were around there somewhere, but I seemed to be feeding him and giving him his medicine. And there's one thing that sticks in my mind — a view of a spoon, an ordinary tablespoon, leaning up against something — in jelly or something along that line, something gelatinous. And I thought I was sort of half awake and I thought: "Well, Jesus Christ what am I doing — what can I say to that dream? it means that I am being my mother; I'm carrying out the functions of my mother, taking care of my father." And this is what I know it means: I have a desire or fear of being homosexual, I'm taking my mother's place. It hit me hard between the eyes and I almost fainted. And the next night I dreamt about a hasp, kind of a lock — you know, the kind where the hasp drops over a part when you drop a padlock into it. And I thought there was something about the hasp, and I thought I'm on this side of it; somebody is on the other side and can't get in, and I can't get over there. I could be turned around the other way. I could be over there, couldn't get in and, he could be here and not get out. It was not in any way a menace or anything like that, but it was that I'm here, and the presence of this hasp keeps him out and keeps me in. I can't get to him and he can't get to me. It's possible that you can turn it around, and the same thing would be true. In other words, it's an equation. (pause)

Therapist   What are your associations to this dream?

Pt.   That is, if I were on the other side, the hasp would prevent me from getting inside. He would be inside, and he would be prevented from getting outside. I just remembered that I had another dream. I dreamed about a man I worked for about the time I got married the second time. I had worked for him once before. He was very fond of me, and I of him. Now I suspect there was a funny component in that relationship. He was, himself, in analysis. We had a lot in common for artistic reasons, philosophic and political reasons. However, in the end he turned out to be a heel. In spite of this guy's glowing promises, and so on and so on, I hadn't been married a month before I was fired. It wasn't his fault; he was just going broke. But the slob didn't even buy me a drink when I got married. This was a pal, wept on my shoulder when his wife left him, and I used to go up there to spend all the evenings with him. When he was very bad I'd stay over, you know, that kind of thing. He was going through what I went through with Anna, only I didn't know it then. You know I'd get flashes — now I know what they mean — that maybe he and I would be better off without women.

The last major feature of what Freud termed his therapy of "psychoanalysis" followed from his observation that patients often expressed totally unwarranted attitudes toward the therapist. Freud noted that these seemingly irrational emotions and thoughts reflected hidden attitudes toward significant persons of the past. This "transference" phenomenon, which illuminated important aspects of the repressed unconscious, could be made easier if the therapist remained a totally neutral object; by assuming this passive role, the therapist "forced" the patient to attribute traits to him drawn from earlier relationships with parents or other significant childhood figures. The transference process is well illustrated in this excerpt; here, a female patient gains insight into the childhood roots of the inability to express aggressive feelings (Wolberg, 1954).

Patient   I want to talk about my feeling about you.

Therapist   Mm hmm.

Pt.   You sit here, a permissive person who lets me go on. I want to do something now, but I'm afraid you will be disappointed in me if I upset the apple cart, if I explode. I think we are too nice to each other. I'm ready not to be nice. My greatest fear of you is that you are potentially going to be severe with me if I let loose. Also, I fear I will let you down by not performing well, by not being nice. I feel I will gain your disapproval. And yet I see you don't condemn and don't criticize. It is still important to me to gain a nod from you or a smile. (pause)

Th.   It sounds as if you would like to let loose with me, but you are afraid of what my response would be. (summarizing and restating)

Pt.   I get so excited by what is happening here. I feel I'm being held back by needing to be nice. I'd like to blast loose sometimes, but I don't dare.

Th.   Because you fear my reaction?

Pt.   The worst thing would be that you wouldn't like me. You wouldn't speak to me friendly; you wouldn't smile; you'd feel you can't treat me and discharge me from treatment. But I know this isn't so, I know it.

Th.   Where do you think these attitudes come from?

Pt.   When I was nine years old, I read a lot about great men in history. I'd quote them and be dramatic. I'd want a sword at my side; I'd dress like an Indian. Mother would scold me. Don't frown, don't talk so much. Sit on your hands, over and over again. I did all kinds of things. I was a naughty child. She told me I'd be hurt. Then at fourteen I fell off a horse and broke my back. I had to be in bed. Mother then told me on the day I went riding not to, that I'd get hurt because the ground was frozen. I was a stubborn, self-willed child. Then I went against her will and suffered an accident that changed my life, a fractured back. Her attitude was, "I told you so." I was put in a cast and kept in bed for months.

CASE 3-3   Th. You were punished, so to speak, by this accident.

Continued   Pt. But I gained attention and love from mother for the first time. I felt so good. I'm ashamed to tell you this. Before I healed I opened the cast and tried to walk to make myself sick again so I could stay in bed longer.

Th. How does that connect up with your impulse to be sick now and stay in bed so much? (The patient has these tendencies, of which she is ashamed.)

Pt. Oh . . . (pause)

Th. What do you think?

Pt. Oh my God, how infantile, how ungrown up, (pause) It must be so. I want people to love me and be sorry for me. Oh, my God. How completely childish. It is, is that. My mother must have ignored me when I was little, and I wanted so to be loved. (This sounds like insight.)

Th. So that it may have been threatening to go back to being self-willed and unloved after you got out of the cast. (interpretation)

Th. Perhaps if you go back to being stubborn with me, you would be returning to how you were before, that is, active, stubborn but unloved.

Pt. (excitedly) And, therefore, losing your love. I need you, but after all you aren't going to reject me. The pattern is so established now that the threat of the loss of love is too overwhelming with everybody, and I've got to keep myself from acting selfish or angry.

To Freud, psychopathology represented the persistence of repressed instinctual drives that had generated severe conflicts during psychosexual development. Not only did the individual expend energies to control these memories, but since the conflicts remained unresolved, they persisted into adulthood and caused the individual to act as if he were living in the past. The task of therapy was to uproot the unconscious and to free potentially constructive energies that had been tied up in the task of keeping it repressed. To do this, Freud employed the procedures of free association, dream interpretation and most importantly, the analysis of the "transference neurosis."

The feature which distinguishes the classical procedure from other methods is the central role given to the resolution of the *transference neurosis*. All psychoanalytic therapists recognize that patients attribute to the therapist attitudes and emotions that derive from past relationships. Classical analysts go one step further; they consider these transference phenomena to represent the essence of the patient's infantile conflicts and pathological essence Accordingly, classical therapists seek to foster the expression of transference materials, revealing not only their current manifestations, but exposing, analyzing and reworking their infantile roots. Unless these origins are thoroughly resolved, treatment is considered incomplete.

CHARACTER ANALYSIS

"Character analysts" pay less heed to matters of the past than they do to the resolution of present difficulties. Moreover, according to these theorists, psychopathology does not arise from conflicts or deficiencies associated with instinctual sources, but from the interpersonal character of early experience. In another deviation from the doctrines of Freud, they assert that adult pathology is not simply a repetition of "nuclear" infantile neuroses. Early experiences are recognized as the basis for later difficulties, but intervening events are thought to modify their impact. Coping behaviors learned early in life promote new difficulties which, in turn, provoke new adaptive strategies. By adulthood, then, important intervening events have occurred, making present behaviors and attitudes far removed from their initial childhood origins. Consequently, "character analysts" consider it wasteful to reconstruct either the infantile neuroses of the id or the adaptive deficiencies of the infantile ego. In their stead, efforts can more fruitfully be expended in uncovering and resolving *current* unconscious attitudes and strategies.

Karen Horney (1937, 1950), although preceded by Alfred Adler and Wilhelm Stekel in this philosophy, was the most successful theorist in pointing out the importance of current life conflicts. As conceived by Horney, neuroses were rooted in infantile anxieties. Stress in childhood led initially to the development of a wide variety of coping behaviors. Ultimately, these early behaviors were narrowed down to a single ingrained "character trait" that became the core of the patient's style. However, a "basic conflict" remained as to which coping behaviors should be employed. To resolve this conflict, the patient repressed the distracting alternatives, and formed an "idealized self-image." This fictional self-concept forced the patient to misrepresent the true variety of his inner feelings and thoughts. In his struggle to retain this false image, the patient's available energies for constructive growth were drained, and he was caught in vicious circles that intensified his difficulties and estranged him further from his "real" self.

Character analysis consists of breaking through the patient's idealized self-image by exposing him to the true variety and contradictory nature of the impulses and attitudes that rage within him. To achieve this, the therapist puts the patient through a self-disillusioning process in which the "neurotic pride" with which he holds his idealized self is shown to be both irrational and self-destructive.

Although face to face discussion is the more typical treatment procedure, free association is often used to uncover the character of the patient's repressed conflicts. Similarly, relevant childhood experiences are probed and unraveled, but not for the purpose of resolving them, as in classical analysis. Rather they are exposed to demonstrate both the foundations of current difficulties and the repetitive sequence of destructive consequences they have caused. The therapist actively interprets the patient's transference distortions, not only in the treatment interaction, but as they are expressed in the patient's everyday relationships with others. The focus on the current ramifications of character trends and the direct mode of attack upon the vicious circles they engender, further distinguish Horney's treatment approach from classical analysis.

TRANSACTIONAL ANALYSIS

A shift from a biological to a more social orientation may be seen as we progress. The classical approach concentrates on the primitive instincts of the id; in character analysis, it is the person as a complete entity rather than that segment associated with his instinctual drives and potentials that is the focus of attention; and in transactional analysis, to be discussed below, the progression continues toward the sociocultural end of the continuum by directing attention to the "roles" assumed by the patient in societal groups.

Employing patient-therapist communications as their data and drawing their models from social role theorists such as Mead (1934), a number of recent therapists have formulated approaches to treatment that they depict by the label "transactional analysis." Eric Berne (1961; 1964) is perhaps the best known of these men, due largely to the witty and

Figure 3–12   Eric Berne (Grove Press).

phrase-making character of his popular works. We shall summarize Berne's ideas to illustrate the transactional approach.

According to Berne, patient-therapist interactions provide insight into the patient's characteristic interpersonal maneuvers and mirror the several varieties of his everyday social behaviors. These maneuvers are translated into caricature forms known as "pastimes" or "games," each of which highlights an unconscious strategy of the patient to defend against "childish" anxieties or to secure other equally immature rewards. This analytical process is akin to that contained in the analysis of transference phenomena, although Berne dramatizes these operations by tagging them with rather clever and humorous labels (e.g., "schlemiel," "ain't it wonderful" or "do me something").

Berne contends, as did Horney, that contradictory character trends coexist within the patient; however, in contrast to Horney, no single trend or "ego state" as Berne puts it, achieves dominance. Rather, these ego states are fluid, with one or another coming to the fore depending on the nature of the social maneuvers of others. Three ego states may be elicited as a consequence of these reciprocal maneuvers or "transactions": archaic or infantile behaviors, known as the *child* state within the patient; attitudes reflecting his parent's orientation, termed the *parent* ego state; and mature qualities the patient has acquired throughout life, termed the *adult* state.

The unconscious attitudes and strategies of these conflicting ego states are exposed and interpreted in transactional analyses. In order to promote insight into the patient's more immature maneuvers, the therapist allows his own parent, child and adult states to transact with those of the patient. This procedure strengthens the patient's adult state since it serves to teach him to withstand manipulations by others that formerly evoked his child and parent trends. As a consequence of these therapeutic transactions, the patient gains insight into the foolish "games" he "plays" in current relationships, and reinforces those skills and attitudes that comprise his mature adult state.

EVALUATION

Psychoanalytic therapists contend that treatment approaches designed "merely" to reduce behavioral symptoms and complaints fail to deal with the root source of pathology and are bound therefore to be short-lived. Reworking the source of the problem rather than controlling its effects is what distinguishes psychoanalytic therapy as a treatment procedure. Once the unconscious roots of the impairment are dislodged, the patient will no longer create new difficulties for himself and will be free to develop strategies that are consonant with his healthy potentials.

No one can question the goals of psychoanalytic therapy; they are highly commendable, if difficult to achieve. It is not the goals which are viewed critically; rather, dissent arises with regard to the theoretical rationale, technique and feasibility of these methods. Let us note several of the objections.

First, and perhaps the most persistent criticism, is the assertion that unconscious data are both vague and inaccessible. Therapists are expected to manipulate "metaphysical" entities whose very existence is unverifiable and whose modification can never be confirmed. Exerting efforts to alter these unobservable processes is considered nothing less than foolishness, and claiming success in such ventures is nothing but an article of faith. In short, dealing with matters of the unconscious is a throwback to the days when mysticism flourished, a continuation of a prescientific way of thinking from which abnormal psychology must be liberated.

Second. The process of psychoanalytic treatment is considered unnecessarily involved and digressive, dredging up facts and events which are irrelevant to the nature of the patient's problem. Rather than focusing directly on the difficulty, as do therapists of other schools, the psychoanalytic therapist pursues a host of activities that turn the patient's attention to his past, his unconscious mechanisms and his "deeper" motivations. Such pathways to the resolution of pathology are seen as wasteful and time consuming.

Third, even if psychoanalytic therapies were shown to be successful, few patients are able to devote the time or expend the funds required to pursue a full course of treatment. Most analytical techniques demand at least three or four sessions per week over a two to five year span. Assuming treatment was feasible on these accounts, problems would arise since there are too few trained therapists to make this approach available to the masses. In short, psychoanalytic therapies must be relegated to a secondary position among treatment techniques on wholly practical grounds, if on no other.

Pablo Picasso — *Seated Woman*

4 PHENOMENOLOGICAL APPROACHES

INTRODUCTION

The major distinction between the psychoanalytic and phenomenological schools of thought lies in their respective emphasis upon unconscious versus conscious processes. Psychoanalytic theorists believe that the most important aspects of functioning are those factors which a person cannot or will not say about himself. In contrast, phenomenologists believe that the person's introspective reports, taken at their face value, are most significant.

Phenomenologists stress that the individual reacts to the world only in terms of his unique perception of it. No matter how transformed or unconsciously distorted it may be, it is the person's way of perceiving events which determines his behavior. Concepts and propositions must be formulated, therefore, not in terms of objective realities or unconscious processes, but in accordance with how events actually are perceived by the individual; concepts must not disassemble these subjective experiences into depersonalized or abstract categories.

According to most phenomenologists, disorder arises when the individual's own needs conflict with values imposed upon him by others. Thus, disorder is an estrangement from self, an inconsistency between attitudes the person feels are right but which others have told him are wrong. For example, a young man may have been taught to think that masturbation is bad, but his body senses pleasure and gratification in it. The inconsistency between what is phenomenologically felt to be right, and the judgments of others creates an internal discord. This inner disharmony, in turn, leads to anxiety, and anxiety produces defensive reactions which alienate the person further from his "natural" feelings. By adopting social evaluations that deny or distort his natural feelings, the individual experiences a sense of inner emptiness and purposelessness.

EARLY VIEWPOINTS

PHILOSOPHICAL ORIGINS

The foundation for the modern movements of both existentialism and phenomenology may be traced to the writings of several European philosophers, most notably Edmund Husserl (1856–1938), Soren Kierkegaard (1813–1855), Martin Heidegger and Jean-Paul Sartre.

Husserl, who may be viewed as the father of phenomenology, stressed a simple research principle, that of viewing events from a totally unbiased approach. In what he termed the *epoche* method of observation, all phenomena of life were to be contemplated free from any judgment of value or intellectual consideration. Simple, and perhaps as naive as this viewpoint might be, it served to stimulate a wealth of psychological studies, particularly the work of the introspectionists who dominated American and German research early this century.

Kierkegaard stressed another aspect of what has come to characterize the existential-phenomenological approach. In his numerous essays, Kierkegaard contended that man becomes what he makes of himself. This he does through a series of choices, most particularly the choice between an *inauthentic* and an *authentic* modality of existence. Inauthentic choices are those in which the person allows himself to be shaped by the "tyranny of the plebs," that is, by the demands and expectations of others. Authentic existence, by contrast, is that choice in which the person assumes full responsibility for his own fate and existence. It was Kierkegaard's belief that all men must suffer the ordeal of "existential anxiety"; this occurs when he struggles to free himself from an inauthentic existence and faces the awesome responsibilities for self that are required to achieve authenticity.

Heidegger, and later Sartre, sought to bridge the views of Husserl and Kierkegaard by focusing on the theme that each man must approach experience on his own terms, to contemplate the events of his life from his unique personal perspective and make choices for the direction of his future on that basis as well.

EMERGENCE OF EXISTENTIAL PSYCHIATRY

Between the first and second World Wars, numerous European psychiatrists were stimulated by the philosophical writings of the phenomenologists and began to approach their patients from this frame of refer-

Figure 4–1 A, Sören Kierkegaard; B, Jean Paul Sartre.

A   B

Figure 4-2 (Cartoon by Herbert Goldberg. Copyright 1969 Saturday Review Co. First appeared in Saturday Review, March 1, 1969. Used with permission.)

"Try not to think of this as a traumatic experience— think of it as an unforgettable existential moment."

SR/March 1, 1969

ence. Among the more notable of these were Karl Jaspers, Eugene Minkowski and Ludwig Binswanger.

Jaspers, a well-known psychological theorist (1913) as well as philosopher, adopted the phenomenological method in his studies of patients. He sought to describe as accurately as possible the subjective experiences of his mentally disturbed patients and to sense and empathize as closely as he could with them. In contrast with the psychoanalysts, who attempted to probe "beneath the surface" of a patient's verbal reports so as to uncover their unconscious roots, Jaspers focused on the patient's conscious self-description of his feelings and experiences, believing that the patient's phenomenological reports were the best source to achieve a true understanding of the world of the abnormal.

Following similar lines, Minkowski attempted to examine the subjective experiences of his patients in the hope of deducing repetitive themes and connections. In what he termed *structural analysis,* he sought to identify the *basic disturbance* of each major syndrome. Thus, in depressed patients he believed that the experience of time lacked a forward direction. Hence, the basic disturbance in this syndrome was a blocking of the capacity to think about and anticipate the future, with a consequent loss of hope for growth or change.

Binswanger (1973) formulated his notions in a series of books and papers published over a 40-year period. In what he termed the theory of "existential analysis," he states that progress and growth depend on a balance among three modes of experience: the *Unwelt,* signifying the world of biological energies and physical reality: the *Mitwelt,* representing the world of other people; and the *Eigenwelt,* or the inner world of phenomenological experience. Mental health results when the individual can come to terms with all three; disorder results when he fails to do so.

Disorder, according to Binswanger's thesis, reflects more than an inability to fulfill biological urges, as Freud stressed, or to establish significant

A   B

Figure 4–3   A, Karl Jaspers; B, Ludwig Binswanger.

interpersonal relationships, as Sullivan and Horney stressed. Pleasure, interpersonal security, even survival itself, are viewed as subsidiary to the need to relate to self, that is, to the *Eigenwelt*. Without self, the individual lacks an identity and cannot experience what is termed *being-in-the-world*.

MODERN THEORIES

EXISTENTIAL THEORY

The ideas described above, originally formulated by early European philosophers and psychiatrists, have been adopted with minor variations by a number of contemporary psychologists, perhaps the best known of which are Viktor Frankl, Ronald Laing and Rollo May.

Frankl drew upon his own personal suffering in concentration camps during the second World War as the basis of his particular views of existentialism (1962, 1973). Expanding on Kierkegaard's views of the previous century, Frankl stressed man's responsibility for choosing his own values in life. He focused on the concept *will to meaning* as the central motive for existence. To him, each person must find a set of "creative, experiential and attitudinal" values that are consonant with his individuality; without such personal values, man will experience "existential frustration and neurosis."

Although similar in outlook to Frankl, who concerned himself primarily with neurotic disorders, Laing (1967, 1973), a British theorist, directed his attention to the more severe pathologies of schizophrenia. As with others of the existential persuasion, Laing considers the primary problem to be one in which the patient has denied his own values and has

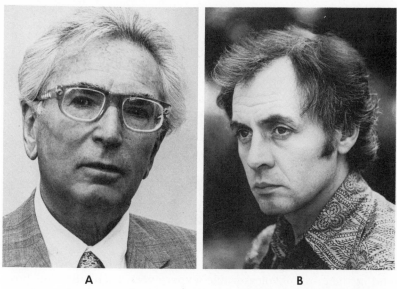

A   B

Figure 4–4 A, Viktor Frankl; B, Ronald Laing.

submerged his very being in an effort to live by the rules of others (Gordon, 1971). Failing to relate meaningfully to himself, the individual cannot satisfy his instinctual drives and cannot establish satisfying relationships with others. Unable to sense his own inner world, he cannot sense the inner world of others, and without meaningful social interaction, he cannot break the vicious circle to expand experience and develop a sense of identity. As this circle continues, he experiences an *ontological anxiety*, that is, a frightening estrangement from self. This anxiety further isolates him from others and makes him incapable of acting in ways which could alter his existence. Eventually, he succumbs to *nothingness*.

Rollo May (1958, 1969, 1973), an American psychologist, although differing from Frankl and Laing on details, agrees that psychological abnormality results from man's estrangement from self. He agrees further that man's capacity for conscious awareness enables him to make choices and to control his existence; man has a unique power to transform events to suit his needs and to create his own distinctive world. The decisions he makes determine whether or not he will progress toward the fulfillment of his inner potentials.

SELF THEORY

There are many commonalities among the ideas of the existentialists and those of the American psychologist, Carl Rogers (1959). However, Rogers is optimistic about man's capacity to fulfill himself, whereas the existentialists express a tragic and pessimistic attitude. To Rogers, man is disposed naturally to be kindly, self-accepting and socially productive. Only if this innate potential is restricted, and feelings of personal worth damaged, will he become ineffective, antagonistic and disturbed.

The principal features of Rogers' theory may be summarized as follows: Every individual is the center of a changing world of experience. Experience is understood only in terms of the individual's perception of his life; thus, Rogers opts explicitly for the phenomenological approach.

Figure 4-5 Carl Rogers.

Rogers proposes that man is motivated by a single basic drive, that of extending the range of "pleasurable" experiences. Each individual possesses an innate potential for these experiences and is motivated by a *self-actualizing tendency* to develop and exercise them. This self-actualizing tendency is guided by an *innate valuing process,* that is, an inborn capacity to judge which experiences "feel right" for him and which do not. If the individual develops according to his inherent self-actualizing tendency he will mature as a healthy and well-integrated adult.

When the individual replaces his innate valuing process with the values of others, he has acquired what Rogers refers to as the *need for self-regard.* This second system for appraising experience may supplant or repress his natural valuing process. As a consequence, he will no longer judge his experiences in terms of his own senses, but will use a set of socially learned criteria. Should these conflict with his innate criteria, he will suffer anxiety and threat.

Anxieties often lead to further difficulty, according to Rogers, since they restrict the person's freedom of action and gratification. Thus, he is not only trapped now by the split between his innate judgments and those of others, but because of his anxieties he may be incapable of finding solutions to his dilemma. For example, many young girls who had been cautioned about the "sins" of sex, experience intense anxieties when they wish to express their rather natural affectionate feelings toward boys. The confusion and anguish they experience only complicates their conflict, and therefore decreases the likelihood that they will resolve the problem satisfactorily.

Two major strategies are employed, according to Rogers, to decrease dissonance and anxiety: *denial,* which consists of ignoring the contradictions between self and social judgments, and *distortion,* which refers to the process by which the contradictions are misinterpreted or falsified so as to make them appear consonant. Should these strategies fail, the person's self-structure will *break down* or become *disorganized,* that is, his behavior will become increasingly erratic and unpredictable.

HUMANISTIC THEORY

As with Rogers and self theory, one man stands out as the primary exponent of humanistic theory: Abraham Maslow (1908–1970). Maslow's

Figure 4-6 Abraham Maslow.

views are similar to Rogers in that both assume that man is inherently good and is motivated to "actualize" this potential; this he would do were it not for the frustrations and distortions imposed upon him by destructive experiences and social values (1973).

In contrast with most of his colleagues, Maslow chose to study not the troubled and emotionally ill, but the healthy and creative. He believed strongly that our present view of personality was limited and negatively oriented because psychologists were preoccupied with the pathological; as an antidote, Maslow directed his efforts to an understanding of the more virtuous and attractive aspects of man, his creativity, love and joy (1962, 1971).

In line with his focus on the constructive potentials of man, Maslow found it necessary to study also those aspects of life which dampened and undermined their development. Thus, he believed that children who experienced intense anxieties while seeking to meet such *basic needs* as hunger, affection, security and self-esteem could not turn their energies to fulfill such *metaneeds* as justice, beauty and goodness.

Trapped throughout life in a search for basic needs, these persons are unable to free themselves to achieve their mature potentials. In other cases, there is an unwillingness to chance seeking self growth for fear of losing what security and safety has been attained. And others forego efforts to actualize themselves because they have been frightened or forced to follow the values and dictates of the non-humanistic society in which they live. Unable to develop in accord with their own nature, each of these persons ultimately becomes disenchanted, alienated, cynical and deeply unfulfilled. It is this state of "nonbeing" that Maslow views to be the essence of psychological abnormality.

CONCEPTIONS OF THERAPY

There are few bonds of strength among phenomenological therapists equal to those that hold the psychoanalysts or the behaviorists together. Phenomenologically oriented therapists inherit their views from widely divergent sources; some are offshoots of psychoanalysis; others are strongly influenced by one or another learning theory; many derive their impetus from existential philosophies.

There are two factors, however, which phenomenological therapists exhibit in common, and which set them apart from other schools.

First, in contrast to behaviorists and in common with psychoanalytic therapists, phenomenologists place heavy emphasis on internal processes that underlie overt actions. Behaviors are viewed to be but "surface" derivations of *internal* dispositions.

Second, in contrast to behaviorists *and* psychoanalysts, phenomenologists concern themselves with the data of *conscious perceptions and attitudes,* believing that these cognitive processes are crucial to both the development and perpetuation of abnormal behavior. Therapy, then, is directed to the reorientation of consciously disturbing feelings and erroneous beliefs, and not to the modification of behaviors or to unconscious forces.

Phenomenologists consider "depth" probing to be both unnecessary and time consuming. They believe that a reorientation of the patient's conscious assumptions and feelings, without exploring their historical origins or dissolving their unconscious roots, will more than suffice to enable him to resolve his difficulties and find a more constructive way of life.

Phenomenological therapists employ the face to face discussion interview as their principal treatment format. Despite important differences in patient-therapist interaction styles and treatment goals, the sequence and content of the therapeutic process are essentially the same; these may be subdivided into the following five steps.

Establishing Rapport. An important part of all therapies, especially face to face interview procedures, is the patient's feeling of comfort and trust in his therapist. This is achieved by providing a congenial treatment atmosphere and by the therapist's genuine concern for the patient's well-being and respect for his potential as a valued person.

Exploration of Thoughts and Feelings. By word and gesture, the therapist conveys to the patient that he can express his concerns, knowing that they will be fully accepted and sympathetically understood. At this stage of treatment, the therapist serves as an interested listener whose efforts are limited to encouraging the patient to explore any thoughts and feelings related to this difficulty. At most, the therapist will act to prompt the flow of ideas or interrupt the patient's discourse to have a point clarified or elaborated.

Selective Focusing. Once the "clinical picture" takes shape in the therapist's mind, he attempts to orient the patient to certain core themes whose further exploration is considered essential to treatment progress. Selective focusing may be achieved in several ways: by pointed questioning, by reflecting or rephrasing certain of the patient's "passing comments" and by planning discussion topics prior to sessions.

Developing Insight. Therapists have at their disposal a number of maneuvers by which they assist the patient to translate his reflections into crystallized formulations called "insight"; which of these maneuvers are emphasized depends on the therapist's "school" of treatment. Some guide the patient gently and indirectly by bringing his attention to certain themes time and again until their significance and meaning gradually unfold. Others facilitate insight by providing tentative interpretations that "suggest" connections between events that seem unrelated in the patient's eyes. Still others are direct, bringing the "reasons" for his difficulties clearly and forcefully to the patient's attention.

Promoting Constructive Alternatives. As insight develops, the patient begins to recognize the possibility that he can assume attitudes and employ strategies that are different than those of his past. However, awareness of these possibilities is not often sufficient in itself to motivate change. To promote change, some therapists assure the patient that these new alternative behaviors are both reasonable and feasible, leaving it entirely to him, however, to decide if and when he will carry them out. Other therapists take a more vigorous role, exhorting the patient to stop dallying, to "get on the ball" and initiate some positive action.

Differences arise among phenomenologists as to the style or manner of the therapist-patient interaction, and whether the therapist or the patient determines the goals of treatment. On the basis of these two elements of the therapeutic relationship, we find sufficient divergences to categorize three variants of the phenomenological approach: self-actualization, confrontation-directive and cognitive-learning.

SELF-ACTUALIZATION METHODS

The chief goal of treatment, according to this approach, is not to understand the causes or to remove the symptoms of psychopathology, but to "free" the patient to develop a confident image of his self-worth. This will enable him to explore and test his own values in the world, unconstrained by the conventions of mass society. Liberated in this manner, the patient will learn to act in ways that are "right" for him, and thereby "actualize" his inherent potentials. Two "schools" of phenomenological therapy stress the goal of self-actualization — the *client-centered* and the *existential* approaches.

CLIENT-CENTERED THERAPY

Carl Rogers (1942, 1951, 1961, 1967) developed the notion of "client-centered" therapy most clearly and effectively. According to Rogers, patient "growth" is a product neither of special treatment procedures nor professional know-how; rather, it emerges from the quality and character of the therapeutic relationship. More specifically, it occurs as a consequence of certain attitudes of the therapist, notably his: *genuineness*, that is, his ability to "be himself" in therapy and to express his feelings and thoughts without pretensions or the cloak of professional authority; *unconditional positive regard*, that is, his capacity to feel respect for the patient as a worthy being, no matter how unappealing and destructive his behaviors may be; and *accurate empathic understanding*, that is, his sensitivity to the patient's subjective world, and his ability to communicate this awareness to the patient.

In line with these three attitudes, the patient assumes full responsibility for the subject and goals of therapeutic discussion; the therapist reflects rather than interprets the patient's thoughts and feelings and encourages, but does not recommend, efforts toward growth and individual expression. The nondirective therapist's willingness to allow the patient to determine his own goals is nicely illustrated in the following (Rogers, 1951).

CASE 4–1

Client-centered Therapy

S (Subject or Client): I've never said this before to anyone — but I've thought for such a long time — This is a terrible thing to say, but if I could just — well (short, bitter laugh; pause), if I could just find some glorious cause that I could give my life for I would be happy. I cannot be the kind of a person I want to be. I guess maybe I haven't the guts — or the strength — or I would be in an accident — I — I — just don't want to live.

C (Counselor):   At the present time things look so black to you that you can't see much point in living —

S: Yes — I wish I'd never started this therapy. I was happy when I was living in my dream world. There I could be the kind of person I wanted to be — But now — There is such a wide, wide gap — between my ideal — and what I am. I wish people hated me. I try to make them hate me. Because then I could turn away from them and could blame them — but no — It is all in my hands — Here is my life — and I either accept the fact that I am absolutely worthless — or I fight whatever it is that holds me in this terrible conflict. And I suppose if I accepted the fact that I am worthless, then I could go away someplace — and get a little room someplace — get a mechanical job someplace — and retreat clear back to the security of my dream world where I could do things, have clever friends, be a pretty wonderful sort of person —

C: It's really a tough struggle — digging into this like you are — and at times the shelter of your dream world looks more attractive and comfortable.

S: My dream world or suicide.

C: Your dream world or something more permanent than dreams —

S: Yes. (A long pause. Complete change of voice.) So I don't see why I should waste your time — coming in twice a week — I'm not worth it — What do you think?

C: It's up to you, Gil — It isn't wasting my time — I'd be glad to see you — whenever you come — but it's how you feel about it — if you don't want to come twice a week — or if you do want to come twice a week? — once a week? — It's up to you. (Long pause.)

S: You're not going to suggest that I come in oftener? You're not alarmed and I think I ought to come in — every day — until I get out of this?

C: I believe you are able to make your own decision. I'll see you whenever you want to come.

S: (Note of awe in her voice.) I don't believe you are alarmed about — I see — I may be afraid of myself — but you aren't afraid of me — (She stands up — a strange look on her face.)

C: You say you may be afraid of yourself — and are wondering why I don't seem to be afraid for you?

S: (Another short laugh.) You have more confidence in me than I have....I'll see you next week — (That short laugh) maybe. (Her attitude seemed tense, depressed, bitter, completely beaten. She walked slowly away.)

Self-actualization unfolds gradually. We may condense the several stages of this progression into two broad phases. First, the patient, sensing the therapist's complete and unshakable belief in his worth, begins to value himself, as well. Second, as he adopts this new self-image, he is increasingly willing to test, in reality, behaviors that are in keeping with his "true" feelings, without fear of censure and humiliation; hence, he begins to "actualize himself."

EXISTENTIAL THERAPY

Therapists of this persuasion are committed to the view that man must confront and accept the inevitable dilemmas of life if he is to achieve a measure of "authentic" self-realization. As noted earlier in the chapter, themes such as these were first formulated in the philosophical writings of Kierkegaard, Nietzsche, Husserl, Heidegger and, more recently, in

A B

Figure 4–7 A, Rollo May; B, Medard Boss.

those of Jaspers, Buber, Sartre and Tillich. From these sources also, may be traced the foundations of existential therapy, notably those advanced by Ludwig Binswanger (1942, 1947, 1956), Medard Boss (1957, 1963), Viktor Frankl (1955, 1965) and Rollo May (1958, 1963). Despite differences in terminology and philosophical emphasis, these existential variants are very similar insofar as their approach to therapy.

Important to all existential therapists is the "being-together encounter" between patient and therapist. This encounter, characterized by mutual acceptance and self-revelation, enables the patient to find an authentic meaning to his existence, despite the profound and inescapable contradictions that life presents. The focus both in *logo-therapy* (Frankl) and *daseinsanalyse* (Binswanger and Boss), the two major variants of existential treatment, is to utilize the insoluble predicaments and suffering of life as a way of discovering self-meaning and purpose. By facing the "inevitable" with equanimity, the patient rises above petty frustrations and discovers the fundamentals upon which his genuine self can unfold.

CONFRONTATION-DIRECTIVE PROCEDURES

The philosophy underlying confrontation-directive procedures contrasts sharply with that of self-actualization methods. Patients are viewed to be inept, irresponsible or sick, and therefore unwilling or unable to choose the course they must take for their own well-being. The therapist not only assumes full authority for deciding the objectives of treatment, but confronts the patient with the irrationalities of his thinking; moreover, he employs commanding tactics to indoctrinate the patient with a value system that is considered universally beneficial.

In the mid-1940's, Thorne (1944, 1948), viewing the growth of what he considered to be the narrow-minded and sentimentalistic practices of nondirective client-centered therapy, proposed an approach that revived modern confrontation-directive procedures. Thorne induced conflicts deliberately by confronting the patient with his contradictory and self-defeating attitudes. Provoked in this manner, the patient was forced to examine his destructive habits and to explore more adaptive alternatives.

Two features distinguish confrontation-directive approaches from other phenomenological procedures: the practice of "forcefully" exposing the patient's erroneous or irrational attitudes and "imposing" a particular philosophy of life in its stead. Of interest in this regard are the diametrically opposite philosophies espoused by the two approaches to be next discussed.

RATIONAL-EMOTIVE THERAPY

This approach has been most clearly formulated by Ellis (1958, 1962, 1967, 1973), although its origins may be traced to the writings of Alfred Adler. Ellis considers the primary objective of therapy to be countering the patient's tendency to perpetuate his difficulties through illogical and negative thinking. The patient, by reiterating these unrealistic and self-defeating beliefs in a self-dialogue, constantly reaffirms his irrationality and perpetuates his distress. To overcome these implicit but pervasive attitudes, the therapist confronts the patient with them and induces him to think about them consciously and concertedly and to "attack them" forcefully and unequivocally until they no longer influence his behavior. By revealing and assailing these beliefs and by "commanding" the patient to engage in activities which run counter to them, their hold on his life is broken and new directions become possible.

The following transcript, in which a patient recounts an experience in which his golf partners expressed their dislike of him, illustrates the technique nicely (Ellis, 1962).

CASE 4–2	Therapist: You think you were unhappy because these men didn't like you?
Rational-emotive Therapy	Patient: I certainly was!

Th. But you weren't unhappy for the reason you think you were.

Pt. I wasn't? But I was!

Th. No, I insist: you only think you were unhappy for that reason.

Pt. Well, why was I unhappy then?

Th. It's very simple—as simple as A, B, C, I might say. A, in this case, is the fact that these men didn't like you. Let's assume that you observed their attitude correctly and were not merely imagining they didn't like you.

Pt. I assure you that they didn't. I could see that very clearly.

Th. Very well, let's assume they didn't like you and call that A. Now, C is your unhappiness—which we'll definitely have to assume is a fact, since you felt it.

Pt. Damn right I did!

Th. All right, then: A is the fact that the men didn't like you, C is your unhappiness. You see A and C and you assume that A, their not liking you, caused your unhappiness, C. But it didn't.

Pt. It didn't? What did, then?

Th. B did.

Pt. What's B?

Figure 4–8 Confrontation-directive procedure.

CASE 4–2

Continued

Th. B is what you said to yourself while you were playing golf with those men.

Pt. What I said to myself? But I didn't say anything.

Th. You did. You couldn't possibly be unhappy if you didn't. The only thing that could possibly make you unhappy that occurs from without is a brick falling on your head, or some such equivalent. But no brick fell. Obviously, therefore, you must have told yourself something to make you unhappy.

Pt. But I tell you . . . Honestly, I didn't say anything.

Th. You did. You must have. Now think back to your being with these men; think what you said to yourself; and tell me what it was.

Pt. Well . . . I . . .

Th. Yes?

Pt. Well, I guess I did say something.

Th. I'm sure you did. Now what did you tell yourself when you were with those men?

Pt. I . . . Well, I told myself that it was awful that they didn't like me, and why didn't they like me, and how could they not like me, and . . . you know, things like that.

Th. Exactly. And that, what you told yourself, was B. And it's always B that makes you unhappy in situations like this. Except as I said before, when A is a brick falling on your head. That, or any physical object, might cause you real pain. But any mental or emotional onslaught against you—any word, gesture, attitude, or feeling directed against you—can hurt you only if you let it. And your letting such a word, gesture, attitude, or feeling hurt you, your telling yourself that it's awful, horrible, terrible—that's B. And that's what you do to you.

Pt. What shall I do then?

Th. I'll tell you exactly what to do. I want you to play golf, if you can, with those same men again. But this time, instead of trying to get them to love you or think you're a grand guy or anything like that, I want you to do one simple thing.

Pt. What is that?

Th. I want you merely to observe, when you're with them and they don't love you, to observe what you say to you. That's all: merely watch your own silent sentences. Do you think you can do that?

Pt. I don't see why not. Just watch my own sentences, what I say to me?

Th. Yes, just that.

When the patient came in for his next session, I asked him if he had done his homework and he said that he had. "And what did you find?" I asked. "It was utterly appalling," he replied, "utterly appalling. All I heard myself tell myself was self-pity; nothing but self-pity."

"Exactly," I said. "That's what you keep telling yourself—nothing but self-pity. No wonder you're unhappy."

Ellis contends that patients exhibit certain almost universal self-defeating assumptions. Among them are the following: that it is necessary to be loved and approved; to be worthwhile as a person, one must be thoroughly good and competent; many people are wicked and sinful and should be blamed and censured for their villainy.

Underlying these destructive attitudes, according to Ellis, is the tendency of patients to blame themselves for their limitations and wrong-doings; that is, to subscribe to the false and self-defeating assumption that they are "no good and therefore deserve to suffer." The principal goal of therapy is to challenge and destroy this belief, to liberate the patient, to free him from such irrational notions as shame and sin and to live life to the fullest despite social shortcomings or the disapproval of others.

REALITY-INTEGRITY THERAPY

The underlying theme of "rational-emotive therapy" is that man is too harsh with himself, tending to blame and judge his actions more severely than is necessary. No more opposite a philosophy could be found than that espoused in Glasser's "reality therapy" (1961, 1965) or Mowrer's "integrity therapy" (1961, 1965, 1966). In effect, these men claim that patients are sick because they are irresponsible; they are *not* "oversocialized" victims of too rigid standards, but "undersocialized" victims of a failure to adhere to rigid moralistic standards. Anguish stems not from too much guilt, but from an unwillingness to admit guilt, sin and irresponsibility.

The task of therapy, according to this view, is to confront the patient with his past misbehaviors and irresponsibilities and make him "confess" his wrongdoings. The therapist does not accept the patient's rationalizations or other efforts to find scapegoats for his misfortunes. Only by facing and admitting the "reality" of his deceit and guilt can the patient regain self-integrity and learn to deal with the future truthfully and ob-

Figure 4-9   O. H. Mowrer.

jectively. No longer needing to hide his sins, he can make up for past mistakes and find a more responsible style of life without shame or the fear of being discovered.

COGNITIVE-LEARNING TECHNIQUES

Therapists grouped in this category are neither directive nor nondirective insofar as treatment goals or style of therapeutic interaction is concerned. Rather, therapist and patient conjointly agree that the latter possesses attitudes which promote and perpetuate his difficulties in life.

Cognitive-learning therapists are more active in the treatment process than those who follow the self-actualization philosophy; they encourage the patient to alter his self-defeating perceptions and cognitions instead of allowing him to work things out for himself. In contrast to confrontation-directive therapists, however, they do not prejudge the patient's problem in accord with a fixed philosophy such as "integrity" or "rationality"; they have no particular "axe to grind," so to speak, no set of beliefs they wish to convey. Rather, they plan merely to reorient the patient's misguided attitudes, whatever these may be and toward whatever direction may prove constructive, given his personal life circumstances.

We shall limit our discussion to two such approaches, those known as expectancy-reinforcement (Rotter, 1954, 1973) and assertion-structured (Phillips, 1956) therapies.

EXPECTANCY-REINFORCEMENT THERAPY

Formulated by Rotter (1954, 1962, 1972), this approach seeks to alter the patient's expectancies (cognitive anticipations) that particular forms of behavior are followed by positive or negative reinforcements of varying strengths. Maladaptive behaviors stem from the presence of erroneous expectancies, learned largely as a consequence of faulty past reinforcements which generalize into current situations and relationships.

Therapy is viewed as a specially arranged process of unlearning and relearning that is no different in its fundamental character and principles than that of other learning settings. In fact, as Rotter notes, formal therapy, despite its concentrated and focused nature, is often a less efficient vehicle for change than repetitive everyday experiences, since it is limited to a few hours a week at most and takes place in a setting that is appreciably different than that to which its effects must be generalized.

Therapeutic processes are designed to change maladjustive reinforcement-expectancies, or as Rotter has put it (1973):

lowering the expectancy that a particular behavior or behaviors will lead to gratifications or increasing the expectancy that alternate or new behaviors would lead to greater gratification in the same situation or situations. In general learning terms we might say we have the choice of either weakening the inadequate response, strengthening the correct or adequate response, or doing both.

Of utmost importance as a therapeutic goal is strengthening the expectancy that problems can be resolved, which Rotter formulates as follows:

It is the purpose of therapy not to solve all of the patient's problems, but rather to increase the patient's ability to solve his own problems. . . . From a social learning point of view, one of the most important aspects of treatment, particularly face to face treatment, is to reinforce in the patient the expectancy that problems are solvable by looking for alternative solutions.

ASSERTION-STRUCTURED THERAPY

According to Phillips' model (1956), behavior is best understood in terms of the person's "assertions" concerning himself and others. These assertions, which are essentially cognitive hypotheses or assumptions about the world in which the person lives, have varying probabilities of "confirmation" (correctness) or "disconfirmation" (incorrectness). Should these assertions be disconfirmed frequently, as occurs in persons inclined to psychopathology, the individual will experience "tension," with its accompanying symptoms. Rather than resolving these tensions. Phillips believes that the disturbed person reiterates his faulty assertions more strongly than before. This results in a self-defeating vicious circle termed "redundancy" and leads to a progressive inflexibility and narrowing of behavior alternatives.

Phillips illustrates the pathological sequence in the following example (1956):

1.   Assertion. Child's expectations are for constant attention, accord, interest; he expects to get his way; expects to have others give in to him in the interest of his comfort and his immediate demands.

2.   Disconfirmation. The school and other out-of-the-home environments cannot treat the child in this way; therefore they act to disconfirm the child's expectations. These social facts conflict with the expectations themselves.

3.   Tension. At school or in other atypical situations (i.e., not typically like the home setting) tensions develop from this conflict.

4.   Redundancy. Child redoubles efforts to get attention, refuses to make academic effort, becomes a behavior problem owing to tension and partly to his fighting back at disconfirming experiences. The child now falls behind in school work in real and formidable ways; this failure, in turn, becomes more disconfirming to him and his original assertions. Thus the vicious circle proceeds; and until it is entered into in effective ways, it continues.

The chief task of therapy is to discover the nature of these faulty assertions, and then to "interfere" with their perpetuation by teaching the patient alternative beliefs and hypotheses that have a greater probability of confirmation. Thus, therapeutic interference reduces the vicious and evernarrowing circle of redundancy, thereby enabling the person to explore on his own increasingly effective problem-solving attitudes and behaviors.

EVALUATION

The variety of philosophies, goals and therapeutic procedures which differentiate the several phenomenological-existential approaches make it difficult to group and evaluate these therapies as a unit. Despite these differences, however, there are certain merits and criticisms which may be assigned in common to all of these methods. Let us note them briefly.

Among the *merits* ascribed by proponents are the following.

First, the language of phenomenological concepts represents events in terms that are "meaningful" to patients rather than in the obscure language of psychoanalytic therapies or the overly objectivized terminology of behavioral schools. Consequently, patients understand what is "going on" in the consulting room, and can readily translate into reality what they have learned. Discussions at the phenomenological level, then, help both the acquisition of insight and its application to current realities.

Second, phenomenological therapies are carried out in a face to face interpersonal interaction that resembles "normal" extratherapeutic relationships to a greater degree than those of other therapeutic schools. Consequently, what is learned in the setting of phenomenological treatment should more readily generalize to the natural interpersonal settings for which they are ultimately intended.

Third, phenomenological approaches focus on internal processes that "underlie" behavior. Consequently, they are more efficient instruments for solving complex difficulties than are behavior therapies which deal primarily with isolated or well-circumscribed symptoms. Similarly, phenomenological therapies can grapple with such nebulous symptom clusters as "existential dilemmas" and "identity crises" that are obscured by the conceptual language of psychoanalytic schools and resist formulation in the overly precise language of behavior therapies.

Among the many *criticisms* leveled at phenomenological therapies, we might note the following.

First, phenomenologists formulate their therapy techniques in a vague and unsystematized manner. Upon careful analysis, these procedures prove to possess no more substance than those of psychological reassurance and persuasion, although they are cloaked in pretentious philosophies. Critics note that all psychotherapies employ the processes that phenomenological therapists consider essential; thus, phenomenologists make a virtue out of the commonplace.

Second, phenomenological therapies fail to deal with the historical course and the unconscious roots of psychological abnormalities. According to psychoanalytic therapists, consciously acknowledged attitudes and feelings, which characterize the data of phenomenological therapy, are but "superficial" verbalizations that cloak deeper motives and emotions. As they see it, unless the patient comes to grips with these "hidden" events, "true" insight will constantly be undermined and therapeutic progress will be blunted.

Third, phenomenological approaches are of minimal value in cases of marked anxiety or with patients who otherwise are unable to face or analyze their attitudes and emotions. In short, these procedures are limited to relatively stable and moderately intelligent adults whose capacities are sufficiently intact to enable them to engage in calm self-exploration.

Kathe Kollwitz—*Study*

5 BIOPHYSICAL APPROACHES

INTRODUCTION

There are many psychiatrists and psychologists today who hold the view that a biological defect, or perhaps a subtle combination of defects, will be found ultimately for all mental disorders. Analogies are made with biological medicine where bacteria and viruses have been shown to underlie overt symptoms of disturbance. This notion has a long and stormy history. Theories have been propounded, tested and found wanting. Significant discoveries have been hailed with much acclaim only to sink into obscurity. Despite this checkered history, there have been enough valid findings to maintain a continued vigorous search through the centuries.

EARLY VIEWPOINTS

The view that mental disorders are processes of the nervous system and not abstract spiritual phenomena was first proposed clearly in the work of Hippocrates. In *Sacred Disease*, Hippocrates wrote (Grimm, 1838):

Men ought to know that from the brain and from the brain only arise our pleasures and joys as well as our sorrows, pains, griefs and tears. . . . It is the same thing which makes us mad or delirious and inspires us with dread and fear.

In the Middle Ages, all studies of anatomy were forbidden. By the seventeenth and eighteenth centuries scientific progress overrode the influence of both Hippocrates' theories and theological supernaturalism. The great English clinician, Thomas Sydenham (1624–1689) enunciated the view that the primary function of diagnosis was to identify the essential disease underlying the overt symptom. He wrote (Latham, 1848):

Nature in the production of disease, is uniform and consistent . . . the self-same phenomena that you would observe in the sickness of a Socrates you would observe in the sickness of a simpleton.

Sydenham's desire to organize accurate symptom patterns was prompted by the belief that specific diseases or bodily dysfunctions could

A   B

Figure 5-1   A, Hippocrates (From Singer and Underwood: A Short History of Medicine, Oxford University Press). B, Thomas Sydenham (From Veith's Hysteria, University of Chicago Press).

be found to account for them. This view was given a firm foundation in the extraordinary accomplishments of the early nineteenth century by Pierre Louis in pathological anatomy, Louis Pasteur and Joseph Lister in infectious diseases and Rudolf Virchow on cellular pathology.

DISCOVERY OF GENERAL PARESIS

Impressive as these accomplishments were, no tangible proof existed that disease did in fact account for any mental disorder. It was not until the painstakingly slow discovery of *general paresis*, that medical science uncovered a biological cause in psychopathology.

The first inkling that a common pattern existed, to be called *dementia paralytica* at first, was noted by John Haslam in 1798. He reported a frequent association between delusions of grandeur and general dementia usually followed by a progressive paralysis. In 1805, Esquirol added his observation that this pattern invariably had a fatal outcome. Credit for a clear description of the symptom constellation goes to A. L. J. Bayle in 1822. In postmortem studies of these patients during the mid-nineteenth century, it was discovered that they had marked inflammation and degeneration in brain tissue. By 1869, Argyll-Robertson noted that patients afflicted with syphilis were unable to react with proper pupillary reflexes. It was not until 1894 that Fournier produced evidence that 65 per cent of all patients classified as dementia paralytica had a history of syphilis. Since the figure of 65 per cent was short of a convincing relationship, doubts arose that syphilis was the cause of dementia paralytica. An ingenious experiment was carried out by Krafft-Ebing in 1897 to dispel these doubts. He took nine paretic patients who had denied a prior syphilitic infection, and demonstrated their failure to develop syphilis when given an inoculation dose. Their immunity was conclusive proof that in fact they had been previously infected. In 1905 Schaudinn discovered that a spirochete. *Treponema pallidum,* was the cause of syphilis; this was followed in 1913 by Noguchi and Moore in their conclusive verification of this spirochete in the paretic's nerve tissue.

DEVELOPMENT OF DISEASE CLASSIFICATIONS

The growth of knowledge in anatomy and physiology strengthened the trend toward disease-oriented classifications. Wilhelm Griesinger (1817–1868), a young German internist and psychiatrist with little direct patient experience, employed the disease concept in his classic text, *Mental Pathology and Therapeutics,* published in 1845. His statement, "Mental diseases are brain diseases," shaped the course of German systematic psychiatry for more than 40 years. Griesinger's contention that classifications should be formed on the basis of underlying brain lesions was not weakened by the fact that no relationship had been established in his day between brain pathology and mental disorders.

The German psychiatrist, Karl Ludwig Kahlbaum (1828–1899), developed a classification system in which disorders were grouped according to their course and outcome. In a series of monographs published between 1863 and 1874, Kahlbaum not only established the importance of longitudinal factors, but described the newly observed disorders of *hebephrenia* and *catatonia,* and coined the modern terms *symptom-complex* and *cyclothymia.*

It was not until the preeminent German synthesist, Emil Kraepelin (1856–1926), that the views and observations of Kahlbaum and Griesinger were brought together. In his outstanding text, revised from a small compendium in 1883 to an imposing two-volume ninth edition in 1927, Kraepelin built a system which integrated the descriptive and longitudinal approach of Kahlbaum with the somatic disease system proposed by Griesinger. Kraepelin constantly revised his system, elaborating it at times, simplifying it at others. In the sixth edition of 1899, he established the definitive pattern of two modern major disorders: *manic-depressive psychosis* and *dementia praecox.*

Within the manic-depressive group he brought together the excited conditions of mania and the hopeless melancholia of depression, indicating the periodic course through which these moods alternate in the same pa-

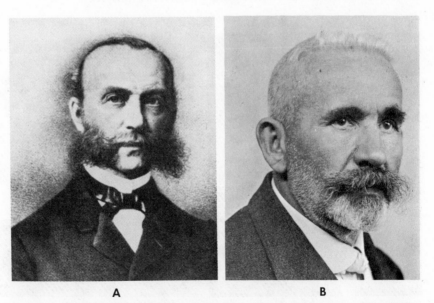

A   B

Figure 5–2   A, William Griesinger (From Alexander and Selesnick's History of Psychiatry, Harper and Row). B, Emil Kraepelin (National Library of Medicine, Bethesda, Maryland).

tient. Consistent with his disease orientation, he proposed that this disorder was caused by an irregular metabolic function transmitted by heredity.

Kraepelin included a wide range of previously known disorders within the category of dementia praecox. He observed two major commonalities which he felt would justify a synthesis among them: each began early in life and then progressed to an incurable dementia. The cause of these disorders, according to Kraepelin, were biologically defective sex glands which led to chemical imbalances in the nervous system. Since puberty was a crucial period in sexual development, defects arose most often at this stage. This fact accounted for the frequency with which dementia praecox occurred in adolescence.

As early as 1905, Adolf Meyer (1866–1950), a major figure in American psychiatry, proposed the view that a true understanding of the patient could be derived only by a study of the individual's total reaction to his organic, psychological and social experience. Although Meyer was the most prominent psychiatrist to introduce the Kraepelinian system in this country, he believed that these disorders were not disease entities, but "psychobiological reactions" to environmental stress (1973). Through his work, Meyer bridged the physiological orientation of the late nineteenth century and the psychodynamic orientation of the twentieth.

The interrelationship of biological and psychological factors in classifying disorders was stressed also by Meyer's contemporary, the Swiss psychiatrist Eugen Bleuler (1856–1935). Although committed to Kraepelin's view that dementia praecox was primarily an organic disease, Bleuler emphasized the presence of psychological ambivalence and disharmony in this impairment, entitling it *schizophrenia*, to signify the "split" he observed between the intellectual and emotional functions in these patients (1973).

Together, Meyer's notion of reaction-types and Bleuler's focus on cognitive and emotional experience (Bleuler, 1950) reshaped Kraepelin's original system into our contemporary psychiatric nosology. In this

A   B

Figure 5–3   A, Adolf Meyer; B, Eugen Bleuler (National Library of Medicine, Bethesda, Maryland).

"traditional" classification, Kraepelin's clinical categories are retained as the basic framework, and Meyer's and Bleuler's psychological notions provide guidelines to the patient's inner processes and social reactions.

EVOLUTION OF SOMATIC THERAPIES

In psychiatric somatic therapy it is assumed that the overt behaviors and feelings of the patient are expressions of an underlying biological affliction best treated at its source. The fact that few if any biological causes have been identified has not deterred the search for such therapies. Somatic treatments that have proved useful have resulted from *serendipity* — the art of accidental discovery. Perhaps the most striking fact about the history of physiological therapy is its progress through error and misconception.

Somatic therapy for a disorder should require that a disease be clearly identified. After syphilis had been established as the cause for general paresis, Julius Wagner-Jauregg, operating more on the basis of a hunch than scientific logic, inoculated paretic patients with malaria in 1917 and successfully cured them of their disease. It was in the mid-1930's, however, that the era of somatotherapies started its major growth with the almost simultaneous development of insulin-coma therapy, convulsion treatment and cerebral surgery.

Insulin was first administered to mental patients to increase their weight and inhibit their excitement. Manfred Sakel (1900–1957) observed that unintentional comas induced by excessive insulin benefited mental patients. From this observation Sakel was led to the hypothesis that psychotic behavior resulted from an overproduction of adrenalin which caused cerebral nerve cells to become hyperactive. Sakel's hypothesis was a simple one and easy to test. In brief time it was established that psychotic patients do not overproduce adrenalin. Furthermore, adrenalin is increased rather than decreased during insulin coma.

In 1934 Laszlo Joseph von Meduna (1896–1964) reported the successful treatment of schizophrenia by inducing convulsions with a camphor mixture, known in its synthetic form as *metrazol*. Meduna's thesis was derived from two observations which had been noted frequently in psychiatric literature: that epilepsy and schizophrenia rarely coexist, and that schizophrenic symptoms often disappear following spontaneous convulsions. Subsequent research has entirely disproved Meduna's thesis. First, epilepsy and schizophrenia are neither related nor opposed. Second, clinical experience has shown convulsive treatment to be useful primarily in depressive disorders and only rarely in schizophrenia.

Figure 5-4 A, Manfred J. Sakel; B, Laszlo J. Meduna; C, Egas Moniz; D, Ugo Cerletti.

Prior to the advent of pharmacologic agents in the mid-1950's, *electrocon-vulsive therapy* was the most widely used method of biological treatment in psychiatry. The technique of electrical convulsion, developed as early as 1900 by Leduc and Robinovitch with animals, was well known to Ugo Cerletti (1877–1963) when he first used it with psychotic subjects in 1937. After his initial success Cerletti formulated his own theory regarding its effectiveness. He speculated that the convulsion brought the patient close to a state of death. This aroused extraordinary biological defenses which led, in turn, to therapeutic recovery.

Egas Moniz (1874–1955) developed a surgical treatment in 1935 known as the *prefrontal leucotomy*. This surgical separation of the frontal lobes (thought) from the thalamus (emotion) was believed to minimize emotional preoccupations. Although the technique was used extensively in this country in the 1940's and 1950's its effectiveness was always in doubt.

MODERN THEORIES

Biophysical theories assume that factors such as anatomy and biochemistry are the primary determinants of psychopathology. Ample evidence from medical science exists to justify this assumption. In the present section we will examine the orientation of theorists who hold this view. Research and data in support of their views will be presented and evaluated in detail in chapter 7.

HEREDITY THEORIES

The role of heredity in abnormal behavior is usually inferred from evidence based on correlations in mental disorder among members of the same family. Most psychopathologists admit that hereditary factors play a role in personality and behavior, but insist that genetic dispositions can be modified substantially by the operation of environmental factors. This moderate view states that heredity operates not as a constant, but as a disposition which takes different forms depending on the circumstances of an individual's upbringing. Hereditary theorists take a more inflexible position. They refer to a body of data supporting a genetic factor in a variety of pathologies such as "schizophrenia" and "manic-depressive" psychoses. Although they admit that variations in these disorders may be produced by environmental conditions, they are convinced that these are "superficial" influences which cannot prevent the individual from succumbing to his hereditary defect.

The first authority to initiate a series of systematic investigations of the coincidence of disorders among relatives of mental patients was the German psychiatrist, E. Rüdin. Because of Rüdin's difficulty in separating the role of heredity from that of environment in his human pedigree studies, two German investigators, J. Lange and H. Luxenburger, devised the method of comparing identical and fraternal twins; identical twins had identical genes and, therefore, the specific role of heredity could be isolated partially from environment.

Studies of twins were continued in the mid-1930's by the research psychiatrist, Franz Kallmann (1973). Kallmann argued that coincidence in disorder varies directly with degree of genetic similarity. He hypothesized specifically that schizophrenia and manic-depressive disorders arise from the effects of a single gene and are transmitted according to

Figure 5-5   Franz Kallmann.

normal hereditary processes. His data are impressive, but several serious questions have been raised about his genetic hypothesis and methodology: these will be elaborated later, in Chapter 7. For the moment let us note that the fact that genetic factors may serve as a predisposition to certain forms of mental disorder does not mean that disordered individuals will not display differences in their symptoms or developmental history. It certainly does not mean that these disorders cannot be helped by psychological therapies, or that similar forms of disorder could not arise without a genetic disposition.

CONSTITUTIONAL THEORIES

Scientists of this persuasion assume that heredity accounts in large part for temperamental and behavioral dispositions. However, these theorists are not interested in the genetic process itself; rather, they focus on the end product of hereditary action, namely, constitutional variations among individuals and the correlation of these variations with abnormal behavior.

The majority of studies undertaken by this group of theorists deals with constitutional measures of adult physique or body structure. Although the belief that relationships exist between pathology and body build goes back to early Greek and Roman writings, the first of the modern studies was initiated by the German psychiatrist, Kretschmer. He proposed that slender individuals with poor muscular development were prone to introspective and schizophrenic disorders, whereas those with heavy or rotund physiques were vulnerable to mood-alternating and manic-depressive disorders. The American physician, Sheldon, modified both Kretschmer's measurement techniques and hypotheses in his own work, the best known of which relates body type, temperament and delinquency. Details of his research, and that of other body build theorists will be presented in detail in a later chapter.

Constitutional theorists often assume that an underlying hereditary linkage system accounts for the consistencies they observe between body physique and pathological behavior. Despite the plausibility of the linkage thesis, alternate interpretations for the correspondence between biophysical and behavioral traits also are plausible. For example, the possession of certain biophysical characteristics may lead an individual to certain experiences and these experiences may, in turn, be the real determinant of his behavior. To illustrate, a muscular individual may learn that assertive and aggressive behavior on his part will succeed in getting him what he wants, whereas a thin and weakly individual may find that

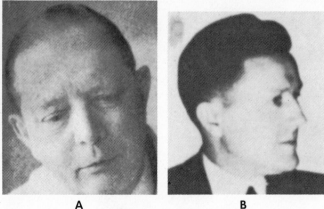

A   B

Figure 5-6   A, Ernst Kretschmer; B, William Sheldon.

withdrawal and devious maneuvers are best for him. In these illustrations, any correlation found between the individual's physical make-up and his personality is not the result of an inborn genetic linkage, but a function of learning and experience.

NEUROPHYSIOLOGICAL THEORIES

In contrast to constitutional theorists, who are concerned primarily with relationships between normal biophysical variability and abnormal behavior, neurophysiological theorists tend to focus on irregularities and errors in functioning, or what we shall refer to as diseases, dysfunctions and defects.

Theories proposing that brain defects underlie abnormal behavior have found many adherents since William Greisinger's assertions to that effect in the mid-nineteenth century. In the 1930's and the 1940's, eminent neuroanatomists presented evidence of atrophy of brain cells in patients classified as schizophrenic. Others have discovered parasitic microorganisms, inflammations and other disease processes.

Several theorists in the last decade proposed specific areas within the brain whose dysfunction may account for various forms of psychopathology. Two sites have been referred to repeatedly: the *reticular formation* and the *limbic system.* These two regions serve as biophysical bases for activating and integrating motivational and emotional responses.

Theoretical work of Magoun and Hebb has shown that the reticular formation plays a key role in the arousal and activation of the central nervous system. The components of this complex system alert or orient awareness and contribute to the selective focusing of attention. In addition to these experimentally established functions, a number of theorists have suggested that it also plays the important function of integrating neural processes. If the functions of both arousal and integration are ascribed correctly to the reticular formation, lesions in this system could very well underlie many mental disorders.

Theoretical notions involving the limbic system likewise are highly speculative. A substantial body of research has been gathered by Olds (1965, 1962) and Delgado (1954, 1966) to the effect that this system is deeply involved in the expression and control of both emotional and motivational processes. It is proposed that damage to the limbic system may suppress, magnify or otherwise distort affective reactions and lead, therefore, to pathologic emotions and behavior. There is no direct evidence to date, however, to correlate limbic system defects with any of the traditional categories of psychopathology. Despite this lack of supporting evidence, there is reason to think that defects in either the reticular or limbic systems may be related to a number of different mental disorders.

Studies have been undertaken on diverse functions such as general metabolic rate, liver reactions, circulatory system patterns and thyroid activity. The belief that physio-chemical dysfunctions might underlie abnormal behavior has been supported by findings of greater biophysical variability among the mentally ill than among normals.

Hoskins (1946), reviewing the early literature on endocrine functions, suggested that thyroid dysfunctions were a central factor in schizophrenia. The failure of schizophrenics to exhibit an adequate response to stress suggested further that their adrenal glands may also be performing deficiently.

Other investigators have attempted to study chemical substances involved in neural transmission. This body of research centers on neuro-hormones, chemical secretions of nerve cells which either facilitate or inhibit synaptic thresholds. *Norepinephrine*, from which epinephrine is derived, is present in a small quantity within the brain. Osmond, Smythies and Hoffer (1952, 1954) have suggested that schizophrenics suffer from a faulty metabolism of norepinephrine leading to the production of two derivatives, adrenochrome and adrenolutin, which ostensibly create hallucinations. Interesting as this line of speculation may be, the theory lacks adequate empirical support.

Heath (1958, 1966) has proposed that schizophrenic symptomatology may be due to the operation of a brain antibody, termed taraxein, which presumably interferes with neural transmission by disrupting the activity of *acetylcholine*. This speculative thesis remains unverified.

Other theorists have avoided committing themselves to specific hypotheses, preferring to speculate only that a general dysfunction in chemical balance exists in mental disorders. Rubin (1962), for example, has proposed that the inability of psychotics to respond effectively to stress may stem from a variety of different hormonal imbalances. According to him, a matrix of different mental disorders may arise as a function of different patterns of hormonal imbalance, excess or deficiency.

CONCEPTIONS OF THERAPY

No relationship need exist between the belief in a biogenic cause of abnormal behavior and the use of biological methods of treatment. Nevertheless, most biologically oriented therapists favor the "disease model." They contend that abnormal behavior is an overt manifestation of underlying anatomical lesions or biochemical aberrations; from this view it follows quite logically that methods that remedy the defect directly (e.g., altering chemical thresholds or rearranging neural circuitries) would be the most successful treatment technique.

We need not be committed to the view that abnormal behavior is of biogenic origin in order to believe that biological therapies may be usefully employed. Biological methods may prove effective in conditions in which the cause is clearly psychological. For example, pharmacological "tranquilizers" may be fruitfully employed to ease "psychological" tension caused by the loss of a job or the death of a relative.

Let us be clear at the start, then, that the therapeutic approach to be described in this chapter does *not* assume a biological basis to abnormal behavior. These techniques are distinguished from other methods only by the fact that their primary mode of action is at the biological level. We will concentrate in this section on the psychopharmacological drugs. In addition, we will elaborate briefly on several of the other biophysical therapies, notably electroconvulsive and surgical procedures.

PSYCHOPHARMACOLOGICAL AGENTS (CHEMOTHERAPY)

The aimless advance of somatotherapies progressed in its course with the discovery of two psychopharmacological agents: chlorpromazine and reserpine. In 1952, Delay and Deniker reported the general "tranquilizing" effects of chlorpromazine, a drug synthesized for use with surgical and hypertensive patients. During the same year, reserpine, an extract of the Rauwolfia Snakeroot plant, which had been used for general medical purposes since the 1920's by Indian physicians, was noted to be effective in calming hyperactive and assaultive patients. Because of the ease of administration, the economy and the highly impressive early reports of their efficacy, these two pharmacological substances ushered in a new wave of optimism in psychiatric medicine. Although this early period of enthusiasm has since subsided, these as well as other drugs have taken a solid place in the physician's kit. A secondary consequence of this boom in psychopharmacological interest has been the growth of sophisticated studies of brain biochemistry and a correlated development of new compounds designed to alter neurophysiological functioning. In recent years, scientific rationales and experimental research rather than aimless chance discoveries have begun to play an increasing role in the design of pharmacological agents.

Because of the varied questions that can be posed regarding the nature of pharmacological action, and because of the complexity of the factors involved, theorists have had a relatively open field to speculate on "why" and "how" these drugs produce their effects (Overall and Henry, 1973). These formulations have been grouped into three categories: *neurohormonal defect theories*, which hypothesize that drugs overcome chemical dysfunctions in synaptic transmission; *neurophysiological imbalance theories*, which assume that these agents reestablish equilibrium among ill-matched functional systems; and *psychological reaction theories*, which propose that these substances result in energy and temperament changes that alter the patient's coping competencies and lead him to modify his self-image. The details of the biophysical theories are too complicated for a text such as this; the interested student may turn elsewhere for extended discussions (Millon, 1969).

Although the direct action of pharmacological drugs is chemical, there are those who believe that the crucial variable is not chemical or neurophysiological, but psychological. To them, the factors that determine the patient's response are his prior psychological state and the environment within which he currently functions. According to this view, biophysical changes induced by drugs take on a "meaning" to the patient, and it is this meaning which determines his "final" clinical response.

Theorists of this persuasion note that barbiturates, which typically produce sedation, often produce excitement and hyperactivity. Similarly, many persons exhibit a cheerful state of intoxication when given sodium amytal in a congenial social setting, but succumb to a hypnotic state when the drug is administered to them in a therapeutic environ-

Figure 5–7 (Drawing by C. Saxon; © 1971 The New Yorker Magazine, Inc.)

"I grant your point, but not because I agree with you. I'm under sedation."

ment. Of even greater significance than social factors according to this view, is the patient's *awareness* of the energy and temperamental changes that have taken place within him as a consequence of drug action. As Sarwer-Foner remarks (1959):

If the pharmacologic effect threatens the patient by interfering with vital defenses, new waves of energy are produced, alerting and disturbing him. Here these arise *precisely because of the medication* he is receiving. . . . When the changes produced affect the patient, physician, hospital, and their interrelations in a way that makes the patient feel *less* inferior, worthless, and dangerous, a new opportunity for a more adult level of functioning is produced. When this situation continues for a sufficiently long time, further ego reintegration can take place. The symptomatic action of the drugs leads therefore to a variable therapeutic effect.

TRANQUILIZERS

As was noted earlier, the discovery of the clinical utility of *chlorpromazine* and *reserpine*, reported in 1952, ushered in a new wave of optimism in psychiatric medicine. Many investigators, spurred by the impressive results of these two agents, began to manipulate their basic molecular structure in the hope of discovering variants that would be even more effective than the parent models. Modifications of these, as well as other, chemical substances have resulted in over 100 new psychopharmacological products in the past 20 years. Despite differences in structure, most of these agents affect essentially the same clinical behaviors as do chlorpromazine and reserpine, that is, they are "tranquilizers."

Tranquilizers may be distinguished from a variety of compounds termed sedatives that have been used for over a century to moderate tension and agitation. Tranquilizers, in contrast to sedatives, relieve anxiety and reduce hyperactivity without markedly dulling cognitive alertness and clarity. They appear more selective in their dampening effects than sedatives, focusing on emotional and motor functions and operating minimally on cognitive functions. Let us briefly discuss the major subtypes of the tranquilizer group.

Chlorpromazine was the first and is still thought to be the most effective phenothiazine for handling markedly disturbed patients characterized by emotional tension, cognitive confusion and motor hyperactivity. Numerous structural modifications of the basic chlorpromazine molecule have been made, producing drugs that differ from the parent model in both potency and side effects. In general, the greater the potency, the more severe and dangerous are the toxic consequences. For example, additions to the basic molecule can result in a compound that is five to ten times more potent than chlorpromazine, but increases the incidence of severe secondary complications. At the other end of the scale significant alterations are made in the basic nucleus of chlorpromazine, decreasing both the potency of the compound and its associated side effects.

In the main, the various phenothiazine derivatives are alike in their clinical utility. Their primary indication is with the more severe reactions, disorders and patterns in which a reduction in activity level and a dampening of heightened moods, such as anxiety and hostility, is desired.

The *rauwolfia* tranquilizers are extracted from the *rauwolfia serpentina* plant, named after the sixteenth century German botanist, Leonhard Rauwolf. Although used for centuries as a medicinal, it was not until 1951, when a crystalline alkaloid termed *reserpine* was extracted from the plant, that its utility in psychopathology received recognition. Early reports on the drug were extremely enthusiastic, especially in psychotic syndromes characterized by anxiety and agitation. However, with increased clinical experience, it became evident that the drug often produced dangerous psychological as well as physiological side effects; severe depressive disorders were precipitated all too frequently. As a consequence, the drug's use has diminished, giving way to the less troublesome phenothiazines. Efforts to modify the structural composition of the basic reserpine molecule have not proved successful in eliminating the depression complication. Recently, rauwolfia alkaloids have reverted to their original use in treating hypertensive diseases, especially in cases where anxiety is a component.

In 1949 an Australian physician (Cade, 1949) accidentally rediscovered an old Greek remedy for manic or overly excited states of irrational euphoria (Gattozzi, 1970). This natural chemical, *lithium salts*, had been employed in the fifth century by administering alkaline spring water to patients. Little interest was shown in these early reports since it was not believed that a common natural element could prove so effective. However, recent studies (Schan, 1970; Goodwin, et al., 1972) have shown lithium to be especially useful in manic disturbances. Relatively small doses appear to relax and subdue the excessive enthusiasms of these patients without dulling them into insensitivity, a consequence often associated with other tranquilizing agents.

For the most part, drug agents other than the phenothiazine derivatives are both less potent and produce fewer troublesome side effects. These drugs are of lesser utility than phenothiazines in treating markedly disturbed patients, but they do fulfill a function with moderately anxious

TABLE 5–1
MAJOR PSYCHOPHARMACO-LOGICAL AGENTS

TRANQUILIZERS

Phenothiazine Derivatives

Dimethylamine Series

Chlorpromazine (Thorazine)*
Methoxypromazine (Tentone)
Promazine (Sparine)
Promethazine (Phenergan)
Propiomazine (Largon)
Triflupromazine (Vesprin)
Trimeprazine (Temaril)

Piperazine Series

Acetophenazine (Tindal)
Carphenazine (Proketazine)
Fluphenazine (Permitil)
Perphenazine (Trilafon)
Prochlorperazine (Compazine)
Thiopropazate (Dartal)
Thiothixene (Narvane)
Trifluoperazine (Stelazine)

Piperidine Series

Mepazine (Pacatal)
Thioridazine (Mellaril)

Rauwolfia Alkaloids

Alseroxylon (many trade names)
Deserpidine (Harmonyl)
Rescinnamine (Moderil)
Reserpine (many trade names)

Substituted Diols

Emylcamate (Stratran)
Mephenesin (Tolserol)
Meprobamate (Miltown, Equanil)
Phenaglycodol (Ultran)

Miscellaneous Compounds

Azacyclonol (Frenquel)
Benactyzine (Suavitil)
Buclizine (Softran)
Captodiamine (Suvren)
Chlordiazepoxide (Librium)
Chlormezanone (Trancopal)
Diazepam (Valium)
Ectylurea (Nostyn, Levanil)
Ethchlorvynol (Placidyl)
Haloperidol (Haldol)
Hydroxyzine (Atarax, Vistaril)
Mephenoxalone (Trepidone)
Oxanamide (Quiactin)
Oxazepam (Serax)
Promoxolane (Dimethylane)
Tybamate (Solacen)

ANTIDEPRESSANTS

MAO Inhibitors – Hydrazines

Iproniazid (Marsilid)
Isocarboxid (Marplan)
Nialamide (Niamid)
Phenelzine (Nardil)
Pheniprazine (Catron)

MAO Inhibitors – Nonhydrazines

Etryptamine (Monase)
Pargyline (Eutonyl)
Tranylcypromine (Parnate)

Iminodibenzyl Derivatives

Amitryptyline (Elavil)
Desipramine (Norpramin)
Imipramine (Tofranil)
Nortryptaline (Aventyl)
Opripramol (Ensidon)

Miscellaneous Compounds

Deanol (Deaner)
Methylphenidate (Ritalin)
Pipradol (Meratran)

* Names listed in parentheses are trade names.

and agitated patients. They influence the same spectrum of symptoms as do the phenothiazines, but to a lesser degree.

ANTIDEPRESSANTS

An early report indicating that the antitubercular drug, isoniazid, produced a beneficial stimulant effect in a psychiatric patient was drowned in the vast sea of medical literature (Flaherty, 1952). It was not until the late 1950's that the role of a similar drug, *iproniazid,* was recognized as an agent that could produce "euphoric" behaviors. Evidence was gathered shortly thereafter that these drugs inhibit monoamine oxidase, an enzyme centrally involved in brain metabolism.

Also in the late 1950's several Swiss chemists synthesizing new variants of phenothiazine noted that one of their compounds, *imipramine,* produced an effect opposite to what they anticipated; it did not decrease tension or control hyperactivity as was expected, but did brighten the mood of depressed patients. New "antidepressant" compounds were quickly formulated on the basis of modifications of the iproniazid and imipramine molecules.

Antidepressants should be distinguished from compounds known as stimulants that have been employed for over a century to increase motor activity and mental alertness. In contrast to stimulants, the effects of antidepressants begin slowly and last appreciably beyond the termination of treatment. Also, and more important, antidepressants not only activate cognitive alertness and motor behavior, but favorably influence the mood of the patient; stimulants, in contrast, often aggravate negative moods. Let us briefly outline the major categories of antidepressant drugs.

MISCELLANEOUS AGENTS

This section includes several drugs grouped according to the symptoms they influence. Some, the *sedatives* and *stimulants,* are less effective and selective than tranquilizers and antidepressants, although they act on the same clinical features. Others, the *anticonvulsants,* have a very narrow band of clinical utility. The last group, *psychotomimetics* and *hallucinogens,* are discussed because of their potential value as experimental tools.

Sedatives. These compounds, previously employed to calm anxiety and agitation, have been replaced in the past 20 years by tranquilizers. *Barbiturates* are the most frequently prescribed and useful of the sedatives. However, they dampen sensory, cognitive and motor functions, and therefore are not as selective in their effects as are the minor tranquilizers; moreover, problems of addiction may ensue as a result of prolonged use. For the most part, the shorter-acting barbiturates are employed to induce sleep whereas the long-acting barbiturates are used primarily as calmatives and anticonvulsants. Some of the short-acting barbiturates are administered intravenously for purposes of "narcotherapy"; in this procedure, a hypnotic state is induced by the drug, allowing the therapist to explore otherwise unconscious memories and emotions.

Stimulants. The major group of stimulants is the *sympathomimetic amines* (amphetamine, dextroamphetamine and methamphetamine). These act directly on the nervous system; their effects are rapid and brief and wear off in a matter of a few hours. During their brief period of chemical action, they tend to accelerate motor behavior and increase energy; this momentary surge is short lived and deceptive, and patients often slump

**TABLE 5–2
PHYSIOCHEMICAL
EFFECTS OF
VARIOUS PSYCHO-
PHARMACEUTICAL
DRUGS***

BRAIN AREA	FUNCTIONS	PHYSIO-CHEMICAL EFFECT	ILLUSTRATIVE DRUGS
Neocortex	Thinking and reasoning	Excitatory	Amphetamines and methylphenidate
		Inhibitory	Barbiturates
Thalamus	Integration of sensation, transmission and modulation of alerting	Excitatory	Barbiturates and phenothiazines
		Inhibitory	Meprobamate
Reticular Formation	Arousal, integration of emotional responses to stimuli	Excitatory	Rauwolfia alkaloids (Small doses)
		Inhibitory	Phenothiazines, barbiturates and iminodibenzyl derivatives
Limbic System	Regulation of emotions	Excitatory	Phenothiazines and rauwolfia alkaloids
		Inhibitory	Meprobamate, calordiazepoxide, diazepam, oxazepam, tybamate and hydroxyzine
Hypothalamus	Control of autonomic and endocrine functions	Excitatory	MAO inhibitors and amphetamines
		Inhibitory	Phenothiazines and rauwolfia alkaloids
Synapses	Nerve impulse transmission	Excitatory	Rauwolfia alkaloids
		Inhibitory	Amphetamines, iminodibenzyl derivatives, LSD and mescaline
Interneuronal Circuits	Coordination of neuronal masses	Inhibitory	Meprobamate
Neurohormonal Depots (Serotonin and Norepinephrine)	Regulation of brain metabolism	Excitatory	MAO inhibitors and iminodibenzyl derivatives
		Inhibitory	Phenothiazines and rauwolfia alkaloids

*Modified from Wolberg (1967)

into a more acute depressive mood when the drug is withdrawn. Despite its many limitations, not the least of which is the problem of addiction, these drugs are of occasional clinical utility as "energizers."

Anticonvulsants.   Numerous drugs have been used to control epilepsy. Bromides, noted previously among the sedatives, were introduced in 1857 to moderate the symptoms of this syndrome. Unfortunately, this agent has a wide inhibitory effect on the nervous system, producing a clouding of consciousness and a pervasive dampening of behavior and mood. It was not until 1912 that a more effective anticonvulsant was synthesized, phenobarbital. With the synthesis of *sodium diphenyl hydantoinate* (Dilantin) in 1937, a major advance took place in treatment of epilepsy.

Psychotomimetics and Hallucinogens.   Although commonly viewed as "mind-expanding" drugs by the public, clinicians consider hallucinogens such as LSD, mescaline and psilocybin to be experimental tools that stimulate psychotic behaviors; thus, professionals have dubbed these drugs "psychotomimetics."

Numerous investigators have created experimental "model psychoses" with these agents in the hope of gaining insight into the cause and treatment of "real" psychopathologies. Early enthusiasms concerning the value of "model psychoses" have waned in recent years since these states do not faithfully duplicate either the physical processes or the subjective experiences of a true psychosis.

Some therapists have claimed that hallucinogens boost the value of other treatment techniques (Cholden, 1956; Shlien et al., 1968). Schmneige (1963) summarized the rationale for their therapeutic use as follows: it helps the patient recall and vent repressed early experiences; it intensifies the patient's affectivity; and it allows him to observe and better understand his distortions and so on.

Despite these commendable features and frequent subjective reports by patients of new "transcendental" feelings following repeated hallucinogen intake, there have been few well-controlled studies proving their effectiveness either as a form of therapy or as an adjunct to other therapeutic methods.

EVALUATION

There are several advantages of psychopharmacological therapy that are not shared by other treatment techniques:

1.   The ease of administration, minimal time demands upon professional personnel and the small financial cost of these agents allow more patients to be treated more efficiently and economically than with other forms of therapy.

2.   Therapeutic regimens can be programmed with considerable precision since dose levels and rates can be administered exactly as desired and regulated to produce optimum effects.

3.   Pharmaceuticals can be used not only as an adjunct to other therapeutic techniques, but to enhance or counteract effects produced by other techniques.

4.   The efficacy of drugs can be evaluated more rapidly than other therapies since their effects are usually evident within a few days.

5.   In contrast to other treatment methods, detrimental effects can readily be reversed by the simple step of withdrawing the drug.

6. Since the chemical composition of pharmacological drugs can be deciphered quickly, modifications in molecular structure can be devised and tested rapidly to see if they are superior to established agents.

ELECTROCONVULSIVE THERAPY

Electroconvulsive therapy (ECT), one of the few genuine techniques to emerge from the long medical history of "electrotherapy," developed not as a form of electrical treatment, but as an incidental method to induce therapeutic convulsions. In other words, the convulsion and not the electricity is the therapeutic agent.

Despite minor variations in method, the basic ECT technique has remained essentially unchanged since Cerletti and Bini originally devised it. The patient rests comfortably on a well-padded mattress. To avoid unpleasant associations with treatment, patients are administered a quick-acting anesthetic such as intravenous sodium pentothal. A reversible muscular relaxant such as anectine may also be injected to minimize the intensity of seizure activity, decreasing thereby the danger of dislocations or fractures. Electrodes are attached to the head and a current from 70 to 130 volts is administered for a period of 0.1 to 0.5 seconds, permitting between 200 to 1600 milliamperes to flow through the brain. When the convulsion begins, a resilient mouth piece is inserted to avoid serious tongue bite. Trunk and upper extremities are gently restrained during the seizure to prevent undue or dangerous movements. The convulsion is of the *grand mal* variety; there is a sudden flexion of the body, followed by a rigid phase lasting about ten to 15 seconds; next, the clonic phase ensues, characterized by rapid jerking movements lasting about 30 seconds. Following the convulsion, most patients remain unconscious from five to 30 minutes and awake in a somewhat hazy and confused state with minor and generalized aches, but with no recall for the episode. This experience is repeated from eight to 20 times in a typical course of therapy, with sessions spaced usually at three per week.

ECT has several advantages as a method of inducing convulsions when compared to pharmacological convulsants. As Kalinowsky and Hoch have put it (1961):

(1) the method is technically simpler and cleaner than the repeated intravenous injections of a drug which easily lead to thrombosis of the veins; (2) there is an immediate loss of consciousness which spares the patient any discomfort; (3) failure to respond with the desired convulsive manifestations can be avoided.

Since the advent of oral pharmacological agents (tranquilizers and antidepressants), however, the use of ECT as a treatment technique has sharply declined. Even with muscular relaxants and anesthetics, ECT patients still experience postconvulsion discomforts, memory loss and possible brain damage.

Despite the small number of well-executed studies, enough data have been gathered over the years to enable us to draw fairly reliable conclusions of ECT efficacy (Huston and Locher, 1948; Alexander, 1953; Staudt and Zubin, 1957; Kalinowsky, 1967).

First, the *short-term* benefits of ECT in *depressive disorders* are highly impressive, making it the treatment of choice, especially in cases of "involutional melancholia" and in episodes of "agitated depression." Rapid improvement figures are in the vicinity of 60 to 90 per cent. Long-

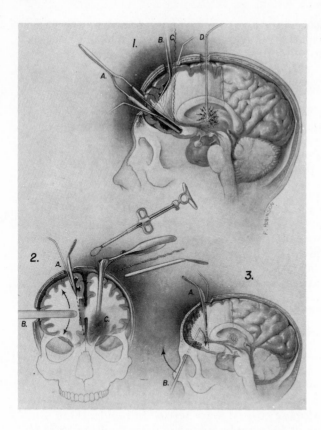

Figure 5–8 Psychosurgical techniques. 1.A, Orbital undercutting. B, Undercutting of superior convexity. C, Electrocoagulation of inferior median quadrant. D, Electrocoagulation of thalamic nucleus. 2.A, Cingulate gyrus undercutting. B, "Closed" standard lobotomy. C, Electrocautery method and suction and spatula method. 3.A, "Open" standard lobotomy. B, Transorbital lobotomy. (Entire set, courtesy of Dr. William B. Scoville.)

term improvement levels, however, do not support the superiority of ECT treatment over matched controls. It appears, then, that ECT only hastens recovery time in those cases that it benefits. On the negative side, patients who improve with ECT relapse more frequently than do those who recover spontaneously.

Second, except for cases of markedly severe depression, the evidence of ECT efficacy is minimal or negative. Where it does bring about recovery in nondepressed cases, these patients are likely to have profited equally well under less drastic therapeutic regimens.

PSYCHOSURGICAL PROCEDURES

At the Second International Neurological Congress in London, Fulton and Jacobsen (1935) described the elimination of experimentally induced "neuroses" in two chimpanzees following the surgical removal of large segments of the frontal brain lobes.

Egas Moniz, a Portuguese psychiatrist, later to receive the Nobel Prize for his work, attended the 1935 Congress. Together with Almeida Lima, a neurosurgeon, Moniz was able to devise several sophisticated surgical methods; they finally selected what they termed the *prefrontal leucotomy* technique (1936), a procedure that severed connections between the frontal lobes (alleged thought center) and the thalamus (alleged emotion center).

Psychosurgery was given a marked impetus in this country by Walter Freeman and James Watts (1942) who reported rather striking results with procedures similar to those of Moniz and Lima. Patients who had for years been confined to institutions as uncooperative or utterly hopeless were reported to have become manageable, capable of working efficiently by themselves and even improved enough in some cases to take on jobs and assume a normal social life. The surgical procedure employed by Freeman and Watts, which they termed the *prefrontal lobotomy*, differed slightly from that of Moniz. They refined Moniz's general statement that mental difficulties were pathologically "fixed" neural pathways, claiming that psychopathology was a product of the patient's tendency to overelaborate, by means of the processes of the frontal lobes, emotions generated in the thalamic region. In accord with this theoretical rationale, they assumed that severing the pathways between these centers would prevent the patient from "worrying" about his emotional discomfort; as a consequence, he could no longer expand minor distresses into pathological proportions.

Since Moniz's original procedure, numerous techniques have been fashioned in the hope of both maximizing the effectiveness of psychosurgery and minimizing its troublesome complications.

The first and most widely employed psychosurgical techniques include the *prefrontal leucotomy* of Moniz, the *prefrontal lobotomy* of Freeman and Watts and the *transorbital lobotomy* devised by Fiamberti in 1937. The primary intent of these operations is to sever nerve tracts between the frontal cortex and the thalamus. In both prefrontal leucotomy and lobotomy methods, small drill holes are made on the side or top of the skull and a sharp instrument is inserted and rotated in about a 35 degree arc just back of the frontal lobes. The transorbital technique differs from the others in that the cutting instrument is inserted through the thin, bony structure separating the eye and the brain; it has the advantage, relative to other methods, that it is simpler to execute surgically and tends to produce fewer postoperative complications.

There is a rather confusing mass of research on the effectiveness of these techniques. From them, we may conclude that psychosurgery has as its primary consequence the reduction of intense affect. Thus, it should be of greatest value with patients characterized by severe anxiety and agitation or by emotional impulsiveness and hostility. However, since the advent of psychopharmacological agents, the need to employ so radical a technique as surgery for these cases has been markedly reduced. It would appear, then, that psychosurgery can be justified only when all other therapeutic procedures have failed. Even then, it should be employed with great reluctance since its effects are irreversible, and the possibility always exists that less drastic and more effective methods may soon be discovered.

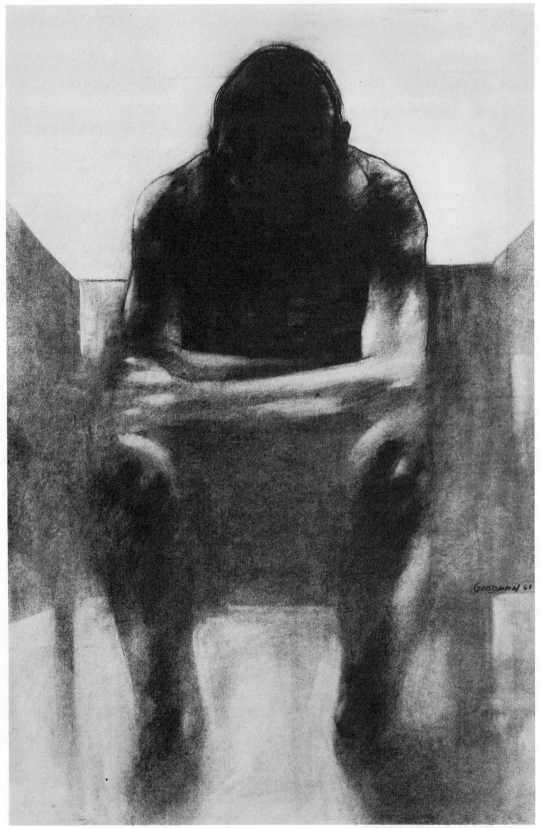

Sidney Goodman—*Man Waiting*

6 SOCIOCULTURAL APPROACHES

INTRODUCTION

Whether or not the label "the third mental health revolution" applies appropriately to the approaches described in this chapter, there is little doubt they represent a striking departure in orientation from those described previously. The individual patient is no longer the prime focus; rather it is the wider social setting, the forces which impinge upon the patient, and which he in turn influences that have taken over center stage. Many innovations in thinking and practice have emerged to reflect this changing orientation: the therapeutic community, family therapy, social action research and so forth. The "clinical model" has been supplanted by the "public health" model, with a consequent shift toward preventive programs and a renewed concern for the underprivileged. These transitions present dilemmas to both fledgling and mature mental health professionals. As Hume has put it (1966):

... If he changes too little, he may attempt to apply the familiar doctor-patient model to the diagnosis and solution of community mental health problems for which it is unsuitable; if he transforms himself too completely or suddenly in order to deal with social issues, he may lose his clinical perspective.

EARLY VIEWPOINTS

The origins of social and community approaches are more divergent than those described in earlier chapters, drawing their impetus not only from psychiatric and psychological thought, but from the demands of public spokesmen, on the one hand, and the compelling data of anthropological and sociological theorists, on the other.

MENTAL HYGIENE MOVEMENT

Support for a public health approach to physical disorders has grown consistently since the mid-1800's. With success in overcoming such diseases as tuberculosis and yellow fever, it was merely a matter of time before a social-preventive approach would draw the interest of professionals concerned with mental disorders.

A   B

Figure 6-1   A, Dorothea L. Dix. B, Clifford W. Beers.

Although the roots of the "mental hygiene" movement can be traced to
the early ideas of Philippe Pinel in France and Benjamin Rush in
America, the first effective leadership came from a Massachusetts school
teacher, Dorothea Lynde Dix (1802–1887). Until her investigations in
1841 into the neglect and brutality prevalent in asylums, these so-called
treatment institutions for the mentally ill were privately funded and,
despite their deplorable conditions, existed only for the wealthy. Miss
Dix contended that "insanity" was a product of inhumane conditions in
society; hence, society should assume full responsibility for the care of its
victims. She continued her crusade for more than 40 years, influencing
the building of 30 state-supported hospitals and, more importantly, establishing firmly the modern principle of public responsibility for the
mentally ill. It is sad to note that this product of her enlightened work,
our great state hospital system, is now viewed a burden to current community mental health efforts.

Although care for the mentally ill had improved as a consequence of
Dix's labors, more was needed than the construction of fortress-like
asylums to calm the suspicions and fears of the general public. Prompted
by repeated mistreatment as a patient in three such institutions, Clifford
W. Beers (1876–1943), wrote a penetrating account of his experiences in
the now famous book *A Mind That Found Itself*. When published in 1908,
it aroused intense public reaction and the support of such eminent men
as William James and Adolf Meyer. With his founding of the Society for
Mental Hygiene shortly thereafter, Beers inaugurated a world-wide
movement designed not only to encourage improved hospital conditions, but to educate the public on the importance of prevention, and
dispel the prevalent belief that mental disorders were a stigma of
disgrace and incurable.

ROOTS IN SOCIAL SCIENCE

As mental health professionals were drawn to social concerns about abnormal behavior, their need to explore the ideas of social scientists grew
increasingly. Meanwhile, social scientists had begun to turn their attention to issues of social pathology and gradually found their focus shifting
to the relationship connecting society to mental health.

The first major theorist to bridge these fields was the eminent French
sociologist Emile Durkheim (1858–1917). Shortly before the turn of the
century he proposed the concept of *anomie* to signify a widespread disintegration of a society's standards and norms. When a high degree of
anomie occurs, the rules which previously served to guide social behav-

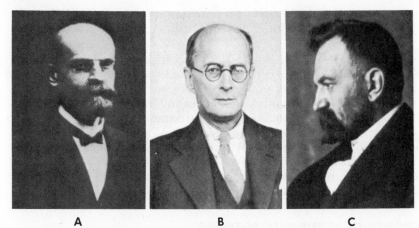

Figure 6-2 A, Emile Durkheim. B, Bronislaw Malinowski. C, George H. Mead.

ior lose their power to maintain group solidarity and individual direction. Durkheim was particularly intrigued by the relationship between anomie and suicide. On the basis of his studies, he concluded that suicide is infrequent during periods when the standards of a society are firm and unchanging; conversely, what he called anomic suicide rose sharply at times of active social change. Although Durkheim's specific thesis has long been challenged, it did serve to stimulate others to explore the connection between social events and mental disorders. Thus, by 1922, a major annual section of the meetings of the American Sociological Society was devoted specifically to this topic.

Interest in abnormal behavior developed concurrently among sociologists and cultural anthropologists. The works of two major figures, George H. Mead (1863–1931) and Bronislaw Malinowski (1884–1942), were especially significant in stimulating a synthesis between anthropological thinking and abnormal behavior. Numerous studies were reported during the mid-1920's comparing the incidence and characteristics of behavior patterns among different cultures. Similarly, a steady stream of articles in anthropological and psychiatric journals utilized the concepts of theories of both fields (Kroeber, 1934). Particularly fruitful

Figure 6-3 A, Alexander Leighton. B, Margaret Mead. C, Abram Kardiner. D, Ruth Benedict.

contributions during this and later periods were made by Ruth Benedict (1934), Alexander Leighton, Abram Kardiner and Margaret Mead.

Not only were the sociologists and anthropologists of the twenties and thirties providing new insights for what was to be known later as the field of "social psychiatry," but another social science discipline, that of epidemiology, began to provide new data and insights as well. Studying the migration, mobility and regional distribution of psychiatric disorders among specific population groups, epidemiologic researchers such as C. R. Shaw, Robert Faris and H. W. Dunham offered impressive data demonstrating the close correspondence between a wide number of cultural variables (e.g., residence, race, socioeconomic status) and the prevalence of abnormality (e.g., schizophrenia, delinquency, alcoholism).

GROWTH OF COMMUNITY AGENCIES

The expansion of the state mental hospital system was a logical outgrowth of the commonly held view at the turn of the century that people were either "sane" or "insane"; if a person was deemed insane, and therefore permanently incapable of assuming responsibility for his actions and welfare, then the "kindest" course of action was to remove him to a custodial asylum and let him live out his days under the guidance of others. It was not long, however, before the notion that mental disturbances were of an all-or-none nature became a matter of dispute among sophisticated professionals and laymen. Sociologists and anthropologists, as noted earlier, provided convincing evidence that man's behavior was a product of his social environment and amenable to change if that environment could be modified. As this viewpoint grew in prominence, it was proposed that institutions be located in the "social communities" where patients lived, rather than in the remote areas where most asylums had been built. Moreover, in their own communities, patients would be treated close to their families and natural life settings rather than isolated for custodial care.

One of the first of these new community mental institutions was the so-called "psychopathic hospital," initially associated with University medical schools such as Michigan, Harvard and Johns Hopkins. These new hospitals not only focused on the treatment of patients but served both to elicit community interest in mental health and reinforce the view that social factors were central elements in the development of mental illness.

Along similar lines, Lightner Witmer, the founder of clinical psychology, established an agency in 1896 at the University of Pennsylvania to serve children with learning and emotional difficulties. Here, too, the focus was on preventive and remedial techniques, with primary attention given to those who continued to function in their normal life settings. A major step in promoting community-based clinics for children was taken when William Healy was provided with state funds in 1909 to establish the Chicago Psychopathic Institute for children, later renamed the Institute for Juvenile Research. Numerous community agencies were founded soon thereafter; although most were affiliated with hospitals, nearly 400 "mental clinics" for adults and children were in operation by 1925.

Throughout this period several women who had functioned as charitable volunteers at mental hospitals recognized the need to systematize the training of others in their many and diverse activities, a step which ultimately led to the formalization of the field of psychiatric social work.

Although conceived initially as a welfare and aftercare service for patients discharged from mental hospitals, the role of this new profession expanded gradually over the years until it assumed primary leadership among the mental health professions in directing attention to the varied social forces involved both in causation and rehabilitation.

MODERN THEORIES

The second World War was a turning point dividing earlier and modern views of mental health. Although social and community approaches gradually took hold among advanced professionals in the 1930's and 1940's, it was not until the late fifties and sixties that this orientation surged into its current prominence. Today, in the seventies, it stands among the most vital of approaches in the field. In this section we will turn to three formulations that reflect this growth: social systems, consultation and crisis theories.

SOCIAL SYSTEMS THEORY

Although Newbrough (1964) has pointed out that the "community mental health movement" lacks the kind of formal theory that typifies other approaches to the field, there is one overriding point of view that is expressed in common among professionals of this persuasion: that known as "social systems" or "ecological" theory. Most clearly formulated by James Kelly (1966, 1968, 1971), the social systems model completely redefines traditional concepts of abnormal behavior. The perspective is no longer the individual himself, but the interrelationship among the complex social settings within which the person functions (Berrien, 1968). Kelly outlines several types of problems that emerge from this ecological frame of reference. At the broadest level, social ecologists ask about relationships between physical environmental forces and individual behavior, probing such areas as the density of the population within which the person lives or the effects of changes in housing patterns or urban life settings. Next, and on the assumption that social structure and individual behavior have reciprocal influences, their studies focus on the impact of culture and community groups, their shifting values, institutionalized roles, status differentials, available resources for behavioral expression, patterns of family life and so forth.

It is central to the ecological orientation that appraisal of mental health problems take as its primary subject the total social context and population rather than the person who at present receives formal clinical service. It is the community that is the client, not the individual. The varied psychosocial forces of a specific community are analyzed in detail so as to highlight those distinctive patterns of behavior that typify that environment. The responsibility of the mental health professional is to identify those forces of the system that support psychological well-being and those that work against it. By clarifying which aspects of the environment are health-producing and which are health-detracting, the ecological analyst can formulate a sound basis for changing the system.

Numerous practical problems arise when the analyst attempts to implement the changes he has specified. Ingrained social systems are self-perpetuating, and those with vested interests in them are resistant to incursions upon their established power and status. Although leadership roles for a community's indigenous nonprofessional population fits logically in an ecological model, the "old guard" political and professional establishment dies hard and often acts to undermine system changes that threaten their authority. The task of the social systems theorist must include, then, an analysis of these rigidities and constraints, and he must reckon with them before his model for change can be effective.

CONSULTATION THEORY

A second, more sharply focused model than social systems theory, yet one also reflecting the sociocultural approach to mental health, is that termed "consultation" theory. Most clearly formulated in the work of Gerald Caplan (1964), the consultation model rests on two basic facts; first, there exist in all communities numerous nonmental health professionals and workers (termed *caregivers),* such as educators, physicians, policemen and clergymen, whose daily activities involve them in frequent, responsible and often close relationships with people in emotional distress; second, there is a marked shortage of fully-trained mental health professionals available to provide needed clinical services. Consultation theory attempts to formulate a means by which nonmental health professionals can develop a measure of expertise to enable them to function in productive mental health roles (Roe, 1970). In effect, consultation is a formal procedure in which mental health professionals advise and guide these caregivers to identify, prevent and solve the emotional problems of those who seek their assistance.

Not only does consultation spread mental health knowledge, and thereby increase the scope and impact of effective service to wider populations, but these caregivers can intervene at early stages of distress and do so in arrangements that are more "natural" to the person seeking help, often with greater confidence and trust. Moreover, the everyday involvement of caregivers in the routine social life of their clients enables them to play a unique role in influencing family affairs and community support. Stated differently, caregivers can often shape sociocultural health-promoting activities in a manner that is not only especially effective but is also integrated within the natural life experiences of those who seek them. Thus, by encouraging and strengthening the expertise of these community-based caregivers, consultation serves to disseminate knowledge and produce a new cadre of mental health workers, especially in areas previously deprived of such services. Furthermore, these activities also develop within communities a foundation for engineering psychologically-minded social change. Indigenous caregivers, in this model, often become committed advocates to the cause of mental health planning and preventive intervention. Consultation, then, can be seen as an operational phase of social systems thinking; it seeks to effect a wide range of interrelated changes that emerge from and evolve naturally within the context of everyday social life.

CRISIS THEORY

As we progress from social systems to consultation and, in this section, to crisis theory, our sociocultural orientation becomes increasingly narrow and focused, from the broad sweep of complex community structure and power to that of specific individuals who are undergoing acute emotional distress. Crisis theory was brought to the foreground as a significant mental health service by Erich Lindemann (1944) following his study of survivors of the disastrous Coconut Grove Nightclub fire. In recent years, providing immediate psychological support for crisis victims in the community has become a major model not only of rehabilitation but of preventive intervention. Thus, crisis thinking is geared

Figure 6-4 A, Gerald Caplan. B, James Kelly.

A   B

today to the task both of forestalling potentially more severe consequences of acute distress and of building within the individual psychological resources which enable him to withstand future psychological strains. As Zax and Cowen (1972) have stated,

Crises are thus significant crossroads — far more important than their brief moment in time would imply. Exertion of effort toward constructive handling of crises is an important challenge for the mental health professions.

Central to the sociocultural theme of the crisis approach is that psychological problems be dealt with directly and promptly as they arise in the community, not following bureaucratic complications and sequences of frustrating referrals and belatedly at the doorstep of an office clinician. To achieve this means establishing "storefront" and "walk-in" clinics (Tannenbaum, 1966), that is, mental health agencies that are located in the community where people live and where they can receive immediate assistance or therapy. By eliminating the obstacles of distance, referrals and long waiting lists, problems can be dealt with at these walk-in centers on an emergency basis. Increasingly prominent and useful in underprivileged communities, where high-priced professionals rarely locate, these crisis-oriented clinics offer a wide range of services, from simple opportunities to vent one's feelings and gain reassurance and support to assistance in managing more specific personal problems such as family disputes, job difficulties and economic and housing questions. Although these seemingly more mundane personal problems appear not to require the services of trained mental health professionals, they are often the forerunners of later, more serious pathology. Hence, through effective early handling, the crisis worker can fulfill the major tenet of preventive intervention so central to the sociocultural approach.

CONCEPTIONS OF THERAPY

Although the major thrust of recent sociocultural thinking has been toward effecting systems changes and developing preventive programs, it has generated a wide variety of remedial therapies over the years. As noted earlier, the impact of social factors in molding and sustaining behaviors and attitudes has been thoroughly studied for several decades. During this same period, we noted that there has been a growing awareness of the shortage of trained personnel to meet the increasing need for therapeutic services. Spurred by practical considerations, psychopathologists sought to devise new and more efficient ways of treating patients for whom individual therapy was neither feasible nor available. The combination of "group dynamics" research in the 1940's and 1950's and the need for more expedient forms of therapy led to a rapid growth of what we have termed the "sociotherapies." In this section we will turn to four such therapeutic techniques: casework, milieu, group and family.

CASEWORK THERAPY

The profession of "social work" has traditionally played a central role in planning and controlling elements of patient life which influence the progress of formal treatment; appropriately enough, social workers are viewed as integral members of the total "therapeutic team."

There are two goals of casework. First, to assist either the patient or his family in removing destructive economic and interpersonal conditions and, second, to help the patient cope with the affairs of his life.

Achieving these ends may require direct counseling on practical matters such as daily habits and routines and the budgeting of family finances. More importantly, caseworkers can be of considerable assistance in pointing out to relatives how they may be contributing to interpersonal tensions and resentments within the family. The one or two hours of face to face therapy with the patient may be completely negated by the attitudes of relatives whose good intentions are no guarantee that they will be carried out. Where necessary, then, direct intervention in the form of weekly counseling sessions may be recommended for relatives who create difficulties.

Where occupational or social problems exist, caseworkers may be instrumental in arranging patient participation in community agencies such as sheltered workshops and recreational centers. In sheltered occupational programs, the patient may learn to cope with tensions he may have previously experienced in relating to fellow employees and employers; the understanding and tolerant attitudes of the professional supervisory staff at these centers ensure against harsh reprimands for poor performance which reinforce feelings of self-inadequacy (Olshansky, 1960). For essentially similar goals, caseworkers may recommend participation in recreational clubs so as to remotivate social interests and develop interpersonal skills; these settings are relatively free of the personal and competitive tensions of normal group relationships (Bierer, 1948; Lerner, 1960).

Caseworkers can be of invaluable service in smoothing the transition of patients from hospital to home and community. Practical arrangements may be made for the patient's employment, follow-up therapy and guidance to the family as to their expectations and ways of reacting to the patient. To ease the strain of resuming normal responsibilities that may be too taxing for the patient, arrangements may be made for *halfway house* or *night or day* hospital programs. In a halfway house, the patient lives with other former patients in a home within the community that is supervised by professional personnel. In this setting, he may begin to relearn the skills of normal social life without facing undue family expectations and occupational pressures (Wechsler, 1960). Similarly, in night hospital programs, patients begin their re-entry to community life by

A   B   C
Figure 6–5   A, Maxwell Jones. B, Jacob L. Moreno. C, Nathan W. Ackerman.

working at a "regular job" during the day, but still have the refuge and support of hospital services and personnel in the evening (Harris, 1957). In a parallel day program, the pattern of transition to community life is reversed; here, patients live at home, but spend their days in the sheltered environs of the hospital where deviant behaviors are tolerated and where they can continue to be helped in coping with everyday problems (Odenheimer, 1965).

MILIEU THERAPY

Until the last two or three decades, hospitalized patients were provided with kind and thoughtful custodial care at best and at worst, were incarcerated in filthy wards, shackled, crammed together and isolated from the interests and activities of the larger community. Even among the better hospitals, little effort was expended to see that the setting, routines and personnel of the institution provided more than a comfortable asylum, a refuge from strains of everyday existence, a place where patients could withdraw quietly into themselves. Despite the pioneering efforts of Pinel in the eighteenth century and Dorothea Dix in the nineteenth century, Deutsch (1948) could report in his book, *The Shame of the States*, that most hospital patients in the mid-twentieth century sat out their lives in dreary environments, abandoned by unsympathetic families and exposed to uninterested personnel.

Today, the well-run mental hospital is no longer a place of incarceration or a refuge for social invalids, but a total "therapeutic community," a miniature environment that simulates the life and activities of the outside social world. Stimulated by the work and writings of Maxwell Jones (1953, 1973), the modern hospital milieu differs from a "true society" only in that it is designed intentionally to assist its members to learn to replace maladaptive and deficient behaviors with more appropriate ones.

Two aspects of institutional life promote these ends.

The first is the simple act of removing the patient from normal environmental stresses and placing him in a quiet and tolerant setting. "Safe" from external sources of humiliation and hostility, and able to "act out" his disturbed feelings without condemnation, the patient's anxieties subside and he may begin to regain a measure of composure.

The achievement of this first goal prepares the patient for the second and more important one of milieu therapy, developing increased social competence. Every facet of hospital life, e.g., cafeteria routine, housekeeping schedules, recreational programs and so on, becomes a therapeutic experience. Two aspects of institutional therapy have been stressed to achieve the goal of increased competence, occupational rehabilitation and the group planning of shared activities.

In years past, occupational therapy served the function of keeping patients busy by using them as cheap labor to reduce the costs of institutional management. At the very best, these activities countered the tendency of patients to disintegrate into idleness and invalidism. Such limited aims have been repudiated. Occupational programs are designed today with the patient's special rehabilitative needs in mind. Industrial training is meaningful and goal-oriented, suited to the talents and interests of the patient and arranged to provide him with new skills that will enhance his self-esteem and prepare him to find a rewarding vocation in the larger social community.

The former practice of isolating patients from each other and from the larger community is a thing of the past. Modern day hospitals not only practice "open ward" policies, but encourage social contact among patients and the outside world. Moreover, patients who live together in ward units establish their own "governments" through which they plan daily routines and recreational activities (Denker, 1960; Rapaport, 1963). Through these self-organized and administered groups, patients begin to gain a sense of citizenship and social responsibility, achieve a renewed sense of self-respect, acquire a modicum of interpersonal skills and learn to assume a participant role in an environment that parallels the give-and-take interactions of normal community life. Although group ventures such as these can prove a strain upon the fragile controls of certain patients, for the greater number it furnishes an opportunity to regain the perspective of shared living that was lost during earlier phases of their illness.

GROUP THERAPY

In the most common form of group therapy, usually six to ten patients participate in leader-directed or non-directed discussions; some groups focus on specific topics whereas others have open discussions in which "anything goes." Usually, the therapist plays a passive role, assuming a congenial and nonjudgmental attitude that encourages patients to expose and explore their feelings until they discover better ways than before to resolve them.

Central to most group therapies is the exposure of each member's attitudes and feelings (Yalom, 1970). As topics and events unfold, each person brings into the open, as candidly as he can, the various emotions and thoughts he experiences toward other members. The patient becomes aware of his particular sensitivities by contrasting his reactions with those of others to the same set of circumstances. Not only does he become aware of his selective distortions, but he begins to see how these reactions perpetuate his difficulties and create new ones.

Another feature that characterizes discussion groups is the way in which patients interpret each other's difficulties; this interpretive interplay is well illustrated in the following transcript (Hinckley and Hermann, 1951).

Therapist.   Will you review for us what happened last time, Alice?

Alice.   I was scared. I didn't like getting together with people I hardly knew. Telling things about myself was awful.

June.   Well, I felt just the opposite. I loved it. I suppose the lesson of the session was that by listening to others and helping them, we learn about ourselves.

Ellen.   I'm having a bad day. Someone bumped my car, and I've been fuming. I'm not sure I can contribute much today at all.

June.   Now that I think about it, I don't know where to start in regard to my problems. I'm too fat. I know it's from eating too much, but there must be some reason behind it, I know. Why do I pick at food all the time?

Therapist.   Tell us something more about your background, if you will.

June.   Well, everybody in our family have beautiful figures. They all disapprove of my overeating.

Sara.   You mean you have to fight it? You don't look overweight to me.

June (in great surprise)   Won't you all come home with me?

Alice.   Are you hungry all the time? Are you hungry when you're happy and satisfied?

June.   No, I guess not. I was with a fellow over the weekend and had a wonderful time, and I wasn't hungry at all.

Therapist.   Sounds psychological. Perhaps you know something of the psychology of overeating.

Alice.   My little niece has the same sort of trouble.

June.   Well, I suppose when you keep on eating all the time and never really get satisfied, it can't be food you want at all. (Silence) Maybe — maybe — the eating is a substitute for something else that is lacking.

Therapist.   You feel something else is lacking?

Alice.   She is right. Something else probably is lacking. She wants something, but it's not food. She feels OK — at least not hungry — when she is with her boyfriend. (Laughing) maybe it's love she is looking for.

June (surprised).   Why, yes, that could be, couldn't it? How reasonable that seems! But why should I need to look for love?

Alice.   Guess I can't help there. I don't know.

June.   There must be something wrong in the family — something lacking. Can it be love there, too? Oh, I'm getting confused.

Sara.   No, I think you are on the right track. I've got trouble along that line, too, but I don't try to solve mine by eating. I do it in other ways.

Karen.   Well, what is this trouble at home? I've got troubles with my boy friend, and I never can get along at home. My mother nags if I don't jump when she wants me to. My boy friend used to take my part, but since my father died, he sides with my mother when he knows about our arguments. My mother ends up crying all the time. Something is wrong.

Therapist.   Conflict with parents sometimes does cause painful behavior symptoms.

CASE 6–1

Group Therapy

Another model of the group approach is Jacob Moreno's technique of *psychodrama* (1934, 1946), a method designed to bring to the open one's deeper attitudes and emotions through spontaneous playacting. In a typical procedure, several patients and therapists enact an unrehearsed series of scenes in which they assume the roles of people that are significant in their real lives. Patients are encouraged to relive and express with dramatic intensity feelings and thoughts that could not be expressed through normal conventional methods.

Let us note some of the advantages of group therapy as seen by its exponents. *First,* and perhaps most significant, is the fact that the patient acquires his new learnings in a setting that is similar to his "natural" interpersonal and social world. It is easier to "generalize" to the outside world what one learns in peer-group settings since it is closer to "reality" than is the individual treatment setting. *Second,* since the patient must cope with a host of different personalities in his group, he acquires a range of flexible interpersonal skills. He learns to relate not only to a single therapist, but to a variety of different personality types. *Third,* the semi-realistic atmosphere of the group provides the patient with ample opportunities to try out his new attitudes and behaviors. Group therapy serves, then, as a proving ground, an experimental laboratory within which the formative stages of new learnings can be rehearsed and refined. *Fourth,* by observing that his feelings are shared by others, the patient is not only reassured that he is not alone in his suffering, but regains some of his former self-confidence and self-respect. *Fifth,* no longer ashamed of his thoughts and emotions, he can give up the barriers he has placed between himself and others, enabling him to relate to them without fear and embarrassment. *Sixth,* able to accept criticism and

A

C

B

Figure 6–6   A, Family therapy. B, Psychodrama. C, Group therapy.

defenses, he begins to see himself as others do and develops a more realistic appraisal of his social strengths and weaknesses. *Seventh,* along with increased accuracy of self-perception, he learns to observe others more objectively and gradually gives up his previous tendencies to distort his social judgments.

FAMILY THERAPY

The patient who seeks therapy is often but one member of an abnormal family unit. Not uncommonly, interactions between family members form a complex of shared psychopathology, the patient being merely its most dramatic "symptom." The "primary" patient is caught in a system of attitudes and behaviors that not only intensify his illness, but maintain the pathological family unit. Each member, through reciprocal distortions, reinforces pathogenic reactions in others, thus creating a vicious circle. It follows that therapy must intervene not only with the patient himself, but with the total family (Boszormenyi-Nagy and Framo, 1965). In short, what is needed is family therapy, not individual therapy.

Several variants in technique have been developed to achieve the goal of disentangling these pathological family relations; best known among these are the views of Nathan Ackerman (1958) and Virginia Satir (1964, 1967). Essentially, the therapist brings several members of the family together, explores major areas of conflict and exposes the destructive behaviors that have perpetuated their difficulties. The therapist clarifies misunderstandings, dissolves barriers to communication and neutralizes areas of prejudice, hostility, guilt and fear. In this manner, he gradually disengages the pathogenic machinery of the family system and enables its members to explore healthier patterns of relating. By recommending new, more wholesome attitudes and behaviors and by supporting family members as they test out these patterns, the therapist may succeed in resolving not only the difficulties of the primary patient, but pathological trends that have taken root in all members.

The following transcript illustrates a typical interchange in family therapy. It is drawn from the fourth session of a group that was formed because of the mother's concern that her son (Dick), a 13 year old boy, was becoming increasingly rebellious and potentially delinquent. The treatment unit consists of the therapist, the mother and father (Mr. and Mrs. Clay), Dick and his ten year old sister, Janet (Sundberg and Tyler, 1962).

CASE 6–2

Family Therapy

Therapist. I think last time one thing that was mentioned was that we need a lot more understanding, and that's our task here — to try to understand each other. The purpose of this kind of meeting is to help the family to talk together and to see how each other feels about things.

Mrs. Clay. I felt that something was brought out last time that was really helpful to me and that is that I spend too much time moralizing and talking. I think I have overdone that.

Therapist (to Dick and Janet). How did the rest of you feel about that? Do you agree with Mom on that? (Janet laughs.) On the moralizing and talking? Both of you?

Janet. Well, I think that she talks a little bit too much, but not too much. I mean she talks a little too much at times, but it isn't too bad.

Mrs. Clay. Janet felt this week that I dug into her about eating too much and gaining weight. (Laughs.)

Therapist. Oh, is that right? Would you tell us about that?

Janet.   Oh, it was yesterday at the party. I had some cookies and I started to eat them. She'd say, "Now Janet, don't you eat any of those."

Mrs. Clay.   I said, "Now don't eat all of them." (Laughs.) She had a whole pile of them. (Laughs again.)

Therapist.   And this is something that you would just as soon not be reminded of.

Janet.   Oh, I might be reminded but not every single second.
(Pause.)

Therapist.   How about you Dick. How have you been?

Dick.   Oh, I wasn't home hardly any of the time. When she (the mother) was home, I wasn't and when I was home, she wasn't, so I didn't have hardly any trouble.

Mr. Clay.   I think that it has been a little easier week this time. I don't know how Dick is coming out on his school problems, but I think that it has been a little better, partly because he has had his own way.

Dick.   The teachers sent me five times to the office this week. That's an improvement.

Mr. Clay.   Improvement? Do you mean that you've gone to the office more times? How many times? Once a day?

Dick.   No, I went three times in one day. Twice. One time in two different days.

Mr. Clay.   The average has been worse than that?

Dick.   It's usually been about two times every day.

Mr. Clay.   Do they come from the same or different teachers?

Dick.   Oh, it's usually the same one. I have my ideas and I'm not going to back down. If you do back down you are a lost soul. You've got to have your own head.

Mr. Clay.   You have a point there. But sooner or later you back up against something you can't control and then what are you going to do?

Dick.   I'm going to just push right forward.

Mr. Clay.   You can't sometimes.

Dick.   Hmmm.

Mr. Clay.   I wonder what the answer is. It seems to me that everyone is going to have to knuckle down some place sometime. It's just a matter of when and how much.

Mrs. Clay.   It has been awful easy for me to have a high standard in life. I have it for myself as well as others, but I think that I am coming to realize that I can't influence others — that if I keep my standard for myself that then I'll have to let others choose their standards. I think I have been getting a little more peace in my mind and realizing that I am responsible to God for myself and to train others, but the results are not my — —

Dick (interrupts).   Mother, this isn't church. Good night!

Mrs. Clay.   Well, those things have to be said.

Dick.   She can do it in church — not here. A bunch of preaching!

Mr. Clay.   Most people have to learn the hard way, but they'd like you to learn some other way than the hard way, but I kind of think that you are going to have to learn the hard way, however hard it is. If you're going to fall, you'll just have to fall.

Mrs. Clay.   Well, I've just wanted to prevent that, but I don't think that can be done.

Therapist.   Is it that you feel irritated with Dick or that you feel that the children need to learn on their own?

Mr. Clay.   I kind of feel, maybe I'm sounding off here against Dick, but that's not necessarily the case, that not the last couple of years but previous to that he didn't get all that was coming to him, not only him but the rest of us in this room. Their discipline wasn't as tough as it might have been. And now that it is starting to tighten up again, they are kind of behind the eightball and they don't know what to do about it. They don't want to give in — they have had their own way for a while — and now the fun begins.

Therapist.   How do you feel about this, Dick?

Dick.   I'm not backing down.

Therapist.   That seems to be your theme, doesn't it?

Dick.   Boy, there's going to be something that's really going to come up. Someone is going to have to work hard. I'm not going to back down.

Therapist.   It's important for you to keep your own head all the way.

Dick.   Yeah.

CASE 6–2
Continued

EVALUATION

The advantages and disadvantages of individual and group therapies have been debated for years. Obviously, these two approaches are different and can be justified on rational grounds by their exponents. Group methods save personnel time and if effective can expedite the treatment of a greater number of patients than can individual methods. Decisions as to their special spheres of utility cannot truly be made since there have been few studies demonstrating their comparative effectiveness. Therapists make their choices on the basis of theoretical or personal preferences; on these dubious grounds, some utilize one or the other treatment approach exclusively for all patients.

Among the few studies, note may be made of two that satisfy certain minimal criteria of sound research design. Powdermaker and Frank (1953) compared two groups, one receiving individual therapy only, the other receiving both individual and group therapy. The results were not notably different. Using physician judgments as a criterion, 52 per cent of the former group were improved as contrasted to 62 per cent of the latter. In a population of hospital patients, Fairweather et al., (1960) studied the effectiveness of four therapeutic regimens: a nontherapy control, individual therapy, group therapy and group living with periodic group therapy. Notable in the design was the systematic differentiation and matching of patient "types," the use of a battery of several objective criterion measures and periodic follow-up evaluations. The results were complicated. Essentially, all therapeutic modalities proved superior to the control group. Differences among treatment procedures were minimal, although they appeared to favor the group-living and individual therapy approaches.

As is true with most types of individual therapy, virtually no studies of a systematic and properly designed nature have been published on group treatment approaches. Although good reasons can be cited for the lack of sound research (e.g., the complexity and number of the variables involved or the difficulty in matching patients), it is the responsibility of group treatment proponents to show that the value of their preferred method is more than an article of faith.

PART 2

DETERMINANTS OF ABNORMAL BEHAVIOR AND PERSONALITY

Willem DeKooning—*Woman I. Collection, The Museum of Modern Art, New York*

7

BIOLOGICAL INFLUENCES

INTRODUCTION

Behavioral scientists tend to depict the brain as a passive target receiving and storing a barrage of incoming stimuli. In contrast, biological scientists know that the nervous system cannot be viewed merely as a faithful follower of what is fed into it from the environment. The brain maintains a rhythm and activity of its own regardless of external stimulation. Moreover, it plays an active role in regulating the sensitivity, and in controlling the amplitude of what is picked up by the peripheral sense organs. Unlike a machine which passively responds to all sources of external stimulation, the brain determines substantially what, when and how events will be experienced.

Each individual's nervous system selects, transforms and registers the objective events of its life in accordance with its distinctive biological sensitivities. Unusual sensitivities or gross abnormalities in this delicate orienting and selecting system can lead to marked distortions in perception and behavior.

Although the exact mechanisms by which brain functions influence abnormal behavior will probably remain obscure for some time, the belief that biological factors are intimately involved in mental disorders is not new. Hippocrates, more than 2000 years ago, attributed most forms of pathology to blood disturbances and to imbalances in the bodily humors. In the mid-nineteenth century, Greisinger claimed that brain lesions would be found to underlie all mental diseases, and Thudichum, the father of modern neurochemistry, in the late nineteenth century, stated that "insanity" was unquestionably the external manifestation of the effects of bodily poisons upon the brain.

The confidence and stature of these men stimulated researchers to explore every nook and cranny of man's anatomy and physiology. The questions raised in this chapter are whether their vague beliefs have been refined into precise theoretical hypotheses and whether recent biological research has produced findings to substantiate their faith.

Pertinent data have been gathered by applying a wide variety of research methods across a broad spectrum of biophysical and behavioral functions. The number of techniques used and the number of variables studied is legion. In the present chapter, we will organize this large and growing body of research into three categories: heredity, infantile reaction patterns and morphological structure.

HEREDITY

In 1962, Paul Meehl included the following query in his Presidential address to the American Psychological Association:

Let me begin by putting a question which I find is almost never answered correctly by our clinical students on PhD orals, and the answer to which they seem to dislike when it is offered. Suppose that you were required to write down a procedure for selecting an individual from the population who would be diagnosed as schizophrenic by a psychiatric staff; you have to wager $1,000 on being right; you may not include in your selection procedure any behavioral fact, such as a symptom or trait, manifested by the individual. What would you write down? So far as I have been able to ascertain, there is only one thing you could write down that would give you a better than even chance of winning such a bet—namely, 'Find an individual X who has a schizophrenic identical twin.'

The notion that mental disorders are inherited has been among the most controversial of topics in psychopathology. Many theorists are convinced that heredity is the crucial determinant of pathology. Others assert with equal conviction that social and interpersonal experiences are primary.

Behavioral scientists have been conditioned to stress environmental learning. Most notable in this regard was J. B. Watson's aggressive denial of the role of heredity back in the 1920's. His disciples and their students retained this viewpoint. At the other extreme are biologically trained theorists who have been conditioned to think that genetic causality is so obvious a factor in behavior as not to require systematic proof through controlled investigation.

In the past decade there has been a rapid growth of theorizing and research in the field of behavioral genetics (Gottesman and Shields, 1973). We will not attempt to persuade the student to accept one or another of the polar views noted previously. Several of the more prominent hypotheses will be outlined and the results of recent research will be critically evaluated. Before we begin this phase of our presentation, however, it will be useful to provide a review of some of the basic terms and methods of genetics.

BASIC CONCEPTS OF GENETICS

The assertion that a trait is subject to genetic influence is a grossly simplified expression of a highly complex physiochemical process, the details of which, for the most part, are beyond our purposes. A few are relevant, however.

The basic units of hereditary transmission are termed *genes*. The existence of the gene as a distinct physical entity is a matter of dispute among geneticists, but it remains a convenient concept for an intricate mosaic of chemical strands arranged in an orderly sequence along a small threadlike body called a *chromosome*. Estimates are that man possesses between 2000 and 80,000 genes. Chromosomes are grouped into 23 pairs. During reproduction each parent supplies, on an entirely random basis, one member of each of their respective pairs of chromosomes. These are combined such that the offspring will possess a new complement of 23 pairs of chromosomes consisting exactly of half from each parent. Because of the random nature of these pairings, the number of combinations possible from any set of parents can be calculated as greater than 8 million. The 46 parental chromosomes are transmitted from one generation to the next unchanged, unless altered by some aberration.

Genetic endowment serves as a foundation which predisposes the individual to particular traits. These dispositions are referred to as *genotypes*. Genotypes which do develop into manifest traits are termed *phenotypes*. Many genotypes remain latent or suppressed, however, and are never expressed in the form of overt physical or psychological characteristcs. Whether or not a genotype becomes manifest depends on the nature of the gene itself, the modifying influences of other genes and the individual's environmental experiences. Two types of genes currently are distinguished by genetic theorists: *major genes* and *polygenes*.

Major Genes.   Only one type of hereditary effect was known in early genetic research, namely transmission by single major genes. Current researchers can now identify many of these genes by their precise locus on a chromosome and their frequent correspondence with conspicuous phenotypic traits, e.g., eye color or pigmentation.

Gregor Mendel, the founder of genetics, observed that certain inherited traits were not manifested except under special conditions. He made a simple distinction among genes to represent this difference in visibility, a distinction conventionally known today as dominant and recessive genes.

Dominant genes reveal themselves even if they occur only in single doses, that is, when they have been inherited from only one parent. *Recessive genes* are discernible only when paired in a double dosage, that is, they must be inherited from both parents to show their effects. If a recessive gene is matched with a dominant gene, the trait with which the recessive gene is normally associated is suppressed by the dominant gene.

Polygenes.   It is increasingly evident that Mendelian major genes cannot account for the full range of genetic variability that has been observed. According to Mendelian notions, major genes are displayed in an all-or-none fashion according to patterns of dominance and recessivity. But we know that most physical and psychological traits (e.g., height, weight, intelligence and blood pressure) fall into continuous or normally shaped distributions. Continuous distributions cannot be explained in terms of the all-or-none operation of major genes.

As an alternative means of explaining the normal distribution of traits, theorists have proposed the operation of multiple minor genes, or what are generally termed polygenes. Polygenes have individually minute, quantitatively similar and cumulative effects. When a large number of such polygenes have equal probabilities of exerting a small and additive effect upon a particular trait, the resulting distribution within the population will be a normal bell-shaped frequency.

The fact that the precise effect of each polygene is too slight to be identified accounts, in part, for why most theorists have avoided them for genetic predictions. Perhaps as the science progresses, their effects will be better known and their role as a research variable will become operational.

METHODS OF GENETIC RESEARCH

Considerable precision is possible when animals are selectively bred to test the genetic origins of a particular trait. Unfortunately for science this is not possible with humans. Studies of human heredity are dependent on an essentially random pattern of social mating, and such naturalistic studies are far from ideal as a means of testing specific genetic hypotheses. Nevertheless, the investigation of correlations among parents, siblings and other relatives of patients has enabled researchers to obtain fairly reliable estimates of the role of genetic influences. The role of heredity in psychopathology has been researched in two ways among humans.

Correspondence Among Relatives. The rationale of this first method as a technique for exploring genetic hypotheses is rather straightforward. The coincidence of a disorder among family members, whose degree of genetic similarity is fairly well established, can pinpoint the operation of a particular type of genetic agent. For example, if all children of a family with one severely disordered parent were similarly and equally disordered, we would have to conclude that their illness stemmed from the operation of a dominant gene. On the other hand, if all the children were disordered, but varied in intensity from mild to moderate severity, we would be inclined to suggest a polygenic hypothesis. If none of the children were ill, a recessive explanation would be in order. It should be evident then, that the results of a carefully planned family study could supply information about the nature of the genetic agent involved in a disorder.

When the family method was first adopted, researchers fell prey to serious methodological biases and errors. Striking cases of family pathology which caught the eye of curious observers were reported. No attempt was made to check on the possible contribution of common environmental experiences. Briefly then, cases were selected in a biased fashion. Families which "proved" the point of heredity were reported; others were not. No effort was made to control for experiential determinants when they clearly played a role.

Concordance Among Twins. Certain interpretive complications which arise in genetic family studies can be avoided by comparing the *concordance* rates among identical and fraternal twins, that is, the degree to which they share a disorder in common. Identical (monozygotic) twins have identical genotypes. As such, differences between them result from environmental sources. Fraternal (dizygotic) twins have similar but not identical genotypes. In these pairs, differences can be attributed either to heredity or environment. A genetic hypothesis is supported when a disorder is shared more often between identical than between fraternal twins. However, we must assume that both types of twins have comparable environmental experiences. This assumption has been questioned. It is pointed out that identical twins often cling together and are treated alike by their parents, whereas fraternal twins experience different reactions from others and tend to develop independently.

As a partial antidote to this objection, researchers have investigated twins who were separated in early life and who were reared in different homes. Under these unusual conditions, where environmental similarities are diminished, a higher concordance rate between identical than fraternal pairs would add more convincing support to a genetic hypothesis. From the viewpoint of research design, however, it is unfortunate that twins raised apart from early life are few and far between.

RESULTS OF RESEARCH

Both adherents and dissenters of genetic hypotheses have undertaken the study of heredity in psychopathology. Table 7–1 offers a capsule summary of the results of a number of major investigations with patients diagnosed as having schizophrenic and manic-depressive disorders.

One feature worthy of note is the rather wide range of percentages recorded by different researchers. This can be attributed largely to three factors: (1) investigators designed their studies to test specific hypotheses and selected their methods and population samples to maximize the probability of supporting that hypothesis, e.g., Tienari (1963) set out to discover identical twins who were not concordant for schizophrenia; (2) by chance and circumstance, investigators selected patient populations that differed in age, socio-economic status and culture, and thereby confounded their findings with a number of extraneous factors; and (3) different investigators used different criteria in selecting their patients. It is well known that the criteria for classifying the syndromes of psychopathology differ in different institutions, e.g., a case which one investigator might classify as schizophrenic might be diagnosed as manic-depressive by another.

In short, the findings reported in Table 7–1 represent data gathered with noncomparable patient populations. Whether the findings of these studies would have been more consistent had there been greater uniformity in patient selection cannot be assessed. Despite these methodological complications, Table 7–1 offers strong support for the view that pathology among relatives is substantially higher than in the general population, and that it decreases roughly in proportion to decreasing genetic similarity.

TABLE 7–1 CORRESPONDENCE IN PSYCHOPATHOLOGY AMONG RELATIVES*

Relationship	Range of Correspondence Reported in the Literature* (Per Cent)	Theoretical Expectancy (Per Cent)	
		Completely Dominant Gene	Completely Recessive Gene
Schizophrenic Groups			
Nonrelated general population	approx. 1.0		
First cousins	2.6	13	3
Nephews and nieces	3.9	25	5
Half siblings	7.1	25	15
Parents	1.0–9.2	50	9
Full siblings	5.2–14.2	50	30
Dizygotic twins	3.7–17.6	50	30
Children: one schizophrenic parent	4.0–16.4	50	2
Children: two schizophrenic parents	39.2–68.1	75	100
Monozygotic twins	0–91.5	100	100
Manic-Depressive Groups			
Nonrelated general population	approx. 0.5		
Parents	2.0–24.4	50	9
Full siblings	1.5–29.1	50	30
Dizygotic twins	16.4–23.6	50	30
Children with one or two disturbed parents	12.8–38.7	50–75	2–100
Monozygotic twins	66.7–92.6	100	100

*From Kallmann (1938, 1953); Shields and Slater (1961); Slater and Shields (1953); Essen-Möller (1952); Fuller and Thompson (1960); Tienari (1963); Kringlen (1964, 1966); Gregory (1960, 1968); Rosenthal (1968, 1971); Vandenberg (1966); Gottesman and Shields (1966, 1970, 1973).

Two questions must be raised, however: can environmental influences be discounted, and can psychogenic hypotheses "explain" the data in Table 7–1 as well as genetic hypotheses?

Psychogenic theorists note that there is a close correlation between genetic similarity and similarity in environmental experience. For example, siblings share parents in common and are exposed to similar patterns of child rearing; in contrast, cousins and nephews experience appreciably less commonality in these early interpersonal relationships. Likewise, identical twins share not only a common set of genotypes but a common uterine environment and a common pattern of reactions from parents and others.

The plausibility of the psychogenic hypothesis is weakened by a number of facts. Most investigators have found the concordance rate among monozygotic twins, whether reared apart or together, to be four to five times greater than among dizygotic twins. The suggestion made by psychogenic theorists that this difference reflects the greater similarity in environmental experience among identical as opposed to fraternal twins cannot be argued persuasively. If environmental factors are primary, the concordance rate among fraternal twins, who share highly similar experiences, should be close to identical twins and appreciably greater than ordinary siblings. This expectancy is not supported by the data. Rates for dizygotic twins and siblings are very similar, whereas the difference between monozygotic and dyzgotic twins is substantial.

Two studies (Rosenthal, 1959; Gottesman and Shields, 1966, 1968, 1971, 1973) demonstrate that genetic research in psychopathology is growing in methodological and interpretive sophistication. Additionally, the data of these studies suggest an important refinement in the assessment of the role of heredity.

Rosenthal reanalyzed Slater's monozygotic twin data on schizophrenia (1953) and found a substantial history of schizophrenia in the families of concordant pairs (13 out of 22) and a minimal history in discordant pairs (1 out of 13). These results were interpreted as meaning that the classification of schizophrenia consists of biologically heterogeneous individuals. More specifically, these data pointed to a different etiologic basis for the concordant twins than the discordant pairs. The fact that a high rate of pathology was found among relatives of concordant twins indicated that their disorder was based on a hereditary defect. Conversely, pathology in the disordered member of discordant pairs resulted from their environmental experiences.

Gottesman and Shields followed up Rosenthal's work in an impressive and well-designed study. They carefully selected 57 monozygotic twins and divided them into four categories graded in terms of degree of concordance with respect to schizophrenia. What they uncovered was a striking relationship between concordance and severity of illness. High concordance corresponded with severe schizophrenic symptomology and vice versa.

If we combine the findings of Gottesman and Shields and Rosenthal, we may deduce the following: severe cases of schizophrenia are attributable largely to a genetic defect; milder forms of the disorder may be attributed only in part, if at all, to genetic factors. There are many more refinements in our understanding of the role of heredity in schizophrenia to be derived from future studies as well designed as these.

If we accept the evidence that genetic factors do operate in some forms of schizophrenia, we may then ask the question: what kind of genetic transmission (dominant or recessive) fits the data best?

Gregory (1960) and Odegard (1971), reviewing the empirical evidence in terms of several alternative theoretical models, concluded that no single or major gene hypothesis is compatible with the data, They suggest two alternate genetic hypotheses: (1) that these syndromes are heterogeneous, that is, they include several subvarieties, each of which is produced by a different genetic mechanism, or (2) that at least part of the genetic component is polygenic in nature. In recent thorough reviews of the literature, Gottesman and Shields (1967, 1973) and Rosenthal (1971) conclude that the greater body of evidence supports some variant of a polygenic theory. Although they recognize that a small number of pathologies may arise as a consequence of major gene effects, for the most part it appears likely that multiple minor genes cumulate to produce "dispositions" to psychopathology.

INFANTILE REACTION PATTERNS

Each infant enters the world with distinctive behavior dispositions and sensitivities. Every nurse knows that babies differ from the moment they are born, and every mother notices differences in the behavior of her successive offspring. Some infants suck vigorously from the start; others seem indifferent, hold the nipple freely and learn to suck slowly. Some infants have a definite cycle of hunger, elimination and sleep, whereas others vary unpredictably from one day to the next. Some twist and turn fitfully in their sleep, while others lie awake peacefully in the most hectic surroundings. Some are robust and energetic; others seem fearful and cranky.

Proving that babies are different may seem to be laboring the obvious, but the implications of the obvious may be overlooked. Scientists, for example, have been preoccupied with demonstrating common developmental patterns among infants (Gesell et al., 1940), whereas practitioners have focused on the unique attributes of their individual patients. In recent years, however, an effort has been made to bridge the gap between these two approaches. This new work reflects an interest not only in different patterns of infantile development but in the implications of these differences for later development. The questions posed by these recent investigations may be divided as follows:

1.   Are there stable individual differences before postnatal experiences exert their influence, and do these differences persist into childhood?

2.   Do these initial patterns have any bearing on the course of later personality characteristics or the development of psychopathology?

Both questions are pertinent to our study. We wish to know not only whether infants differ but whether a whole sequence of subsequent life experiences is associated with these initial differences. Infantile differences would be of little significance if they did not persist and establish a lifelong pattern of functioning.

Among other questions we must ask are (1) whether the experiences a child has are determined by his inborn capacities, temperament and energy; (2) whether his unique characteristics evoke distinctive reactions from his parents and sibs; and (3) whether these reactions have a beneficial or a detrimental effect upon his development. In short, rather than ask what effects the environment has upon the child, we might ask what effect he has on his environment and what the consequences of these are upon his personality development.

RECENT RESEARCH

Stable patterns of behavior observed in the first few months of life are likely to be of biogenic rather than psychogenic origin. Thomas et al. (1963, 1968) speak of these infantile patterns as *primary* because they appear before postnatal experience can account for them. They have been labeled as *reaction patterns* rather than behavior patterns because they are characterized by the way the child reacts to stimuli, not by the content of behavior. The content of behavior changes with learning, but the basic style or pattern of reactions tends to remain constant.

Several investigators have turned their attention in recent years to the relationship between the overt behavior of infants and later personality development. The studies of two groups of collaborators, one associated with New York Medical School (Thomas et al., 1963, 1968) and the other with the Menninger Foundation in Kansas (Escalona and Leitch, 1953; Escalona and Heider, 1959; Murphy et al., 1962; Escalona, 1968), have been especially comprehensive and fruitful. They have contributed knowledge not only to an understanding of personality development in general but also to the development of psychopathology in particular. The ensuing discussion will focus on the findings and implications of their work.

Over a hundred infants were observed from birth through the early years of schooling. Reports were made on sleeping, eating, eliminating and a host of other ordinary situations common to infants. As they developed, these children were observed in their reactions to toilet training, learning to drink from a cup, starting to walk, reactions to strangers, trips to a store, being sick, playing with others, getting a pet and so on. With few exceptions, it was found that each infant had a recognizable and distinctive way of behaving in his first weeks of life which persisted through early childhood.

Some babies seemed to have been born with built-in alarm clocks; they did everything on a predictably regular schedule. Others followed a chaotic sequence in which their pattern of sleeping, waking, eliminating and eating changed from day to day. Some reached out for everything presented to them. Others avoided anything new, be it food, people or toys. Some jumped at the turn of a door handle, whereas others were indifferent to overloud voices, hot milk and rough handling. Differences were noted in persistence and distractibility. Some babies could be turned from their hunger pangs by cooing and soothing, while others remained adamant in their demands through all diversionary tactics.

Although infants could be differentiated on several specific features of behavior, one descriptive term seemed to summarize or tie together a number of the characteristics relevant to later development: the infant's *activity* pattern (Murphy et al., 1962). Marked differences in vigor, tempo, smoothness and rhythm colored the infant's style and frequency of relating to his environment, and influenced the character of responses he evoked from others. Of course, all children displayed both active and passive tendencies but in most, one pattern predominated.

Active infants displayed decisiveness, selectivity and vigor. They maintained a continuous relatedness to their environment and were insistent that these relationships should be experienced in accordance with their desires. In contrast, passive infants displayed a more placid and receptive orientation. They appeared to be content to wait and see what was going to be done to meet their needs, and accepted matters until their desires were fulfilled. Of particular interest was the observation that the pattern of activity or passivity shaped the way in which the child learned to manipulate his environment. Active youngsters, for example, came into contact with more aspects of their environment, had more opportunities to develop relationships and interests and developed more ways of coping with frustration, but also encountered more obstacles and risked more failures.

Although early patterns were modified only slightly from infancy to childhood, it was made clear by both groups of researchers that this continuity could not be attributed entirely to the persistence of the infant's innate endowment. Subsequent experiences tend to reinforce characteristics which the infant displayed in early life. The impact of the infant's initial behavior transforms his environment in ways that intensify and accentuate these behaviors. An elaboration of this important notion will comprise our next topic.

IMPLICATIONS FOR PERSONALITY DEVELOPMENT

There has been little systematic attention to the child's own contribution to the course of his development. Environmental theorists of psychopathology have viewed disorders to be the result of detrimental experiences that the individual has had no part in producing himself. This is a gross simplification. Each infant possesses a biologically based pattern of reaction sensitivities and behavioral dispositions which shape the nature of his experiences and may contribute directly to the creation of environmental difficulties.

It is a stubborn but inescapable fact that the interweaving of biological dispositions with environmental experience is not a simple and readily disentangled web. It is a complicated and intricate feedback system of criss-crossing influences in which the role of each specific etiological agent must be viewed in light of its relationship to the others. Two facets of this interactive system will be elaborated because of their special pertinence to the development of pathology: the relationships between infantile reaction patterns and (1) adaptive learning and (2) social reinforcement.

ADAPTIVE LEARNING

The biological dispositions of the maturing child are important because they strengthen the probability that certain kinds of behavior will be learned (Seligman and Hager, 1972). Highly active and responsive children relate to and learn about their environment quickly. Their liveliness, zest and power may lead them to a high measure of personal gratification. Conversely, their energy and exploratory behavior may result in excess frustration if they overaspire or run into insuperable barriers.

Adaptive learning in constitutionally passive children also is shaped by their biological equipment. Ill-disposed to deal with their environment assertively and little inclined to discharge their tensions physically, they may learn to avoid conflicts and step aside when difficulties arise. They are less likely to develop guilt feelings about misbehavior than active youngsters who more frequently get into trouble, receive more punishment and are therefore inclined to develop aggressive feelings toward others. But in their passivity, these youngsters may deprive themselves of rewarding experiences and relationships. They may feel "left out of things" and become dependent on others to fight their battles and to protect them from experiences they are ill-equipped to handle on their own.

SOCIAL REINFORCEMENT

It appears clear from studies of early patterns of reactivity that *infantile behaviors evoke counterreactions from others which accentuate these initial dispositions.* The child's biological endowment shapes not only his behavior but that of his parents as well (Bell, 1968; Bijou, 1970.)

If the infant's primary disposition is cheerful and adaptable and has made his care easy, the mother will tend quickly to display a positive reciprocal attitude; conversely, if the child is tense and wound up, or if his care is difficult and time consuming, the mother will react with dismay, fatigue or hostility. Through his own behavioral disposition then, the child elicits a series of parental behaviors which reinforce his initial pattern. The manner in which minor features of initial behavior can be strengthened and magnified is illustrated in this quotation (Chess et al., 1960):

It is not infrequently apparent that the disturbed functioning represents an accentuation and distortion of characteristics of primary reactivity to the point of caricature. For example, there are many cases in which the parents respond with growing annoyance and pressure to the manifestations of initial negative mood and withdrawal. The child's response of negativism and increased negative mood to these parental attitudes can produce a vicious cycle which can finally lead to defensive hostility with constant projections of derogation and aggression. Thus we may obtain as an end product an individual with motivated aggressive and hostile behavior who shows a highly suspicious reaction to anything new, be it a person, place or activity. He makes contact by attacking and assumes that every personal contact must involve an overt or hidden antagonism on the other person's part.

Unfortunately, the reciprocal interplay of primary patterns and parental reactions has only recently begun to be explored systematically (Harper, 1971; Osofsky, 1971, 1972; Yarrow et al., 1971). It may prove to be one of the most fruitful spheres of research concerning the social learning of psychopathology and merits the continued serious attention of investigators. The *biosocial-learning approach* that characterizes much of this book stems largely from the thesis that the child's primary reaction pattern shapes and interacts with his social reinforcement experiences.

MORPHOLOGICAL STRUCTURE

Shakespeare, a notably perceptive observer of human character, wrote these words in *Julius Caesar:*

Let me have men about me that are fat;
Sleek-headed men and such as sleep o'nights:

Yon Cassius has a lean and hungry look;
He thinks too much; such men are dangerous.

Observant men since times of antiquity have noted that bodily form and
structure (morphology) were related to particular dispositions and patterns of behavior. What rationale can be offered to account for this relationship?

Biogenic theorists are inclined to believe that correlations between physique and behavior result from the joint operation of linked genes. Body
morphology and tempermental disposition may be coupled on the same
chromosome or may be produced by the combined action of a single set
of genes. Sex-linked characteristics (e.g., height, body form and hir-
suteness) arising from associated genetic sources are a well-known phenomenon. In the same manner, associated genes may produce correlated bodily and behavioral attributes. For example, the thesis of a joint

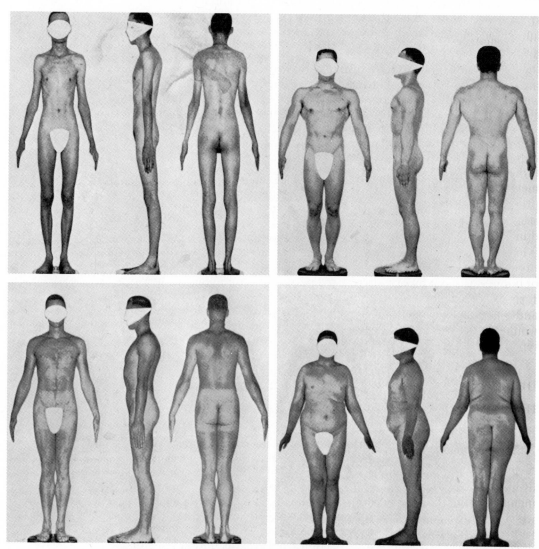

Figure 7–1   Photographs of somatotype extremes. (From Sheldon, W. H.: Atlas of Men.
New York, Hafner Publishing Co., 1970.)

genetic basis for morphology and behavior may be illustrated in the
disorder known as Down's syndrome (mongolism). Here, distinct physical attributes (slanted eyes and a short squat build) are associated with a
particular form of mental retardation; both the morphological and behavioral aspects of this syndrome are consequences of a single anomaly
in chromosomal structure.

The constitutional biogenic thesis can be summarized simply: specific biological determinants simultaneously influence both physique and behavior. These determinants account for correlations observed between
them.

MORPHOLOGICAL MEASURES

A question arises as to which features of body structure and form best
characterize an individual's constitutional make-up. Despite differences
in detail, there is a consensus among constitutional theorists as to the significance of three major dimensions: fat, muscularity and linearity.
Before this century, these three features of morphology were put into a
three-fold typology in which individuals were classified in accordance
with the dominant feature they display.

In recent years, theorists have recognized the naiveté of dividing people
into distinct body types. There are a few individuals, of course, who
display a marked dominance of one of these morphological features, but
the greatest part of the population displays a mixture of all three in varying combinations. It appeared wise, therefore, to devise methods by
which the proportionate relationship among these components could be
gauged.

Best known among these methods are Sheldon's photographic techniques (1940, 1942, 1949, 1954) in which the magnitude of each of the
three body dimensions is rated (anthroscopy) or measured (anthropo-
metry). Sheldon refers to these dimensions as *endomorphy*, in which a
predominance or roundness and softness in body structure is evident;
mesomorphy, which is characterized by muscular and connective tissue
dominance; and *ectomorphy*, in which a linearity and fragility of structure
is manifest without fat or muscular strength. Each component is measured on a seven point scale, resulting in a *somatotype*, or quantified index
of body physique. Extreme endomorphs, for example, are listed as 7–1–
1, signifying their marked obesity, minimal endowment of muscularity
and a lack of linearity or delicacy of structure. A well-balanced physique
would be rated as 4–4–4 somatotype. As is evident, a variety of physical
types can be incorporated in this tripolar scheme.

THEORIES OF MORPHOLOGY

Hippocrates, the forerunner of many contemporary ideas in medicine,
separated men into two categories: the short, heavy and strong and the
tall, slight and weak. These physical types, he felt, differed in their sus-
ceptibility to diseases. Hippocrates suggested also that men could be
divided into four basic temperaments according to their dominant bodily humors, but he failed to connect his body typology to these temperamental categories. Several centuries later, Galen formulated a scheme in
which Hippocrates' four humors were related to variations in body
form. This suggestive thesis was not completed and the notion remained
dormant until recently. Proposals were made in the intervening years in

which Hippocrates' two-fold body typology was extended and refined (Rostan, 1828; Viola, 1932). The work of Lombroso on criminal types (1889, 1911) was the first systematic attempt, however, to revive Galen's hypothesized relation between behavior and physical consitution.

Kretschmer. The modern trend in constitutional psychology began with the ideas and research of Ernst Kretschmer (1925). In his practice as a psychiatrist, Kretschmer observed a frequent association between certain physical types and particular forms of mental disorder. Prompted by this impression, he set out to categorize individuals according to their dominant physical build and to relate these categories to the two major Kraepelinian disorders of schizophrenia and manic-depressive psychosis. As a third objective, Kretschmer sought to relate physique to normal behavior dispositions.

His physical classification scheme resulted in four types: the *pyknic*, which he described as a compact individual with a large, round head, large thorax and abdomen, soft and poorly muscled limbs and a marked tendency to obesity; the *athletic*, noted for his extensive muscular development and broad skeletal endowment; the *asthenic*, viewed as a fragile individual possessing thin muscularity and a frail bone structure; and the *dysplastic*, which reflected Kretschmer's recognition that the first three types may be mixed in an awkwardly constructed physique.

Using his constitutional system as a basis, Kretschmer rated the physiques of 175 schizophrenics and 85 manic-depressives. His results, presented in Table 7–2, led him to conclude that there was a clear biological affinity between manic-depressives and the pyknic body build, and a comparable relationship between schizophrenia and the asthenic, athletic and dysplastic types.

To Kretschmer, psychotic disorders were accentuations of normal personality types. He suggested a gradation of temperamental dispositions progressing from pathological schizophrenia to moderately afflicted schizoids to adequately adjusted schizothymic personalities. In a like fashion, cycloids were viewed as moderately ill variants of manic-depressive psychosis, and cyclothymic personalities as essentially normal individuals displaying mild features similar to the more severe types.

Kretschmer's proposal of a gradated relationship between body build and behavioral disposition was an imaginative extension of previous constitutional ideas. Unfortunately, he offered no systematic or quantifiable evidence in support of this assertion, nor did he offer an explanation of why one individual of a particular physique remained normal while a

TABLE 7–2 KRETSCHMER'S PHYSIQUE TYPES AND PSYCHO-PATHOLOGY*

Type	Number of Cases	
	Manic-Depressive	Schizophrenic
Asthenic	4	81
Athletic	3	31
Asthenic-athletic mixed	2	11
Pyknic	58	2
Pyknic mixture	14	3
Dysplastic	–	34
Deformed and uncategorized	4	13
	85	175

*From Kretschmer (1925).

similarly built individual succumbed to a psychosis. Other criticisms have been leveled at Kretschmer's hypotheses and methodology. For example, he failed to control for the typical age difference between patients classified as schizophrenics and those diagnosed as manic-depressives: the older manic-depressive may be heavier since age usually is associated with an increment in weight. Thus, schizophrenics may have been found to be thinner (asthenic) because they are younger; and manic-depressives fatter (pyknic) because they are older.

Sheldon. The most notable figure in contemporary constitutional psychology is the research psychiatrist, William H. Sheldon. A brief review of his morphological schema was presented in an earlier section. Here we will outline his hypotheses concerning the relationship between body physique, temperament and psychopathology.

Sheldon contends that the diversity and complexity of man's manifest behavior should be viewed as surface features of a small number of underlying factors. In his search for these basic dimensions he constructed a typology of *temperaments,* that is, persistent dispositions and reaction patterns to the environment that are rooted in the individual's make-up. The temperament scale devised by Sheldon was constructed and rated in a fashion similar to his somatotype system. He narrowed an original list of over 650 traits by correlational analysis to a group of 60 items divided into three clusters of 20 each. Table 7–3 outlines the final items included in the scale.

Sheldon termed the three temperament clusters, viscerotonia, somatotonia and cerebrotonia. They were viewed as parallel to his three basic somatotypes.

The *viscerotonic* component, which parallels endomorphy in Sheldon's theory, is characterized by gregariousness, easy expression of feeling and emotion, love of comfort and relaxation, avoidance of pain and dependence on social approval. *Somatotonia,* the counterpart to mesomorphy, is noted by assertiveness, physical energy, low anxiety, indifference to pain, courage, social callousness and a need for action and power when troubled. *Cerebrotonia,* corresponding to ectomorphy, is defined by a tendency toward restraint, self-consciousness, introversion, social awkwardness, and a desire for solitude when troubled.

How does Sheldon relate these measures of somatotype and temperament to psychopathology?

Sheldon attempted at first to correlate measures of morphology with the traditional system of psychiatric diagnosis and found that the traditional system of diagnosis was inadequate for his purposes (1949). In particular, he rejected the conventional notion in psychiatry of discrete diagnostic categories (e.g., patients were classified as suffering *either* from manic-depressive psychosis, *or* paranoid schizophrenia *or* catatonic schizophrenia). He proposed, in their stead, that a series of continuous or gradated dimensions should be substituted for the notion of discrete disease entities. Toward this end, he developed three primary components of psychopathology which coexist, in varying proportions, in each disturbed individual. These components parallel not only his somatotype and temperament measures but also psychotic categories found in the traditional classification system (Figure 7–2).

The first psychiatric component is termed *affective;* it is found in its extreme form among manic-depressive patients. Sheldon postulates

**TABLE 7-3
SHELDON'S
TEMPERAMENT
SCALE***

Viscerotonia	Somatotonia	Cerebrotonia
( )† 1. Relaxation in posture and movement	( ) 1. Assertiveness of posture and movement	( ) 1. Restraint in posture and movement, tightness
( ) 2. Love of physical comfort	( ) 2. Love of physical adventure	( ) 2. Physiological over-response
( ) 3. Slow reaction	( ) 3. The energetic characteristic	( ) 3. Overly fast reactions
( ) 4. Love of eating	( ) 4. Need and enjoyment of exercise	( ) 4. Love of privacy
5. Socialization of eating	5. Love of dominating. Lust for power	5. Mental overintensity. Hyper-attentionality. Apprehensiveness
6. Pleasure in digestion	6. Love risk and chance	6. Secretiveness of feeling, emotional restraint
( ) 7. Love of polite ceremony	( ) 7. Bold directness of manner	( ) 7. Self-conscious mobility of the eyes and face
( ) 8. Sociophilia	( ) 8. Physical courage for combat	( ) 8. Sociophobia
( ) 9. Indiscriminate amiability	( ) 9. Competitive aggressiveness	( ) 9. Inhibited social address
10. Greed for affection and approval	10. Psychological callousness	10. Resistance to habit and poor routinizing
11. Orientation to people	11. Claustrophobia	11. Agoraphobia
( ) 12. Evenness of emotional flow	( ) 12. Ruthlessness, freedom from squeamishness	12. Unpredictability of attitude
( ) 13. Tolerance	( ) 13. The unrestrained voice	( ) 13. Vocal restraint and general restraint of noise
( ) 14. Complacency	14. Spartan indifference to pain	14. Hypersensitivity to pain
15. Deep sleep	15. General noisiness	15. Poor sleep habits, chronic fatigue
( ) 16. The untempered characteristic	( ) 16. Overmaturity of appearance	( ) 16. Youthful intentness of manner and appearance
( ) 17. Smooth, easy communication of feeling, extraversion of viscerotonia	17. Horizontal mental cleavage, extraversion of somatotonia	17. Vertical mental cleavage, introversion
18. Relaxation and sociophilia under alcohol	18. Assertiveness and aggression under alcohol	18. Resistance to alcohol and to other depressant drugs
19. Need of people when troubled	19. Need of action when troubled	19. Need of solitude when troubled
20. Orientation toward childhood and family relationships	20. Orientation toward goals and activities of youth	20. Orientation toward the later periods of life

*From Sheldon (1942).
†The 30 traits with parentheses constitute collectively the short form of the scale.

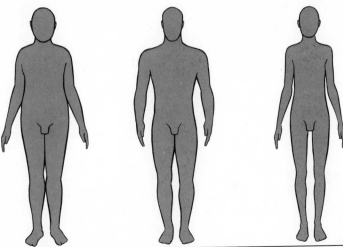

SOMATOTYPE	ENDOMORPHY	MESOMORPHY	ECTOMORPHY
	Soft and round	Muscular and solid	Lean and fragile
TEMPERAMENT	VISCEROTONIA	SOMATOTONIA	CEREBROTONIA
	Comfort-loving, pleasure and people oriented	Assertive and competitive, socially callous, action oriented	Emotionally restrained, apprehensive, solitude oriented
PSYCHIATRIC COMPONENT	AFFECTIVE	PARANOID	HEBOID
	Fluctuates between elation and Depression	Has hostility and delusions of persecution	Is socially withdrawn and indulges in autistic fantasy

Figure 7-2 Relationships between Sheldon's three somatotypes, temperaments and psychiatric components.

a high relationship between this component, the endomorphic physique, and the viscerotonic temperament. According to his formulation, the affective component is characterized by a low threshold of behavioral reaction and emotional expression resulting from a weakened or feeble inhibitory capacity. Sheldon speaks of this defect as a pathologically uncontrolled expression of the viscerotonic temperament. With minimal prompting these individuals display either marked elation or intense dejection, depending on the nature of their immediate environment. The depressed patient is slowed down, overrelaxed, overdependent and overly expressive of his melancholy feelings. During a manic stage, the patient is keyed up, uninhibited, maladaptively hyperactive, euphoric, and overly suggestible.

The *paranoid* component corresponds both in title and in its most intense form of expression with the traditional diagnostic category of the same name. Sheldon proposes that this component corresponds both with mesomorphy and somatotonia. It reflects a "fighting against something," a driving antagonism and resentment which is projected against the environment. Thus, the persecution delusions which characterize paranoid psychotics can be seen as extremes of this dimension. The patient views his associates as persecutors and as legitimate objects for his scorn and defiance.

The third component, referred to by Sheldon as *heboid,* is typified by marked withdrawal, features characteristic of the traditional psychiatric diagnosis hebephrenic schizophrenia. It is found in ectomorphic or cerebrotonic individuals, according to Sheldon since these individuals lack both energy and affect. The drive to act, to accomplish and to compete is deficient. In extreme form, the patient learns to relinquish what little affect and energy he may possess as a means of avoiding the disastrous consequences of his feeble efforts to utilize these attributes. Rather than chance continued failure with his ill-equipped constitution, he withdraws from active social participation and regresses into an infantile state of dependency.

RECENT RESEARCH

Few of the empirical studies relating physique to pathology have been well designed. Some of the methodological defects in Kretschmer's work were noted earlier. Similar design problems have plagued researchers since. Despite these faults, the results of morphological research have been so impressive that dismissing their findings on methodological grounds alone would appear unwise.

In one of the few well-designed studies relevant to psychopathology, Sheldon set out to explore the correspondence between somatotype and his three psychiatric components (Wittman, Sheldon and Katz, 1948). He devised a checklist for rating each of these components after carefully screening the descriptive records of hospitalized patients. The items finally selected were then organized in terms of his three-fold cluster schema. Two clinicians reviewed and rated the records of 155 psychiatric patients while Sheldon *independently* somatotyped each of these patients. Neither the clinicians nor Sheldon saw the patients personally, nor did they have access to each other's judgments. A remarkable consistency was shown in the independent ratings of the clinicians (correlations of +.78 to +.91.). Of greater significance, however, were the impressive correlations found between the rated psychiatric components and the independently measured somatotypes. The results are presented in Table 7–4.

Although three of Sheldon's minor expectations were not supported, the major hypotheses of significant relations between endomorphy-affective, mesomorphy-paranoid and ectomorphy-heboid were confirmed. As Sheldon anticipated, there was a complicated pattern of the correlations among these variables, signifying that pathology and morphology are related neither in a simple nor a clear-cut fashion.

Rees (1957, 1961), reviewing the research literature on morphology and psychopathology, concluded that a well-established relationship exists between schizophrenia and ectomorphy and between manic-depressive disorders and endomorphy. He noted further that ectomorphs appear to succumb to their illness at an earlier age, display more marked regres-

TABLE 7–4 CORRELATIONS BETWEEN SHELDON'S SOMATOTYPES AND PSYCHIATRIC COMPONENTS*

| Somatotype | Psychiatric Component | | |
	Affective	Paranoid	Heboid
Endomorphy	+.54	−.04	−.25
Mesomorphy	+.41	+.57	−.68
Ectomorphy	−.59	−.34	+.64

*From Wittman, Sheldon and Katz (1948).

sive and withdrawal behavior and follow a more progressive course of deterioration than either endomorphs or mesomorphs.

In the sphere of antisocial behavior, Sheldon (1949) and Glueck and Glueck (1962) conducted longitudinal studies of delinquent youngsters, and found impressive correlations with morphology. Sheldon reported the majority of delinquents to be either mesomorphs or endomorphic-mesomorphs. Glueck and Glueck, comparing delinquents with matched normals, discovered 60 per cent of the delinquents to be mesomorphic, a figure twice that of the normal group. Less than 15 per cent of the delinquents were ectomorphic, whereas more than 40 per cent of the normals were so grouped. Each of these studies as well as some recent work (Cortes and Galti, 1970), supports the general thesis that body build and deviant forms of behavior are related.

The association between morphology and behavior which Sheldon interprets on a constitutional basis can be explained, as well, by a number of psychogenic hypotheses. Let us enumerate three such alternative interpretations.

1.   Environmental influences may have a simultaneous effect upon both behavior and physique. For example, overprotective mothers tend to train their children to be emotionally responsive and dependent. Overprotectiveness often leads also to excessive feeding and consequent obesity. Thus, this type of maternal behavior can produce both an endomorphic physique and a viscerotonic (emotionally expressive and socially dependent) temperament. As another example, economic deprivation may give rise to self-consciousness and social withdrawal (cerebrotonic characteristics), as well as to nutritional deficiencies which lead to an ectomorphic physique. This formulation bypasses the contribution of biogenic determinants entirely by proposing that specific environmental conditions can account fully for both physique and behavior.

2.   Another psychogenic explanation stresses the influence of social stereotypes and role expectations (Lerner, 1969; Lerner and Korn, 1972). Individuals whose physical characteristics fit certain commonly held notions and superstitions such as the "fat, jolly man" or the "mean-tempered redhead" will be expected to play the behavioral role expected of them. Many individuals, reinforced by social expectations, and given implicit sanction to display the expected behaviors, learn to conform to the stereotype. For example, the rotund and cherubic endomorph is not only expected to be jolly and gregarious but he finds that this behavior is rewarded handsomely. Thus, the congruence we observe between physique and behavior may be the result of reinforcing social stereotypes rather than common biological influences.

3.   A third psychogenic interpretation recognizes the fact that physical structure can either encourage or limit the kinds of behaviors an individual will learn. In other words, to be endowed with a certain body build increases the probability that certain types of behaviors will be successful, while others will fail (Seligman and Hager, 1972). Just as it is unlikely for an intellectually deficient youngster to find advanced mathematics rewarding, so too is it improbable that a frail ectomorph will find his efforts at aggression successful. No matter how persistent a "97 pound weakling" may be, he cannot expect to be able "to push around the boys on the beach." Conversely, it would be quite easy for an ener-

getic and robust mesomorph to adopt this assertive and domineering behavior. Clearly then, physique does facilitate or limit the range and types of reactions that an individual can — and therefore will — learn. According to this thesis, associations between morphology and behavior do not arise from some biogenic linkage but from adaptive learning.

It seems reasonable to conclude that the psychogenic interpretations just enumerated account in some part for the high correlations found between physique, behavior and psychopathology. The relative contributions of psychogenic and biogenic factors will not be disentangled easily; at this stage in our knowledge it will suffice to say that both types of etiological mechanisms intertwine in a complicated developmental sequence.

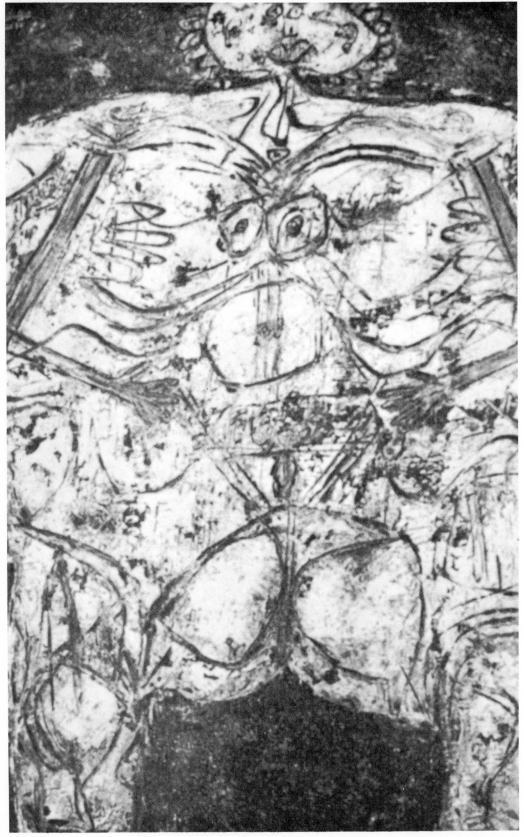

Jean Dubuffet — *Corps de dame*

8

EARLY DEVELOPMENT AND LEARNING

INTRODUCTION

A major theme of this chapter is that abnormal behavior develops as a result of an intimate interplay of biological and psychological forces. Such interactions start at the time of conception and continue throughout life. Individuals with similar biological potentials emerge with different personality patterns depending on the environmental conditions to which they were exposed. These patterns unfold and change as new biological maturations interweave with new environmental encounters. In time, these patterns stabilize into a distinctive hierarchy of behaviors which remain *relatively* consistent through the everchanging stream of experience.

In the previous chapter we examined a number of ways in which biological factors can shape the nature of the individual's experiences and learning. For example, the constitutional structure of an individual will strengthen the probability that he will learn certain forms of behavior. Not only will his body build, strength and energy influence the stimuli he will seek or be exposed to, but they will determine which types of behaviors he will find are successful for him in dealing with these encounters (Seligman and Hager, 1972).

We must recognize further, that the interaction between biological and psychological factors is not unidirectional such that biological determinants always precede and influence the course of learning and experience. The order of effects can be reversed, especially in the early stages of development. From recent research we learn that biological maturation is largely dependent on favorable environmental experience. The development of the biological substrate itself, therefore, can be disrupted, even completely arrested, by depriving the maturing organism of stimulation at sensitive periods of rapid neurological growth. The profound effect of these experiences upon biological capacities will be a central theme in this chapter. We will contend that the sheer quantity as well as the quality of these early experiences is a crucial aspect in the development of patterns of personality.

Beyond the crucial role of these early experiences, we will argue further that there is a circularity of interaction in which initial biological dispositions in young children evoke counter-reactions from others which accentuate their disposition (Bell, 1968; Yarrow et al., 1971; Osofsky and O'Connell, 1972). The notion that the child plays an active role in creating environmental conditions which, in turn, serve as a basis for reinforcing his biological tendencies is illustrated well in this quote from Cameron and Magaret (1951):

. . . the apathy that characterizes an unreactive infant may deprive him of many of the reactions from others which are essential to his biosocial maturation. His unresponsiveness may discourage his parents and other adults from fondling him, talking to him or providing him with new and challenging toys, so that the poverty of his social environment sustains his passivity and social isolation. If such a child develops behavior pathology, he is likely to show an exaggeration or distortion of his own characteristic reactions in the form of retardation, chronic fatigue or desocialization.

This thesis suggests, then, that biological tendencies are not only perpetuated but intensified as a consequence of their interaction with experience.

EARLY DEVELOPMENT

Deeply rooted personality traits need not signify the presence of an innate disposition, nor need they stem from the effects of a biological trauma or disease. Embedded patterns of behavior may arise entirely as a product of psychological experience, experience which shapes the development of biological structures so profoundly as to transform it into something substantially different from what it might otherwise have been.

Under what circumstances can psychological experience exert so profound an effect?

An answer that enjoys a great degree of acceptance among abnormal psychologists is experience during infancy and early childhood. This view can be traced to the writings of Freud at the turn of this century. The observations of ethologists on the effects of early stimulation in animals have added naturalistic evidence to support this position.

Why is early experience crucial, and, more specifically, how does this experience shape the biological substrate of personality?

Several answers advanced in response to these questions will be discussed in this chapter. For the moment we will concentrate on one: the dependence of maturation on early environmental stimulation. The thesis may be stated simply: certain biological capacities will fail to develop fully as a result of impoverished stimulation; conversely, these same capacities may be overdeveloped as a consequence of enriched stimulation.

MATURATION

Maturation refers to that sequence of development in which initially diffuse structures of the body unfold into functional units. It was once believed that the course of maturation arose exclusively from forces laid down in the genes. Maturation was thought to evolve according to a preset timetable that operated independently of environmental conditions. This view no longer is tenable. Maturation progresses not in a fixed course leading to a predetermined level, but is subject to numerous variations which reflect the character of the organism's environment (Simmel, 1970).

The answer to why early experiences are more crucial to development than later experiences derives from the fact that the peak period of maturation occurs from the prenatal stage through the first years of postnatal life. The organism is subject to more alteration in the early, or more plastic years, than when it has fully matured. An example in the sphere of body structure may illustrate this point well. Inadequate nutrition in childhood may result in stunted bone development, leading to a permanently shortened stature. No amount of nutrition in adult life can compensate to increase the individual's height. However, had adequate nutrition been given during the formative or maturing years, the child might have grown to his full potential. Similarly, in the nervous system, prenatal deficiencies in nutrition will retard the differentiation of gross tissue into separable neural cells. However, deficiencies arising later in life will have little or no effect on the development of these neural structures.

STIMULUS NUTRIMENT

The concept of nutrition must be viewed more broadly than we commonly view it if we are to understand its role in the development of biological maturation. Nutrition should be conceived as including not only obvious supplies such as those found in food, but in what Rapaport had termed "stimulus nutriment" (1958). This notion of nutrition suggests that the simple impingement of environmental stimuli upon the maturing organism has a direct bearing on the chemical composition, ultimate size and patterns of neural branching within the brain. Stated simply, the sheer *amount* of stimulation to which the child is exposed has an effect on the maturation of his neural capacities.

The belief that the maturing organism must receive periodic stimulus nutriments for proper development has led some theorists to suggest that the organism actively seeks an optimum level of stimulation. Just as the infant cries out in search of food when deprived, or wails in response to pain, so too may it display behaviors which provide it with sensory stimulation requisite to maturation. Thus, in the first months of life, infants can be seen to track auditory and visual stimuli. As they mature further, they grasp incidental objects, and then mouth, rotate and fondle them. Furthermore, we observe that the young of all species engage in more exploratory and frolicsome behavior than adults. These seemingly "functionless" play activities may not be functionless at all. They may be essential to growth, an instrumental means of self-stimulation that is indispensable to the maturation and maintenance of biological capacities.

Sensitive Developmental Periods

Certain types of stimuli have an especially pronounced effect upon the organism at particular and well-circumscribed periods of maturation (Thompson and Grusec, 1970; Kovach, 1970). At these periods or stages, the organism is unusually responsive to and substantially influenced by the action of these stimuli.

The contention that stimuli produce different effects at different ages can scarcely be questioned, e.g., the shapely legs of an attractive girl catch the eye of most young and middle-aged men but rarely draw the attention of preadolescent boys and senile men. The concept of sensitive periods of development states more than this, however. It argues, first, that there are limited time periods during which particular stimuli are necessary for the full maturation of an organism and, second, that if these stimuli are experienced either before or after the sensitive period, they will have minimal or no effects. Thus, if critical periods pass without proper stimulus nourishment, the organism will suffer certain forms of maldevelopment which are irremediable, that is, cannot be compensated for by the presentation of the "right" stimuli at a later date.

The rationale for the sensitive period concept was presented initially in the field of experimental embryology. One of the early researchers, Child (1941), found that rapidly growing tissues of an embryo are especially sensitive to environmental stimulation. The structure of bodily cells was determined, in large part, by the character of the stimulus environment within which it was embedded. At later stages, where growth had slowed down, these same cells were resistant to environmental influences. These embryological findings suggested that the effects of environmental stimuli upon bodily structure are most pronounced *when tissue growth is rapid.*

The notion that brief early experiences may produce a permanent modification of functions has been theorized by scientists in fields other than embryology. Lorenz (1935), the eminent European ethologist, has discovered critical periods during which primary social bonds are permanently established in birds. In human research, McGraw (1943) and Bayley (1970) demonstrated the existence of peak periods for learning specific skills, and illustrated the resistance of these skills to subsequent extinction. Murphy (1947) reports a number of studies to support the concept of canalization, a notion signifying an irreversible initial learning process.

Developmental theorists have proposed, either by intention or inadvertently, schemas based on a concept of sensitive periods. Few, however, have formulated this notion in terms of neurological growth stages.

Freud's theory of discrete stages of psychosexual development, in which particular early experiences at specified times in development have deeply etched and lasting effects, may be viewed as the first major psychopathological theory based on a concept of sensitive periods. Despite Freud's early training as a neurologist, his schema was founded *not* in terms of internal neurological maturation, but in terms of a peripheral sphere of maturation, that of sexual development. His concern lay with variations in external sensory erogenous zones (e.g., oral, anal and genital), not with the more central neurological structures which underlie and are basic to them.

It would appear from recent neurological and behavioral research that a more profitable basis for organizing a system of developmental periods would be in terms of internal neurological growth potentials. Relationships certainly will exist between these inner variables and other less centrally involved variables, such as Freud's concept of erogenous zones. But to focus on peripheral spheres of maturation as did Freud, is, from our view, to put the proverbial "cart before the horse."

It is appropriate, before we progress further, to ask a simple but important question: how precise is our knowledge of the character and sequence of neurological maturation? The simplest and most direct answer, given our present state of empirical research, is that we have little knowledge that is clear and relevant. We grasp only the barest outline of the diverse and intricate features which unfold in the developing nervous system. At best, we can make only a few rough distinctions for separating the developmental sequence into identifiable periods of rapid neurological growth. These neurologically sensitive periods must be inferred from sketchy odds and ends gathered from fields as diverse as embryology, neurophysiology, ethology, behavior development and childhood psychopathology. The framework we shall employ to divide these neurological stages will be revised, no doubt, as research progresses.

How shall we divide the maturational sequence, then, given the sketchy knowledge we possess today?

Keeping in mind the tentative nature of the proposed divisions, and the substantial overlapping which exists between successive stages (all aspects of growth occur simultaneously, though in varying degrees), current theory and research suggests three broad periods of development in which an optimal point of interaction occurs between neurological maturation and environmental stimulation:

Stage 1: Sensory-Attachment

The first year or two of life is dominated by *sensory* processes. These functions are basic to later development in that they enable the infant to construct some order out of the initial diffusion and chaos he experiences in his stimulus world. This period may also be termed that of *attachment* because the infant cannot survive on his own, and must affix himself to others who will provide the protection, nutrition and stimulation he needs.

Development of Sensory Capacities.   The early neonatal period has been characterized as one of undifferentiation. This descriptive term suggests that the organism behaves in a diffuse and unintegrated way. Recent research indicates that certain sensory functions are well matured at birth and that they progress rapidly in their development shortly thereafter. Experimental studies support the view that the near receptors, involving touch, taste, smell and temperature, are dominant in the neonate. This evidence is not inconsistent with Freud's belief in the importance of the oral region, since the mouth, lips and tongue are especially rich in several of these receptor capacities. However, tactual and kinesthetic sensitivities pervade the entire body, and there is every reason to believe that the infant can discriminate and respond to subtle variations in temperature, texture and general physical comfort.

The primacy in the first months of life of touch, taste, temperature and smell recedes as the distance receptors of vision and audition come to the foreground. Whereas the near receptors are limited to bodily contact stimuli in the immediate environment, the distance receptors expand the scope of the infant's experiences by enabling him to survey and explore a far-ranging and infinitely more elaborate sphere of stimuli.

Development of Attachment.   The neonate does not differentiate between objects and persons. Both are experienced simply as stimuli. How does this initial indiscriminateness become transformed into specific attachments to particular stimuli, especially the stimulus of the mother?

The newborn, for all essential purposes, is helpless and dependent on others to supply its needs. Separated from the womb at birth, the neonate has lost its "attachment" to the mother's body, and the nurturance it provided. It now must turn toward other sources of attachment if it is to survive, be comforted and obtain stimulation for further development. The infant's attachment behavior may be viewed, albeit figuratively, as an attempt to reestablish the intimate and gratifying unity lost at birth. Since it will be some years before it can provide these needs on its own, the infant progressively discriminates, through its developing sensory capacities, those objects which have a high nurturant and stimulus value. Attachments may occasionally be made to inanimate objects, such as the odor of a doll's hair or the texture of a favorable blanket, but the infant, under normal conditions, will center his attachments to the complexly stimulating and rewarding object of his mother. Gradually distinguishing her as a stimulus source providing warmth, softness, food and comfort, he begins to seek her touch, her odors and her soothing voice: thus, his attachment to her (Maccoby and Masters, 1970).

What systematic evidence is there to support the view that sensory processes play a central role in the development of specific attachments? In large measure, this support is obtained from research on subhuman species. These data are extrapolated or analogized then to similar behaviors displayed among humans.

One body of animal research deals with what has been referred to as "imprinting" behavior. Young birds and sheep, for example, are first attracted to the sight of moving objects, then track or follow them as they locomote (Lorenz, 1935; Hess, 1959, 1970; Moltz, 1968, 1970). The second body of research, referred to as "the establishment of primary affectional and social bonds," has concentrated on the early behaviors of dogs and monkeys (Scott, 1960, 1968; Harlow, 1960, 1963, 1965, 1970; Cairns, 1966, 1972; Fuller, 1970); for example, these animals demonstrate attachments to surrogate mother objects who provide soft tactual stimulation.

Attachment behavior studies with humans lean heavily on naturalistic evidence. Ribble (1943), Spitz (1965), Bowlby (1952, 1969), Gewirtz (1963, 1972) and Rheingold (1963, 1970), though differing in their interpretation of the mechanisms involved, all conclude that the tactile and kinesthetic stimulation provided by the mother serve as the basis of the infant's attachment. Aspects of their work will be elaborated more fully in later sections.

Maladaptive Consequences of Impoverishment.   A wealth of clinical evidence is available to show that humans, deprived of adequate maternal care in infancy, display a variety of pathological behaviors. Of course, we cannot design studies to tease out precisely which of the complex of variables that comprise maternal care account for these irreparable consequences. The lives of babies cannot be manipulated to satisfy our scientific curiosity. The value of animal research is clear here since it is possible in these studies to arrange conditions necessary for a more precise analysis of the problem.

Gewirtz (1972), Palmer (1969), Melzack (1965), Riesen (1961) and Beach and Jaynes (1954) have provided extensive reviews of the consequences in animals of early stimulus impoverishment. Briefly, sensory neural fibers atrophy and cannot be regenerated by subsequent stimulation. Al-

Figure 8-1   A and B. Frightening objects such as a mechanical teddy bear caused almost all infant monkeys to flee to the cloth mother. C and D. After reassurance by pressing and rubbing against the cloth mother they dared to look at the strange object. (Courtesy of Professor Harry F. Harlow.)

most any means of stimulation (e.g., stroking, tossing, shaking or shocking) will provide the necessary activation for neural development. Inadequate early stimulation in any of the major sensory functions results in marked decrements in the capacity to utilize these and other sensory processes in later life.

Assuming the infant animal has an adequate base of *physical* stimulation, what consequences will follow if it is deprived of *social* stimulation?

The profound effects of social isolation have been studied most thoroughly by Harlow and his associates (1960, 1963, 1965). In a series of studies in which monkeys were totally or partially deprived of social contact, they found that the longer and more complete the social isolation, the more devastating were the behavioral consequences. Deprived monkeys were incapable at maturity of relating to their peers, of participating effectively in sexual activity and of assuming adequate roles as mothers.

Many theorists have sought to relate stimulus impoverishment in human infants to aberrations in later behavior. Most notable in this regard are the views of Bowlby (1952, 1969), Goldfarb (1955), Spitz (1965), Sears (1972) and Ainsworth (1972). According to their observations, an inadequate supply of stimuli from a caretaking environment results in marked deficits in social attachment behaviors. Quite often, there are gross developmental retardations, limited capacities for human relationships and a pervasive apathy and depression. These children display inadequate use of their visual and auditory functions. For example, experimenters often are unable to achieve visual contact with these youngsters, and they appear to "look through" observers when approached frontally. Yarrow (1961, 1965, 1973) and O'Connor (1968) have furnished amply documented surveys of these findings.

Little has been said in the literature about the potential effects of less severe degrees of early sensory impoverishment (Caldwell, 1970). We should not overlook the fact that degree of sensory impoverishment is a gradient or continuum, not an all-or-none effect. There is every reason to believe that children who receive less than an optimum degree of sensory stimulation (an amount that will vary, no doubt, in accord with individual differences) will grow up to be less "sensory oriented" and less "socially attached" than those who have experienced more.

Maladaptive Consequences of Enrichment. What are the consequences of too much early sensory stimulation? Unfortunately, data and theories on this score are few and far between; researchers have been preoccupied with the effects of deficient sensory stimulation rather than excess sensory stimulation. There is a substantial body of theory, but little research, describing the process of overattachment.

It is not unreasonable to hypothesize that excess stimulation during the sensory-attachment stage would result in an overdevelopment of associated neural structures (Thompson and Grusec, 1970). The work of Rosenzweig et al. (1962), for example, has shown that enriched early environments produce increments in certain neurochemicals. It would be plausible to hypothesize, further, that an abundance of these chemicals would prove detrimental to subsequent development. Thus, just as too little stimulation may lead to deficit sensory capacities, so too may superfluous stimulations lead to receptor oversensitivities and, in turn, to a maladaptive dominance of sensory functions. We would expect these individuals to be characterized by their seeking of sensory stimulation, their boredom of routine and their capricious searching for excitement and adventure. For example, a 14 year old hyperactive girl seemed incapable of "being satisfied" and made inordinate demands upon her parents to "take me here" and "take me there" and "buy me this" then "buy me that." No sooner would she go somewhere or get something than she would be bored and want to do or get something new. A review of her early history showed that she was a "happy and good baby," but indulged excessively with warm affection and playful stimulation by doting parents and grandparents.

Turning briefly to attachment behaviors, it would seem reasonable to assume that excess stimulation, anchored exclusively to the mother, would result in an overattachment to her. This consequence is demonstrated most clearly in the pathological disorder known as the *symbiotic child*, where we find an abnormal clinging by the infant to the mother, an unwillingness to leave or allow her out of sight and a persistent resistance to stimulation from other sources (Mahler, 1952). Feelings of catastrophe, isolation and panic often overtake these children if they are sent to nursery school, or "replaced" by a newborn sibling.

The need to sever the ties of early attachments, so deeply troubling for the symbiotic child, is experienced in some measure by all children. The progression from the first to the second neuropsychological stage is a gradual and overlapping one. A progressive unfolding of newly matured capacities encourage the shift, however. We next will turn to the characteristics and consequences of this second stage.

Stage 2: Sensorimotor-Autonomy

All infants possess basic motor capacities at birth. However, it is not until the end of the first year that they are sufficiently mature to act independently of parental support. A holding of the drinking cup, purposeful crawling, the first steps or a word or two, all signify a growing capacity to act autonomously of others.

Development of Sensorimotor Capacities. The unorganized gross movements of the neonate progressively give way to focused muscular activity. These newly developed functions coordinate with previously matured sensory capacities to enable the child to explore, manipulate, play, sit, crawl, babble, throw, walk, catch and talk.

The innately maturing fusion between sensory and motor functions is strengthened by the child's exploratory behavior (Bayley, 1970). His absorption in manipulative play, or the formation of babbling sounds, are methods of self-stimulation. He is building a neural foundation for progressively more complicated and refined skills such as running, handling utensils, controlling sphincter muscles and articulating precise speech. His intrinsic tendency to "entertain" himself is not merely "something cute to behold," but a necessary step in establishing capacities that are more substantial than maturation alone would have furnished. Stimulative experiences, either self-provided or through the actions of others, are requisites then for the development of normal sensorimotor skills. Unless retarded by environmental restrictions, by biological handicaps or by deficits in early sensory development, the toddler's growing sensorimotor capacities prepare him to cope with his environment with increasing competence and autonomy.

Development of Autonomy. — Perhaps the most significant aspect of sensorimotor development is that it enables the child to begin to do things for himself, to exert an influence upon his environment, to free himself from parental domination and to outgrow the attachment and dependencies of his first years — in other words, to develop a range of competencies by which he can master his world and establish a feeling of autonomy (Baumrind and Black, 1967).

This developmental progression can be seen in many spheres of behavior (Stone et al., 1973). With his growing skill in locomotion, he can explore new environments. With the advent of speech, he can engage in new social relationships, challenge the thoughts and desires of others, resist, entertain and manipulate his parents. He becomes aware of his increasing competence and seeks to test his mettle in new ventures. Needless to say, conflicts and restrictions inevitably arise as he asserts himself. These may be seen most clearly during the period of toilet training when youngsters often resist submitting to the demands of their parents. A delicate exchange of power and cunning ensues (Feshbach, 1970). Opportunities arise for the child to manipulate his parents and to extract promises or deny wishes. In response, parents may mete out punishments, submit meekly, register dismay or shift inconsistently among all three. Important precedents for attitudes toward authority and feelings of power and autonomy are generated during this and other periods of parent-child conflict.

Maladaptive Consequences of Impoverishment.   The failure to encourage
and stimulate sensorimotor capacities can lead to serious retardations in
functions necessary to the development of autonomy (Fowler, 1970).
This may be seen most clearly in children of overprotective parents.
Spoon-fed, helped in dressing, excused from "chores," restrained from
exploration, curtailed in friendships and protected from "danger," all
illustrate controls which restrict the growing child's opportunities to exercise his sensorimotor skills and develop the means for autonomous behavior (Ferguson, 1970). A self-perpetuating cycle may unfold. The
child may not be able to abandon his overlearned dependency upon his
parents since he is ill-equipped to meet other children on their terms. He
is likely to be timid and submissive when forced to venture out into the
world, likely to avoid the give and take of competition with his peers,
likely to prefer the play of younger children and likely to find an older
child who will protect him and upon whom he can lean. Each of these
adaptive maneuvers intensifies his established sensorimotor retardations
since it prevents him from engaging in activities that will promote
catching up with his peers.

Maladaptive Consequences of Enrichment.   The consequences of excessive enrichment of the second neuropsychological stage are found most
often in children of lax, permissive or over-indulgent parents. Given
free rein to test new skills with minimal restraint, stimulated to explore
at will and to manipulate things and others to his suiting without guidance or control, the child will soon become irresponsibly undisciplined in
his behaviors. When carried into the wider environment, however, these
behaviors normally will run up against the desires of other children and
the restrictions of less permissive adults. Unless the youngster is extremely adept, or the larger community unusually lax, he will find that
his self-centered and free-wheeling tactics fail miserably. For the few
who succeed, however, a cycle of unbridled self-expression and social arrogance may become dominant. To illustrate, a seven year old boy was
completely unmanageable both in kindergarten and first grade, talking
aloud while the teacher spoke, telling her that he knew "the answers"
better than she, intruding and disrupting the play of other children, who
referred to him as a "pest" and "bully"; from the family history it was
learned that this youngster's parents not only believed in "total permis-
siveness" but encouraged their son to "speak up and disagree with them"
and to "do whatever he wished, short of physically hurting others." The
majority of these youngsters will fail to gain acceptance by their peers
and will never acquire the give-and-take skills of normal social relationships.

Stage 3: Intracortical-Initiative

What capacities unfold during this intracortical and initiative stage, and
what consequences can be attributed to differences in the magnitude of
stimulus experience?

Development of Intracortical Capacities.   Progressively complex arrangements of neural cells become possible as the infant advances in maturation. Although these higher order connections begin as early as four to
six months of age, they do not form into structures capable of thought
until the youngster has fully developed his more basic sensorimotor
skills. With these capacities as a base, he is able to differentiate, arrange
and control the objects of his physical world. As his verbal skills unfold,
he learns to symbolize these concrete objects. Soon he can manipulate

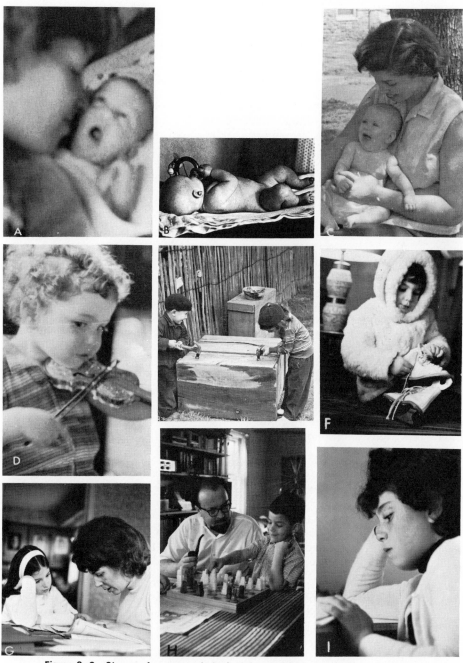

Figure 8–2   Stages of neuropsychological development. A to C. Sensory-attachment. D to F. Sensorimotor-autonomy. G to I. Intracortical-initiative. (Part E, courtesy of L. Stone, parts F to I, courtesy of L. Ross.)

and coordinate these symbols as well as, if not better than, the tangible events themselves (Kuhn, 1972). Free now of the need to make direct reference to the concrete world, he can recall past events and anticipate future ones. As more cortical connections are established, higher powers of abstraction are formulated, enabling him to transfer, associate and co-ordinate these symbols into ideas of increasingly finer differentiation, greater complexity and broader integration (Milton, 1970). It is his own internal representations of reality, his own patterns of symbolic thought and his own constructions of events — past, present and future — which take over as the primary units of his stimulus world.

This process of neural growth toward higher forms of cortical integra-tion depends on, and is stimulated by, both his own growing capacity to fantasize, and the evergrowing diversity of his environmental experi-ences. Without an increase in the complexity in his stimulus environ-ment, and without his own inner symbolic manipulations, the major steps in the growth of potentially more elaborate intracortical connec-tions will fail to materialize.

Development of Initiative.   When the inner world of symbols is mas-tered, giving the elements of reality an order and integration, the grow-ing youngster is able to create some consistency in his life (Aronfreed, 1969). No longer is he buffeted from one mood or action to another by rapidly changing events. He now has an internal anchor, stable cogni-tions which serve as a base and which impose a sameness upon an otherwise fluid environment. Increasingly, as he grows in his capacity to organize his symbolic world, one configuration predominates. Acquired from his experiences with others and from his effects upon them and their reactions to him, an image of the self-as-object takes shape. This highest order of abstraction, the sense of individual identity, becomes the core of personality functioning which guides and influences the indi-vidual's style of behavior. External sources of stimulation no longer have the power they once exerted. The youngster now has an everpresent and stable sphere of internal stimuli which governs his course of ac-tion — he has an established inner base from which *he* initiates events (Masters, 1972).

Maladaptive Consequences of Impoverishment.   The task of attaining in-tegration is not an easy one in a world of changing events and values. What is best? What is right? How shall I handle this or think about that? Questions such as these plague the growing child at every turn (Hoff-man, 1970). How can the everchanging guidelines for behavior be fash-ioned into a well-integrated system of beliefs and actions? From what source can a consistent image of self be consolidated?

Let us elaborate the consequences of understimulation. Erikson (1959) has formulated the concept of *identity diffusion*, a notion we will borrow to represent the effects of inadequate or erratic stimulation during the peak years of intracortical integration. Without direct tuition from his elders, a youngster will be left to his own devices to master the complexi-ties of a varied world, to control intense aggressive and sexual urges which well up within him, to channel his fantasies and to pursue the goals to which he aspires. He may become a victim of his own growth, unable to discipline his impulses or fashion acceptable means for ex-pressing his desires. Scattered and unguided, he cannot get hold of a sense of personal identity, a consistent direction and purpose to his exist-ence. He becomes an "other-directed" person, one who vacillates at every turn, overly responsive to fleeting stimuli and who shifts from one erratic course to another.

Maladaptive Consequences of Enrichment.   The negative consequences of overenrichment at the third stage usually occur when parents are controlling and perfectionistic. The overly trained, overly disciplined and overly integrated youngster is given little opportunity to shape his own destiny. Whether by coercion or enticement, the child who, too early, is led to control his emergent feelings, to focus his thoughts along narrowly defined paths and to follow the prescriptions of parental demands, has been led into adopting the identities of others (Aronfreed, 1968). Whatever individuality he might have acquired is drowned in a model of adult orderliness and virtue. Such oversocialized and rigid youngsters lack the spontaneity, flexibility and creativeness we expect of the young. They have been trained to be old men before their time, too narrow in perspective to respond to excitement, variety and the challenge of new events. Overenrichment at this stage has fixed them on a restrictive course, and has deprived them of the rewards of being themselves.

It would be a gross error if we left our discussion of neuropsychological development with the impression that personality growth was merely a function of volume and timing of stimulation. Impoverishment and enrichment have their profound effects, especially in the first two years of life, but the quality or kind of stimulation the youngster experiences is often of equal, if not greater, importance. The impact of parental harshness or inconsistency, of sibling rivalry or social failure, is more than a matter of stimulus intensity, volume or timing. Different dimensions of experience take precedence as the meaning conveyed by the stimulating source becomes clear to the growing child. We will turn to this complex facet of psychogenesis in the next section. Here the concepts forged in the search for principles and processes of learning will prove most relevant and useful.

EARLY LEARNING

To summarize the previous section, we might say that the basic architecture of the nervous system is laid down in a relatively fixed and orderly manner, but certain refinements in this linkage system do not develop without the aid of stimulative experience. However, environmental experiences not only activate the growth of neural collaterals but selectively prepare these pathways to be receptive to later stimuli which are qualitatively similar. This second consequence of stimulus experience, representing a lowering of the threshold for the transmission of similar stimuli, has been described in the language of psychology as the process of learning. It reflects the observation that perceptions and behaviors which have been subjected to prior experience and training are reactivated with relative ease. The following sections will outline some of the basic concepts, principles and processes of early learning.

LEARNING PRINCIPLES

There are few fields of psychological inquiry that are beset with more theoretical controversy than that of learning. What will be presented in this section represents the author's particular biases. Different approaches have been proposed by other psychologists, and it behooves the serious student to examine their comparative usefulness as tools for psychopathological analysis.

PRINCIPLE OF CONTIGUITY LEARNING

The simplest formulation proposed to account for the acquisition of new behaviors and perceptions has been referred to as contiguity. In essence this principle states that any set of environmental elements which occurs either simultaneously or in close temporal order will become associated with each other. If one of these elements recurs in the future, the other elements with which it had previously been associated will be elicited. Some years ago, for example, the author had the unpleasant experience of running out of gas as his car was crossing a heavily trafficked bridge. For several months thereafter, he sensed an uncomfortable feeling whenever he drove over this particular bridge, and found himself anxiously checking the gas gauge.

The principle of contiguity may be applied to the progressive development of both *response learning* and *expectancy learning*. Response learning refers to associative bonds established between stimulus events and responses. Using the contiguity concept as a model, we can formulate this type of learning as follows: any stimulus pattern accompanying or immediately preceding a response will tend, if it recurs, to elicit that response. Expectancy learning refers to associative bonds established among stimulus events. It does not relate to the learning of responses to stimuli but to the learning of relationships among stimuli. Described in contiguity terms, it states: any environmental stimulus which previously has occurred in temporal or spatial contiguity with other stimuli will, if it recurs, elicit the expectation, i.e., perception, cognition or prediction, that the other stimuli will follow.

ROLE OF MOTIVATION AND REINFORCEMENT

Several subsidiary factors, i.e., neither necessary nor sufficient but associated with conditions of contiguity learning, tend to increase the rapidity and strength with which behaviors and expectancies are acquired. We will briefly describe two of these contributing factors: *motivation* and *reinforcement*. The first condition concerns properties of the environment or the organism which encourage learning by initiating and intensifying behavioral activity; the second term refers to conditions which protect what has been learned by terminating new behaviors that might interfere with or disrupt these learnings.

Motivation signifies a state in which the organism is aroused or stimulated into behavior. Motivation may be prompted by internal bodily conditions such as hunger and thirst, or by external sources such as threats to one's security. Whatever the impetus, the motivated organism is driven to engage in need-fulfilling behaviors, e.g., obtaining food or withdrawing from a threat.

Motivation has other effects upon learning. Specific needs tend to produce a selective focusing upon the stimulus environment. Those features of the stimulus world which are relevant to these needs, that is, that enter the sphere of the organism's selective perceptions, will be strongly bonded to each other or to behavioral responses. Thus, specific motivations narrow the effective stimulus field to particular elements. These elements are most firmly incorporated into learned patterns. For example, a tourist is not likely to register the fact that there were no restaurants along a particular highway if he was not hungry while traveling it. However, if he was searching for a place to eat, the probabilities are high that he would note and remember this fact for future reference.

In a similar manner, attractive environmental stimuli tend to catch the attention and activate the organism. These more striking stimuli have a greater probability than less attractive stimuli of entering the perceptual sphere of the organism, and hence are subject to stronger learning.

Reinforcement is one of the most frequently used, yet one of the most troublesome concepts to define in learning. Historically, the concept of reinforcement has referred to the power of certain events to satisfy the motivational needs of the organism and, thereby, strengthen the associative bond between stimuli and responses (Bijou, 1970). More specifically, the term *positive reinforcement* has been used to signify conditions which, when added to a situation, increase the probability that responses associated with it will be evoked in the future (e.g., food is a positive reinforcer for a hungry animal); the term *negative reinforcement* denotes conditions which, when added to a situation, decrease the probability that responses associated with it will be evoked in the future (e.g., a painful electric shock is a negative reinforcer for all animals).

How do reinforcers (e.g., biological need satisfiers or learned rewards) influence the learning process according to the contiguity point of view?

Briefly, reinforcers serve initially as activators of organismic behavior. Second, once the reinforcement is achieved, the organism usually terminates his behavior. For example, the attainment of a *positive reinforcer* (food) will stop a hungry laboratory animal from continuing his food-searching behaviors (exploring alleys of the maze other than the one in which he found food). In this manner the reinforcer protects the specific alley-food association he learned by preventing new bonds from developing. In other words, the receiving of the reinforcement serves to discontinue exploratory behavior, and the early bond is preserved intact since there are no new associative bonds to interfere with it. *Negative reinforcers* (e.g., pain or punishment), in contrast, stir the organism to continue behaving until such time as he learns an appropriate escape response. Thus, positive reinforcers lead to the termination of behavior, whereas negative reinforcers prompt the continuation of activity. As the organism engages in his escape efforts under conditions of negative reinforcement, he acquires new behaviors that interfere with and break each of the associative bonds he has learned along the way. Eventually, he learns one that enables him to successfully escape the negative reinforcement; this last associative bond remains intact since no subsequent ones are learned to replace it.

PRINCIPLE OF INSTRUMENTAL LEARNING

In time, the organism learns to discriminate between those stimuli which result in pain and those which promise pleasure. This stage of learning takes the form of an expectancy in which he avoids stimuli that lead to discomfort and exposes himself to those that provide rewards. With these cognitions in mind he is able to circumvent future negative reinforcements and invite future positive reinforcements. Moreover, he begins to engage intentionally in a series of acts designed to obtain the reinforcements he seeks. He anticipates and actively manipulates the events of his environment to suit his needs since he has learned that reinforcements are contingent on his performing certain prior acts.

The process of acquiring these anticipations and manipulative behaviors is known as *instrumental learning* or, as Skinner has termed it, operant conditioning. Either through direct tuition or chance events, the organism learns which of his acts ultimately "produces" the desired result of obtaining a positive reinforcement or escaping a negative one. A simple example may prove instructive. A fussy and cranky child is offered candy or ice cream as a means of pacifying him. Although the child has been subdued for the time being, the parent, in effect, has given the child a positive reinforcement consequent to his misbehavior. On subsequent occasions, when the child is desirous of candy or other similar reinforcements, he will engage in cranky and fussy behavior once more since it "succeeded" previously in producing a reward for him.

If these "successful" manipulative acts prove effective in a variety of similar subsequent situations, they may take the form of an ingrained and widely generalized behavior pattern. These learned sequences of instrumental responses serve as the basis for the development of coping strategies, that is, a complex series of manipulative acts, employed in relation to events or people, in which the individual avoids negative reinforcements and obtains positive ones. Instrumental strategies will be elaborated in a later section.

VICARIOUS LEARNING THROUGH OBSERVATION

Human patterns of behavior are extraordinarily complex. For each child to learn the intricacies of civilized behavior by trial-and-error or reinforcement methods alone would be no less possible than it would be for an isolated primitive culture to advance, in one generation, to a full-fledged industrial and scientific society. Rather than struggling to acquire and integrate each of the many components of human behavior piece by piece, the child learns by adopting whole sequences of behaviors provided for him through the incidental actions of older members of his social group. These learnings are acquired in toto merely by observing, vicariously learning and then imitating what others do and think (Hartup and Coates, 1970). It is an efficient and necessary means by which the child becomes a "civilized human" in an amazingly short period of time.

This form of vicarious learning may be acquired quite incidentally by simple contiguity (e.g., being exposed to established associations among stimuli such as are found in social belief systems or observing exemplary forms of behavior) or by complex instrumental strategies (e.g., identifying with and adopting patterns of behavior manifested by parents as a means of obtaining their approval). Thus, intricate sequences of model-matching behaviors and attitudes are learned by incidental exposure to social models, by deliberate parental guidance and reinforcement or by the child's own instrumental maneuvers (Bandura, 1969; Kohlberg, 1969).

IMPLICIT LEARNING THROUGH THINKING

Much of what is learned, especially after the early years of childhood, occurs implicitly, that is, without being a direct consequence of external environmental effects (Baldwin, 1969). Clearly, the "thinking" organism is capable of arranging memories of experiences into new patterns of association. As the child develops an extensive symbolic repertoire of words and images, he no longer is dependent on "real" environmental experience to form and strengthen new learnings. By manipulating his storehouse of symbols and images, he can reinforce himself by fantasy attainments and can concoct new instrumental strategies for dealing with his environment. By reorganizing his internal symbolic world, then, he supplements the objective world with novel thoughts that provide him with new learnings and self-administered reinforcements (Berlyne, 1970; Masters, 1972).

Figure 8-3 Imitative learning. Children from three to six observed either live or filmed presentations of aggressive behavior. (Parts A to C.) After seeing these models, the children underwent mild frustration and then were photographed in a playroom in which various objects and instruments conducive both to aggressive and nonaggressive behavior were available. The influence of the models was clearly demonstrated by several children who imitated the models' behavior almost exactly. (Parts D to I.) (Courtesy of A. Bandura, Department of Psychology, Stanford University, Stanford, California.)

PERSISTENCE OF EARLY LEARNINGS

We have contended in the two preceding sections that childhood experiences are crucially involved in shaping lifelong patterns of behavior. To support this view we elaborated several conditions of early upbringing and their consequences. We will concentrate in this section on the notion of continuity in behavior, since we believe that the significance of early experience lies not so much in its impact but in its durability and persistence. Experiences in early life are not only ingrained more pervasively and forcefully, but their effects tend to persist, and are more difficult to modify, than later experiences.

Part of the continuity we observe between childhood and adulthood may be ascribed to the stability of biological constitutional factors. But there are numerous psychological processes which contribute to this consistency. Because these processes enable us to see more clearly how pathology develops, we cannot afford to merely enumerate them without elaboration.

Acquired behaviors and attitudes usually are not fixed or permanent. What has been learned can be modified or eliminated under appropriate conditions, a process referred to as *extinction*. Extinction usually entails exposure to experiences that are similar to the conditions of original learning but which provide opportunities for new learning to occur. Essentially, old habits of behavior change when new learning interferes with, and replaces, what previously had been learned. Failure to provide opportunities for interfering with old habits means that they will remain unmodified and persist over time. In other words, learnings associated with events that are difficult to reproduce are resistant to extinction.

Are the events of early life experienced in such a manner as to make them difficult to reproduce and, therefore, resistant to extinction? An examination of the conditions of childhood suggests that the answer is yes! The reasons for asserting so have been formulated with extraordinary clarity by David McClelland (1951). We will draw upon several of his ideas in the following sections.

PRESYMBOLIC LEARNING

Biologically speaking, the young child is a primitive organism. His nervous system is incomplete, he perceives the world from momentary vantage points and he is unable to discriminate many of the elements of his experience. What he sees and learns about his environment through his infantile perceptual systems will never again be experienced in the same manner in later life.

The infant's presymbolic world of impressions recedes gradually as he acquires the ability to discriminate and symbolize experience. By the time he is four or five, he views the world in a way quite different from that of infancy. He can no longer duplicate the amorphous experiences of his earlier years. Unable to reproduce early experiences in later life, he will not be able to extinguish what he learned in response to them. No longer perceiving events as initially sensed, he cannot supplant his early reactions with new ones.

RANDOM LEARNING

The young child lacks not only the ability to form a precise image of his environment but the equipment to discern logical relationships among its elements. His world of objects, people and events is connected in an unclear and random fashion. He learns to associate events which have no relationship. Thus, when he experiences fear in response to his father's harsh voice, he may learn to fear not only that voice but the setting, the atmosphere, the pictures, the furniture and a whole bevy of incidental objects which by chance was present at that time. Unable to discriminate the precise source in his environment which "caused" his fear, he connects his discomfort randomly to all associated stimuli. Now each of them can become precipitants for these feelings.

Random associations of early life cannot be duplicated as the child develops the capacity for logical thinking. By the time he is four or five he can discriminate cause-and-effect relationships with considerable accuracy. Early random associations do not "make sense" to him. When he reacts to one of the precipitants derived from early learning, he is unable to identify what it is in the environment to which he is reacting. He cannot locate the source of his difficulty, since he now thinks more logically than before. To advise him that he is reacting to a picture or piece of furniture simply will be rejected. He cannot fathom the true features that evoke his feelings since these sources are so foreign to his new, more rational mode of thought.

GENERALIZED LEARNING

The young child's discriminations of his environment are crude and gross. As he begins to differentiate the elements of his world, he groups and labels them into broad and unrefined categories. All men become "daddy"; all four-legged animals are called "doggie"; all foods are "yum-yum." When the child learns to fear a particular dog, for example, he will learn to fear not only that dog but all strange, mobile four-legged creatures. To his primitive perception, all of these animals are one-of-a-kind.

As the mass of early experiences becomes more finely discriminated, learning gets to be more focused, specific and precise. A ten year old will learn to fear bulldogs as a result of an unfortunate run-in with one, but will not necessarily generalize this fear to collies or poodles, since he knows and can discern differences among these animals.

Generalized learning is difficult to extinguish. The young child's learned reactions are attached to a broader class of objects than called for by his specific experiences. To extinguish these broadly generalized reactions in later life, when his discriminative capacities are much more precise, will require that he be exposed to many and diverse experiences. This may be a difficult point to grasp, and an illustration may be useful to clarify it.

Let us assume that a two year old was frightened by a cocker spaniel. Given his gross discriminative capacity at this age, this single experience may have conditioned him to fear dogs, cats and other small animals. Let us assume further, that in later life he is exposed repeatedly to a friendly cocker spaniel. As a consequence of this experience, we find that he has extinguished his fear, but only of cocker spaniels, not of dogs in general, or cats or other small animals. His later experience, seen through the discriminative eye of an older child, was that *spaniels* are friendly but not dogs in general. The extinction experience applied then to only one part of the original widely generalized complex of fears he acquired. His original learning experience incorporated a much broader range of stimuli than his later experience, even though the objective stimulus conditions were essentially the same. Because of his more precise discriminative capacity, he now must have his fear extinguished in a variety of situations in order to compensate for the single but widely generalized early experience.

These three interlocking conditions — presymbolic, random and generalized learning — account in large measure for the unusual difficulty of reexperiencing the events of early life, and the consequent difficulty of unlearning the feelings, behaviors and attitudes generated by these events.

Edvard Munch—*Isolation*

9 SOCIAL LEARNING AND PERSONALITY

INTRODUCTION

Attitudes and behaviors may be learned as a consequence of instruction on the part of parents, but most of what is learned arises from a haphazard series of casual and incidental events to which the child is exposed. Not only are rewards and punishments meted out most often in a spontaneous and erratic fashion, but the everyday activities of parents provide the child with "unintended" models to imitate. The following quote from Bandura and Huston describes well this incidental feature of learning (1961):

During the parents' social training of a child, the range of cues employed by a child is likely to include both those that the parents consider immediately relevant and other cues of parental behavior which the child has had ample opportunity to observe and to learn even though he has not been instructed to do so. Thus, for example, when a parent punishes a child physically for having aggressed toward peers, the intended outcome of the training is that the child should refrain from hitting others. Concurrent with the intentional learning, however, a certain amount of incidental learning may be expected to occur through imitation, since the child is provided, in the form of the parent's behavior, with an example of how to aggress toward others, and this incidental learning may guide the child's behavior in later social interactions.

Without their awareness or intention, parents suggest, through incidental aspects of their behavior, how "people" think, talk, fear, love, solve problems and relate to others. Aversions, irritabilities, attitudes, anxieties and styles of interpersonal communication are adopted and duplicated by children as they observe the everyday reactions of their parents and older siblings. Children mirror these complex behaviors without understanding their significance and without parental intentions of transmitting them. The old saying, "practice what you preach," conveys the essence of this thesis. Thus, as noted in the quote, a parent who castigates the child harshly for failing to be kind to others may create an intrinsically ambivalent learning experience; the contrast between parental manner and verbalized statement teaches the child simultaneously to think "kindly" but to "behave" harshly.

165

SOURCES OF ABNORMAL LEARNING

The belief that early interpersonal experiences within the family play a decisive role in the development of psychopathology is well-accepted among professionals, but reliable data supporting this conviction are difficult to find. The deficits in these data are not due to a shortage of research efforts. Rather, they reflect the operation of numerous methodological and theoretical difficulties which stymies progress (Yarrow, 1963; Wenar and Coulter, 1962; Roff, 1970). For example, most of the data depend on retrospective accounts of early experience. These data are notoriously unreliable. Patients interviewed during their illness are prone to give a warped and selective accounting of their relationships with others. Information obtained from relatives often is distorted by feelings of guilt or by a desire to uncover some simple event to which the disorder can be attributed. In general, then, attempts to reconstruct the complex sequence of events of yesteryear which may have contributed to pathological learning are fraught with almost insurmountable methodological difficulties (Roff and Ricks, 1970). Nevertheless, in the following sections we will attempt to outline some of the more reliable findings of recent research.

Parental Feelings and Attitudes

The most overriding, yet the most difficult to appraise, aspect of learned experience is the extent to which the child develops a feeling of acceptance or rejection by his parents (Alanen, 1970). With the exception of cases of blatant abuse, investigators have extreme difficulty in specifying, no less measuring, the signs of parental disaffection (Peterson et al., 1959). Despite the methodological difficulties which researchers encounter, the child who is the recipient of rejecting cues has no doubt but that he is unappreciated, scorned or deceived.

To be exposed throughout one's early years to parents who view one as unwanted and troublesome can only establish a deep and pervasive feeling of isolation in a hostile world. Deprived of the supports and security of home, the child may be ill-disposed to venture forth with confidence to face struggles in the outer world. Rejected by his parents, he may anticipate equal devaluation by others. As a defense against further pain, he may learn the strategy of avoiding others. He may utilize apathy and indifference as a protective cloak to minimize the rejection he now expects from others. Different strategies may evolve, of course. Children may imitate parental scorn and ridicule, and learn to handle their disturbed feelings by acting in a hostile and vindictive fashion.

Rejection is not the only parental attitude which may result in insidious damage to the child's personality. Attitudes represented by terms such as seduction, exploitation and deception contribute their share of damage as well. But it is usually the sense of being unwanted and unloved which proves to have the most pervasive and shattering of effects. A child can tolerate substantial punishment and buffeting from his environment if he senses a basic feeling of love and support from his parents. Without them, his resistance, even to minor stress, is tenuous.

Methods of Behavior Control

What training procedures are used to regulate the child's behavior and to control what he learns? As noted earlier, incidental methods used by parents may have a more profound effect than the parent intended, that is, the child acquires a model of interpersonal behavior by example and imitation as well as by verbal precept.

What are some of the pathogenic methods of control? Five will be noted (Sears et al., 1957; Glidewell, 1961; Becker, 1964; Bijou, 1970).

Punitive Methods. Parents disposed to intimidate their offspring, using punitive and repressive measures to control their behavior and thought, may set the stage for a variety of maladaptive patterns (Parke, 1970; Terr, 1970).

If the child submits to pressure and succeeds in fulfilling parental expectations (i.e., learns instrumentally to avoid the negative reinforcement of punishment), he is apt to become an overly obedient and circumspect person. Quite typically, these individuals learn not only to keep in check their impulses and contrary thoughts but, by vicarious observation and imitation, to adopt the parental behavior model, and begin to be punitive of deviant behavior on the part of others. Thus, an otherwise timid and hypertense 16 year old boy, whose every spark of youthful zest had been squelched by harshly punitive parents, was observed to be "extremely mean" and punitive when given the responsibility of teaching a Sunday school class for seven year olds.

Should these youngsters fail to satisfy excessive parental demands, and be subject to continued harassment and punishment, they may develop a pervasive anticipatory anxiety about personal relationships, leading to feelings of hopelessness and discouragement, and resulting in such instrumental strategies as social avoidance and withdrawal. Others, faced with similar experiences, may learn to imitate parental harshness and develop hostile and aggressively rebellious behaviors. Which of these reactions or strategies evolves will depend on the larger configuration of factors involved.

Contingent Reward Methods. Some parents rarely are punitive, but expect certain behaviors to be performed *prior* to giving encouragement or doling out rewards. In other words, positive reinforcements are contingent upon approved performance. Youngsters reared under these conditions tend to be socially pleasant, and, by imitative learning, tend to be rewarding to others. But, quite often, we observe that they seem to have acquired an insatiable and indiscriminate need for social approval. For example, a 15 year old girl experienced brief periods of marked depression if people failed to comment favorably on her dress or appearance. In early childhood she had learned that parental approval and affection were elicited only when she was "dressed up and looked pretty". To her, failure on the part of others to note her attractiveness signified rejection and disapproval. It would appear then that contingent reward methods condition children to develop an excessive need for approval. They manifest not only a healthy social affability but also a dependency on social reinforcement.

Inconsistent Methods. Parental methods of control often are irregular, contradictory and capricious (Bijou, 1970). Some degree of variability is inevitable in the course of every child's life, but there are parents who display an extreme inconsistency in their standards and expectations, and an extreme unpredictability in their application of rewards and punishments (Deur and Parke, 1970). Youngsters exposed to such a chaotic and capricious environment cannot learn consistently, and cannot devise nonconflictive strategies for adaptive behavior.

To avoid the suspense and anxiety of unpredictable reactions, the child may protectively become immobile and noncommittal. Others, imitatively adopting what they have been exposed to, may come to be characterized by their own ambivalence and their own tendency to vacillate from one action or feeling to another. We know that irregular reinforcements build difficult to extinguish behavior patterns. Thus, the immobility or ambivalence of these youngsters may persist long after their environment has become uniform and predictable.

Protective Methods.   Some parents so narrowly restrict the experiences to which their children are exposed that these youngsters fail to learn even the basic rudiments of autonomous behaviors (Ferguson, 1970). Overprotective mothers, worried that their children are too frail or are unable to care for themselves or make sensible judgments on their own, not only succeed in forestalling the growth of normal competencies but, indirectly, give the child a feeling that he is inferior and frail (Levy, 1945). The child, observing his actual inadequacies, has verification of the fact that he is weak, inept and dependent on others. Thus, not only is this youngster trained to be deficient in adaptive and self-reliant behaviors but he also learns to view himself as inferior, and becomes progressively fearful of leaving the protective "womb."

Indulgent Methods.   Overly permissive, lax or undisciplined parents allow children full rein to explore and assert their every whim. These parents fail to control their children and, by their own lack of discipline, provide a model to be imitated which further strengthens the child's irresponsibility. Unconstrained by parental control, and not guided by selective rewards, these youngsters grow up displaying the inconsiderate and often tyrannical characteristics of undisciplined children. Having had their way for so long, they tend to be exploitive, demanding, uncooperative and antisocially aggressive. Unless rebuffed by external disciplinary forces, these youngsters may persist in their habits and become irresponsible members of society.

Family Styles of Communication

Each family constructs its own style of communication, its own pattern of listening, attending and conveying thoughts to others. The styles of interpersonal communication to which the child is exposed serve as a model for reacting to the expressions of others. Unless this framework for learning interpersonal communication is rational and reciprocal, he will be ill-equipped to function in an effective way with others (Feinsilver, 1970). Thus, the very symbolic capacities which enable man to transcend his environment so successfully may lend themselves to serious misdirections and confusions.

The effect of confusing patterns of family communication have been explored by numerous investigators (Singer and Wynne, 1965; Lidz et al., 1958; Bateson et al., 1956; Lu, 1962). Not only are messages attended to in certain families in an erratic or incidental fashion, with a consequent loss of focus, but when they are attended to, they frequently convey contradictory meanings. The transmission of ambivalent meanings produces what Bateson refers to as a *double-bind*. For example, a seriously disturbed ten year old boy was repeatedly implored in a distinctly hostile tone by his equally ill mother as follows: "Come here to your mother; mommy loves you and wants to hug and squeeze you, hug and squeeze you." The contradictory nature of these double-bind messages precludes satisfactory reactions; the recipient cannot respond without running into conflict with one aspect of the message, i.e., he is "damned if he does, and damned if he doesn't." Exposed to such contradictions in communication, the youngster's foundation in reality becomes increasingly precarious.

Content of Teachings

The family serves as the primary socialization system for inculcating beliefs and behaviors. Through these teachings the child learns to think about, be concerned with and react to certain events and people in prescribed ways.

What kinds of teachings lend themselves to the learning of abnormal attitudes and behaviors? Just a few will be mentioned.

1.   The most insidious and destructive of these teachings is training in anxiety. Parents who fret over their own health, who investigate every potential ailment in their child's functioning and who are preoccupied with failures or the dismal turn of events teach and furnish models for anxiety proneness in their children. Few incidents escape the effects of a chronically anxious household. Fantasies of body disease, vocational failure, loss of prized objects and rejection by loved ones, illustrate the range of items to which a generalized disposition to anxiety can become attached. Once learned, this tendency intrudes and colors otherwise neutral events.

2.   Feelings of guilt and shame are produced by the teachings in many homes. A failure to live up to parental expectations, a feeling that one has caused undue sacrifices to be made by one's parents and that one has embarrassed the family by virtue of some shortcoming or misbehavior illustrate events which question the individual's self-worth and produce marked feelings of shame and guilt. Furthermore, the sacrificing and guilt-laden atmosphere of these parental homes provides a model for behavioral imitation. Youngsters who are reproached repeatedly for minor digressions often develop a deep and pervasive self-image of failure. If the child admits his misdeeds, and adopts his parents attitudes as his own, he will come to view himself as an unworthy, shameful and guilty person. To protect against feelings of marked self-condemnation, such children may learn to restrict their activities, to deny themselves the normal joys and indulgences of life and to control their impulses far beyond that required to avoid shame and guilt.

3.   Other destructive attitudes can be taught directly through narrow or biased parental outlooks. Feelings of inferiority and social inadequacy are among the most frequent. Particularly damaging are teachings associated with sexual urges. Unrealistic standards which condemn common behaviors such as masturbation and petting create unnecessary fears and strong guilt feelings. Sexual miseducation may have long-range deleterious effects, especially during periods of courtship and marriage.

Family Structure

The formal composition of the family often sets the stage for learning pathogenic attitudes and relationships. A number of these structural features will be noted (Gregory, 1958; Clausen, 1966).

Deficient Models. The lack of significant adult figures within the family may deprive children of the opportunity to acquire, through imitation, many of the complex patterns of behavior required in adult life. The most serious deficit usually is the unavailability of a parental model of the same sex. The frequent absence of fathers in underprivileged homes, or the vocational preoccupations of fathers in well-to-do homes, often produce sons who lack a mature sense of masculine identity (Biller, 1970; Cortes and Fleming, 1970).

Family Discord. Children subject to persistent parental bickering not only are exposed to destructive models for imitative learning but are faced constantly with upsetting influences. The stability of life, so necessary for acquiring a consistent pattern of behaving and thinking, is shattered when strife and controversy prevail. There is an ever present apprehension that one parent may be lost through divorce. Dissension often leads to the undermining of one parent by the other. An air of mistrust frequently pervades the home, creating suspicions and anxieties. A nasty and cruel competition for the loyalty and affections of children may ensue. Children often become scapegoats in these settings, subject to displaced parental hostilities. Constantly dragged into the arena of parental strife, the child not only loses a sense of security and stability but may be subjected to conflicting and destructive behavior models.

Sibling Rivalry. The presence of two or more children within a family requires that parents divide their attention and approval (Einstein and Moss, 1967; Meissner, 1970). When disproportionate affection is allotted to one child, or when a newborn child supplants an older child as the "apple of daddy's eye," seeds of discontent and rivalry flourish. Intense hostility often is generated and the child may continue to experience deep resentments and a sense of marked insecurity. Such persons often display, in the future, a distrust of affections, fearing that those who express them will prove to be fickle as their parents. Not unlikely also is the possibility that the intense hostility felt toward siblings will generalize into envious feelings toward other "competitors."

Ordinal Position. It seems plausible that the order of a child's birth within the family would be related to the kinds of problems he faces, and the kinds of strategies he is likely to adopt (Toman, 1970). For example, the *oldest child*, once the center of parental attention, experiences a series of displacements as new sibs are born. This may produce a pervasive expectation that "good things don't last." However, to counteract this damaging experience, he may be encouraged to acquire the skills of autonomy and leadership, may be more prone to identify with adult models and may learn, thereby, to cope with the complications of life more effectively than his less mature siblings. The *youngest child*, although petted, indulged and allotted the special affections and privileges due the family "baby," may fail to acquire the competencies required for autonomous behaviors. He may be prone to dependency and prefer to withdraw from competition. The higher incidence of mental disorder among the last-born in families lends support to these interpretations (Gregory, 1958; Dohrenwald and Dohrenwald, 1966). *Only children* appear to be especially resilient to severe emotional difficulty. This may reflect their special status as sole recipient of parental attention, approval and affection. In his singular state, the child may learn to view himself as especially gifted. With this confidence as a base, he may venture into the larger society secure in the conviction that he will be as well-received there as in the parental home. Despite this sound beginning, he is ill-equipped to cope with the give-and-take of peer relationships since he has not experienced the sharing and competition of siblings relationships.

SIGNIFICANT AREAS OF LEARNING

Because of our primary focus at the moment, we may forget that the child's developmental pattern is a biosocial process in which biophysical dispositions such as reactivity, temperament and physical constitution contribute a part. Learning is vitally important, of course, but we must not overlook the fact that the child's biophysical make-up influences the character of these learnings. The interaction between biological factors and the nature of what is learned will be touched upon only briefly in this section, but the intimate interplay between them should be kept in mind at all points in our discussion.

LEARNING INTERPERSONAL AND SELF-ATTITUDES

It will be useful to remind ourselves that experience may have a more profound effect at certain stages in the developmental sequence than at others. Thus, a hypothetical event *A* may have a more deleterious consequence if it occurs at stage 2 than at stage 3, because it affects neurological structures which are developing rapidly at stage 2, but which are relatively dormant at stage 3.

What experiences arise typically at each of the three neuropsychological stages of development presented in Chapter 8 and, more importantly, what are the central attitudes learned during these periods?

Briefly, during the sensory-attachment stage, the central attitude learned deals with one's *trust of others;* the sensorimotor-autonomy stage is noted by the learning of attitudes about *self-competence;* and the intracortical-initiative stage is characterized by learning attitudes regarding one's *personal identity.* A brief elaboration of the character of these learnings is in order.

STAGE 1: LEARNING TRUST OF OTHERS

Trust may be described as a feeling of confidence that one can rely on the affections and support of others. There are few periods in which an individual is so wholly dependent on the good faith and care of others as during the helpless state of infancy. Nothing is more crucial to the infant's survival and well-being than the nurture and protection afforded him by his caretakers. It is through the quality and consistency of this support that deeply ingrained feelings of trust are etched within the child's make-up.

Needless to say, the young infant can make only the grossest of discriminations at this period. It is as a result of this perceptual indiscriminateness, however, that what he does learn is so very significant. Feelings arising from his more specific relationship with his parents are highly generalized, and come to characterize his entire image of his environment. It is precisely because of his inability to make fine discriminations that these early learnings become pervasive and widespread. Were he able to differentiate among experiences more sharply, their effects would not be as generalized as they are.

Generalized early learnings establish a foundation of feelings of trust or mistrust with regard to the environment, feelings which will tinge and color every facet of the child's outlook and relationship with others. Nurtured well and given comfort, affection and warmth, he will acquire a far-reaching sense of trust of others. Should he be deprived of affection, warmth and security or should he be handled severely and painfully, he will learn to mistrust his environment, to anticipate further distress and to view others as harsh and undependable.

STAGE 2: LEARNING SELF-COMPETENCE

During the sensorimotor-autonomy stage the child becomes progressively less dependent on his caretakers. By the second and third years, he is ambulatory and possesses the power of speech and of physical control over many elements in his environment. Increasingly, he acquires the manipulative skills by which he can venture forth within his world and test his competence.

Subtle, as well as obvious, attitudes conveyed by parents will shape the child's confidence in his competencies. These attitudes will markedly influence the child's behavior, since it is not only what he can do which will determine his actions but how he feels about what he can do. The system of rewards and punishments to which he is exposed, and the degree of encouragement and affection surrounding his first performances, will contribute to the child's confidence in himself. Faced with rebuffs and ridicule, the child will learn to doubt his adequacy. Whether he actually possesses the requisite skills to handle events no longer is at issue; he simply lacks the confidence to try, to venture or to compete.

STAGE 3: LEARNING PERSONAL IDENTITY

With the emergence of the intracortical-initiative stage, and its associated capacities of thinking, evaluating and planning, the child begins to formulate a distinct image of himself as a certain "kind of person." Several elements of experience which influence the image of self-as-object were discussed in an earlier description of *Stage 3* and need not be reiterated here. It will suffice to recall that the healthy child must acquire a coherent system of beliefs which will guide him through a changing environment. Properly equipped by successful efforts toward autonomy, he will have confidence that he possesses a direction and purpose in life which is valued by others, and which can safely withstand the buffeting of changing events. Deprived of rewarding experiences in self-action and unable to get a picture of a valued inner identity, he will be incapable of handling the discouraging and divisive forces which may arise within his personal life.

Should there be a lack of an integrated sense of self, the growing adolescent or adult will flounder from one tentative course to another, and be beset with vague feelings of discontent and purposelessness.

LEARNING INSTRUMENTAL BEHAVIOR STRATEGIES

As noted above, children learn complicated sequences of attitudes, reactions and expectancies in response to the experiences to which they were exposed. Initially, these responses are specific to the particular events which prompted them. Over the course of time, however, the child begins to crystallize a stable pattern of instrumental behaviors for handling the events of everyday life. These coping and adaptive strategies come to characterize his way of relating to others, and comprise one of the most important facets of what we may term his personality pattern.

After the first years of groping through trial and error learning, the normal child acquires a set of strategies for coping effectively with the challenges of his environment. The healthy child will display a flexibility in his strategies, using only those behaviors which are suited to the particulars of each challenge. Once a conscious and objective appraisal of the conditions of reality has been made, the person will initiate behaviors which he previously has learned are successful in comparable situations. He may alter destructive elements in his own behavior, remove or circumvent obstacles in his way or compromise his goals and accept substitutes for them. Should all of these previously learned strategies fail, he may devise novel approaches until these prove either adequate or deficient to the task.

Instrumental strategies may be separated into two broad categories: *unconscious mechanisms* and *interpersonal patterns.* The first consists of several intrapsychic and self-deluding processes the child learns as a means of taking the "sting" out of painful events and feelings. The second category is composed of relatively ingrained habits or styles of relating to others learned as a function of the particular reinforcements a child has experienced with people throughout his life (Bijou, 1970).

INSTRUMENTAL UNCONSCIOUS MECHANISMS

Along with more rational instrumental behaviors, the child learns to employ a number of intrapsychic processes which diminish the discomforts he experiences when he is unable to resolve his problems in a more direct fashion. Several instrumental mechanisms may be learned to relieve his anguish. They are useful also in that they enable him to maintain his equilibrium until he can muster a better solution. We should take note, then, that healthy coping may be characterized both by retreat and self-deception *if* the objective conditions of the environment prevent a direct solution to a painful problem. Only when the individual persistently distorts and denies the events of the objective world do these unconscious mechanisms interfere with effective functioning.

Two broad classes of unconscious mechanisms may be differentiated. The first group, the *denial mechanisms,* represents the banishing from consciousness of intolerable memories, impulses and conflicts. By various maneuvers, the person disavows these feelings and thoughts, and thereby avoids acknowledging their painful nature. The second class of defenses, noted as *distortion mechanisms,* represents the misinterpretation of painful thoughts and feelings in order to minimize their impact. A discussion of these mechanisms follows.

Denial Mechanisms.   These concepts represent unconscious processes in which the individual denies the existence of painful or irreconcilable thoughts.

1.   *Repression* is the most common of the mechanisms and is basic to other denial mechanisms. It involves the simple but involuntary process of excluding one's undesirable thoughts and feelings from consciousness. In this way, the individual keeps inaccessible what would otherwise be unbearable.

2.   The mechanism known as *isolation* represents a segmented repression. Here the painful association between a thought and its emotional counterpart is disconnected. By repressing the feeling associated with a

painful event, the individual prevents this feeling from upsetting his equilibrium. For example, a prisoner may isolate his emotional feelings from thoughts about his impending execution; in response to questions about his fate, he may shrug his shoulders and say, "well, that's the way the cookie crumbles." He detaches feeling from the event to protect himself against overwhelming anxiety.

3. *Projection* represents first, a repression of one's own objectionable traits and motives and second, an attribution of these characteristics to others. The failing college student may claim that "his school has a lousy curriculum and stupid professors"; the tax-dodging businessman may state that he was driven to do it by "mercenary union leaders" and "dishonest government investigators"; the sexually driven person may accuse the object of his advances as having seduced him.

4. In *reaction-formation* the individual represses his undesirable impulses and assumes a diametrically opposite conscious attitude. A hostile person may display a facade of exaggerated amiability; a rebellious youngster may become scrupulously polite and gracious; a socially insecure woman puts forth a blasé attitude and gregarious manner.

Reaction-formations not only maintain repression, but strengthen the person's control over his unconscious tendency, e.g., by being scrupulously polite, the youngster is able to keep his rebellious inclination under constant check. Reaction-formations may also give vent to the repressed desire. Thus, persons who condemn public immorality may devote their spare time to "investigating" obscene literature, burlesque houses and neighborhood brothels. They may be gratifying their own unconscious, lascivious desires, while consciously decrying the shameful state of our society.

5. *Undoing* is a self-purification mechanism in which the individual attempts to repent for some misdeed or counteract a repressed "evil" motive. Greedy financiers donate their fortunes to charity; miserly husbands, unable to tolerate their niggardliness, give exorbitant tips to bellhops and waitresses. In more pathological form, undoing may be displayed in bizarre rituals and "magical" acts. The patient who compulsively washes his hands may symbolically be "cleansing his dirty thoughts"; his intolerable feeling of moral impurity is kept unconscious and counteracted by his ritual.

6. *Fixation* denotes the repression of maturing impulses and capacities. The individual refuses to "grow up" and acknowledge feelings and responsibilities appropriate to his age. Thus, in a rather unusual case, an otherwise fully developed and highly intelligent 12 year old boy never learned to drink liquids by any means other than through a nipple; moreover, he refused to wear undershorts, insisting that his parents purchase diapers that fit him.

7. *Regression* is similar to fixation. It differs in that it represents a retreat to an earlier level *after* normal development has progressed. Unable to face the anxieties and conflicts of adult existence, the individual reverts to immature and even infantile behaviors. Thus, disturbed adolescents, fearful of heterosexual impulses and competition, or anxious about their ability to be independent of their parents, often retreat to the safety of an infantile dependency. Their regressive mechanisms may be observed in signs such as incontinence, baby talk, thumbsucking and womb-like postures.

Distortion Mechanisms. These concepts represent processes that misinterpret distressing experiences and feelings in order to make them more bearable.

1. *Fantasy* is a semiconscious process of imagination serving to gratify wishes that cannot be fulfilled in reality. Thus, the daydreams of a shy and withdrawn 15 year old served to "transform" him into an admired and powerful figure, on some occasions, and a noble sufferer whose unjust plight would be redeemed, on others.

2. *Rationalization* is the most common mechanism of reality distortion. It represents an unconscious process in which the individual excuses his behavior or relieves his disappointments with reasons that are plausible but not "true." Rational explanations are concocted to cover up unrecognized and unacceptable motives. Thus, the businessman may justify hostility toward his wife by claiming "a hard day at the office"; the failing college student enhances his self-esteem by attributing his failure to "merciless freshman grading"; the spinster aunt alters her feelings of frustration and loneliness by pointing out how much better her life is than that of "those bickering Smiths next door."

3. *Identification* signifies a distortion of self-image in which the individual assigns to himself the power, achievements and stature of those with whom he associates. In this way he experiences vicariously gratifications which otherwise are not available to him. An alumnus may identify with his college's football team in order to bask in the glory of its athletic victories; an insignificant clerk may read biographies of great men and revel in minor similarities he finds between them and himself. Identification serves important developmental functions in the young, but it may lead to self-repudiation and identity confusion among adults. Thus, every large mental hospital has one or two patients who claim they are "Napoleon," "Jesus Christ" or some other figure of historical eminence.

4. *Compensation* represents a less pathological attempt to disguise one's deficiencies, frustrations or conflicts. In this mechanism, the individual overcomes his weakness by counteracting it or developing substitute behaviors. Short men may counter their feelings of insignificance by aggressive attention-getting behavior; physically unattractive girls may become preoccupied with their academic studies, and thereby cultivate respect for their "brains"; wives who have been cast aside by their husbands may gratify their need for love symbolically by insatiable appetites for sweets and drink. Well-known examples of successful compensation may be found throughout history. Demosthenes surmounted his early stuttering and became a great orator; Theodore Roosevelt overcame his sickly childhood by turning to feats of physical vigor and courage.

5. *Sublimation* usually is a healthy form of self-distortion. It represents the gratification of unacceptable needs by socially approved substitutes. Through this process the individual keeps his selfish and forbidden impulses out of awareness, yet finds acceptable channels for their expression. An aggressive individual may find gratification in an athletic, military or surgical career; unconscious strivings for power may form the basis of a political or business career; unacceptable desires for recognition may underlie success in science, teaching or acting. In none of these does the person consciously recognize that his occupation is a disguised outlet for unattractive needs or motives.

6. *Displacement* signifies the transfer of negative emotions from one object onto a more neutral or safe object. For example, the professor who

displaces upon his students the hostility that originates at home, protects himself from recognizing that he really feels hostility toward his wife and gives vent to his emotions safely. His anger not only is dissipated in this manner but he maintains the illusion that his martial relations are ideal and avoids the possibility of retribution.

INSTRUMENTAL INTERPERSONAL PATTERNS

Each of us has learned a variety of instrumental interpersonal strategies which enable us to reduce our anxieties (avoid negative reinforcements) and gratify our needs (achieve positive reinforcements). These interpersonal patterns, which can be seen as complex forms of learned instrumental behavior, develop as a function of early experiences with parents and siblings. Over time, they become an integral part of our way of relating to all others. Because they are so deeply ingrained, we are generally unaware of their distinctive and automatic character.

The eight instrumental patterns that follow underlie the overt manifestations of many forms of pathology. Although often developed as instrumental means of achieving reinforcements, they frequently prove self-defeating in that they tend to foster problems. The following descriptions are brief summaries of characteristics central to the principal personality patterns to be discussed fully in later chapters.

1.   The *passive-detached* patterns are characterized by social impassivity. Affectionate needs and emotional feelings are minimal, and the individual has learned instrumentally to function as a passive observer detached from the rewards and affections, as well as from the dangers of human relationships.

2.   The *active-detached* patterns represent an intense mistrust of others. The individual fears that his impulses and longing for affection will result in a repetition of the pain he has experienced previously. He has learned instrumentally that only by an active detachment and suspicion can he protect himself from others. Despite desires to relate to others, he has learned that it is best to deny these desires and withdraw from interpersonal relationships.

3.   The *passive-dependent* patterns are characterized by a search for relationships in which one can lean upon others for affection, security and leadership. This patient displays a lack of both initiative and autonomy. As a function of early experience, he has learned instrumentally to assume a passive role in interpersonal relations, accepting whatever kindness and support he may find, and willingly submitting to the wishes of others in order to maintain their affection.

4.   In the *active-dependent* patterns we observe an insatiable search for stimulation and affection. The patient's instrumentally learned gregarious behavior gives the appearance of considerable independence of others, but beneath this lies a fear of autonomy and an intense need for social approval and affection. Affection must be replenished constantly and must be obtained from every source of interpersonal experience.

5.   The *passive-independent* patterns are noted by narcissism and self-involvement. As a function of early experience the individual has learned to overvalue his self-worth. However, his confidence in his superiority may be based on false premises. Nevertheless, he assumes that others will recognize his worth, and he maintains a self-assured distance from those whom he views to be inferior to himself.

6.   The *active-independent* patterns reflect mistrust of others and a desire to assert one's autonomy. The result is an indiscriminate striving for power. Rejection of others is justified because they cannot be trusted. Autonomy and initiative are claimed to be the only means of heading off betrayal by others.

7.   The *passive-ambivalent* patterns are based on a combination of hostility toward others and a fear of social rejection and disapproval. The patient has learned to resolve this conflict by repressing his resentment. To achieve his instrumental goals, he overconforms and overcomplies on the surface. However, lurking behind this front of propriety and restraint are intense contrary feelings which, on rare occasion, seep through his controls.

8.   The *active-ambivalent* patterns represent an inability to resolve conflicts similar to those of the passive-ambivalent. However, these conflicts remain close to consciousness and intrude into everyday life. The individual gets himself into endless wrangles and disappointments as he vacillates between deference and conformity, at one time, and aggressive negativism, the next. His behavior displays an erratic instrumental pattern of explosive anger or stubbornness intermingled with moments of hopeless dependency, guilt and shame.

PERSISTENCE OF LEARNED BEHAVIORS

Several factors which make it difficult to extinguish early learnings are noted in Chapter 8. In this section we will describe several additional influences which contribute to the persistence of what has already been learned.

Self-Perpetuation of Learnings

The residual of the past does more than passively contribute its share to the present. By temporal precedence, if nothing else, memory traces of the past guide, shape or distort the character of current events. Not only are they ever-present, but they transform new stimulus experiences in line with past. We will elaborate two of these processes of perpetuation in this section: perceptual and cognitive distortion and behavior generalization.

Perceptual and Cognitive Distortion.   As noted above, certain psychological processes not only preserve the past but transform the present in line with the past. Cameron (1947) labels this process *reaction-sensitivity*. To him, once a person acquires a system of threat expectancies, he responds with increasing alertness to similar threatening elements in his life situation. Thus, a person who has learned to believe that "everyone hates him" will tend to interpret the incidental and entirely innocuous comments of others in line with this premise.

The role of habits of language as factors shaping one's perceptions are of particular interest. As Whorf (1956) and others have shown, the words we use transform our experiences in line with the meaning of these words. For example, a child who has been exposed to parents who respond to every minor mishap as "a shattering experience" will tend to use these terms himself in the future. As a consequence, he will begin to feel that every setback he experiences is shattering because he has labeled it as such. Instead of interpreting events as they objectively exist, then, the individual selectively distorts them to "fit" his expectancies and habits of thought.

The following quote from Beck illustrates this process well (1963):

A depressed patient reported the following sequence of events which occurred within a period of half an hour before he left the house: His wife was upset because the children were slow in getting dressed. He thought, "I'm a poor father because the children are not better disciplined." He then noticed a faucet was leaky and thought this showed he was also a poor husband. While driving to work, he thought, "I must be a poor driver or other cars would not be passing me." As he arrived at work he noticed some other personnel had already arrived. He thought, "I can't be very dedicated or I would have come earlier." When he noticed folders and papers piled up on his desk, he concluded, "I'm a poor organizer because I have so much work to do."

This distortion process has a cumulative and spiraling effect. By misconstruing reality in such ways as to make it corroborate his expectancies, the individual, in effect, intensifies his misery. Thus, ordinary, even rewarding events, may be perceived as threatening. As a result of this distortion, the patient subjectively experiences neutral events "as if" they were, in fact, threatening. In this process, he creates and accumulates painful experiences for himself where none exists in reality.

Behavior Generalization. We have just described a number of factors which lead individuals to perceive new experiences in a subjective and frequently warped fashion. Perceptual and cognitive distortions may be viewed as the defective side of a normal process in which new stimulus conditions are seen as similar to those experienced in the past. This process, though usually described in simpler types of conditions, commonly is referred to as *stimulus generalization*. In the present section, we will turn our attention to another closely related form of generalization, the tendency to react to new stimuli in a manner similar to the way in which one reacted in the past. We may speak of this process as *behavior generalization*.

Stimulus generalization and behavior generalization often are two sides of the same coin. Thus, if an individual distorts an objective event so as to perceive it as identical to a past event, it would be reasonable to expect that his response to it would be similar to that made previously. For example, let us assume that a child learned to cower and withdraw from a harshly punitive mother. Should the child come into contact with a somewhat firm teacher, possessing physical features similar to those of the mother, the child may distort his perception of the teacher, making her a duplicate of the mother, and then react to her as he had learned to react to his mother.

This tendency to perceive and to react to present events as if they were duplicates of the past has been labeled by intrapsychic theorists as the process of *transference*. This concept signifies the observation that patients in treatment often magnify minor objective similarities between their parents and the therapist, and then transfer to the therapist responses learned within the family setting.

The tendency to generalize inappropriate behaviors has especially far-reaching consequences since it often elicits reactions from others which not only perpetuate these behaviors but aggravates the conditions which gave rise to them. An example may be useful. A person whose past experiences led him to anticipate punitive reactions from his parents may be hyperalert to signs of rejection from others. As a consequence of his suspiciousness he may distort neutral comments, seeing them as indications of hostility. In preparing himself to counter the hostility he expects, he freezes his posture, stares coldly and rigidly and passes a few aggressive comments himself. These actions communicate a message that quickly is sensed by others as unfriendly and antagonistic. Before long, others express open feelings of disaffection, begin to withdraw and display real, rather than imagined, hostility. The person's suspicious behavior has evoked the punitive responses he expected. He now has experienced an objective form of rejection similar to what he received in childhood. This leads him to be more suspicious and arrogant, beginning the vicious circle all over again.

Social Reinforcement of Learned Behaviors

Of the many factors which contribute to the persistence of early behavior patterns, none plays a more significant role than social and interpersonal relationships. As pointed out in an earlier section, ingrained personality patterns develop as a consequence of enduring experiences generated in intimate and subtle relationships with members of one's immediate family. We described a number of events which lead to the acquisition of particular types of behaviors and attitudes. Here our attention will be not on the content of what is learned but on those aspects of relationships which strengthen what has been learned, and which lead to their perpetuation. Three such influences will be described: repetitive experiences, reciprocal reinforcement and social stereotyping.

Repetitive Experiences.   The typical daily activities in which the young child participates are restricted and repetitive. There is not much variety in the routine experience to which the child is exposed. Day in and day out he eats the same kind of food, plays with the same toys, remains essentially in the same physical environment and relates to the same people. This constricted environment, this repeated exposure to a narrow range of family attitudes and training methods, not only builds in deeply etched habits but prevents the child from new experiences that are essential to change. Early behaviors fail to change, therefore, not because they may have jelled permanently but because the same slender band of experiences which helped form them initially, continue and persist as influences for many years.

Reciprocal Reinforcement.   The notion that a child's early behaviors may be accentuated by his parents' response to him was raised in Chapter 7. We noted that a circular interplay often arises which intensifies the child's initial biological reactivity pattern (Bell, 1968). Thus, unusually passive or cranky infants frequently elicit feelings on the part of their mothers which perpetuate their original tendencies (Harper, 1971; Osofsky, 1971).

This model of circular or reciprocal influences may be applied not only to the perpetuation of biological dispositions but to behavior tendencies that are acquired by learning. Whatever the initial roots may have been — constitutional or learned — certain forms of behavior provoke, or "pull" from others, reactions which result in the repetition of these behaviors (Osofsky and O'Connell, 1972). For example, a suspicious, chip-on-the-shoulder and defiant child eventually will force others, no matter how tolerant they may have been initially, to counter with exasperation and anger. An ever-widening gulf of defiance may develop as parents of such children "throw up their hands in disgust." Affections which might have narrowed the gulf of suspicion and hostility break down. Each participant, in feedback fashion, contributes his share and the original level of hostile behavior is aggravated and intensified.

Social Stereotypes.   The dominant features of a child's early behavior form a distinct impression upon others. Once this early impression is established, people expect that the child will continue to behave in his distinctive manner. In time, they develop a fixed and simplified image of "what kind of person the child is." The term "stereotype," borrowed from social psychology, represents this tendency to simplify and categorize the attributes of others.

People no longer view a child objectively once they have formed a stereotype of him. They now are sensitized to those distinctive features they have learned to expect. The stereotype operates as a screen through which the child's behaviors are selectively perceived so as to fit the characteristics attributed to him. Once cast in this mold, the child will experience a consistency in the way in which others react to him (Hartup, 1970). No matter what he does, he finds that his behavior is interpreted in the same fixed and rigid manner. Exposed time and time again to the same reactions and attitudes of others, he may give up efforts to convince them that he can change. For example, if a "defiant" child displays the slightest degree of resentment to unfair treatment, he will be jumped on as hopelessly recalcitrant. Should he do nothing objectionable, questions will be raised as to the sincerity of his motives.

Our discussion of social stereotypes leads us quite naturally to the next section, that dealing with influences arising from the larger social and cultural environment.

SOCIETAL AND CULTURAL INFLUENCES

We would be remiss in our presentation if we failed to recognize that abnormal behavior may be shaped by the institutions, traditions and values of societal living. These cultural forces serve as a common framework of influences which establish guidelines for members of a social group.

In previous sections we noted that for many children the process of cultural training is far from ideal. Methods by which societal regulations are transmitted by parents often are highly charged and erratic, entailing affection, persuasion, seduction, coercion, deception and threat. Feelings of stress, anxiety and resentment may be generated within the young, leaving pathological aftereffects that distort their future relationships. Several of these pathogenic experiences have been dealt with earlier.

Attention in this "sociocultural" section will focus, not on the more private experiences of particular children in particular families, but on those more public experiences which are shared in common among members of a societal group. In a sense, we shall be speaking of forces which characterize "society as the patient."

CONTEMPORARY LIFE

Lawrence K. Frank suggested the following proposal almost forty years ago (1936):

Instead of thinking in terms of a multiplicity of so-called social problems, each demanding special attention and a different remedy, we can view all of them as different symptoms of the same disease. That would be a real gain even if we cannot entirely agree upon the exact nature of the disease. If, for example, we could regard crime, mental disorders, family disorganization, juvenile delinquency, prostitution and sex offenses, and much that now passes as the result of pathological processes (e.g., gastric ulcer) as evidence, not of individual wickedness, incompetence, perversity or pathology, but as human reactions to cultural disintegration, a forward step would be taken.

The notion that many of the pathological patterns observed today can best be ascribed to the perverse, chaotic or frayed conditions of our cultural life has been voiced by many commentators of the social scene (Fromm, 1955; Reisman, 1950; Goodman, 1960; Reich, 1970; Toffler, 1970). These conditions have been characterized in phrases such as "future shock," "the age of anxiety," "growing up absurd" and "the lonely crowd." It is not within the scope of this book to elaborate the themes implied in these phrases. A brief description of three conditions of contemporary life will suffice to provide the student with some idea of what these writers are saying.

ACHIEVEMENT STRIVING AND COMPETITION

Ours has been a culture which has maximized the opportunity of its members to progress, to succeed and to achieve material rewards. With certain notable and distressing exceptions, the young of our society have been free to rise above the socio-economic status of their parents. Implicit in this option to succeed, however, is the expectancy that each person will pursue opportunities, and will be measured by the extent to which he fulfills them. Each aspiring individual is confronted with a precarious choice: Along with the promising rewards of success are the devastating consequences of failure.

Opportunities are shared by most members of our society. This can only bring forth intense competition. The struggle for achievement is geared, therefore, not only to transcend one's past but to surpass the attainments of others. No better illustration can be seen of the consequences of competitive failure and inadequacy than in the constant testing and grading which children experience throughout their school years. This early form of teaching competitiveness persists and pervades every fabric of societal life. It is evident in athletics, in the desire to be accepted by prestigious colleges, in the search for "pretty" dates, for getting a job with a "title," having the highest income, buying "up" to a status car, belonging to the "right" country club and so on. Thus, a depressed man of 47, who had risen from a poor immigrant family background to a respected and financially rewarding career as a lawyer, became despondent and considered himself a failure following his unsuccessful bid for the elective office of county judge.

CONTRADICTORY SOCIAL STANDARDS

Achievement strivings refer to the need to surpass one's past attainments. Competition describes the struggle among individuals to surpass each other in these achievements. What happens, however, if the standards by which people gauge their achievements keep changing or are ambiguous? What happens if people cannot find dependable standards to guide their aspirations?

One of the problems we face today is the pace of social change, and the increasingly contradictory standards to which members of our society are expected to subscribe (Sherif and Sherif, 1965; Toffler, 1970). Under the cumulative impact of rapid industrialization, immigration, urbanization, mobility, technology and mass communication, there has been a steady decline of traditional values and standards. Instead of a simple body of customs and beliefs, we find ourselves confronted with constantly shifting and increasingly questioned standards whose durability is uncertain. No longer can we find the certainties and absolutes which guided earlier generations.

Lacking a coherent view of life, we find ourselves bewildered, swinging from one set of standards to another, unable to find stability and order in the flux of changing events.

DISINTEGRATION OF REGULATORY BELIEFS

There are large segments of our society that find themselves out of the mainstream of American life. Isolated by the unfortunate circumstance of social prejudice or economic deprivation, they struggle less with the problem of achieving in a changing society than with managing the bare necessities of survival. To them, the question is not which of the changing social values they should pursue but whether there are any social values that are worthy of pursuit.

Youngsters exposed to poverty and destitution, provided with inadequate schools, living in poor housing set within decaying communities, raised in chaotic and broken homes, deprived of parental models of "success and attainment" and immersed in a pervasive atmosphere of hopelessness, futility and apathy, cannot help but question the validity of the "good society" (Short, 1966). Reared in these settings one quickly learns that there are few worthy standards to which one can aspire successfully. Whatever efforts are made to raise oneself from these bleak surroundings run hard against the painful restrictions of poverty, the sense of a meaningless and empty existence and an indifferent, if not hostile, world. Thus, the young black people of today reject outright the idea of finding a niche in American society. They question whether a country that has preached equality, but has degraded their parents and deprived them of their rights and opportunities, is worth saving at all. Why make a pretense of accepting patently "false" values or seeking the unattainable goals of the larger society, when reality undermines every hope, and social existence is so evidently and pervasively painful and harsh?

SOCIOCULTURAL CORRELATES OF ABNORMAL BEHAVIOR

Many investigators have attempted to specify particular conditions of social life which contribute to mental illness. Usually, these studies establish precise correlations between single variables such as socioeconomic class, national and racial origin and the presence of psychopathology. In this section, we will describe briefly some empirical findings and conclusions of recent research. Students interested in detailed reviews would do well to read the articles by Scott (1958), Dunham (1966) and Freeman and Giovannoni (1969).

CROSS-CULTURAL STUDIES

It is commonly held that substantial differences in the prevalence (total frequency) of psychopathology exist between cultures. Weinberg (1952), for example, asserts that serious disorders arise less frequently among homogeneous and well-integrated primitive cultures than in those characterized by technological complexities, cultural heterogeneity and intergroup conflict. Ralph Linton (1956) came to a more discriminating conclusion. He noted that specific symptoms are shaped by the customs of different social groups, but that psychopathology can be found with equal frequency throughout the world.

Carothers, in Africa (1953), Stainbrook, in Brazil (1952), and Phillips, in Argentina and Japan (1968), found that the proportions of various forms of psychopathology differed substantially from that found in most Western societies. Along similar lines, Rosen and Rizzo (1961) found appreciable differences in the distribution of disorders between subcultures of a single Western society. In summary, then, there is evidence that cultural factors effect the form of expression, but not the frequency of psychopathology.

RACIAL AND ETHNIC ORIGIN

Problems in the definition of race and ethnic origins make research on these variables difficult to interpret. If we accept the traditional criteria used by investigators in this field, we are led to conclusions such as the following: Blacks show a higher prevalence of severe pathology than whites; Jews have a lower frequency of severe, but a higher frequency of mild, pathology than non-Jews; Chinese have a particularly low rate of alcoholic and sociopathic disorders; Irish Catholics display different patterns of pathology than Italian Catholics; recent immigrants and foreign-born have higher incidence rates than native-born.

In summarizing his review of research on these correlates, Scott states (1958):

Explanations for the differential rates of mental illness among the different racial and ethnic groups tend to be more speculative than empirically demonstrated. In addition to the problem of controlling socioeconomic status when making interethnic and interracial comparisons, there is the likelihood that differential willingness to care for psychotics within the family, rather than within institutions, might be responsible for some of the apparent differences in incidence.

The findings of the extensive Midtown Manhattan Study corroborate Scott's assertion. They found that racial and ethnic differences in psychopathology disappear when these groups are matched on socioeconomic variables (Srole et al., 1962).

RESIDENTIAL LOCALE

The admission rate for all forms of mental illness is substantially higher in urban than rural areas (Malzberg, 1940). Furthermore, the larger the city and the more central, congested and overpopulated the region within it, the higher the incidence (Faris and Dunham, 1939).

Differences between urban and rural rates have been attributed primarily to the more benign environment of country life, and to the ability of rural dwellers to care for their mentally ill at home. Other interpretations are possible; however, there are not sufficient data to enable us to choose among them.

The higher rates found within the central and congested tracts of a city, as compared to the more peripheral regions, appear to apply only to larger urban centers (Clausen and Kohn, 1959). It seems reasonable to ascribe the higher rates of psychopathology in central city areas to the fact that these communities usually are poverty stricken, physically decayed and socially disorganized. Not only do these regions breed conditions conducive to pathology but they tend to attract and serve as a haven for the unstable who drift into their midst.

MARITAL STATUS

Married persons have a lower incidence of mental disorder than single people, especially single males, who, in turn, have lower rates than those who are divorced (Rose and Stub, 1955; Odegaard, 1953, Turner et al., 1970). There are several ways in which these findings have been interpreted. The two most common assert: that marriage protects the individual from distresses associated with loneliness and disaffection, and that those inclined to psychopathology either are ill-disposed, incapable of establishing a marital relationship, or precipitate difficulties which result in its termination (Renne, 1970).

SOCIOECONOMIC CLASS

Numerous studies have sought to demonstrate relationships between socioeconomic conditions and prevalence and type of mental disorder (Zigler, 1970). Despite a sprinkling of negative data, two findings appear to hold up fairly consistently. First, members of the lowest socioeconomic class more often are diagnosed as severely impaired than those of the upper classes. Second, the particular form of psychopathology differs among these classes (Dohrenwald and Dohrenwald, 1969).

Two well-controlled studies, the first based in New Haven, Connecticut (Hollingshead and Redlich, 1958), the other in midtown New York City (Srole et al., 1962), offer evidence that both the prevalence (frequency) and incidence (rate) of serious disorders is greatest among the lowest socioeconomic class, whereas the prevalence of the milder (neurotic) disorders is greatest among the higher social classes. No difference exists between classes in the incidence of milder disorders (Table 9–1). That these data are not merely a result of the proportion of the overall population that fall within these class categories can be seen from Table 9–2; e.g., the lowest socioeconomic class accounts for 18.4 per cent of the general population, but 38.2 per cent of the psychiatric population.

Class	Six-Month Incidence	Prevalence
	Neuroses	
I–II	69	349
III	78	250
IV	52	114
V	66	97
	Psychoses	
I–II	28	188
III	36	291
IV	37	518
V	73	1505

TABLE 9–1

SOCIOECONOMIC CLASS DIFFERENCES IN INCIDENCE AND PREVALENCE OF PSYCHOPATHOLOGY*

*From Hollingshead and Redlich (1958).

TABLE 9–2

SOCIOECONOMIC CLASS PROPORTIONS IN NORMAL AND PSYCHIATRIC POPULATIONS*

Class	Per Cent of Normal Population	Per Cent of Psychiatric Population
I	3.0	1.0
II	8.4	7.0
III	20.4	13.7
IV	49.8	40.1
V	18.4	38.2

*From Hollingshead and Redlich (1958).

Analysis of type of pathology found most frequently among the various social strata indicates that apathy and social detachment (traditionally diagnosed as schizophrenia), as well as the more aggressive and antisocial tendencies (traditionally diagnosed as sociopathic disturbances), characterize the mentally ill of the lower classes, whereas feelings of interpersonal anxiety, inadequacy and guilt (traditionally diagnosed as neuroses and depressive disorders) are seen most often in the middle and upper classes (Frumkin, 1955; Hollingshead and Redlich, 1958; Hardt and Feinhandler, 1959; Srole et al., 1962; Langner and Michael, 1963).

PART 3

ABNORMALITIES OF MODERATE SEVERITY

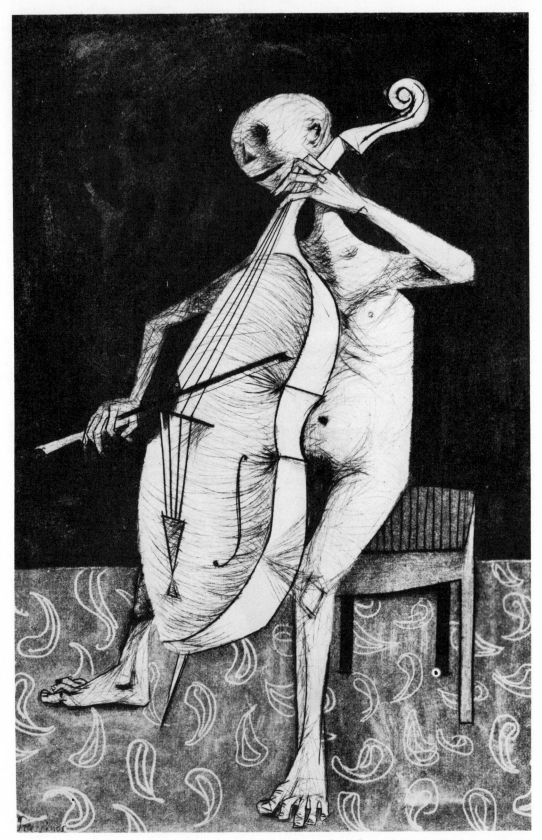

Mario Prassinos — *Cellist. Collection, the Museum of Modern Art, New York*

10 LEARNED BEHAVIOR REACTIONS

INTRODUCTION

Learned abnormal behavior reactions are relatively specific responses that operate independently of the patient's personality. Their form and content are determined largely by the character of external factors and not by the intrusion of complex unconscious or internal influences. Behavior reactions are best understood, then, as simple and straightforward learned responses to specific or circumscribed stimulus conditions (Bernstein, 1973). To paraphrase Eysenck (1959): there are no obscure "causes" which "underlie" pathological behavior reactions, there is merely the reaction itself; modify the reaction, or the conditions which precipitate it, and you have eliminated all there is to the pathology.

These abnormalities, then, consist of relatively permanent pathological behaviors learned in response to ordinarily neutral stimuli. They tend to be stimulus-specific and uniform in their expression since they are free of intruding intrapsychic processes. Many, but not all, develop under rather calm and undramatic conditions, that is, without the presence of a stressful precipitant. For example, certain forms of misconduct (shoplifting, alcoholism and promiscuity) are often learned vicariously as a direct result of simple observation and imitation.

Let us next organize the clinical features of the learned reaction syndrome into three subcategories—fears, sexual deviations and addictions. Other behavior reactions will be discussed in Chapter 19, dealing with abnormalities of childhood.

LEARNED FEAR REACTIONS

We need not elaborate the characteristics of intense fear since they are well known to all of us. These rather common reactions are not considered as pathological unless the response is entirely inappropriate or out of proportion to the objective seriousness of the stimulus that prompted it, as for example in reacting fearfully to the sight of a pine tree or becoming panicky when in the presence of an Oriental person.

Fear reactions are direct, nonsymbolic responses to the actual stimulus the patient has learned to fear, e.g., a fear of Oriental persons that is traceable to distressing encounters in childhood with a Chinese teacher. Some measure of generalization occurs, of course, but the individual tends to respond only to events which are similar or closely associated with the original fear stimulus, e.g., learning to fear a cat in early life may be generalized into a fear of dogs since these are barely discriminable in the eyes of the very young. At most, then, fear reactions reflect simple generalizations based on specific earlier stress situations. Although often appearing irrational to the unknowing outsider, they can be traced directly to these reality-based and well-circumscribed experiences.

Eysenck (1959) provides a classic illustration of how fear reactions are acquired in the following quotation (given the distinctions we will be making between fear reactions and phobic disorders, we should replace the terms "phobia" and "neurotic" in Eysenck's quote with "fear" and "behavior reaction"):

The paradigm of neurotic symptom formation would be Watson's famous experiment with little Albert, an eleven month old boy who was fond of animals. By a simple process of classical Pavlovian conditioning, Watson created a phobia for white rats in this boy by standing behind him and making a very loud noise by banging an iron bar with a hammer whenever Albert reached for the animal. . . .

The fear of the rat thus conditioned is unadaptive (because white rats are in fact not dangerous) and hence is considered to be a neurotic symptom: a similarly conditioned fear of snakes would be regarded as adaptive, and hence not as neurotic. Yet the mechanism of acquisition is identical in both cases. This suggests that chance and environmental hazards are likely to play an important part in the acquisition of neurotic responses. If a rat happens to be present when the child hears the loud noise, a phobia results; when it is a snake that is present, a useful habit is built up.

Eysenck's example demonstrates beautifully what we conceive as learned fear reactions, that is, a simple and direct learned response to an ordinarily innocuous stimulus object.

Let us briefly note a number of conditions which give rise to the acquisition of learned fear reactions.

The simplest of these are situations in which a previously neutral stimulus has been paired, either intentionally or incidentally, with a noxious stimulus. In the example reported in Eysenck's quote, the fear response given "naturally" to the stimulus of a sharp noise was "conditioned" to the stimulus of a white rat by the simple process of pairing the two stimuli.

Learned fear reactions need not have been based on direct prior experience with the fear-producing stimulus. Quite commonly, as in vicarious learning, children have merely seen or read about the "frightening" qualities of certain stimuli, e.g., a TV mystery in which a bloody murder occurs in a bathtub may build a persistent fear of taking a bath. In addition to visual pairings of noxious and neutral stimuli, children often acquire their fears through verbal association. For example, many youngsters who have never seen a snake have a dreadful fear merely of the thought of seeing one. They may have read about the "deadly poisonous" and "nauseatingly slimy" characteristics of these creatures or may have been told, in a tense and agitated voice by a fearful parent, "never to go near, let alone touch one." Along similar lines, children may acquire a variety of fearful attitudes simply by observing and imitating the behaviors, ideas and emotions of an apprehensive parental model. Thus, even though parents may never have directly told their children to be afraid of certain objects or events, children vicariously "soak in" attitudes merely by incidental observation. Through indirect associations such as these, a child may acquire within his behavioral repertoire a fearful expectancy of distress to stimuli that objectively are innocuous, despite the fact that he may never have had a direct or "real" experience with them.

If we think of the many incidental stimuli and chance-like conditions under which fears are learned, and add to it the effects of even simple stimulus generalization, we may begin to understand why so many of these fears appear irrational and peculiar. Despite their strange and nonsensical quality, however, they are a simple product of conditioned and vicarious learning, no more obscure in the manner of their acquisition than most of the attitudes and behaviors we take for granted as "normal."

LEARNED SEXUAL DEVIATIONS

Inclusion in the *sexual deviation reaction* syndrome signifies that the problem does *not* have its roots in personality pathology. Rather, it is a *circumscribed* learned reaction, a bizarre fragment that departs from an otherwise reasonably "normal" personality style. These deviations should be viewed, then, as isolated habits acquired in response to an unusual combination of circumstances that have distorted the learning of normal sexual behaviors, but have not intruded upon other spheres of personality development.

Before we discuss these forms of sexual deviance, let us briefly elaborate how personality factors often are involved in these habits. First, sexual difficulties may reflect a broader pathological pattern. Second, and perhaps more importantly, sexual deviancy, although initially circumscribed, may lead to behaviors and problems that ultimately result in more pervasive problems. In other words, sexual deviance can be both a cause as well as a consequence of personality deviance. For example, a young and otherwise "healthy" homosexual must engage in furtive maneuvering, given the customs of our society, in order to gratify his needs. In addition to becoming sensitive to cues from potential partners, he is often fearful that others may have detected his behaviors. As a consequence of operating in this manner for some time, he may acquire generalized traits of hypersensitivity and suspiciousness concerning the hidden thoughts and feelings of others. These traits may become so ingrained that he begins to behave and think in ways that are similar to those seen in abnormal personalities.

In this section, we will focus our attention on persons whose deviance neither reflects nor has given rise to personality complications. Rather, we will limit ourselves to sexual deviancies that are circumscribed, that is, relatively free of associated personality impairments.

The popular view that sexual deviance is invariably associated with degeneracy, violence or other signs of marked antisocial pathology is grossly mistaken. Certain forms of perversion, such as rape-murders, usually indicate the presence of more general psychopathology, but the great majority of individuals who engage in deviant forms of sexuality are not different from anyone else in their general behaviors and attitudes. If anything, they tend to be socially reserved and timid rather than cruel and violent. Moreover, many deviates evidence only one form of sexual pathology. They repeat the same act time and time again and rarely explore or engage in other types of sexual deviance.

SOCIAL LEARNING OF SEXUAL DEVIANCE

It appears safe to assume that sexual deviance is primarily a product of social learning, a result of some unusual or faulty set of environmental conditions which has blocked or distorted the acquisition of normal sexual attitudes and behaviors. Which one of an almost infinite number of sexual practices will come to the foreground during development depends on the cultural setting within which a child is born and the particular attitudes and experiences to which he is exposed. In some societies, such as early Greece, homosexuality was not only an accepted form of sexual behavior, but a preferred one among the intelligentsia and well-to-do. In contemporary Western societies, however, heterosexual intercourse is the preferred modality and goal of sexual behavior. Any form of sexual activity which does not result in coitus with an adult of the opposite sex as its ultimate objective is viewed as a sign either of immaturity or perversion.

What influences give rise to these deviations?

Sexual deviations, viewed as socially learned habits, are acquired primarily in two ways: by conditioning and by imitative learning. Once acquired, these habits tend to be perpetuated and intensified as a consequence of a number of secondary reinforcing events. Let us elaborate this general thesis.

Neutral stimuli may acquire either sexually attractive or repulsive qualities simply by being paired through contiguity association with stimuli which previously were viewed as sexually attractive or repulsive. This process of learning is the standard paradigm of classical conditioning. For example, a child who was rather indifferent to his mother's undergarments may have his attitude changed when he hears "dirty jokes" about underclothes from his friends or becomes "infected" with sexual excitement as they titillate each other while viewing advertisements for ladies' undergarments.

Preadolescent and adolescent boys are especially prone to sexual arousal and erotic titillation. However, young adolescents rarely experience the act of coitus directly. More often, they associate their maturing sexual feelings with lurid stories, pornographic pictures, peephole observations and the like. Given the diverse and bizarre conceptions of sexuality experienced by adolescents, we should not be surprised that they learn to associate sexual responses with a peculiar array of stimuli. This early and largely incidental pairing of erotic excitement with objectively neutral stimuli may create strong aversions to "real" sexuality and strange misconceptions of the nature of adult sexual activity. For example, if a young girl reads lurid stories in which sex is paired with brutal treatment, she may be conditioned to fear sexual activity, becoming in time not only hesitant in sexual matters, but totally unable to consummate the sexual act in marriage. Another young girl may have learned to believe, through the incidental comments and behaviors of her mother, that women must be "free with their bodies" if they ever wish to get and hold on to a man. This imitative learning may lead the child to pursue a promiscuous course when she begins heterosexual dating.

Sexual attitudes and behaviors need not be acquired in so direct a manner as those just illustrated. For example, a boy raised by an affectionate but controlling mother, and having minimal contact with a busy or rejecting father, may fail to acquire a sense of masculine identity; lacking in feelings of male competence and fearful of asserting himself in relation to women, he may gravitate into the role of a passive or feminine homosexual.

In summary, then, sexually deviant habits are often acquired as a result of faulty conditioning and imitative experiences. We will elaborate other types of learning conditions which foster the major variants of sexual deviance in a later section.

Before proceeding to specifics, let us ask the question: why do early deviant learnings persist? This question must be posed since most youngsters, somewhere along the way, usually acquire rather peculiar conceptions and habits of sexuality which they gradually relinquish in preference to more "mature" and conventional forms of sexual behavior. What factors contribute, then, to the persistence of deviant habits in certain individuals?

A rather general answer to this question was provided in earlier chapters when we outlined several factors which foster the continuity or perpetuation of early patterns of behavior. Let us briefly review several of those points, adapting them to the particular conditions surrounding sexual learning.

Foremost among these perpetuating factors are the consistency and sheer repetitiveness of certain environmental influences. For example, the child who is taught to "beware of sex" hears this admonishment not once but innumerable times, and not only in the form of stated precepts but in incidental ways such as the tone of voice and anxious questions of a worried parent.

Among the various forms of social reinforcement, we might mention the powerful impact of social stereotypes upon the development of homosexual behaviors. For example, an "effeminate" looking, nonathletic boy may be excluded from opportunities to acquire masculine traits and be shamed from attempting to date girls. As this stereotype shapes a feminine self-image within him and as his fears of heterosexual inadequacy grow, he may drift into homosexual relationships in which he neither is ridiculed nor feels inadequate.

It is not only external circumstances which serve to prevent the extinction of early deviant habits; many internal forces tend to perpetuate these behaviors. For example, feelings of fear and guilt often prevent youngsters from exploring new sexual outlets that could help alter their misconceptions and stimulate the acquisition of normal sexual behaviors. Similarly, many youngsters restrict their sexual life to masturbatory fantasies. Unfortunately, these fantasies may be limited to a few youthful misconceptions and distortions based on faulty or perverse experiences. As a consequence, masturbation only reinforces and strengthens their deviant conceptions. Thus, if new real life experiences are not available to extinguish these immature conceptions, these youngsters will con-

tinue, through self-reinforcement, to strengthen the same deviant notions each time they achieve pleasure in masturbation.

In the preceding paragraphs we have noted a few illustrations of how
social reinforcement and self-perpetuation may strengthen early deviant
habits and interfere with the acquisition of normal heterosexual behaviors. We will refer to these processes again when we next discuss the specific variants of sexual pathology.

MAJOR VARIANTS OF SEXUAL DEVIANCE

Although the principles and processes of learning are essentially the
same, it is common practice to differentiate the various forms of sexual
deviance into several categories. Three groups of perversions may
usefully be distinguished.

The *first* includes deviancies in the sexual object; among these are
homosexuality (preferences for same sex mates), *pedophilia* (preferences
for children) and *fetishism* (preferences for nongenital body parts or
inanimate objects).

The *second* category refers to deviances in the mode of sexual gratification: these include *exhibitionism* (exposing one's genitals before members
of the opposite sex), *voyeurism* (observing the genitals or sexual behavior
of others), *transvestitism* (wearing the clothes of the opposite sex) and
sadomasochism (inflicting or suffering pain).

The *third* group pertains to deviancies in the intensity of desire and the
frequency of sexual activity; among these are *nymphomania* in females
and *satyriasis* in males (excessive desire and activity) and *frigidity* in
females and *impotence* in males (deficient desire and activity).

Keep in mind that these categories are not mutually exclusive; for example, many homosexuals (deviant object) suffer also from satyriasis
(deviant intensity and frequency).

HOMOSEXUALITY

Erotic relationships between members of the same sex were recorded in
the earliest of ancient manuscripts. It is mentioned in the Bible, eu-
logized in the writings of the Greeks and Romans, commonly practiced
and tacitly approved in a number of highly cultured civilizations and
found among eminent historical and literary figures such as Alexander
the Great, Michelangelo, Lord Byron, Oscar Wilde and Andre Gide.

Contrary to popular belief, homosexuality is neither a rare phenomenon
nor a characteristic of "queer perverts." As Kinsey (1948, 1953) has
shown, over 37 per cent of all males have had homosexual experiences
to the point of orgasm after the onset of adolescence; 18 per cent of all
males show as much homosexual as heterosexual behavior in their
clinical histories; and 8 per cent have engaged exclusively in homosexual
activities for at least three consecutive years after the age of 16. Although the frequency of homosexual behavior among women is about
half that found among men, these figures are rather substantial and
often come as a shock to those who view homosexuality as a rare phenomenon to be socially condemned and punished. Yet despite the high
incidence of this habit and the fact that homosexuals manifest no greater
degree of psychopathology than that found in the general population

(Hooker, 1957), the view remains fixed in the public mind that these behaviors are a sign of degeneracy that calls for the arrest and incarceration of its practitioners.

Because they are subject to suspicion and potential derogation, many homosexuals live in constant fear that their habit will be exposed, resulting in their public disgrace. Not infrequently, these individuals acquire certain personality characteristics *as a consequence* of the subterfuge they invariably must practice to escape detection and the unusual pressures to which they are subject in their efforts to extract some measure of sexual gratification (Socarides, 1972).

To minimize these tensions, young homosexuals tend to gravitate toward large urban settings where they may find a more congenial "homosexual community" in which to gain the emotional support and sexual outlets they need. Previously hounded and humiliated homosexuals can find in these communities a place to live and a "gay" bar or two where they may establish contacts for pursuing either a brief one night rendezvous or a more enduring "marital" relationship.

The great majority of practicing homosexuals are indistinguishable in speech, manner and dress from other people. Most take great pains to avoid the appearance of effeminacy. Those who achieve the security of regular employment and the emotional gratifications available in a well-knit homosexual community, lead rather "ordinary" lives, preoccupied with the same run-of-the-mill concerns and problems that are found in the society at large. Many, however, have not been able to secure a comfortable niche for themselves in society. They experience prolonged periods of loneliness, remain apprehensive lest they be detected, grow increasingly insecure about their loss of "attractiveness" and so on. These homosexuals are in great conflict, troubled by the implacable nature of a habit they would like to be rid of but cannot.

What kinds of experiences have been shown to be related to the acquisition and the persistence of the homosexual habit? Although data relevant to this question are far from reliable or complete, several conditions, often in combination, appear with fair regularity in the histories of these patients.

Imitation of Opposite Sex Parental Models. Parental relationships which foster the imitation of the opposite sex is a common theme in the upbringing of many homosexuals (Snortum et al., 1969; Evans, 1969). An early investigation of this thesis, carried out by Bender and Paster (1941), found that over 90 per cent of a group of 23 homosexuals were unable to identify with their same-sex parent because these parents were either physically absent from home, or grossly abusive or ineffectual and weak. By default, if nothing else, the opposite sex parent in these cases became the primary model for imitation (Apperson and McAdoo, 1968). Bieber et al. (1962) carried out a large-scale study comparing 106 homosexual males and 100 heterosexual males undergoing psychoanalysis, gave further support to this imitation thesis, and provided some details concerning how parents encourage the development of homosexual behaviors. Table 10–1 may be referred to for a comparative summary of these experiential influences. Basically, Bieber found that homosexual males spent appreciably less time with their fathers and feared and hated them to a greater extent than did equally troubled heterosexual males who suffered different forms of pathological impairments. As to their mothers, the homosexual group experienced less encouragement and more interference with masculine activities than the

Relationship	Homo-sexuals	Hetero-sexuals
Mother	*in per cent*	
Demanded that she be prime center of patient's attention	61	36
Was seductive toward patient	57	34
Spent a great deal of time with patient	65	27
Tried to ally with patient against husband	62	40
Was more intimate with patient than with other male siblings	56	29
Encouraged masculine activities	17	47
Interfered with patient's heterosexual activity during and after adolescence	58	35
Father		
Patient was father's favorite	7	28
Patient spent little time with father	87	60
Patient hated and feared father	57	31
Patient admired father	16	47

TABLE 10–1

PARENTAL RELATIONSHIPS OF HOMOSEXUAL AND HETEROSEXUAL MALE PATIENTS*

*From Bieber (1962).

heterosexual group. In summary, then, male homosexuals appear not only to be deprived of adequate masculine identification, but concurrently are encouraged and even seduced to identify with the feminine role. (As a parenthetical note, we often find an early history among male homosexuals of having been dressed and groomed as little girls.)

Learned Aversion to the Opposite Sex.   Many homosexuals report feelings of disgust and revulsion in response to the thought or sight of the sexual anatomy of the opposite sex. These persons tend to be exclusively homosexual whereas those who experience no such distaste are often *bisexual* (homosexual *and* heterosexual).

Many factors may give rise to this aversive learning. The psychoanalysts refer to castration anxiety, a dreadful shock engendered within males upon first viewing what they believe to be the dismembered female genitalia. Whether, as the psychoanalysts assert, this provokes a fear that they also will suffer castration, leading them to avoid contact with the "mutilated" bodies of females, or whether this experience merely serves to condition an aversion to the strange and bizarre character of the female anatomy, is a point which may be debated endlessly. Rather than engage in this fruitless debate, it seems best to conclude simply that *any* event which connects opposite sex genitalia to aversive feelings will dispose the individual to avoid further contact.

White (1959) illustrates that homosexuality may be an incidental by-product of the typical attitudes conveyed by parents toward their children's early sexual interests. Thus, many a child is punished for his erotic curiosity and play with members of the opposite sex, but is never told in his early years that similar interests and activities with members of his own sex are forbidden. As a consequence, he may selectively learn to avoid heterosexual pursuits, without impairing comparable homosexual interests.

Aversions to heterosexuality may be acquired in more complex ways than simple aversive conditioning or selective punishment. As was previously noted, male homosexuals have often been dominated by affectionate but controlling mothers. The attitudes and feelings they acquire in this relationship are likely to be strong and to generalize to other women; some of these learnings may disincline them to heterosexual relationships. For example, they may have learned to fear women, to see them as demanding and "castrating" figures who control and manipulate men, as their mothers may have done both to them and to their fathers. Other homosexuals may have learned to view women as "saints," creatures who must never be defiled and besmirched by the coarse and lustful desires of men. A third group of homosexuals may have been overly attached to their "protectively loving" mothers, and now prove their endearing loyalty by avoiding the pursuit of a female replacement.

Early Homosexual Experiences. Bieber (1962) reports that more than half of his group of adult male homosexuals had their first homosexual experience prior to the age of 14; this contrasts with a figure of one fifth in a comparable group of adult heterosexuals. We must not conclude from this finding that early homosexual seduction must have been the "cause" of homosexuality since homosexual inclinations may already have been present before the age of 14. However, once such early involvements take place, especially if they occur prior to equivalent heterosexual gratifications, they may serve to reinforce and crystallize a rather weak and inchoate homosexual inclination (Manosevitz, 1970). As we may recall from an earlier chapter, "first experiences" tend to weigh more heavily in shaping behavior than equivalent later experiences. Moreover, if these early homosexual relationships proved repeatedly pleasurable and served additionally as a source of emotional comfort and security, as Greco and Wright (1944) found in their study, then there is an increased likelihood that an early homosexual trend would be strengthened and perpetuated.

Adolescent Alienation. Bieber (1962) found that over half of his group of homosexuals were isolated from normal peer relationships in adolescence. Less than one fifth engaged in competitive sports and social games, and most felt rebuffed and ridiculed by their male age-mates. Experiences such as these not only may have contributed to feelings of masculine inadequacy, but may have built a strong desire and longing for masculine acceptance and approval. Such youngsters may gravitate into homosexual relationships for a variety of reasons. First, among homosexuals they will be totally accepted despite their deficit masculinity. Second, in homosexual affairs they can receive the approval and affection from male peers that were denied them in earlier adolescent relations, as illustrated in the following segment of a more extensive case history.

CASE 10–1

Isaac P., Age 46, Unmarried

Isaac, a lifelong homosexual, was raised on an isolated farm until he was 12 years of age. His father was an alcoholic who ridiculed him for his "sissified" ways; most of Isaac's time was spent at home talking to and helping his mother and three older sisters. Isaac's sole contact with boys during this early period was limited to four hours of "strict academic work each weekday in a one-room schoolhouse" that contained first through sixth grades; there was only one other boy of his age at the school.

Isaac entered a regular junior high school at age 12 when his parents moved to a small city. In no time, he was dubbed a "sissy" since he spoke in an effeminate way and was extremely inept in sports. He recalled his desperate longing to be "like other boys" and to be "accepted by them." Unfortunately, his image was fixed in their eyes and his plight grew worse rather than better.

When he was 14, Isaac met a boy of his own age, similarly stereotyped and seeking male recognition and companionship. They became extremely close and dependent on each other, including the sharing of masturbatory fantasies. In time, they began to masturbate together and, ultimately, to masturbate each other. The "secret" they shared soon included another boy and as time progressed a number of older men. By the time Isaac was 17, his homosexual activities had become a deeply ingrained and highly rewarding pattern.

Before closing this discussion of homosexuality, we should note a few points concerning certain personality correlates of this form of sexual deviance.

A large segment of male homosexuals, but by no means all, exhibited a "soft" and non-assertive temperament in childhood. Of course, these traits in themselves do not produce homosexuality. However, youngsters who display these characteristics are more likely to fall prey to those experiences which Bieber has found to be typical of future homosexuals, e.g., rejection by their fathers, who may be disinclined to identify and associate with their "effeminate" sons, over-protection and identification with their mothers, who may be attracted to the soft and gentle temperament of their sons, and rebuff and ridicule by adolescent peers, who value competitive assertiveness and demean timidity and "weakness."

PEDOPHILIA

This pathological habit focuses on children or young adolescents as sexual objects. The relationship, frequently forced upon the child, may be either of a heterosexual or homosexual nature, and usually involves the reciprocal manipulation of genitalia, or mouth-genital stimulation. Heterosexual penetration is not common except under the influence of alcoholic intoxication, or in cases of severe psychopathology where a marked loss of control is evident.

Statistics on the frequency of pedophiliac offenses are rather sparse, and etiological studies are limited essentially to case histories. Pedophiliacs appear to comprise a highly diverse group in terms of age, education and socioeconomic background. Revitch and Weiss (1962) found a preference for young children among offenders over 50 and a preference for adolescents among those under 40. Kopp (1962) suggests that these men feel markedly deficient in masculine adequacy and turn toward children as a means of achieving gratification without incurring the rejection and ridicule they anticipate with adult partners. The apparent lack of interest in the act of intercourse among these men adds support to the view that they feel inadequate in adult sexuality.

Pedophilia, as a learned habit, appears to represent a process of early conditioning that failed to be extinguished by more rewarding later experiences. The clinical history of most of these deviates indicates that they engaged in childhood and adolescent sexual play. These experiences, however, are not uncommon in the general population. What distinguishes pedophiliacs is the fact that they did not experience sufficient and satisfactory adult-like sexual activities which normally supplant these early behaviors. Whether a function of shyness, heterosexual inadequacy or a simple deficit of adult opportunities, the sexual practices of these individuals were restricted to masturbatory fantasies that fixated on the few satisfying sexual activities they engaged in with their childhood age-mates. The repetitive nature of these fantasies reinforced the immature level of sexual behavior previously enacted in conjunction with childhood partners.

FETISHISM

In this deviant habit the focus of sexual interest is either some nongenital body part, usually the foot, thighs, buttocks and hair or an inanimate object, usually an article of clothing such as undergarments, shoes and stockings. Not uncommonly, these objects acquire special powers of sexual stimulation if they were pilfered.

The origins of the fetishistic habit have been argued for over a century. One of the earliest hypotheses, proposed by Binet in 1888, viewed the perversion as a result of "accidental" circumstances in which incidental objects inadvertently were associated with periods of sexual excitement. Binet's thesis seems as valid today as when it was first formulated. Whether by direct tuition or incidental circumstance, the mere pairing of certain objects with sexual excitement may establish an association that can endure and become the preferred pattern of sexual release. This simple "conditioning" model may also account for the common practice of stealing the fetish as a means of enhancing its stimulating powers. Thus, it is not unusual for adolescents to pilfer undergarments from their mother's or their sister's wardrobes and use them as a tangible stimulus for their secretive masturbation. The whole sequence of stealing and using undergarments becomes conditioned to sexual excitement. Since adolescents usually do not find more mature sexual outlets, they may repeat the stealing prelude to masturbation over and over again, until it becomes a deeply ingrained habit.

EXHIBITIONISM

In this perversion, perhaps second only to homosexuality as the most common of sexual deviations, gratification is obtained by exposing the genitals to members of the opposite sex in public or semipublic places such as parks, theaters, stores, and quite commonly, from a parked car along crowded streets. Children or young adolescent girls are the preferred objects for the great majority of male exhibitionists (female exhibitionists are extremely rare). Many exhibitionists engage in lewd gestures as a means of attracting viewers. Some expose themselves to induce tension and excitement for masturbatory activity. Exhibitionists tend to be consistent in the manner, setting, time of day and type and age of person to whom they expose themselves. A central element leading to the experience of gratification is a response of curiosity, embarrassment or shock on the part of the viewer. Failure to evoke such responses frequently results in feelings of deflation and disappointment; for example, Apfelberg et al. (1944) reported a case of a patient who achieved gratification only if the victim of his exhibitionistic act responded favorably to a question concerning the size of his penis. Exhibitionists often struggle to inhibit their impulse, but find that the more they restrain themselves, the more insistent their impulse becomes. Not uncommonly, they feel both shame and self-disgust following the act.

What experiences contribute to the acquisition and perpetuation of this deviation?

Certain facts strongly support the role of conditioning in acquisition. Once the behavior has been learned, it is reinforced by masturbatory fantasies and protected from extinction by personality traits which make difficult the acquisition of more mature forms of sexual gratification. Let us briefly review these points.

The history of most male exhibitionists reveals a period of either preadolescent exposure to little girls in games such as "doctor and nurse," adolescent sexual play, in which reciprocal exposures take place, or some "accidental" event in which a state of inadvertent exposure gave rise to embarrassment or curiosity on the part of the female viewer.

Henry (1955) reports the following recollections of an exhibitionist that illustrate such "accidents" well.

The exhibitionistic tendencies really started ten years ago. I remember one incident distinctly. I used to go bathing and undress in back of some rocks and shrubbery. While I was undressing, a woman about a block away was looking at me and was interested. I made note of this interest. I couldn't help but notice that she was of the opposite sex and that she had an interest in my body. It made me feel important and secure. Until this experience, I had been very modest and shy about showing any part of my body.

That first experience with the woman on the beach was very, very interesting. I got the impression that all women might feel the same way.

The exhibitionistic conditioning process includes not only the act of exposure itself, but an entire complex of incidental events and objects associated with the original learning experience. Quite often, we can infer the specific circumstances surrounding the initial acquisition of the habit by noting the setting and objects the exhibitionist utilizes repetitively for his act. It should not be surprising that children and adolescent girls are common victims since the original setting in which the habit was learned frequently involved exposure before one's playmates. Furthermore, the characteristic expectation among exhibitionists that their victim will register surprise or embarrassment may be seen as a replica of the curious or shocked response of the little girls to whom they exposed themselves in childhood.

Of course, many youngsters who never become exhibitionists engaged in childhood sex games or were involved in accidental exposures which proved exciting or stimulating. However, in these cases, subsequent experiences may have extinguished or overridden the exhibitionist response. To account for the failure of this habit to be extinguished among future exhibtionists, we must add to our formula a number of secondary factors. First, the experience may have been repeated innumerable times either in fact or in fantasy. Second, the individual may have possessed personality traits such as shyness or feelings of masculine inadequacy which precluded subsequent sexual experiences that could have diverted the exhibitionistic habit toward more adult forms of behavior.

TRANSVESTITISM

The term transvestitism literally means cross-dressing; it refers to the habit of achieving sexual gratification by wearing the clothing of the opposite sex or by genital contact with such clothing.

Fetishism and transvestitism are alike in that both employ objects as instruments of sexual excitement. However, the transvestite has no particular attachment for the object he utilizes; it is merely a means of creating a temporary self-image that he is a member of the opposite sex.

Because of these brief periods of self-identification with the opposite sex and the not infrequent covariation of homosexuality and transvestitism, many authors contend that these perversions are merely two sides of the same coin. However, the great majority of transvestites do not display the cardinal sign of overt homosexuality, that of preferring members of their own sex as their sexual partners (Bentler, 1970; Buckner, 1970).

What are the etiological origins of this deviant habit?

Many of the case studies reported in the literature can be interpreted most readily in accord with the conditioning model provided earlier. Let us illustrate some of the typical features in the following case.

Figure 10-1 Transvestitism. A. As a male. B. As a female. (From Olkon, D.: Essentials of Neuropyschiatry. Philadelphia, Lea and Febiger, 1945.)

CASE 10-2

John T., Age 20, College Student

John reported numerous events in support of the view that he had been the object of maternal seduction, and recalled quite vividly that at the age of 13 or 14 his mother served as his primary source of sexual fantasies. These maternal experiences contrasted with those of a harshly rejecting father with whom he had no rapport. Thus, John was unsure of his masculine adequacy, having been subjected to repeated humiliation by his father; in relation to his mother, however, he felt both secure and wanted.

John recalled his constant state of confusion throughout childhood as to what sex he would rather be. At about the age of 14, he began to "borrow" his mother's undergarments for purposes of masturbation. Clothed in her brassiere and panties, he was able both to be his accepting and kindly mother and, at the same time utilize her as a receptive object for his masculine sexual fantasies. The transvestitic act enabled him to be simultaneously both male and female. This "split" in sexual identification was illustrated nicely in the following description he provided:

"When I masturbate, I try to look at myself in the mirror as if I were two persons. The brassiere and panties make me feel as if I were a woman. At the same time I see my erect penis and know that I am also a man. I sort of switch back and forth so that I am a man masturbating with a woman at his side at the same time."

Whatever the original combination of psychogenic events, and it may be "pure chance" and nothing more, the process of viewing oneself as both a man and woman, as in a split screen, becomes the central focus of sexual fantasy and gratification. This initial habit is strengthened by repeated pleasurable reinforcements through these "mixed" masturbatory images. If the individual lacks the personality disposition or physical opportunities by which new habits can be acquired to supplant the practice, it may persist well into adulthood.

SADOMASOCHISM

In this perversion the infliction of pain is a prerequisite for sexual excitement and gratification. Sadism, a term derived from the Marquis de Sade, refers to the act of inflicting pain upon a sexual partner. Masochism, a term derived from the novelist Leopold von Sacher-Masoch, whose fictional characters were obsessed with the sexual pleasures of pain, refers to the act of accepting and perhaps soliciting punishment as

a necessary element of sexual gratification. It is common to combine
these two deviant habits since they are frequently present in the same
person. Where they do not coexist, sadism usually is found in men
whereas masochism is more common in women. In some cases, sexual
gratification is fully achieved as a consequence of the hostile act alone,
e.g., achieving orgasm while being abused. In others, pain or the act of
inflicting it serves as an exciting and energizing prelude to otherwise
normal coitus.

Sadomasochism, as a learned habit, can be understood well in terms of
the conditioning model presented earlier. Of course, as we have noted
before, these same behaviors may also reflect pervasive personality pathology.

What experiences, then, serve to condition the sadomasochistic habit?
Two types of events are frequently encountered in these cases.

First, many youngsters, either by direct observation or by exposure to
books, TV and newspaper reports or by direct parental tutelage, come to
associate sexuality with brutality and pain. The fear and tension generated by these learnings deeply impress children, and often result in
the distorted image that sex is invariably connected either with the infliction or the suffering of physical and mental abuse. Armed with these
bizarre conceptions, the youngster reinforces them through his own
masturbatory fantasies, and pursues and expects them as an inevitable
and necessary ingredient of the real sexual act.

The second source of this perverted habit may be traced to attitudes of
shame, disgust and guilt toward sexual matters. Conditioned to view sex
as "dirty" or as a sign of degradation and sin, the youngster reinforces
this image through fantasy and carries it with him into the sexual act.
Both sadistic and masochistic habits may arise as a consequence. The
sadist handles his guilt by venting contempt for his partner's willingness
to engage in the despised act; prior to intercourse, he degrades and even
tortures her. The masochist, guilt-ridden for her "lascivious" intentions,
must subject herself to physical and verbal abuse as a prerequisite to the
forbidden and sinful act.

IMPOTENCE AND FRIGIDITY

These disturbances refer to deficits either in the desire for sexual experiences or the capacity to fulfill them. Impotence is the term applied to
men who suffer this impairment, and frigidity is its counterpart in
women.

The difficulty may be relative or absolute, selective or pervasive. Some
individuals not only lack all desire, but even have strong negative reactions merely to the thought of sex. Others desire relations and often
make genuine attempts but succeed only on rare occasions. Many experience no sexual difficulties with certain partners, usually prostitutes or
women they hold in contempt, but are completely blocked and impotent
with their spouses. In short, there are innumerable variations in the pattern and particulars of these impairments.

What are the origins of these deficits of sexual desire or competence?

An extremely common source is faulty training in sex attitudes, especially prominent in the upbringing of girls. The view that sex is bad,
dirty and sinful can establish deeply etched fears and guilt feelings

which not only impair desire, but may create ineradicable aversions toward anything even remotely connected with sex. These distorted childhood habits and attitudes, reinforced throughout adolescence, persist into marriage where sexual relations are fully sanctioned. Even though the person may consciously be desirous, her ingrained fear of detection and punishment or the guilt she associates with sexual "lust and sin" remains unaltered, and results in a frustrating and disheartening frigidity.

Along similar lines, many women carry into marriage the tension and fear of pregnancy they acquired as a result of anxious premarital relationships. The dread and anguish associated with the act of coitus that was built up in these earlier experiences persist, and the grown woman finds herself unable to relax and "let go," despite the fact that it would now be perfectly proper for her to become pregnant.

Attitudes and feelings associated with the first sexual experience or set of experiences can play a crucial role in future sexual relations. As was noted above, a habitual fear of pregnancy may linger as a deterrent to sexual desire long after such concerns should have waned. In a different way, both men and women may have their "romantic" expectations shattered by the realities of a faulty early sexual experience. Intense pain, clumsy awkwardness, feelings of dissatisfaction and incompetence or other forms of unpleasantness and disillusionment, may set the stage for longstanding sexual anxieties and aversions. Once acquired in these initial ventures, these feelings perpetuate themselves in a vicious circle; thus, the mere anticipation of pain, tension or humiliation gives rise to these very feelings and becomes a self-fulfilling prophecy, thereby reinforcing the expectancy and starting the circle over again.

Whether a function of actual distressful experience or a result of a generalized anticipation of personal inadequacy or unattractiveness, many individuals come to the sexual act with fear and trepidation. As was noted above, the presence of worries and tensions precipitates unrewarding and humiliating sexual experiences which, in turn, reinforce the initial anxiety and self derogation and thereby perpetuate the problem.

SATYRIASIS AND NYMPHOMANIA

Exaggerated or insatiable sexual desires is termed satyriasis in men and nymphomania in women. These sexual preoccupations and involvements may be confined to a single marital partner or may be pursued in a variety of premarital and extramarital relations. Although most of these deviates center their attentions on members of the opposite sex, it is not uncommon for homosexuals to be overly engrossed with sexual activities.

These perversions, viewed as circumscribed habits, may be traced to a number of different experiences.

Prominent among them is exposure to models of imitation. In families in which mothers are excessively promiscuous with "strange" men or are sexually seductive with their husbands as a means of "cooling their tempers," the young girl may learn comparable habits and attitudes of sexual behavior. Similar patterns of imitation occur among "delinquent" and "hippie" groups in which promiscuous involvements become a "badge" of ingroup membership, a necessary pastime modeled in accord with group standards and values. Once initiated and reinforced by security and status, the habit may persist either of its own accord or on the basis of some rationalized belief such as "true love" is synonymous with "sexual freedom." Imitation of idealized models also follows from the popular belief among male adolescents that "masculine power and virility" correlate with frequent and varied conquests. The status and reputation of those who succeed in these exploits provide a model to be copied among those who need to "prove their manliness." Insatiable habits may be acquired in this pursuit, and since perfect success cannot be attained in one's pursuits, the person will feel that no matter how successful a "man" he has been, he can always do better.

Similar habits of sexual insatiability may have their origin in homes in which erotic feelings and affection were stimulated, but where strict parental attitudes forbade sex and the overt expression of warmth and tenderness. As a consequence of such deprivations, youngsters may have an acute need for outlets for their bottled-up affectionate emotions. Pained by parental undemonstrativeness, they search not only for an outlet, but for the opposite of that to which they were accustomed. Out of desperation, if nothing else, they stumble upon a relationship in which "no holds are barred" in the expression of warmth, love and passion. The sharp contrast to the barren and cold home environment makes this experience doubly reinforcing; and to it, of course, are added the genuine pleasures of sexual intimacy. So reinforced, these youngsters continue to pursue more of the same, sliding bit by bit into a habitual pattern of nymphomania or satyriasis, as illustrated in the following case.

CASE 10–3

Desi T., Age 16, High School Student

Desi was admitted to the psychiatric ward of a general hospital following an attempted suicide; upon examination, it was found that she was pregnant. Interviews with the girl, her parents, two brothers and one of her boyfriends revealed the following.

Desi's parents were extremely "proper and strict" about sex and gave their children no leeway in dating and attending school dances; home in general was a cold and formal place. Although all the children felt deprived of affection, the two older brothers "accepted" their fate and submitted to their parents' strictures. Desi, however, had "always been sort of rebellious."

When Desi was 13 she met a 15 year old boy with whom she "fell in love." Petting activities began within a few weeks, and after three or four months, Desi experienced coitus for the first time. The event was referred to by her as "marvelous." To keep her parents from being unduly suspicious, she informed them that she was in a "special honors" club that met four times a week after school (Desi was in fact an excellent student). This story enabled her to visit her boyfriend's home almost every afternoon; both his parents worked, and he had no siblings at home. For three years, they engaged in intercourse nearly every school day. When Desi was 15, she met another boy whom she began to see one or two evenings a week for similar purposes. A third, older man had appeared on the scene in recent months and she pursued her pleasures with him as well. Upon learning that she was pregnant. Desi felt her "goose was cooked," thought of running away, became confused and distraught and then tried to "do away" with herself by taking an overdose of sleeping pills.

LEARNED ALCOHOLIC AND DRUG BEHAVIORS

The general literature dealing with drugs has grown rapidly in recent years owing to their increased use among college and high school students. Despite the marked concern of parents and the fascination that young people exhibit with regard to the newer drugs, these chemicals are of little intrinsic interest in themselves to psychopathologists, although their effects and manner of acquisition are worthy of attention. The incidence of alcoholism, fostered largely by public sanction and active promotion, makes it a problem of equal seriousness to that of drugs.

ALCOHOLISM

Upwards of 75 million Americans drink alcoholic beverages in varying degrees. Alcoholism, however, is defined essentially as an insatiable craving and by the fact that an individual's work efficiency and social functioning have been chronically impaired. It occurs in about 5 million cases, ranking the habit as the fourth most prevalent of all behavioral problems. Two hundred thousand new cases are reported each year, and about 15 per cent of first admissions to mental hospitals are diagnosed as suffering from this impairment. Alcoholic behavior is found in all races and nationalities, but its incidence is unevenly distributed; for example, the rate is especially high among the Irish and the French, but rather low among Jews, Chinese and Italians. In general, more men than women are alcoholocs, the ratios varying from 2 to 1 in some countries to as high as 25 to 1 in others.

PHASES

Jellinek, in his authoritative studies of alcoholic addiction (1952, 1960), suggests that the sequence from moderate social drinking to chronic alcoholism follows a fairly predictable sequence, which he breaks down into four stages.

1. The first stage, labeled the *prealcoholic symptomatic phase*, begins with conventional social drinking. Here the individual may be faced with the normal stresses of life, but he learns to his pleasure that alcohol can diminish his tensions and bolster his confidence. Acquainted now with this agreeable means of escape from pressure and tension, he no longer bothers to tolerate or "put up with" the everyday strains which most people take in stride. With but minimal provocation, he turns increasingly to his morale booster, his dissipator of minor as well as major woes. This transition, manifesting itself ultimately in daily indulgence, proceeds imperceptibly, step by step, over a period of several months to two years.

2. The second, or *prodromal phase*, begins with a rather sudden and unexplainable experience in which the individual does not lose consciousness, but has no recall afterward of his actions and surrounding events. These episodes, often repeated, do not necessarily follow a heavy bout with alcohol. As this phase continues, the person begins to engage in surreptitious drinking, becomes preoccupied with plans for his "next" drink, starts to "gulp down" rather than sip his glassful and evidences the first signs of an awareness and concern that his habit has progressed beyond simple social drinking.

3. In the third, or *crucial phase*, the individual has "lost control"; once he takes a drink he does not stop until he is too uncoordinated to hold the bottle, or too ill to imbibe more. Despite his inability to stop once he has started, he is still able to control whether or not to take that first drink. This measure of control enables him periodically to "give up" alcohol for periods of weeks or even months. Ultimately, however, he "gives in" just once, with the inevitable consequence of complete intoxication.

The inevitable downward spiral picks up momentum and the alcoholic begins the practice of drinking heavily during the day. Faced with impaired work efficiency, dismay and criticism from family and friends, he begins to concoct alibis to himself and others to justify his habit and its consequences. His deceptions and alibis lead to exasperation and recrimination from others. His inability to control himself leads not only to guilt but to job dismissals, abandonment by friends, resentments and conflicts at home.

Now he anticipates failure and humiliation, begins protectively to withdraw from social contact and thereby increases his isolation and his dependency on alcohol. This vicious, perpetuating circle of increased alcoholic dependency ultimately involves the deterioration of physical health. Alcohol serves now as the primary source of dietary sustenance, resulting in severe nutritional deficiencies and distressing physical ailments.

When he ventures into those prolonged bouts of intoxication, known as "benders," his limited physical reserves are strained beyond their limits, resulting in his first hospital admission for alcoholism. His dependence on alcohol is no longer merely psychological. He has become a true addict, suffering "withdrawal symptoms" that can be alleviated only by further alcoholic indulgence. Beset by guilt, recrimination and a physical need for alcohol, he no longer is able to abstain, starts the habit of drinking upon awakening each morning and crosses the line into the final phase of addiction.

4.   The fourth, or *chronic phase,* is characterized by continual drinking and repeated benders. Judgment, responsibility and ethical considerations are cast to the wind. Life is composed of drinking and more drinking, with no thought to its consequence upon family and future. A function of habit, expectancy and physiochemical body changes, he is now precipitated into a state of stupor with half the alcohol previously required. Despite prolonged periods of oblivion, he returns to the bottle, not so much to dilute the impact of his memories and his sorry state, as to avoid physical withdrawal symptoms such as "the shakes," violent nausea, hallucinated images and bizarre fears. The circle is now complete; he is totally addicted, both psychologically and physically.

PERSONALITY AND INSTRUMENTAL BEHAVIOR

The question arises, given the devastating effects of alcoholic addiction, of why the habit persists, that is, what functions does it fulfill to compensate for its many inevitable and crushing losses. In contrast to other pathological habits and their disastrous consequences, the solution to the alcoholic habit is so simple and uncomplicated: stop drinking. What propels the addict to persist in his "foolishness' with so simple a solution at hand? Does this perverse habit reflect a deeper and more pervasive pathology, and if so, is there a particular personality pattern disposed to alcoholism? Let us address ourselves to these questions in the following paragraphs.

A literature review (Fenichel, 1945; Menninger, 1938; Levy, 1958; Zwerling and Rosenbaum, 1959; Jones, 1968, 1971; Sanford, 1968) will provide us with an endless number of coping functions associated with the use of alcohol. These varied and diverse aims of the alcoholic habit can be grouped into four categories: *self-image enhancement*, e.g., providing a feeling of well-being and confidence; *disinhibition of restraints*, e.g., allowing previously controlled impulses such as hostility to be released without feeling guilt; *dissolution of psychic pain,* e.g., alleviating the anguish of a "dead-end" job or a hopeless marriage; and *masochistic self-destruction,* e.g., relieving one's sense of guilt by destroying one's career. It is evident, then, that there is no single purpose or function to which the alcoholic habit is directed; in fact, some of them, e.g., dissolution of psychic pain and masochistic self-destruction appear at odds. Given this diversity in alcoholic coping functions, it is not surprising that no one has been able to pinpoint an "alcoholic personality type." Research and clinical observation lead us to conclude that almost all forms of "troubled and maladjusted personalities" may be found among alcoholics, none of them distinctive or unique to alcoholism, and none necessarily a cause rather than a consequence of the habit. In the following section, however, we will offer some tentative hypotheses that are specific to the development of the learned alcoholic habit.

DEVELOPMENTAL BACKGROUND

It is especially difficult to disentangle the interacting causes of behavior habits that involve biochemical properties, such as alcoholism. The interplay between predisposing constitutional factors and experiential determinants is so intricate and subtle that no one as yet has been able to trace its relations. Most studies suggesting a role for biogenic influences either have been poorly designed or achieve results that lend themselves to psychological as well as biological interpretations. As matters now stand, social learning determinants are believed to be primary.

Conceived as a learned habit, although one in which there is an inevitable involvement of biological factors, alcoholism may be traced through a sequence of three etiological influences. *First,* incidental observation and imitation usually serve as the *original* source that gives rise to the practice of drinking. *Second,* a variety of positive reinforcements occur in conjunction with drinking, strengthening the habit and ultimately leading to what may be termed a "psychological addiction." *Third,* prolonged psychological addiction leads to biochemical changes of cell metabolism which result in a physiological craving for alcohol, that is, a "physiological addiction." Let us elaborate this sequential etiological hypothesis.

1. Vicarious learning seems to be a universal source for the original acquisition both of drinking habits and its use as a coping instrument. Most notable in this regard is exposure to parental models and to the well-advertised image of drinking as a social lubricant and dilutor of tension. Youngsters may learn to believe that drinking is sanctioned for purposes of coping with frustration or dissolving guilt and responsibility, simply by observing similar uses on the part of their parents. In a relevant study showing the impact of parental modeling, Roe et al. (1945) found that children who were separated from their alcoholic parents and placed in foster homes were no more likely to become alcoholic than were children of nonalcoholic parents, and much less likely than those who remained with alcoholic parents (this study contradicts the argument that alcoholism is a hereditary disease).

Not to be overlooked among the forces of vicarious learning and imitation are common social stereotypes regarding the drinking habits of certain ethnic groups. Thus, the popular image that "the Irish are drunks" may not only serve as an implicit model to copy for youngsters of Irish descent, but also be a form of encouragement and sanction for drinking. When faced with normal strains of life, an Irish youngster may turn to alcohol rather than to other forms of coping, because he feels that this course of behavior is not only expected, but inevitable among members of his ethnic background.

2.   Once the practice of "normal" social drinking has become established, the powers of positive reinforcement become more significant than those of imitation. Given the presence of any of the various coping needs which alcohol can reward, drinking if practiced repetitively can become deeply ingrained as a habit. Alcohol not only serves as a useful source of reinforcement, but it is especially powerful in this regard since its effects are immediate, in contrast to the slow and delayed character of other, more complicated, forms of coping. Because of this distinctive feature of immediacy, the drinking response preempts all other coping methods. Progressively, then, the individual's alternatives for dealing with tension and discomfort are narrowed to this one preeminent response.

Of course, there are negative consequences of drinking (hangovers, wives' complaints and loss of job), but these negative effects are not as immediately experienced as its positive rewards. Moreover, if the person pauses to reflect on these troublesome consequences, he can quickly turn off these thoughts simply by taking another drink.

Given the rapid and tremendously reinforcing properties of alcohol, why is it that most people who take an occasional drink do not become alcoholics?

For the main part, the answer is that they either have found other, more suitable, ways of coping with their discomforts or are not so troubled in the first place that alcohol proves strongly reinforcing. There is a third explanation, however, one that stems from individual differences in the biological tolerance for alcohol. Although the evidence favoring a constitutional *disposition* to alcoholism is equivocal at best, there is no question that many individuals have a constitutional *aversion* to alcohol, experiencing numerous biological discomforts such as nausea, dizziness and sleepiness. These discomforts are *immediate negative reinforcers* that come more quickly and outweigh the positive rewards, serving therefore to preclude any possible development of the alcoholic habit. In contrast, those who do *not* experience these aversive effects, consume substantial quantities of alcohol, achieve their associated positive reinforcements and find themselves on the road to alcoholism.

3.   The final stage of alcoholism follows a long-term reinforced psychological habit. Ultimately, there are changes in the individual's cell metabolism which result in severe withdrawal symptoms (tremors, nausea, fevers and hallucinations) when drinking is terminated. At this state, alcohol has become more than a psychological habit; it is a substance which the alcoholic craves to ward off a physiologically induced suffering. Now, as the vicious circle expands, he drinks not only for psychologcal reasons, but to avoid the negative reinforcements of physiological withdrawal. He is both a psychological and physiological addict.

DRUG DEPENDENCE

Alcohol has not been the only instrument for facilitating man's need to relieve pain and monotony. Drugs also have served since ancient times to moderate the discomforts of life and to expand its illusory possibilities.

Alcohol is a drug, although Western customs have guided our thinking otherwise. There are as many differences in chemical composition and effects between drugs as there are between alcohol and most drugs. In short, were it not for our customary practices, alcohol would be viewed as just one of a number of chemical substances to which people become habituated and addicted.

In recent years there has been a marked rise in the usage of certain hallucinogens and stimulants, especially among adolescents (Blumer, 1967; Nowlis, 1968). This increased incidence has given rise to a flood of public concern and consternation (Szasz, 1972). For these reasons, it may be instructive to differentiate the major types of drugs and their effects. In addition, we will touch upon certain features of acquisition, coping and personality correlates that distinguish drug dependence from alcoholism.

The World Health Organization has suggested a useful distinction between drug *addiction* and drug *habituation*. The addictive drugs, notably those listed as "narcotics" and "sedatives" in Table 10–2, sooner or later, *always* produce an overpowering craving. Ultimately, there is a need for increased dosages, followed by severe physical symptoms upon drug withdrawal. In contrast, habit-forming nonaddictive drugs, such as those included under the labels "hallucinogens" and "stimulants," do not generate compulsive cravings, although the individual ordinarily acquires a strong inclination to continue the habit. Furthermore, there usually is no increased tolerance for the drug which would produce a need for higher dosages. Crucial to the distinction between addiction and habituation is the fact that the termination of the habituation drugs does not result in physical withdrawal symptoms.

Table 10–2 provides a brief summary of the major types of drugs. These are grouped into four major categories: narcotics, sedatives, hallucinogens and stimulants. The first two meet the criteria of addictive drugs whereas the latter two are viewed as habituation drugs.

Narcotics, and in particular heroin, are notably harmful in that tolerance builds up rapidly and results in an increasing need for this highly expensive addictive. It is not uncommon to find, within an extremely short period, that every aspect of the addict's life is centered on ways to acquire the drug. Because of the expense involved, the heroin addict gives up his few valued belongings, becomes careless about his diet and health and is drawn by a desperate search for funds into illegal activities. *Sedative* addictions produced by barbiturate drugs are more common than generally recognized, especially among middle and upper class adults. In contrast to heroin this addiction can be controlled and stabilized with minimum dosages. However, should the addiction be prolonged, severe brain dysfunctions may result, and marked withdrawal symptoms are inevitable.

Hallucinogens and *stimulants* are associated neither with increased body tolerance, physiological cravings nor severe withdrawal symptoms upon termination, that is, they are not addictive drugs. However, the individual may become psychologically dependent on these agents in the sense that he finds himself unwilling or unable to "chuck the habit" he has built up. Marijuana and cocaine are among the oldest and best known drugs used to induce temporary euphoria and relaxation (cocaine has been listed in some quarters as an addictive drug, but it does not fulfill the criteria of physiological dependence and withdrawal symptoms). In recent years, marijuana, better known as "pot" or "grass," has attained

TABLE 10-2
DRUGS: THEIR SOURCES AND EFFECTS

Drug	Slang Name	Source	Effects
Narcotics			
Opium		Dried, coagulated milk of unripe opium poppy pod	Pain relief; drowsy indifference; aimless and drifting feeling; loss of appetite; temporary impotence; severe withdrawal symptoms such as cramps and tremors lasting four to five days.
Morphine	M; Miss Emma	10–1 Reduction of crude opium	
Heroin	H; Horse; Junk	Converted morphine	
Sedatives			
Nembutal	Yellow jackets		Calm, subdued, relaxed state; dull, depressive mood; incoherency and confusion; withdrawal symptoms such as convulsions and vomiting lasting seven to ten days or more.
Seconal	Red devils	Barbituric acid derivatives	
Luminal	Purple hearts		
Amytal	Blue heavens		
Hallucinogens			
Marijuana	Pot; Grass	Resinous female hemp plant	Euphoric relaxation; altered perceptions; impaired judgment.
Peyote	Cactus	Dried cactus buttons with mescaline	Visual hallucinations; feelings of omnipotence; marked anxieties lasting six to twelve hours.
LSD	Acid; Hawk	Synthetic chemical	Same as above, but more intense and lasting three to four days.
STP		Atropine-like synthetic	
Stimulants			
Cocaine	Coke; Snow	Alkaloid of cocoa leaf	Temporary blissful state preceded by headaches and followed by insomnia
Benzedrine	A; Bennies	Synthetic chemical	Energy and exuberance, followed by hypertension, confusion and anxiety.
Dexedrine	Pep pills; Dexies		
Methedrine	Speed; Crystals	Synthetic chemical	Rapidly mounting exhilaration, followed by marked anxiety and delirium.

great popularity among "liberated" students (Kolansky and Moore, 1972). Here, it is used as a means of "cooling it," that is, gaining a pleasant interlude of mild euphoria to block out what are felt to be the absurd values and oppressive regulations of a dehumanized adult society (Kaufman et al., 1969; Mirin et al., 1971). This drug has no known harmful physical effects, and what psychological difficulties are associated with it appear to precede the habit, rather than result from it (Halikas et al., 1972). LSD (lysergic acid diethylamide), although not a narcotic, has proved a mixed blessing to many youths who have dabbled with it (Blacker et al., 1968; McGlothin and Arnold, 1971). Unquestionably, LSD is an instrument capable of evoking a dramatic experience, a means of expanding and sensitizing conscious awareness, but it may also precipitate extremely frightening hallucinations and emotions that can last well after the chemical residues of the drug have worn off (Katz et al., 1968; Smart and Jones, 1970). Among the various amphetamines — benzedrine, dexedrine and methedrine — the last-named, known as "speed," has recently come into prominence as a source of rapidly induced exhilaration. However, it may also induce severe anxieties and delirium, not uncommonly resulting in homicide, rape and suicide (Ellinwood, 1971).

What instrumental functions are fulfilled by these drugs?

As was stated earlier, drugs and alcohol appear to fulfill essentially similar purposes, although perhaps in somewhat different population groups. Thus, we would include "self-image enhancement," "disinhibition of restraints," "dissolution of psychic pain" and "masochistic self-destruction" among the various coping aims of drug use.

Next, we may ask if there are differences between those who become addicted to alcohol rather than to drugs.

There is a considerable overlap, of course, but it appears that drug reactions, with the exception of sedative addictions, is primarily a problem of the young. Relatively few people over 40 are frequent users of narcotics, hallucinogens and stimulants. This disproportionate difference between age groups reflects in part the relative recency of the discovery and popularity of certain drugs. Thus, older people who were "addictively disposed" years ago could not have been exposed to these agents until well after they had been "hooked" on something else, in all likelihood alcohol. Moreover, until fairly recently, the image of the drug addict was that of a "lower class degenerate," hardly an inviting model for the young of the past to identify with (Gordon, 1973). This contrasts with the "alienated intellectual hippie" image associated with current-day users, an attractive model to be emulated by "ingroup" students. (We might note parenthetically that this model is associated only with the use of marijuana, LSD and other mild or "mind-expanding" drugs; it does not extend to heroin, which still is associated with "lower class degeneracy" or to methedrine, which prompts "mindless" hyperactivity and delirium.)

Are there differences in personality among those who use different drugs?

No clinical research or data have accumulated to provide an answer to this question. From the few unsystematic studies available, it would appear that drug choice may be influenced in part by the characteristic coping style of the individual (Brill et al., 1971). In other words, addicts may "select" a drug that is consonant with and facilitates their preferred mode of dealing with stress.

We have touched previously on some of the instrumental goals associated with the development of drug habits. They appear, essentially, to be the same as those found in alcoholism: imitation as the source of habit origination; positive reinforcement of coping aims as a means of strengthening the habit; and finally, body chemical changes resulting in physiological addiction. Narcotic and sedative addictions often have their origin in medical treatment; thus, morphine may have been prescribed to relieve pain, and seconal recommended to counter insomnia. The hallucinogenic habit is most commonly acquired as an incidental by-product of peer group involvement; thus, "smoking pot" or "tripping with LSD" has come to be expected of everyone associated with the "alienated" adolescent subculture.

TREATMENT OF LEARNED REACTIONS

Despite differences in their form of expression, learned behavior reactions are alike in their stimulus specificity, e.g., an individual suffering a fear reaction behaves "normally," that is, fearlessly, except when confronted with a particular stimulus. Furthermore, each reaction tends to be manifested in a uniform and consistent fashion, e.g., a sexual deviate manifests the same perversion time and again, and usually in the same environmental settings. Each of these response habits is repeated innumerable times until it becomes a deeply ingrained form of behavior. Moreover, these reactions are strongly reinforced upon repetition, e.g., fear and sexual responses are associated with intense activation levels; addiction reactions provide rapid if not immediate gratification. In short, unless it is superseded by stronger incompatible responses or extinguished by deconditioning experiences, it is highly likely that these learned reactions will persist unmodified, as many of them do.

What therapeutic methods can be employed to eliminate or moderate these pathological reactions? Several approaches, either alone or in concert, may be recommended.

First, the stimulus conditions to which the pathological habit is a response may be altered. For example, parents may be counseled in the case of a fearful child to terminate their "destructive" practice of paying excessive attention to the youngster's concerns. Similarly, a severe addict may be removed to a hospital to prevent his being "tempted" by available drugs.

Biophysical methods may usefully be employed in several of these learned disturbances. For example, pharmacological tranquilizing agents may serve to alleviate tensions associated with a patient's fear reaction. Other pharmaceuticals may overcome the uncomfortable side effects and withdrawal symptoms of alcoholic and drug addiction. Methadone drug maintenance has been helpful for a segment of those addicted to heroin (Ramer et al., 1971; Bowden and Maddux, 1972).

Most promising among the therapies for these reactions are techniques based on learning principles associated with various "behavioral modification" methods. These procedures are highly efficient in that they operate on the target habit without becoming involved in personality traits (Abel et al., 1970; McConoghy, 1971; Reitz and Keil, 1971). Various techniques, e.g., systematic desensitization, seek through cognitive suggestion to pair neutral feelings and attitudes, such as relaxation, with formerly provocative stimuli. Similarly, aversive conditioning methods have been used to associate negative reinforcements with responses that previously were positively reinforcing, e.g., drugs such as "antabuse" are given to alcoholics to produce intense physical discomfort in conjunction with drinking (Fookes, 1969; Feldman, 1966). Repetition of this experience will condition pain rather than pleasure with the habit, thereby fostering its extinction (Vogler et al., 1970).

Group methods may be employed with moderate success in reactions that originated as a function of social imitation or that have been reinforced by group activities. Thus, alcoholics and drug addicts often benefit by extinction techniques generated in group settings, e.g., Alcoholics Anonymous or the Synanon for narcotic addicts. The special value of these group procedures is that the individual's habit is negatively reinforced in a setting that previously encouraged and provided reinforcements for it.

George Segal — *Group*

11 ABNORMAL PERSONALITIES IN EVERYDAY LIFE: I

INTRODUCTION

The historical predominance of hospital psychiatry has, in the past, turned the attention of theorists and researchers away from common or everyday psychological problems. In the last quarter-century, however, there has been an increased interest in preventive psychiatry and "mental health," bringing with it a concern with abnormal tendencies in the less severely ill. We now know that the quiet anxieties and minor conflicts of our relatives and friends serve as forerunners of more serious problems. In addition, outpatient clinics, community-based mental health centers and school and family agencies geared to the needs of the less severely troubled have shown us that we must change our views of abnormal psychology to reach beyond those of hospital psychiatry.

Texts in this field no longer bypass or give lip service to milder personality disturbances. Not only are these impairments an integral part of abnormal psychology in their own right, but they are the foundation for understanding the development of more serious disorders. For these reasons, then, we will concern ourselves to a considerable extent with the abnormal personality patterns of "everyday life." With these patterns as a base, we then can grasp better the processes underlying the more severe syndromes and the sequences through which they unfold.

CONCEPT OF PERSONALITY PATTERNS

In the first years of life, children engage in a wide variety of spontaneous behaviors. Although they display certain constitutional characteristics at birth, their way of reacting to others and coping with their environment tends, at first, to be changeable and unpredictable. This seemingly random behavior serves an exploratory function; each child is "trying out" and testing alternative modes for coping with his environment. As time progresses, the child learns which techniques "work," that is, which of these varied behaviors enable him to achieve his desires and to avoid discomforts.

CHAPTER 11

Throughout these years a shaping process takes place in which the range of initially diverse behaviors becomes narrowed, reinforced repeatedly and, finally, crystallized into particular preferred modes of seeking and achieving. In time, these behaviors persist and become accentuated. Not only are they highly resistant to extinction, but they are reinforced by the restrictions and repetitions of a limited social environment and are perpetuated and intensified by the child's own perceptions, needs and actions. Thus, given a continuity in basic biological equipment, and a narrow band of experiences for learning behavioral alternatives, the child develops a distinctive pattern of habits and attitudes that are deeply etched and cannot be eradicated easily. In short, these characteristics *are* the essence and sum of his personality.

When we speak of a personality pattern we are referring to those modes of functioning which emerge from the entire matrix of the individual's social learning history, and which now characterize his perceptions and ways of dealing with his environment. We have chosen the term *pattern* for two reasons: first, to focus on the fact that these behaviors and attitudes arise from a complex interaction of both biological dispositions and learned experience; and second, to denote the fact that these personality characteristics are not just a scattered collection of random behavior tendencies, but a learned, repeated and predictable structure of needs, attitudes and behaviors. Possessing a personality pattern, however, does *not* mean that the individual responds in a uniform manner to diverse environmental situations (Mischel, 1968); rather, the person responds differently to different stimulus events but displays a consistency in his responses to the *same* events.

We stress the centrality of personality patterns in order to break the deeply entrenched habit of thinking that all forms of abnormal behavior are "diseases." This archaic disease notion can be traced back to such prescientific ideas as demons, spirits and witches, which "possessed" the person and cast spells upon him. The recognition in modern medicine of the role of infectious agents has reawakened this archaic view. No longer do we see "demons," but we still think, although we use current medical jargon, that malevolent and insidious forces undermine the patient's otherwise healthy status. This view is a comforting and appealing simplification to the layman. He can attribute his discomforts, pains and irrationalities to the influence of some external agent, something he ate or caught, or some foreign object he can blame that has assaulted his normal and "true" self. This simplification of "alien disease bodies" has its appeal to the physician as well. It enables him to believe that he can find a malevolent intruder, some tangible factor he can hunt down and destroy.

The disease model carries little weight among informed and sophisticated psychiatrists and psychologists today. Increasingly, in both medicine and psychology, disorders and disturbances are conceptualized in terms of the patient's *total capacity to cope* with the environment he faces. In medicine, it is the patient's overall constitution — his vitality and stamina — which determine his proclivity to, or resistance against, ill health. Likewise, in psychology, it is the patient's personality pattern, his coping skills, outlook and objectivity, which determine whether or not he will be characterized as mentally ill. Physical ill health, then, is less a matter of some alien disease than it is an imbalance or dysfunction in the overall capacity to deal effectively with one's physical environment. In the same manner, psychological ill health is less the product of an intrusive psychic strain or problem than it is an imbalance or dysfunction in the overall capacity to deal effectively with one's psychological environment. Viewed this way, the individual's personality pattern becomes the foundation for his capacity to function in a mentally healthy or ill way.

DISTINCTIONS BETWEEN NORMAL AND ABNORMAL PERSONALITY PATTERNS

Normality and abnormality are relative concepts. They represent arbitrary points on a continuum or gradient. Abnormal behavior is shaped according to the same processes and principles as those involved in normal development and learning. However, because of differences in the character, timing, intensity or persistence of certain influences, some individuals learn maladaptive habits and attitudes, whereas others do not.

When an individual displays an ability to cope with his environment in a flexible and adaptive manner and when his characteristic perceptions and behaviors foster personal gratification, he may be said to possess a normal and healthy personality pattern. Conversely, when average responsibilities and everyday relationships are responded to inflexibly or defectively, or when the individual's characteristic perceptions and behaviors foster personal discomfort or curtail his opportunities to learn and grow, then an abnormal personality pattern may be said to exist. Of course, no sharp line divides normality and abnormality. Not only are personality patterns so complex that certain spheres of functioning may operate "normally" while others do not, but environmental circumstances may change such that certain behaviors and strategies prove "healthy" one time but not another.

Despite the variable nature of the normality-abnormality distinction, it may be useful to elaborate some criteria by which it may be made. We will not concern ourselves with gross aberrations whose pathological character is easily identified. Rather, it is in that nebulous category of *apparently normal* personality that we wish to alert ourselves to subtly concealed signs of an insidious and pervasive abnormal process.

Three signs, mentioned briefly in Chapter 1, may be noted again:

1. First, the individual displays an *adaptive inflexibility*. This means that the alternative instrumental strategies he employs for relating to others and for coping with conflict are practiced rigidly and imposed uniformly upon conditions for which they are ill suited. Not only is he unable to adapt to events but he seeks to change the conditions of his environment so that they do not call for behaviors beyond his meager behavior repertoire.

2. Of course, all individuals instrumentally manipulate their environment to suit their needs. What distinguishes abnormal from normal personality patterns is not only their rigidity and inflexibility but their *tendency to foster vicious circles*. Thus, abnormal personality patterns are, themselves, pathogenic; the individual himself perpetuates his difficulties, provokes new ones and sets in motion self-defeating experiences which cause his discomforts to persist and become intensified.

3. The third distinguishing feature of these patterns is their *tenuous stability*, that is, their fragility or lack of resilience under conditions of stress. (This notion has often been referred to in the literature as weak "ego strength.") Given the ease with which past sensitivities can be re-

activated, and the inflexibility and relative paucity of the coping strategies they have at their command, these individuals are extremely
susceptible to disruptions or breakdowns in their established patterns.

FOCUS ON LEARNED INTERPERSONAL BEHAVIORS

Traditionally, diagnostic categories constitute convenient ways of
grouping each variant of abnormality. Additionally, they should further the accomplishment of the important clinical goals of determining diagnosis, etiology, prognosis and the nature of therapy. The
question which we must ask ourselves, then, is, What system of labeling
will best accomplish these goals for the abnormal personalities we see
in everyday life?

Numerous writers have suggested that the interpersonal behavior
dimension provides particularly useful information for diagnostic and
prognostic decisions (Leary and Coffey, 1955). Along the same line,
there are others who suggest that interpersonal behaviors should take
primacy over other symptoms, since interpersonal variables play a
crucial role in therapy (Lorr, 1965). It has been proposed, further, that
interpersonal classifications would clarify the study of the social background of abnormal behavior (Haley, 1959): for example, if one
specifies the particular manner in which a patient interacts with others,
then one would have a useful basis for tracing the kinds of learning
experiences in which he acquired these behaviors. It appears from the
above that the interpersonal dimension may provide a focus for abnormal personalities that lends itself to the significant clinical goals of
diagnosis, etiology, prognosis, and therapy.

The logic for this interpersonal thesis applies especially to the less
severe abnormal personalities. These individuals remain in their normal social environment, operating daily in a variety of interpersonal
relationships. The style of learned interpersonal behavior exhibited
in these relationships in large measure will determine the future
course of their impairments. The strategies an individual uses to
achieve his goals and resolve his conflicts with others will evoke counter-
reactions that will influence whether his problems stabilize, improve
or lead to stress and further decompensation.

It is with the preceding considerations in mind that we have designated the mild abnormal personality syndromes, to be discussed in
this and the following chapters, largely in terms of those learned
interpersonal behaviors which perpetuate the very problems they were
designed to resolve. It is important to recognize that the patterns to
be described characterize people who maintain moderately adequate
adjustments to life. The "abnormal" traits they possess often escape
observation and, if noted, are difficult to differentiate from those
considered to be "normal;" these individuals rarely seek therapy,
since their behaviors usually are not viewed to be especially peculiar
by others or discomforting to themselves.

ASTHENIC PERSONALITY: PASSIVE-DETACHED PATTERN

It will be useful to differentiate personalities that display detached patterns into two broad subclasses — the *passive* and the *active* (Millon, 1969).
These persons should be distinguished because they possess basically

different developmental histories, behavioral orientations, self-concepts and interpersonal strategies. Neither of these subcategories is entirely homogeneous, of course, but the individuals grouped in each exhibit common clinical features. One group, the *passive*-detached, to be discussed in this section under the label "asthenic personality" (DSM-II),* is composed of persons who exhibit emotional and cognitive deficits that hinder the development of close interpersonal relationships. The other, *active*-detached group, to be described in the following section of this chapter, is composed of individuals whose experience of interpersonal anxiety has led them to avoid close relationships.

Asthenic personalities are found in every walk of life. They appear untroubled and function adequately in their chosen professions, but are rather colorless and shy, prefer to remain by themselves and seem to lack the need to communicate or relate affectionately to others. Asthenic personalities remain in the background of social life, work quietly at their jobs and rarely are noticed or thought about by those who have contact with them. They would fade into the passing scene, to live their lives in undisturbed inconspicuousness, were it not for the fact that there are persons who expect them to be more vibrant, alive and involved. According to Millon (1969), an appropriate label for these individuals would be *asocial personalities*. The following case portrays an individual with this pattern who might not have come to the attention of a clinician were it not for his wife's discontent.

Roy was a successful sanitation engineer involved in the planning and maintenance of water resources for a large city; his job called for considerable foresight and independent judgment but little supervisory responsibility. In general, he was appraised as an undistinguished but competent and reliable employee. There were few demands of an interpersonal nature made of him, and he was viewed by most of his colleagues as reticent and shy and by others as cold and aloof.

Difficulties centered about his relationship with his wife. At her urging they sought marital counseling for, as she put it, "he is unwilling to join in family activities, he fails to take an interest in the children, he lacks affection and is disinterested in sex."

The pattern of social indifference, flatness of affect and personal isolation which characterized much of Roy's behavior was of little consequence to those with whom a deeper or more intimate relationship was not called for; with his immediate family, however, these traits took their toll.

In the early years of marriage, his wife maneuvered Roy into situations which might interest him, getting him involved in bridge clubs, church activities, sports and so on. These not only proved of no avail in activating Roy, but they seemed to make him grumpy and antagonistic.

Eventually, it was she who became discontent and irritable, and in time, she began to cajole, hound and intimidate Roy. Finally, sensing the grave changes that were beginning to take place within herself, she beseeched him to seek help, not so much "because of his behavior, but because I felt I was turning into a frustrated and irritable shrew." It soon became apparent that her difficulties stemmed from Roy's impassivity and self-absorption.

CASE 11-1

Roy L., Age 36, Married, Two Children

CLINICAL PICTURE

The brief case presentation of Roy touches upon just a few of the cardinal features of the asthenic personality.

---

*The DSM-II refers to the official American Psychiatric Association nosology (1968).

Figure 11-1 Humorous portrayal of asthenic personality. (Drawing by Mirachi; ©1972 The New Yorker Magazine, Inc.)

"I don't know when he disappeared. I just happened to notice that his chair in front of the TV was empty."

In general, these individuals lack the equipment for experiencing the finer shades and subtleties of emotional life. They appear especially insensitive to the feelings and thoughts of others. Their interpersonal passivity may often be interpreted by others as signs of hostility and rejection. In fact, it merely represents a fundamental incapacity to sense the moods and needs which others experience. These individuals are unfeeling, then, not by intention or for self-protective reasons but because they possess an emotional blandness and interpersonal insensitivity.

Because they experience few rewards in social interaction, asthenic personalities often turn their talents and interests toward things, objects or abstractions. In childhood these individuals typically evidence a disinclination toward the competitive games and frolicsome activities of the young, preferring to concentrate their energies on hobbies such as stamp- or rock-collecting, mechanical gadgets, electronic equipment or academic pursuits such as mathematics or engineering. They may find considerable gratification with these nonhuman activities and may develop rather intricate fantasy lives with them. Moreover, the drab and withdrawn characteristics of these youngsters often make them easy targets for teasing and condemnation by their peers, leading frequently to an intensification of their withdrawal and self-absorption activities.

The asthenic personality evidences a steady, even state of under-responsiveness to all sources of external stimulation. Events which might provoke anger, elicit joy or evoke sadness in others appear to fall on deaf ears. He is minimally introspective, since the rewards of self-evaluation are relatively few for those incapable of experiencing deep inner emotions. This diminished introspectiveness, with its attendant lowering of insight, derives from another feature of the asthenic pattern, that of "cognitive slippage." This is a vagueness and impoverishment of thought and a tendency to skim the surface of events, along with the tendency to convey confused notions, especially regarding interpersonal phenomena. Several of these features are demonstrated in the following case.

Chester, an engineering professor of my acquaintance, would stop by my office repeatedly to chat about "our mutual interests in psychology and philosophy," oblivious of the fact that I thought his ideas obscure and archaic, at best, and that I found him personally tiresome and boring. Despite his obvious competence in engineering and mathematical matters, he seemed completely incapable of formulating his thoughts in a logical manner, let alone of conveying them to others. His superficial grasp and naivete regarding worldly and social affairs were quite striking, and he appeared totally devoid of any recognition that people might "feel" one way or another about him as a person. He was an extremely inept teacher, a fact he could not understand but nevertheless accepted.

CASE 11–2

Chester A., Age 39, Married, No Children

This style of amorphous communication appears related to another trait, which we will refer to as "defective perceptual scanning." This is characterized by a tendency to blur the varied elements of experience. Instead of differentiating events, sensing their distinctive attributes, the individual "mixes them up," intrudes irrelevant features and perceives them in a cluttered fashion. This inability to attend, select and regulate one's perceptions of the environment seems especially pronounced with regard to social phenomena.

There are few complicated unconscious processes in these personalities. Untroubled by intense emotional experiences, insensitive to interpersonal relationships and difficult to arouse and activate, they hardly feel the impact of events and they have little reason to devise complicated intrapsychic defenses and strategies. Of course, they do possess past memories and emotions, but in general, the inner world of the passive-detached personality is lacking in the complexities typically found in other abnormal patterns.

DEVELOPMENTAL BACKGROUND

Four interrelated features stand out in the clinical picture of the passive-detached personality; for the sake of simplicity we shall term them: *affectivity deficit* (emotional blandness; inability to experience intense feelings), *cognitive slippage* (obscurity and irrelevance in thought and communication that is inappropriate to the intellectual level), *complacent self-image* (lack of self-insight; unclear but untroubled concept of self) and *interpersonal indifference* (minimal interest in social relationships). The following case may be helpful in illustrating these characteristics:

Margaret was an extremely pretty, petite brunette, who personified the young college coed in appearance. She sought counseling on the urging of her dormitory room-mate because both felt she might have latent homosexual tendencies. This concern proved unjustified, but there were other characteristics of a pathological nature that clearly were evident.

CASE 11–3

Margaret L., Age 20, College Junior, Unmarried

Margaret rarely enjoyed herself on dates; not that she found herself "disgusted" or "repelled" with necking and petting, but she simply "didn't experience any pleasure" in these activities (affectivity deficit). She went out of her way to avoid invitations to parties, preferring to stay in her room, either watching TV or working at her studies. She was an excellent student, majoring in geology and hoping for a field career in forestry, petroleum research or archeology.

Margaret was viewed as rather distant and aloof by her classmates. She rarely engaged in social activities, turned down an opportunity to join a sorority and had no close friends, in fact, few friends at all, except for her room-mate and one girl back home. Despite her good looks, she was asked to date infrequently; when she did date, it usually was a one or two date affair in which either the boy failed to ask again or she refused to accept the invitation. The little reputation she had on campus was that she was a "cold fish" and "a brain," someone who would rather talk about her courses and career plans than dance, drink and be merry.

One relationship with a boy lasted several months. He seemed to be a quiet and introversive young man who joined her in taking hikes, in demeaning the "childish" behaviors of their classmates and in discussing their mutual interest in nature, trees and rock formations. Their relationship faltered after ten to 12 outdoor hiking dates; they seemed to have nothing more to say to each other. Margaret would have liked to continue this friendship, but she experienced no dismay over its termination (interpersonal indifference).

Further explorations showed that Margaret rarely experienced either joy, dismay or anger. She seemed content to "let matters ride along," sitting on the sidelines while others became perturbed, ecstatic or hostile about "silly little things between them." This viewpoint, however, reflected less a well-reasoned philosophy of life than an inability to grasp "what it is that got people so excited."

In describing her few relationships, past and present, she seemed to be vague, superficial and naive, unable to organize her thoughts and tending to wander into irrelevancies such as the shoes certain people preferred or the physical characteristics of their parents (cognitive slippage).

What background factors can account for the emotional and social deficits portrayed in cases such as Margaret's?

Numerous influences may operate singly or in combination to produce the picture we see. Several contributing factors will be highlighted in this section, but let us keep in mind that these influences do not act independently of one another in the natural course of development. Biogenic and psychogenic determinants, though separated for pedagogic purposes, interact in a complex, reciprocal and circular fashion.

BIOLOGICAL INFLUENCES

Heredity.   Since children inherit many overt physical features from their parents, it would seem safe to assume that features of internal morphology and physiochemistry may similarly be inherited. Extrapolating further, it would seem plausible that parents who are biologically limited in their capacity to experience intense emotions, or to be vigorous and active, possess certain associated structural and physiological deficiencies which they may transmit genetically to their children. What we are proposing, then, is that the passive-detached pattern may arise because an individual is at the low end of a genetically based continuum of individual differences in neurological structures and physiochemical processes which underlie affectivity, interpersonal sensitivity, activation and so on.

Passive Infantile Reaction Pattern.   We believe that a substantial number of these personalities displayed in infancy and early childhood a low sensory responsivity, motor passivity and a generally placid mood. They may have been easy to handle and care for, but it is likely that they provided their parents with few of the joys associated with more vibrant and expressive youngsters. As a consequence of their undemanding and unresponsive nature, they are likely to have evoked minimal stimulation and overt expressions of affectivity from their caretakers. This deficit in sheer physical handling may have compounded their initial tendencies toward inactivity and emotional flatness. The following case illustrates this early pattern and some of its potential consequences.

Gerald's difficulties came to the attention of a therapist after his parents previously brought his eleven year old brother to a mental health clinic; Gerald's brother was excessively aggressive, and Gerald was among his prime targets.

Intense sibling rivalry feelings were engendered at Gerald's birth. Gerald was a "good" baby, gave his parents little trouble, hardly had to be attended and was undemanding and quiet. Gerald's placid temperament was a welcome relief to a harried mother with five other young children. As she put it, "It was a pleasure never to have to be concerned with him."

Gerald's "ideal" behavior was used repeatedly as an example for his brother to emulate. Needless to say, this accomplished little other than to further provoke the brother's general hostile behavior. Gerald's mother was pleased that Gerald "never seemed to mind" his brother's animosity, needling and occasional physical assaults. Only slowly did she realize that Gerald seemed indifferent to all normally provoking emotional situations. She was so pleased with the little he demanded of her, however, that she let this observation pass.

Subsequent clinical study of Gerald indicated that his flatness was not a defense against deeper emotional distress, or an attempt to live up to the "idealistic" model he was made to be, but simply a pervasive apathy and insensitivity to feelings, either his own or others.

CASE 11–4
Continued

Ectomorphic Body Structure. Numerous theorists have proposed that individuals with thin and fragile body builds typically are shy and introversive. It is debatable, however, as to whether this correlation can be attributed primarily to an intrinsic genetic linkage between these physical and psychological traits. A more plausible interpretation suggests that persons who possess the frail ectomorphic build tend to conserve their energies, and lack the physical competencies, resilience and mechanical wherewithal to engage in vigorous and assertive behaviors. Given these physical limitations, they may learn quickly to become indifferent to, and to avoid, emotionally charged situations and physically demanding activities.

SOCIAL LEARNING HISTORY

The number and variety of influences which shape personality are legion. Only with great difficulty have theorists been able to assign more weight to some influences than others. However, when the basic principles of learning are grasped, we should be able to correctly assess which conditions give rise to which behaviors.

Stimulus Impoverishment During the Sensory-Attachment Stage. One of the conditions which appear to set the stage for later learning of interpersonal behaviors is the quantity of stimulus nourishment received by the child in his first year of life. Insufficient stimulation during this crucial period is likely to result in various maturational and learning deficits, as well as failure of development of the "emotional" centers of the brain. Constitutionally unresponsive infants who evoke few reactions from their environment experience a compounding of this process. Such children receive little attention and cuddling from their parents and, as a consequence, are deprived of the social and emotional cues necessary to learn human attachment behaviors. Although they may provide stimulation for themselves, their objects of attachment are likely to be dolls, blankets, blocks and so forth rather than other human beings.

Formal or Impassive Family Atmospheres. Children learn to imitate the pattern of interpersonal relationships to which they are exposed. Learning to be stolid, reticent and undemonstrative can be a by-product of observing the everyday relationships within the family. Families characterized by interpersonal reserve and formality, or those possessing a bleak and cold atmosphere, are likely breeding grounds for asthenic children.

The following brief sketch portrays this background feature.

CASE 11-5

Lester M., Age 19, College Student

Lester "wandered in" the door of his college's counseling service, and stood about for over an hour before arranging an appointment. In his first counseling session, he spoke of his inability "to feel" and his awareness that he could not carry on a conversation with his peers of more than a few words at a time. In later sessions, he recounted the impersonal atmosphere of his childhood home. Rarely was he allowed to speak unless spoken to, and he could not recall any occasion when he experienced or witnessed affection or anger among the members of his family.

Fragmented Family Communications.   Family styles of communicating in which ideas are aborted, or are transmitted in circumstantial or amorphous ways, are likely to shape the growing child's own manner of communication (Wynne, 1968). The child's pattern of relating to others will assume the vague and circumstantial style of his home. Moreover, exposed to disrupted and murky patterns of thought, he will, both by imitation and by the need to follow the illogic which surrounds him, learn to attend to peripheral aspects of human communication, that is, to signs and cues that most people would view as irrelevant and distracting (Hirsh and Leff, 1971). This way of attending to, of thinking about and reacting to events, if extended beyond the family setting, will give rise to perplexity and confusion on the part of others. As a consequence, a vicious circle of disjointed and meaningless transactions may come to characterize his interpersonal relations.

Deficient Coping Behaviors.   The notion of coping behaviors implies an instrumental course of action designed either to fulfill certain drives or to resolve certain conflicts; in other words, to seek positive reinforcements and avoid negative reinforcements.

Asthenic personalities are essentially devoid of these instrumental behaviors since their drives are meager, and they lack the interpersonal involvements conducive to severe emotional conflicts. This is not to say that they possess no drives or conflicts, but that the few they do experience are of mild intensity and of little consequence. Thus, one of their distinctions as a personality type is the paucity, rather than the character or direction, of their coping strategies.

If any factor in their generally feeble hierarchy of motives can be noted, it is their preference for remaining socially uninvolved. This, however, is not a "driving" need, as it is with the active-detached personality, but merely a comfortable and preferred state. When social circumstances press them beyond comfortable limits, they simply retreat and withdraw to themselves. If the strain of social demands is intense and persists, these individuals may adopt more severe pathological coping patterns such as are found in the "schizoid" or "schizophrenic" syndromes. These advanced states of the detached pattern will be presented in later chapters.

Socially Insensitive Behaviors.   The impassivity and lack of color of the passive-detached personality enables him to maintain a comfortable distance from others. But this preferred state of detachment is itself pathogenic, not only because it fails to elicit reactions which could promote a more vibrant and rewarding style of life but because it fosters conditions conducive to more serious forms of psychopathology. The lack of color and general unresponsiveness of asthenic individuals is not attractive to others, and people tend to overlook their presence in social settings. Of course, the fact that others view him as a boring and colorless individual suits the passive-detached person's desire to remain apart and alone.

The asthenic person not only is socially imperceptive but tends, in general, to "flatten" all emotional events, i.e., to blur that which is intrinsically distinct and varied. In short, he projects his murky cognitions upon discriminable and complex social experiences. As a consequence of his own perceptual diffusiveness, he precludes learning from experiences which could lead him to a more varied and socially discriminating life.

The passive-detached person perpetuates his own pattern by restricting to a minimum his social contacts and emotional involvements. Only those activities necessary for performing his job or fulfilling his family obligations are pursued with any diligence. By shrinking his interpersonal milieu in this way, he prevents new and different experiences from coming to bear upon him. This, as we have said, is his preference, but it fosters the continuation of his isolated existence since it excludes events which might modify his personality pattern.

TREATMENT APPROACHES

Should passive-detached personalities come to the attention of a therapist, his efforts would best be directed toward countering their withdrawal tendencies. The primary therapeutic task is to prevent the possibility that these patients will isolate themselves entirely from the support of a benign environment. Furthermore, the therapist should seek to ensure that they continue some measure of social activity so as to prevent them from becoming lost in fantasy preoccupations and separation from reality contacts. Efforts to encourage excessive social activity should be avoided, however, since their capacities in this area are limited.

Biophysical treatment methods may be indicated. Trial periods with a number of the pharmacological "stimulants" may be explored to see if they "perk up" energy and affectivity. These should be used with caution, however, lest they activate feelings that the patient is ill-equipped to handle.

Attempts to reorient the patient's attitudes may be made for the purpose of developing self-insight, and for motivating greater interpersonal sensitivity and activity. Group activity methods may prove useful in enabling them to acquire healthier social attitudes. In these settings, they may begin to alter their social image and develop both motivation and skills for normal interpersonal relations.

AVOIDANT PERSONALITY: ACTIVE-DETACHED PATTERN

In terms of surface behavior, the *active*-detached pattern appears very much like the passive-detached personality. Closer inspection, however, reveals that these persons are quite dissimilar. Active-detached or *avoidant personalities* (Millon, 1969) are highly alert to social stimuli and are oversensitive to the moods and feelings of others, especially those which may lead to rejection and humiliation. Their extreme anxiety in this matter intrudes and distracts their thoughts, interferes with effective behavior and disposes them to avoid, that is, to detach themselves from others as a protection against the stress they anticipate.

The following case portrays an avoidant personality, referred for counseling through the personnel office of a large industrial concern.

James was a bookkeeper for nine years, having obtained this position upon graduation from high school. He spoke of himself as a shy, fearful and quiet boy ever since early childhood. He currently was living with his mother, a socially insecure and anxious woman who kept her distance from others. His father, described as an alcoholic, was "mean to his mother" and deprecating to his children. He died when James was 14. A sister, four years older than James, lives in another city, had recently been divorced and was referred to by James as "being just like my father."

James was characterized by his supervisor as a loner, a peculiar young man who did his work quietly and efficiently. They noted that he ate alone in the company cafeteria and never joined in coffee breaks or in the "horsing around" at the office. Some years back he signed up for a company-sponsored bowling league, but withdrew after the first session.

As far as his social life was concerned, James had neither dated nor gone to a party in five years. He dated a girl "seriously" while in high school, but she "ditched" him for another fellow. After a lapse of about three years, he dated a number of different girls rather sporadically, but then stopped "because I didn't know what to say to them, and I thought they must have liked someone else." He now spent most of his free time reading, watching TV, daydreaming and fixing things around the house.

James experienced great distress when new employees were assigned to his office section. Some 40 people worked regularly in this office and job turnover resulted in replacement of four or five people a year. He feared constantly that he was going to be "fired," despite the fact that his work was competent and that the firm almost never dismissed its employees.

In recent months, a clique formed in his office. Although James very much wanted to be a member of this "in-group," he feared attempting to join them because "he had nothing to offer them" and thought he would be rejected. In a short period of time, he, along with two or three others, became the object of jokes and taunting by the leaders of the clique. After a few weeks of "being kidded," he began to miss work, failed to complete his accounts on time, found himself unsure of what he was doing and made a disproportionate number of errors. When his supervisor discussed with him his increasingly poor performance, James displayed extreme anxiety and complained of being "nervous, confused, tired and unhappy much of the time." Although he did not connect his present discomfort to the events in his office, he asked if he could be reassigned to another job where he might work alone.

The counselor to which he was directed found him to be of average intelligence and extremely conscientious, but lacking in confidence and fearful of competition. It became clear in further discussions that many of his traits could be traced to the humiliation and deprecation he suffered at the hands of his father, the rejection he experienced with his peers and in dating and his life-long identification with, and exposure to, his mother's fearful attitudes which he imitated unconsciously.

CLINICAL PICTURE

The case of James touches briefly on a number of points distinguishing the avoidant from the asthenic personality. *Active*-detached individuals are acutely sensitive to social deprecation and humiliation. They feel their loneliness deeply, experience being out of things and have a strong, though often repressed, desire to be accepted.

Despite this longing to relate and to be an active participant in social life, they fear placing their welfare in the hands of others, or trusting and confiding in them. Thus, their social detachment does not stem from deficit drives and sensibilities, as in the asthenic personality, but from an active self-protective restraint. Although they experience a pervasive estrangement, they do not expose themselves to the defeat and humiliation they anticipate, as can be seen in the repeated withdrawal behavior that characterizes the social life of James M.

Since their affective feelings cannot be expressed overtly, they cumulate and are vented in an inner world of rich fantasy and imagination. Their need for affect, contact and relatedness may pour forth in poetry, be sublimated in intellectual pursuits or a delicate taste for foods and clothing or be expressed in finely detailed and expressive artistic activities.

Their isolation, that is, their protective withdrawal from others, results, however, in a variety of secondary consequences which compound their difficulties. Their apparently tense and fearful demeanor often "pulls" ridicule and deprecation from others, that is, they leave themselves open to persons who gain satisfaction in taunting and belittling those who dare not retaliate.

To most observers who have superficial contact with them, avoidant personalities appear simply to be timid and withdrawn or perhaps cold and strange — not unlike the image covered by the asthenic personality. However, those who relate to them more closely recognize that they are touchy, evasive and mistrustful.

The avoidant personality is alert to the most subtle feelings and intentions of others. Although this vigilance serves to protect him against potential danger, it floods him with excessive stimuli and distracts him from attending to the ordinary features of his environment. Thus, even in the course of an ordinary day, James M. was so attuned to matters that might have a bearing on how others felt toward him that he could attend to little other than the routine aspects of his job.

Cognitive processes of the avoidant personality are not only interfered with by this flooding of irrelevant environmental details but are complicated further by an inner emotional disharmony. These feelings upset his cognitive processes and diminish his capacity to cope effectively with many of the ordinary tasks of life. This "cognitive interference," one of the cardinal features of the avoidant personality, is especially pro-

Figure 11–2 Humorous portrayal of avoidant personality. (Drawing by Booth; ©1971 The New Yorker Magazine, Inc.)

BOOTH

"All the pieces in this room are for sale except the chifforobe. The chifforobe is not for sale."

nounced in social settings. It is here that he must protect himself from the anticipated humiliation of rejection, and so avoidance becomes the guiding force behind his social behavior.

Avoidant personalities are beset by conflict. They cannot act on their own because of marked self-doubt. On the other hand, they cannot depend on others because of social mistrust. Positive reinforcements cannot be obtained from themselves or others; both sources provide only pain and discomfort.

The vigilance which characterizes the avoidant personality may signify a high level of somatic arousal (Venables, 1968; Epstein and Coleman, 1970). The behavioral sluggishness and inactivity is deceptive, since it may overlay an extremely low threshold for alertness and reactive readiness.

DEVELOPMENTAL BACKGROUND

The dominant features of the personality we have termed the avoidant pattern may be summarized in these four traits: *affective disharmony* (confused and conflicting emotions), *cognitive interference* (persistent intrusion of distracting and disruptive thoughts), *alienated self-image* (feelings of social isolation; self-rejection), and *interpersonal distrust* (anticipation and fear of humiliation and betrayal).

As we have stated previously, the concept of personality represents an individual's basic and pervasive style of functioning. It arises as a consequence of the intricate interplay of both biological and psychological influences.

BIOLOGICAL INFLUENCES

As noted earlier, propositions about biological determinants are highly speculative, given our present state of knowledge.

Heredity.   Genetic predispositions to avoidant behavior cannot be overlooked, despite the lack of empirical data. Many physiological processes comprise the biophysical substrate for complex psychological functions. It would be naive to assume that these biophysical substrates do not vary from person to person. Studies which demonstrate a higher than chance correspondence within family groups in social apprehensiveness and withdrawal behavior can be attributed in large measure to learning, but there is reason to believe, at least in some cases, that this correspondence may partially be assigned to a common pool of genotypic dispositions within families.

Fearful Infantile Reaction Pattern.   Infants who display hyperirritability, crankiness, tension and withdrawal behaviors from the first days of postnatal life may not only possess a constitutional disposition toward an avoidant pattern but may prompt rejecting and hostile attitudes from their parents. Such tense and frightened infants typically induce parental dismay, an attitude which may create a stereotype of a difficult-to-manage child. In these cases, an initial biophysical tendency toward anxiety may be aggravated further by parental rejection.

Neurological Imbalances.   Quite possibly, avoidant personalities experience aversive stimuli more intensely and more frequently than others because they possess an especially dense substrate in the "aversive" center of the nervous system. Another plausible speculation regarding the aversive feature of the active-detached pattern centers on a possible functional dominance of the sympathetic nervous system. Excess adrenalin may give rise to the hypervigilance, affective disharmony and cognitive interference found among these personalities.

Individual differences in brain anatomy and physiology have been well demonstrated, but we must recognize that speculations attributing complex forms of clinical behavior to biophysical variations is not only conjectural but also rather simplistic. Even if differences in biological aversiveness ultimately were found, the psychological form and content of these tendencies would take on their specific character only as a function of the individual's particular life experiences and learnings.

SOCIAL LEARNING HISTORY

Parental Rejection and Deprecation.   Even normal, attractive and healthy infants may encounter parental devaluation and rejection. Reared in a family setting in which they are belittled and censured, youngsters will have their natural robustness and optimism crushed, and acquire in its stead attitudes of self-deprecation and feelings of social alienation. We can well imagine the impact of these experiences upon a child who was not especially robust and competent to start with.

The consequences of parental rejection and humiliation are many and diverse (Heilbrun, 1972). In the following discussion we will outline them as they might arise during each of the three neuropsychological stages of development.

1.   The opportunity for creating the basis for tension and insecurity through mismanagement is greatest at the *sensory-attachment* stage of life. Infants of cold, rejecting parents will acquire a diffuse sense that the world is harsh and unwelcoming. They will learn, in their primitive and highly generalized way, to avoid attaching themselves to others. They will acquire a sense of mistrust of their human surroundings and, as a result, feel helpless and alone.

2.   Parents who scorn their offspring's first stumbling efforts during the *sensorimotor-autonomy* stage will diminish markedly feelings of self-competence and the growth of confidence. Although normal language skills and motor control may develop, the youngster will often utilize these aptitudes in a hesitant and self-doubting manner. He may accept as "valid" his parents' criticisms and, in time, begin to turn against himself.

3.   The roots of self-deprecation begun earlier in life take firm hold during the period of *intracortical-initiative*. The image of being a weak, unlovable and unworthy person now takes on a strong cognitive base. He becomes increasingly aware of himself as unattractive, a pitiful person, one who deserves to be scoffed at and ridiculed. Little effort may be expended to alter this image, since nothing the youngster attempts can succeed, given the deficits and inadequacies he sees within himself.

Peer Group Alienation.   The give and take of normal friendship, school, athletic competitions and eventually heterosexual dating, make demands that the healthy youngster is prepared to meet. Others, less fortunate, approach this era of life convinced of their own inadequacy (Barthell and Holmes, 1968). The feeling is conveyed to peers and is in turn reinforced by them. Peer group interaction, at this stage of life, can be devastating for the future avoidant personality. Many such youngsters feel shattered daily by constant humiliation in the exposure of their scholastic, athletic, physical or social inadequacies. Unable to prove themselves, they may not only be derided and isolated by others but become sharply critical toward themselves for their lack of worthiness and esteem. Their feelings of loneliness and rejection are now compounded further by severe self-judgments of personal inferiority and unattractiveness. They are unable to turn either to others for solace and gratification or to themselves.

Aversive Coping Behaviors.   The active-detached person is guided by a need to put distance between himself and others, that is, to minimize involvements that can reactivate or duplicate past humiliations. Any desire or interest which entails personal commitments to others constitutes a threat to his security.

To avoid the anguish of social relationships requires remaining vigilant and alert to potential threat. This contrasts markedly with the strategy of the asthenic personality who is perceptually insensitive to his surroundings. The avoidant person is keenly attentive to and aware of variations and subtleties in his stimulus world. He has learned through past encounters with threats that the most effective means of avoiding them is to be hyperalert to cues which forewarn their occurrence.

Self-Derogating Thinking.   Turning away from one's external environment brings little peace and comfort, however. The avoidant personality finds no solace and freedom within himself. Having acquired an attitude of self-derogation and deprecation, he not only experiences little reward in his accomplishments and thoughts but finds in their stead, shame, devaluation and anguish.

There may be more pain being alone with one's despised self than with the escapable torment of others. Immersing oneself in one's thoughts and feelings presents a more difficult challenge since the person cannot physically avoid himself, cannot walk away, escape or hide from his own being. Deprived of feelings of self-worth, he suffers constantly from painful thoughts about his pitiful state, his misery and the futility of being himself. Efforts as vigilant as those applied to the external world must be expended to ward off the distressing ideas and feelings that well up within him. He muddles his own emotions and thoughts: better to experience diffuse disharmony than the sharp pain and anguish of thinking about oneself.

Restricted Social Experiences.   Avoidant personalities assume that the atypical experiences to which they were exposed in early life will continue to be their lot forever. In defense, they narrow the range of activities in which they allow themselves to participate. By circumscribing their life in this manner, they preclude the possibility of corrective experiences, experiences which may show them that "all is not lost," that there are kindly and friendly persons who will not disparage and humiliate them.

Moreover, by detaching themselves from others they are left to be preoccupied with their own thoughts and impulses. Limited to these inner stimuli, they can only reflect about past events, with all the discomforts they bring forth. Since experience is restricted largely to thoughts of their past, life becomes a series of duplications. They relive the painful events of earlier times rather than experience new and different events which might alter their attitudes and feelings.

TREATMENT APPROACHES

Because of the active-detached person's basic mistrust of others, he is unlikely to be motivated either to seek or to sustain a therapeutic relationship. Should he submit to treatment, it is probable that he will engage in maneuvers to test the sincerity and genuineness of the therapist's feelings and motives. In most cases he will terminate treatment long before remedial improvement has occurred. The potential positive rewards of therapy not only may fail to motivate the avoidant personality but may actually serve as a deterrent. It reawakens what he views will be false hopes. It may lead him back to the dangers and humiliations he experienced with others when he tendered his affections, but received rejection. Now that he has carved out a modest degree of comfort by detaching himself from others, he would rather leave matters stand, stick to his accustomed level of adjustment and not "rock the boat" he so tenuously learned to sail.

A first therapeutic approach would be to assist the patient in managing a more wholesome and rewarding environment. Here we might seek to assist in the discovery of opportunities which might enhance self-worth. Supportive therapy may be all the patient can tolerate until he is capable of dealing comfortably with his more painful feelings and thoughts. Biophysical treatment may be used to diminish or control anxieties. Behavior modification techniques may prove useful as a means of learning less fearful reactions to formerly threatening situations. As the patient progresses in trust and security with the therapist, he may be amenable to methods which alter erroneous self-attitudes and distorted social expectancies. No doubt, deeper and more searching procedures can be useful in reworking unconscious anxieties and mechanisms which pervade every aspect of his behavior. Lastly, group therapy may be employed, where feasible, to assist the patient in learning new attitudes and skills in a more benign and accepting social atmosphere than normally encountered.

INADEQUATE PERSONALITY: PASSIVE-DEPENDENT PATTERN

Docility, a clinging helplessness and a search for support and reassurance characterize *inadequate* personalities. They are self-depreciating, feel a sense of marked inferiority and avoid initiative and self-determination. Except for their need for signs of belonging and acceptance, they refrain from making any demands of others. They submerge their individuality, subordinate their desires, and often submit to intimidation, all in the hope of avoiding the dread of loneliness and abandonment. They feel paralyzed and empty if left to their own devices. They search for guidance in fulfilling simple tasks or making routine decisions.

Passive-dependent individuals often seek a single, all-powerful "magic helper," a partner in whom they can place their trust, depend on to supply the few comforts they want and to protect them from having to assume responsibilities or face the competitive struggles of life alone. Supplied with a dependable partner, they may function with ease, be sociable and display warmth, affection and generosity to others. Deprived of these supports, they may withdraw and become tense, dejected, despondent and forlorn.

CASE 11-7

Harry G., Age 57, Married, Four Children

Mr. G. was a rather short, thin and nicely featured but somewhat haggard man who displayed a hesitant and tense manner when first seen by his physician. His place of employment for the past 15 years had recently closed and he had been without work for several weeks. He appeared less dejected about the loss of his job than about his wife's increasing displeasure with his decision to "stay at home until something came up." She thought he "must be sick" and insisted that he see a doctor; the following picture emerged in the course of several interviews.

Mr. G. was born in Europe, the oldest child and only son of a family of six children. As was customary of his ethnic group, the eldest son was pampered and overprotected. His mother kept a careful watch over him, prevented him from engaging in undue exertions and limited his responsibilities; in effect, she precluded his developing many of the ordinary physical skills and competencies that most youngsters learn in the course of growth. He was treated as if he were a treasured family heirloom, a fragile statue to be placed on the mantlepiece and never to be touched for fear he might break. Being small and unassertive by nature, he accepted the comforts of his role in a quiet and unassuming manner.

His life was uneventful and inconspicuous until he was called to serve in the army. Despite all kinds of maneuvers on the part of his mother, he was physically removed from his home and trundled off to a training camp. No more than a week elapsed, during which time he experienced considerable anguish, than his eldest sister bribed her way into the camp and spirited him to the home of a distant relative. The records of the government whose army he was to serve were so ill kept that he was able to return to his home several months thereafter with no awareness on the part of local officials that he had failed to fulfill his service obligations.

A marriage was arranged by his parents. His wife was a sturdy woman who worked as a seamstress, took care of his home and bore him four children. Mr. G. performed a variety of odds-and-ends jobs in his father's tailoring shop. His mother saw to it, however, that he did no "hard or dirty work," just helping about and "overlooking" the other employees. As a consequence, Mr. G. learned none of the skills of the tailoring trade.

Shortly before the outbreak of World War II, Mr. G. came to visit two of his sisters who previously had emigrated to the United States; when hostilities erupted in Europe he was unable to return home. All members of his family, with the exception of a young son, perished in the war.

During the ensuing years, he obtained employment at a garment factory owned by his brothers-in-law. Again he served as a helper, not as a skilled workman. Although he bore the brunt of essentially good-humored teasing by his co-workers throughout these years, he maintained a friendly and helpful attitude, pleasing them by getting sandwiches, coffee and cigarettes at their beck and call.

He married again to a hard-working, motherly type woman who provided the greater portion of the family income. Shortly thereafter, the son of his first wife emigrated to this country. Although the son was only 19 at the time, he soon found himself guiding his father's affairs, rather than the other way around.

Mr. G. was never troubled by his "failure" to mature and seemed content to have others take care of him, even though this meant occasional ridicule and humiliation. His present difficulty arose when the factory closed. Lacking the wherewithal of a skilled trade and the initiative to obtain a new position, he "decided" to stay at home, quite content to remain dependent on others.

CLINICAL PICTURE

The absence of self-confidence is apparent in the posture and mannerisms of inadequate persons. They tend to be overly acquiescent and prefer to yield and placate rather than assert themselves. Their self-image, on the surface, is that of a considerate, thoughtful and cooperative person, prone to be unambitious and modest in achievement. Deeper probing, however, will evoke marked feelings of personal inadequacy and insecurity. They tend to downgrade themselves, claiming a

Figure 11-3 Humorous portrayal of inadequate personality. (Drawing by Weber; ©1972 The New Yorker Magazine, Inc.)

"Hi. I'm Herb Armstrong. Uncertainty is my thing."

basic lack of abilities, virtues and attractiveness. They magnify their failures and defects. In any area of comparison, they minimize their attainments, underplay their attributes, note their inferiorities and assume personal blame for problems they feel they have brought to others. Much of this self-belittling has little basis in reality.

By claiming weakness and inferiority, the passive-dependent absolves himself of the tasks and responsibilities he knows he should assume, but would rather not. Likewise, self-deprecation evokes sympathy, attention and care from others, for which he feels guilt.

These maneuvers and conflicts cannot be tolerated consciously. To experience harmony with one's self, the dependent must deny the feelings he experiences and the "deceptive" strategies he employs. He must cover up his fundamental need to be dependent by rationalizing his inadequacies, that is, by attributing them to physical illnesses, unfortunate circumstance and the like.

Inadequate personalities often suffer a chronic state of fatigue. Any form of exertion brings on the need to rest and recuperate. Many wake up exhausted, ready to turn over for another night's sleep. Concerted effort, or work out of the ordinary routine, exhausts them. They hesitate engaging in new activities or in any task which may prove demanding or taxing. They frequently lack sexual interest, and often experience impotence. The mere thought of extending themselves beyond their usual narrow boundaries may invite anticipatory feelings of weakness, anxiety and a sense of being "weighted down."

DEVELOPMENTAL BACKGROUND

We shall label the central traits of the inadequate personality as follows: *gentle affectivity* (having kind, soft and humanitarian impulses), *cognitive denial* (showing a Pollyanna-like refusal to admit discomforting thoughts), *inadequacy self-image* (viewing self as inferior, fragile and unworthy) and *interpersonal compliance* (willing to submit and oblige others). Let us next turn to hypotheses that refer to the developmental background of these traits.

BIOLOGICAL INFLUENCES

Heredity.   The thesis that dispositions to behavior may in part be rooted in genetic factors is no less plausible in the passive-dependent pattern than in any other. Convincing empirical evidence is lacking, however. Similarities among members of a family group suggest the operation of hereditary determinants, but these findings may reflect environmental influences as well. Passive-dependency *per se* is never inherited, of course, but certain types of genetic endowments have high probabilities of evolving, under "normal" life experiences, into the inadequate personality pattern.

Placid Infantile Reaction Patterns.   If the assumption is correct that one's constitutional make-up is moderately consistent throughout life, it would seem reasonable to conclude that many inadequate personalities would have displayed a tendency to be gentle and placid in infancy and early childhood. A soft and somewhat solemn quality may have characterized their early moods. Similarly, they may have shown a reticence, a hesitance to assert themselves, a restraint in new situations and a fear of venturing forth to test their growing capacities.

SOCIAL LEARNING HISTORY

Parental Attachment and Overprotection.   Every infant is helpless and entirely dependent upon his caretakers for protection and nurturance. During the first few months of life, the child acquires a vague notion of which objects surrounding him are associated with increments in comfort and gratification. He becomes "attached" to these objects since they provide him with positive reinforcements. All of this is natural. Difficulties arise, however, if the attachments the child learns are too narrowly restricted, or so deeply rooted as to deter the growth of competencies by which he can obtain reinforcements on his own. Let us follow the course of these pathological attachments through the three stages of neuropsychological development.

1.   The first stage of neuropsychological development, referred to as sensory-attachment, serves as a foundation for future growth. Supplied with adequate amounts of beneficial stimulation, the child is likely to develop both interpersonal sensitivity and trust.

It seems plausible that infants who receive an adequate amount of reinforcing stimulation, but obtain that stimulation almost exclusively from one source, usually the mother, will be disposed to develop passive-dependent traits. They experience neither stimulus impoverishment nor enrichment, but rather stimuli from an unusually narrow sphere of objects. As a consequence of this lack of variety, the infant will form a singular attachment, a fixation if you will, upon one object source to the exclusion of others.

Any number of factors may give rise to this exclusive attachment. Unusual illnesses or prolonged physical complications in the child's health may prompt a normal mother to tend to her infant more frequently than is common at this age. On the other hand, an excessively worrisome and anxious mother may be over-alert to real and fantasied needs she sees in her normal child, resulting in undue attention, cuddling and so on. Occasionally, special circumstances surrounding family life may throw the infant and mother together into a "symbiotic" dependency. The following case, not uncommon during wartime, illustrates the consequences of events such as these.

CASE 11–8

Paul R., Age 7

Paul was born while his father served overseas in the armed forces. Until the age of three he lived in an apartment alone with his mother. With the exception of his mother's parents, both of whom worked, he had little opportunity to relate to anyone other than his mother. Supported by a government allotment, and her parent's gifts, Paul's mother had little to do but devote her attention to, and heap her affections upon him. Two evenings a week, and on Sundays, Paul went with his mother to visit his grandparents. Except for brief and infrequent excursions to a zoo or a park, his contact with people was limited to mother and grandparents.

When Paul's father returned from service he was met by a frightened and withdrawn son. No matter what his father attempted, Paul would turn away, cry and run to his mother. It took several months of good will and considerable patience to get Paul to stay alone with his father. However, the moment mother came upon the scene, Paul fled to her.

Entrance to kindergarten was traumatic. Paul simulated a variety of ailments each morning. He would develop headaches, vomit or simply cry so intensely that his mother often decided to let him remain at home. After several weeks of this behavior, which often continued in school on those days when he did attend, his mother insisted that he be allowed to remain home for the semester.

The advent of a second child, when Paul was six and ready to enter first grade, further aggravated his attachment and dependency behavior. He could hardly be contained when his mother went to the hospital. Only the comforting of his grandparents could assuage his anxiety. Upon his mother's return, Paul began to wet his bed. He had been fully toilet trained two years earlier. His school phobia began again. This time his father insisted that Paul attend despite the morning battles and the teacher's distress over his sulking and weepy behavior in class. The persistence of his resistance to school led to a recommendation for psychological study and treatment.

2. An infant who retains his exclusive attachment to the mother during the second neuropsychological stage, that known as sensorimotor autonomy, will have his earlier training in dependency behaviors strengthened and perpetuated. However, there are many youngsters who were not especially attached to their mothers in the first stage who also develop the inadequate pattern. Experiences conducive to the acquisition of dependency behaviors can arise independently of an initial phase of exclusive maternal attachment.

Barring the operation of constitutional dispositions and physical deficits, the average youngster in this stage will assert his growing capacities, and strive to do more and more things for himself. This normal progression toward self-competence and environmental mastery may be interfered with by excessive parental anxieties or other harmful behaviors. For example, some parents may discourage their child's independence for fear of losing "their baby." They place innumerable barriers and diverting attractions to keep him from gaining greater autonomy. These parents limit the child's ventures outside the home, express anxiety lest he strain or hurt himself, make no demands for self-responsibility and provide him with every comfort and reward so long as he listens to mother. Rather than let him stumble and fumble with his new skills, his parents do things for him, make things easier, carry him well beyond the walking stage, spoon feed him until he is three, tie his shoelaces until he is ten and so on. Time and time again he will be discouraged from his impulse to "go it alone."

3.   Parental pampering and overprotection, continued into the third neuropsychological stage, often have a devastating effect upon the child's growing self-image.

First, he may fail to develop a distinct picture of himself apart from his caretaker. His excessive dependence upon others for the execution of everyday tasks of life has denied him the opportunity to do things for himself, to form an impression of what *he* is good at and who *he* is. Second, it is implicit in parental overprotection that the child cannot take care of himself. The pampered child is apt to view himself as his parents do, as a person who needs special care and supervision because he is incompetent. Third, when he is forced to venture into the outside world, he finds that his sense of inferiority is confirmed, that he objectively is less competent and mature than others of his age. Unsure of his identity and viewing himself to be weak and inadequate, he has little recourse but to perpetuate his early pattern by turning to others again to arrange his life and to provide for him. The case of Harry G. illustrates these points well.

Competence Deficits.   Let us briefly note some non-parental factors alluded to in the last paragraph which may dispose the child to the passive-dependent pattern. The major theme to be noted here concerns events or relationships that lead the individual either to believe that he cannot compete with others or to learn that a submissive rather than an assertive role will assure less discomfort and greater reward for him.

Feelings of unattractiveness and competitive inadequacy, especially during adolescence, may result in social humiliation and self-doubt. These youngsters, however, are more fortunate than the active-detached adolescent since they usually can retreat to their home where they will find both love and acceptance. In contrast, the active-detached youngster receives little solace or support from his family. Although the immediate rewards of affection and refuge at home are not to be demeaned, they may, in the long run, prove a disservice to the child since ultimately he must learn to stand on his own.

It may appear strange and paradoxical that the genuine affection and acceptance experienced in childhood by the passive-dependent should dispose him to abnormal behavior. Childhood, for most of these individuals, was a time of warmth and security, a period marked by few anxieties and discomforts that were not quickly relieved by parental attention and care. Certainly, the early life of the passive-dependent was idyllic when contrasted to the indifference and humiliation to which the active-detached child was exposed.

But too much of a "good" thing can turn bad. Excessive parental shielding and attachment may establish habits and expectancies which prove detrimental in the long run since they ill prepare the child to cope on his own with the strains and discouragements of later life. Accustomed to support from others and ill-equipped to obtain rewards without them, he remains rooted to the deep attachments of his childhood.

Unable to free himself from his dependence, the passive-dependent is faced with the constant danger of loss and desertion. Beneath his pleasant and affable exterior, then, lie a sense of helplessness and incompetence and a fear of abandonment.

Submissive Interpersonal Behavior. The inadequate personality feels that it is best to abdicate self-responsibility, to leave matters to others and to place his fate in their hands. They are so much better equipped to shoulder responsibilities, to navigate the intricacies of a complex world and achieve the few pleasures to be found in the tough competitions of life.

To accomplish this goal of dependency, he learns to attach himself to others and to submerge his individuality — in other words, to assume an attitude of helplessness and compliance. By acting weak, expressing fear and self-doubt, and displaying a willingness to trust and submit, he may elicit the protection he seeks.

Learned Self-Deprecation. Not only does the passive-dependent observe real deficits in his competence but he deprecates what virtues and talents he may possess so as to prevent others from expecting him to assume responsibilities he would rather avoid. Successful as this maneuver may be as a shield against discomfort and in the service of fulfilling his dependency needs, it is achieved at the cost of lessening of self-respect and esteem.

Rationalizations of frailty and weakness, offered for the benefit of others, have an impact on the person himself. Each time he announces his defects, he convinces himself as well and deepens his self-image of personal incompetence. Trapped by his own persuasiveness, he feels increasingly the futility of standing on his own, and tries less and less to overcome his sense of inadequacy. As a consequence of his strategy, then, he fosters a vicious circle of increased helplessness and dependency.

TREATMENT APPROACHES

Passive-dependents not only are receptive to therapy but are disposed to seek assistance wherever they can find it. The strength and authority of the therapist comforts them, gives them the assurance that an all-powerful and all-knowing person will come to their rescue and nuture them with the kindness and helpfulness they crave. The task of unburdening their woes to a therapist calls for little effort on their part. Unfortunately, the patient's receptiveness and the auspicious beginning of therapy create a misleading impression that future progress will be rapid. The patient desires a dependency relationship with his therapist. Despite "promises" to the contrary, the dependent person will resist efforts to assume independence and autonomy.

Behavior modification procedures may be employed to maximize growth and to minimize situations which foster continued dependency. Biophysical treatment, notably certain stimulants, may prove useful toward the end of promoting increased alertness and vigor, since passive-dependents often are plagued by undue fatigue and lethargy, a state that inclines them to postpone efforts at independence. The relationship between therapist and patient must not reestablish the dominance-submission pattern that has characterized the history of these patients. Nondirective approaches are more likely to foster the growth of autonomy and self-confidence than more directive methods. Group therapeutic techniques can often be pursued fruitfully as a means of learning autonomous social skills and assisting in the growth of social confidence.

HYSTERICAL PERSONALITY: ACTIVE-DEPENDENT PATTERN

Dependent personalities experience few positive reinforcements from themselves, and look to others to protect them and provide the rewards of life. Beneath their good-natured affability lies an intense need for attention and affection. They require constant affirmation of approval and acceptance, are exceedingly vulnerable to withdrawal from those upon whom they depend and experience a sense of helplessness, even paralysis, when left alone.

Every dependent personality is different from every other, but two basic groups may usefully be distinguished — the passive and the active (Millon, 1969). In the previous section we described the passive type, who contrasts markedly with the hysterical or active-dependent pattern. Hysterical personalities may be no less dependent upon others for reinforcements, but they do not surrender the initiative for achieving these reinforcements. Rather than placing the fate of their needs in the hands of others, and thereby having their security in jeopardy, they actively manipulate others in their interpersonal behaviors so as to assure receipt of the stimulation and esteem they need. They develop an exquisite sensitivity to the moods and thoughts that others experience. This hyperalertness enables them to appraise what reactions will succeed in attaining the ends they desire. Their extreme "other-directedness," devised in the service of achieving approval, results, however, in a life style characterized by a shifting pattern of behaviors and emotions (Halleck, 1967). Unlike the passive-dependent, who anchors himself often to one object of attachment, the active-dependent lacks fidelity and loyalty, that is, turns repeatedly from one source of affection and approval to another. The dissatisfaction he experiences with single attachments, combined with his constant need for stimulation and attention, often results in the development of a seductive pattern of personal relationships and a flair for the dramatic. According to Millon (1969), a better descriptive label for these hysterical types would be the "gregarious" or "histrionic" personality.

In the case presented below we can trace some of the features of this pattern in a "successful" woman.

CASE 11–9

Suzanne D., Age 34, Twice Divorced, Married, One Child

Suzanne, an attractive and vivacious woman, sought therapy in the hope that she might prevent the disintegration of her third marriage. The problem she faced was a recurrent one, her tendency to become "bored" with her husband and increasingly interested in going out with other men. She was on the brink of "another affair" and decided that before "giving way to her impulses again" she had "better stop and take a good look" at herself. The following history unfolded over a series of therapeutic interviews.

CASE 11–9
Continued

Suzanne was four years older than her sister, her only sibling. Her father was a successful and wealthy business executive for whom children were "display pieces," nice chattels to show off to his friends and to round out his "family life," but "not to be troubled with." Her mother was an emotional but charming woman who took great pains to make her children "beautiful and talented." The girls vied for their parents' approval. Although Suzanne was the more successful, she constantly had to "live up" to her parents' expectations in order to secure their commendation and esteem.

Suzanne was quite popular during her adolescent years, had lots of dates and boyfriends and was never short of attention and affection from the opposite sex. She sang with the high school band and was an artist on the school newspaper, a cheerleader and so on.

Rather than going to college, Suzanne attended art school where she met and married a fellow student—a "handsome, wealthy ne'er-do-well." Both she and her husband began "sleeping around" by the end of the first year, and she "wasn't certain" that her husband was the father of her daughter. A divorce took place several months after the birth of this child.

Soon thereafter she met and married a man in his forties who gave both Suzanne and her daughter a "comfortable home, and scads of attention and love." It was a "good life" for the four years that the marriage lasted. Her husband was wealthy and had interesting friends. Suzanne attended a dramatic school, took ballet lessons, began to do free-lance artwork and, in general, basked in the pleasure of being the "center of attention" wherever she went. In the third year of this marriage she became attracted to a young man, a fellow dancing student. The affair was brief, but was followed by a quick succession of several others. Her husband learned of her exploits, but accepted her regrets and assurances that they would not continue. They did continue, and the marriage was terminated after a stormy court settlement.

Suzanne "knocked about" on her own for the next two years until she met her present husband, a talented writer who "knew the scoop" about her past. He "holds no strings" around her; she is free to do as she wishes. Surprisingly, at least to Suzanne, she had no inclination to venture afield for the next three years. She enjoyed the titillation of "playing games" with other men, but she remained loyal to her husband, even though he was away on reportorial assignments for periods of one or two months. The last trip, however, brought forth the "old urge" to start an affair. It was at this point that she sought therapy.

Suzanne felt that she had attained what she wanted in life and did not want to spoil it. Her husband was a strong, mature man who "knew how to keep her in check." She herself had an interesting position as an art director in an advertising agency, and her daughter seemed finally to have "settled down" after a difficult early period. Suzanne feared that she would not be able to control her tendency to "get involved" and turned to therapy for assistance.

CLINICAL PICTURE

The case of Suzanne demonstrates what our society tends to foster and admire in its members — to be well liked, successful, popular, extraverted, attractive and sociable. Unless one examines her life more closely, Suzanne would appear to epitomize the American ideal: intelligent, outgoing, charming and sophisticated, liberated from the traditions of the past, married to an interesting and able person and pursuing a career commensurate with her talents. But beneath this surface veneer we see a driving quality, a consuming need for approval and a desperate striving to be conspicuous, to evoke affection and attract attention at all costs. Despite the frequent rewards these behaviors produce, the needs they stem from remain inflexible, repetitious and persistent.

Hysterical personalities impress one, at first, by the ease with which they express their thoughts and feelings, by their flair for the dramatic and by their seemingly natural capacity to draw attention to themselves. They are highly capricious, however, and intolerant of frustration. The words and feelings they express appear shallow, fraudulent and simulated, rather than deep or real.

The active-dependent is more than merely friendly and helpful in his interpersonal relationships; he is actively solicitous of praise, "markets" his appeal to others and is entertaining and often sexually provocative. Since affection and attention are his primary goals, he engages in a wide variety of maneuvers to elicit favorable responses. Women typically are charming or coquettish; men are generous in praise and overtly seductive.

Their preoccupation with external rewards and approvals has left them without an identity apart from others. They describe themselves *not* in terms of their own intrinsic traits, but in terms of their social relationships and their effects upon others. They behave like "empty-organisms" which react more to external stimuli than to promptings from within.

Active-dependents evidence an extraordinarily acute sensitivity to the thoughts and moods of those from whom they desire approval and affection. This well-developed "radar" system serves them in good stead for it not only alerts them to signs of impending rejection but enables them to manipulate the object of their designs with consummate skill. It does not, however, provide them with self-knowledge and depth in personal relationships. This the hysterical personality studiously avoids, for real insights might upset his strategy of facile superficiality.

DEVELOPMENTAL BACKGROUND

Using the format of characteristics which has served to summarize the principal features of previous personality patterns, the following distinguishing attributes may be noted in the active-dependent pattern: *labile affectivity* (uncontrolled and dramatic expression of emotions), *cognitive dissociation* (failure to integrate learnings; massive repression of memories), *sociable self-image* (perception of self as attractive, charming and affectionate) and *interpersonal seductiveness* (a need to flirt and seek attention). Next we turn to the question of how these attributes came to pass.

BIOLOGICAL INFLUENCES

Heredity.   The role of heredity cannot be overlooked in searching for the biological origins of the active-dependent pattern. The neural and chemical substrate for tendencies such as sensory alertness and autonomic or emotional reactivity may logically be traced to genetic influences. Evidence demonstrating a high degree of family correspondence in these traits is suggestive of physiological commonalities, of course, but such tendencies can be explained also as a function of experience and learning. The need for research is obvious, not only in establishing factually the presence of family correspondence but in tracing the manner in which such alleged genetic factors unfold and take shape as psychological traits.

Figure 11–4 Humorous portrayal of hysterical personality. (Drawing by Price; © 1972 The New Yorker Magazine, Inc.)

Hyperresponsive Infantile Reaction Patterns.   It would seem reasonable to expect that active-dependent adults would have displayed a high degree of alertness and emotional responsiveness in infancy and early childhood. This inference derives from the assumption not only that constitutional traits are essentially stable throughout life but that an active and responsive child will tend to foster and intensify his initial responsiveness by evoking varied and stimulating reactions from others.

SOCIAL LEARNING HISTORY

Biogenic influences appear less relevant in the development of the hysterical pattern than in the personality types previously described. It is logical, then, to focus our attention on psychological experience and learning as the primary etiological variables.

Stimulus Enrichment and Diversity.   Constitutionally alert and responsive infants will experience greater and more diverse stimulation in the first months of life than dull and phlegmatic infants. As a consequence of these early stimulus gratifications, their tendency is reinforced to look "outward" to the external world for rewards rather than "inward" into themselves. In a similar manner, normally alert infants may develop this attitude if their caretakers expose them to excessive stimulation during the sensory-attachment stage.

Both passive and active-dependents exhibit a focus upon external rather than internal sources of reinforcement. But there is a basic difference between them, one that may be traced in part to differences in the diversity, intensity and consistency in early sensory attachment learning.

Passive-dependents appear to have received their enriched stimulation from a single, perhaps exclusive, source which provided a consistent level of gratification. In contrast, active-dependents appear to have been exposed to a number of different sources that provided brief, highly charged and irregular stimulus reinforcements. Such experiences may not only have built a high level of sensory capacity, which requires constant "feeding" to be sustained, but may also have conditioned them to expect stimulus reinforcements in short concentrated spurts from a variety of different sources. The shifting from one source of gratification to another, so characteristic of the hysterical personality, their search for new stimulus adventures, their penchant for creating excitement and their inability to tolerate boredom and routine, all may represent the consequences of these unusual early experiences (Zuckerman et al., 1972).

Parental Control by Contingent and Irregular Reward.   In addition to differences in the variety, regularity and intensity of stimulus enrichments in the sensory-attachment stage, the experiences of the active-dependent child may be distinguished from those of the passive-dependent both during and after the sensorimotor-autonomy stage.

Passive-dependent children continue to receive attention and affection from their caretakers *regardless* of their behavior; it is *not* necessary for them "to perform" in order to elicit parental nurturance and protection. As a consequence of sitting idly by and passively waiting for their parents to tend to their needs, they fail to develop adequate competencies and autonomy.

The active-dependent child, in contrast, appears to learn that he must engage in certain sanctioned behaviors, and must satisfy certain parental desires and expectations in order to receive attention and affection. Thus, Suzanne D. knew that parental approval was contingent on her "looking pretty," or "showing them my latest artistic masterpiece" or the "fancy ballet steps" she had just learned in dancing school. In her quest for attention, she gradually acquired the set of strategies we have described as active-dependent.

What are the conditions of learning which shape these strategies into the active-dependent form?

They seem to be characterized by the following three features: minimal negative reinforcement, e.g., Suzanne's parents rarely criticized or punished her; positive reinforcement contingent upon performance of parentally approved behaviors, e.g., favorable comments were conveyed to Suzanne only if she "was pretty" or "performed"; and irregularity in positive reinforcement, e.g., Suzanne's parents often failed to take cognizance of her "productions" even when she attempted to attract their attention. Stated in conventional language, parents of the future active-dependent rarely punish their children and distribute rewards only for what they approve and admire, but often fail to bestow these rewards even when the children behave acceptably.

This pattern of experiences has three personality consequences: strategies designed to evoke rewards, a feeling of competence and acceptance *only* when others acknowledge one's performances and a habit of seeking approval for its own sake. All three of these traits are characteristic of the active-dependent personality.

Histrionic Parental Models.   There is little question that children learn, quite unconsciously, to mimic what they are exposed to. The prevailing attitudes and feelings, and the incidental daily behaviors displayed by family members serve as models which the growing child imitates and takes as his own long before he is able to recognize what he is doing or why. This process of vicarious learning is made especially easy if parental behaviors and feelings are unusually pronounced or dramatic. Under these circumstances, when parents call attention to themselves and create emotional reactions in their child, the child cannot help but learn clearly how people behave and feel. Thus, Suzanne D. reported that she was "just like" her mother, an emotionally labile woman who was "bored to tears with the routines of home life," flirtatious with men and "clever and facile in her dealings with people." The presence of a gregarious and histrionic parent, who exhibits feelings and attitudes rather dramatically, provides a sharply defined model for vicarious and imitative learning.

Learned Seductive Behavior.   It may be useful to recall that the interpersonal behavior of mild abnormal personalities is not strikingly different from that seen among "normal" individuals. Its distinction lies not in its uniqueness, but in its inflexibility and persistence.

The hysterical personality is often successful in accomplishing the aims of his instrumental behaviors, that of eliciting the stimulation and excitement he craves, or captivating others and winning their attention and approval. His strategies are pathological, however, because he does not limit their use to situations in which they are appropriate or promise success. Rather, they are applied indiscriminately and relentlessly; for example, he seeks to please the most insignificant of people with whom he comes into contact and pursues his strategies with the most unlikely prospects and under the most unsuitable circumstances.

To achieve his goals and avoid his fears, the hysterical personality has learned with considerable skill to manipulate others to his suiting. More than being merely agreeable and friendly, he learns to "sell" himself, that is, to employ his talents and charm to elicit approval. This he does by presenting an attractive front, by seductive pretensions, and by a dilettante sophistication and knowledgeability. Exhibitionistic displays and histrionics, dramatic gestures, attractive coiffures, frivolous comments, clever stories and shocking clothes — all are designed *not* to "express himself," but to draw interest, stimulation and attention to himself. In short, he uses himself as a commodity and as a "personality" with a bag of tricks, a conspicuous talent that corners all of the attention of those with whom he comes into contact.

Despite his charm and his talent for "pleasing" others, the active-dependent does not provide others with real and sustained affection. In fact, the converse is true. All that is offered in return for the approval he seeks are fleeting and superficial displays of affection. Having failed throughout life to develop any depth and richness of inner feelings and lacking in resources from which he can draw, he is unable to sustain a meaningful and stable relationship with others. Moreover, he senses the disparity between the favorable but superficial impression he gives to others, and his real lack of inner substance. As a consequence, he shies from prolonged contact with others for fear that his fraudulence will be uncovered.

Orientation to External Stimuli.   We have noted that the hysteric orients his attention to the external world and that his perceptions tend to be fleeting, impressionistic and undeveloped. This scattered preoccupation with incidental and passing details prevents events from being digested and embedded within his inner world. As a result, there is no integration, no well-examined reflective process, that intervenes between perception and action. Although the active-dependent is sharply attuned to the outside world, the disadvantages of hyperalertness and hypersensitivity may outweigh their advantages. Unless experience is digested and integrated, the individual gains little from them. Events and transactions with others pass through the person as if he were a sieve. There is no development of inner skills, no construction of memory traces against which future experience may be evaluated.

Fleeting Social Attachments.   One of the consequences of the fleeting and erratic relationships so characteristic of the hysterical personality is that he can never be sure of securing the affection and support he craves (Jordan and Kempler, 1970). By moving constantly from one adventure to another and by devouring the affections of one person and then another, he places himself in jeopardy of having nothing to tide him over the times between. He often is left high and dry, alone and abandoned with no one "to love," nothing to do and no excitement with which to be preoccupied. Unlike the passive-dependent who opts for the security of a single and stable relationship, the active-dependent ravenously consumes his source of nourishment. Once it is gone, he will frantically search for new sources of stimulation and approval, only to start the futile and vicious circle again.

TREATMENT APPROACHES

Hysterical personalities rarely seek therapy. When they do, it usually follows a period of prolonged deprivation of stimulation and approval. Their complaints take the form of rather vague feelings of boredom, restlessness, discontent and loneliness. The person often reports a growing disaffection with his mate, a feeling that the interest and vitality, which characterized their earlier years together, have now palled. Sexual interest may have faded, and the frequency of relations may have dropped markedly due to a growing impotence or frigidity. As this disaffection continues, conflicts and tension may arise, prompting the patient to feel not only a sense of loss but rejection and hostility from his mate. Life begins to take on a purposeless and meaningless quality. He begins to dramatize his plight, feeling that matters are hopeless and futile.

A first step in therapy is to curtail the patient's tendency to indulge, overemotionalize and thereby aggravate his distraught feelings. Once calmed and more objectively oriented, it is best not to further weaken the patient's previously successful, but currently flagging, gregarious strategy.

In the early stages of treatment, the therapist must be prepared to be viewed by his patient as an object possessing magical powers. This illusion is transient; nevertheless, it may be used to reestablish the patient's equilibrium. It is best to terminate treatment once equilibrium is established, unless more extensive therapy is indicated. Also, few active-dependents retain long term motivation for therapy; either they again feel capable of securing affection and approval on their own, or they begin to experience intense anxieties upon therapeutic efforts and self-exploration.

Supportive therapy may be indicated to tide them over the "rough periods." If the patient is sufficiently inclined, insight-oriented procedures may prove of assistance in developing deeper self-understanding and a richer inner life. Of frequent value, also, are behavior modification and group methods designed to aid the person in developing more genuine and sustaining ways of relating to others.

Mare Chagall—*I and the Village. Collection, the Museum of Modern Art, New York*

12 ABNORMAL PERSONALITIES IN EVERYDAY LIFE: II

Let us proceed directly from where we left off in Chapter 11 and discuss the remaining four abnormal personality patterns seen in everyday life.

NARCISSISTIC PERSONALITY: PASSIVE-INDEPENDENT PATTERN

In contrast to dependent personalities, who look to others to provide the reinforcements of life, independent patterns turn inward for gratification, relying on themselves both for safety and comfort. Weakness, inferiority and dependency are threatening. They are overly concerned with matters of adequacy, power and prestige. Differences in status and superiority must always be in their favor. They fear the loss of self-determination, are proud of their achievements, strive to enhance themselves and to be ascendant, stronger, more beautiful, wealthier or more intelligent than others. In short, it is what they themselves possess, not what others say or can provide for them, which serves as the touchstone for their security and contentment.

The independent style of life may usefully be divided into two subtypes (Millon, 1969). The *passive-independent,* to be discussed in this secton, is confident of his self-worth and needs to be merely himself to feel content and secure; the *active-independent,* to be described in the following section, struggles to "prove" himself, insists on his rights and will be cunning and ruthless if necessary to gain power over others. For the passive type, self-esteem is based on a blind and naive assumption of personal worth and superiority. For the active-independent, self-determination is a protective maneuver, a means of countering, with his own power and prestige, the hostility, deception and victimization he anticipates from his surroundings.

The label "narcissistic" connotes more than mere egocentricity. Narcissism signifies, more particularly, that the individual overvalues his personal worth, directs his affections toward himself, rather than others, and expects that they will recognize and cater to the high esteem in which he holds himself. This rather fascinating pattern, though well known in contemporary life, and depicted so well in literary writings, has been given but scant theoretical and clinical attention (Kohut, 1970). For example, the recent DSM-II has no diagnostic category that approximates the clinical features of this personality type.

Narcissistic individuals display a benign form of arrogance and a disdainful indifference to the standards of shared social behaviors. They feel themselves to be "above" the conventions and ethics of their cultural group, and exempt from the responsibilities that govern and give order and reciprocity to societal living. Others are expected to submerge their desires in favor of the narcissist's comfort and welfare. He operates on the rather fantastic assumption that *his* mere desire is justification enough for possessing whatever he seeks. In short, he possesses illusions of an inherent superior self-worth, and moves through life with the belief that it is his inalienable right to receive special considerations. Some of the features of this pattern are illustrated in the following case.

CASE 12–1

Steven F., Age 30, Artist,
Married, One Child

Steven came to the attention of a therapist when his wife insisted that they seek marital counseling: According to her, Steve was "selfish, ungiving and preoccupied with his work." Everything at home had to "revolve about him, his comfort, moods and desires, no one else's." She claimed that he contributed nothing to the marriage, except a rather meager income. He shirked all "normal" responsibilities and kept "throwing chores in her lap," and she was "getting fed up with being the chief cook and bottle-washer . . . tired of being his mother and sleep-in maid."

On the positive side, Steve's wife felt that he was basically a "gentle and good-natured guy with talent and intelligence." But this wasn't enough. She wanted a husband, someone with whom she could share things. In contrast, he wanted, according to her, "a mother, not a wife"; he didn't want "to grow up . . . he didn't know how to give affection, only to take it when he felt like it, nothing more, nothing less."

Steve presented a picture of an affable, self-satisfied and somewhat disdainful young man. He was employed as a commercial artist, but looked forward to his evenings and weekends when he could turn his attention to serious painting. He claimed that he had to devote all of his spare time and energies to "fulfill himself," to achieve expression in his creative work. His wife knew of his preoccupation well before they were married; in fact, it was his self-dedication and promise as a painter that initially attracted her to him. As Steve put it "what is she complaining about . . . isn't this what she wanted, what she married me for?"

Exploration of Steve's early history provided the following. Steve was an only child, born after his mother had suffered many miscarriages; his parents had given up hope of ever having a child until he came along, "much to their surprise and pleasure." His parents doted upon him. He never assumed any household or personal responsibilities. He was given music and art lessons, discovered to have considerable talent in both and given free rein to indulge these talents to the exclusion of everything else. He was an excellent student, won several scholarships and received much praise for his academic and artistic aptitudes. To his family he was "a genius at work." Life at home revolved entirely around him.

Socially, Steve recalled being "pretty much of an isolate," staying home "drawing and reading, rather than going outside with the other kids." He felt he was well liked by his peers, but they may have thought him to be a "bit pompous and superior." He liked being thought of this way, and felt that he was "more talented and brighter" than most. He remained a "loner" until he met his wife.

His relationships with his present co-workers and social acquaintances were pleasant and satisfying, but he did admit that most people viewed him as a "bit self-centered, cold and snobbish." He recognized that he did not know how to share his thoughts and feelings with others, that he was much more interested in himself than in them and that perhaps he always had "preferred the pleasure" of his own company to that of others.

CLINICAL PICTURE

Rather typically the passive-independent conveys a calm and self-assured quality in his social behavior. His seemingly untroubled and self-satisfied air is viewed, by some, as a sign of confident equanimity. Others respond to it less favorably. The narcissist appears to them to lack humility and to be overly self-centered and ungenerous. He exploits others, takes them for granted and expects them to serve him, but is unwilling to give in return. Moreover, his self-conceit often is viewed as unwarranted.

The passive-independent, however, feels justified in his claim for special status. He has little conception that his behaviors may be unjustified and even irrational. His self-image is that of a superior person, someone "extra-special," entitled to unusual rights and privileges. This view is fixed so firmly in his mind that he rarely questions whether his assumption is valid. Anyone who fails to respect him is viewed with contempt.

Narcissistic individuals place few limits upon their fantasies and rationalizations. Their imagination runs free of the constraints of reality or the views of others. They exaggerate their powers, freely transform failures into successes, construct lengthy and intricate rationalizations to inflate their self-worth, justify what they feel is their due and depreciate those who refuse to accept or enhance their self-image.

Passive-independents suffer few conflicts. Their past experiences have supplied them, perhaps too well, with affection and encouragement. As a consequence, they are disposed to trust others and to feel a high degree of confidence that matters will work out well for them.

As will be detailed later, this outlook upon life is founded on an unusual set of early experiences that rarely can be duplicated in later life. The narcissist was misled by his parents into believing that he was lovable and perfect, regardless of what he did and how he thought. Such an idyllic life cannot long endure.

Reality bears down heavily at times. Even the demands of shared everyday responsibilities can prove troublesome to the narcissist. Such responsibilities are demeaning. They shatter the cherished illusion of his godlike qualities. Alibis to avoid such pedestrian tasks as "taking out the garbage" or "diapering the baby" are easy to muster since he is con-

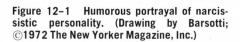

Figure 12–1 Humorous portrayal of narcissistic personality. (Drawing by Barsotti; ©1972 The New Yorker Magazine, Inc.)

"By George, I like that! Yes, I like that very much!"

vinced of the superiority of *his* logic; what he believes is true, and what he wishes is right.

Since the passive-independent cares little for the opinions of others, his defensive maneuvers are transparent, a poor camouflage to a discerning eye. This failure to bother "covering up" more thoroughly accounts in part for his overt appearance of immodesty and obvious arrogance.

DEVELOPMENTAL BACKGROUND

Bringing together the clinical features noted above suggests the following primary characteristics of the passive-independent pattern: *elevated affectivity* (buoyant, optimistic and carefree), *cognitive expansiveness* (boundless in imagination; facile in rationalization), *admirable self-image* (egotistic; self-assured) and *interpersonal exploitation* (presumptuous in expectation of special considerations and good will). In this section we will attempt to trace some of the influences which shape these traits.

BIOLOGICAL INFLUENCES

The role of biogenic influences in the narcissistic personality seems especially unclear. Although evidence adduced in support of biogenic determinants for most of the other personality patterns was largely of a speculative nature, there was some, albeit tenuous, logic for these speculations. In the case of the passive-independent pattern, however, where the existence of distinctive biophysical traits seems lacking, conjectures would have unusually weak grounding; thus, none will be proposed.

SOCIAL LEARNING HISTORY

Parental Overvaluation and Indulgence.   For many reasons, some parents will view their child as "God's gift to man." They pamper, and indulge the youngster in such ways as to teach him that his every wish is a command to others, that he can receive without giving and that he deserves prominence without effort. In short order, the child learns to view himself as a special being, learns to expect subservience from others, begins to recognize that his mere existence is sufficient to provide pleasure to others and that his every action evokes commendation and praise. On the other hand, however, he fails to learn how to cooperate and share or to think of the desires and interests of others. He acquires no sense of interpersonal responsibility and no skills for the give-and-take of social life. The world revolves about him. He is egotistic in focus, and narcissistic in the expression of love and affect.

Exposed repeatedly to acquiescent parents, he expects comparable treatment from others, and learns to employ the demanding strategies which effected favored reactions in the past. Should desire be frustrated, he can act only in one way — to demand and exploit. He has learned no alternative and has no recourse but to assume that his wishes automatically will be met.

Learned Exploitive Behavior.   We can easily understand why the instrumental behaviors of the narcissist are so gratifying to him. By treating himself kindly, by admiring and imagining his own prowess, beauty and intelligence, and by reveling in his superiority and talents, he gains, through self-reinforcement, the rewards that most people must struggle to achieve through genuine attainments. He need depend on no one else to provide gratification.

Satisfying though it may be to reinforce oneself, it is all the more satisfying to arrange one's environment so that others will contribute to these reinforcements. The narcissist seeks to accomplish this with minimal effort and reciprocity on his part. Thus, in contrast to the passive-dependent, who must submit and acquiesce to evoke favorable rewards, or the active-dependent, who must perform and be attractive and seductive in order to win praise from others, the passive-independent contributes little or nothing to others in return for the gratifications he seeks.

The sheer confidence displayed by the narcissist often elicits the admiration and obedience of others. Furthermore, he sizes up those around him and quickly trains those who are so disposed to pay tribute to him, e.g., the narcissist often will select a passive-dependent mate, one who will be solicitous and subservient, without expecting anything in return except his strength and assurances of fidelity.

Self-Reinforced Illusions of Competence.   Narcissists act as if belief in their superiority will suffice as its proof. Conditioned to think of themselves as capable, they refuse to expend effort to really become so. At some deeper level, however, they may sense a failure to "live up" to their self-made publicity, and consequently avoid facing the genuine challenges of the real world. In this way they can retain their illusion of superiority without fear of disproof.

Unwilling to expend the effort, the narcissist may slip increasingly behind others in realistic attainment. In due course, his deficits become pronounced, making him, as well as others, aware of his shortcomings. Since his belief in his intrinsic superiority is the bedrock of his existence — the underpinning of his coping strategy — the disparity between his genuine and illusory competence becomes increasingly painful. The strain of maintaining his false self-image may blossom to serious proportions, and result in the emergence of more severe pathological disturbances.

The narcissist's illusion of competence is only one facet of a more generalized disdain for reality. These personalities are neither disposed to stick to objective facts nor to shape their actions and thoughts in accord with social custom or the demands of cooperative living. Unrestrained by parental discipline in childhood, and confident of his worth and prowess, he takes liberties with rules and reality, and prevaricates and fantasizes at will. Apart from others and free to wander in his private world of fiction, he may begin to lose touch with reality, lose his sense of proportion and think along peculiar and deviant lines.

Deficient Social Responsibility.   If the narcissist were able to respect others, allow himself to value their opinions or see the world through their eyes, he would stand a good chance of having his tendencies toward illusion and unreality checked. But the narcissist has learned to devalue others, not to trust their judgments and capacities, and to think of them as fools and knaves. Rather than questioning the correctness of his own actions and beliefs, he assumes that it is theirs that are at fault. The more disagreement he has with others, the more convinced he is of his own superiority, and the more isolated and alienated he becomes.

These difficulties are magnified by his inability to participate gracefully in the give-and-take of shared social life. His characteristic selfishness often "pulls" condemnation and disparagement from others. These reactions, unfortunately, drive him further into his world of fantasy, only to strengthen his alienation and his illusion of superiority.

TREATMENT APPROACHES

Passive-independents are not inclined to seek therapy. Their arrogant pride disposes them to reject the "weakness" implied in the role of a patient. They are convinced that they can get along well on their own. How demeaning it would be to admit their shortcomings. Why consider changing if one already is perfect. And to add insult to injury, why should one be guided by some less talented being, namely the therapist. The passive-independent consents to therapy unwillingly. He maintains a well-measured distance from the therapist, resists the searching probes of therapeutic exploration, becomes indignant over implications of deficiencies on his part and seeks to shift the responsibility for them to others. His denials and evasiveness and his unwillingness to examine his illusions and destructive behaviors, intrude and interfere with progress. The treatment situation may become a struggle in which he attempts to outwit the therapist and to assert dominance and superiority. Only with great patience and equanimity can the therapist establish a spirit of confidence and respect.

Narcissists are precipitated into therapy usually after a particularly painful blow to their pride. A severe occupational failure, an embarrassing loss of public esteem or a sudden change of attitude on the part of a previously idolizing marital partner illustrate the kinds of events which may prompt the voluntary acceptance of therapy.

Once involved in carrying out treatment, the therapist may hold the narcissist's interest by allowing him to focus attention upon himself. Furthermore, by encouraging discussions of his past achievements, he may enable him to rebuild his recently depleted self-esteem. Not infrequently, the patient's self-confidence is restored merely by talking about himself, by recalling and elaborating his attributes and competencies in front of a knowing and accepting person.

If support is all that the therapist seeks as his goal, this can often be achieved in a few sessions. But the goals of therapy usually are more substantial, especially since the rebuilding of the patient's superiority illusions may prove, in the long run, to be a disservice to him.

As more fundamental goals, the therapist should seek to assist the patient in acquiring greater self-control, becoming more sensitive and aware of reality and learning to accept the constraints and responsibilities of shared social living. But first, the therapist must strengthen the patient's capacity to confront his weaknesses and deficiencies. Until he can accept himself on a more realistic basis than heretofore, it is not likely that the narcissist will be able to develop socially cooperative attitudes and behaviors.

AGGRESSIVE PERSONALITY: ACTIVE-INDEPENDENT PATTERN

Independent personalities exhibit in common an inclination to view themselves as the primary source for achieving reinforcement. However, a major distinction must be drawn between the passive and active subtypes. Passive-independents are characterized by their sublime self-confidence and their deeply rooted faith in themselves as superior beings. In contrast, active-independents, referred to as aggressive personalities, are driven by a need to assert and prove their superiority. Independence for them stems not so much from a belief in self-worth, as from a fear and mistrust of others. They have faith only in themselves and are secure only when they are independent of those who may undo, harm and humiliate them.

The *antisocial personality* diagnosis in the DSM-II parallels to some extent the "aggressive personality" syndrome described here. The DSM designation, we believe, places too great an emphasis on the undesirable social consequences of the patient's behavior, overlooking in great measure his "basic" personality style. In a later chapter, we will discuss those aggressive personalities who are openly and flagrantly hostile in their social behavior. Other aggressive personalities, however, "fit in" to the mainstream of the larger society, and are much more subtle in the expression of their hostile impulses. Aggressive individuals often are commended and endorsed in our competitive society, where tough, hard-headed "realism" is admired as an attribute necessary for survival. Thus, most aggressive personalities find a socially valued niche for themselves in the rugged side of the business, military or political world. This pattern often is found in the arrogant patriotism of nationalists, militarists and demagogues.

Aggressive personalities grab as much control and power as they can so as to prevent others from using it to exploit and harm them. Once having seized power, however, they become ruthless and vindictive themselves and employ their acquired strength for retribution directed at those who mistreated and betrayed them in the past.

The following case illustrates the development of a number of these features of the aggressive pattern:

CASE 12–2

John W., Age 42, Production Supervisor, Married, Two Children

The company for whom Mr. W. worked recently contracted with a management consulting firm to have their middle and senior level executives "talk over their personal problems" on a regular basis with visiting psychologists. Mr. W. was advised to take advantage of the arrangement because of repetitive difficulties with his subordinates. He had been accused of being "rough" with his secretaries, and excessively demanding of engineers and technicians directly responsible to him. The validity of these accusations was attested to by a rapid turnover in his department, and the frequent requests for transfer on the part of his professional staff.

Mr. W. was seen as a tall, broad-shouldered, muscular, but slightly paunchy, man with a leathery, large-featured face, large hands and brusque manner. He was the third child in a family of four. The oldest child was a girl, the others were boys. He recalled that his mother spoke of him as a strong-willed and energetic baby, one who fought to have his way right from the start. Until he left for college at 18 he lived with his family on a small ranch in Montana. His father struggled to "make a go of things" through the depression, and died just as he was "starting to make ends meet." Mr. W. spoke of his father as a tough, God-fearing man. He dominated the household, was a "mean" disciplinarian and showed no warmth or gentility. Toward the end of his life, while Mr. W. was in his teens, his father "got drunk three or four times a week," and often would come home and try to "beat up the kids and mom." He hated his father, but recognized that he served as a model for his own toughness and hardheaded outlook.

Mother was a background figure. She cooked, cleaned and helped out on the ranch when father asked her to do so. She never interfered with her husband's wishes and demands, turning over all decisions and responsibilities to him. Mr. W.'s older sister was quiet like his mother. They both "sort of faded into the wall." The three brothers were quite different. They fought "tooth and nail" ever since they were young. Mr. W. proudly boasted, "I could beat up my older brother when I was ten and he was 12." He remained the dominant sibling from then on.

Mr. W. was given a "paid scholarship" to play college football, but was drafted into the Army between his freshman and sophomore years. He served in the final European phase of World War II and recalled his harrowing experiences with consider-

CASE 12-2
Continued

able pride. He currently is an active member of a veterans organization. Upon returning home, he continued his education on the G.I. Bill of Rights, played football for two seasons and majored in business economics. Upon graduation he joined, as a field production assistant, the oil firm in which he is currently employed, married a girl he "picked up" some months before and moved about from one field location to another as assigned by his company.

On the job, Mr. W. was known as a "hard boss"; he was respected by the field hands, but got on rather poorly with the higher level technicians because of his "insistence that not a penny be wasted, and that nobody shirk their job." He was an indefatigable worker himself, and demanded that everyone within his purview be likewise. At times he would be severely critical of other production chiefs who were, as he saw it, "lax with their men." Mr. W. "couldn't stand lazy, cheating people"; "softness and kindness were for social workers"; "there's a job that's to be done and easy-going people can't get it done the way it should be." Mr. W. feared "the socialists" who were "going to ruin the country." He had a similar distaste for "lazy and cheating" minority and racial groups.

Mr. W. was assigned to the central office of his company on the basis of his profitable production record. For the first time in his occupational life he had a "desk job." His immediate superior liked the way Mr. W. "tackled problems" but was concerned that he alienated others in the office by his gruffness and directness. It was only after considerable dissension within his department that Mr. W. was advised, as he put it, "to unload on someone other than my secretaries and my pussy-footing engineers."

CLINICAL PICTURE

Many people shy away from aggressive personalities, feeling intimidated by their brusque and belligerent manner. They sense that the aggressive individual is cold and callous, insensitive to the feelings of others and that he gains pleasure by competing with and humiliating anyone he can get his hands on.

Figure 12-2 Humorous portrayal of aggressive personality. (Drawing by Lorenz; ©1972 The New Yorker Magazine, Inc.)

"Of course, Nibriski's only a first-year man, but he's got one thing going for him—desire."

Aggressive personalities tend to be argumentative and contentious. On occasion, they are abusive and cruel. They insist in discussions on being viewed as "right," tend to be dogmatic in their views and rarely give in on points.

Aggressive personalities behave as if the "softer" emotions were tinged with poison. They avoid expressions of warmth and intimacy and are suspicious of gentility, compassion and kindness.

When matters go their way, they may act in a gracious and clever manner. But more characteristically, their behavior is guarded and resentful. Moreover, they have a low tolerance for frustration, and fear being viewed as indecisive and inadequate. When crossed or embarrassed, they respond quickly and become furious and revengeful. They are easily provoked to attack, to demean and to dominate.

Many are perceptually alert and finely attuned to the subtle elements of human interaction. The great majority, though appearing to be coarse and imperceptive, are in fact quite often aware of the moods and feelings of others. Their seeming insensitivity stems from their tendency to use what they see for purposes of upsetting the equilibrium of others; that is, they take advantage of their social perception to be intentionally callous or manipulative.

The active-independent views himself as assertive, energetic, self-reliant and perhaps hard-boiled, but honest, strong and realistic. If we accept his premise that ours is a tough, dog-eat-dog world, we can understand why he values himself for being hard-headed, forthright and unsentimental. In a jungle philosophy of life, where "might makes right," the only valid course for a person is to be on guard, suspicious, aggressive and at times ruthless.

He is adept at pointing out the hypocrisy and ineffectuality of do-gooders. He notes the devastating consequences of appeasement and compromise, equates this with weakness, and dreads the thought of being weak as well as being deceived and humiliated. He expects no greater kindness from others than they should expect from him. He projects his own hostility, sees others as arrogant and claims that he must be aggressive to defend himself. Personal feelings are irrelevant, at best. At worst, they are signs of weakness and of maudlin and sloppy sentimentality. No one can make a go of it in this life if he lets his feelings get in the way.

DEVELOPMENTAL BACKGROUND

Following the format laid down in discussing the previous patterns, we might note the following characteristics as typical of the aggressive personality: *hostile affectivity* (irritable and easily provoked to anger), *cognitive projection* (tending to ascribe one's own malicious motives to others), *assertive self-image* (proud of his energy, "realism," and hard-headedness) and *interpersonal vindictiveness* (socially blunt, intimidating and punitive). Let us next turn to those aspects of their developmental background which may give rise to these features.

BIOLOGICAL INFLUENCES

Heredity.   The high frequency of overt hostile behavior commonly observed among family members suggests that constitutional dispositions traceable to genetic origins may play a role in the development of the aggressive pattern. Of course, observed similarities in family behaviors can be accounted for in large measure by shared experiences and common training methods. Nevertheless, it seems reasonable to posit that if there are biophysical substrates for aggressive tendencies, they may in part be transmitted by heredity.

Energetic and Fearless Infantile Reaction Patterns.   Parents who bring their acting out and aggressive children to clinics often report that their youngsters "always were that way." A common complaint is that their child displayed temper tantrums even as an infant, would get furious and turn "red" when frustrated, either when awaiting the bottle or feeling uncomfortable in his wet diaper. As the child matured he is described as having had a "hot temper," and a bullying and demanding attitude toward other children. Not uncommonly, parents remark that these children seemed undaunted by punishment, unimpressionable, unbending and unmanageable. Furthermore, they evidenced a daring and boldness, an audacious and foolhardy willingness to chance punishment and physical harm. They seemed thick skinned and unaffected by pain.

The possession of temperamental attributes from early life are significant not only in themselves but for the experiences they produce, and the reactions they evoke from others. Aggressive children explore the challenges and competitions of their environment more assertively than others. Moreover, they intrude themselves and upset the peaceful existence that others seek. Not only are they likely to encounter more trouble than most children, but their seeming recalcitrance in the face of punishment results in their receiving more punishment than that required to control most children. Thus, given a "nasty" disposition and an "incorrigible" temperament from the start, these children provoke a superabundance of exasperation and counterhostility from others. Their constitutional tendencies may, therefore, initiate a vicious circle in which they not only prompt frequent aggression from others, but, as a consequence, learn to expect frequent hostility.

SOCIAL LEARNING HISTORY

Although aggressive characteristics may be traced in part to biogenic dispositions, psychogenic factors will shape the content and direction of these dispositions. Moreover, psychogenic influences often are sufficient in themselves to prompt these behaviors. The following hypotheses focus on the role of experience and learning, but let us keep in mind that as far as personality patterns are concerned biogenic and psychogenic factors interweave in a complex sequence of interactions.

Parental Hostility.   Infants who, for constitutional reasons, are difficult to manage, are likely to provoke negative and rejecting reactions from their parents. It does not take long before a child with this disposition will be stereotyped as a "miserable, ill-tempered and disagreeable little beast." Once categorized in this fashion, momentum builds up and we may see a lifelong cycle of parent-child feuding.

Parental hostilities may stem from sources other than the child's initial disposition. For example, children often are convenient scapegoats for displacing angers that have been generated elsewhere. Thus, in many cases, a vicious circle of parent-child conflict may have its roots in a parent's occupational, marital or social frustrations. Whatever its initial source, a major cause for the development of an aggressive personality pattern is exposure to parental cruelty and domination.

Hostility breeds hostility, not only in generating intense feelings of anger and resentment on the part of the recipient, but, perhaps more importantly, in establishing a model for vicarious learning and imitation. It appears to make little difference as to whether or not a child desires consciously to copy parental hostility. Mere exposure to these behaviors, especially in childhood when alternatives have as yet not been observed, serves as an implicit guide to how people feel and relate to one another. Thus, impulsive or physically brutal parents arouse and release strong counter feelings of hostility in their children. Moreover, they demonstrate in their roughshod and inconsiderate behavior both a model for imitation and an implicit sanction for similar behaviors to be exhibited whenever the child feels anger or frustration.

Deficient Parental Models and Social Ostracism.   Children who are exposed to parental hostility acquire enduring resentments toward others, and incorporate the parental model of aggression as a guide for venting these feelings. This background is among the most common found in the aggressive personality, but by no means is it the only psychogenic source for the development of this pattern.

Another set of experiences conducive to the aggressive personality is one in which there is a lack of parental models. In these cases, parents provide little or no guidance for the child, and he is left to fend for himself, to observe and to emulate whatever models he can find to guide him.

Broken families, especially those in which the father has abandoned his wife and children, characterize this state of affairs. With the model and authority of the breadwinner out of sight, and the mother harassed by overwork and financial insecurity, the youngster often is left to roam the streets, unguided and unrestrained by the affection and controls of an attending parent. The disappearance of the father and the preoccupations of a distracted mother are felt implicitly as signs of rejection. To find a model, a credo by which his fate can be mobilized and given meaning, he must often turn to his peers, to those other barren and lost souls bereft of parental attention, and wander aimlessly in a hostile world.

Together with their fellow outcasts, these youngsters quickly learn that they are viewed as misfits in society, that their misfortunes will be compounded by closed-minded attitudes of the larger community. They learn also that it is only by toughness and cunning that they will find a means of survival. But this adaptive strategy sets into play a vicious circle. As the youngster asserts himself, as he ventures into the deviant remains left for him and his fellow scavengers by the larger society, that very same society castigates and condemns him. His resentment mounts, and the circle of hostility and counterhostility gains momentum. With no hope of changing his fate, no promise of advancement, and struggling throughout to keep a foothold in the dog-eat-dog world into which he has been cast, he is driven further into an aggressive and vindictive style of life.

Learned Vindictive Behavior.   The aggressive person's strategy is clear: You cannot trust others. They will abuse and exploit their power, they will dispossess you, strip you of all gratifications and dominate and brutalize you, if they can. To avoid this fate, one must arrogate all the power one can to oneself, one must block others from possessing the means to be exploitive and harmful. Only by alert vigilance to threat, only by vigorous counteraction can one withstand and obstruct their malice and hostility. Getting close to others, displaying weakness and being willing to appease and compromise, are fatal concessions to be avoided at all costs. Given these fears and attitudes, we can readily see why the aggressive person has taken the course of the active and independent strategy. Only through self-sufficiency and decisive action can he forestall the dangers of the environment and achieve the bounties of life.

The aggressive act serves more than the function of counteracting hostility for the active-independent. He is driven to aggress by a desire to dominate and humiliate others, to wreak vengeance upon those who have mistreated him. Not only does he covet possessions and powers but he gains special pleasure in taking from others. What he can plagiarize, swindle and extort are fruits far sweeter than those he can earn through honest labor. And once having drained what he can from one source, he turns to others to exploit and then cast aside.

Perception of Hostile Intentions.   In the active-independent there is an everpresent undertone of anger and resentment. There is a persistent suspicion that others are devious and hostile. Because of the enduring nature of these moods and expectancies, the aggressive personality has learned to distort the incidental remarks and actions of others so that they appear to be deprecating him. He misinterprets what he sees and hears, and magnifies minor slights into major insults and slanders.

By perceiving hostility where none exists he prevents himself from recognizing the objective good will of others. Phenomenologically speaking, *his* reality is what *he* perceives, not what factually exists. Thus, his vulnerability to threat blocks him from recognizing the presence of non-threatening experiences, that is, experiences which might prove gratifying and thereby change the course of his outlook and attitudes. Moreover, these distortions aggravate his misfortunes by creating, through mood and anticipation, fictitious dangers which duplicate the past. Rather than avoiding anguish, his hypersensitivity uncovers dangers where, in fact, they do not exist. In effect, then, his moods and defensive strategies create dangers through his own actions, dangers from which he cannot escape since they derive from within himself.

Demeaning of Affection and Cooperative Behavior.   The aggressive personality is suspicious of sentimentality, tenderness and social cooperativeness. He lacks sympathy for the weak and oppressed, and displays contempt toward those who express compassion for the underdog.

By denying tender feelings, the active-independent protects himself against the memory of painful parental rejections. Furthermore, feelings of sympathy and warmth would be entirely antithetical to the militant credo he has carved out for himself as a philosophy of life. But this very attitude creates a vicious circle. By restraining positive feelings toward others and by repudiating cooperative social behaviors, he provokes others to withdraw from him. His arrogant manner intimidates them and blocks them from expressing warmth and affection. Thus, once again, through his own actions, he creates experiences which perpetuate the frosty, condemning and rejecting environment of his childhood.

Creation of Realistic Antagonisms.   The aggressive personality evokes hostility, not only as an incidental consequence of his behavior and attitude but because he often intentionally provokes others into conflict. He carries a "chip on his shoulder," seems to be spoiling for a fight and appears to enjoy tangling with others to prove his strength and to test his competencies and powers. By looking for a fight and by irrational arrogance, he has created not only a distant reserve on their part but intense and well-reasoned animosity. Now he must face real aggression, and now he has a real basis for fearing retaliation. Objective threats and resentments do exist in his environment, and the vicious circle has been perpetuated anew. His vigilant state of mobilization cannot be relaxed. He must ready himself, no longer for suspected threat and imagined hostility, but for the real thing.

TREATMENT APPROACHES

The aggressive personality is not a willing participant in therapy. The submissive, help-seeking role of patient is unappealing to these power-oriented people. When they come for therapy it is usually under the pressure of marital discord or vocational friction. They may be in a jam as a consequence of undue harshness with subordinates, as in the case of John W., or as a result of incessant quarrels with and occasional brutality toward their spouse or children. Rarely do they experience guilt or accept blame for the turmoil they cause. To them, the problem can be traced to the other fellow's stupidity, laziness and hostility. Even when they voice some measure of responsibility for their difficulties, one senses an underlying defiance, a resentment and scorn toward their "do-gooder" therapist.

Aggressive personalities challenge the therapist and seek to outwit and defeat him. They set up situations to test the therapist's skills, to catch him in an inconsistency, to arouse his ire, to belittle and humiliate him. It is no mean task for the therapist to restrain his impulse to "do battle," or to express a condemning or disapproving attitude; great effort may at times be expended to control these counterhostile and rejecting feelings. The therapist may have to remind himself periodically that his client's plight was not of his own doing, that he was the unfortunate recipient of a harsh and unkind upbringing and that only by a respectful and sympathetic approach can he ever be helped to get back on the right track.

To accomplish this goal the therapist must be ready to see things from the patient's point of view, he must convey a sense of trust, a feeling of sharing and alliance. It is imperative, however, that this building of rapport not be interpreted by the patient as a sign of the therapist's capitulation, of his having been intimidated by bluff and arrogance. He must maintain a balance of professional firmness and authority, mixed with understanding and a tolerance of the patient's less attractive traits. By building an image of a kind yet strong authority figure for himself, the therapist may guide the patient to change his expectancies. In his quiet manner and his thoughtful comments, the therapist may serve as a model of power, restraint and kindness, a model he desires to have his client learn to emulate. Hopefully, by this process, the patient may begin to develop more wholesome attitudes toward others, and be led to direct his energies into more constructive channels than he has in the past.

COMPULSIVE PERSONALITY: PASSIVE-AMBIVALENT PATTERN

Ambivalence is conflict, an opposition between contrary tendencies. In his conflict, the passive-ambivalent, or what has been termed the compulsive personality, represents an unresolved mixture of feeling and behaviors seen in several of the other patterns previously discussed. He is like the active-independent in that he possesses a strong, although unconscious, desire to assert himself and act autonomously of regulations imposed by others. Yet, at the same time, he consciously submits to others and submerges his individuality, not unlike the passive-dependent. To secure the support and comforts which others provide, he rigidly controls his impulses toward independence. Aggressive tendencies remain unconscious, and to the outside world he often looks like the inadequate personality.

To assure that his aggressive impulses do not break through, the passive-ambivalent becomes overconforming and oversubmissive. In fact, in another classification system (Millon, 1969), these individuals are referred to as "conforming personalities." The passive-ambivalent overorganizes and over-regulates his life in an effort to bind his unconscious oppositional urges. Moreover, he not only accepts societal rules and customs but vigorously defends them. He becomes moralistic, legalistic and righteous.

Certainly, morals and ethics are requisites to the civilized life, but the compulsive is so inflexible in his pursuit of them that one begins to wonder if he "protests too much." His insistence that life be systematized and regulated, whether appropriate or not, becomes a caricature of the virtues of order and propriety.

All these behaviors and attitudes are necessary to the passive-ambivalent's aim of controlling the antagonisms which lie beneath the surface (Rosenwald, 1972). He must cling grimly to the prescriptions and rules of society. They are his protection against himself. He does not deviate from an absolute adherence to these injunctions lest his impulses burst out of control, and he expose to others and himself what he "really" feels.

In the following case we can trace the development and clinical features of this common personality type.

CASE 12–3

Wayne B., Age 40, College Dean, Married, No Children

Wayne was advised to seek assistance from a therapist following several months of relatively sleepless nights and a growing immobility and indecisiveness at his job. When first seen, he reported feelings of extreme self-doubt and guilt and prolonged periods of tension and diffuse anxiety. It was established early in therapy that he always had experienced these symptoms. They were now merely more pronounced than before.

The precipitant for this sudden increase in discomfort was a forthcoming change in his academic post. New administrative officers had assumed authority at the college, and he was asked to resign his deanship to return to regular departmental instruction.

In the early sessions, Wayne spoke largely of his fear of facing classroom students again, wondered if he could organize his material well, and doubted that he could keep classes disciplined and interested in his lectures. It was his preoccupation with these matters that he believed was preventing him from concentrating and completing his present responsibilities.

At no time did Wayne express anger toward the new college officials for the "demotion" he was asked to accept. He repeatedly voiced his "complete confidence" in the "rationality of their decision." Yet, when face-to-face with them, he observed that he stuttered and was extremely tremulous.

Wayne was the second of two sons, younger than his brother by three years. His father was a successful engineer, and his mother a high school teacher. Both were "efficient, orderly and strict" parents. Life at home was "extremely well planned," with "daily and weekly schedules of responsibility posted" and "vacations arranged a year or two in advance." Nothing apparently was left to chance. Both boys were provided with the basic comforts of life, enjoyed the rewards of a well-run household, but knew exactly what was expected of them, and knew that their parents would be punitive and unyielding if they failed to adhere to these expectations.

CASE 12–3
Continued

Wayne perceived his brother as the more preferred and dominant child in the family. He felt that his brother "got away with things," was a "show-off" and knew how to "get around his mother." Begrudgingly, Wayne admitted that his brother may have been a brighter and more attractive child. Nevertheless, he asserted that there was "not much of a difference" between them, and that he had been "cheated and overlooked by the fraud." This latter comment spilled forth from Wayne's lips much to his surprise. Obviously, he harbored intense resentments toward his brother which he desperately tried to deny throughout his life. He feared expressing hostility in childhood since "mother and father would have nothing to do with emotions and feelings at home, especially angry feelings toward one another." The only way in which Wayne could express his resentment toward his brother was by "tattling"; he would experience great pleasure when able to inform his parents about things his brother had done of which they would disapprove. Not until therapy, however, did Wayne come to recognize that these self-righteous acts were less a matter of "sticking to the rules" than of trying to "get back at him."

Wayne adopted the "good boy" image. Unable to challenge his brother either physically, intellectually or socially, he became a "paragon of virtue." By being punctilious, scrupulous, methodical and orderly, he could avoid antagonizing his perfectionistic parents, and would, at times, obtain preferred treatment from them. He obeyed their advice, took their guidance as gospel and hesitated making any decision before gaining their approval. Although he recalled "fighting" with his brother before he was six or seven, he "restrained his anger from that time on and never upset his parents again."

Peer experiences were satisfactory throughout schooling, although he was known as a rather serious and overconscientious student. With the exception of being thought of as "a sort of greasy grind," his relationships during adolescence were adequate, if not especially rewarding.

At 27, Wayne completed his doctorate in political economics, married a rather plain but "serious-minded" girl and obtained his first regular academic appointment at a small college. Two years later he moved to his present institution. His "fine work" in advising freshmen students led to his appointment as Dean of Freshmen, and eventually to that of Dean of Students, a position he has held for seven years.

Although Wayne demonstrated a talent for "keeping the rules" and for assuming his responsibilities with utmost conscientiousness, he had been accused by both students and faculty as being a "stuffed shirt," a "moralist" with no real sympathy or understanding for the young. His lack of warmth and frequent, harshly punitive decisions with students were out of keeping with the new administration's policies and led to the request that he step down.

CLINICAL PICTURE

One is often struck by the grim and cheerless character of the passive-ambivalent. Posture and movement reflect an underlying tightness, a tense control of emotions kept well in check.

Socially, they are viewed by others as industrious and efficient, though lacking in flexibility and spontaneity. They appear stubborn, stingy, possessive, uncreative and unimaginative. They tend to procrastinate, seem indecisive and are easily upset by the unfamiliar or by deviations from routines to which they have become accustomed.

Compulsive personalities seem most content with their "nose to the grindstone," working diligently with activities that require being tidy and meticulous. Some people perceive this as a sign of being orderly and methodical; others judge them as small-minded. They are especially concerned with matters of organization, and tend to be rigid about rules and procedures. This often leads to the view that they are perfectionistic and legalistic.

Figure 12–3 Humorous portrayal of conforming personality. (Drawing by Farris; ©1972 The
New Yorker Magazine, Inc.)

*"I practiced what you preached, Reverend,
and thank you very much."*

The interpersonal behavior of passive-ambivalents may be characterized
as polite and formal. They appear to view and relate to others primarily
in terms of rank and status. Although often ingratiating with their superiors, they are quite autocratic when dealing with subordinates. This
deprecatory attitude usually is hidden behind rules, regulations and
legalities. Thus, they attempt to justify their aggressive intent by leaning
on some authority higher than themselves.

The passive-ambivalent takes great pains not to recognize contradictions
between his unconscious impulses and his overt behaviors. He protects
himself from recognizing this disparity by avoiding self-exploration. As
a consequence, he exhibits little or no insight with regard to his motives
and feelings. Thus, despite his high intelligence, Wayne B. had no conscious awareness of the obvious source of his recent difficulties.

The compulsive individual is a good "organization man" and typifies
what has been termed the "bureaucratic personality." His self-image is
that of a conscientious, selfless, loyal, dependable, prudent and responsible person. Not only does he "willingly" accept the expectations and
beliefs of institutional authorities but he believes that their coercive
demands and expectations are for the "greatest good." His vigorous
defense of institutional authority often brings him commendation and
support, rewards which serve to reinforce his inclination toward obedience, autocratic behavior and self-righteousness.

The compulsive personality bases his reactions to others, then, according
to the conventional values and customs of his group, claiming to make
no "personal" judgments in his appraisal of others. What he fails to
recognize, however, is that he judges others in accordance with rules that
he himself unconsciously detests. It is as if he must impose harsh criteria

upon others to convince *himself* that these rules can be adhered to. If he restrains the rebellious impulses of others, perhaps he can have confidence in being able to restrain his own.

Although appearing on the surface to be deliberate and well-poised, the passive-ambivalent sits atop an internal powder keg. He is beset by intense conflicts, an inner turmoil that threatens to upset the delicate balance he has so carefully wrought throughout his life. He must preserve that balance and protect himself against the intrusion into awareness and behavior of explosive contrary impulses and feelings. He must avoid events which might unleash these forces and cause him to lose favor with those in authority. Having opted for a strategy in which reinforcement is to be gained from those in power, he must, at all costs, prevent losing this primary source of reward and protection.

To accomplish this, he must take no risks, and operate with absolute certainty that no unanticipated event upsets his equilibrium. This avoidance of external disruptions is difficult enough. But his greatest task is to control his own emotions, that is, to submerge the impulses that surge from within and from which he cannot escape.

DEVELOPMENTAL BACKGROUND

The four features we would abstract from the foregoing as characterizing the conforming personality are: *restrained affectivity* (emotionally controlled; grim and cheerless), *cognitive constriction* (narrow-minded; overly methodical and pedantic in thinking), *conscientious self-image* (practical, prudent and moralistic) and *interpersonal respectfulness* (ingratiating with superiors; formal and legalistic with subordinates). Let us trace some of the roots of these and other traits of the passive-ambivalent pattern.

BIOLOGICAL INFLUENCES

There is little evidence to suggest that biogenic influences contribute in any distinctive manner to the development of the compulsive personality. Stated differently, a wide variety of overt physical traits, infantile reaction patterns and so on may be found among passive-ambivalents; no biological features are especially discriminable or highly correlated with this style of life.

SOCIAL LEARNING HISTORY

Parental Overcontrol by Contingent Punishment. The notion of overcontrol as a concept of child rearing may best be understood by comparing it to other rearing practices. Let us contrast it to practices associated with several of the pathological patterns that were previously described.

It differs from "overprotection" in that it stems from an attitude of parental firmness and repressiveness. Overprotection, as seen in the passive-dependent pattern, usually reflects a gentle and loving parental concern. Overcontrolling parents, in contrast, may be "caring," but display this concern with the attitude of "keeping the child in line," of preventing him from causing trouble not only for himself but for them. Thus, overcontrolling parents, as illustrated in the case of Wayne B., frequently are punitive in response to transgressions whereas overprotective parents restrain the child more gently, with love, and not with anger and threat.

Overcontrol is similar in certain respects to the techniques of parental hostility, a training process more typical of the history of the active-in-dependent pattern. But there is an important distinction here, as well. The hostile parent is punitive *regardless* of the child's behavior, whereas the overcontrolling parent is punitive *only if* the child misbehaves. Thus, Wayne's parents expected him to live up to their expectations, and con-demned him only if he failed to achieve the standards they imposed. We may speak of overcontrol as a method of contingent punishment, that is, punishment is selective, occurring only under clearly defined conditions.

The major learning experiences of the passive-ambivalent may be sum-marized as follows.

First, the child learns instrumentally to avoid punishment by agreeing to parental demands and strictures. He has been "shaped" by fear and in-timidation to be obedient and to conform to the expectations and stand-ards set down by his elders.

Second, the child learns vicariously and by imitation. He models himself after the parental image. He incorporates "whole hog" the rules and inhibitions which characterize his parents' behaviors. Moreover, he learns to make a virtue of necessity; he becomes proud and self-satisfied in being a "good" and "proper" young man. This enables him not only to master his fear of parental rejection but to gain their approval and com-mendation. Adoption of the parental model has its seamy side, however. Along with their air of adult propriety, he incorporates his parents' strictness and punitive attitudes. He learns to place himself in a role par-allel to theirs, and becomes a stern, intolerant and self-righteous tyrant who condemns the "immaturity and irresponsibility" of others.

The third characteristic of the passive-ambivalent's learning is its insuf-ficiency, its narrow range of competencies and its inadequacies for dealing with novel and unforeseen events. Thus, the compulsive person-ality not only is fearful of violating rules but lacks the wherewithal to chance the unknown. His behavioral rigidity is partly a matter of in-strumental choice and partly a matter of having no alternatives.

Guilt and Responsibility Training.   Another feature found commonly in the developmental history of the compulsive personality is his exposure to conditions which teach him a deep sense of responsibility to others, and a feeling of guilt when these responsibilities have not been met. These youngsters often are "moralized" to inhibit their natural inclina-tions toward frivolous play and impulse gratification. They are im-pressed by the shameful and irresponsible nature of such activities, and are warned against the "terrifying" consequences of mischief and sin.

The driving force behind the behavior of the compulsive personality is his intense fear of disapproval and his concern that his action will be frowned upon and punished. This fear can well be understood given his history of exposure to perfectionistic and condemnatory parents. One would think, however, that by "toeing the line" and by behaving prop-erly and correctly at all times, he could put this concern aside and be relaxed and untroubled. But this does not prove to be the case since lurking behind his facade of submissiveness and propriety are deeply re-pressed and intense urges toward self-assertion and rebellion. It is the presence of these internal contrary impulses which causes him concern. It is the everpresent threat that these impulses will break into the open that serves as the basis for his fear of disapproval.

The passive-ambivalent is extraordinarily careful to pay proper respect to authorities; he is not only polite and orderly but also ingratiating. He takes great pains to display his loyalty to those in power. His conduct is beyond reproach, ever punctual and meticulous in fulfilling the duties and obligations expected of him.

Learned Emotional and Behavioral Rigidity.   The problems faced by the compulsive personality cannot be resolved by conformity alone. Regardless of the success with which he complies with the demands and expectations of others, he continues to experience contrary inner impulses which remain a constant source of threat to the facade he presents. He must restrain these hostile urges for fear they will upset the security he has achieved. He cannot give up his dependence on others for he recognizes full well that he is totally inadequate without them. In short, he cannot give up his attachment to stronger authorities since he possesses no personal identity, and lacks the courage and means to act with initiative on his own.

The passive-ambivalent dreads making mistakes and fears taking risks lest these provoke disapproval and punishment. As a defensive maneuver, he restricts himself to those situations with which he is familiar, and to those actions he feels confident will be approved. He operates within narrow boundaries and confines himself to the repetition of the familiar. He rarely allows himself to wander or to look at things with a different perception than he has in the past.

The compulsive personality is single minded, has sharply defined interests and can stick to "the facts" without distraction or deviation. To avoid the ambiguity of the unknown, that is, the potentially dangerous, he maintains a tight, well-structured orientation toward life. He holds fast to the "tried and true" and keeps his nose to familiar grindstones.

By the time the passive-ambivalent has reached adolescence, he has learned to incorporate the rules and regulations of his elders. Thus, even if he could "get away with it," even if he could be certain that no external power would judge him severely, he now has a merciless internal "conscience," a ruthless and inescapable inner gauge that serves to evaluate and intimidate him, one that intrudes at all times to make him doubt and hesitate before acting. These inner controls hinder him from new and more venturesome actions, and thereby perpetuate the bonds and constraints of the past.

TREATMENT APPROACHES

The passive-ambivalent often seeks therapy as a result of psychophysiological discomforts. These persons are frequently beset with psychosomatic difficulties since they have been unable to discharge their internal tensions; repressed impulses churn away within them, giving rise to numerous physical ailments.

Among the other reasons these personalities seek therapy are severe attacks of anxiety, and periodic spells of immobilization, sexual impotence or excessive fatigue. Symptoms such as these threaten the passive-ambivalent's facade of efficiency and dedicated responsibility. They prefer, however, to view these symptoms as the product of an isolated physical "disease," failing to recognize, to the slightest degree, that they represent the outcroppings of internal ambivalence and repressed resentments.

The compulsive is likely to regard therapy as an encroachment upon his defensive armor. He seeks to relieve his symptoms but at the same time seeks desperately to prevent self-exploration and self-awareness. The patient's defensiveness in this matter must be honored by the therapist; probing and insight should proceed no faster than he can tolerate. Only gradually, and after building trust and self-confidence, may the therapist begin to bring to the open the patient's anger and hostile impulses.

As is evident from the foregoing, therapy is a major vehicle for treating these patients. Several psychopharmacological tranquilizing agents may prove beneficial in alleviating periods of marked anxiety. These should be kept to a minimum, however, lest they cause the patient to feel a decrement in efficiency and coping alertness.

Quite useful also are behavioral modification techniques designed to desensitize the patient to previously discomforting or anxiety-provoking situations. To rework the foundations of their strategy may require long-term therapy; however, personality change in these patterns is a slow and often fruitless process. Passive-ambivalents are not especially amenable to group therapy. Either they ally themselves too readily with the therapist, refusing to participate wholeheartedly as patients, or experience extreme threat and anxiety if forced to relinquish their defenses under the cross-examination of their fellow patients.

NEGATIVISTIC PERSONALITY: ACTIVE-AMBIVALENT PATTERN

The active-ambivalent pattern is perhaps the most frequent of the milder forms of pathological personality. It arises in large measure as a consequence of inconsistency in parental attitudes and training methods, a feature of experience that is not uncommon in our complex and everchanging society. What distinguishes life for the active-ambivalent child is the fact that he is subject to appreciably more than his share of contradictory parental attitudes and behaviors. His erraticism and vacillation, his tendency to shift capriciously from one mood to another, may be viewed as mirroring the varied and inconsistent reinforcements to which he was exposed.

The overt picture of the active-ambivalent is strikingly dissimilar from that of the passive-ambivalent. Both share intense and deeply rooted conflicts about themselves and others, but the passive-ambivalent vigorously suppresses his ambivalence, and appears, as a consequence, to be self-assured and single minded in purpose. In contrast, the active-ambivalent fails either to submerge or to otherwise resolve his conflicts. As a consequence, his ambivalence and indecisiveness intrude constantly into the stream of everyday life. He cannot decide whether to seek reinforcements from others or from himself, whether to be dependent or independent or whether to take the initiative or sit idly by. He vacillates, then, like the proverbial donkey, first moving one way, and then the other, never quite reaching either bale of hay.

There are two diagnostic syndromes in the DSM-II that relate to the principal clinical features of the active-ambivalent pattern: the *explosive personality* and the *passive-aggressive personality*. The characteristics described under these separate labels represent, we believe, the same basic coping pattern, and should be combined, therefore, into one syndrome. Excerpts from the DSM-II are quoted below; the first paragraph describes the "explosive" type, and the second that of the "passive-aggressive." Together, they provide a brief portrait of the typical behavior of the active-ambivalent pattern as we have conceived it.

This behavior pattern is characterized by gross outbursts of rage or of verbal and physical aggressiveness. Such outbursts are strikingly different from the patient's usual behavior, and he may be regretful and repentant for them. These patients are generally considered excitable, aggressive and over-responsive to environmental pressures. It is the intensity of the outbursts and the individual's inability to control them which distinguishes this group.

The aggressiveness may be expressed passively, for example by obstructionism, pouting, procrastination, intentional inefficiency or stubbornness. This behavior commonly reflects hostility which the individual feels he dare not express openly. Often the behavior is one expression of the patient's resentment at failing to find gratification in a relationship with an individual or institution upon which he is overdependent.

As we perceive it, the active-ambivalent displays an everyday "passive-aggressive" style, punctuated periodically by "explosive" outbursts for which he is subsequently regretful and repentant (Small et al., 1970).

We shall refer to the active-ambivalent pattern as the negativistic personality since it is their general contrariness, their resistance to doing things which others wish or expect of them, their grumbling and sulky, unaccommodating and fault-finding pessimism that best characterize these people. Negativists dampen everyone's spirits; they tend to be sullen malcontents, "sourpusses" and perennial complainers, whose very presence demoralizes and obstructs the efforts and joys of others.

The following case illustrates some of these features and their historical development.

For many years Ann had periodic "spells" of fatigue, backaches and a variety of discomforting gastrointestinal ailments. These recurred recently and, as in the past, no physical basis for her complaints could be established. In his interviews with her, Ann's physician concluded that there was sufficient evidence in her background to justify recommending psychiatric evaluation.

In his report, her physician commented that Ann had withdrawn from her husband sexually, implored him to seek a new job in another community despite the fact that he was content and successful in his present position, disliked the neighborhood in which they lived and had become increasingly alienated from their friends in past months. He noted the fact that a similar sequence of events had occurred twice previously, resulting in her husband's decision to find new employment as a means of placating his wife. This time Ann's husband was "getting fed up" with her complaints, her crying, her sexual rebuffs, her anger and her inability to remain on friendly terms with people. He simply did not want to "pick up and move again, just to have the whole damn thing start all over."

When Ann first was seen by her therapist she appeared contrite and self-condemning; she knew that the phsycial problems she had been experiencing were psychosomatic, that she caused difficulties for her husband and that she precipitated complications with their friends. This self-deprecation did not last long. Almost immediately after placing the burden of responsibility on her own shoulders, she reversed her course, and began to complain about her husband, her children, her parents, her friends, her neighborhood and so on. Once she spilled out her hostility toward everyone and everything, she recanted, became conscience-smitten and self-accusing again.

CASE 12-4
Ann W., Age 27, Married, Three Children

The first item to which Ann referred when discussing her past was the fact that she was an unwanted child, that her parents had to marry to make her birth "legitimate." Her parents remained married, though it was a "living hell much of my life." A second girl was born two years after Ann, and a third child, this time a boy, five years thereafter. In the first two years of life, Ann was "clung to" by her mother, receiving a superabundance of mother's love and attention. "It seems as if my mother and I must have stuck together to protect ourselves from my father." Apparently, parental bickering characterized home life from the first day of their marriage. Ann's father remained antagonistic to her from the very beginning, since Ann represented for him the "cause" of his misery.

The protection and affection that Ann received from her mother in her first two years was substantially reduced with the advent of her sister's birth. Mother's attention turned to the new infant and Ann felt abandoned and vulnerable. She recalled the next several years as ones in which she tried desperately to please her mother, to distract her from her sister and recapture her affection and protection. This "worked at times." But as often as not, Ann's mother was annoyed with her for demanding more than she was able to provide.

By the time the third child appeared on the scene, parental conflicts were especially acute, and Ann was all the more demanding of support and attention as a means of assuaging her increased anxieties. It was not long thereafter that she began to hear the same comment from her mother that she had heard all too often from her father: "you're the cause of this miserable marriage." Mother would feel pangs of guilt following these outbursts, and would bend over backwards for brief periods to be kind and affectionate. But these moments of affection and love were infrequent. More common were long periods of rejection or indifference.

Ann never was sure what her mother's attitude would be toward her, nor what she could do to elicit her love and attention. Thus, at times when she attempted to be helpful, she gained her mother's appreciation and affection; at other times, when mother felt tired, distraught or preoccupied with her own problems, the same behavior would evoke hostile criticism.

Ann hated her sister "with a vengeance," but feared to express this hostility most of the time. Every now and then, as she put it, she would "let go," tease her unmercifully or physically attack her. Rather interestingly, following these assaults, Ann would "feel terrible" and be contrite, becoming nurturant and protective of her sister. She quickly recognized in therapy that her behavior with her sister paralleled that of her mother's. And, in time, Ann observed that this vacillating and ambivalent pattern served as the prototype for her relationships with most people.

Until college, Ann's peer relationships were not unusual, although she reported never having been a member of the "in group." She had her share of friends nevertheless. Ann attended an all-girls college where she frequently experienced problems in social relationships. She had a sequence of ill-fated friendships. For example, during her first two years, she had four different room-mates. Typically, Ann would become "very close" to her room-mate. After a short period, usually less than a semester, she would become disillusioned with her friend, noting faults and finding her disloyal. Eventually, Ann would become "blue," then "nasty" and hostile.

When Ann met her future husband, during the first semester of her junior year, she decided to move into a single room in her dormitory. Though not a total isolate, she rarely mingled socially with the other girls. The courtship period with her boyfriend had its trying moments. Ann was inordinately jealous of his friends, and feared that he would leave her. Quite often, she would threaten to break off the romance so as not to be hurt should it progress further. This threat served to "bring him back" to her.

Ann's marriage has mirrored many of the elements she experienced and observed in her childhood. She is submissive and affectionate, then sickly, demanding and intimidating of her husband, a pattern not unlike the one she saw her mother use to control her father. Ann's husband spent much of his energies trying to placate her, but "Ann is never content." During the six years of their marriage, she seemed satisfied only when they first moved to a new location. But these "bright periods" dimmed quickly, and the same old difficulties emerged again. This time, however, her husband would have "none of this," and refused to budge. Ann again began to experience her physical symptoms, to withdraw affection, vent anger and vacillate in her moods.

CLINICAL PICTURE

The negativistic person displays a rapid succession of moods and seems restless, unstable and erratic in his feelings. These persons are easily upset, offended by trifles and can readily be provoked into being sullen and contrary. There is a low tolerance for frustration. They seem impatient much of the time and are irritable and fidgety unless things go their way. They vacillate from being distraught and despondent, at one time, to being petty, spiteful, stubborn and contentious, another. At times they may appear enthusiastic and cheerful, but this mood is short lived. In no time, they again become disgruntled, critical and envious of others. They begrudge the good fortunes of others and are jealous, quarrelsome and easily piqued by indifference. Their emotions are "worn on their sleeves." They are excitable and impulsive and may suddenly burst into tears and guilt or anger and abuse.

The impulsive and unpredictable reactions of the negativist make it difficult for others to feel comfortable in his presence, or to establish reciprocally rewarding relationships. Although there are periods of pleasant sociability, most acquaintances of these personalities feel "on edge," waiting for them to display a sullen and hurt look or become obstinate and nasty.

The active-ambivalent can be quite articulate in describing his subjective discomfort, but rarely does he display insight into its roots. In speaking of his sensitivities and difficulties, he does not recognize that they reflect, in largest measure, his own inner conflicts.

Figure 12–4 Humorous portrayal of negativistic personality. (Drawing by Steig; ©1972 The New Yorder Magazine, Inc.)

"Your bones should break, you should get leprosy, and your stocks should drop as low as possible!"

Self-reports alternate between preoccupations with their own personal inadequacies, bodily ailments and guilt feelings, on the one hand, and resentments, frustrations and disillusionments, on the other. They voice their dismay about the sorry state of their life, their worries, their sadness, their disappointments, their "nervousness" and so on. They express a desire to be rid of distress and difficulty, but seem unable, or perhaps unwilling, to find any solution to them.

Negativists feel that the obstructiveness, pessimism and immaturity which others attribute to them reflect their "sensitivity," the pain they have suffered from persistent physical illness or the inconsiderateness that others have shown toward them. But here again, the negativist's ambivalence intrudes. Perhaps, they say, it is their own unworthiness, their own failures and their own "bad temper" which is the cause of their misery and the pain they bring to others. This struggle between feelings of guilt and resentment permeates every facet of the patient's thoughts and feelings.

Their behaviors are even more erratic than we might expect from the negativists' reinforcement history, since they have long labored under a double handicap. Not only were they deprived of external sources of consistency and control in childhood, but as a consequence of these experiences they never acquired the techniques of internal control. Unsure of what to expect from their environment, and unable themselves to impose discipline and order, these persons seem adrift in their environment, and bob erratically up and down from one mood to another.

DEVELOPMENTAL BACKGROUND

As in the discussions of earlier patterns, we will list four major characteristics that distinguish the personality type under review. Several of these have been described in the "clinical picture"; others will be developed in later sections. These characteristics have been labeled as follows: *irritable affectivity* (is moody, high-strung and quick-tempered), *cognitive ambivalence* (holds incompatible ideas and shifts erratically among them), *discontented self-image* (feels misunderstood, disillusioned, a failure) and *interpersonal vacillation* (is impatient and unpredictable with others; switches from resentment to guilt). Let us next look at several etiological factors which may have contributed to their development.

BIOLOGICAL INFLUENCES

Heredity.   Many clinical features of the negativistic personality may be observed in common among family members. No doubt, this commonality can arise entirely from the effects of learning. But equally reasonable is the thesis that the biophysical substrate for affective irritability and for a sullen, peevish and testy temperament may be transmitted by genetic mechanisms.

Erratic Infantile Reaction Pattern.   Infants whose behaviors and moods vary unpredictably may develop rather normal and stable patterns as they mature. The possibility arises, however, that a disproportionately high number of such "difficult to schedule" infants will continue to exhibit a "biologically erratic" pattern throughout their lives, thereby provoking confusion and inconsistency in parental training methods. Such "irregular" children may set into motion erratic and contradictory reactions from their parents which then serve, in circular fashion, to reinforce their initial tendency to be spasmodic and variable.

Uneven Maturation.   Children who mature in an unbalanced progression, or at an uneven rate, are more likely to evoke inconsistent reactions from their parents than normally developing children. Thus, a "very bright" but "emotionally immature" youngster may precipitate anger in response to the "childish" dimensions of his behavior, but commendation in response to the "cleverness" he displayed while behaving childishly. Such a child will be confused whether to continue or to inhibit his behavior since the reactions it prompted were contradictory. Additionally, such children may possess "mature" desires and aspirations but lack the equipment to achieve these goals; this can lead only to feelings of discontent and disappointment, features associated with the active-ambivalent pattern.

SOCIAL LEARNING HISTORY

Parental Inconsistency.   The central role of inconsistent parental attitudes and contradictory training methods in the development of the negativistic personality has been referred to repeatedly in our discussions. Although every child experiences some degree of parental inconstancy, the active-ambivalent youngster is likely to have been exposed to appreciably more than his share. His parents may have swayed from hostility and rejection, at one time, to affection and love another. This erratic pattern has probably been capricious, frequent, pronounced and lifelong.

As a consequence, the child may develop a variety of pervasive and deeply ingrained conflicts such as trust versus mistrust, competence versus doubt and initiative versus guilt and fear. His self-concept will be composed of contradictory appraisals. Every judgment he makes of himself will be matched by an opposing one. Is he good or is he bad, is he competent or is he incompetent? Every course of behavior will have its positive and its negative side. He is in a bind; he has no way of knowing which course of action on his part will bring him relief; he has not learned how to predict whether hostility or compliance will prove instrumentally more effective. He vacillates, feeling hostility, guilt, compliance, assertion and so on, shifting erratically and impulsively from one futile action to another.

Unable to predict what kinds of reactions his behavior will elicit and having learned no way of reliably anticipating whether his parents will be critical or affectionate, the negativist takes nothing for granted. He must be ready for hostility when most people would expect commendation. He may experience humiliation when most would anticipate reward. He remains eternally "on edge," in a steady state of tension and alertness. Keyed up in this manner, his emotions build up and he becomes raw to the touch, overready to react explosively and erratically to the slightest provocation.

We may summarize the effects of parental inconsistency as follows. *First,* the child learns vicariously to imitate the erratic behavior of his parents. *Second,* he fails to learn what "pays off" instrumentally; he never acquires a reliable strategy that achieves the reinforcements he seeks. *Third,* he internalizes a series of conflicting attitudes toward himself and others. For example, he does not know whether he is competent or incompetent. He is unsure whether he loves or hates those upon whom he depends. *Fourth,* unable to predict the consequences of his behaviors, he gets "tied up in emotional knots," and behaves irrationally and impulsively.

Contradictory Family Communications.   Closely akin to parental inconsistency are patterns of intrafamilial communication which transmit simultaneously incompatible messages. Such families often present a facade of cooperativeness which serves to cloak hidden resentments and antagonisms. This may be illustrated by parents who, although smiling and saying, "Yes, dear," convey through their facial expression and overly sweet tone of voice that they mean, "No, you miserable child." Overt expressions of concern and affection may be disqualified in various subtle and devious ways. A parent may verbally assert his love for the child, and thereby invite the child to demonstrate reciprocal affection, but the parent always may find some feeble excuse to rebuff the affectionate response.

These children constantly are forced into what are termed approach-avoidance conflicts. Furthermore, they never are sure what their parents really desire, and no matter what course they take, they can never be sure of getting parental approval. This latter form of entrapment has been referred to as a *double-bind*. Thus, the child may be condemned for selecting either of the two alternatives available in a given situation.

Family Schisms.   Contradictory parental behaviors often are found in "schismatic" families, that is, in families where the parents are frequently in conflict with each other. Here, there is constant bickering, and an undermining of one parent by the other through contradicting statements. A child raised in this setting not only suffers from the constant threat of family dissolution, but, in addition, often is forced to serve as a mediator to moderate tensions generated by his parents. He constantly switches sides and divides his loyalties. The different roles he must assume to placate his parents are markedly divergent. As long as his parents remain at odds, he must engage in behavior and thoughts that are irreconcilable.

This state of affairs prevents the child from identifying consistently with one parent; as a consequence, he ends up modeling himself after two intrinsically antagonistic figures, with the result that he forms opposing sets of attitudes, emotions and behaviors. As is evident, schismatic families are perfect training grounds for the development of an ambivalent pattern.

Learned Vacillating Behavior.   It would appear from first impressions that the erratic course of the active-ambivalent pattern would fail to provide the individual with reinforcements; if this were the case, we would expect these persons to quickly decompensate into severe forms of pathology. Obviously, most do not, and we are forced to inquire, then, as to what instrumental gains, supports and rewards an individual can achieve in the course of behaving in the erratic and vacillating active-ambivalent pattern.

Being "difficult," unpredictable and discontent can both produce a variety of positive reinforcements and avoid a number of negative reinforcements. It may be instructive to look at some examples, drawn from the sphere of marital life, of the ingenious, though unconscious, "games" these personalities "play."

1.   An active-ambivalent woman who cannot decide whether to "grow up" or remain a "child," explodes emotionally whenever her husband expects "too much" of her. She then expresses guilt, becomes contrite and pleads forbearance of his part. By being self-condemning, she

evokes his sympathy, restrains him from making undue demands and maneuvers him into placating rather than criticizing her.

2.   Another wife, feeling both love and hate for her husband, complains and cries bitterly about his loss of interest in her as a woman. To prove his affection for her, he suggests that they go on a "second honeymoon," that is, take a vacation without the children. To this proposal, she replies that this plan indicates that he is a foolish spendthrift, but, in the same breath, she insists that the children come along. That evening, when he makes affectionate advances to her, she abruptly turns him down, claiming that all he is interested in is sex. No matter what he does, it is wrong; she has him trapped and confused. Her ambivalence has maneuvered him, first one way, and then the other; it keeps him on his toes, always alert to avoid situations which may provoke her ire, yet never quite succeeding in doing so.

The strategy of negativism, of being discontent and unpredictable, of being both seductive and rejecting and of being demanding and then dissatisfied, is an effective instrumental weapon not only with an intimidated partner but with people in general. Switching back and forth among the roles of the martyr, the affronted, the aggrieved, the misunderstood, the contrite, the guilt-ridden, the sickly and the overworked, is a clever tactic of interpersonal behavior which gains the active-ambivalent the attention, reassurance and dependency he craves, while at the same time, it allows him to subtly vent his angers and resentments. Thus, for all the seeming ineffectuality of vacillation, it attracts affection and support, on the one hand, and provides a means of discharging the tensions of frustration and hostility, on the other. Interspersed with periods of self-deprecation and contrition, acts which relieve unconscious guilt and serve to solicit forgiveness and reassuring comments from others, this strategy proves *not* to be a total instrumental failure.

Emotional and Behavioral Undercontrol.   The active-ambivalent is noted for his lack of controls. Deprived of the necessary life conditions for acquiring self-controls, and modeling themselves after undisciplined parents, these personalities never learn to conceal their moods for long, and cannot bind or transform their emotions. Whatever inner feelings they sense, be it guilt, anger or inferiority, it rises quickly to the surface in pure and direct form.

This weakness of control would not prove troublesome if the active-ambivalent's feelings were calm and consistent, but they are not. Rooted in deep personal ambivalences, the negativist experiences an undercurrent of inner turmoil and anxiety. His equilibrium is extremely unstable. His lack of clarity as to what the future will bring gives rise to a constant state of insecurity. Moreover, the frustrations and confusions he senses within himself turn readily to anger and resentment. And guilt often comes into play as a means of curtailing this anger. In short, the negativist suffers a wide range of intense and conflicting emotions which surge to the surface because of his weak controls and self-discipline.

The inconstant "blowing hot and cold" behavior of the active-ambivalent prompts other persons into reacting in a parallel manner. By prompting these reactions he recreates the same conditions of his childhood that led to the development of his unstable behavior. People weary quickly of the unpredictable behaviors of the active-ambivalent. They are goaded into exasperation and into feelings of futility when their efforts to placate the negativist invariably meet with failure. Eventually, these persons express hostility and disaffiliation, reactions which then serve to intensify the dismay and anxiety of the negativistic personality.

Anticipation and Creation of Disappointment.   Not only does the active-ambivalent prompt real difficulties through his negativistic behaviors, but he often perceives and anticipates difficulties where none in fact exists. He has learned from past experience that "good things don't last," that the pleasant and affectionate attitudes of those from whom he seeks love will abruptly come to an end and be followed by disappointment, anger and rejection.

Rather than be embittered again, rather than allowing himself to be led down the "primrose path" and to suffer the humiliation and pain of having one's high hopes dashed, it would be better to put a halt to illusory gratifications, to the futility and heartache of short-lived pleasures. Protectively, then, he refuses to wait for others to make the turnabout. He "jumps the gun," pulls back when things are going well and thereby cuts off experiences which may have proved gratifying, had they been completed. His anticipation of being frustrated prompts him into creating a self-fulfilling prophecy. Thus, by his own hand, he defeats his own chances to experience events which may promote change and growth.

TREATMENT APPROACHES

One of the major goals of therapy is to guide the patient into recognizing the sources and character of his ambivalence, and to reinforce a more consistent approach to life. Since these patients often come for treatment in an agitated state, a first task of treatment is to calm their anxieties and guilt. Once relieved of their tensions, however, many lose their incentive to continue treatment. Motivating the patient to pursue a more substantial course of therapy may demand formidable efforts on the part of the therapist since negativistic personalities are ambivalent about dependency relationships. They may desire to be nurtured and loved by a powerful parental figure, but such submission poses a threat to their equally intense desire to assert their independence.

A seesaw struggle often develops between patient and therapist; the negativist may exhibit an ingratiating submissiveness, at one time, and a taunting and demanding attitude, the next. Similarly, he may solicit the therapist's affections, but when these are expressed in the form of verbal assurances, the patient rejects them, voicing doubt about the genuineness of the therapist's feelings. In a different vein, when the therapist points out the patient's contradictory attitudes, the patient will show great verbal appreciation but not attempt to alter his attitudes at all.

Undue environmental pressures which aggravate the patient's anxieties or increase his erratic behaviors should be removed. Intense anxieties often preoccupy the patient in the early phases of treatment; supportive therapy may usefully be employed in their relief, as may the pharmacological tranquilizing agents. If depressive features predominate, an antidepressant drug should be prescribed.

The more directive behavioral and insight-oriented techniques may be used to confront the patient with the obstructive and self-defeating character of his interpersonal relations; this approach must be handled with caution, however, lest the patient become unduly guilt ridden, depressed and suicidal. Perhaps the greatest benefit derived through these directive approaches is to stabilize the patient, to "set him straight" and put reins on his uncontrollable vacillations of mood and behavior.

Because of the deep-rooted character of his problems and the high probability that resistances will impede the effectiveness of other therapeutic procedures, it often is necessary to recommend the more extensive and prolonged techniques of therapy. A thorough reconstruction of personality may prove to be the only means of altering this deeply rooted pattern. Short of that, group therapy may prove useful in highlighting the negativist's erratic social behavior. With adequate support from fellow group members, the patient may learn a more consistent way of relating to others.

Edvard Munch—*The Shriek*.

13 NEUROTIC DISORDERS

INTRODUCTION

In this chapter we shall outline and describe what have been termed the "neurotic disorders," those dramatic, but not severely disabling, signs of personality malfunctioning which stand out sharply against the background of the patient's everyday style of personality functioning. To be consistent with our thesis that personality is the foundation for understanding all forms of pathology, we shall relate neurotic disorders to the major personality patterns described in the previous two chapters. *Disorder* syndromes should be viewed as extensions or disruptions in the patient's characteristic personality style. They are anchored to the patient's past history, and take on significance and meaning largely in that context. They contrast with the "learned behavior reactions", described in Chapter 10, which are isolated and dramatic symptoms that crop up in otherwise normal persons and which are largely unrelated to their general personality style. To clarify distinctions among the major types of abnormal syndromes described in this text, it will next be useful to differentiate more sharply than before the "symptom disorders" from both the "abnormal personality patterns" and "learned behavior reactions."

The behaviors which characterize "personality patterns" persist as permanent features of the individual's way of life and seem to have an inner momentum and autonomy of their own. They continue to exhibit themselves with or without external stimulation. In contrast, "symptom disorders" arise as a reaction to stressful external stimulation, tend to be of brief duration and disappear shortly after these conditions are removed. We have chosen the label "disorder" to signify the fact that these symptoms occur when the patient's basic personality pattern has been *upset*.

The clinical features of the personality pattern are highly complex, varied and widely generalized, with many attitudes and habits exhibited only in subtle and indirect ways. In contrast, behaviors which characterize the symptom disorders tend to be isolated and dramatic, often simplifying, accentuating and caricaturing the everyday features of the patient's personality style; they stand out in sharp relief against the background of the patient's more enduring and typical mode of functioning.

The symptoms of "learned behavior reactions" tend to be stimulus-specific, that is, linked to particular environmental events. They are isolated behaviors, largely separated from the general pattern of personality functioning and elicited only in response to a particular stimulus. Although "symptom disorders" are also prompted by external events, they are rooted *in addition* to the complex pattern of the individual's personality traits; these generalized traits intrude upon and complicate what otherwise might be a simple response to an external cause.

Learned behavior reactions tend to be durable and unvarying, displaying themselves in a uniform and consistent way each time the external stimulus appears. This is not the case with symptom disorders. The clinical picture of disorders is contaminated not only by secondary symptoms, but entirely different symptoms may emerge and become dominant over time. At any one point, several subsidiary symptoms may covary simultaneously with the dominant symptom, e.g., in "phobic" cases one may find in addition to the phobia a mixture of depressive, obsessive and other features. Moreover, the dominant symptom may subside and be replaced by previously unseen symptoms. This fluidity in the clinical picture of symptom disorders can be attributed to intrusions stemming from the patient's basic personality. As the varied elements of his habitual instrumental strategies become involved, waxing and waning over time, different symptoms may emerge and subside. Behavior reactions do not display these complications and fluidities since complicating personality processes do not intrude upon them.

Neurotic disorders occur primarily in abnormal personality patterns, since these individuals possess unusual vulnerabilities to certain objectively innocuous environmental experiences. Moreover, they have a history of established instrumental behaviors which they characteristically employ in response to these experiences. Faced with extreme stress — sufficient to upset or "disorder" their equilibrium — they are forced to apply their typical behaviors in an extreme form. What we observe, then, are "neurotic" symptoms. Although these symptoms are similar to those seen in the "learned behavior reactions," those of the latter syndrome are less a product of complicated feelings and habits than they are of narrowly circumscribed learnings.

Neurotic disorders should be seen as learned forms of instrumental behavior. More specifically, these neurotic behaviors serve instrumentally to avoid social derogation and to elicit support and sympathy from others. For example, a neurotically depressed person not only may be relieved of family responsibilities, but through his subtly aggressive symptom makes others feel guilty. He limits their freedom while eliciting concern, yet does not provoke anger. In another case, a hypochondriacal person experiences diverse somatic ailments which preclude sexual activity; he not only gains compassion and understanding, but does so without his recognizing that his behavior is a subtle form of punishing his mate. He is so successful in this maneuver that his frustration of his mate's sexual desires is viewed, not as an irritation or a sign of selfishness, but as an unfortunate consequence of his physical illness. His "plight" evokes more sympathy for him than for his mate.

Why do the symptoms of neurotic disorders take this particular, devious route? Why are hostile or otherwise socially unacceptable impulses masked and transformed so as to appear not only socially palatable but evocative of support and sympathy?

As we previously stated, a full understanding of symptom disorders requires study of the instrumental behaviors that characterize the patient's basic personality. Symptoms are but an outgrowth of deeply rooted sensitivities and learned instrumental behaviors. What events a person perceives as threatening or rewarding and what behaviors he employs in response to them depend on the reinforcement history to which he was exposed. *If we wish to uncover the reasons for the particular symptoms a patient "chooses," we must first understand the source and character of the reinforcements he seeks to achieve.* As elaborated in earlier chapters, the character of the reinforcements a patient chooses has not been a last minute decision, but reflects a long history of interwoven biogenic and social learning factors which have formed his basic personality pattern.

In analyzing the distinguishing reinforcement goals of neurotic behaviors, we are led to the following observations: neurotic patients appear especially desirous of avoiding the negative reinforcers of social disapproval and rejection. Moreover, where possible, they wish to evoke the positive reinforcers of attention, sympathy and support.

There are reasons for us to be cautious and not to overstate the correspondence between general personality traits and specific neurotic symptoms. *First,* neurotic-like symptoms, often indistinguishable from those exhibited by pathological personalities, arise in normal persons. These were discussed in Chapter 10 under the label of "learned behavior reactions." *Second,* there are endless variations in the specific experi-

Figure 13–1 Humorous portrayal of the near universality of neurotic symptoms. (Drawing by Weber; ©The New Yorker Magazine, Inc.)

"I'm just looking for somebody who's not neurotic."

ences to which different members of the same personality syndrome have been exposed. Let us compare, for example, two individuals who have been "trained" to become compulsive personalities. One may have been exposed to a mother who was chronically ill, a pattern of behavior which brought her considerable sympathy and freedom from many burdens. With this as a background factor, the person may be inclined to follow the model he observed in his mother when he is faced with undue anxiety and threat, thereby displaying hypochondriacal symptoms. A second compulsive personality may have learned to imitate a mother who expressed endless fears about all types of events and situations. In his case, there is a greater likelihood that phobic symptoms would arise in response to stressful and anxiety-laden circumstances. In short, *the specific "choice" of the neurotic symptom is not a function solely of the patient's personality pattern, but may reflect more particular and entirely incidental events of prior experience and instrumental learning.*

Let us terminate our review of the general features of neurotic syndromes, and turn our attention to the specific subvariants, both old and new.

ANXIETY DISORDERS

Among the most unpleasant yet common experiences is anxiety. Discomforting though it may be, anxiety plays a central role in the adaptive repertoire of all organisms. As a signal of danger, it mobilizes the individual's coping reaction to threat.

Anxiety is involved in all forms of abnormal behavior, either as a symptom of psychological tension or as a stimulant to adaptive coping. Because of its universality, however, we must restrict the usage of the term to conditions in which extreme apprehension and diffuse emotional tension are dominant features of the clinical picture.

In the "anxiety disorders," as we shall describe them, the utility of anxiety as an alerting signal has been destroyed. The anxious patient is unable to locate the source of his apprehension. He experiences such unbearable distress as a consequence that his coping efforts become disorganized. Thus, once anxieties are aroused, they continue to mount. Unable to identify a reason for his fearful expectations, his anxiety generalizes and attaches itself to incidental events and objects in his environment. In this way, anxiety not only is disruptive in its own right, but it plants the seeds for its own perpetuation and growth.

The DSM-II, under the label *anxiety neurosis*, provides a succinct description of the syndrome as follows:

. . . anxious over-concern extending to panic and frequently associated with somatic symptoms . . . may occur under any circumstances and is not restricted to specific situations or objects. This disorder must be distinguished from normal apprehension or fear, which occurs in realistically dangerous situations.

We have begun our discussion of the "disorders" with anxiety since most of the other symptom syndromes are instrumental maneuvers used to diminish anxiety. In the other disorders, patients utilize devious and often complicated instrumental mechanisms to maintain their psychological balance against the effects of anxiety.

CLINICAL PICTURE

The elements of which anxiety is composed are numerous, lending themselves to varied definitions and measures. Some clinicians focus on the subjective or *phenomenological* elements of the anxiety experience (reported feelings of diffuse fears and panic). Others concentrate on more objective *behavioral* signs (tremulousness, fidgeting and restless pacing). A third group attends to and defines the disorder with reference to its *biophysical* concomitants (excessive perspiration and rapid heart rate). The fourth group of clinicians prefers to represent anxiety in terms of repressed *intrapsychic* impulses that disrupt the individual's coping controls (upsurge of erotic and aggressive id instincts). Clearly, the concept of anxiety is not a single dimension that can easily be pinpointed. It will be useful, however, to describe three general forms in which anxiety is experienced. These distinctions reflect differences in the duration and intensity of the anxiety experience.

Chronic Anxiety.   This is the most common of the anxiety disorders, characterized by prolonged periods of moderately intense and widely generalized apprehension and strain. The coping behaviors of these patients are barely adequate to the challenges and impulses they must handle. Thus, they always seem on edge, unable to relax, easily startled, tense, worrisome, irritable, excessively preoccupied with fears and calamities and prone to nightmares and insomnia, have poor appetites and suffer undue fatigue and minor, but discomforting, physical ailments. Many patients learn to "adjust" to their chronic state, but their lives tend to be unnecessarily limited and impoverished, restricted by the need to curtail their activities and relationships to those few which they can manage with relative comfort.

Acute Anxiety.   Brief eruptions of extreme and uncontrollable emotion often occur in patients who suffer a chronic state of anxiety. For varied reasons, traceable to some basic personality sensitivity or coping inadequacy, the patient feels a sense of impending disaster; he feels that he is disintegrating and powerless against forces which surge from within him. These feelings often climax a period of mounting distress in which a series of objectively trivial events were viewed as devastating and crushing. At some point, the patient's fears and impulses are reactivated, breaking through his crumbling controls and resulting in a dramatic upsurge and discharge of emotions. As the attack approaches its culmination, the patient's breathing quickens, his heart races, he perspires profusely and feels faint, numb, nauseous, chilly and weak. After a brief period, lasting from a few minutes to one or two hours, the vague sense of terror and its frightening sensations subside, and the patient returns to his more characteristic level of composure.

Panic.   Here there is a sweeping disorganization and an overwhelming feeling of terror; the patient's controls completely disintegrate, and he is carried away by a rush of irrational impulse and bizarre thought, often culminating in wild sprees of chaotic behavior, violent outbursts of hostility, terrifying hallucinations, suicidal acts and so on. These transitory states of severe anxiety and decompensation terminate after a few hours, or at most after one or two days, following which the patient regains his "normal" equilibrium. Should these shattering eruptions linger or recur frequently and their bizarre behaviors and terrifying anxieties persist, it would be proper to categorize the impairment as a psychotic disorder.

The following brief sketch outlines a typical anxiety patient.

CASE 13–1

Simon B., Age 27,
Unmarried

This chronically anxious young man began to experience, for no apparent reason, a mixture of intense anger and sexual impulses each morning as he entered the elevator that took him up to his office. The upsurge of these confusing emotions added a new dimension to his general state of anxiety. Not only was Simon unable to fathom their sources, but being unable to identify them he could not counteract them; what was especially distressing about these unwarranted urges was the fear that they would provoke severe condemnation from others. Although he did not know from where these feelings arose, he did know that these surging impulses of rage and lust would destroy his tenuous personal and social stability. Simon's anxiety was compounded then by the very real consequences he could anticipate should these impulses find expression.

In the chronic anxious state, bizarre thoughts and emotions churn close to the surface, but manage to be kept under control. If these feelings overpower the patient's tenuous controls, we will observe either an acute or a panic attack. These attacks often exhibit a mixture of terror and fury. In the less severe acute attack, there is more terror than fury. Violent urges are partially controlled or neutralized in these eruptions. In panic, however, these unconscious impulses rise to the foreground and account for the bizarre and turbulent picture seen during these episodes.

Although there is a marked loss of control during acute and panic episodes, these eruptions often serve as a useful safety valve. By discharging otherwise hidden and pent-up feelings, the patient's tensions may subside temporarily, and he may be able to relax for a while. For a fleeting moment, he has vented emotions and engaged in acts which he dares not express in the normal course of events. Chaotic and destructive as they appear and as they basically are, these temporary "flings" serve a minor adaptive function.

Some patients instrumentally utilize their chronic moderate tensions as a source of surplus energy. These individuals may be characterized by their seeming indefatigability, their capacity to "drive" themselves tirelessly toward achievement and success. There are others, however, who draw upon their tension surplus to intrude and disrupt the lives of their friends and families; they often become persistent and troublesome social irritants. Whether and how these tensions will be exploited depend on the basic personality pattern of the patient.

PERSONALITY AND INSTRUMENTAL BEHAVIOR

As was noted before, the label "anxiety disorder" is reserved for anxiety states found in abnormal personality patterns. The term "fear reaction," described in Chapter 10, refers to similar states arising in essentially normal individuals. The primary distinction between these two impairments is that the fear reaction is stimulus-specific, anchored to an observable and circumscribed object or event whereas the anxiety disorder is unanchored, free floating and precipitated by unobservable and essentially unidentifiable memories or impulses. Thus, in abnormal personalities, minor and objectively insignificant stimulations not only reactivate past memories and emotions, but stir up and unleash a variety of associated secondary thoughts and impulses. These memory residuals of the past surge forward and become the primary stimulus that threatens the stability of the person, giving rise, then, to acute states of anxiety.

What are the *specific* causes of anxiety in abnormal personalities? To specify the source of anxiety we must look not so much to the objective conditions of reality, though these may in fact exist, as to the social learning history of the patient. The task of identifying these historical roots is a highly speculative one. The best we can do is to make intelligent guesses as to which attitudes in each of the major personality types are likely to give rise to their anxiety proneness. This we shall attempt to do in the following paragraphs.

It should be evident by now that there is no single "cause" for anxiety disorders, even in patients with similar personality patterns. Moreover, not only do anxiety sources differ from patient to patient, but different sensitivities may take precedence from time to time within a single patient. Let us proceed with this caution in mind.

1. *Asthenic personalities* (passive-detached) are characterized by their flat and colorless style. Intense emotions are rarely exhibited, and states of chronic anxiety are almost never found. Either of two diametrically opposite sets of circumstances, however, may prompt a flareup of acute anxiety or panic: excess stimulation or marked understimulation. Hence, they may "explode" when they feel encroached upon or when they sense that they are being surrounded by oppressive social demands and responsibilities. Similar anxiety-provoking consequences follow from marked understimulation. Here, the patient may experience a frightening sense of emptiness and nothingness, a state of self-nonexistence and unreality.

2. *Avoidant personalities* (active-detached) may be precipitated into anxiety in the same manner as their passive-detached counterparts. But, in addition, their social learning histories have made them hypersensitive to social humiliation. They have acquired a marked distrust of others, but lack the self-esteem to retaliate against insult and derision. When repeated deprecations occur, reactivating past humiliations and resentments, these patients cannot respond or fear responding as they would like. Their frustration and tension may mount, finally erupting into acute anxiety or panic. The following case points up a number of these elements.

This man, employed as a clerk in a large office, normally performed his work in a quiet and unobtrusive manner, keeping to himself and rarely speaking to anyone except to return a "hello" to a passing greeting. Every several weeks or so, Gerald would be found in the morning at his office to be sitting and "quaking" in a small back room, unable to calm himself or to describe why he felt as he did. Upon repeated probing, it was usually possible to trace his anxiety to some incidental slight he experienced at the hands of another employee the day before.

CASE 13-2

Gerald Y., Age 31, Unmarried

3. *Inadequate personalities* (passive-dependent) are extremely vulnerable to separation anxieties. Having placed their eggs in someone else's basket, they have exposed themselves to conditions that are ripe for chronic anxieties. They may now experience the everpresent worry that they will be forsaken, abandoned by their sole benefactor and left to their own meager devices. Another potent factor, often giving rise to an acute anxiety attack, is the anticipation and dread of new responsibilities. Their deep sense of personal inadequacy and the fear that new burdens may tax their limited competencies, thereby bringing forth disapproval and rejection from others, often precipitate a dramatic change from a

calm and relaxed state to one of marked anxiety. Some of these features are illustrated in the following case.

CASE 13-3

Joanne L., Age 22, Unmarried

Joanne was to be married shortly: she had been overprotected throughout her life and felt generally ill-equipped to assume the various roles of a housewife. Her fiancé was a strong-willed man some 20 years her senior whose wife had died several months earlier. Joanne was advised to see a therapist for premarital counseling; it was clear, however, that her presenting problem was that of an anxiety disorder.

In recent weeks Joanne was unable to sleep and woke up frightened, tense and crying. She would sit at home in her favorite chair, anxious and fretful, preoccupied with a variety of "strange" thoughts, notably that her fiancé would die before the date of their planned marriage. She noticed that her hands trembled; she felt nauseated much of the time and had heart palpitations, feelings of dizziness and irregularities in her menstrual cycle. These symptoms began about ten days after her fiancé asked her to marry him, which she quickly agreed to do on the advice of her parents.

After several sessions, Joanne began to see that her anxiety was founded on her fear of leaving the protective security of her family and her dread that she might not be able to perform her new responsibilities in accord with her fiancé's expectations. As she gained some insight into the roots of her present state, and with adequate assurances of affection and support from her fiancé, Joanne's anxieties abated.

It should be noted that anxiety in these patients often serves as a means of evoking supporting responses from others. In addition, it may become an instrumental ploy by which they can avoid the discomforting responsibilities of autonomy and independence.

4.   *Hysterical personalities* (active-dependent) are vulnerable to separation anxiety only to a slightly less extent than passive-dependents. However, the specific conditions which precipitate these feelings are quite different. Hysterical personalities promote their own separation anxieties by their tendency to seek diverse sources of support and changing sources of stimulation. They quickly get "bored" with old attachments and excitements. As a consequence, they frequently find themselves alone, stranded for extended periods with no one to lean on and nothing to be occupied with. During these "empty" times they are "at loose ends" and experience a marked restlessness and anxiety until some new excitement or attraction draws their interest. These patients experience genuine anxiety during these vacant periods, but they tend to overdramatize their distress as a means of soliciting attention and support. The use of anxiety histrionics as an instrumental tool of attention-getting is most notable in these patients.

5.   *Narcissistic personalities* (passive-independent) characteristically do not exhibit anxiety disorders. However, anxiety may be manifested for a brief period before these patients cloak or otherwise handle the expression of these feelings. The image of "weakness" conveyed in the display of this symptom is rejected by these persons. Thus, it is rarely allowed to be expressed overtly, tending to be neutralized by other symptoms.

The precipitants of anxiety in these patients usually relate to such matters as failures to manipulate and exploit others, or the growing disparity between their illusions of superiority and the facts of reality. Although they are not accustomed to inhibit emotions and impulses, their anxiety is manifested not in pure form but in an alloy of anxious hostility and resentment, as illustrated in the following brief history.

This narcissistic man was recently berated, and his work disparaged, by his employer. In previous years, discomforting events such as these were moderated by his adoring mother who assured him of the "stupidity" of others and, by contrast, his "brilliance and ability." Unfortunately, Alan's mother passed away several months prior to this work incident. Unable to replenish his self-esteem, Alan's feelings of anxiety began to mount. However, rather than admit his faults or "show" his inner tension, Alan began to criticize his boss to others in an agitated, bitter and deprecating tone.

CASE 13-4

Alan P., Age 34, Unmarried

6. *Aggressive personalities* (active-independent) may experience appreciably greater and more frequent anxiety than their passive counterparts. The dread of closeness, of being controlled, punished and condemned by others is much more intense, and events which reactivate these memories evoke strong mixtures of anxiety and hostility. Severe attacks of panic will occur if the patient feels particularly powerless or at the mercy of the hostile forces he sees about him. In contrast to the "free-floating" anxiety found in most other personality patterns, these patients quickly find an external source to which to ascribe their inner discomfort.

7. *Compulsive personalities* (passive-ambivalent), along with their active-ambivalent counterparts, are, of all pathological patterns, the most frequent candidates for anxiety disorders. First, they experience a pervasive dread of social condemnation. Every act or thought which may digress from the straight and narrow path is subject to the fear of punitive reactions from external authority. Second, this dread is compounded by their deeply repressed hostile impulses, which threaten to erupt and overwhelm their controls. Without these controls, the tenuous social facade they have struggled to maintain may be torn apart at the seams. Thus, ever concerned that they will fail to fulfill the demands of authority, and constantly on edge lest their contrary inner impulses break out of control for others to see, these patients often live in a constant state of anxiety.

8. *Negativistic personalities* (active-ambivalent) experience frequent and prolonged states of anxiety. In contrast to their passive counterparts, however, their discomfort and tension are exhibited openly and are utilized rather commonly as a means either of upsetting others or of soliciting their attention and nurture. Which of these two instrumental functions takes precedence depends on whether the dependent or the independent facet of their ambivalence comes to the foreground.

Typically, these patients color their apprehensions with depressive complaints, usually to the effect that others misunderstand them and that life has been full of disappointments. These complaints crystallize and vent their diffuse tensions and at the same time are subtle forms of expressing intense angers and resentments. Most commonly, these patients discharge their tensions in small and frequent doses, thereby decreasing the likelihood of a cumulative build up and massive outbursts. It is only when they are unable to discharge their hostile impulses or experience threatening separation, that these patients may be precipitated into a full-blown anxiety attack. Having learned to utilize anxiety as an instrument of subtle aggression or as a means of gaining attention and nurture, they often complain of anxiety for manipulative purposes, even when they do not genuinely feel it.

TREATMENT APPROACHES

Patients suffering from anxiety disorder typically seek therapy for the sole purpose of relieving their distressing symptom. Should this be the primary goal, the therapist may focus his efforts appropriately, and utilize a variety of symptomatic treatment methods. Most prominent among these are the psychopharmacological tranquilizing agents. In conjunction with these, especially where objective precipitants are present, the therapist may engage in social life changes, advising, where feasible, the changing of jobs, taking of vacations, moving and so on. In addition, the direct procedures of behavioral modification therapy are especially effective in extinguishing anxiety-producing attitudes. These techniques often achieve this goal in a relatively brief treatment course.

Should any of the aforementioned measures of symptom removal prove successful, the patient is likely to lose his incentive for further therapy. There is no reason to pursue treatment if the patient seems content, and experiences no secondary complications. However, should the patient desire to explore the "deeper" roots of his disorder, or should symptom removal efforts have failed, it may be advisable to embark on more extensive and probing therapeutic techniques. Attention is directed here not to the relief of symptoms or to teaching the patient to accept and utilize his anxiety. Rather, the task is to uncover the residuals of the past which have sensitized the patient to anxiety, and then to resolve or reconstruct these memories and feelings.

PHOBIC DISORDERS

Pathological fears were first reported in the writings of Hippocrates. Shakespeare referred to phobic reactions in *The Merchant of Venice* when he spoke of "Some, that are mad if they behold a cat." John Locke, in the early eighteenth century, speculated on their origin in his *Essays on Human Understanding*. In 1872, Westphal reported on three cases of peculiar fears of open public places. It was not until the writings of Freud, however, that the concept of phobia was presented, not as a simple although peculiar fear reaction, but as a displacement of an internal anxiety onto an external object. Phobias were seen by Freud as the outcome of unconscious transformations and symbolic externalizations of inner tensions.

CLINICAL PICTURE

Phobias are unrealistic fears, that is, they appear to be unjustified by the object or event which prompts them. For example, most people would agree on the inherent danger and appropriateness of keeping distance from a large and wild animal or from a blaze that had gotten out of control. But it is not situations like these which evoke the phobic reaction. Rather, anxiety is prompted by such innocuous events as crossing a bridge, passing a funeral home, entering an elevator and so on.

Phobias signify perhaps the simplest of all unconscious instrumental transformations. The patient does not neutralize or dilute the experience of anxiety but simply displaces it to a well-circumscribed external source. In this way he blocks from conscious awareness the real "internal" reason for its presence, and by the simple act of avoiding the substitute or phobic object prevents himself from experiencing anxiety. In ad-

Figure 13–2 Humorous portrayal of the frequent co-existence of different phobic behaviors. (Cartoon by Charles Schulz. ©1961 United Features Syndicate, Inc.)

dition to mastering discomforting inner tensions, his symptom often achieves instrumental gains such as avoiding responsibilities, gaining sympathy, controlling the lives of others, finding rationalizations for failures and so on (Smith, 1968).

Entirely incidental experiences of the past may determine the particular focus of a neurotic symptom. But simple conditioned learning is not sufficient in itself to account for the presence of phobias. Phobias arise in abnormal personalities, not in normal personalities, where conditioned fear reactions occur. In the abnormal patterns, the objects or events to which the phobic response is displaced have a "symbolic" significance, that is, the external source of fear crystallizes a range of more widely generalized anxieties that have roots in past experiences.

Among the more common forms of phobia are the following:

Acrophobia: fear of heights
Agoraphobia: fear of open places
Claustrophobia: fear of closed places
Mysophobia: fear of dirt and germs
Xenophobia: fear of strangers
Zoophobia: fear of animals

PERSONALITY AND INSTRUMENTAL BEHAVIOR

The following paragraphs survey the typical precipitants and instrumental functions of those personality patterns which have a high probability of suffering a phobic disorder. In this and subsequent sections, an attempt will be made to present these personality patterns in descending order of probability of symptom formation, e.g., in phobic disorders, as listed subsequently, passive-dependents are the most vulnerable to this symptom, active-dependents are next and so on. In this and the following sections on neurotic disorders, you will find only five personality patterns described: the two dependent patterns, the two ambivalent patterns and the active-detached pattern. These listings are based on limited observations and deductions from clinical theory (Millon, 1969), not on systematic empirical research.

1. *Inadequate personalities* (passive-dependent) develop phobic symptoms when their dependency needs are threatened or when demands are made which exceed their feelings of competence. They dread responsibility, especially that which requires self-assertion and independence. For similar reasons of dependency security, they are instrumentally motivated to transform any impulse which may provoke social rebuke.

Not only does the phobic symptom externalize anxiety and avoid threats to security, but by anchoring tensions to tangible outside sources the patient may prompt others to come to his assistance. Thus, phobias, as external threats, may be used to solicit protection. Clearly, then, the phobic instrumental maneuver can serve a variety of functions consonant with the patient's basic passive-dependent orientation.

2. *Hysterical personalities* (active-dependent) exhibit phobic symptoms somewhat less frequently than their passive counterparts. Here, feelings of emptiness, unattractiveness and aloneness or the upsurge of socially unacceptable aggressive or erotic impulses, tend to serve as the primary sources of phobic symptom formation.

These symptoms often are displayed exhibitionistically, instrumentally utilized as "dramatic" vehicles to gain attention and support from others. Active-dependents are quite open about their symptom, therefore, and try to get as much mileage out of it as they can, as is evident in the following case history.

CASE 13–5 *Charlotte B., Age 27,* *Divorced, Two Children*	**This recently divorced active-dependent woman suddenly developed panic reactions while driving alone in a car. At home, Charlotte spent her days with her mother and two children; at work, she was busily engaged with fellow employees and customers. Charlotte was "isolated," however, without needed attention and support from others, when driving herself to and from work. To avoid these anxieties, she arranged to be picked up and driven home by a man whom she "found quite attractive." Her phobia symbolized her dread of aloneness; her resolution not only enabled her to travel without anxiety, but brought her into frequent contact with an "approving" and comforting companion.**

3. *Compulsive personalities* (passive-ambivalent) develop phobias primarily as a function of three anxiety precipitants: stressful decision-making situations in which they anticipate being faulted and subjected to criticism; actual failures which they seek to rationalize or avoid facing again; and surging hostile impulses which they wish to counter, transform or externalize lest they overwhelm the patient's controls and provoke social condemnation.

In contrast to dependent personalities, these patients "hide" their phobias since their self-image would be weakened by such "foolish" and irrational symptoms. Similarly, they fear that these symptoms may provoke social ridicule and criticism. Thus, unbeknown to others, they displace their tensions onto a variety of external phobic sources. This enables them not only to deny the internal roots of their discomfort, but to make it tangible and identifiable, and thereby subject to easy control.

4.   *Avoidant personalities* (active-detached) are similar to passive-ambivalents in that their phobias tend to be private affairs. For them, the symptom does not serve as a means of evoking social attention, since they are convinced that attention will bring forth only ridicule and abuse. More commonly, it is a symbolic expression of feeling encroached upon or of being pressured by excessive stimuli and demands. Crystallized in this fashion, these patients possess an identifiable and circumscribed anxiety source which they can actively avoid. In a similar manner, phobias enable these patients to control the eruption of surging feelings of resentment and hostility which they dare not express openly. Dreading social rebuke, they must find some innocuous external source to keep their resentments in check. Through displacement and condensation, the phobic object comes to represent the true source of their anxieties and resentments. This feature of the phobic problem is illustrated in the following case.

Nelson, an avoidant personality, experienced sudden surges of anxiety whenever reference was made to the name of a major shopping center in his home town. Crowded areas made him feel insignificant and worthless, and also often stimulated frightening erotic and hostile impulses. For some unknown reason, the shopping center came to symbolize these unwanted feelings. By avoiding the shopping center or reference to its name, Nelson felt as if his fears and impulses could be kept in check.	**CASE 13–6** *Nelson C., Age 19, Unmarried*

5.   *Negativistic personalities* (active-ambivalent) tend to be more open about discharging their feelings than other neurotically disposed personalities. This ready and diffuse discharge of anxiety and emotion has its self-defeating side. By venting tensions openly and connecting them freely to any and all aspects of their life, these individuals increase the likelihood that many formerly innocuous objects and events will become anxiety-laden. Moreover, these patients instrumentally utilize their phobic symptoms to draw attention to themselves and as a tool to control and manipulate the lives of others, as portrayed in the following case.

This woman, with a history of two brief depressive episodes that required hospitalization, developed an "unreasonable" dread of entering the kitchen of her home. During a series of therapeutic sessions, it became clear that her phobia symbolized her growing feeling of incompetence as a wife, and enabled her to avoid facing her general fear of failure. Moreover, the phobia served to bring her sympathy and to punish her husband by forcing him to prepare most of the family's meals and to wash and dry the dishes, a chore he had always detested.	**CASE 13–7** *Hermione K., Age 40, Married, One Child*

CONVERSION DISORDERS

The concept of conversion disorder, in which physical symptoms serve as vehicles to discharge psychological tension, may be traced to the early Greeks. They identified a disease, termed by them *hysteria*, which represented a malady found in women, and which they attributed to abnormal movements of the uterus (hystera). A wandering uterus, they believed, could result either in the total loss of sensation in any of several body regions or in the experience of peculiar sensations and involuntary movements. The first major breakthrough in understanding this disorder came in the late nineteenth century through the work of Charcot and the subsequent clinical studies of Janet, Breuer and Freud.

Freud proposed an entirely psychological theory of hysterical symptom formation. On the basis of a few cases, he claimed that the symptom represented repressed emotions caused by a traumatic incident, which failed to be discharged at the time of the trauma. These emotions and their associated thoughts were "dammed up" because they were morally repugnant to the patient's conscience. By disconnecting them from the mainstream of consciousness, the person was spared the pain of recognizing their contrary or immoral character. However, through the operation of several intrapsychic mechanisms, these emotions could be vented in disguised form. Phobias were one outcome; here, emotional energy was detached from its original source or idea, and displaced to some innocuous external object or event. In hysteria, the energy was displaced, converted and discharged through a body symptom. The hysterical symptom, though quite obscure in its psychic significance, did convey elements of the original unacceptable thought or impulse. To Freud, it symbolically represented the repressed and forbidden idea. His work on the "dynamics" of conversion disorders, presented at the turn of the century, became the cornerstone of all of his subsequent contributions. Alternative psychological interpretations of the conversion process have been proposed from a straightforward behavioral-learning approach (Liebson, 1969).

CLINICAL PICTURE

Among the major overt symptoms of these disorders are the following (rarely is more than one evident in any patient): *loss of speech* — mutism, persistent or repetitive laryngitis or prolonged speech stammers; *muscular paralyses* — loss of voluntary control of major limbs or fingers; *tactile anesthesias* — total or partial loss of sensitivity in various external body parts; *visual or auditory defects* — total or partial loss of sight or hearing; and *motor tics* or *spasms* — eye blinks, repetitive involuntary grimaces and erratic movements or muscular or intestinal cramps. The list can be expanded endlessly since there is a tremendous number of body parts and functions which can be used as the focus of conversion displacement. The few we have noted are the most common and distinctive of these transformations. Other less frequent symptoms reflect the operation of the same instrumental processes. What is significant in these bodily ailments is the fact that there is no genuine physical basis for the symptom (Guze, 1967).

PERSONALITY AND INSTRUMENTAL BEHAVIOR

In the following paragraphs we shall by-pass extensive reference to the typical precipitants of conversion disorder. The events that trigger conversions are no different than those found in most other neurotic syndromes. These have been amply referred to in discussions of the anxiety and phobic disorders.

What does differentiate the conversion disorder from these other syndromes is the instrumental strategy the patient utilizes to cope with his distress. The discussion that follows will focus on instrumental behaviors which achieve significant reinforcers. Which reinforcers are sought and which strategies are used to attain them derive from a long history of social learning experiences that have shaped the individual's personality pattern.

1.   *Inadequate personalities* (passive-dependent) may develop conversions as an instrumental means of controlling an upsurge of forbidden impulses. However, more commonly, these symptoms serve to avoid onerous responsibilities and to recruit sympathy. By demonstrating their physical helplessness, these patients often succeed in eliciting attention and care. Conversion symptoms may also represent self-punishment in response to feelings of guilt and worthlessness. However, these patients tend not to be too harsh with themselves. As a consequence, their conversion symptoms often take the form of relatively mild sensory anesthesias such as a generalized numbness in the hands and feet. Also notable is the observation that their symptoms are often located in their limbs. This may be a means of demonstrating to others that they are "disabled" and incapable of performing even the most routine of chores.

2.   *Hysterical personalities* (active-dependent) tend to exhibit rather open and dramatic conversion symptoms. This is consistent with their basic instrumental style of attracting attention to themselves. Common symptoms among these patients are mutism and persistent laryngitis. This serves to prevent them from verbalizing hostile and erotic thoughts which might provoke social criticism. Moreover, these are extremely eye-catching symptoms, enabling the patient both to dramatize his plight and to draw total attention to his gesticulations and pantomime.

3.   *Compulsive personalities* (passive-ambivalent) succumb to conversion symptoms primarily as a means of containing the upsurge of hostile or other forbidden impulses. The conversion disorder is not an easy "choice" for these patients, since to be ill runs counter to their image of self-sufficiency. However, in contrast to phobic symptoms, which prove especially embarrassing in this regard, conversions enable the patient to assume that his illness is of physical origin. Thus, it not only allows him to achieve dependence and nurture, but it enables him to continue to believe that he is basically self-sufficient, merely an unfortunate victim of a "passing" sickness.

These patients tend to underplay their ailment, acting rather indifferent and even comfortable with it. However, because of their instrumental need to cloak the pleasure they gain in their dependency and to rigidly seal off the intense but forbidden impulses which well up within them, the symptoms they exhibit tend to be rather severe. Thus, in these personalities we often find the total immobilization of some body function, e.g., blindness, mutism or complete paralysis of both legs. These symptoms frequently represent, in addition, self-punishment for intense guilt feelings. By becoming blind or disabling their limbs, they sacrifice a part of themselves as penance for their "sinful" thoughts and urges.

4.   *Avoidant personalities* (active-detached) display a wide variety of conversion symptoms, ranging from minor tics, generalized sensory anesthesias and motor paralyses to the total loss of vision or hearing.

The loss of vision and hearing in these patients may be seen as an extension of their habitual avoidance strategy. By eliminating all forms of sensory awareness, they no longer see or hear others deriding them. Severance of body functions, by means of either sensory anesthesia or motor paralysis, may represent the displacement of depersonalization anxieties. Rather than experience a total sense of "nothingness," the patient may crystallize and contain this dreadful feeling by attaching it to one part of his body. Conversion symptoms may also reflect an instrumental act of self-repudiation. Since these patients tend to view themselves with derision and contempt, they may utilize conversion as an expression of self-rejection. By disconnecting some part of themselves, they symbolize their desire to disown their body.

The following case illustrates some of these elements.

CASE 13–8

James L., Age 19, Unmarried

This avoidant young man was seen for several years by his family physician in conjunction with periodic complaints of breathing difficulties associated with a numbness in the nasal region. Subsequent neurological examination proved negative, and he was referred on for psychiatric evaluation. The presence of an ingrained avoidant pattern was evident. The specific referring symptom of breathing difficulty remained a puzzle. Interviews revealed that James was extremely sensitive, and had frequently been taunted by his peers for his rather long and misshapen nose.

Once James began to trust his therapist, he voiced frequent derogatory remarks about his own unattractive physical appearance, particularly the humiliation he experienced when his fellow students called him "the anteater," a term of derision designed to poke fun at his long nose. The basis for his nasal anesthesia and its attendant breathing difficulties was soon apparent. The nose symbolized the source of both social and self-rejection. By conversion desensitization, he disowned it. Breathing difficulties naturally followed the failure to use his nasal musculature. But more significantly, it represented a hidden obsessive thought that he might "breathe in" ants.

After several sessions of behavior modification therapy, both conversion and obsessive symptoms receded. However, other features of his basic personality remained unmodified.

5. *Negativistic personalities* (active-ambivalent) express their feelings rather openly and directly. Thus, there is little build up of tension. What tension does occur, is rarely camouflaged. When conversion symptoms form, they tend to be fleeting and exhibited in transitory intestinal spasms, facial tics or laryngitis. These represent sporadic efforts to control intense anger and resentment, which typically give way to more overt outbursts.

Many of these patients have been "trained" to use physical ailments as instruments for manipulating others. Complaints of vague sensations of bodily pain often draw attention and create guilt in others. These behaviors, however, are difficult to distinguish from the neurotic syndrome of hypochondriasis, to which we will address our attention in a later section.

DISSOCIATION DISORDERS

Dissociation is closely linked to both phobias and conversions; in fact, they are often grouped together under the more general label of "hysteria." Despite an overlapping in the personalities who exhibit them, as well as in the underlying instrumental strategies which give rise to them, these disorders are sufficiently distinct in other regards to justify their separation. For example, in both phobias and conversions, inner tensions are displaced and discharged through a symbolic object or body part that both the patient and others are fully conscious of. In dissociation, however, the patient neither crystallizes his tensions into tangible forms nor gives evidence of being conscious of their expression. Rather, he vents his tension through transitory behavioral acts and does so in a dream-like state, that is, while completely unaware of what he is doing.

CLINICAL PICTURE

For our purposes, the varieties of dissociation may be grouped into two categories: *minor dissociations,* including relatively prolonged dream-like states, in which events are experienced as hazy or unreal, and briefer states, in which the individual seems divorced from himself and his surroundings; *major dissociations,* including cases in which there is a sweeping amnesia of the past and cases known as multiple personality, in which entirely different features of the individual's psychic make-up separate and become autonomous units of functioning.

Minor Dissociations. These include experiences of *estrangement* from self or environment (Seidman, 1970). Here the patient senses familiar objects and events as strange or foreign or views himself to be unreal or unknown (depersonalization). *Trance-like states* are akin to estrangement, but here the patient's awareness is merely dimmed; he seems to be in a "twilight" dreamworld, totally immersed in inner events and entirely oblivious of his surroundings. *Somnambulism* refers to sleepwalking, a process of carrying out acts that are consistent with concurrent dream fantasies. In these states, the individual often searches for desired objects and relationships or works out tensions and conflicts that normally are unconscious. For example, a young man wanders nocturnally to the foot of the bed of his sleeping parents, seeking comfort and security; a woman runs every so often to the basement of her home to escape a nightmare fantasy of being taunted by her neighbors; a wealthy and respected man gets fully dressed, strolls into neighboring streets looking into trashcans and then returns home to sleep. Although somnambulists are able to get to wherever they are going, their thought processes tend to be hazy and incoherent during these episodes, and they rarely recall any of the events that happened. To be included also in the minor dissociations are *frenzied states* in which sudden, brief and totally forgotten bizarre behaviors erupt in the course of otherwise normal events. In these cases the person usually acts out forbidden thoughts and emotions which previously had been repressed.

Major Dissociations. These include total amnesia in which the patient usually forgets both his past and his identity. These may occur in conjunction with a flight from one's normal environment, an event referred to as a *fugue.* Whether or not physical flight occurs, the amnesic patient has genuinely lost cognizance of his identity and the significant persons and places of his life. Most amnesic episodes terminate after several days, although a few prove to be permanent. *Multiple personalities* are extremely rare cases in which the patient's psychic make-up is reorganized into two or more separate and autonomously functioning units; the fictional characters of Doctor Jekyll and Mr. Hyde are a dramatic and simplified portrayal of the coexistence of diametrically contrasting features which often characterize the two personality units. In most cases, the patient's "normal self" is the dominant personality unit. It periodically gives way to, and is totally amnesic for, a contrasting but subsidiary unit of personality functioning. Appreciably less frequent are cases in which two equally prominent personality units alternate on a regular basis and with some frequency.

PERSONALITY AND INSTRUMENTAL BEHAVIOR

The personality patterns disposed to dissociative episodes are the same as those found in most other neurotic disorders. The theme which unifies them in this regard is their common desire to avoid social disapproval. Other personalities, both abnormal and normal, may exhibit dissociative symptoms, but the probability of such episodes in these cases is rather small. As noted earlier, our presentation will proceed in the order of the most to the least vulnerable of the five patterns in whom the disorder is most frequently exhibited.

1.   *Avoidant personalities* (active-detached) experience frequent and varied forms of dissociative phenomena. Feelings of estrangement may arise as instrumental maneuvers designed to diminish the impact of excessive stimulation or the pain of social humiliation. These symptoms may also reflect the consequences of the patient's devalued sense of self. Without an esteemed and integrated inner core to which experience can be anchored, events often seem disconnected and unreal.

Self-estrangement, termed depersonalization, may be traced to a characteristic instrumental maneuver of cognitive interference, which not only serves to disconnect normally associated events, but deprives the person of meaningful contact with his own feelings and thoughts.

Experiences of amnesia may occur as an expression of self-rejection. Forever to be oneself is not a cheerful prospect for these persons, and life may be started anew by disowning one's past identity.

Frenzied states are a common dissociative disorder in these patients; for a brief period, the patient may act out his frustrated impulses, as illustrated in the following case.

CASE 13–9

Dolores J., Age 29, Unmarried

Dolores was seen after a series of "hysterical fits" at home. She lived alone with an elderly mother, had been unemployed for several years and spent most of her days sitting by the window, staring blankly. Her mother reported that Dolores had always been a quiet girl. However, since her older brother left home some two years earlier, Dolores rarely spoke to anyone, and often hid in her room when visitors came.

Her "fits" were repeated on an average of once a week while she was hospitalized. They would begin when Dolores shouted aloud, "I don't want to, I don't want to"; she then fell on her bed, vigorously fighting an unseen assailant who, she believed, sought to rape her. As she fended off her hallucinated attacker, Dolores would begin to tear at her clothes; finally, half denuded, she submitted to his desires, enacting a rather bizarre form of masturbation. After a brief period, mixed with tears and laughter, Dolores became quiet and subdued. Conscious awareness gradually returned, with no recall of the episode.

It is only in accord with tradition that we include these frenzied dissociative states among the neurotic disorders. There is no question but that the bizarre behavior and loss of reality evident during these episodes are severe enough to merit viewing them as psychotic. Custom and perhaps the brevity of the eruption and the rapid return to former functioning are the only justifications for placing them in the neurotic categories.

2.   *Compulsive personalities* (passive-ambivalent) succumb to dissociative episodes for a variety of reasons. Experiences of estrangement stem primarily from their characteristic overcontrol of feeling. By desensitizing their emotions or withdrawing them as a part of everyday life these patients may begin to experience the world as flat and colorless, a place in which events seem mechanical, automatic and unreal.

Episodes of total amnesia may occur if the patient is otherwise unable to control intense ambivalent feelings. The coexistence of conflicting habits and emotions may be too great a strain. Not only will the eruption of hostile and erotic impulses shatter the patient's self-image of propriety, but they may provoke the severe condemnation he dreads from others. Unable to restrain these urges, he must disown his identity and in the process obliterate all past associations and memories. The following brief sketch summarizes a typical case.

This rather overcontrolled and highly tense police officer had recently become involved in an extramarital affair. After a few weeks, he began to suffer marked insomnia and unbearable guilt feelings. Unable to share his thoughts and emotions and refusing to go to confession at his church, he became increasingly disconsolate and depressed. One morning, he "forgot" who he was while driving to work, rode some 200 miles from his home town and was found three days later in a motel room, weeping and confused as to his whereabouts.

CASE 13–10

George T., Age 38, Married, Four Children

A frenzied state may be another form of discharge when tensions become unbearable. These allow the patient to vent his contrary impulses without conscious awareness.

Although rare, multiple personality disorders may be formed, enabling the patient to retain his "true" identity most of the time while gaining periodic release through his "other" self.

3. *Hysterical personalities* (active-dependent) generally lack an adequate degree of personality integration, making it difficult for them even in normal times to unify the disparate elements of their lives. At times of strain and discord, this integrative deficiency may readily result in a dissociative state.

Somnambulism, a nighttime phenomenon, is not uncommon and usually takes the form of a search for attention and stimulation, when these patients feel otherwise deprived. Daytime trance-like episodes are rather unusual, however, since these patients desire to be alert to their environment. Also rare are amnesic fugues and multiple personality formations. When they do occur, they usually represent an instrumental attempt to break out of a confining and stultifying environment. Faced with internal poverty and external boredom or constraint, they may seek the secondary gains of a more exciting and dramatic life in which they can achieve the attention and approval they crave. These elements are nicely illustrated in the following brief history.

This active-dependent woman had begun to feel "boxed in" by her suspicious husband; she suddenly disappeared from her home and was not located for several months. Brenda was found more than 1000 miles away working as a chorus girl in a run-down burlesque house, returning thereby to her vocation prior to marriage five years earlier. Although her claim that she had "blacked out" was doubted at first, further study revealed that she was totally amnesic for her life since her marriage, but recalled with great clarity her activities and relationships prior to that time.

CASE 13–11

Brenda S., Age 30, Married, No Children

4. *Inadequate personalities* (passive-dependent) may develop dream-like trance states when faced with responsibilities and obligations that surpass their feelings of competence. Through this instrumental maneuver they effectively fade out of contact with threatening realities. Amnesic episodes, however, are extremely rare since these would prompt or intensify separation anxieties.

Brief frenzied states may arise if the patient experiences an upsurge of intense hostile impulses that may threaten his dependency security. In this way, contrary feelings may be discharged without the patient knowing it and therefore without having to assume blame. These irrational acts are so uncharacteristic of the patient that they tend to be seen by others as a sign of "sickness," often eliciting thereby supporting responses.

5.   *Negativistic personalties* (active-ambivalent) are accustomed to expressing their contrary feelings rather directly, and will exhibit dissociative symptoms only if they are unduly constrained or fearful of severe retaliation. Even under these circumstances, the frequency of these disorders is rather low. Temper tantrums, which approach dissociative frenzied states in their overt appearance, are rather common. However, in these eruptions the patient does not lose conscious awareness and usually recalls the events that transpired.

OBSESSION AND COMPULSION DISORDERS

Most people find themselves overly concerned and preoccupied when facing some real and troubling problem; they experience an inability to "get their mind off it" and turn to other matters. These events are similar to obsessive experiences, but in these cases the idea the person mulls over is rather picayune, absurd or irrational, yet it intrudes with such persistence as to interfere with his normal daily functioning. Compulsions are similar to obsessions. However, here the patient cannot resist engaging in certain acts, in performing some trivial behavioral ritual which he recognizes as ridiculous, humiliating or disgusting, but which he must execute to avoid the anxiety he experiences when he fails to do it.

Both obsessions and compulsions are similar to other neurotic symptoms. Each disorder instrumentally protects the individual from recognizing the true source of his anxieties, yet allows the anxiety a measure of release without damaging his self-image or provoking social rebuke. In phobias, the inner tension is symbolized and attached to an external object; in conversions, it is displaced and expressed through some body part; in dissociative symptoms, there is a blocking or splitting off of the anxiety source; in obsessions and compulsions, tension is controlled, symbolized and periodically discharged through a series of repetitive acts or thoughts (Goodwin et al., 1969).

CLINICAL PICTURE

Since several features of the obsessive-compulsive syndrome have already been elaborated, we need only detail in more systematic fashion what has been said.

Obsessions tend to be exhibited in two forms. The first, *obsessive doubting*, represents a state of perpetual indecision in which the patient continually reevaluates a series of alternatives, rarely makes a clear-cut choice, and if he does, rescinds that choice, only to waver again. The uncertainty he feels leads him to brood about past actions and reexamine them endlessly, to believe that they were ill conceived or poorly executed, and then to undo or recheck them repeatedly, e.g., a woman lies awake, uncertain whether she turned off the gas jets on the stove, proceeds to check them, finds them closed, returns to bed, thinks she may have inadvertently put them on, doubts that she could have done so, but must go and check again. *Obsessive thoughts* are intrusive ideas which the person cannot block from consciousness. Some are mean-

Figure 13-3   Humorous portrayal
of obsessive doubting. (Drawing by
Modell; ©1972 The New Yorker
Magazine, Inc.)

"Well, Mr. Decision Maker! We're waiting."

ingless (e.g., "where did I see a chair with one leg cut off?") and are experienced without emotion, but nonetheless are so persistent and distracting as to upset even the most routine of daily activities (Salzman, 1968). Other recurrent thoughts are affect and tension-laden, pertain to forbidden aggressive impulses or to prohibited sexual desires and are experienced with shame, disgust or horror. The more desperately the patient tries to rid himself of these repugnant ideas, the more tormenting and persistent they become, e.g., a passing thought of poisoning a wayward husband becomes fixed in a wife's mind; no matter how much she seeks to distract her attention from it, the thought returns to hound her at every meal.

Compulsions are behavior sequences, usually in the form of some ritual that is recognized by the patient as absurd or irrational, but which, if not executed, will provoke anxiety. These rituals express themselves most frequently as bizarre stereotyped acts, e.g., touching one's nose with one's pinky before washing; repetition of normal acts, e.g., tying one's shoelace exactly eight times before feeling satisfied with the outcome; or insisting on cleanliness and order, e.g., being unduly concerned that ashtrays remain spotless or that one's books never be out of alphabetical sequence.

PERSONALITY AND INSTRUMENTAL BEHAVIOR

Obsessions and compulsions are instrumental acts exhibited by several abnormal personalities. In the following we will list the five most common patterns, ranging from the most to the least vulnerable.

1.   *Compulsive personalities* (passive-ambivalent) exhibit these symptoms with appreciably greater frequency than any of the other pathological patterns. In these individuals, the obsessive-compulsive symptomatology is not so much a matter of "disordered" coping as it is a deeply ingrained and learned instrumental strategy utilized throughout their lives to contain the upsurge of intense socially forbidden impulses. In essence, they have learned not only to control their contrary inclinations, but to present a front of complete conformity and propriety.

Obsessive doubting may be so ingrained that these patients reevaluate and reexamine even the most trivial decisions and acts. This excessive preoccupation with minor irrelevancies enables them to distract their attention from the real source of their anxieties. Although doubting is a habitual aspect of their daily functioning, it may become quite distinctive as a symptom if there is a sudden eruption of feelings that may "give them away." Their pretense of control is often disrupted by bizarre thoughts, usually of a hostile or erotic character. These stir up intense fears of social condemnation, which may be handled by a series of compulsive rituals, e.g., each morning, by washing his face three times and knotting his tie five times, a patient assured himself of his purity; moreover, by repeating some insignificant act in which he feels competent, he strengthened his confidence in his ability to control his impulses.

2.   *Avoidant personalities* (active-detached) develop these symptoms for various instrumental purposes. Obsessions may serve as substitute thoughts to distract these patients from reflecting on their "true" misery. Similarly, these thoughts may counter feelings of estrangement by providing ideas and events that serve to assure them that life is real. Compulsive acts accomplish similar coping aims. They "fill up" time, diverting patients from self-preoccupations. Moreover, these acts keep them in touch with real events and thereby help deter feelings of depersonalization and estrangement. Certain of these repetitive and superstitious acts may reflect attempts to cope with anticipated social derision. For example, a 30 year old active-detached patient made a complete 360 degree turn each time prior to his walking through a door. This, he felt, would change his personality, which in turn would disincline those he subsequently met from ridiculing him. These ritualistic behaviors often signify also a bizarre method of controlling socially condemned thoughts and impulses. Thus, the patient noted above put the index finger of his right hand to his lips, and then placed both hands in the back pockets of his trousers, whenever he felt the urge to shout obscenities or touch the breasts of women passers-by.

3.   *Inadequate personalities* (passive-dependent) are often preoccupied with obsessive doubts. These usually derive from feelings of inadequacy and are precipitated by situations in which they must assume independence and responsibility. Here, they weigh interminably the pros and cons of the situation, thereby postponing endlessly any change in the status quo of dependency. Obsessional thoughts and compulsive acts frequently are manifested when feelings of separation anxiety or repressed anger come to the fore. Here, the instrumental maneuver serves to counter tensions that would arise as a consequence of discharging their impulses. The symptoms displayed often take the form of "sweet" thoughts and approval-gaining acts, as illustrated in Case 13–12.

4.   *Hysterical personalities* (active-dependent) are disposed to have their thoughts and emotions rather scattered and disconnected as a function

This woman could not rid herself of the obsessive image that her husband's face was "the most beautiful in the world"; she also took great pains each night to wash, iron and prepare every item of clothing he planned to wear the next day. Upon clinical study, she revealed an intense fear that her husband might discover that she once allowed a neighbor to kiss her while he was away on an extended business trip. Her obsessive symptom enabled her to block the visualization of her neighbor's face. Her compulsive acts of caring for her husband were an attempt to "prove" her faithfulness and devotion to him.

CASE 13–12

Myrna H., Age 32, Married, One Child

of their weak personality integration. They characteristically exhibit dramatic emotional feelings over matters of minimal import and significance. Conversely, they may discuss serious topics and problems with a rather cool detachment. This ease with which feelings and thoughts can be isolated from each other is a primary factor in contributing to their obsessive symptoms. Thus, with little strain or tension, they readily disconnect an emotion from its associated content.

5. *Negativistic personalities* (active-ambivalent) tend to vent their contrary impulses rather openly. However, these feelings may be transformed into obsessions and compulsions if they are especially intense and likely to provoke either separation anxieties or severe social reproval. Obsessive thinking is a common resolution of this conflict, e.g., a normally outspoken patient was quietly obsessed with the thought that her husband's clothes were stained with lipstick and sperm. This symbolized her fear that he was having an affair and that others would discover this "fact," much to her shame. She did not dare confront him with her obsessive suspicion, dreading that he would admit it and leave her.

DEJECTION (NEUROTIC DEPRESSION) DISORDERS

Dejected patients alter their true feelings for fear that they might provoke social rejection and rebuke if openly expressed. Forbidden feelings are transformed in such ways as to recruit attention, support and nurture instead of reproval and condemnation. Although their "play for sympathy" may be seen through by some, these patients convey their sad plight with such genuineness or cleverness as to evoke compassion and concern from most.

CLINICAL PICTURE

The form in which dejection is expressed depends largely on the instrumental style and personality of the patient. Some exhibit their depressive mood with displays of dramatic gesture and pleading commentary. Others are demanding, irritable and cranky. Some verbalize their thoughts in passive, vague and abstract philosophical terms. Still others seem lonely, quiet, downhearted, solemnly morose and pessimistic. Common to all, however, is the presence of self-deprecatory comments, feelings of apathy, discouragement and hopelessness and a marked decline of personal initiative. Their actions and complaints usually evoke sympathy and support from others, but these reassurances provide only temporary relief from the prevailing mood of dejection.

All persons succumb, on occasion, to periods of gloom and self-recrimination, but these feelings and thoughts are usually prompted by

Figure 13-4   Humorous portrayal of the circular nature of dejection. (Drawing by Handelsman; ©1972 The New Yorker Magazine, Inc.)

"After all these years, you still feel guilt? You should be ashamed of yourself."

conditions of objective stress, and tend to pass as matters take a turn for the better. In contrast, dejection, as a neurotic disorder, appears either as an uncalled for and intense response of despondency to rather trivial difficulties or as an unduly prolonged period of discouragement following an objective, distressful experience.

A distinction must be made between the neurotic disorder of "dejection" to be described in this section and the psychotic disorder termed "depression" to be discussed in a later chapter. This distinction is largely a matter of degree. No sharp line can be drawn to separate what is essentially a continuum. Nevertheless, when the patient's moods and oppressive thoughts are so severe as to prevent meaningful social relationships or to foster total dependency or to be accompanied by grossly bizarre behaviors, we may justly categorize the disorder as a psychotic depression.

PERSONALITY AND INSTRUMENTAL BEHAVIOR

What instrumental aims are served by the patient's symptoms of morose hopelessness, ineffectuality and self-recrimination?

First and foremost, the moods and complaints of the dejected person summon supportive responses from others. He recruits from both family and friends reassurances of his lovability and value to them, and gains assurances of their faithfulness and devotion.

As with other neurotic disorders, the dejection symptom may serve also as an instrument for avoiding unwelcome responsibilities. Dejection with its attendant moods and comments is especially effective in this regard since the patient openly admits his worthlessness and demonstrates his state of helplessness for all to see.

Along similar lines, some of these patients develop their impairment as a rationalization for indecisiveness and failure. Here, their complaints are colored with subtle accusations and claims that others have not supported or cared for them, thus subtly shifting the blame elsewhere.

Overt expressions of hostility, however, are rarely exhibited by these patients, since they fear that these actions will prove offensive and lead others to reject them. As a consequence, feelings of anger and resentment may be discharged only in indirect ways. This often is done by overplaying one's helplessness and futile state. His "sorrowful plight" may not only create guilt in others, but cause them no end of discomfort as they attempt to fulfill the patient's "justified" need for attention and care. The varieties of dejection exhibited in these patients reflect the particular sensitivities and coping strategies they acquired in the past. To better grasp these distinctions we must turn to the different personality backgrounds conducive to this syndrome.

1. *Inadequate personalities* (passive-dependent) are especially susceptible to separation anxiety. Feelings of helplessness and futility readily come to the fore when they are faced either with burdensome responsibilities or the anticipation of social abandonment. The actual loss of a significant person often prompts severe dejection, if not psychotic depression.

Anticipation of abandonment may prompt these patients to admit openly their weaknesses and shortcomings as a means of gaining reassurance and support. Expressions of guilt and self-condemnation typically follow since these verbalizations often successfully deflect criticism from others, transforming their threats into reassurance and sympathy.

2. *Negativistic personalities* (active-ambivalent) display an agitated form of dejection; they characteristically vacillate between anxious futility, despair and self-deprecation on the one hand, and a bitter discontent and demanding attitude toward friends and relatives on the other (Derogatis et al., 1972). Accustomed to the direct ventilation of impulses, these patients restrain their anger and turn it inward only when they fear that its expression will result in total rejection. One senses a great struggle between acting out and curtailing resentments. They exhibit a grumbling and sour disaffection with themselves and with others. Moody complaints and an attitude of generalized pessimism pervade the air. These serve as a vehicle of tension discharge, relieving them periodically of mounting inner and outer directed hostilities.

Instrumentally, the sour moods and complaints of these patients tend to intimidate others, and enable them to gain partial retribution for past disappointments by making life miserable for others. These manipulative characteristics and their consequences are illustrated in the following case.

Anna employed a variety of complaints and intimidating maneuvers with her husband and children as a means of extracting attention and nurture from them, but she knew that these attentions were provided without genuine affection and compassion. Moreover, these expressions of support were received by her with a mixed welcome since Anna learned all too well from the past that people were inconsistent and fickle in their affectionate overtures. It was the unsureness of the durability and genuineness of support which, in large measure, gave her dejection its anxious and apprehensive coloring. This insecurity combined with Anna's restrained anger and mixed feelings of guilt to shape the restless and agitated character of her dejection.

CASE 13-13

Anna F., Age 50, Married, Two Children

---

3. *Compulsive personalities* (passive-ambivalent) exhibit a pattern of tense and anxious dejection that is similar to, but more tightly controlled than, that of their active-ambivalent counterparts. Faced with difficult decisions but unable to obtain either clear direction or approval from others, these patients experience a strong upsurge of anger and resentment toward themselves for their weakness and toward others for their

unyielding demands and their unwillingness to provide support. They are fearful, however, of exposing their personal shortcomings and hostile feelings to others. On the other hand, they have been trained well to express and feel guilt. Thus, rather than vent their resentments toward others and suffer the consequences of severe social rebuke, these patients turn their anger toward themselves. Their agitated and apprehensive dejection reflects, then, both their struggle to contain resentments and their fear that weakness will prompt derision.

4. *Hysterical personalities* (active-dependent) overplay their feelings of dejection, expressing them through rather dramatic gestures and in fashionable jargon. This contrasts to the flat and somber picture of the passive-dependent, and the tense, guilt-ridden and agitated quality seen in the ambivalents. The histrionic coloring of their mood is a natural outgrowth of their basic instrumental style of actively soliciting attention and approval.

Episodes of dejection in these patients are prompted less by a deep fear of abandonment than by a sense of inner emptiness and inactivity. It arises most often when they feel stranded between one fleeting attachment and another, or between one transitory "exciting" preoccupation and the next. At these times of noninvolvement, they sense a lack of direction and experience a fearful aloneness.

Dejection in active-dependents tends to be expressed in popular jargon. The patient philosophizes about his "existential anxiety" or the alienation that one must inevitably feel in this "age of mass society" (Maddi, 1967). Their use of fashionable terms provides them with a bridge to others. It gives them a sense of belonging during those moments when they feel most isolated from the mainstream of active social life in which they so desperately crave to be.

5. *Avoidant personalities* (active-detached) are not viewed by most theorists as being among those who display the mood of dejection. This contention reflects, no doubt, the characteristic effort of these patients to flatten their affect. For purposes of self-protection, they suppress or otherwise interfere with the experience of any and all emotions. Despite the validity of this analysis, there are times when these patients sense genuine feelings of emptiness and loneliness. Periodically, they express a vague yet hopeless yearning for the affection and approval they have been denied. Adding to this mood are the contempt these patients feel for themselves and the self-deprecation they experience for their unlovability, weakness, ineffectuality and their failure to assert themselves and stand up for their rights. Though hesitant to express this self-contempt before others, lest it invite a chorus of further derision, close inquiry or tactful probing will frequently elicit both the self-deprecatory comments and moods of dejection that we more commonly associate with other patterns.

HYPOCHONDRIACAL AND NEURASTHENIC DISORDERS

Interspersed between TV commercials for headache tablets, muscular relaxants, intestinal tonics and the like, we manage to see a few of the other forms of entertainment provided to meet the public demand. It has often been noted that more ingenuity is invested in attracting the American populace to remedies for their non-existent ailments than in

Figure 13-5   Typical coexistence of dejection and several psychophysiologic disorders. (Courtesy of Geigy Pharmaceuticals.)

filling their impoverished imaginations. There are many reasons for the vast and continuous commercial success of these nostrums. Primary among them is the need of millions of Americans to find magical elixirs and balms by which they hope, rather futilely, to counter their lack of energy and a bevy of minor physical discomforts. These perennial states of fatigue and the persistence of medically undiagnosable aches and pains signify another of the neurotic disorders, one that runs to endless expenditures for drugs and physicians and disables, in one form or another, a significant portion of our populace.

Hypochondriacal disorders, as formulated in this text, include two separate syndromes listed in the DSM-II: *hypochondriacal neurosis* and *neurasthenic neurosis*. The following excerpts summarize their principal characteristics:

[Hypochondriacal neurosis] is dominated by preoccupation with the body and with fear of presumed diseases of various organs. Although the fears are not of delusional quality as in psychotic depressions, they persist despite reassurance.

[Neurasthenic neurosis] is characterized by complaints of chronic weakness, easy fatigability, and sometimes exhaustion.

It is our belief that hypochondriacal and neurasthenic symptoms represent two facets of the same syndrome; in one, the patient complains of *specific* bodily ailments and in the other, he complains of a *general* bodily weariness. Both symptoms often covary in a single patient since they serve essentially identical instrumental functions.

CLINICAL PICTURE

The clinical features of the hypochondriacal and neurasthenic disorders are difficult to narrow down. Not only are the types of reported discomfort many and varied, but they almost inevitably combine with, complicate and blend into several other neurotic and psychophysiologic syndromes. They are given special note by the presence of prolonged periods of weariness and exhaustion, undiagnosable physical sensations, persistent insomnia, a state of diffuse irritability and reported pain in different, unconnected and changing regions of the body.

Phenomenologically, these patients experience a heaviness and a drab monotony to their lives. Despite this lethargy, they are exquisitely attuned to every facet of their normal physiology and are markedly concerned with minor changes in bodily functioning.

Many patients, despite their preoccupation and concern with aches and pains, manage to function actively and with considerable vigor in the course of everyday life. Here, we may speak of hypochondriasis without neurasthenia. Other patients, however, are easily exhausted and cannot perform simple daily tasks without feeling that they have totally drained their meager reserves. This state of perpetual weariness, unaccompanied by specific body anxieties or discomforts, may be referred to as neurasthenia without hypochondriasis.

PERSONALITY AND INSTRUMENTAL BEHAVIOR

Among the principal instrumental goals of the hypochondriacal strategy are the patient's desires to solicit attention from others and to evoke reassurances that he will be loved and cared for, despite his weaknesses

"May I please be excused? I have a tension headache."

and inadequacies. By his "illness," the patient diverts attention from the true source of his dismay, usually the lack of interest and attention shown to him by others. Thus, without complaining directly about his disappointment and resentment, he still manages to attract their interests and devotions. Moreover, these physical complaints are employed as a means of controlling others, making them feel guilty, and thereby retaliating for the disinterest and mistreatment the patient feels he has suffered (Kenyon, 1966).

In certain cases, these symptoms represent a form of self-punishment, an attack upon oneself disguised in the form of bodily ailments and exhaustion, as illustrated in the following case.

CASE 13–14

Ned R., Age 36, Married, Two Children

Ned, a passive-ambivalent personality, had recently begun to feel that his work at the office was "measurably" less than his colleagues' and that his exhaustion at the end of the day prevented him from being a "proper" father to his children. Although he voiced guilt for his failures, he was unable to face the real source of his recent distressing and depressing thoughts, the fact that he had begun to "fake" data to keep up with his associates; it was easier to tolerate weakness in his body than in his mind. Thus, he chose some symbolic physical substitute to punish himself for his guilt, "arthritic" aches in his fingers that made it increasingly difficult to write or to punch the keys of a calculator.

Not to be overlooked are such instrumental goals as avoiding responsibilities that threaten the patient's life style. Also prominent in this regard is the use of physical illness as a rationalization for inadequacies. Which of these varied coping aims are likely to be dominant in a particular patient depends on his basic personality.

As with most of the previously discussed neurotic disorders, we find the same five personality patterns to be most susceptible to hypochondriacal and neurasthenic symptoms. Let us be mindful again that these disorders are exhibited in other personalities, both normal and abnormal, but that they occur with appreciably greater probability in the five following groups.

1.   *Negativistic personalities* (active-ambivalent) often display these symptoms in conjunction with a variety of psychophysiologic disorders. These basically discontent and irritable individuals use their physical complaints as a weak disguise for hostile impulses, a veil to cloak anger and resentment. Feelings of revenge for past frustrations often lie at the root of their excessive demands for special treatment. As household tyrants, they not only create guilt in others, but control the lives of family members and cause them considerable emotional anguish and financial cost.

Most of these patients were subjected in childhood to inconsistent parental treatment. Many learned, however, that they could evoke reliable parental attention and support when they were ill or complained of illness. As a consequence, whenever they feel the need for care and nurture, they revert back to this instrumental ploy of physical complaints as a means of evoking it.

Other patients, less successful in extracting the care and sympathy they desire, learn to nurture themselves and to attend to their own bodily needs. Disillusioned by parental disinterest or inconsistency, they provide, by a hypochondriacal ministering to themselves, a consistent form of self-sympathy and self-gratification.

2.   *Inadequate personalities* (passive-dependent) have been well trained to view themselves as weak and inadequate. Overdependency and excessive parental solicitousness in childhood have taught them to protect themselves against overwork, not to exert their frail bodies and not to assume responsibilities that may strain their delicate physical equipment.

All sources of tension, be they externally precipitated or based on efforts to control forbidden inner impulses, lead to an anxious conservation of energy. Moreover, having learned that frailty and weakness elicit protective reactions from others, they allow themselves to succumb to physical exhaustion and illness as an instrumental device to ensure these desired responses.

Genuine guilt feelings may crop up when these patients recognize how thoughtless and ineffectual they have been in carrying their responsibilities. But here again, their physical state of weariness and bodily illness come to the rescue as a rationalization to exempt them from assuming their share of family chores.

3.   *Compulsive personalities* (passive-ambivalent) also utilize these symptoms to rationalize failures and inadequacies. Fearful of being condemned for their shortcomings, they maintain their self-respect and the esteem of others by ascribing their deficiencies to a "legitimate" physical illness. This instrumental maneuver not only shields them from rebuke, but often evokes praise from others for the few meager accomplishments they have achieved. How commendable they must be for their conscientious efforts and attainments in the face of their illness and exhaustion!

Passive-ambivalents frequently suffer real fatigue as a consequence of

TABLE 13-1		*Symptoms*	*Typical Instrumental Functions*
DISTINCTIVE FEATURES OF SPECIFIC NEUROTIC DISORDERS	PHOBIA	Strange and irrational fears that are recognized as absurd by the patient, but which must be avoided.	Distract self from inner sources of anxiety by displacing them to an external symbolic equivalent which can readily be avoided; deny and control forbidden impulses; solicit protection; avoid responsibilities.
	CONVERSION	Bodily symptoms which simulate organic ailments, e.g., muscular paralysis; tactile anesthesia, mutism, visual and auditory defects, tics and spasms.	Crystallize and symbolize psychic tensions by displacement to body substitute; avoid responsibilities; control impulses; self-punishment by sacrificing body function.
	DISSOCIATION	Estrangement, trance-like states, somnambulism, frenzied states, total amnesia, multiple personality.	Isolate and control ambivalent elements of a conflict; disown unacceptable feelings and memories; withdraw from environment; act out impulses.
	OBSESSION-COMPULSION	Persistent and intrusive thoughts, repetitive and irresistible stereotyped acts, self-doubts, indecisiveness, need for orderliness.	Isolate and displace anxiety-producing thoughts to innocuous substitute; distract from and counteract forbidden feelings; discharge guilt by ritualistic undoing.
	DEJECTION	Self-deprecation, feelings of futility, guilt and moroseness.	Solicit compassion; avoid responsibilities; create guilt in others; disguise expression of hostility.
	HYPOCHONDRIASIS	Undiagnosable aches and pains, persistent complaints of physical discomfort, morbid concern over health, fatigue and weakness.	Attract attention; control others; rationalize failures and inadequacies; provide self-punishment and self-nurturance.

their struggle to control their anger and resentment. Not infrequently, these ailments are a displaced and symbolic form of self-punishment, a physical substitute to vent feelings of guilt and self-reproval. Suffering not only discharges tension, then, but serves the function of expiation.

4. *Hysterical personalities* (active-dependent) utilize hypochondriacal symptoms largely as an instrument for attracting attention. It also elicits approving comments for achievements which would not be offered were the patient well. To be fussed over and showered with favors is a rewarding experience for most individuals. In the active-dependents, however, this need for approval is "like a drug" that is required to sustain them. Because they feel a sense of emptiness and isolation without it, they seek a constant diet of attention and approval. If nothing else "works," illness can be depended on as a sure means to achieve these ends. When life becomes humdrum and boring, physical ailments not only evoke interest and attention, but provide these patients with a needed source of stimulation. Bodily pains and aches are a preoccupation that can fill the empty moments.

5. *Avoidant patients* (active-detached) exhibit hypochondriacal symptoms to achieve a variety of different instrumental goals. For many it is a means of countering feelings of depersonalization. They may be overly alert to bodily sounds and movements to assure themselves that they are

"real" and alive. Not uncommonly, because of their habitual social isolation and self-preoccupation, they elaborate these bodily sensations into bizarre and delusional experiences.

Discomforting bodily sensations may be a symbolic expression of self-punishment. Thus, these symptoms often represent the disgust active-detached patients feel toward themselves.

Fatigue in these personalities may be viewed as an extension of their basic detachment strategy. It can serve as a rationalization justifying withdrawal from social contact.

TREATMENT APPROACHES

Most neurotic patients exhibit a blend of several symptoms that rise and subside over time in their clarity and prominence. This complex and changing picture is further complicated by the fact that it is set within the context of the patient's broader personality pattern of attitudes and instrumental strategies. In planning a remedial approach, the therapist is faced, then, with an inextricable mixture of symptoms that are embedded in a pattern of more diffuse and permanent traits.

Separating this complex of clinical features for therapeutic attention is no simple task. To decide which features comprise the "basic personality" and which represent the "neurotic symptomatology" cannot readily be accomplished since both are facets of the same system of vulnerabilities and strategies. Even when clear distinctions can be drawn, as when a symptom suddenly emerges in clear and sharp relief, a judgment must be made as to whether therapeutic attention should be directed to the focal symptom or to the "underlying" pattern from which it sprung. In certain cases, it is fruitful to concentrate solely on the manifest symptom disorder; in other cases, however, it may be advisable to rework the more pervasive and ingrained personality pattern.

Our interest in this chapter lies in the focal symptom, and we will now discuss some of the remedial approaches utilized in its relief. Recourse may be had to other techniques when more extensive personality changes appear appropriate.

Despite their instrumental efforts, many patients with neurotic disorders continue to experience considerable anxiety and tension. In these cases, any one of a number of biophysical tranquilizing agents may prove beneficial. In dejection, however, these drugs may have an adverse effect; it is advisable in these cases to utilize the pharmacological stimulants or antidepressants. At all times, the use of drugs should be considered with great care since they often upset the patient's own coping efforts and may result, thereby, in disturbances that are more serious than the one they were designed to alleviate. For example, dejection may serve to help the patient control his angry impulses, thereby preventing him from acting them out and experiencing serious repercussions such as separation and abandonment; by using a biophysical stimulant, hostile impulses may be released, precipitating fears of retribution and severe separation anxieties.

Behavior modification techniques are particularly promising as remedial measures for several of the neurotic disorders (Bandura, 1969; Mather, 1970; Parry-Jones et al., 1970). These therapeutic procedures are especially suited for readily identifiable symptoms which patients may be highly motivated to extinguish, such as anxiety (Paul and Shannon, 1966). Phobias and many of the obsessions and compulsions meet these basic criteria. Notable success has been reported in these syndromes with little or no deleterious consequences. Certain of the conversions (e.g., mutism, tics and some of the anesthesias and visual defects) have also been found amenable to behavior modification methods.

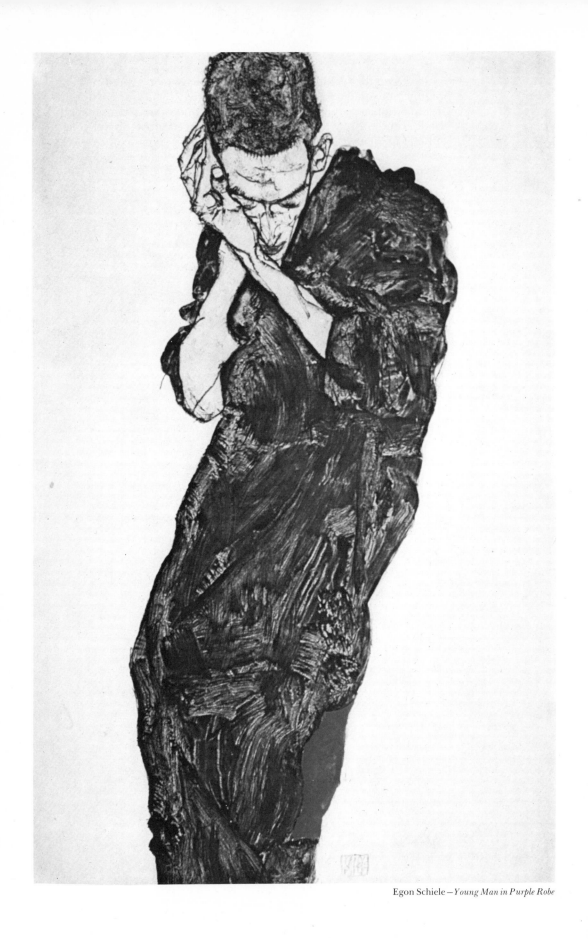

Egon Schiele — *Young Man in Purple Robe*

14 PSYCHOPHYSIOLOGIC (PSYCHOSOMATIC) DISORDERS

INTRODUCTION

It is at times of illness or under conditions of excitement and stress that we become aware of many of the bodily functions we normally take for granted. If we stop to think for a moment we will recognize that each of the several systems which comprise our biophysical make-up—cardio-vascular, gastrointestinal, respiratory, genitourinary and so on—is quietly carrying out a variety of functions requisite to organic survival.

Faced with threat, these systems are quickly activated to release and reg-ulate energies which prepare the organism to cope efficiently with danger. Most frequently, the energy and tension that build up in response to these threats are discharged in the coping process. At other times, however, these physiological energies mount and persist since the individual is unable or unwilling to vent them. For example, fear and anger precipitate, among other things, a sharp rise in blood pressure, which normally will subside if tension is expressed in the form of a rapid flight or a direct attack upon the threatening source. If fear or anger persists and tension is restrained and undischarged, a state of chronic high blood pressure may ensue, with eventual permanent tissue or organ damage.

Circumstances such as these are referred to as psychophysiologic dis-orders; the persistence of unrelieved physiological energies, precipitated initially by psychogenic agents, ultimately results in a fundamentally al-tered biological state. The central feature of these disorders, then, is the buildup of unexpressed protective physiological reactions. This upsets normal bodily balance and leads to irreversible organic diseases such as ulcer, hypertension and asthma. Thus, individuals who are subjected to persistent environmental stress or who are unable to resolve basic conflicts, may be afflicted with bodily ailments that are no less severe than many that are caused by hereditary defects and infectious agents.

Psychophysiologic and neurotic disorders display many similarities, and often coexist or covary in the same patient. Also, both sets of disorders tend to crop up in the same five pathological personality patterns. However, psychophysiologic disorders are especially prominent in the two ambivalent personality types.

Psychophysiologic symptoms tend to differ from neurotic symptoms in that they do not represent a psychological form for expressing the patient's problems. Moreover, these symptoms reflect the failure of the patient to avoid the sources of his problems and to discharge tensions generated by them. In contrast, neurotic behaviors are instruments, though indirect ones, to avoid or to dissipate the buildup of physiological tensions. The psychophysiologic patient is unable to avoid psychic distress or to vent the cumulation of psychic tensions. Thus, his physiological reactions are bottled up and churn away until they create irreversible bodily damage.

Psychophysiologic disorders are similar to anxiety disorders in that both signify failures to avoid the sources of emotional tensions. However, in anxiety, the patient is quite conscious of his tension and discharges the buildup of physiological reactions through restless hyperactivity. By contrast, the psychophysiologic patient neither experiences acute conscious apprehension nor vents his bodily tensions. He manages both to block awareness of his psychic discomfort and to suppress and somaticize his physiological reactions. In this way he remains unaware both of the psychic source of his tension and the anxieties they generate.

CLINICAL PICTURE

More than 20 psychosomatic disorders have been ascribed, at least in part, to psychological causes. Which ones are influenced substantially by emotional factors remains a matter of dispute to be decided by future research. In the following paragraphs we shall list and briefly describe the symptoms of six psychophysiologic disorders which have been subjected to numerous theoretical and research studies.

1.   The *gastrointestinal system* is a frequent locale for psychophysiologic impairment.

Particularly common are *peptic ulcers* in which the patient exhibits a crater-like lesion in the stomach or the upper part of the small intestine. Normally, a mucous lining protects the surface of these organs by blocking the corrosive effects of acid secretions that are necessary for digestion. However, should the lining be perforated or should excess secretions be produced, the patient will experience "burning" sensations, nausea and vomiting about one or two hours following meals. In these cases, the corrosive action of acids continues to dissolve the unprotected stomach and intestinal tissue. Where large open perforations are present there may be severe internal bleeding that may result in death. The following case history illustrates life history data for a typical peptic ulcer patient.*

---

*From Gregory, I.: Fundamentals of Psychiatry. 2nd edition. Philadelphia. W. B. Saunders Co., 1968, p. 383.

This man was admitted to a psychiatric hospital immediately after having been discharged from a senior executive position in a large company because of excessive drinking and unreliability in keeping appointments. Apart from a few years in military service Fred had been with this company for the preceding 25 years, had worked extremely hard, and felt personally responsible for much of the company's growth and expansion during the preceding 15 years. He had spent much time away from home traveling on company business and had worked evenings and weekends, and had not taken a vacation with his family for some years. However, Fred had come to feel that his talents and dedication were not appreciated or adequately rewarded. During the preceding five years he had perceived his future as bleak, with little or no opportunity for further advancement financially or in terms of prestige. Every morning he would feel sick over the dismal prospect of another day's exhausting demands. He would not express his feelings of frustration and resentment directly at work, but became increasingly irritable at home with his family. Fred started to drink excessively to relieve his tension and he developed peptic ulcers which were treated medically. He was given some sedative medication, but remained dependent on alcohol and became increasingly depressed, although he never reached the point of considering suicide.

Fred was born the fourth child in a family of five boys, and his father was an unsuccessful farmer whom he never respected and disliked from an early age. He felt much closer to his mother, who was nervous and physically frail, with numerous chronic bodily complaints that the family regarded as 90 per cent emotional. This hypochondriacal mother, however, dominated her husband, criticized him, and nagged her sons into striving for the success that their father had never achieved.

Poverty and small physical stature contributed to making Fred feel inferior to other children in the neighborhood, but he overcompensated for this by striving for academic distinction. In spite of having to work in a store during noon hours, after school, and on Saturdays, he remained at the top of his class in school and graduated as valedictorian. He left home soon afterward, worked in an office during the daytime, and attended night school, where he claimed to have completed four years of college work, including two years of law school, although he never obtained a degree. At the age of 24 he married, and subsequently had three children, who he hoped would all go to college. It was a bitter blow to Fred when his eldest daughter got married shortly after leaving high school. Although his work always came ahead of his family, there was little conflict between him and his wife until the last few years during which he had been resentful, depressed, irritable, and drinking excessively.

At the time Fred was admitted to hospital after losing his job he was angry, tense, tremulous, and unhappy, but he showed no evidence of organic intellectual impairment, was in good contact with reality, and his depression appeared to be of neurotic intensity. The MMPI was valid and none of the clinical scales were elevated with the exception of scale 2 (depression). For several years he had been dissatisfied with his way of life, and the loss of his job freed him from its obligations and confronted him with the necessity of reevaluating his patterns of behavior and goals in life. Fred participated actively in individual and group psychotherapy, and rapidly acquired considerable insight into developmental psychodynamics. His tension and depression diminished, his excessive smoking decreased, and he gained about seven pounds in weight. Fred was given a mild tranquilizing drug and after six weeks he left hospital much improved. There was no recurrence of his former symptoms during the next two years.

CASE 14–1

*Frederick B., Age 46,
Married, Three Children*

A similar disease, known as *colitis,* represents an inflammation of the colon (large intestine) and is typically accompanied by severe cramps and diarrhea.

2.   The *cardiovascular system* exhibits two prominent psychophysiologic disorders.

Essential hypertension consists of chronically elevated blood pressure, without organic cause, often resulting in serious circulatory and kidney ailments (Davies, 1970).

Migraine refers to repeated headaches, lasting several hours, attributable to arterial spasms; it is characterized by severe throbbing or pressure on one side of the head, and frequently is accompanied by nausea and other gastrointestinal upsets.

3.   Certain *respiratory system* disorders are attributed in part to psychogenic influences.

Bronchial asthma is characterized by episodic attacks of wheezing, panting, gasping and a terrifying feeling of imminent suffocation (Knapp, 1969). These symptoms reflect marked contractions or spasms in the bronchial muscles which cause the passages of the bronchi (lung tubes) to shrink, thereby creating a severe reduction in air intake. The background and experiences of an asthmatic woman with depressive inclinations are illustrated in the following history.*

---

*From Gregory, I.: Fundamentals of Psychiatry. 2nd edition. Philadelphia, W. B. Saunders Co., 1968, p. 380.

CASE 14–2

Leah V., Age 34, Married, Four Children

This woman was admitted to a psychiatric hospital with a history of asthmatic attacks which had been increasing in frequency and severity during the preceding twelve years, together with feelings of fatigue, insomnia, and depression which had been increasing progressively over the preceding three months. She reported that her maternal grandmother and one maternal aunt had suffered from severe asthma, and she claimed that she was allergic to several fruits and vegetables. However, she had had extensive medical investigations and sensitivity tests but no program of desensitization had ever been recommended by the physicians caring for her, and her asthmatic attacks tended to be precipitated and aggravated by emotional stress.

Leah was the eldest of eight children and her mother was pregnant with her at the time of her marriage. This probably led to unconscious resentment and partial rejection of the patient by her mother who appeared to discriminate against the patient and favor some of the younger children. She perceived no such discrimination or favoritism on the part of her father who was a conscientious man, regularly employed, and well liked by everyone. In this home, however, he was rather passive and ineffectual, whereas the mother was dominant and aggressive. Leah described her mother as being moody and "a martyr type" who was critical and demanded high standards of behavior from all members of the family. During her childhood, Leah was given a great deal of responsibility in caring for her younger siblings and during adolescence she was frequently deprived of social activities with her friends in order to help at home. The patient was never able to express anger as a child and at the age of 34 she still felt that the opinion of her parents was as important as when she was a child.

Leah obtained little sexual information from her mother but started dating about the age of 15 and had a number of boy friends. During her junior year in high school she started going steady with a boy slightly older than herself and within six months she began a pregnancy which led to a forced marriage. Her parents disapproved of her husband, who was not a Catholic, but after marriage he changed his religion and their children were raised in this faith. During the first 12 years of her marriage the patient was pregnant 11 times. Six of these pregnancies terminated in spontaneous abortions and one child died a few days after birth, so that she was left with four living children. Pregnancy was always stressful for her and her first attack of asthma occurred shortly after the birth of her second child. The attacks became more frequent and severe during subsequent pregnancies, and after 12 years of marriage she submitted to a sterilization operation which freed her from this particular source of stress. However, a couple of years prior to this Leah became aware that her husband was going out with another woman. This made her feel nervous and angry inside, but she never confronted him with the fact or expressed her anger directly. Instead she punished him by denying him sexual relations, which she had in fact feared from the time of her first spontaneous abortion. Her husband's interest in the other woman was of very brief duration, but she continued to deny him sexual relations until about two years after her sterilization operation at which time he was involved in an automobile accident and sustained a whiplash injury to his neck. He felt unable to work and began drawing regular unemployment insurance which probably prolonged his disability. In addition, Leah became more solicitous of him and went out to work to supplement the family income. When the husband's insurance payments ran out, he looked for work sporadically but remained unemployed. He visited various employment offices and was offered several jobs, but turned them down for various reasons such as poor wages, no chance for getting ahead, or simply because he did not feel he would like the work.

In this situation Leah was unable to express resentment directly to the husband, but felt obliged to continue providing for the family and became increasingly worried about their financial situation. She became tired, had difficulty in sleeping, lost interest in her usual recreations, lost her appetite and some weight, and felt miserable. At interview she was in good contact with reality, and projective tests indicated neurotic constriction of personality with some hysterical denial and evidence of depression. Leah maintained that her husband and children were wonderful and initially she denied the marital conflict already outlined. During several weeks of psychotherapy, however, she was able to verbalize freely her sources of frustration and conflict and to gain considerable insight into previously unconscious psychodynamics. She also received antidepressive medication and gained about ten pounds in weight. Her husband was seen on several occasions, and eventually found employment. Leah left hospital much improved and was felt to be somewhat less vulnerable to developing overt psychopathology than formerly.

CASE 14–2
Continued

4. The *skin* is a major system of bodily functioning, centrally involved in mediating the organism's contact with the environment. As such, it is highly reactive not only to physical stimuli but to a whole range of psychologically significant events (e.g., blushing in embarrassment or blanching in fear).

Among the more prominent psychophysiologic skin disorders is *neurodermatitis,* a chronic and nonallergenic inflammation accompanied by severe itching (Musaph, 1969).

All psychophysiologic symptoms mimic diseases that can be ascribed entirely to physical causes; thus, bronchial asthma or peptic ulcer may have its basis in hereditary defects or infectious agents. Many theorists contend that even where known psychogenic factors operate as causal agents, they merely aggravate and make manifest a latent biological vulnerability. Regardless of cause, the final clinical picture is essentially the same, making the task of differential diagnosis an extremely difficult one at best. We label these diseases as psychophysiologic when psychogenic factors are considered to play a significant role.

Let us next turn to some of the historical ideas which have shaped our understanding of the psychogenic roots of these disorders.

THEORETICAL VIEWS

The label "psychosomatic" was first applied to cases of insomnia by Heinroth in 1818. This term remains a common synonym for psychophysiologic disorders. Until the early twentieth century, however, little was known about the psychological mechanisms involved in these ailments, other than the fact that they appear to be related to emotional stress.

EARLY PSYCHOANALYTIC CONCEPTS

Current thinking about psychophysiologic disorders may be traced to two notions first formulated by Freud.

In the concept of the "actual neuroses," Freud spoke of symptoms which were a direct consequence of the "damming up" of body energies. Here he included anxieties, neurasthenia and hypochondriasis, viewing them to be the simple result of a failure to discharge physiological sexual instincts. Although the three ailments he specified as resulting from this damming up process do not correspond to our present day list of psychophysiologic disorders, the notion that they reflect a blockage of physiological tensions may clearly be traced to Freud's "actual neurosis" hypothesis.

Several of Freud's disciples utilized the symbolism which he observed among the neurotic conversion disorders as a means of explaining psychosomatic symptoms, or what they called the "organ neuroses." To them, these symptoms symbolized, through a form of "body language," the character of the patient's repressed intrapsychic conflicts. For example, Ferenczi (1926) considered diarrhea to be an aggressive form of giving to others which substituted for real performance, and Garma (1950) conceived peptic ulcers to be symbolic attacks upon the mucous lining by the patient's hostile mother. This symbolic conversion hypothesis for psychophysiologic disorders has been seriously questioned. It has been believed in the past that the visceral organs, from which these symptoms arise, may not be connected to higher cortical processes, and therefore do not lend themselves to the expression of symbolic ideas. Recent work by Miller (1969) and DiCara (1970) does suggest, however, that visceral organs can be "conditioned" psychologically. Should their work be verified and extended, it is possible that symbolic learning can take place in these organs, thereby making the psychoanalytic conversion hypothesis at least a tenable one.

DUNBAR'S PERSONALITY PROFILE THEORY

The conversion model utilized by Freud's disciples attempted to account for the "specificity" of the symptom, that is, why patients with specific types of psychological problems developed certain psychophysiologic disorders rather than others. Since it was believed that the conversion model of symbolic symptom expression was inapplicable to the visceral organs, alternate hypotheses had to be devised. This seemed necessary since many investigators had observed a correlation between particular experiences and particular somatic disorders.

The first of these alternative models was provided by Flanders Dunbar (1935). As a consequence of her exhaustive studies of psychosomatic diseases, she was led to conclude that there was a direct correspondence between *personality types* and specific psychophysiologic symptoms. For example, she proposed that ambitious and hard-driving executive personalities were especially vulnerable to coronary artery disease. Other personality profiles were found according to Dunbar to correlate specifically with migraines, peptic ulcers and so on.

Despite the plausibility and superficial validity of her thesis, subsequent evidence has indicated that there is no simple one to one correspondence between specific personality types and specific psychophysiologic disorders. Each psychosomatic symptom has been found in a variety of different personality profiles.

ALEXANDER'S CONFLICT-REGRESSION THEORY

Franz Alexander (1950, 1968) agreed with Dunbar that psychophysiologic disorders should not be conceived as symbolic conversions, but disagreed with her view that direct correlations existed between particular personality types and specific somatic diseases. Instead, Alexander proposed that each psychosomatic disorder reflected a *specific* type of *unconscious conflict* which could be found not in one but in a variety of different personality types.

Central to his thesis was the belief that a specific and different configuration of physiological reactions was activated in conjunction with each of several types of emotional states, e.g., rage was specifically associated with cardiovascular responses, dependency needs characteristically stimulated gastrointestinal activity and respiratory functions were notably involved in problems of communication. To Alexander, then, whatever correspondence existed between specific organs and specific psychological difficulties reflected neither a symbolic conversion process nor a personality style, but rather the presence of a specific emotional conflict. Since certain physiological responses correlated with these emotions, patients with particular conflicts will, according to Alexander, suffer corresponding physiological disorders.

In attempting to explain how the psychophysiologic symptom arose in particular patients, Alexander invoked the Freudian concept of "regression," stating that psychosomatic patients had experienced traumatic conflicts in childhood which were "fixated," persist and are reactivated in the present. Current threats that stir up these fixated unconscious conflicts not only set into motion the person's "immature" psychological defenses, but in addition activate the *specific* physiological reactions that had been associated with these conflicts in childhood. Thus, to Alexander, adult psychophysiologic disorders reflect the consequence of chronic reactivations of the physiological reactions of childhood. For example, ulcer patients ostensibly suffered fixated dependency conflicts during the oral stage of psychosexual development. When present events reactivate this conflict, the patient's body responds with the same physiological reaction as when the conflict originally occurred in infancy. Specifically, these reactions took the form of excess gastrointestinal secretions since these occurred as a consequence of the infant's search for the security provided through maternal nutrition. Since "mother's milk" is not forthcoming in adulthood, the stomach and upper intestine are subjected, as a consequence of these physiological reactions, to a repeated flooding of gastric acids, causing the destruction of mucous lining and resulting in a peptic ulcer.

The logic of Alexander's thesis has been modified by other theorists and extended to a variety of psychosomatic syndromes.

1. Margolin (1953) has been among those who have argued for the view that psychophysiologic illnesses can best be understood as regressions to infantile modes of physiological functioning. However, he does not accept fully the specific conflict aspect of Alexander's theory. Rather, Margolin views the psychosomatic ailment as a consequence of the persistence of a *generally immature* physiological coping response which, though once appropriate in infancy, is now inappropriate for dealing with adult stress. He equates these inflexible and generalized infantile physiological reactions with immature and maladaptive childhood psychological coping maneuvers, both of which are equally inappropriate to present circumstance.

2. Ruesch (1946) has formulated another variant of Alexander's regression theory. In this proposal, he revives the conversion thesis that psychosomatic symptoms are a symbolic expression of unconscious conflicts transformed into the "language of the body." According to Ruesch, psychosomatic patients are either immature in their ways of

communicating to others, having failed to learn to express ideas and feelings verbally, or have regressed as a consequence of stress to the use of primitive bodily forms of communication. As a consequence of his verbal inadequacies, the individual reverts to psychosomatic symbolism as a way of telling others about his psychological needs and conflicts. For example, chronic nausea would express an inability to "stomach" the unpleasant things which the person feels he must take from others; persistent back pains would be interpreted as a way of saying that he feels "overloaded" with pressure; neurodermatitis conveys the thought that others are "getting under his skin" and so on.

Table 14–1 provides a summary of some of the causes, personality characteristics and aims which theorists such as Alexander, Margolin and

Disorder	Social Learning History, Personality Characteristics and Instrumental Aims
Peptic Ulcer	Feels deprived of dependency needs; is resentful; represses anger; cannot vent hostility or actively seek dependency security; characterizes self-sufficient and responsible "go-getter" types who are compensating for dependency desires; has strong regressive wish to be nurtured and fed; revengeful feelings are repressed and kept unconscious.
Colitis	Was intimidated in childhood into dependency and conformity; feels conflict over resentment and desire to please; anger restrained for fear of retaliation; is fretful, brooding and depressive or passive, sweet and bland; seeks to camouflage hostility by symbolic gesture of giving.
Essential Hypertension	Was forced in childhood to restrain resentments; inhibited rage; is threatened by and guilt-ridden over hostile impulses which may erupt; is a controlled, conforming and "mature" personality; is hard-driving and conscientious; is guarded and tense; needs to control and direct anger into acceptable channels; desires to gain approval from authority.
Migraine	Is unable to fulfill excessive self-demands; feels intense resentment and envy toward intellectually or financially more successful competitors; has meticulous, scrupulous, perfectionistic and ambitious personality; failure to attain perfectionist ambitions results in self-punishment.
Bronchial Asthma	Feels separation anxiety; was given inconsistent maternal affection; has fear and guilt that hostile impulses will be expressed toward loved persons; is demanding, sickly and "cranky" or clinging and dependent; symptom expresses suppressed cry for help and protection.
Neurodermatitis	Has overprotective but ungiving parents; has craving for affection; has conflict regarding hostility and dependence; demonstrates guilt and self-punishment for inadequacies; is a superficially friendly and oversensitive personality with depressive features and low self-image; symptoms are atonement for inadequacy and guilt by self-excoriation; displays oblique expression of hostility and exhibitionism in need for attention and soothing.

TABLE 14–1

SOME HYPOTHE-SIZED PSYCHO-LOGICAL CORRELATES OF PSYCHOPHYSIO-LOGIC DISORDERS

Ruesch, as well as others, have proposed as correlated with the six psychophysiologic disorders described earlier. We will comment on the validity of these hypotheses following our presentation of a number of alternate theories which reject the notion that psychosomatic symptoms are correlated with *specific* psychological needs or experiences.

NONSPECIFICITY THEORIES

A number of theorists (Mahl, 1953; Kaplan and Kaplan, 1959) state that there is insufficient evidence to warrant acceptance of any of the various "specificity" models that have been proposed. Despite impressive and intriguing theorizing, no clear-cut empirical relationship has been found to indicate that specific psychogenic factors are correlated with specific forms of psychophysiologic disorder.

The nonspecificity theorists offer an alternative. *First,* they contend that all sources of psychogenic stress, ranging from external realistic events (e.g., face to face warfare) to unconscious conflicts (e.g., repressed childhood hostilities), produce essentially similar *diffuse* physiological reactions. *Second,* should these generalized physiological states be prolonged or frequently repeated, one or several of a number of psychosomatic ailments may result. *Third,* the particular ailment that the patient finally displays *cannot* be predicted by reference either to the content or to the source of the problem.

The nonspecificity model has been criticized by many clinicians on the grounds that it fails to correlate psychosomatic disorders with psychological difficulties. This criticism is inaccurate. The model claims merely that the *specific* form of the psychophysiologic disorder cannot be predicted by the *specific* type of emotional difficulty experienced. The nonspecificity model asserts, quite clearly, that psychosomatic ailments *in general* are found to be associated with psychogenic problems. More specifically, its proponents claim that patients who are chronically unable to reduce anxiety are strongly disposed to exhibit *some form* of psychophysiologic disorder. This aspect of the nonspecificity view is nicely summarized in the following quote (Kaplan and Kaplan, 1959):

We believe that as long as a patient can deal with unpleasant emotions and with the anxiety engendered by his conflicts by means of various psychological defenses and mechanisms, there will be no abnormal psychogenic physical functioning nor resultant psychosomatic illness. If, however, a patient's psychological defenses are inadequate to reduce his excited or anxious state of emotional tension, then a variety of psychosomatic diseases may be produced in constitutionally susceptible individuals as a result of the physiological concomitants of chronic tension. According to this view, many psychosomatic diseases are a consequence of the *breakdown* of psychological defenses. It should be added that we do not consider the aforementioned mechanism to account for all instances of psychosomatic illness; other mechanisms, such as conditioning, may play a role in certain diseases. Nor do we believe that there is sufficient evidence to indicate that the nature of the psychological stimulus setting off the emotional tension determines the type of disease that develops. The problem of "organ selection," i.e., what accounts for the type of disease suffered by a particular patient, is unsolved as yet.

CONSTITUTIONAL SPECIFICITY THEORIES

The criticism that most psychological models fail to take account of constitutional differences as a factor in psychophysiologic disorders has led a number of researchers to propose the following alternate hypothesis: although specific psychogenic factors have not been shown to correlate with specific psychosomatic ailments, patients with distinctive and different physiological reaction patterns are disposed to develop specific types of ailments. This proposal may be spoken of as a "response specificity" thesis, resting on the well-accepted notion of intrinsic constitutional differences among individuals.

It was Adler, Freud's early disciple, who first spoke of the role of "organ inferiorities" in psychological illness. However, Adler did not concern himself particularly with psychosomatic ailments; rather, he drew upon the notion of bodily weaknesses to demonstrate mechanisms of compensatory striving.

It has only been in recent years, through the systematic experimental research of several investigators (Lacey and Lacey, 1958; Mirsky, 1958; Malmo, 1962), that evidence has accrued to show that individuals exhibit rather distinctive and stable types of physiological reactions to stress. For example, it has been shown that some individuals characteristically react with muscular rigidity to such varied conditions as embarrassment, pain and frustration whereas others react to the same variety of stressful events with intense gastrointestinal upsets. According to this thesis, the dominant sphere of physiological reactivity in an individual will dispose him to develop a specific type of correlated psychosomatic disorder; for example, "cardiovascular reactors" tend to experience heart palpitations and chest pains whereas "muscle reactors" are inclined to develop severe headaches.

The question may be posed as to whether these physiological reactivity patterns are acquired as a consequence of social learning or whether they are inborn. As reported in Chapter 7, studies by Murphy et al. (1962) and Thomas et al. (1964) indicate that distinctive autonomic behavioral patterns are exhibited shortly after birth and persist for many years thereafter. Since these styles of responding were evident prior to the effects of socialization, it would appear safe to assume that later patterns of reactivity are *in part* attributable to intrinsic constitutional tendencies.

Among the virtues of the constitutional specificity theory is that it rescues the notion of "symptom choice" from oblivion. Rather than depending on unverified clinical hypotheses, this theory is based on experimentally validated research, although much remains to be done in correlating physiological reaction patterns and vulnerabilities to particular psychosomatic ailments. It should be noted, further, that the constitutional thesis does not eliminate the role of social learning influences. Combined with certain social learning hypotheses, it can account for which patients experience psychosomatic ailments in the first place, and which specific ailments they eventually will display. In short, psychophysiologic disorders are likely to reflect the interaction of both psychological experience and constitutional vulnerabilities; more on this point will be discussed in the following theory.

AUTONOMIC RESPONSE LEARNING THEORY

Lachman (1972) has recently published a model of psychosomatic development based essentially on social learning theory. He does not minimize the significance of constitutional specificity — that is, organ vulnerability — but gives it a secondary role to social reinforcement history. His view is that when positive reinforcements become associated with responses of the autonomic nervous system, the probability is increased that these autonomic responses will, in similar situations, be produced again. The following quote summarizes Lachman's thesis:

Not only are autonomic responses learned on the basis of their being conditioned to new stimuli, but also particular autonomic responses are selectively learned on the basis of differential reward or reinforcement. A specific rewarded autonomic response tends to be differentiated out of the emotional response constellation and to be selectively strengthened. Thus, the individual who is rewarded for his expression of gastrointestinal pain by being permitted to stay home from school or from work and who is given special attention, consideration, and love under those circumstances is likely to have strengthened gastrointestinal reactions that led to the gastrointestinal pain, that is, increased gastric acid secretion. This is a statement of the idea that *rewarded autonomic responses may be selectively learned.*

The concept of *vicious-circle effects* is also necessary to understand certain psychosomatic phenomena. Once initiated, a psychosomatic event may produce stimuli that lead to implicit reactions, which rearouse or intensify the psychosomatic event, and so on. For example, the noxious stimulation from a gastric ulcer may elicit implicit reactions including facilitated stomach-acid secretion, which intensifies that ulcerous condition, which leads to further emotional reaction and further irritation of the ulcer.

COMMENT

What conclusions can we draw concerning the determinants of psychophysiologic disorders from the many alternate theories and data just reviewed.

1. Although the issue is not a closed one and is awaiting further and more detailed investigations for final judgment, the greater body of research evidence to date indicates that the *specific* type of psychophysiologic disorder exhibited by a patient *cannot* be predicted from the *specific* character of his psychological problem.

2. A fairly substantial body of data has accrued to the effect that psychosomatic disorders, *in general,* arise as a consequence of the failure to dissipate tensions, regardless of the content or source of these tensions. Individuals whose personality styles lead them into repeated tension producing situations or prevent them from discharging the cumulative build-up of tensions are likely to succumb to one or several of a number of different psychophysiologic disorders.

3. Essentially identical difficulties have been postulated as the cause of a wide variety of psychosomatic problems. A review of the literature, as summarized in Table 14–1, indicates that diverse psychosomatic disorders such as hypertension, ulcers, asthma and neurodermatitis, appear to derive from a single basic conflict, i.e., suppressing hostile impulses for fear that they may endanger dependency security. It is extremely difficult to uncover different etiologies among these disorders. The conflict between dependency security and hostile assertion seems to apply to all. This uniformity leads us to conclude that most psychosomatic patients are trapped in an unresolvable dependency-independency ambivalence. They are unable to express feelings associated with one part of their conflict without increasing tensions in the other. As a consequence, their overall level of tension continues to mount and churn internally until it finally results in an irreversible psychophysiologic disorder.

4. Recent research indicates that the specific type of psychosomatic

symptom the patient develops is likely to depend either on constitutional vulnerabilities or on his dominant physiological reaction pattern.

5.   We are led to conclude that the pathway which leads to a psycho-physiologic disorder derives from both social learning and constitutional influences. We must envision, then, a sequence of interactions in which the individual's learned instrumental behaviors *either* produce autonomic disturbances to gain support, attention and so forth *or* fail to dissipate physiological tensions. A constitutionally predisposed individual will develop a specific type of psychosomatic disorder since his psychological problems, whatever their source or content, will have a selective physiological effect upon certain vulnerable organ systems.

6.   Definitive conclusions concerning the specific interplay of social learning and physiogenic factors must await further empirical research. Most of what has been published in the field of psychosomatic medicine can be faulted on a number of methodological grounds (Freeman et al., 1964). At the very best, these studies provide some rough guidelines for future systematic research.

PERSONALITY AND INSTRUMENTAL BEHAVIOR

It may be possible from what we have reviewed thus far to deduce which of the various abnormal personality patterns are most susceptible to psychophysiologic disorders. Toward this end, it will be useful to examine first the various instrumental functions that underlie psychosomatic symptom formation.

One purpose of the psychosomatic patient's strategy is to block from awareness the content and source of his tensions. This aim, however, is neither distinctive to psychophysiologic disorders nor to any particular personality type. Since it is a basic instrumental function of most disorders, we must look to other factors to account for the psychosomatic symptom and its personality correlates.

Two other coping functions fulfilled by the psychosomatic symptom are the control or inhibition of hostile impulses and the eliciting of attention, sympathy and nurture. However, these instrumental functions are also found in neurotic disorders, and are characteristic of the entire group of five personality patterns that are subject to these disorders, notably the two dependent patterns, the two ambivalent patterns and the active-detached pattern (Millon, 1969). Since various instrumental functions are found in common among these five personality patterns and two disorder syndromes, we are led to believe that psychosomatic symptoms would covary with neurotic symptoms in each of these personality patterns. Stated differently, we would hypothesize that psychophysiologic disorders will be found, not exclusively in one personality type, but in the five types that share these common instrumental goals. Further, we would hypothesize that neurotic and psychosomatic symptoms will coexist or fluctuate interchangeably in the same patient. This latter finding has regularly been reported in the literature, but has not been systematically researched. It may reflect the fact that neurotic disorders often only partly discharge physiological tensions, therefore leaving a residue which may take the form of a psychosomatic ailment.

We believe not only that psychophysiologic disorders will arise most frequently in the five personality patterns mentioned previously, but that they are particularly characteristic of two types, the passive and active-ambivalents. Ample evidence exists for this view in the literature, but let us examine our reasons for believing it.

Among the central features of psychosomatic causation are repetitive upsets of the body's physiological balance and a chronic failure to dissipate physiological tensions. These events will arise most often in patients who repeatedly find themselves in conflict situations, especially those in whom the discharge of tensions created by one side of the conflict will increase tensions created by the other. This state of affairs describes, in effect, the experiences of ambivalent personalities; they are trapped between submissive dependency on the one hand, and hostile independence on the other. When they allow themselves to submit to the wishes of others, they experience deep resentments and angers for having displayed weakness and given up their independence. Conversely, if they assert their independence and express hostility, they experience intense anxieties for fear they will have further endangered their security.

Let us next examine how this conflict develops into psychophysiologic disorders in each of the five vulnerable personality patterns.

1. The *compulsive personality* (passive-ambivalent) keeps under close wraps most of the tensions generated by his dependence-independence conflict. His resentments and anxieties are tightly controlled and infrequently discharged. As a consequence, his physiological tensions are not dissipated, tend to cumulate and result in frequent and persistent psychophysiologic ailments, as illustrated in the following brief sketch.

CASE 14–3

Peter S., Age 23, Married, No Children

This passive-ambivalent graduate student was admitted to the college infirmary following a recurrence of an old ulcer ailment. Peter's early history showed intense rivalries with an alcoholic but "brilliant" father who constantly demanded superior performances on the part of his son in both academic affairs and athletics. However, no matter how well Peter would perform, his father demonstrated "how much better he could do it now—or did it when he was young." Although Peter "quietly hated" his father, he dared not express it for fear of "being publicly humiliated by him."

In recent weeks, Peter's thesis proposal had been severely criticized by his departmental advisor. Peter believed that the professor was completely wrong in his judgments and suggestions, but dared not express these thoughts for "fear of further condemnation." Unable to vent his resentments, which were so much like those he felt toward his father, Peter's repressed emotions churned away inside and resulted in a flareup of his ulcer.

2. The precipitants and sequence of physiological tensions take a somewhat different turn in the *negativistic personality* (active-ambivalent). Here, the patient periodically discharges his tensions, but because of his hypersensitivities and irritable behaviors, he creates an endless sequence of one troublesome problem after another. In other words, he accumulates tension faster than he dissipates it. Moreover, because of his fretful and disagreeable behaviors, his body is subject to constant vacillations in mood and emotion. As he swings erratically from one intense feeling to another, his equilibrium, so necessary for proper physiological functioning, is kept constantly off balance. Not only is he likely to experience, then, an excess of chronic or repeated tension, but his system rarely settles down into a smooth and regularized pattern. As a consequence, the active-ambivalent is kept churning and sets himself up for a variety of psychosomatic disorders.

3. Although *inadequate* and *hysterical personalities* (passive- and active-dependents) are subject to psychophysiologic ailments, they are not faced with the severe and unresolvable conflict that confronts ambivalents. In their case, dependency needs can be pursued without intensify-

ing tensions associated with independence. Furthermore, although they are similar to ambivalents in their fear of expressing forbidden hostile impulses, the anger and resentment they feel are appreciably less. At a more severe level, however, dependents have suffered frequent rebuffs and carry within them resentments no less intense than those found more characteristically in ambivalents.

4. *Avoidant personalities* (active-detached) have strong but unexpressed resentments which may lead them to suffer psychosomatic ailments. However, the likelihood that they will experience these disorders is less than that of ambivalents since their detached strategy enables them to avoid most anger arousing situations.

In conclusion, then, all five personalities are disposed to psychosomatic disorders, the specific form of which appears to depend on their particular constitutional vulnerabilities and social learning experiences. As we have noted, the two ambivalent types seem especially susceptible to these disorders since their dependent-independent conflict disposes them to tensions which cannot either readily be resolved or easily be dissipated through behavioral discharge.

TREATMENT APPROACHES

Of all the abnormalities described we can see most clearly the close interweaving of biological and psychological functions in the psychophysiologic disorders. Of course, every abnormality derives in part from the operation of both psychic and somatic factors. Psychophysiologic disorders are notable in this regard only because they give evidence of this inseparable fusion in manifest physical form.

Therapeutic attention must be directed first to remedying whatever physical impairments have occurred in conjunction with the disorder. Body pathology, as in ulcer perforations or severe hypertension, should be dealt with promptly by appropriate medical, nutritional or surgical means. When the physical disease process is under adequate control, attention may be turned to the management of environmental stresses and to the modification of detrimental attitudes and habits.

As we have said, psychosomatic symptoms arise as a consequence of the patient's instrumental learning and/or his inability to resolve conflicts and discharge tensions. Because of the patient's fear that these emotions will overwhelm him if released, the therapist must move slowly before exposing these conflicting attitudes or "opening the floodgates" to the onrush of these feelings. Quite evidently, the patient has been willing to suffer considerable physical discomfort as the price for achieving his instrumental goals and containing his unacceptable impulses. The danger of provoking a crisis is great if the patient gains insight too quickly or if his previously hidden feelings are uncovered and unleashed too rapidly. Such exposure and release must be coordinated with a parallel strengthening of the patient's capacity to cope with these feelings.

The warning just noted points to the important role of supportive techniques in the early stages of treatment. At first, care should be taken to diminish tension and to help dissipate the cumulation of past tensions. Psychopharmacologic tranquilizers may be useful in softening the response to tension sources. In addition, arrangements should be made where feasible to have the patient avoid those aspects of everyday living which prompt or aggravate unresolvable anxieties and conflicts.

Turning to the formal psychotherapeutic measures, behavior modification approaches may be used to extinguish attitudes and habits which have generated tensions, and to build in new ones which may help in discharging, avoiding or otherwise coping with them (Mitchell and Mitchell, 1971; Schwartz et al., 1971). Group therapy often serves as a valuable adjunct to help the patient explore his feelings, learn methods of resolving conflicts and liberate tensions. The probing and uncovering methods of psychoanalytic therapy should not be utilized in the early phases of treatment since they may prompt the surge of severely upsetting forbidden thoughts and impulses. However, should other procedures prove unsuccessful in alleviating tension or in diminishing the disturbing symptomatology, it may be necessary to employ this technique and to begin a slow and long-term process of reconstructing the patient's personality pattern.

PART 4

ABNORMALITIES OF MARKED SEVERITY

Conrad Marca-Relli—*Seated Figure*

15 SCHIZOPHRENIC DISORDERS AND PATTERNS

INTRODUCTION

This chapter is the first of three that make up our study of the more severe types of abnormal behavior. Each chapter focuses on one of the traditional "psychotic" classifications: the schizophrenic, affective and paranoid syndromes. Several empirically-based or theoretically-derived alternatives have been proposed to replace this tripartite classification of severe pathologies (Lorr and McNair, 1963; Garmezy, 1968; Millon, 1969); despite their merits, these proposals are of too recent vintage to supplant the traditional model.

One recent refinement of the traditional classification, referred to as the process-reactive distinction, has achieved a modest degree of acceptance and will be employed as a means of separating the subvarieties of each of the three syndromes (Higgins, 1964, 1969; Kantor and Herron, 1966). In essence, "reactive" subtypes correspond to what we have termed earlier in the text as "symptom disorders"; they have been described as relatively brief pathological states that are prompted largely by external events and differ significantly from the patient's more usual behavior style. The "process" level corresponds to the term "personality pattern" as used in previous chapters. These pathologies characterize the patient's typical, ingrained and enduring style of psychological functioning. In the following chapters, what might be termed "reactive schizophrenia" will be referred to as an *acute psychotic disorder,* schizophrenic type; and a "process schizophrenia" will be noted as a *severe personality pattern,* schizophrenic type. Before elaborating the various schizophrenic syndromes, which make up the body of this chapter, it may be useful to note briefly several additional features distinguishing "disorders" and "patterns."

Concept of Acute Psychotic Disorders

Psychotic disorders are extremely severe forms of psychopathology and normally require inpatient or hospital treatment. The rather baffling symptoms we observe in these patients either represent extreme and bizarre efforts on their part to cope with threat and anxiety or signify the collapse of their habitual coping strategies. These disorders contrast with the severe personality patterns, in which corrosive pathological processes have permeated the entire psychological structure. In psychotic disorders the pathology tends to be episodic and reversible, and not as permanent and ingrained as the patterns.

The term "psychosis" has been in use for less than two centuries. Only since the classic texts of Kraepelin, in the first quarter of this century, has it been applied as a label to represent severe mental impairments. There is no need to discuss the history of these disorders. To all intents and purposes, it is one and the same with the history of psychopathology itself. Reference should be made to earlier chapters for a detailed exposition of both ancient and recent concepts and theories.

The official DSM-II nomenclature refers to the *psychoses* as follows:

Patients are described as psychotic when their mental functioning is sufficiently impaired to interfere grossly with their capacity to meet the ordinary demands of life. The impairment may result from a serious distortion in their capacity to recognize reality. Hallucinations and delusions, for example, may distort their perceptions. Alterations of mood may be so profound that the patient's capacity to respond appropriately is grossly impaired. Deficits in perception, language and memory may be so severe that the patient's capacity for mental grasp of his situation is effectively lost.

The range and variety of clinical features associated with psychotic psychopathology cannot be encompassed by a summary listing. Equally difficult and problematic are attempts to classify the complex and infinitely diverse clusters into which these symptoms may form. We will address ourselves to some of the issues connected with specific symptom clusters in conjunction with our later presentation of clinical types and their personality dispositions. For the present, we will note in general several features which justify the psychotic disorder label.

The two distinguishing characteristics of the markedly severe states are a *diminished reality awareness* and a *cognitive* and *emotional dyscontrol*. As the tide of uncontrollable anxieties and impulses surges forward, these patients begin to sink into a hazy world of fleeting, distorted and dreamlike impressions in which subjective moods and images become fused with, and ultimately dominate, objective realities. Overt behaviors, stimulated primarily by these internal states, appear purposeless, disjointed, irrational, stereotyped and bizarre. There is a disunity and disorganization to their communications. Ideas and thoughts are conveyed in a jumbled fashion, often taking the form of delusions or projected onto the world as hallucinatory perceptions. Controls are rendered useless or are abandoned as emotions break loose. There is no instrumental purpose or goal other than the ventilation of impulse and anxiety. Unable to grasp objective reality or coordinate feelings and thoughts, these patients regress into a totally helpless state.

To delineate more clearly the features of the psychotic disorders, it may be useful to differentiate them from those of the severe personality patterns, other symptom disorders and the behavior reactions.

The distinction between psychotic disorders and severe personality patterns is difficult to make on the basis of overt clinical features alone. The principal distinction between them lies in the developmental history of the impairment. The emergence of psychotic disorders is usually of rapid onset and follows a period of reasonably adequate functioning.

Another distinction between disorders and patterns is the role played by external precipitants. In the severe patterns, the patient's disturbance reflects the operation of internal and ingrained defects in his personality make-up whereas in the psychotic disorders there is evidence that current behaviors are, at least in part, a product of external or environmental stress. Furthermore, as the intensity of stress is reduced, the disordered patient begins, albeit slowly, to recoup his coping powers and to regain his former level of functioning. This is not in evidence among the severe patterns. Thus, disorders are distinguished by their transitory character. They tend to be of relatively short duration, whereas patterns are more permanent and fixed as a style of life.

The patterns evolve slowly, growing bit by bit into the very fabric of the personality make-up. In contrast, psychotic disorders come rather abruptly and are experienced as a marked disruption of the accustomed or "normal" mode of functioning. Either the symptoms stand out as isolated and dramatic deviations from a more typical style of behavior or they erupt as a bizarre accentuation or caricature of the more prosaic personality style.

Despite the distinctions noted, the line between psychotic disorders and the severe personality patterns is often a blurred one. Man does not readily accommodate us in our desire for a simple system of classification. This diagnostic complication is compounded further in these cases by the fact that episodes of psychotic disorder may gradually blend into a more chronic personality pattern. Thus, for a variety of reasons—persistent stress, the "comforts" of hospitalization and so on—a patient may "get caught" in the web surrounding his psychosis and fail to "pull out" of what may otherwise have been a transitory episode.

Distinctions between psychotic disorders and milder symptom disorders are not difficult to make. Psychotics evidence two central symptoms not found in less severe impairments, notably the loss of reality awareness and cognitive and emotional dyscontrol. Although psychotics often exhibit neurotic or psychophysiologic symptoms, they manifest in addition a variety of symptoms not found in these less severe disorders, such as perceptual hallucinations, irrational excitement, delusions, total apathy and profound depression. With their coping strategies upset or shattered, their behaviors take on a chaotic and disorganized quality rarely seen in those who are able to maintain a moderate level of personality cohesion.

Psychotic disorders, although often prompted by external precipitants, are not as stimulus-specific as *learned behavior reactions* are. The disorders occur in response to a wide variety of stimulus conditions since they reflect the operation of pervasive personality sensitivities and vulnerabilities. Behavior reactions tend to be consistent in their form of expression, manifesting themselves rather uniformly and predictably each time the distressing precipitant appears. In contrast, psychotic disorders tend to be inconsistent and contaminated with a mixture of different and interchangeable symptoms since they derive from a complex network of reactivated feelings, attitude and strategies.

Learned behavior reactions are often totally understandable when viewed in terms of the precipitating stimulus. Furthermore, they tend to subside quickly when the disturbing event is removed. In contrast, the responses of psychotic disorders appear extremely complicated and irrational when viewed in terms of the precipitating event, and tend to "drag on" after the precipitant has been removed. The baffling, obscure and symbolic nature of "disordered" responses contrasts markedly with the relatively simple and straightforward responses seen in the behavior reactions.

Psychotic disorders are precipitated when mild abnormal personalities are unable to control or discharge their tensions by means of a neurotic or psychophysiologic resolution. We must point out that it is extremely difficult to predict the *particular* symptoms a patient will manifest when he succumbs to a psychosis. The first complication we face in this regard is the fact that the experiences of each individual are unique. The specific content and form of his symptoms will reflect the idiosyncratic character of his learnings. Thus, it will be evident in the following chapters that we have *not* asserted that a one-to-one correspondence exists between a particular personality pattern and a particular psychotic disorder. Rather, as the evidence of our own preliminary research suggests, certain personality patterns are *more likely* to exhibit certain disorders than they are others. This loosely fitting model of pattern-disorder correspondence was presented in our chapter on the neurotic disorders.

Concept of Severe Personality Patterns

In previous chapters, we referred to patterns of abnormal personality as deeply pervasive characteristics which unfold as a product of the interplay of constitutional and experiential influences. The attitudes, behaviors and strategies which derive from this transaction are embedded so firmly within the individual that they become the very fabric of his make-up, operating automatically as his style or way of life. So much are they a part of him that the person often is blind to their fixed and self-destructive character. Present realities merely stir up longstanding habits and memories; he acts as he learned to act in the past, persisting inflexibly in his attitudes and strategies, irrespective of how maladaptive these behaviors may be. Sooner or later his actions prove his undoing. His behaviors are self-defeating and promote vicious circles which involve him in difficulties that reactivate and aggravate the less favorable conditions of earlier life.

Is there some line we can draw, some criteria we can use by which certain pathological patterns may be categorized as more severe than others? Can we clearly distinguish between degrees of pathology in personality, when all of them display adaptive inflexibility, promote vicious circles and hang on a tenuous balance?

Personality structure is best conceived of as a complex series of traits which lie on a continuum of adaptiveness. Adaptiveness, then, is a gradient, a matter of degree, and not a dichotomy. Health versus disease, abnormal versus normal or psychotic versus nonpsychotic are polar extremes of a continuum that evidences many intervening shades and gradations between them. Moreover, the course of a patient's impairment may vary from time to time, progressing toward greater health in one period, and regressing toward greater illness the next.

As far as clinical behavior is concerned, moderately and markedly ill patients differ from mild patients in the frequency with which certain unusual and bizarre symptoms arise, such as explosive emotional outbursts, delusions and hallucinations. Control has weakened in the more severe patient, and he employs rather extreme measures to maintain his homeostatic balance and psychological cohesion. These individuals cannot effectively mobilize their instrumental strategies, are less able to appraise the threats they face and are less flexible in drawing upon their coping resources. They become overly rigid and constrictive in their behaviors or, conversely, so confused and scattered as to nullify their chances for achieving their goals.

Markedly ill patients frequently lose whatever insight they had into their difficulties, and may fail to discriminate between their inner subjective world and that of external reality. They are less and less able to fulfill their social responsibilities, or respond appropriately in terms of conventional group standards and expectations. As reality recedes further into the background, rational thought and action is lost. Previously repressed emotions erupt and are acted out, and an overwhelming sense of disintegration and demoralization may take hold.

At the first stage of personality deterioration, most patients mobilize their resources, shore up their strategies and take a more active role than before to secure the reinforcements to which they are accustomed. In each case the individual is driven to reinstate more actively the equilibrium and rewards he achieved in the past. Individuals who stabilize at this exceedingly uncomfortable, *moderately severe,* state of personality functioning will be referred to as displaying a *borderline personality pattern.*

At the second stage of personality decompensation the borderline patient's coping efforts have begun to fail. He achieves little or no positive reinforcement from reality experiences, and he begins to turn increasingly to the world of inner fantasy. But as the inner world becomes his world of experience, his already tenuous hold on reality slips increasingly. He sinks into the muddy and boundless world of illusion, submerged in a sea of bewildering impulses and fluid fantasies. As in dreams, he finds himself in a whirling abyss of confusion and irrationality, a frightening phantasmagoria of ethereal images and primitive feelings in which illusions dissolve, impulses surge forth, events seem suspended and objects have no meaning.

It is an odd, detached and unreal world to which the patient now has decompensated. At this more advanced state, all patients, regardless of initial distinguishing features, become more and more alike. Although their premorbid personality patterns continue to color their behaviors and perceptions, they have drawn increasingly into themselves, adrift from social reality. We shall refer to these *markedly severe* forms of deterioration as the *decompensated personality patterns.*

In this chapter, we shall limit our attention to the various acute psychotic disorders and severe personality patterns traditionally labeled as "schizophrenic." Chapters 16 and 17 will focus, respectively, on those disorders and patterns usually listed as "affective" and "paranoid" syndromes.

ACUTE SCHIZOPHRENIC DISORDERS

It will be instructive to review the history and clinical conditions associated with the syndrome label "schizophrenia."

This term has been applied to almost 50 per cent of all hospitalized mental patients; such a striking statistic may signify either the impressive prevalence of this particular impairment or the indiscriminate lumping into one gross category of equally disturbed but basically different patients. It is our contention that the traditional category of "schizophrenia" should be subdivided. Many severely disturbed patients diagnosed as "schizophrenic" should be assigned to a psychotic "disorder" category since their impairments are only of brief duration (Birley and Brown, 1970). Other "schizophrenics" possess deeply ingrained personality patterns, and should be separated from the former group. In this section, we shall limit our attention to those patients who experience only periodic and acute states of schizophrenic *disorder*.

The English neurologist Willis, in 1674, made note of a pathological sequence in which "young persons who, lively and spirited, and at times even brilliant in their childhood, passed into obtuseness and hebetude during adolescence." The Belgian psychiatrist Morel, in 1856, described the case of a 14 year old boy who had been a cheerful and outstanding student, but who progressively lost his intellectual capacities and increasingly became melancholy and withdrawn. Morel considered cases such as these to be irremediable, ascribing them to a decline in brain development stemming from hereditary causes. He gave the illness the name *dementia praecox* (démence précoce) to signify his observation that deterioration occurred at an early age.

Between 1863 and 1874, the German psychiatrists Kahlbaum and Hecker described two other forms of mental deterioration. They applied the term *hebephrenia* to conditions, arising in puberty and adolescence, that started with a quick succession of erratic moods, were followed by a rapid enfeeblement of all functions, and finally progressed to an unalterable psychic decline. The label *catatonia,* representing "tension insanity," was introduced for cases in which the patient displayed no reactivity to sensory impressions, lacked "self-will" and sat mute and physically immobile. Ostensibly, these symptoms reflected structural brain deterioration.

Prior to 1896, the great German synthesist Emil Kraepelin considered hebephrenia and dementia praecox to be synonymous. However, in the fifth edition of his classic psychiatric text he concluded that the diverse symptom complexes of catatonia and hebephrenia, as well as certain paranoid disturbances, displayed a common theme of early deterioration and ultimate incurability. As he saw it, these illnesses were variations of Morel's original concept of dementia praecox. By subordinating the disparate symptoms of these syndromes to the common factor of an early and inexorable mental decline. Kraepelin brought order and simplicity to what previously had been diagnostic confusion and psychiatric dissension.

Following the tradition of German psychiatry, Kraepelin assumed that a biophysical defect lay at the heart of this syndrome. In contrast to his forebears, however, he hypothesized sexual and metabolic dysfunctions as probable causal agents rather than anatomical lesions.

Kraepelin's observations and syntheses were soon challenged and modified. Eugen Bleuler in Switzerland and Adolf Meyer in the United States were notable in this regard.

After observing hundreds of dementia praecox patients in the early

1900's, Bleuler concluded that it was entirely misleading to compare the type of deterioration they evidenced with that found among patients who were known to be suffering from brain deficiencies or degeneration. He observed that the reactions and thoughts of his patients were highly complex and differentiated, in marked contrast to the simple and gross behaviors of the feebleminded and organically diseased. Furthermore, many patients first displayed their illness in adulthood rather than adolescence, and others evidenced none of the signs of progressive deterioration which Kraepelin considered central to the syndrome. To Bleuler, then, the label "dementia praecox" seemed misleading as a designation since it characterized an age of onset and a course of development that were not supported by the evidence he had gathered. The significant features, as Bleuler saw it, were a "loosening of associations" and a "disharmony among affects." The patient's characteristic fragmentation of thought, feeling and action led Bleuler, in 1911, to propose the label "schizophrenia" to signify what he saw as a split (schism) within the patient's mind (phrenos).

Bleuler retained the Kraepelinian notion that the impairment was a unitary disease attributable to organic pathology. All schizophrenics shared a common neurological ailment which resulted in a common set of "primary" symptoms, notably that of loosened thoughts and disharmonious emotions. Beyond these, patients possessed a group of "secondary" symptoms, such as the content of their hallucinations and delusions, which Bleuler ascribed to the patients' distinctive life experiences and to their efforts to adapt to their neurological disease. Although Bleuler conceded that psychogenic influences shaped the particular character and color of the schizophrenic impairment, he asserted that these experiences could not in themselves "cause" the disturbance.

In 1906, Adolf Meyer suggested that dementia praecox was not an organic disease at all but a maladaptive way of "reacting" to stress, fully understandable in terms of the patient's life experiences. These maladaptive reactions led to a progressive "habit deterioration." Thus, these impairments reflected "inefficient and faulty attempts to avoid difficulties," and symptoms were seen as end products of abortive and self-defeating efforts to reestablish psychic equilibrium. Meyer did recognize, however, that constitutional weaknesses may prove to be serious handicaps to psychological adaptation, and thereby dispose the individual to future mental illness. His eclectic but well-reasoned "psychobiological" approach to schizophrenia (which he preferred to call "paregasia" to signify its distorted or twisted character) represented the first systematic recognition of the interactive and progressive nature of pathogenesis.

The system of classification currently used in psychiatry retains the basic typology of dementia praecox as formulated by Kraepelin in the fifth edition (1896) of his text. However, for the greater part of this century, the label dementia praecox was replaced by the term "schizophrenic reaction types," representing modifications in accord with the thinking of Bleuler and Meyer. In the recently revised DSM-II, the nomenclature was simplified to that of "schizophrenia."

Despite the fact that Kraepelin's categories rested on dubious assumptions regarding etiology and prognostic course, they have been retained with minimal change, though clothed in more fashionable language. For many and divergent reasons, few diagnosticians are satisfied with the

Kraepelinian typology. It remains in popular usage today largely as a result of habit and inertia.

The term schizophrenia is applied in current practice to almost all patients who evidence chronic personality decompensation, without regard to the character of their premorbid traits. In addition, it is used as a designation for almost all acute impairments that are noted by the primacy of disorganized thinking. The following descriptive statements are excerpted from the DSM-II classification of schizophrenia:

This large category includes a group of disorders manifested by characteristic disturbances of thinking, mood and behavior. Disturbances in thinking are marked by alterations of concept formation which may lead to misinterpretation of reality and sometimes to delusions and hallucinations, which frequently appear psychologically self-protective. Corollary mood changes include ambivalent, constricted and inappropriate emotional responsiveness and loss of empathy with others. Behavior may be withdrawn, regressive and bizarre.

We consider the application of the schizophrenic term to so wide a spectrum of ailments to be a serious limitation of the Kraepelinian system (Grinker, 1969). Although an alternative formulation has been published in the literature (Millon, 1969), its complexity and length are such that we best forego presenting it in a text designed for the beginning student. It will suffice for the present simply to underline the important distinction already drawn between acute disordered states and chronic personality patterns. We will turn next to a discussion of four schizophrenic "disorders."

HEBEPHRENIC (FRAGMENTATION) DISORDER

CLINICAL PICTURE

These patients are identifiable by their incongruous and disorganized behavior. They seem disoriented and confused, unclear as to time, place and identity. Many exhibit grimacing, inappropriate giggling, mannerisms and peculiar movements. Their speech tends to ramble into incoherent irrelevancies. The content of their ideas is colored with fantasy and hallucination and scattered with bizarre and fragmentary delusions that have no apparent logic or function. Regressive acts such as soiling and wetting are common, and these patients often consume food in an infantile or ravenous manner.

PERSONALITY AND INSTRUMENTAL BEHAVIOR

For most patients, this disordered state signifies a surrendering of all coping efforts. In some personalities, however, it may represent an active instrumental maneuver. Although all personalities may succumb to this disorder, some are more likely to do so than others. The following list includes these more vulnerable patterns.

1.   *Avoidant personalities* (active-detached pattern) are especially inclined to this disorder not only because they can easily be overwhelmed by external and internal pressures, but because fragmentation is an extension of their characteristic protective maneuver of interfering with their own cognitive clarity. By blocking the normal flow of thoughts and memories, they distract themselves and dilute the impact of painful feelings and

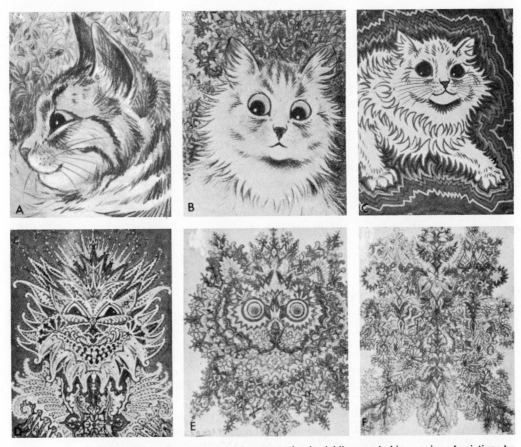

Figure 15-1 The process of fragmentation is vividly revealed in a series of paintings by an English artist, Louis Wain, an eccentric bachelor who had made a specialty of making portraits of his 17 cats before suffering a breakdown in middle life. The cat becomes more horrifying and the background more bizarre and abstract until finally the cat disappears entirely. © Guttmann Maclay Collection, Institute of Psychiatry, University of London.)

recollections. Hebephrenia may arise, then, as a direct product either of intolerable pressures, self-made confusion or both. What we see as a result is a picture of "forced" absurdity and incoherence and a concerted effort to disrupt cognitive clarity and emotional rationality. The following portrays such an episode.

Greta displayed an avoidant pattern ever since early adolescence. She was shy, somewhat fearful of all people, even those she had known all of her life, and preferred to spend her days at home helping her mother cook and clean for her father and younger brothers. One morning she became "silly and confused," began to talk "gibberishly," as her mother put it, became incontinent, grimaced and giggled for no apparent reason. When the family physician arrived, he noted that Greta placed herself into a series of contorted positions on the floor, sang incoherent songs and cried fitfully for brief periods. Greta continued this behavior, although more sporadically, for several weeks after institutionalization, following which she became quiet and withdrawn. About three months after hospitalization, she returned home and resumed her "normal" pattern of behavior.

CASE 15-1

Greta S., Age 22, Unmarried

---

2.   Both *inadequate* and *hysterical personalities* (passive- and active-dependents) are disposed to hebephrenia when faced with situations that

seriously tax their limited capacity to function independently. Without external security and support and lacking a core of inner competence and self-determination, they may easily crumble and disintegrate, usually into regressive or infantile behaviors. Beneath their confusion and bizarre acts we often see remnants of their former instrumental strategies. For example, their regressive eating and soiling may reflect a continued seeking of care and nurture. Their stereotyped grimacing and giggling may signify a forced and pathetic effort to capture the good will and approval of those upon whom they now depend.

3.   In *compulsive* and *negativistic personalities* (passive- and active-ambivalents), hebephrenia usually follows the shattering of controls previously employed to restrain deeply repressed conflicts. Unable to keep these divisive forces in check, these patients are torn apart, engulfed in a sea of surging memories and contrary feelings that now spew forth in a flood of incoherent verbalizations and bizarre emotions and acts. In their case, grimacing and mannerisms often signify feeble efforts to contain their impulses or to dampen the confusion and disharmony which they feel.

IMPASSIVE CATATONIC DISORDER

CLINICAL PICTURE

Most striking among these psychotics is their lethargy and seeming indifference to their surroundings. They move listlessly, are apathetic and even stuporous. Clothes are drab and their faces appear lifeless and mask-like. Speech is slow, labored and often blocked, whispered or inaudible. They seem passively withdrawn and unresponsive to their environment, cannot participate or feel involved and tend to perceive things about them as unreal and strange. There is an emotional poverty, a dreamy detachment, a tendency to stand immobile or fixed in one place for hours. They habitually sit in cramped, bent-over and peculiar positions, to which they return repeatedly if they are momentarily distracted or dislodged. Some not only show a total lack of initiative, but display an automatic obedience to the requests of others, even when these directives could result in severe physical discomfort or danger. Others are so profoundly detached that they fail to register reactions of distress to painful stimuli such as a slap or a pinprick.

All these behaviors signify a protective withdrawal, a retreat into indifference and a purposeful uninvolvement and insensitivity to life so as to avoid the anguish it has produced. By disengaging themselves totally, they need no longer feel the painful emotions they experienced before, no longer suffer the discouragement of struggling fruitlessly and no longer desire and aspire, only to be frustrated and humiliated again. Faced with a sense of hopelessness and futility, they have given up, become uncaring, neutral, flat, impassive and "dead" to everything.

PERSONALITY AND INSTRUMENTAL BEHAVIOR

Psychotic impassivity occurs in all personality patterns. The shutting off of emotions and the retreat into indifference are protective devices that can be employed easily by all individuals who have been overwhelmed by a sense of hopelessness and futility. Despite its ease as an instrumental maneuver, it appears with greater frequency among patients whose life-long strategies dispose them to emotional detachment and withdrawal.

1. As a "logical" extension of their instrumental coping style, we find the impassive disorder arising often in *asthenic* and *avoidant personalities* (passive- and active-detached patterns). Unable to handle even minor degrees of overstimulation, be it from unexpected responsibilities, objective threat or reactivated anxiety, they may overemploy their coping strategies and withdraw into an impassive, unresponsive and unfeeling state. These cases can usually be identified by their total muteness and their complete "tuning out" of the world, traits which result in an inner void and a picture of mask-like stupor, as portrayed in the following:

Arthur, an avoidant personality, was admitted to the psychiatric section of a general hospital after being found by a hotel chambermaid sitting on the edge of his bed, staring vacantly at a wall. When brought to the ward, he sat impassively in a chair, was unresponsive to questioning, indifferent to his surroundings and well-being, disinterested in food and unwilling to feed himself. He remained mute, withdrawn and immobile for several days, following which he slowly began to take care of himself without assistance, although he failed to speak to anyone for almost a month.

CASE 15–2

Arthur O., Age 29, Unmarried

2. *Inadequate personalities* (passive-dependent pattern) succumb on occasion to catatonic impassivity, but here we often see a coloring of sadness, a tone of inner softness, an inclination to "be nice" and to acquiesce in the wishes of others in the hope of maintaining some measure of affection and support from them. It is in these patients that we often observe a cataleptic waxy flexibility, that is, a tendency to maintain bodily positions into which others have placed them. This willingness to be molded according to the whims of others signifies their total abandonment of self-initiative and their complete dependence and submission to external directives. At the heart of their acquiescent impassivity is the deep need they have to counter their separation anxieties and to avoid actions which might produce disapproval and rejection.

3. In *hysterical personalities* (active-dependent pattern) catatonic impassivity usually reflects a collapse of their lifelong instrumental style of actively soliciting attention and approval. Rather than face failure and rejection, these patients may "retire" from their habitual strategy, disown their need for stimulation and excitement and temporarily reverse the course of their life style. Impassivity is usually of short duration in these patients, and can be relieved by genuine assurances from others of their care, interest and affection.

RIGID CATATONIC DISORDER

CLINICAL PICTURE

This syndrome is similar both to "catatonic impassivity" and "retarded depression," to be discussed in a later chapter, in that all three groups of patients exhibit minimal motor activity and often appear to be totally withdrawn and stuporous. The feature which distinguishes the "catatonic rigidity" disorder from the others lies in the patient's purposeful uncooperativeness (Morrison, 1973). One senses that beneath the quiet and restrained exterior lies a seething but controlled hostility. The patient is not only mute and immobile, then, but "bullheaded" and adamant about remaining in certain fixed and preferred positions, oppos-

Figure 15-2 Two catatonic states. Credits noted. (From Mayer-Gross, W., Slater, E., and Roth, M.: Clinical Psychiatry. London, Cassell, 1960.)

ing all efforts to alter them. This rigidity and resistance are manifest in his body tension. For example, his fists may be clenched, his teeth gritted and his jaw locked tight and firm. Breaking periodically through his physical immobility, however, are stereotyped repetitive acts, bizarre gestures and grimaces and peculiar tics, grins and giggles. It appears that every now and then his inner impulses and fantasies emerge briefly to be discharged or enacted through strange symbolic expression. Evidently, there are active although confused thoughts and emotions churning beneath the passive exterior.

PERSONALITY AND INSTRUMENTAL BEHAVIOR

Periods of motor rigidity may be exhibited, in passing, by all personality patterns. In general, however, they occur rather infrequently and arise as a dominant symptom primarily in two pathological types.

1. *Compulsive personalities* (passive-ambivalent patterns) are especially subject to this form of psychotic disorder. Their physical uncooperativeness is a passive expression of their deeply felt resentments and angers. Their body tightness reflects an intense struggle to control against the outbreak of seething hostility, and their physical withdrawal helps them avoid contact with events that might provoke and unleash their aggressive impulses. Thus, rigidity both communicates and controls their anger, without provoking social condemnation. It may be viewed, then, as a bizarre extension of their habitual instrumental style, a means of controlling contrary impulses by protective restraint and rigid behaviors. The stereotype gestures and grimaces seen in these patients usually convey symbolically an abbreviated and immediately retracted expression of their intolerable aggressive and erotic urges. Features of this disorder are illustrated in the following case history.

CASE 15-3

Arnold N., Age 28, Married, One Child

Arnold, a passive-ambivalent personality, was found one morning by his wife to be "staring in a funny way" outside his bathroom window. Not only did he refuse to reply to her concerned questions regarding his health, but he remained in a rigid position and refused to budge; no amount of pleading on her part was adequate to get him to relax or lie down. A physician was called to examine him shortly thereafter, but he was equally unable to penetrate Arnold's mutism or to alter his taut and unyielding physical posture.

Although Arnold did not resist being carried into an ambulance, he refused to change the body position in which his wife found him that morning.

Arnold's physical rigidity gave way under sedation and he spoke during these periods in a halting and confused manner. As soon as the effects of the drug wore off, however, he again was mute and resumed his immobile stance. Only after several weeks did he loosen up and begin to divulge his thoughts and feelings, both of which indicated a struggle to contain the rage he felt toward his father and his wife for the excessive demands he believed they imposed upon him.

CASE 15-3
Continued

2. *Avoidant personalities* (active-detached patterns) exhibit motor rigidity for reasons similar to those found in the passive-ambivalent. Here, however, the patient is motivated more by his desire to withdraw from external provocation than by the need to control his aggressive impulses, not that the latter is to be overlooked as a factor. Faced with unbearable derogation and humiliation, he draws into a shell, resistant to all forms of stimulation which may reactivate his past misery. The grimaces and giggling often observed in these patients clue us to their rather chaotic fantasy world.

EXCITED CATATONIC DISORDER

CLINICAL PICTURE

In contrast to the rather cheerful and buoyant hyperactivity typically seen in "manic excitement," to be discussed in the next chapter, these patients move about in a surly and truculent manner and explode into uncontrollable rages during which they threaten and occasionally physically assault others with little or no provocation. They may unleash a torrent of abuse and storm about defiantly, cursing and voicing bitterness and contempt for all. Quite unpredictably, they may lunge at and assail passers-by and shout obscenities at unseen hallucinated attackers and persecutors. It is this quality of irrational belligerence and fury, the frenzied lashing out, which distinguishes this disorder from others. We might note, parenthetically, that since the advent of the major psychopharmacological tranquilizers, the incidence of such acting out in hospitalized patients has been markedly reduced.

PERSONALITY AND INSTRUMENTAL BEHAVIOR

Brief outbursts of catatonic hostile excitement may be observed in many of the pathological patterns. However, it arises with greater frequency and persistence in independent and ambivalent personalities.

1. *Aggressive personalities* (active-independent patterns) are particularly prone to this disorder since they are hypersensitive to betrayal and have learned to cope with threat by acting out with hostility. Faced with repeated failures, humiliations and frustrations, their limited controls may be overrun by deeply felt and undischarged angers and resentments. These forces, carrying with them the memories and emotions of the past, surge unrestrainedly to the surface and break out into wild and irrational displays and uncontrollable rage, as exemplified in the following case.

CASE 15-4

Barry J., Age 32, Divorced, No Children

This aggressive personality was remanded by the court to a psychiatric hospital after attempting to run down and shoot several innocent passers-by from his car. Barry was subdued after a violent struggle with several police officers who had side-swiped his auto off the road; fortunately, he had no ammunition left in his revolver at this point. For several hours after imprisonment, Barry continued to shout obscenities and to flail about in a strait jacket, finally succumbing to the effects of intravenously administered tranquilizers. No clear precipitant appeared to have set off his maniacal outburst, although it was learned that he had recently "been ditched" by a girlfriend. Despite the tempering effects of drugs, Barry was difficult to manage, would curse at hallucinated assailants and periodically attempt to assault the psychiatric aides that attended him.

2.   *Compulsive personalities* (passive-ambivalent patterns) may exhibit brief but highly charged hostile outbursts should adverse circumstances lead them to drop their normal controls. The buildup of repressed resentments, concealed for years under a veneer of conformity, occasionally erupts into the open when they have felt betrayed by those in whom they have placed their faith. During their rage, it is not unusual for these patients to brutalize themselves as well as others. For example, they may tear off their clothes, smash their fists and lacerate their bodies, thereby suffering more themselves than do their assailants and betrayers. Their violent discharge of pent-up animosity is usually followed by a return to their former controlled state. In many cases, however, these patients may begin to exhibit one of the other psychotic disorders following their hostile episode.

3.   *Negativistic personalities* (active-ambivalent patterns) also exhibit brief episodes of hostile excitement, often associated with self-mutilation. Their behaviors, however, do not come as a total surprise to former associates since the symptoms of the disorder are but extreme variants of their lifelong pattern of hostile irritability and behavioral unpredictability.

4.   In *narcissistic personalities* (passive-independent patterns) we observe less of the physically vicious and cruel forms of excited hostility than is seen in the patterns noted previously. Rather, we observe an arrogant grandiosity characterized by verbal attacks and bombast. Anger and fury in these patients tend to take the form of oral vituperation and argumentativeness. There is a flow of irrational and caustic comments in which they upbraid and denounce others as inferior, stupid and beneath contempt. This withering onslaught has little objective justification, is chaotic and highly illogical, often colored by delusions and hallucinations, and is directed in a wild, scathing and hit or miss fashion in which they lash out at those who have failed to acknowledge the exalted status in which they view themselves.

5.   *Avoidant* and *asthenic personalities* (active- and passive-detached patterns) often experience brief hostile episodes, usually as a consequence of excessive social demands and responsibilities or events that threaten to reactivate the anguish of the past. As in the case of the ambivalent patterns, these patients often brutalize themselves during their aggressive fury as much as they do others.

SCHIZOPHRENIC PERSONALITY PATTERNS

Detachment from others and alienation from self are the principal features of these personalities. Using concepts provided in earlier chapters we might say that these patients neither anticipate receiving nor are capable of experiencing positive reinforcements either from themselves or others. The *passive-type* is generally insensitive to feelings. As a consequence, he often experiences a separation between his thoughts and his physical body, a strange sense of nonbeing or nonexistence, as if he carried along with his floating conscious awareness some depersonalized or identity-less human form. For the *active-type*, who depreciates his self-worth, there is an abandonment of self and a disowning and remoteness from feeling and desire. His "real" self has been devalued and demeaned, something split off and rejected as valueless. Not only are they alienated from others, then, but they find no refuge and comfort in turning to themselves. Thus, their isolation is two-fold; they gain little from others and experience a despairing sense of emptiness and isolation with themselves. Without these positive reinforcements to spur them, they drift into apathy and social withdrawal.

Denied the power or desire to experience the joy, love and vibrancy of a "personal" life, these patients become devitalized and numb, wander in a dim and hazy fog and engage in activities and thoughts which have minimal purpose or meaning. Why should they participate in social activity, why should they desire, aspire or seek to achieve when nothing in life can spark their flat and spiritless existence or provide them with the feeling of personal pleasure and joy? Thus, they move through life like automatons, possessing impenetrable barriers to shared meanings and affections and estranged from the purposes and aspirations of society, or the spontaneity, delight and triumph of selfhood.

In the following sections we shall describe the two levels of severity found among these patients: the borderline or moderately severe *schizoid* personality, and the decompensated or markedly severe *schizophrenic* personality.

BORDERLINE SCHIZOID PERSONALITY

Several features are found in common among patients classed in the schizoid category. These will be noted before specifying some of the characteristics that differentiate the active and passive subvarieties.

The deficient affect of these patients deprives them of the capacity to relate to persons with warmth and comfort. Moreover, they feel themselves to be more dead than alive, insubstantial, foreign and disembodied. As existential phenomenologists might put it, schizoids are threatened by "nonbeing." Detached observers of the passing scene, these patients remain uninvolved, looking from the outside not only with regard to others but with regard to themselves, as well.

The slippage and interference in thought processes which characterize the milder detached patterns are even more pronounced in the schizoid. When motivated or prompted to relate to others, they are frequently unable to orient their thoughts logically and they become lost in personal irrelevancies and in asides which have no pertinence to the topic at hand. They lack "touch" with others and are unable to order their ideas in terms relevant to reciprocal, social communication.

The colorfulness of personality is lost in the schizoid. There is a listlessness and a lack of spontaneity, ambition and interest in life. These patients are able to talk about only a few relatively tangible matters, usually things that demand immediate attention. Rarely do they initiate conversation, or pursue it beyond what is necessary to be civil. Not only do they lack the spark to act and participate, but they seem enclosed and trapped by some force that blocks them from responding and empathizing with others. This inability to take hold of life, to become a member of society and to invest one's energies and interests in the world of others is well illustrated in the following case.

CASE 15–5

Jane W., Age 27, Unmarried, Hospitalized

Jane was the youngest of three sisters. Since early life, she was known to be quiet and shy, the "weakest" member of the family. Jane's father was a chronic alcoholic who, during frequent drinking sprees, humiliated and regularly beat various members of his family. Her mother seemed detached from Jane, but she often would be critical of her for being "stupid and slow."

Jane completed the tenth grade with better than average grades; however, she had to leave school shortly thereafter because of her mother's death. Jane was given a job as a seamstress as a means of contributing to the family income since her father had abandoned his family two years prior to his wife's death, never to be heard from again.

Unfortunately, Jane was unable to hold her position since the factory in which she worked had closed down; she failed to keep the next three jobs her sisters got for her over a two year period; as Jane put it, "I was not interested and slow."

Following dismissal from her last position, Jane simply withdrew from work, becoming entirely dependent on her older sister. Jane claimed that work was too difficult for her and, more significantly, that she thought that everyone felt, "I was stupid and would mess up the job." In a similar vein, several young men sought to court her, but she persistently refused their overtures since she knew "they wouldn't like me after they took me out."

For the next seven years, Jane took care of the house for her unmarried sister; however, Jane felt that she had never done a "good job" since, "I spent most of my time sleeping or watching TV." She reported further, "I don't like to read or to watch TV, but it's better than thinking about people or myself."

Upon her older sister's marriage, it was decided that Jane, who was both afraid and incapable of being on her own, should be institutionalized. The decision, made by both her sisters, was not responded to by Jane as a painful rejection; she accepted it, at least overtly, without protest.

Upon entrance to the hospital, Jane seemed hazy and disconnected, although she evidenced no hallucinations or delusions. She spoke minimally, answered questions with a yes or no, seemed rational, took care of herself reasonably well and fitted quietly into the admissions ward. She voiced relief to an attendant at being away from the expectations and demands of the outer world; however, she established no personal relationships with other patients or with the hospital personnel.

Were it not for the fact that no one wanted to assist her in making the transition back to society, Jane would have been recommended for discharge. Lacking such environmental support and recognizing her inability to relate easily with others or to assume independence, there was no option but to keep her hospitalized.

Let us next note some of the clinical features differentiating passive from active schizoids.

Passive-schizoids are drab, sluggish and inexpressive. They display a marked deficit in affectivity, are bland and appear untroubled, indifferent, unmotivated and insensitive to the external world (Broen and Nakamura, 1972). Their cognitive processes seem obscure, vague and tangential. They are either impervious to, or miss the shades of, interpersonal and emotional experiences. Social communications are responded to minimally or in a confused manner. Their speech is monotonous, listless or inaudible. Most people consider these schizoids to be unobtrusive and strange persons who fade into the background and are self-absorbed, aloof or lethargic.

Figure 15–3 Typical features of schizoid personalities. (Courtesy of Geigy Pharmaceuticals.)

Active-schizoids are restrained, isolated, apprehensive, guarded and shrinking. Protectively, they have sought to "kill" their feelings and desires. They bind their impulses, withdraw from social encounters and prevent themselves from feeling the pain and anguish of interpersonal relationships. Thus, the apathy, indifference and impoverished thought we observe are not, as it is in the passive-schizoid, owing to an intrinsic lack of sensitivity but to an attempt to control, damp down or deaden excessive sensitivity.

Having given up the hope of gaining affection and security, the active-schizoid defensively denies feelings and aspirations. His cognitive processes are intentionally confused in an effort to disqualify rational thought and the distressful elements they contain. Thus, we see disharmonious affects, irrelevant and tangential thoughts and an increasing social bankruptcy and isolation produced as a function of building a tight armor of indifference around himself.

DECOMPENSATED SCHIZOPHRENIC PERSONALITY

The schizophrenic is a markedly decompensated variant of the mild and moderately severe detached patterns. Though the schizophrenic's clinical appearance is clearly more deteriorated than his schizoid counterparts, he still retains many of their attributes in addition to those he shares with the other decompensated patterns. His lack of social relatedness and competence is most striking. Cognitive processes are markedly disorganized, evidencing both autistic and fragmented qualities. Speech frequently is incoherent, and tends to be scattered with neologisms mixed into rambling word salads. Behavior is extremely bizarre and spotted with peculiar mannerisms. Emotional affect either is totally lacking, creating a drab and flat appearance, or is characterized by its inappropriateness and incongruity. Hallucinations and delusions are quite common, tending to be fleeting, unconnected and totally illogical.

In the *passive-detached* schizophrenic pattern there is a premorbid affectivity deficit, cognitive slippage and interpersonal insensitivity (Ax, 1970). These patients always appeared perplexed, vacant and drab and were drawn within themselves, unable to communicate clearly and with feeling toward others. As conditions led them to retreat to what we have termed the schizoid pattern, they began to experience feelings of depersonalization and became even more unresponsive, socially inadequate, detached and inarticulate. Thus, prior to their advanced schizophrenic decompensation, they evidenced clear signs of cognitive disjunctiveness, depersonalization anxieties and deficient social behaviors, each of which parallels the cardinal traits of the markedly severe personality level. It is for these reasons that disintegration into the decompensated pattern occurs with greater frequency and at an earlier age among detached personalities than among other premorbid personality types. Thus, we would expect to find that a major proportion of institutionalized psychotic patterns would be classified as schizophrenic personalities; similarly, the age at which the psychosis first becomes evident in these patients should be appreciably earlier than in that of other decompensated personality patterns.

Although the premorbid clinical picture of the *active-detached* schizophrenic pattern differs in certain fundamental respects from that of the passive-detached, these patterns progressively become more alike as they decompensate. As in the passive patterns, the active-detached is disposed to a rapid and early development of schizoid and schizophrenic features. His affective disharmony, alienated self-image, cognitive interference and interpersonal aversiveness are early forerunners of the decompensated level (Kish, 1970). The road toward schizophrenic disintegration has been well laid since childhood, and requires little external prompting to be traveled fully and rapidly in early life.

Although many more mildly detached personalities remain well compensated, a substantial proportion falter along the way, either deteriorating to the schizoid level, with its periodic psychotic eruptions, or decompensating further to the more chronically maladaptive schizophrenic pattern. At this stage of abject surrender and instrumental collapse, we see behavioral regressions, a frightening depersonalization and estrangement, bizarre and fragmented thinking and a marked social invalidism. The following case history depicts the development and the clinical characteristics of such an unfortunate being.

CASE 15–6

Harold T., Age 27, Unmarried

Harold was the fourth of seven children. His father, a hard-drinking coal miner, had been on relief throughout most of Harold's early life; his mother died giving birth to her seventh child when Harold was eight. The family was raised by two older sisters, ages 15 and 11 at the time of their mother's death; partial household assistance was provided by a widowed maternal aunt with eight children of her own.

"Duckie," as Harold was known, had always been a withdrawn, frightened and "stupid" youngster. The nickname "Duckie" represented a peculiar waddle in his walk; it was used by others as a term of derogation and ridicule. Harold rarely played with his sibs or neighborhood children; he was teased unmercifully because of his "walk" and his fear of pranksters. Harold was a favorite neighborhood scapegoat; he was intimidated even by the most innocuous glance in his direction.

His father's brutality toward the other children of the family terrified Harold. Although Harold received less than his share of this brutality, since his father thought him to be a "good and not troublesome boy," this escape from paternal hostility was more than made up for by resentment and teasing on the part of his older siblings. By the time Harold was ten or 11, his younger brothers joined in taunting and humiliating him.

Harold's family was surprised when he performed well in the first few years of schooling. He began to falter, however, upon entrance to junior high school. At about the age of 14, his schoolwork became extremely poor, he refused to go to classes and he complained of a variety of vague, physical pains. By age 15 he had totally withdrawn from school, remaining home in the basement room that he shared with two younger brothers. Everyone in his family began to speak of him as "being tetched." He thought about "funny religious things that didn't make sense"; he also began to draw "strange things" and talk to himself. When he was 16, he once ran out of the house screaming "I'm gone, I'm gone, I'm gone . . .", saying that his "body went to heaven" and that he had to run outside to recover it; rather interestingly, this event occurred shortly after his father had been committed by the courts to a state mental hospital. By age 17, Harold was ruminating all day, often talking aloud in a meaningless jargon; he refused to come to the family table for meals.

The scheduled marriage of his second oldest sister, who had been running the household for five years, brought matters to a head. Harold, then 18, was taken to the same mental hospital to which his father had been committed two years previously.

When last seen, Harold had been institutionalized for nine years; no appreciable change was evident in his behavior or prognosis since admission. Most notable clinically is his drab appearance, apathy and lack of verbal communication; on rare occasions he laughs to himself in an incongruous and peculiar manner. He stopped soiling, which he had begun to do when first admitted, and will now eat by himself. When left alone with pencil and paper, he draws strange religious-like pictures but is unable to verbalize their meaning in a coherent fashion. Drug therapy has had no effect upon his condition; neither has he responded to group therapeutic efforts.

DEVELOPMENTAL BACKGROUND

We shall not review in detail the background of schizoid and schizophrenic personalities since their histories essentially duplicate conditions already discussed in our presentations of the mild detached patterns in earlier chapters.

As has been stressed throughout the text, severe patterns lie at one extreme of a continuum of pathology, with the other extreme occupied by the mild personality types. The same complex of etiological factors that is found in mild pathologies is seen in the background of more severe variants. The principal differences are the greater intensity and frequency of pathogenic elements in the latter. Thus, where constitutional factors are operative, the presence of a severe biophysical impairment is more likely to result in a marked rather than a mild pathological pattern (Stein, 1971; Pollin, 1972). Similarly, in the severely disabled patterns we are likely to discover a social learning history of persistent and unrelieved environmental adversity (Rodnick, 1968). Let us briefly note some of the pathogenic elements associated with the passive- and active-patterns of schizoid and schizophrenic development.

1.   There is a reasonable likelihood that genetic tendencies conducive to affective and cognitive deficits are present in the biogenic background of *passive schizoid* and *schizophrenic personalities.* Many have shown a passive reaction pattern in infancy, which in turn may have initiated a sequence of impoverished stimulation and parental indifference.

In their social learning background, there is a reasonable probability of marked stimulus impoverishment during the sensory-attachment stage, reflecting either parental neglect or indifference. These experiences may lay the groundwork for an underdevelopment of affectivity and a deficit learning of interpersonal attachment behaviors. A family atmosphere of cold formality may have served as a model for imitative learning, resulting in a lifelong style of social reticence and a discomfort with personal closeness (Cheek, 1967). Fragmented and amorphous styles of parental communication may have prompted the development of disjointed and unfocused patterns of thinking (Laing and Esterson, 1970).

Repeated exposure to these conditions and to peer experiences which aggravate them may grow to produce a complex web of pathology. Once established, early styles of behavior and coping may perpetuate and intensify past difficulties (Offord and Gross, 1969). Social detachment, emotional impassivity and cognitively obscure thinking will progressively alienate the youngster from others and lead him to subordinate overt activity to autistic fantasy; unchecked by social contact, these inner thoughts begin to lose their logic and coherence, causing a new spiral of self-defeating processes that further the decompensation trend.

2.   The biogenic background of *active schizoid* and *schizophrenic personalities* will often give evidence of apprehensive or cognitively obscure relatives, indicating the possible contribution of genetic factors to pathology. Hypertense infantile patterns are common, often precipitating parental tension and derogation, which then aggravate the established temperament. Irregularities in maturation may frequently be noted, producing uneven competencies, difficult to handle emotions and notable social "peculiarities."

Their social learning histories typically show a background of parental deprecation and peer group humiliation, resulting in lowered self-esteem and social distrust. These experiences often begin as early as the first or sensory-attachment stage of development, leading the youngster to protectively insulate his feelings. Ridicule in response to second-stage autonomy efforts contributes markedly to a sense of personal inadequacy and incompetence. The persistence of belittling and derogating attitudes through later childhood and adolescence leads eventually to self-criticism and self-deprecation. For example, Harold T. was subjected to relentless harassment and humiliation both at home and at school. By the time he was 13 or 14, Harold had "accepted" the inevitability of his fate, referred to himself as "stupid and ugly" and ultimately withdrew protectively from all social contacts.

The learned instrumental strategies these persons employ to protect against further social ridicule only perpetuate and intensify their plight. Thus, Harold denied himself opportunities for remedial experiences, perceived threat where none existed and preoccupied himself with fantasies that focused on past misfortunes. To counter these oppressive thoughts, he began to block or destroy his cognitive clarity, thereby fostering further self-estrangement and social incompetence. As feelings of unreality grew, periodic psychotic episodes blended into one another, and he deteriorated gradually into a more permanent decompensated state (Brown, Birley and Wing, 1972).

Schizoid and schizophrenic personalities lack sources of positive reinforcement, and have disengaged themselves from reality and the controls of social interaction. Without positive reinforcements to motivate them and without the support and controls of social life, the prospects are high that they will undergo rapid personality decompensation. For these reasons, we find the schizophrenic personality pattern emerging typically early in life, usually, but not invariably, between the ages of 15 and 25. It is this same lack of developed social skills and sense of deep unworthiness and incompetence that account for the fact that these patients often remain in a permanent decompensated state; schizophrenic personalities comprise the greater bulk of the chronic or "hard-core" patients in most mental institutions.

TREATMENT APPROACHES

In the following discussion we will differentiate, as we have before, the passive- and active-schizoid and schizophrenic varieties.

Passive-types have poor prognoses for several reasons. Many are limited in their constitutional capacity for affectivity and activation. Cognitive dysfunctions and interpersonal insensitivities may have their roots in irremediable biophysical deficiencies and few are motivated to seek or sustain a therapeutic relationship. Left to their own devices they isolate themselves increasingly from social activities, thereby diminishing environmental controls and precluding beneficial interpersonal experiences.

The primary focus of therapy is the prevention of the self-defeating and deleterious consequences of social isolation. Through environmental management and various behavior modification procedures (Ayllon and Azrin, 1965; Smith and Carlin, 1972; Carlson et al., 1972), the therapist may seek to increase the patient's awareness and involvement in interpersonal activities. Toward this end also, several psychopharmacological agents may be prescribed to stimulate activation and affectivity. However, efforts to enhance social interest must be undertaken in a slow, step by step manner, so as not to press the patient beyond tolerable limits.

Among cognitively obscure patients, a clearer and more orderly style of thinking may be fostered by employing careful and well-reasoned therapeutic communications. Since passive types are not totally devoid of feeling, the therapist would do well to alert himself to those spheres of life in which the patient possesses constructive emotional inclinations, seeking to encourage activities that are consonant with these tendencies. Involvement in therapeutic groups may facilitate the development of social skills. It is wise, however, to precede or combine group therapy with individual sessions, so as to forestall undue social discomforts.

Active-types also have poor prognostic prospects. Their pattern is deeply ingrained; rarely do they live in an encouraging or supporting environment. Probing into personal matters often is painful, even terrifying. They have a marked distrust of close personal relationships, such as is inevitable in most forms of psychotherapy. Furthermore, therapy sets up false hopes, and often necessitates painful self-exposure. They would rather leave matters be, keeping to themselves, insulated from "unnecessary" humiliation and anguish. Should they engage in treatment, they will tend to be guarded, and constantly test the therapist's sincerity; a "false" move will be interpreted as verification of the disinterest and deprecation they have learned to anticipate from others.

Trust is the essential prerequisite to therapeutic progress. Without a feeling of confidence in the genuineness of the therapist's interests and motives, the patient will block his efforts and, ultimately, terminate treatment. Equally important is that the patient be settled in a supportive social environment. Treatment will involve a long and uphill battle unless external conditions are favorable.

The primary focus of therapy with active-types should be to enhance the patient's self-worth and to encourage him to recognize and utilize his positive attributes. The development of pride in self, that is, of valuing one's constructive capacities and feelings, is a necessary first step in rebuilding the patient's motivation to face the world. No longer alienated from himself, he will have a basis for overcoming his alienation from others. With a sense of valued self begun, the therapist may guide the patient into positively reinforcing social activities. The experience of positive reinforcements is what was lacking in the life of the active type. Initiating such experiences may prove to be the crucial turning point in what otherwise may have been an inexorable downward progression.

Both passive and active-types should be aided to strengthen their controls and to curb the expression of irrational impulses. Any precipitant of bizarre and socially destructive episodes, such as prolonged isolation, too rapid and intense personal relationships or the use of alcohol should be avoided when possible.

As far as specific techniques are concerned, behavioral methods are primary in the early stages of therapy; insight and group techniques (O'Brien et al., 1972) are best employed in the midphases of treatment, that is, after adequate rapport and trust have been established. Psychoanalytic therapy should not be considered until schizoid detachment is well under control. Analytic procedures such as free association, the detached attitude of the therapist or the focus on dreams may only foster the patient's tendency to autistic reveries and social withdrawal. Institutionalization, when necessary, should be brief, if possible; hospital settings too often breed isolation and reward "quiet" behaviors, thus resulting in increased detachment and fantasy preoccupations (Braginsky et al., 1969).

How, then, do schizoids and schizophrenics learn new, more adaptive styles of behavior? In a nutshell, by acquiring a trust of the therapist, learning to relate to, and identify with, a receptive and encouraging person and hopefully, generalizing these experiences to others. With these learnings as a model, and with an increased sense of self-esteem, the patient may begin to test his newly acquired attitudes and skills beyond the therapeutic setting.

Vincent Van Gogh — *Sorrow.*

16 AFFECTIVE DISORDERS AND PATTERNS

INTRODUCTION

From the earliest literary and medical history, writers have recognized the coexistence within single persons of intense and divergent moods such as euphoria and depression. Both Homer and Hippocrates described with great clarity the related character of mania and melancholia, noting both the periodic vacillation between these "spells" and the personality types likely to be subject to them. However, as with most medical and scientific knowledge, these early formulations were lost or suppressed in medieval times. With the advent of the Renaissance, the observations of Greek and Roman physicians were brought to light, and new systematic studies of the mentally ill were begun anew.

The first to revive the notion of the covariation between mood extremes in a single syndrome was Bonet, who applied the term *folie maniaco-mélancolique* in 1684. Schacht and Herschel noted similar patterns in the eighteenth century. In 1854, Falret published the results of thirty years' work with depressed and suicidal persons. He found that a large proportion of these patients showed a course of extended depression, broken intermittently by periods of marked elation and normality. He termed this syndrome *la folie circulaire* to signify its contrasting and variable character. It was Kahlbaum, however, whose genius for perceptive clinical classification has too often been overlooked, who clearly described in 1882 the typical covariation of mania and melancholia; to him, they were facets of a single disease which manifested itself in different ways at different times.

Although Kraepelin borrowed heavily from Kahlbaum's formulations, he rejected Kahlbaum's important distinction between mild and severe circular types. This reflected his attempt to find a set of simple common denominators for large groups of mental disorders. Thus, in 1896, he proposed the name manic-depressive insanity for "the whole domain of periodic and circular insanity," including such diverse disturbances and "the morbid states termed melancholia . . . [and] certain slight colorings of mood, some of them periodic, some of them continuously morbid."

Asserting his conviction of the unitary character of this disease, Kraepelin wrote:

I have become convinced all these states only represent manifestations of a single morbid process. It is certainly possible that later a series of subordinate groups may be . . . entirely separated off. But if this happens, then according to my view those symptoms will certainly not be authoritative which hitherto have usually been placed in the foreground.

Kraepelin left no doubt that he viewed the "circular insanity" to be a unitary illness. Every disorder which gave evidence of mood disturbances was conceived to be a variant or "rudiment" of the same basic impairment. The common denominator for this group of disturbances was an constitutional metabolic dysfunction that was "to an astonishing degree independent of external influences."

To contrast these mood disorders with dementia praecox, which he characterized as progressing to an inevitable state of total personality disintegration, Kraepelin asserted that the manic-depressive had a favorable outcome. To reinforce this distinction more sharply, Kraepelin drew upon a valid but by no means consistent observation and made it into an irrefutable rule. It is well known that patients with mood disorders generally but not always have good prognoses. Kraepelin took this observation as a basis for claiming that *all* mood disorders have good prognoses. By a curious twist of logic, he then asserted that if a patient did deteriorate, he could not have had a mood, that is, a manic-depressive disorder, but rather dementia praecox. To fit the facts into his system, Kraepelin and his followers often changed their diagnoses.

It is our contention that patients with severe mood disorders can deteriorate, that is, display a chronic and persistent pattern of divergent and changing emotions (Bunney et al., 1972). Since this pattern becomes the very fabric of their personality make-up, it would seem logical to characterize them as displaying what may be termed an *affective personality pattern*. Others, who exhibit these erratic intense emotions infrequently, may be said to display *affective symptom disorders* (Paykel, 1972). Hence, as in the previous chapter, we will separate our presentation into these two major subcategories (Kendall, 1968; Millon, 1969; Eysenck, 1970; Mendels, 1970). The first to be described, the acute affective disorders, may be further differentiated by the major symptom displayed, e.g., depression, excitement and so forth; the second, the severe affective patterns, are differentiated into the borderline (moderate) and decompensated (marked) levels of severity.

ACUTE AFFECTIVE DISORDERS

MANIC (EUPHORIC EXCITEMENT) DISORDER

CLINICAL PICTURE

Certain commonalities may be noted between the "hebephrenic" (see Chapter 15) and "manic" disorders. Most notable among these is that patients in both disorders tend to be rather disorganized, scattering their ideas and emotions in a jumble of disconnected thoughts and aimless behaviors. However, there is an exuberance, a zestful energy and jovial mood among manics that is lacking in hebephrenic patients. Furthermore, their ideas and hyperactivity, although tending to be connected only loosely to reality, have an intelligible logic to them and are colored by a consistent mood of affability which evokes feelings of sympathy and good will on the part of others. In contrast, the behaviors and ideas of hebephrenic patients are extremely vague, disjointed and bizarre. Moreover, their emotional moods are varied and changeable, inconsistent with their thoughts and actions and difficult to grasp and relate to, let alone empathize with.

Manic euphorics tend, albeit briefly, to infect others with their conviviality and optimism. Many are extremely clever and witty, rattling off puns and rhymes and playing cute and devilish tricks (Janowsky et al., 1970). However, their humor and mischievousness begin to drain others, who quickly tire of the increasingly irrational quality of their forced sociability. In addition to frenetic excitement and their impulsive race from one topic to another, these patients often display an annoying pomposity and self-expansiveness as well. The boundless boastfulness and self-aggrandizement become extremely trying and exasperating, and often destroy what patience and good will these patients previously evoked from others.

PERSONALITY AND INSTRUMENTAL BEHAVIOR

Manic excitement occurs with reasonable frequency in several personality patterns. In most, it tends to last for periods of less than two to three months.

1. *Hysterical personalities* (active-dependents) are particularly susceptible to this disorder since it is consistent with their characteristic gregarious behavior style. Confronted with severe separation anxieties or anticipating a decline or loss of social approval, these personalities may simply intensify their habitual strategy until it reaches a rather forced and frantic congeniality. Here we observe a frenetic search for attention, a release of tension through hyperactivity and a protective effort to stave off depressive hopelessness, as illustrated in the following brief history.

This active-dependent woman had been living alone for several months following the break up of an affair that had lasted five years. Jeri had been mildly depressed for some weeks thereafter, but claimed that she "was glad it was all over with." Her co-workers at the department store in which she was employed as a buyer began to notice a marked brightening of her spirits several weeks prior to her "breakdown." Jeri's "chipper mood" grew with each passing day until it became increasingly extreme and irrational. She would talk incessantly, skipping from one topic to the next and be uncontainable when telling lewd stories and jokes, not only to fellow employees but to customers as well. Her indiscretions and the frightening quality of her exuberance prompted her supervisor to recommend that she be seen by the store nurse, who then suggested psychiatric treatment.

CASE 16–1

Jeri T., Age 37, Unmarried

2. In *inadequate personalities* (passive-dependent patterns) we see a marked, although usually temporary, reversal of these patients' more subdued instrumental style. Their hyperactivity, their happy go lucky air, their boundless energy and optimism comprise a front, an act in which they try to convince themselves as well as others that "all will be well." In short, it is a desperate effort to counter the beginning signs of hopelessness and depression, a last-ditch attempt to deny what they really feel and to recapture the attention and security they fear they have lost (Korner, 1970).

Figure 16-1 Euphoric excitement. These pictures show the sequence of events during the first two days of a euphoric excitement episode in a 57 year old man. A. One day, while working on his farm, he suddenly jumped up shouting that the "spirit" had overtaken him. B. He said later that he had begun to get commands to jump up and roll over like a wheel, and then "to holler and praise the Lord and make a noise enough so He can hear you." C. He tried to get others to follow his lead, and eventually fell down exhausted. D and E. The next morning he started out to walk to a neighbor's house but was forcibly detained by his son, who carried him back. He told the doctors later, "I was joy at heart—That is why I couldn't stay still. I had to go talk with somebody and tell them how much joy." He was sent home from the hospital soon thereafter. (Reprinted from the American Journal of Psychiatry, 100(2):781–787, 1944. Copyright, 1944, The American Psychiatric Association.)

3. *Narcissistic personalities* (passive-independents) evidence a self-exalted and pompous variant of manic excitement. Faced with realities that shatter their illusion of significance and omnipotence, they become frightened, lose their perspective and frantically seek to regain their status. No longer secure in their image of superiority, they attempt through their euphoric behaviors to instill or revive the blissful state of their youth, when their mere existence was of value in itself. Thus, passive-independents are driven into their excited state in the hope of reestablishing an exalted status and not to recapture support and nurture from others, as is the case among the dependents.

4. *Avoidant* and *asthenic personalities* (active- and passive-detached) exhibit brief and rather frenzied episodes of manic excitement in an attempt to counter the frightening anxieties of depersonalization. Here, for a fleeting period, they may burst out of their more usual retiring and unsociable pattern and into a bizarre conviviality. The wild, irrational and chaotic character of their exuberance tends to distinguish their manic episodes from those of others.

RETARDED DEPRESSION DISORDER

CLINICAL PICTURE

There are several similarities between "impassive catatonic" and "retarded depression" disorders. Both exhibit a generalized psychomotor inactivity, e.g., heavy and lugubrious movements, slow or dragged out speech and an everpresent air of fatigue and exhaustion. Careful observation, however, will uncover areas of considerable difference, even at the gross clinical level. For example, the retarded depressive patient experiences deep feelings, contrasting markedly with the emotional flatness of the withdrawn catatonic. His gloom and profound dejection are clearly conveyed as he slumps with brow furrowed, body stooped and head turned downward and away from the gaze of others, held in his hands like a burdensome weight. Various physical signs and symptoms further enable us to distinguish these disorders from the impassive catatonic. Retarded depressives lose weight and look haggard and drained. In their nighttime habits they follow a characteristic pattern of awakening after two or three hours of sleep, turn restlessly, have oppressive thoughts and experience a growing dread of the new day. Notable, also, is the content of their verbalizations, meager though they may be. They report a vague dread of impending disaster, feelings of utter helplessness, a pervasive sense of guilt for past failures and a willing resignation to their hopeless fate. As will be noted shortly, retarded depressions occur most often among passive-dependent personalities whereas catatonic impassivity is more typical of the passive-detached type.

PERSONALITY AND INSTRUMENTAL BEHAVIOR

1. *Inadequate personalities* (passive-dependent) are especially susceptible to this disorder; *hysterical personalities* (active-dependent) are only slightly less vulnerable. Both patterns manifest these symptoms in response to essentially similar sources, notably a loss or the anticipated loss of an important source of their dependency security, e.g., the death of a parent or spouse or dismissal from a steady job. Their depression often represents a logical but overly extreme response to real or potentially threatening events. However, there is no question that the reaction is pathological. The depth of the response and the tendency to succumb to profound dejection, even before difficulties have arisen, clearly point to the presence of an unusual personality vulnerability.

Despite the genuineness of the depressive mood, dependent personalities do not give up their coping aims in their disordered state. Their displays of contrition and the deep gravity of their mood solicit attention, support and nurture from others (Shapiro, 1972). Moreover, their coping aims enable them to avoid unbearable responsibilities and provide them with the comforts and security of dependent invalidism. Aspects of this syndrome are depicted in the following brief example.

CASE 16–2

Alma F., Age 34, Married, Two Children

This markedly dependent woman was admitted to the psychiatric wing of a general hospital with her third depressive episode in eight years. When first seen she was markedly underweight, had been "unable" to eat for weeks and sat limply at the edge of her chair, weeping quietly and stating, over and over again, "What have I done to my family. . . ." Alma was observed to be quiet, although downcast when she was left alone. However, as soon as someone appeared, she began to moan aloud, deprecating herself for the harm and shame she had brought to her family. Needless to say, these lamentations evoked sympathetic and reassuring responses from others.

2. Both *compulsive* and *negativistic personalities* (passive- and active-ambivalents) succumb with some frequency to retarded depressions although, more characteristically, they lean toward the agitated form of depressive expression, to be discussed later. In the retarded form, ambivalents have managed to gain a measure of control over their conflicts and hostile impulses. This they have done by turning their feelings inward, that is, by taking out their hatred upon themselves. Thus, they persist in voicing guilt and self-disparagement for their failures, antisocial acts, contemptuous feelings and thoughts. In this self-punitive depressive disorder, they manage to cloak their "real" contrary impulses and seek redemption for their past behaviors and forbidden inclinations. Moreover, their illness solicits support and nurture from others. In a more subtle way it also serves as a devious means of venting their hidden resentment and anger. Their state of helplessness and their self-derogation make others feel guilty and burden them with extra responsibilities and woes.

AGITATED DEPRESSION DISORDER

CLINICAL PICTURE

The features of this disorder are rather mixed and erratic, varying in quality and focus in accord with the patient's basic personality pattern. In many respects, it is a composite of previously described "retarded depression" and "catatonic excitement" disorders, although not as extreme as either in their respective dominant characteristics. In all cases there is an incessant despair and suffering, an agitated pacing to and fro, a wringing of hands and an apprehensiveness and tension that are unrelieved by comforting reassurances. In some cases, the primary components are hostile depressive complaints and a demanding irritability in which the patient bemoans his sorry state and his desperate need for attention. In other cases, the depressive picture is colored less by critical and demanding attitudes and more by self-doubting, expressions of self-hate, a preoccupation with impending disasters, suicidal thoughts, feelings of unworthiness and delusions of shame and sin (Mendels et al., 1972).

PERSONALITY AND INSTRUMENTAL BEHAVIOR

As was noted previously, the overall tone and subsidiary clinical details observed among the disorders depend on the particular social learning history and personality pattern of the patient. Some of these differences may be noted in the following survey of the more vulnerable personality types.

1. *Negativistic personalities* (active-ambivalent) are especially prone to agitated depressions. These disorders can be seen as an extension of

Figure 16-2 Typical features of agitated depression. (Courtesy of Geigy Pharmaceuticals.)

their premorbid personality style—complaints, irritability and a sour
grumbling discontent, usually interwoven with hypochondriacal preoccupations and periodic expressions of guilt and self-condemnation.
Their habitual style of acting out their conflicts and ambivalent feelings
becomes more pronounced, resulting in extreme vacillations between
bitterness and resentment on the one hand (Kendall, 1970) and self-
deprecation on the other. Self-pity and bodily anxieties are extremely
common and may serve as a basis for distinguishing them from other
agitated types. The following illustrates a typical case.

CASE 16–3 *Ethel S., Age 53, Married,* *Three Children*	Ethel, a markedly ambivalent personality with a prior history of several psychotic breaks, became increasingly irritable, despairing and self-deprecating over a period of one or two months: no clear cause was evident. She paced back and forth, wringing her hands and periodically shouting that God had forsaken her and that she was a "miserable creature, placed on earth to make my family suffer." At times, Ethel would sit on the edge of a chair, nervously chewing her nails, complaining about the disinterest shown her by her children. Then, she would jump up, move about restlessly, voicing irrational fears about her own and her husband's health, claiming that he was a "sick man," sure to die because of her "craziness." Ethel's agitated and fretful behavior took on a more contentious and hypochondriacal quality in the hospital to which she was brought. During a course of electroconvulsive treatments and a regimen of antidepressant drugs, Ethel's composure gradually returned, and she came home seven weeks following hospitalization.

2. *Compulsive personalities* (passive-ambivalent) exhibit the traditional
form of agitated depression, noted by diffuse apprehension, marked
guilt feelings and a tendency to delusions of sin and unworthiness.
These patients do not exhibit the whining qualities seen in their active-
ambivalent counterparts. Instead, they turn the aggressive component
of their conflict toward themselves, claiming that they deserve the
punishment and misery which they now suffer.

3. *Inadequate* and *hysterical personalities* (passive- and active-dependent)
evidence agitated depressions less frequently than the ambivalents. In
their case, the primary stimuli tend to be anticipated losses in dependency security. They generally wail aloud and convey feelings of hope
lessness and abandonment, all in the hope of soliciting support and nurture. Their agitation does not reflect an internal struggle of hostility
versus guilt, as in the case of the ambivalents, but a more direct and
simple expression of worrisome apprehension.

AFFECTIVE PERSONALITY PATTERNS

The most obvious feature of affective patients is the depth and variability
of their moods (Roth et al., 1972). All these patients experience periods
of dejection and disillusionment, frequently interspersed with temporary periods of elation or hostility. For example, some experience a
sense of helplessness and hopelessness, interspersed periodically with
frantic efforts to stand on their own, or to recapture, by a cheerful
outgoingness, the affections they need. Similarly, others may reach a fe-
verish pitch of euphoric excitement, only to fall into the depths of despondency and self-deprecation, should their efforts fail. Unsure of external approval and troubled by surging inner impulses, some may
vacillate among marked self-condemnation, protestations of piety and
good intentions, impulsive outbursts of hostility and feelings of intense

guilt for their shortcomings. Others swing into profound gloom, at one time, and irrational negativism and chaotic excitement, at another. It is their extreme vacillation of behavior and mood and their common desperate seeking for esteem and approval from others that justifies thinking of these patients as members of this major syndrome. As discussed earlier, we have differentiated this larger group into two broad categories, the disorders, already described, and the chronic personality patterns, to be divided into two levels of severity, borderline *(cycloid [or cyclothymic] personality)* and decompensated *(cyclophrenic personality)*.

BORDERLINE CYCLOID (CYCLOTHYMIC) PERSONALITY

Cycloid (cyclothymic) personalities are exceedingly dependent. Not only do they require a great deal of protection, reassurance and encouragement from others to maintain their balance, but they are vulnerable to separation from these external sources of support.

Separation and isolation can be terrifying not only because cycloids do not value themselves or use themselves as a source of positive reinforcement, but because they lack the know-how and equipment for independence and self-determination. Unable to fend for themselves, they not only dread signs of potential loss, but they anticipate it, and distort their perceptions so that they "see it" happening when, in fact, it is not. Any event which stirs up these feelings may prompt a psychotic episode, most notably those of depression or excitement, as illustrated in the following brief case history.

This cycloid woman was admitted into a general hospital following a brief period of severe depression. For several years, Ruth would "go into a blue funk" whenever her husband was required to take short business trips away from home. In recent episodes, she could not perform even the simplest household chores and would sit in her bedroom with her two year old son and cry all day. Since this last episode, her husband requested a demotion to a job that required no traveling. However, in recent months, Ruth has again begun to exhibit her depressive moods whenever her husband would come home late from work or spend a few hours on a Sunday afternoon golfing with his friends.

CASE 16–4

Ruth S., Age 27, Married, One Child

Matters are bad enough for the cycloid given his separation anxiety, but these patients are also in conflict regarding their dependency needs, and often feel guilt for having tried to be self-assertive. Moreover, to assert himself would endanger the rewards he so desperately seeks from others and perhaps even provoke them to totally reject and abandon him. Moreover, given his past experiences, he knows he can never fully trust others nor hope to gain all the affection and support he needs. Should resentments be discharged, even in so mild a form as displays of self-assertion, his security may be undermined and severely threatened. Thus, he finds himself in a terrible bind; should he "go it" alone, no longer depending on others who have been so unkind, or should he submit for fear of losing what little security he can eke out?

To secure his anger and constrain his resentment, the cycloid often turns against himself and is self-critical and self-condemnatory. He begins to despise himself and to feel guilty for his offenses, his unworthiness and his contemptibility (Beck, 1971).

The most striking feature of the cycloid is the intensity of his moods and the frequent changeability of his behaviors, as illustrated in the following case history.

CASE 16–5

Leo P., Age 42, Married, Two Children

Leo has shown a lifelong development typical of the cycloid. He claimed that he was never fully appreciated by anyone, especially his wife and his employers.

Desirous of seeking affection and approval from others, yet unsure of their feelings toward him, smothered by deep resentments, yet fearful of the consequences of assertion and anger, Leo would be in a state of turmoil, in an unresolvable conflict that prevented finding a single and stable course of action. Thus, for short periods, he would be submissive, but as soon as he felt unsuccessful, unloved and deserted he would burst into rage. When he momentarily felt confident and successful again, he became euphoric and was up in the clouds, making grandiose plans for the future; with his high hopes dashed shortly thereafter, he again became overtly hostile; then, protectively, he would turn his resentments inward and feel worthless and guilty, but to counter the oppressiveness of these feelings, he would divert his thoughts from himself, seek to lift his spirits, run frenetically here and there and speak hurriedly and without pause, changing excitedly from one topic to another.

These *rapid* swings from one mood and behavior to another are *not* typical of the cycloid. They characterize periods in which there is a break in control or what we have referred to as a psychotic episode. More commonly, these patients exhibit a single dominant mood, usually a depressive tone that, on occasion, gives way to brief displays of anxious agitation, euphoric activity or outbursts of hostility.

The cycloid's typical, everyday mood and behavior reflect his basic personality pattern (Chodoff, 1972). In the following paragraphs we will note some of the clinical features that differentiate the four subvariants of the cycloid syndrome (Grinker et al., 1961). These parallel the two dependent and two ambivalent milder personality types described in Chapters 11 and 12.

1. *Passive-dependent cycloids* typically are self-effacing, sweet and Pollyanna-like individuals who shun competition, are lacking in initiative and are easily discouraged. They attach themselves usually to one or two other persons upon whom they depend, with whom they can display affection and to whom they can be loyal and humble.

However, the cycloid's strategy of cooperation and compliance, in contrast to his less pathological counterpart, has not been notably successful. He has put all his eggs in one basket, a specific loved one to whom he is excessively attached. But this attachment has not proved secure. His lifeline is connected to an unreliable anchor and his psychic equilibrium hangs on a thin thread and is in constant jeopardy. As a consequence, these patient exhibit a perennial preoccupation and concern with security. Their pathetic lack of inner resources and their marked self-doubts lead them to cling to whomever they can find, and to submerge every remnant of autonomy and individuality they possess (Koran and Maxim, 1972).

This insecurity often creates conflict and distress. These cycloids easily become depressed and feel powerless to overcome their fate. Everything becomes a burden. Simple responsibilities demand more energy than they can muster, life seems empty but heavy, they cannot go on alone, and they begin to turn upon themselves, feeling unworthy, useless and despised (Loeb et al., 1971). Should their sense of futility grow, they may regress to a state of marked apathy and infantile dependency, requiring others to tend to them as if they were babies.

2. *Active-dependent cycloids* are similar to their mildly pathological counterparts. Both are charming, extravert, flighty, capricious, superficial and seductive. However, the cycloid's strategies are instrumentally less successful than those of the hysterical personality. Deprived much of the time of the attentions and reinforcements they crave, these cycloids may intensify their learned habits of gregariousness and seductiveness, and become dramatically histrionic and exhibitionistic. At these times, extreme hyperactivity, flightiness and distractibility are often evident. They exhibit a frenetic gaiety, an exaggerated boastfulness and an insistent and insatiable need for social contact and excitement. Frightened lest they lose attention and approval, they display a frantic conviviality, an irrational and superficial euphoria in which they lose all sense of propriety and judgment, and race excitedly from one activity to another.

At other times, they experience repeated rebuffs, or their efforts to solicit attention simply prove futile. Fearing a permanent loss of attention and esteem, they succumb to hopelessness and self-deprecation. Having lost confidence in their seductive powers, dreading a decline in vigor, charm and youth, they begin to fret and worry, to have doubts about their worth and attractiveness.

3. *Passive-ambivalent cycloids* are extreme variants of the mildly pathological compulsive personality. Both are methodical, rigid, industrious, conscientious and orderly persons. They overcomply to the strictures of society, display an air of moral rectitude, are overly respectful and deferential to authority and tend to be small-minded, perfectionistic, grim and humorless. They have learned to look to others for support and affection, but such rewards are contingent on compliance and submission to authority. They know that one *must* be good "or else." However, the passive-ambivalent cycloid is less certain than the compulsive personality that he will receive rewards for compliance. Try as he may, he is not confident that diligence and acquiescence will forestall desertion and that he will not be left adrift, alone and abandoned even when he submits and conforms.

The resentment and anger these cycloids feel for having been coerced into submission and then betrayed, churns within them and presses hard against their usually strong controls. Periodically, these feelings break through to the surface, erupting in an angry upsurge of fury.

Whether resentments are discharged overtly or kept seething near the surface, these cycloids experience them as a threat. Feelings such as these signify weakness and emotionality, traits which run contrary to their self-image of propriety and control. Moreover, such impulses create anxiety because they jeopardize their security, that is, their basic dependency on others.

To counter these hostile impulses, the passive-ambivalent cycloid may become excessively constrained and rigid, and engage in ritualistic and compulsive precautions to control all traces of resentment. Struggling feverishly to control their aggressive impulses, these patients often turn their feelings inward, and impose upon themselves severe punitive judgments and actions.

4. *Active-ambivalent cycloids* are difficult to distinguish from their less severe counterpart, the negativistic personality. At best, we can say that the cycloids' overt symptoms are more intense and that their occasional psychotic episodes occur with somewhat greater frequency than in the

negativist. Both groups may be characterized by their high unpredictability and by their restless, irritable, impatient and complaining behaviors. Typically, they are disgruntled and discontent, stubborn and sullen and pessimistic and resentful. Enthusiasms are short lived. They are easily disillusioned and slighted, tend to be envious of others and feel unappreciated and cheated in life.

Unable to get hold of themselves and unable to find a comfortable niche with others, these cycloids may become increasingly testy, bitter and discontent. Resigned to their fate and despairing of hope, they oscillate between two pathological extremes of behavior. For long periods, they may express feelings of worthlessness and futility, become highly agitated or deeply depressed, develop delusions of guilt and be severely self-condemnatory and perhaps self-destructive. At other times, their habitual negativism may cross the line of reason, break out of control and drive them into maniacal rages in which they distort reality, make excessive demands of others and viciously attack those who have trapped them and forced them into intolerable conflicts.

DECOMPENSATED CYCLOPHRENIC (SCHIZO-AFFECTIVE) PERSONALITY

The label "cyclophrenia" is a relatively new term (Millon, 1969) coined to represent a syndrome whose decompensation is deeply ingrained and pervasive. Its distinguishing feature as a personality pattern is that it overlies a lifelong style either of dependency or of ambivalence. The invalidism and cognitive disorganization of these patients emerge following the disintegration of a cycloid pattern of coping. Thus, the syndrome reflects one further step in pathological severity that began with a mild dependent, or ambivalent, personality pattern.

There is no term in the psychiatric literature for severely deteriorated patients whose earlier life style is noted by dependence strivings. It has been customary in psychiatric circles to label as "schizophrenic" all markedly decompensated patients, regardless of their premorbid personalities. We reject this common practice. It is our contention that distinctions should be made in accord with premorbid personality styles.

The official DSM-II classification does include a clinical syndrome that is roughly comparable to cyclophrenia. Not surprisingly, it is categorized under the schizophrenic rather than the affective label; it is listed as *schizophrenia, schizo-affective type*. The descriptive text for this impairment in the detailed 1952 manual states:

For those cases showing significant admixtures of schizophrenic and affective reactions. The mental content may be predominantly schizophrenic, with pronounced elation or depression. Cases may show predominantly affective changes with schizophrenic-like thinking or bizarre behavior.

This brief description represents in crude form some of the overt clinical features of what we have termed the cyclophrenic. In essence, these patients exhibit cognitive disorganization, estrangement and invalidism (which are features of all decompensated patterns). In addition, they display both a strong affective tone and a social relatedness which are *not* found in schizophrenic personalities. The affectivity and sociability of cyclophrenics reflect their lifelong basic strategy of seeking interpersonal support, approval and nurture. Thus, cyclophrenics possess both the features of decompensated personalities and those of dependent or dependent-ambivalent strategies.

Most notable at this stage of impairment is the emergence of a persistent social invalidism, as is evident in his inability to assume responsibility for his own care, welfare and health. Thinking is difficult and speech may be limited, hesitant and indecisive. Cognitive processes tend to be confused, manifesting themselves either in sudden and erratic changes in focus or as inaudible and incoherent ramblings. Behavior and emotion tend either toward the bizarre, with bursts of energy and irrational exuberance, or toward the sluggish. There may be little or no motor activity, and a physical inertia, weighty and stooped posture and downcast and forlorn expression may come to dominate the clinical picture. Fragmented as contrasted to systematized delusions and hallucinations are not uncommon, usually reflecting obsessive fears of impending disaster or strange and undiagnosable bodily ailments. Self-deprecation, remorse and guilt are prominent as the content of their disorganized and fleeting delusions.

The following brief history depicts a number of these features.

CASE 16–6

Louis M., Age 53, Married, Two Children

Louis, an institutionalized cyclophrenic, would sit in his more typical daily behavior in a stooped manner, quietly bemoaning the fate of God, to whom he claimed he spoke the night before, and who had told him that because of his and God's sins, life for everyone would soon be even more "hellish" than living in a state hospital. Every several weeks, and rather unpredictably, Louis would suddenly be buoyed up, begin clapping his hands, and loudly sing to a cheerfully melodic refrain, a song with pleasant neologistic words (e.g., goody dum dum, happimush), but one that was otherwise totally incomprehensible. Following these brief euphoric episodes, Louis would succumb to his more usual depressive agitation, moaning incoherently about the wretched state of man's sinfulness, the coming of doomsday, the "tastelessness" of the weather, his "dramink" of hundreds of little girls and so on.

Acceptance of social invalidism as a way of life has not been difficult for these patients, given their lifelong orientation toward dependency. As the effort to maintain contact with the mainstream of social life is finally abandoned, they readily succumb to a state of helpless dependence.

Any withdrawal into self increases the probability of cognitive disorganization. In dependent patterns this process is accentuated. These personalities have habitually lacked the capacity to "think for themselves." Thus, they have great difficulty on their own in achieving self-reinforcements and in finding a consistent direction and order for thinking. Furthermore, whatever thoughts they do possess are colored by an oppressive and melancholy tone. To avoid these preoccupations, cyclophrenics may attempt to focus on deviant, cheerful thoughts. This accounts, in part, for their capricious and erratic ramblings. But these cognitive digressions cannot be sustained. Sensing the futility of these efforts to change their mood, these patients may block or retard all thought processes, thereby producing the slow and laborious responses which often characterize them. Should these latter efforts fail, they may simply disorganize their thoughts as a protective maneuver against the anguish which they evoke.

Next, we will note some of the symptomatological features which distinguish the four basic personality types that decompensate to cyclophrenia.

1. *Passive-dependent cyclophrenics* tend to be consistent in their helpless invalidism and depression. Convinced of their unworthiness and the inevitability of abandonment and desertion, they crumble and sink into a state of utter hopelessness. Though frightened by their separation from past sources of dependency, they quickly learn that they can gain a more consistent security in the "womb" of a totally nurtural hospital. Here they can comfortably regress to a child-like dependency, to a limpet-like attachment to whoever supplies their needs for protection and nurture.

2. The picture of the *active-dependent cyclophrenic* tends at times to be distinctly different from that of the passive-dependent. Despite their social invalidism and the bizarre character of their thinking and behavior, these patients frequently make an effort to be charming, gay and attractive. Their lifelong pattern of soliciting attention and approval reemerges periodically in displays of irrational conviviality, often accompanied by garish clothes and ludicrous make-up. In the following case we may note several of these features.

CASE 16-7

Olive W., Age 49, Separated, Three Children

Olive has been institutionalized three times, the first of which, at the age of 24, was for eight months; the second, at 31, lasted about three years; this third period has continued since she was 37.

Olive was the fifth child, the only girl, of a family of six children. Her early history is unclear, although she "always was known to be a tease" with the boys. Both parents worked at semiskilled jobs throughout Olive's childhood; her older brothers took care of the house. By the time she entered puberty, Olive had had sexual relations with several of her brothers and many of their friends. As she reported it in one of her more lucid periods, she "got lots of gifts" that would not otherwise have been received for "simply having a lot of fun." Apparently, her parents had no knowledge of her exploits, attributing the gifts she received to her vivaciousness and attractiveness.

A crucial turning point occurred when Olive was 15; she became pregnant. Although the pregnancy was aborted, parental attitudes changed, and severe restrictions were placed upon her. Nevertheless, Olive persisted in her seductive activities, and by the time she was 17 she again had become pregnant. At her insistence, she was married to the father of her unborn child. This proved to be a brief and stormy relationship, ending two months after the child's birth. Abandoned by her husband and rejected by her parents, Olive turned immediately to active prostitution as a means of support. In the ensuing six years, she acquired another child and another husband. Olive claims to have "genuinely loved" this man; they had "great times" together, but also many "murderous fights." It was his decision to leave her that resulted in her first, clear, psychotic break.

Following her eight month stay in the hospital, Olive picked up where she left off—prostitute, dance-hall girl and so on. Periods of drunkenness and despondency came more and more frequently, interspersed with shorter periods of gay frivolity and euphoria. For a brief time, one that produced another child, Olive served as a "plaything" for a wealthy ne'er-do-well, traveling about the country having "the time of her life." She fell into a frantic and depressive state, however, when he simply "dumped her" upon hearing that she was pregnant.

Hospitalized again, this time for three years, Olive's personality was beginning to take on more permanent psychotic features. Nevertheless, she was remitted to the home of her father and older brother; here she served as a housemaid and cook. Her children had been placed in foster homes; her mother had died several years earlier.

The death of her father, followed quickly by the marriage of her brother, left Olive alone again. Once more, she returned to her old ways, becoming a bar-girl and prostitute. Repeated beatings by her "admirers," her mental deterioration and her growing physical unattractiveness, all contributed to a pervasive despondency which resulted in her last hospitalization.

For the past several years she has been doing the work of a seamstress in the institution's sewing room; here, in addition to her mending chores, she makes rather garish clothes for herself and others. Every now and then, she spruces herself up, goes to the beauty parlor, puts on an excess of make-up and becomes transformed into a "lovely lady." More characteristically, however, her mood is somber; though responsive and friendly to those who show interest in her, her ideas almost invariably are bizarre and irrational.

CASE 16–7
Continued

3.   Turning next to the *passive-ambivalent cyclophrenic*, we observe a much tighter and restrained picture than that found in either of the types discussed previously. The woebegone look has an air of tension. Behaviors are more rigid and all sorts of mannerisms and grimaces may be displayed. On rare occasions they may exhibit explosive outbursts of rage directed at unseen persecutors. At other times they may assault themselves viciously. Many remain mute and unresponsive for long periods. Cognitive processes generally are labored, emitted in a slow and deliberate manner and tending to be self-deprecatory and tinged with delusions of persecution and guilt. Their cognitive distortions usually are more organized or systematic than those of other cyclophrenics.

4.   The clinical picture of the *active-ambivalent cyclophrenic* is similar to that of the passive-ambivalent. However, tension and inner agitation are more manifest. Conflicts and impulses are frequently acted out, and a stream of complaints is often voiced in irritable and disorganized commentaries. Behavior varies from listless pacing to hostile immobility. Delusions of guilt and self-condemnation may prompt periodic flareups of violence and bickering. Most times, however, the patient is subdued and downcast, complaining in a quiet, almost unfeeling and automatic manner, as if by sheer habit alone. His sour pessimism, although now dissipated, still colors his attitudes and behaviors, making relationships with fellow patients and hospital workers difficult to sustain.

DEVELOPMENTAL BACKGROUND

We find the same complex of determinants in the cycloid and cyclophrenic syndrome as we do in their less severe counterparts. The primary differences between them are the intensity, frequency, timing and persistence of pathogenic factors. They may begin with less adequate constitutional equipment, or be subjected to a series of more adverse early experiences. As a consequence, they may fail to develop an adequate instrumental style in the first place or decompensate slowly under the weight of repeated and unrelieved difficulties.

We shall review next the developmental history of the four basic personalities that serve as foundations for the cycloid and cyclophrenic syndromes.

1.   The biogenic background of *passive-dependent cycloids* and *cyclophrenics* includes a disproportionately high number of bland and unenergetic relatives. A melancholic, infantile reaction pattern is not infrequent (Winokur et al., 1969).

The central social learning influence appears to have been parental overprotection, leading to an unusually strong attachment to, and dependency on, a single caretaking figure. The perpetuation of overprotection throughout childhood fostered a lack in the development of autonomous behaviors and a self-image of incompetence and inadequacy. The growing child's own coping style accentuated these weaknesses.

By abdicating self-responsibility and by clinging to others, they restricted their opportunities to learn skills for social independence.

In contrast to personalities who stabilize at the milder levels of pathology, future cycloids and cyclophrenics found themselves frequently rebuffed by those upon whom they depended. The intense separation anxieties that these experiences created led to the cycloid pattern, characterized by mood vacillations, marked self-disparagements and guilt, and frequent psychotic episodes, as illustrated in the following case study.

CASE 16–8

Helen A., Age 32, Married, No Children

This cycloid woman decompensated over several years into a cyclophrenic pattern following persistent quarrels with her exasperated husband, a man she married in her teens who began to spend weeks away from home in recent years, presumably with another woman. For brief periods, Helen sought to regain her husband's affections, but these efforts were for naught, and she became bitterly resentful, guilt-ridden and self-deprecating. Her erratic mood swings not only increased feelings of psychic disharmony, but further upset efforts to gain her husband's attention and support. As she persisted in vacillating between gloomy despondency, accusatory attacks and clinging behaviors, more of her sources of support were withdrawn, thereby intensifying both separation anxieties and the maladaptive character of her behaviors. The next step, that of a regression to invalidism, was especially easy for her since it was consistent with her lifelong pattern of passive-dependence. Along with it, however, came discomforting feelings of estrangement and the collapse of all self-controls, as evidenced in her ultimate infantile-like behaviors and the total disorganization of her cognitive processes.

2. *Active-dependent cycloids* and *cyclophrenics* often have numerous close relatives who exhibit high autonomic reactivity (Dorzab et al., 1971). Other evidence suggesting a biological predisposition is hyperresponsivity in early childhood. This temperamental factor not only exposed them to a high degree of sensory stimulation, but tended to elicit more frequent and intense reactions from others.

Among the more important social learning influences in this syndrome is an unusually varied and enriched sequence of sensory experiences in the first neuropsychological stage that built in a "need" for stimulus diversity and excitement. Parental control by contingent and irregular reward may also have occurred, establishing in these children the habit of feeling personally competent and accepted only if their behaviors were explicitly approved by others. Many of these youngsters were exposed to histrionic parental models. Another background contributor may have been exposure to variable and rapidly changing parental and societal values, resulting in an extreme of exteroceptivity, that is, an excessive dependence on external cues for guiding behavior. The emergent pattern of seductiveness in interpersonal relations fostered rather than resolved difficulties. Their emotional shallowness and excessive demands for attention and approval often resulted in a deficit in enduring relationships.

Unable to sustain a consistent external source of nurture and fearful that their capacity to elicit attention and support was waning, these patients began to evidence the cyclical mood swings that are characteristic of the cycloid level of functioning. Persistent shifts between brooding dejection, simulated euphoria and impulsive outbursts of resentment and hostility only resulted in further interpersonal complications and a mounting of separation anxieties. As these self-defeating behaviors and coping efforts failed repeatedly, there was a pervasive decompensation of all personality functions, and a gradual slipping into the more permanent cyclophrenic pattern.

3.   The major social learning influence in *passive-ambivalent cycloids* and *cyclophrenics* is likely to have been parental control by contingent punishment and the resulting dread of abandonment should authority expectations fail to be heeded. This dread may have been compounded by ambiguity in parental demands. Thus, the young, future cyclophrenic, unsure of what is and what is not approved, stood in constant fear of making errors. Many learned to model themselves as closely as they could to approved authority figures. They sacrificed all inclinations toward autonomy and independent action as a means of avoiding parental condemnation. In time, they came to judge themselves as harshly as their parents had done. To protect themselves against reproach, they vigorously repressed their assertive and hostile impulses, kept carefully within conventional guidelines, and even criticized themselves for minor digressions. A strong sense of guilt served as a further protection against error. Their coping strategy proved self-defeating. They became alienated from their own feelings and were unable to act decisively and confidently.

The sequence of decompensation in these patients is well illustrated in the following case study.

Thomas, a passive-ambivalent cycloid, had a previous history of several brief depressive episodes, two of which required hospitalization. Shortly before his last institutionalization, he had been fired from his job and abandoned by his wife and children. According to the reports of other relatives, Thomas turned against himself at first. Quite obviously, with the mounting of his objective failures and shortcomings, his insecurity and guilt increased; Thomas felt like a fraud, a worthless creature who could not perform up to the expectations of others. The gloom and hopelessness of his mood was broken, however, by periodic eruptions of previously repressed anger and resentment. With his grip on reality wearing thin, he began to attack his "accusers" viciously, projecting onto them the weaknesses and defects which he felt within himself. In a constant state of tension, his prideful sense of order shattered, his dread of condemnation and rejection turning to reality and his rigid coping systems crumbling bit by bit, he slipped progressively into a state of confusion and invalidism; now his cognitive processes were in total disarray, and he was estranged both from self and reality. In time, left to drift alone in the back wards, he succumbed to the cyclophrenic pattern.

CASE 16–9

Thomas P., Age 45, Married, Two Children

4.   *Active-ambivalent cycloids* and *cyclophrenics* often display both an erratic infantile reaction pattern and an uneven course of development, thereby increasing the likelihood of inconsistent treatment at the hands of others.

Primary among social learning influences was the role of parental inconsistency in upbringing. As youngsters, these patients are likely to have been exposed to extreme oscillations between smothering or guilt-laden affection on the one hand, and indifference, abuse or castigation on the other. Many were products of schismatic families. In addition to the emotional consequences of these experiences, parents served as models for learning erratic and contradictory behaviors.

Patients who decompensated beyond the mild level continued to be subjected to marked conflicts and disappointments. These difficulties were fostered by their own sullen and vacillating behaviors. Rarely could they sustain a prolonged harmonious relationship. As a consequence of their negativism and moodiness, they turned away the very affections and support they so desperately needed. This only intensified their erratic and troublesome behaviors. At this point, the cycloid pattern emerged in the form of violent and irrational outbursts of revenge. Interspersed with these bizarre episodes were periods characterized by severe self-reproaches and pleas for forgiveness.

Unable to "get hold" of themselves, control their churning resentments and conflicts or elicit even the slightest degree of approval and support from others, guilt-ridden and self-condemnatory, these patients slide from the cyclical episodes of the cycloid pattern into the more permanent abyss of cyclophrenia. Here they linger as invalids, away from the turmoil of reality. Disorganized cognitively and estranged from themselves, they sink into the sheltered obscurity of institutional life.

TREATMENT APPROACHES

The cycloid and cyclophrenic classifications refer to a deeply ingrained personality pattern. Nothing but the most prolonged and intensive therapy can produce substantial changes in basic patterns. Should the attention and indulgence these patients require be withdrawn, should their strategies prove wearisome and exasperating to others, prompting anger and unforgiveness, their tenuous hold on reality will disintegrate. At these times, they may succumb either to a somber depression or to an erratic and explosive surge of assertion and hostility. Care must be taken to head off the danger of suicide during these episodes.

Efforts should be made to boost the patient's sagging morale, to encourage him to continue functioning in his normal sphere of activities, to build up his confidence in his self-worth and to deter him from being preoccupied with his melancholy feelings. Care must be taken, however, not to press him beyond his capabilities, or to tell him to "snap out of it," since his failures to achieve such goals will only strengthen his growing conviction of his own incompetence and unworthiness.

Should a deeper melancholy take hold, it is advisable to prescribe one of the many antidepressant agents which may help in buoying his flagging spirits (Simpson et al., 1972; Dekin and DiMascio, 1972; Himmelbach et al., 1972). These may be supplemented, where indicated, by a course of electroconvulsive treatments, a procedure notably useful in abbreviating depressive periods. During a manic stage, particularly promising results often are obtained with lithium (Cade, 1949; Goodwin et al., 1972).

It is only during more quiet periods that serious efforts to alter the basic psychopathology can be instituted. A primary aim in this regard is the construction of capacities for autonomy, the building of confidence and initiative, and the overcoming of fears of self-determination and independence. No doubt, this will be resisted. These patients often feel that the therapist's attempt to aid them in assuming self-responsibility is a sign of rejection, an effort to "be rid" of them. The anxiety this creates may evoke feelings of disappointment, dejection and even rage. These reactions must be anticipated and dealt with if fundamental personality changes are to be achieved.

Once a sound and secure therapeutic relationship has been established, the patient may learn to tolerate his contrary feelings and anxieties. Learning to face and handle these emotions must be coordinated, however, with behavioral techniques designed to strengthen healthier self-attitudes and instrumental strategies (Lazarus, 1968; Burgess, 1969).

This will be fostered if the therapist serves as a model to demonstrate how conflicts and uncertainties can be approached and resolved with equanimity and foresight. Group therapeutic methods may be utilized for purposes of testing these newly learned attitudes and strategies, and in refining them in a more natural social setting than is found in individual treatment.

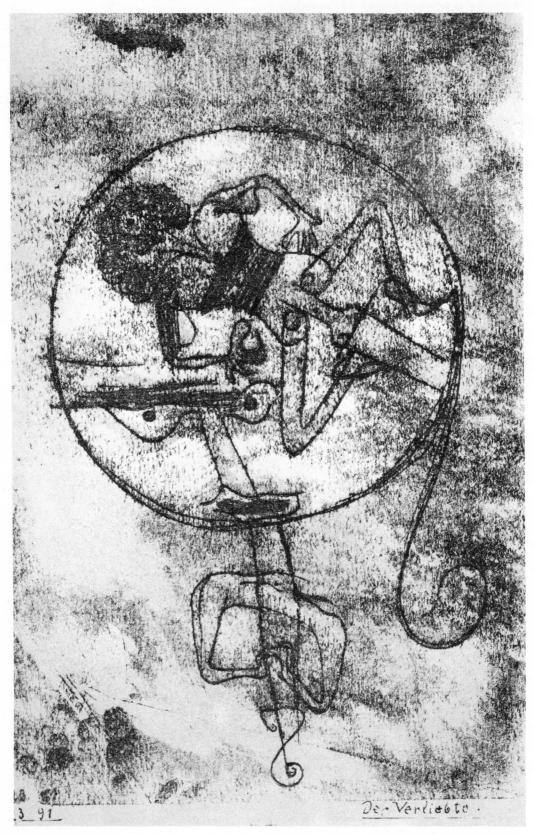

Paul Klee — *A Man in Love*

17 PARANOID DISORDERS AND PATTERNS

INTRODUCTION

The term "paranoia" can be traced back over 2000 years in medical literature, antedating the writings of Hippocrates. Translated from the Greek it means "to think beside oneself," and was used in ancient times as a general designation for any and all forms of serious mental disturbance. The word disappeared from the medical vocabulary in the second century and was not revived again until the eighteenth century. Heinroth, following the logic of Kantian psychology, utilized the term in 1818 to represent disorders of the intellect. Greisinger drew upon it in 1845 to signify pathological thought processes, and applied it to cases which exhibited persecutory and grandiose delusions. In 1863, Kahlbaum suggested that this label be reserved exclusively for delusional states. Kraepelin further refined its usage in 1893, restricting it to highly systematized and well-contained delusions in patients lacking other signs of a general personality deterioration. Despite the numerous subvarieties formulated in recent years, the correspondence between the diagnostic label of paranoia and symptomatic delusional thinking has been firmly established (Cameron, 1959; Salzman, 1969; Sarvis, 1962; Schwartz, 1963).

There are several listings in the DSM-II which resemble the syndromes described in this chapter. Most relevant are *paranoia, paranoid states* and *schizophrenia, paranoid type* (Hay and Forrest, 1972). All three syndromes are distinguished by the presence of persecutory and grandiose delusions. The DSM-II description of the *paranoia* category states that "this extremely rare condition is characterized by gradual development of an intricate, complex and elaborate (delusional) system . . . [that] does not seem to interfere with the rest of the patient's thinking and personality." The *paranoid state* is differentiated in the detailed 1952 manual from paranoia by the fact that "it lacks the logical nature of (delusional) systematization . . . yet it does not manifest the bizarre fragmentation and deterioration of the schizophrenic reactions." And finally, the syndrome noted as *schizophrenia, paranoid type* is described in the 1952 manual by its "strong tendency to deterioration . . . autistic, unrealistic thinking, with mental content composed chiefly of delusions." Distinctions between these three subvarieties are difficult to draw in clinical practice (Swanson et al., 1970). For our purposes, the essential difference lies in whether the delusional symptoms are of a relatively recent or of a chronic and long-standing nature. The former will be dealt with in the first section of this chapter under the title "acute paranoid disorders"; the latter are discussed in the second section under the label "paranoid personality patterns."

ACUTE PARANOID DISORDERS

CLINICAL PICTURE

Many psychotic disorders exhibit delusions. For the most part, however, delusions are subsidiary features in other impairments, an element that emerges as a secondary consequence following the effects of the primary disturbance, e.g., during "hebephrenic-fragmentation" (see Chapter 15) the patient confuses his fantasy world with reality, producing quite incidentally a variety of distorted impressions, which may then persist as delusional beliefs. In what we are terming the paranoid disorder, however, the false belief usually takes shape first, leading in time to a cluster of secondary symptoms, e.g., for various reasons, the patient believes he possesses certain special powers and rights; these delusions may lead him to react to events in an excited, fragmented or otherwise irrational manner. Thus, in these episodes, the delusional system, no matter how disorganized it may be or become, is the primary component of the disorder, an intrinsic element producing subsidiary psychotic features, the most notable of which are the perceptual distortions of hallucination.

As implied above, delusions in these patients have a coherence and focus, in contrast to the more fragmented and incidental distortions which arise in other psychotic states. The focus of these delusions (persecutory or grandiose) and the tone and character of the secondary symptoms with which they are associated, depend largely on the patient's longstanding habits, needs and attitudes, that is, his prepsychotic personality pattern.

PERSONALITY AND INSTRUMENTAL BEHAVIOR

The foundation for paranoid disorders is usually well established in the patient's characteristic mode of behaving and thinking. In the following survey of vulnerable personalities we will deal only with those patterns in which delusions are both dominant and an intrinsic part of the psychosis.

1. *Narcissistic* and *aggressive personalities* (passive- and active-independents) are well disposed to misinterpret events and to exhibit delusional beliefs. Unable to accept constraints on their independence and unwilling to accept the viewpoints of others, these patients isolate themselves from the corrective effects of shared thinking. Alone, they begin to weave their suspicions into a network of fanciful and totally invalid beliefs. Among narcissists, delusions often take form after a serious challenge or setback in which their image of superiority and omnipotence has been upset. These patients tend to exhibit compensatory grandiosity and jealousy delusions, in which they reconstruct reality to suit the image they cannot give up. The delusional system of aggressive personalities typically occurs following failures in their efforts to dominate

others or as a result of having felt betrayed and humiliated. In these cases we are likely to see a rapid unfolding of persecutory delusions, as portrayed in the following case.

CASE 17–1

Carl F., Age 40, Married, No Children

This aggressive personality, characterized throughout his life as arrogant and suspicious, was brought to a hospital following his refusal for several weeks to leave his bedroom at home. Carl had been in a competitive business, and over recent months had lost both money and important contracting jobs to another company that consistently underbid him. Forced to lay off many of his employees and feeling humiliated by the turn of events, Carl began to accuse others of having conspired to destroy him and his business. The more he accused others, the more his reputation and reliability were questioned. Unable to stem the tide against him by veiled threats and intimidation, Carl locked himself in his room at home "to think things over." His thoughts, however, turned increasingly irrational. After a few days, he "figured out" the plot that was "schemed up" by his competitors. He then sent a series of "blistering" letters to numerous city and state officials insisting that they "investigate the illegal methods" used against him. He refused to leave his room "until justice was done."

2. *Compulsive* and *negativistic personalities* (passive- and active-ambivalent) may be sent into a delusional psychosis as a consequence of anticipating or experiencing real mistreatment from those to whom they have turned for support and security. Shocked by betrayal and having foregone the hope of fulfilling their dependency needs, the repressed resentments and suspicions of the compulsive overwhelm their former rigid controls, break to the surface and quickly take delusional shape. During these episodes, usually brief and rather chaotic, the patient releases his anger and at the same time rids himself of guilt by projecting his hostility upon others. Thus, his delusions tend to be persecutory. Negativistic personalities are accustomed to discharging their emotions more readily than are compulsives. Thus, their tensions do not mount and burst out of control, as in the case of the passive type. Rather, they continue to be touchy and irritable. Their typical suspicions merely are aggravated until they form into a mixture of persecutory and jealousy delusions. The following detailed case illustrates a typical course with periodic delusional episodes (Rosen and Gregory, 1965).

CASE 17–2

Magda A., Age 42, Married, No Children

This woman was admitted to the psychiatric ward of a general hospital six months after separation from her husband when she left home and moved into a single room. A few days prior to admission she told her sister that her food and cigarettes were being poisoned. In the hospital Magda said she could hear the voices of men and women engaged in sexual intercourse and she claimed her food was being doped so that she could be used sexually. She was extremely agitated by these hallucinations and delusions and felt anxious and miserable. After a few days she walked out of the hospital without permission. Magda went to a hotel, locked herself in her room and refused to let anyone in. The police were called and they broke down the door and took her to a state hospital.

Magda was born in Roumania. Her father died when she was nine years old. Her mother remarried two years later; the patient could not get along with her stepfather and claimed that he mistreated her. When she was 13 the whole family emigrated. She left school at 14 and worked in a factory until marriage at 18 to a much older man. She claimed that he was irresponsible and did not pay their bills so that she too had to work. Their sexual relationship was unsatisfying to her; in complete contrast to the erotic content of her delusions, she claimed that she had never wished to have intercourse with her husband or anyone else.

In the state hospital Magda was restless and agitated. She paced the floor and talked to herself or wept uncontrollably. In an evaluative interview her eyes were averted, her voice was quiet and monotonous, and at times she spoke inaudibly or answered questions with irrelevant comments. She was disoriented. Asked if she had inquired where she was, she replied, "I don't know whether they would tell me the truth or not. I locked the doors at my mother's and left the light on all night because I thought they were going to poison me and rob me when I was locked in that room. They asked me how I could talk, different ones, and I don't know how they could see me because the blinds were drawn. They were going to burn me to prove that I am what they say I am. You know what they are saying about me. I guess everybody does. They are saying that I am a prostitute and a bitch." She said she had been unhappy for a long time because she had been alone and added, "If you are not with the one you love, you are unhappy." Asked whom she loved, she replied, "Ray." (She was slightly acquainted with a man named Ray.) Asked how his name was spelled she said, "W-r-a-y, I think. There is x-ray, too. I don't know. They are forcing me to holler so they can say I am crazy."

Magda responded only temporarily to ECT and insulin coma therapy (her hospitalization occurred before tranquilizers were in general use). A year after admission, a lobotomy was performed; Magda's symptoms disappeared and she returned home to live with her husband. A few months later, however, her hallucinations and delusions reappeared. She was readmitted to the hospital and given chlorpromazine. She kept hearing voices, but they ceased to agitate her and she went home again, with instructions to continue the medication indefinitely. Soon Magda became seclusive and hostile again and then developed delusions of grandeur. She believes that she has been divorced from her husband and has married a king named Raymond; she herself was a princess, her father was Jesus, and she had given birth to quintuplets.

3.   *Avoidant personalities* (active-detached) exhibit less systematic and coherent delusions than those seen among other personality types. Distortions of reality are almost inevitable during periods of marked social isolation. An abrupt delusional formation may occur if these patients are thrust into situations of excessive responsibility and stimulation. In general, however, other psychotic symptoms tend to predominate in the detached patterns. Their delusions, usually bizarre or nonsensical, are subsidiary features for the most part.

PARANOID PERSONALITY PATTERNS

The most prominent feature of these personalities is their mistrust of others, and their desire to remain free of close personal relationships in which they may lose the power of self-determination. Characteristically, they are suspicious, resentful and hostile, tend to misread the actions of others and respond often with anger to what they interpret as deception, deprecation and betrayal. Their readiness to perceive deceit and aggression provokes many social difficulties, which then confirm and reinforce their expectations. Their isolation from others, combined with their tendency to magnify minor slights, results ultimately in distortions that cross the boundary of reality. At this point, their thinking takes the form of delusions, a clinical sign traditionally associated with these patients.

BORDERLINE PARANOID PERSONALITY

CLINICAL PICTURE

The paranoid detests being dependent not only because it signifies weakness and inferiority, but because he is unable to trust anyone. To lean upon another is to expose oneself to ultimate betrayal and to rest on ground which will only give way when support is needed most. Rather than chance deceit, the paranoid aspires to be the maker of his own fate, free of entanglements and obligations. Any circumstance which prompts feelings of helplessness and incompetence, decreases his freedom of movement or places him in a vulnerable position subject to the powers of others, may precipitate a psychotic episode. Trapped by the danger of dependency, struggling to regain his status and dreading deceit and betrayal, he may strike out aggressively, accuse others of seeking to persecute him, and ennoble himself with grandiose virtues and superiority.

Paranoids are oversensitive, ready to detect signs of hostility and deception, tend to be preoccupied with them and actively pick up, magnify and distort the actions and words of others so as to confirm their expectations. Moreover, they assume that events that fail to confirm their suspicions "only prove how deceitful and clever others can be." In their desire to uncover this pretense, they explore every nook and cranny to find justification for their beliefs, constantly testing the "honesty" of their "friends." Finally, after intimidating others, the paranoid provokes them to exasperation and anger.

A number of these features are exemplified in the following graphic account.

CASE 17–3

Raymond R., Age 46, Married, One Child

This paranoid male was brought to a state hospital by the police following his merciless beating of his wife and 14 year old daughter. For some weeks prior to this event, he had been harboring the suspicion that his wife was in love with his best friend and had been poisoning his (Raymond's) food to be rid of him. On the evening of this episode, Raymond noticed that his wife served him a different meal than she took for herself and their daughter. Upon questioning, his wife informed him that she was merely, and quite obviously, eating the leftovers of the night before; knowing Raymond's dislike for leftovers, she had prepared him a fresh dinner. Raymond claimed that this was a ruse; no matter how his wife protested, Raymond twisted and distorted her words so as to make them reinforce his belief that she was, in fact, poisoning his food. When she refused to "prove her honesty" by eating the remains of his serving, and, then, exasperated, turned to leave the room, Raymond leaped up from the table, threw her to the floor and brutally attacked her; after rendering her bloody and unconscious, he assaulted his frightened daughter.

In short, the preconceptions of the paranoid rarely are upset by facts. They disregard contradictions, confirm their expectations by seizing upon real, although minute and irrelevant facts, or create an atmosphere which provokes others to act as they anticipated.

Paranoids are constantly on guard, mobilized and ready for any emergency or threat. Whether faced with real dangers or not, they maintain a fixed level of preparedness and an alert vigilance against the possibility of attack. There is an edgy tension, an abrasive irritability and an ever-present defensive stance from which they can spring to action at the slightest hint of threat. This state of rigid control never seems to abate. Rarely do they relax, ease up or let down their guard.

Beneath the surface mistrust and defensive vigilance in the paranoid lies a current of deep resentment toward others who "have made it." To the paranoid, most people have attained their status unjustly. Thus, he is bitter for having been overlooked, treated unfairly and slighted by the "high and mighty," "the cheats and the crooks" who duped the world. Only a thin veil hides these bristling animosities.

There are no universal attributes which may be spoken of as making up the "essence" of the paranoid personality. In what follows we shall describe some of the features which differentiate the four basic patterns of the paranoid personality. Despite the distinctions we shall draw, we must be mindful that distinctions are not well defined in reality. There are overlappings, with traces of the more distinctive features of each subvariety found often in the others.

1.   *Passive-independent paranoids* are similar to their less severe counterparts, the narcissistic personalities. They seek to retain their admirable self-image, act in a haughty and pretentious manner, are naively self-confident, ungenerous and presumptuous.

In contrast to the narcissist, who has achieved a modicum of success with his optimistic veneer and exploitive behaviors, the paranoid has run hard against reality. His illusion of omnipotence has periodically been shattered, toppling him from his vaulted image of eminence. Accustomed to being viewed as the center of things and to being a valued and admired figure among others, he cannot tolerate the lessened significance now assigned to him. His narcissism has been wounded.

Not only must the paranoid counter the indifference, the humiliation and the fright of insignificance generated by reality, but he must reestablish his lost pride through extravagant claims and fantasies. Upset by assaults upon self-esteem, he reconstructs his image of himself and ascends once more to the status from which he fell. To do this, he endows himself by self-reinforcement with superior powers and exalted competencies. He dismisses events which conflict with his newly acquired and self-designated importance. Flimsy talents and accomplishments are embellished, creating a new self-image that supplants objective reality. The following brief case illustrates this sequence of events in a passive-independent paranoid.

CASE 17–4

Charles W., Age 36, Married, No Children

Charles, an only child of poorly educated parents, had been recognized as a "child genius" in early school years. He received a Ph.D. degree at 24, and subsequently held several responsible positions as a research physicist in an industrial firm.

His haughty arrogance and narcissism often resulted in conflicts with his superiors; it was felt that he spent too much time working on his own "harebrained" schemes and not enough on company projects. Charles increasingly was assigned to jobs of lesser importance than that to which he was accustomed. He began to feel, not unjustly, that both his superiors and his subordinates were "making fun of him" and not taking him seriously. To remedy this attack upon his status, Charles began to work on a scheme that would "revolutionize the industry," a new thermodynamic principle which, when applied to his company's major product, would prove extremely efficient and economical. After several months of what was conceded by others as "brilliant thinking," he presented his plans to the company president. Brilliant though it was, the plan overlooked certain obvious simple facts of logic and economy.

Upon learning of its rejection, Charles withdrew to his home where he became obsessed with "new ideas," proposing them in intricate schematics and formulas to a number of government officials and industrialists. These resulted in new rebuffs which led to further efforts at self-inflation. It was not long thereafter that he lost all semblance of reality and control; for a brief period, he convinced himself of the grandiose delusion that he was Albert Einstein.

2.   *Active-independent paranoids* may be seen as more severe variants of the aggressive personality described in earlier chapters. They are characterized best by their power orientation, their mistrust, resentment and

envy of others, and by their autocratic and belligerent manner. Underlying these features is a ruthless desire to triumph over others, and vindicate themselves for past wrongs by cunning revenge or callous force, if necessary.

In contrast to his less severe counterpart, the paranoid has found that in his efforts to outwit and frustrate others, he had only prompted them to inflict more of the harsh punishment and rejection to which he was subjected in childhood. His strategy of arrogance and brutalization has backfired too often, and he now seeks retribution, not as much through action as through fantasy.

Repeated setbacks have confirmed the paranoid's expectancy of aggression from others. By his own hand, he stirs up further hostility and disfavor. Because of his argumentative and "chip-on-the-shoulder" attitudes, he provokes much antagonism from others. Isolated and resentful, he increasingly turns to himself, to mull over his fate. Left to his own thoughts, he begins to imagine a plot in which every facet of his environment plays a threatening and treacherous role. Moreover, through the intrapsychic mechanism of projection, he attributes his own venom to others, ascribing to them the malice and ill will he feels within himself. As the line draws thin between objective antagonism and imagined hostility, the belief takes hold that others intentionally are persecuting him. Alone, threatened and with decreasing self-esteem, the suspicions of the active-independent paranoid now have been transformed into delusions.

3. *Passive-ambivalent paranoids* are similar both to the mildly severe compulsive personality and to the moderately severe passive-ambivalent cycloid personality. However, in contrast to these patients, who retain the hope of achieving protection through others, the passive-ambivalent paranoid renounces his dependency and assumes a stance of independence. Despite his growing hostility and his repudiation of conformity as a way of life, he retains his basic rigidity and perfectionism.

In his new found independence, this paranoid frees himself from submission. He begins to discharge the hostility he previously had repressed and imposes his standards upon others, attacking them with the same punitive attitudes to which he himself was earlier subjected. Impossible regulations set for others allow him to vent hostilities and condemnation for their failures to meet them. Now he can give to others what he himself has received. He can despise and hate them for their weaknesses, their deceits and their hypocrisy — precisely those feelings which he previously had experienced within himself, had once sought to repress and which he still tries to conceal by condemning them in others. The following brief example portrays a number of these characteristics.

This passive-ambivalent paranoid, although known as a harsh, perfectionistic and overly legalistic probation officer, managed to maintain a moderately acceptable veneer of control and propriety in his relationships with his neighbors. In recent years, however, he became convinced that youngsters who "smoked pot" were part of a "communist plot to undo this great country." Whenever a "hippie" was brought to court on any charge, he would "make it his business to talk to the judge" about the plot, and attempt to ensure that he would impose a "proper jail sentence." After repeated failures to persuade the judge to see things his way, he began a personal campaign in the community to impeach the judge and to place "all hippies in a federal jail."

CASE 17–5

Martin D., Age 50, Married, No Children

4. *Active-ambivalent paranoids* may be differentiated from their less severe counterparts, the negativistic personality, and the equally ill active-ambivalent cycloid, by the presence of both overt hostility and frank delusions. All three categories are noted by their discontent, pessimism, stubbornness and vacillation. However, the paranoid is more aggressively negativistic and faultfinding, appears sullen, resentful, obstructive and peevish at all times and openly registers his feelings of jealousy, of being misunderstood and of being cheated (Dupont, 1968). As a consequence, he rarely can sustain good relationships, creating endless wrangles wherever he goes. Demoralized by these events, he foregoes all hopes of gaining affection and approval from others, and decides to renounce these aspirations in preference for self-determination.

Erotic delusions are not uncommon among these patients. Although conciously repudiating his need for others, the active-ambivalent paranoid still seeks to gain affection from them. Rather than admit to these desires, however, he defensively projects them, interpreting the casual remarks and actions of others as subtle signs of their amorous intent. However, the paranoid is unable to tolerate these "attentions" since he dreads further betrayal and exploitation. Thus, in conjunction with these erotic delusions, the paranoid insists that he must be "protected". He may accuse innocent victims of commiting indignities, making lewd suggestions or molesting him, as illustrated in the following case.

CASE 17–6

Belle G., Age 40, Divorced, No Children

This active-ambivalent paranoid woman, currently unmarried, but divorced twice following rather embittered and stormy marriages, began to accuse several men in her neighborhood of "peeking in" her bedroom windows while she slept at night. Despite their suspicion that her accusations were nothing more than fantasy, the local police, without her knowledge, assigned two officers to check her home several times each night. One evening, the two officers heard strange sounds within Belle's home (these turned out to be scuffling between her two cats); they quickly shined their flashlights into her open bedroom window, the one through which she claimed the accused men would peek, and found Belle sleeping nude and uncovered on her bed, a most unusual behavior for someone who anticipated and condemned the presence of voyeurs, but not surprising in pathologically ambivalent paranoid personalities.

DECOMPENSATED PARAPHRENIC PERSONALITY (PARANOID SCHIZOPHRENIA)

The label "paraphrenia" was first used by Kraepelin in 1893 to describe an insidiously developing pathology which he viewed as lying halfway between the paranoid conditions and dementia praecox (schizophrenia). The term shall be revived in this text since it seems especially appropriate for those cases of markedly severe personality decompensation which have been preceded by a premorbid history of strivings for independence, power and recognition. Paraphrenia parallels both schizophrenia and cyclophrenia in its progressively slow course of decompensation, and in the pervasiveness and severity of deterioration; it differs from these syndromes in that it applies to cases of paranoid deterioration rather than to cases of schizoid or cycloid deterioration.

As noted earlier, it is customary in current psychiatric practice to apply the label of "schizophrenia" to *all* cases of personality decompensation, regardless of differences in premorbid styles of functioning. This practice, we believe, has been most unfortunate since it unwisely groups widely divergent personalities into a single syndrome, causing endless diagnostic complications.

The closest approximation to what we have termed paraphrenia may be found in the DSM-II descriptive text of "schizophrenia, paranoid type." However, as noted above, we do not consider the paraphrenic syndrome to be a variant of schizophrenia; rather, it is a parallel and equally decompensated personality pattern. It has its roots in a developmental history of independence strivings and follows the moderately severe paranoid pattern as the last of a series of personality decompensations of the independent instrumental strategy.

CLINICAL PICTURE

The contrast in the clinical picture between the paranoid and paraphrenic patterns is more striking than that found between other borderline patterns and their decompensated counterparts. Although the transition is a gradual one, spotted along the way with several "disordered" episodes, the final decompensated state appears to reflect a major transformation. Actually, this is not the case. Certain fundamental changes have taken place, of course, but superficial appearances tend to accentuate them. It is this overt and dramatic clinical difference which may, in part, have accounted for Kraepelin's decision to subsume these cases, which he originally termed "dementia paranoides," under the dementia praecox label.

The air of independence and self-assertion which characterizes so many paranoid personalities is sharply deflated when they succumb to the paraphrenic pattern. In contrast to schizoids and cycloids, who have always appeared more or less ineffectual, weak or vacillating, the paranoid has fostered the image of being cocky, self-assured, willful and dominant. He falls a far distance when he finally topples, and the contrast is quite marked.

Though cognitively disorganized, the paraphrenic remains defensively on guard against influence, coercion or attachments of any kind. He still is mistrustful and suspicious, ever fearful that those upon whom he now must depend for his survival will be deceitful or injurious. Through the haze of his disorganized thought processes, he still distorts objective reality. Not only is he estranged from others, and therefore unable to share a common social perspective, but he continues his habit of actively resisting the other person's viewpoint. And despite the general collapse of his instrumental strategy, he persists, however feebly, in the struggle to retain his independence and to keep intact the remnants of his shattered self-image.

These traces of the paraphrenic's past assertiveness and self-assurance are submerged, however, in the confusions of severe decompensation. Where self-determination and independence had characterized earlier behavior, we now observe a pervasive invalidism and dependence on others, an inability to assume responsibility for even the most mundane tasks of self-care and survival. Although cognitive processes were always distorted, delusional and narrow in focus, they possessed intrinsic order and logic to them. Now they are fragmented and irrational. Previously, ideas were conveyed in a self-confident and often articulate manner. They now tend to be stated with hesitation and doubt. Remarks frequently are tangential, expressed in incoherent phrases or scattered in disjointed flights of fancy. Emotions still retain their quality of veiled hostility but the "fight" is lacking, words of anger seem devoid of feeling and the spark of intense resentment has burned out. Behavior, once dominant, intimidating or contemptuous, has become aversive, secretive and bizarre. The whole complex of paranoid self-assurance and social belligerence has disintegrated, leaving an inner vacancy, a fearful hesitation and a fragmented shadow of the former being.

Let us next distinguish the clinical features of each of the four basic personality patterns that often decompensate to paraphrenia.

1.   Before their final stage of decompensation, *passive-independent paraphrenics* usually construct delusional self-pictures of grandiose omnipotence as a means of countering the painful reality of their failures and embarrassments. But these efforts have not been supported or encouraged. The patient has repeatedly been rebuffed and humiliated. As he progressively disengages himself from reality, sinking further into a state characterized by autistic fantasy and feelings of futility, his overt behavior begins to lose its former color and his grandiose statements lack the flavor of self-confidence. His delusional beliefs no longer seem inspired, suggesting that the patient himself may sense their emptiness and invalidity.

2.   Despite their common degree of disorganization, *active-independent paraphrenics* exhibit a more hostile appearance than passive-independents. Though repeatedly humiliated and deflated, an undercurrent of suspicion and resentment remains in these patients and pervades their every mood and behavior. Each setback to their aspirations for power and revenge has only reinforced their persecutory delusions, and there is no diminishment in their tendency to project their anger upon others. However, because of their hospital confinement and their growing doubts of omnipotence, these paraphrenics become relatively subdued, usually working out their hostility and desire for retribution through fantasy and hallucination. Unconscious impulses may periodically erupt into bizarre and violent behavior. More often, however, these feelings are directed toward hallucinated images.

The following case portrays this deteriorated pattern.

CASE 17–7

Joseph M., Age 52, Separated, Four Children

Joseph lived in foster homes since the age of three months; at 8 years of age he settled with one family, remaining there until he was 15, when he left to go on his own. Eventually enlisting in the Navy, he was given a medical discharge on psychiatric grounds, after three years of service.

As a child, Joseph was known to be a "bully"; he was heavy, muscular, burly in build, had an inexhaustible supply of energy and prided himself on his physical strength and endurance. Though quite intelligent, Joseph was constantly in trouble at school, teasing other children, resisting the directives of teachers and walking out of class whenever he pleased.

Joseph was the foster son of a manager of a coal mine, and spoke with great pride of his capacity, at the age of 12, to outproduce most of the experienced miners. When he was 14, his foster mother died, leaving Joseph alone to take care of himself; his foster father, who lived periodically with a mistress, rarely came home. Joseph worked at the mine and quarreled bitterly with his father for a "fair" wage; when he was 15, he got into one of his "regular fights" with his father and beat him so severely that the man was hospitalized for a month. After this event, Joseph left his home town, wandered aimlessly for two years and enlisted in the Navy. In the service, Joseph drank to excess, "flew off the handle at the drop of a hat" and spent an inordinate amount of time in the brig. The persistence of this behavior and the apparent bizarre features which characterized some of these episodes resulted in his discharge.

CASE 17–7
Continued

For several years thereafter, Joseph appeared to make a reasonable life adjustment. He married, had four sons and started a small trash collecting business. Drinking was entirely eliminated, though Joseph remained a "hot-headed" fellow who happily "took on all comers" to prove his strength.

Greater success — and difficulty — followed when Joseph "took up" with a teen-age girl; this younger woman was quite attractive and built up Joseph's self-image. More importantly, she bore him, illegitimately, what his own wife failed to — a little girl. With mistress and child in hand, he left his legal family, moving some 600 miles to a new city where he "started life again." Within three years, Joseph founded a successful contracting company and became moderately wealthy; at 36, he ran for a local political office, which he won.

Trouble began brewing immediately thereafter. Joseph was unable to compromise in the give-and-take of politics; he insisted at public meetings, to the point of near violence, that his obviously impractical and grandiose plans be adopted. After many outbursts, one of which culminated in the assault of a fellow official, Joseph was asked to resign from office, which he refused to do. To assure his resignation, as he put it, "They dredged up all the dirt they could get to get rid of me"; this included his Navy psychiatric discharge, his abandonment of his legal family, his illicit "marriage," illegitimate child and so on. The final collapse of his world came when his present "wife," in whose name alone his business was registered, rejected him, sold the company and kept all of the proceeds.

Joseph became physically violent following these events, and was taken to a state institution. Here, his well-justified feelings of persecution were elaborated until they lost all semblance of reality. Joseph remained hospitalized for two years during which time he managed gradually to reorient himself, although still retaining his basic, aggressive paranoid pattern. Upon remission, he returned to his legal family, working periodically as a driver of heavy contracting equipment. He began drinking again and got involved in repeated fist fights in local bars. When Joseph came home after a night's drinking, he frequently attempted to assault his wife. To his dismay, his teen-age sons would come to their mother's defense; Joseph invariably was the loser in these battles.

After living with his family for four years, Joseph disappeared, unheard from for about 18 months. Apparently, he had lived alone in a metropolitan city some 90 miles from his home; the family learned of his whereabouts when he was picked up for vagrancy. After he was bailed out, it was clear that Joseph was a beaten and destitute man. He returned to the state hospital where he has since remained. Although subdued and generally cooperative, Joseph is still suspicious, tends to be easily affronted and occasionally flares up in a hostile outburst. He ruminates to himself all day, occasionally speaking in an angry voice to hallucinated images. The decompensation to the paraphrenic level now seems deeply entrenched.

3.   The clinical picture of the *passive-ambivalent paraphrenic* is difficult to distinguish from the passive-ambivalent cyclophrenic, discussed in Chapter 16. Although the basic passive-ambivalent style often splits in separate directions at the borderline level, taking either a cycloid or paranoid form, this divergence terminates as patients decompensate to the markedly severe or decompensated personality level. Basically alike in their personalities from early life, these ambivalent patients took different directions when faced with the threat of separation and abandonment. Some asserted their independence, thereby turning in the paranoid direction. Others clung to the hope of reestablishing their security through dependence on others, thus turning toward the cycloid pattern. Now, sharing a common fate of failure and personal devastation, they revert to similar decompensated characteristics. The clinical features they exhibit are essentially those of the passive-ambivalent cyclophrenic. We maintain a distinction at this level primarily to indicate differences in the developmental course during the borderline, or moderate, stage of personality disintegration.

4.   What has just been said about the clinical similarity between passive-ambivalent paraphrenics and their cyclophrenic counterparts is also true of *active-ambivalent paraphrenics* and their cyclophrenic counterparts. Reference should be made to Chapter 16 for a description of this clinical picture.

DEVELOPMENTAL BACKGROUND

As should be evident from the general thesis presented in the text, the determinants that shape the development of the paranoid and paraphrenic pattern are similar to those found in their less severe counterparts, differing essentially only in their intensity, frequency, timing and persistence. The roots of these difficulties may be traced to a variety of sources: constitutional defects, adverse early experiences, periodically severe or unrelieved stress and so on. Thus, the patient's capacity to cope with his environment may never have been adequately developed, or it may have crumbled under the weight of persistent misfortune.

We shall next summarize the developmental background of the four variants of the paraphrenic personality.

1.   An early pattern of parental overvaluation and indulgence is common among *passive-independent paranoids* and *paraphrenics.* Many fail to learn interpersonal responsibility, rarely think of the desires and welfare of others and seem markedly deficient in group sharing and social cooperation. Undisciplined by parental controls and given an illusory sense of high self-worth, these youngsters place no reins on their imagination. They tend through excessive self-reinforcement to weave glorious fantasies of their own power and achievements. Most of them, however, lack true substance to support their illusions and aspirations. Once beyond the confines of home, their haughty and selfish orientation provokes repeated ridicule, humiliation and ostracism by peers. Unwilling to adjust to reality and accept a lowered self-esteem, they begin to withdraw from direct social competition and find consistent gratification in the refuge of fantasy. A vicious circle of rebuff, increased isolation and fantasy develops.

As these patients revert to the instrumental style characterizing the paranoid level, they harshly reject all forms of dependence, refuse to ally themselves with those whom they view as "inferior," and begin to suspect that others will undo them the first moment they can. Their resentment toward others for failing to appreciate them or to be willing subjects for their exploitation comes to the surface in the form of overt anger and vituperation. Unable to gain recognition and humiliated time and again, they reconstruct reality to suit their desires and illusions. As fantasy supplants reality and as their delusions lead them further astray from others, the decompensation process speeds up.

The final shameful collapse to the role of hospital invalid is a further blow to their once vaunted self-image. All that remains is a thin thread connecting the present to memories of a happier yesteryear. These few mementos they hold fast to, turning them over and over again in their thoughts, embellishing and nurturing them, lost in the distant past which now becomes their only reality.

2.   The background of the *active-independent paranoid* and *paraphrenic*

may include a number of biogenic factors. This is suggested by the frequent presence among family members of high levels of activation and energy and irascible and fearless temperaments. Along these lines, many of these patients as young children exhibited a vigorous aggressive and thick-skinned obtrusiveness. Witness the early history of Joseph M.

Many active-independent paranoids and paraphrenics have been exposed to harsh parental treatment. As a consequence, they acquire a deep mistrust of others, a desire for self-determination and a confident sense of competence and autonomy. With this as a base, they frequently reject parental controls and social values, developing in their stead an impulsive, aggressive, and often hedonistic style of life.

The expectations of attack and the chip on the shoulder attitudes of these youngsters provoke new tensions and conflicts, and thereby reactivate old fears and intensify new mistrusts. In decompensated cases, we see either deficiencies in the skill with which aggressive and vindictive strategies were learned or a gradual weakening of them as a result of repeated setbacks, as in the case of Joseph M. Under these conditions, suspicions of deceit gradually are transformed into irrational delusions of persecution. Unable to cope directly with the threats that surround them, their tensions either erupt into overt hostile attacks or are resolved in increasingly delusional fantasies. This paranoid stage with its periodic psychotic episodes may disintegrate further.

Unrelieved stress may prompt a marked withdrawal from social contact. The shock of hospitalization, the loss of self-determination and the terrifying dependence on others may shatter the last remnants of their delusional self-image. As they protectively withdraw further, they sink into a primitive world of fantasy. The former logic of their delusional system loses its coherence. Disorganized fantasies blur into objective reality. Hallucinations are projected and dismembered; bizarre feelings and a sense of disorientation come to the fore as these patients now pass the line into paraphrenic decompensation.

3.   With the exception of a divergency in coping aims during the borderline level of decompensation, the developmental history of the *passive-ambivalent paranoid* and *paraphrenic* and the passive-ambivalent cycloid and cyclophrenic is essentially alike. Reference should be made in this regard to Chapter 16, since there is no need to repeat this earlier discussion.

4.   The parallel noted above also applies to the developmental course of the *active-ambivalent paranoid* and *paraphrenic* and the active-ambivalent cycloid and cyclophrenic. Again, the major distinction lies in directions taken during the borderline period. Reference may be made to Chapter 16 for a brief description of the characteristic background of these patients.

In general, the prognostic picture for paranoids and paraphrenics is grave. This is true of all four variants. The chronic and pervasive nature of their decompensation augurs a poor future adjustment. However, because of their earlier self-confidence and capacity to draw self-reinforcements, their prognosis is somewhat better than that of schizoids and schizophrenics. But circumstance has devastated their self-image, leaving but a few remnants of self-esteem in its wake. Moreover, the undercurrent of mistrust and hostility in these patients makes it extremely difficult to establish therapeutic relationships which might alter the course of their illness.

As with all personality patterns, the prospects for a "thorough cure" of the paranoid and paraphrenic are poor. Habits and attitudes are deeply ingrained and pervade the entire fabric of personality functioning. Modest inroads are possible, of course, but these only diminish the frequency of psychotic episodes rather than revamp the personality style.

Therapy with these patients is a touchy proposition at best. Few come willingly for treatment in the first place, for it signifies weakness and dependency, both of which are repellent to the paranoid. Furthermore, the therapist may fall into the trap of disliking and rejecting his patient since the suspicions and veiled hostility of the paranoid and paraphrenic easily provoke displeasure and resentment. Also, the therapist must resist being intimidated by the patient's arrogance and demeaning comments. Weakness is the last trait the paranoid could accept in one with whom he finally has placed his trust. There are other problems which can complicate the therapist's efforts. He must not display excessive friendliness and overt consideration. These behaviors often connote deceit to the patient, a seductive prelude to humiliation and deprecation. As the paranoid sees it, he has suffered undue pain at the hands of deceptively "kind" people. Nor can the therapist question the patient about his delusional beliefs. At best, this will drive the patient to concoct new rationalizations and distortions. At worst, it may intensify his distrust.

What approach and tactic then can the therapist take?

Essentially, he must aim to build trust through a series of slow and progressive steps. He must evidence a quiet, formal and genuine respect for the patient as a person; he must accept, but not confirm, his patient's beliefs, and allow him to explore his thoughts and feelings at whatever pace he can tolerate. Thus, the major goal of therapy is to free the patient of mistrust by showing him that he can share his anxieties with another person without the dread of humiliation and maltreatment to which he is accustomed. If this can be accomplished, the patient may learn to share with others, to look at the world not only from his own perspective but through the eyes of others. Trusting the therapist, he can begin to relax, relinquish his defensive posture and open himself to new attitudes and points of view. Once he has accepted the therapist as a trusted friend, he will be able to lean on him and accept his thoughts and suggestions. This can become the basis for a more generalized lessening of suspicions and for a wider scope of trusting and sharing behaviors.

As regards specific modes of therapy, it is simplest to say that techniques are wholly secondary to the building of trust. Nevertheless, psychopharmacological drugs may be of value as calmatives during anxious or acting out periods. Institutionalization is required when reality controls break down. It is best, however, not to place the patient in too confining a setting for too long, since this will only reinforce his anticipation of injustice and maltreatment.

During outpatient treatment, it is mandatory that environmental irritants be reduced. Otherwise, therapy becomes an uphill battle. Behavioral and psychoanalytic therapies cannot be employed without the prior development of trust; their effectiveness is dubious in any event. Nondirective insight-oriented approaches are often useful, to be followed, where appropriate, by other measures. The choice of specific second-stage therapeutic methods depends on practical considerations and ultimate goals. As noted earlier, therapy is likely only to moderate rather than reverse the basic personality pattern.

PART 5

OTHER ABNORMALITIES

Ben Shan—*Incubus*

18 BRAIN DEFECTS

INTRODUCTION

The syndromes discussed in preceding chapters may be traced, in large measure, to social learning factors. Where biological influences were involved, they neither assumed a paramount role in creating the impairment nor were necessary elements in shaping the character of the disturbance. Rather, they were either entirely subsidiary, as in the learned behavior reactions, or interwoven with learning experiences, as in the personality patterns and symptom disorders.

To contrast with these impairments, our attention shall turn in this chapter to syndromes in which biological factors are preeminent. Social learning influences color the particular form and content of these aberrations, but the basic pathology itself has been shaped by neurological defects or physiochemical dysfunctions. Nevertheless, the consequences of biological disturbances often depend less on the type, location or extent of the brain defect than on the personality of the patient and the environment within which he continues to function (Amante et al., 1970). For example, the same type of brain tumor may lead to a morose and withdrawn depression in one person, to hypochondriacal irritability in a second, severe delusions in a third and a quiet but cognitively confused set of responses in a fourth.

CLINICAL SIGNS

Some patients exhibit no signs of illness, despite the presence of a clear-cut brain disease. There are limits, however, to the degree to which psychological compensation can camouflage the defect. At some point in brain dysfunction, differing from person to person, the individual begins to display abnormal features. These clinical signs may be manifested in any of a variety of functions, and may range from mild disturbances to the most markedly severe. In this section, we will focus on some of the more common signs that reflect the organic process itself, apart from its more personal "psychological" components. These clinical signs may be grouped conveniently into three categories: those associated with the loss of *general integrative functions*, those reflecting a loss of *specific functions* and those representing the patient's *compensatory coping efforts*. In no single case should we expect to find more than a few of the signs mentioned.

GENERAL INTEGRATIVE IMPAIRMENTS

Certain processes are prerequisites to wakeful brain activity. Others represent the brain's capacity to coordinate its diverse functions. Defects that disrupt these fundamental operations of the nervous system shall be termed losses of general integrative functions. We shall divide them into three subcategories: those concerned with levels of activation, manifesting themselves in *impairments of consciousness;* those associated with the brain's monitoring and regulating functions, exhibiting themselves in *impairments of control;* and those relating to the processes of memory retrieval and cognitive learning, displaying themselves in *impairments of abstraction.*

Impairments of Consciousness.   A prerequisite to all higher forms of brain functioning is a minimal level of central nervous system arousal. Various injuries, toxins and infections may result in the rapid or progressive faltering of neural activation, leading to decrements in attentiveness and awareness. These vary in intensity from the relatively mild forms of "clouding of consciousness" to the severe, stuporous states of coma. Clouded consciousness is signified by a hazy level of awareness in which the patient is awake but extremely difficult to reach. He seems unable to attend to external stimuli, to think clearly or to maintain a consistent focus on one set of ideas or events without "drifting off" into a dream-like state. At the extreme end of these impairments are states of coma in which even dream processes, as well as those of conscious awareness, are suspended.

Impairments of Control.   Activation and consciousness, although prerequisites to higher brain functioning, are no assurance that the brain will monitor and order the events to which it attends. Any number of disturbances may impair the overall mastery and control of thoughts, emotions and behaviors. The basic processes of inhibiting, separating and directing the concurrent streams of impression, memory and impulse which bombard the brain may be either mildly or markedly disrupted. This general breakdown in the regulation of perceptions and behaviors ranges from mild distractibility to the markedly severe state of delirium.

Less severe degrees of brain dyscontrol are seen in such clinical signs as labile emotions, perceptual distractibility and physical hyperactivity. These patients attend in rapid succession to one or another element of the multiple stimuli that surround them and are unable to focus on anything for too long a period. In addition, they are typically restless, shift capriciously from one activity to another and exhibit sudden outbursts of impulsive and changeable emotions. In short, they seem incapable of stemming or otherwise governing the flow of both external and internal stimulation, responding to these stimuli as if they were short-circuited through the brain without benefit of assimilation or control.

In the milder states of disorientation, this disorganized and drifting process may be sustained for extended periods; although flustered and distractible, the patient has some measure of control and some cognizance of reality. In the more severe states of delirium, however, brain dyscontrol is marked, and the patient seems utterly confused.

Impairments of Abstraction.   Consciousness and control are but preliminaries to the distinctively human capacity of abstraction. The vast network of intracortical systems in the brain allows for the coordination, retrieval and synthesis of diverse memories and cognitive processes. Damage to higher cerebral centers may cause a marked decrement in this integration of symbolic material.

In less severe form, the loss of abstraction is seen in an inability both to grasp and to retain new information. Old memories are functionally operative in these patients, but new learnings fail to be registered with clarity and tend not to be recalled, even in their simplest form. With severe injury, the patient succumbs to the "concrete attitude," noted by the tendency to be oriented only by the immediate and tangible, without recourse to memory retrieval and cognitive reflection.

SPECIFIC FUNCTIONAL IMPAIRMENTS

All parts of the nervous system work together as a unit. The scientist's separation of "general" versus a variety of different "specific" functions is largely artificial, a distinction representing his need to organize his subject matter into convenient categories. Although there is some basis in the differentiated structures of the brain for making these distinctions, any defect in one part of the brain usually alters in some manner other psychological functions. There is a "gradient of neural specialization," however, such that focal brain defects impair certain functions to a greater extent than others. Only in this sense of a specialization gradient can we speak of impairments as *specific* rather than general.

Let us briefly review a few of the many and varied specific psychological processes which may be disturbed by biophysical defects. We shall group them into three categories: *single function impairments, perceptual-motor impairments* and *cognitive-language impairments.*

Single Function Impairments. In addition to paralyses of *motor* capacities, patients often exhibit a variety of spontaneous involuntary movements, e.g., rhythmic tremors in the extremities known as parkinsonism, slow writhing and twisting movements of the hands and feet, referred to as athetosis, or rapid, irregular, asymmetrical jerking motions in extremities, termed chorea.

Innumerable *sensory* and *perceptual* dysfunctions may be diagnosed through neurological, visual and auditory examinations. The labels and details of these clinical symptoms are beyond the province of this textbook. It will suffice to note that specific sensory defects usually stem from damage to the peripheral regions of the nervous system, those concerned with the initial receipt of stimuli. Perception is a more complex function than sensation; in these processes, the central nervous system is involved in the organization of sensory stimuli into "meaningful" patterns or units. Disturbances in those regions of the brain underlying the perception of organized stimulus patterns and relationships may be evident in numerous pathological distortions.

Disturbances of *gross motor coordination* may reflect nervous system defects in regions necessary for body equilibrium; among their consequences are sudden losses of balance and tendencies to drift to one side in walking.

Perceptual-Motor Impairments. The attempt to coordinate one's motor responses in line with one's perception of stimuli is a higher order activity of the brain that is basic to a wide variety of psychological functions. In certain respects, impairments of this type may properly be viewed as "general integrative" disturbances. However, in many cases, the injury is relatively circumscribed, affecting only activities which require the sequential act of perceiving an event and reacting to it in a manner consonant with one's desires. Thus, the individual may be able to abstract what he perceives and may possess the capacity to understand what he wishes to accomplish, but be incapable of producing the desired response. It is as if some segment of internal wiring is missing, resulting in repetitive digressions in the progression from sensory input to motor output. Not uncommonly, these persons are extremely awkward or deficient in physical coordination, speech articulation, reading and writing. Many also exhibit disturbances of body image, weakly established handedness and right-left confusions.

Cognitive-Language Impairments.   The major category of cognitive language defects is labeled *aphasia.* This disorder arises primarily from impairments in the left cerebral hemisphere. The diagnosis of aphasia assumes that sensory and motor mechanisms are intact. Several subvarieties of aphasia have been differentiated, each of which represents a different aspect of disturbance in the complex process of symbolic verbalization.

Motor or expressive aphasia refers to an inability to verbalize spontaneously letters, words or sentences. The ability to comprehend language remains intact in pure cases. Quite commonly, expressive aphasia, which refers to vocalized speech, is often accompanied by an inability to write, known as *agraphia.*

Sensory or receptive aphasia denotes an inability to understand words and sentences. In some cases, the spoken word can be understood, but written symbols are experienced as obscure and meaningless. This latter impairment is referred to as *alexia.*

Amnestic aphasia is signified by an inability to recall the names of familiar objects and events. Other types of aphasia have been differentiated, but the list we have supplied covers the major varieties.

Before concluding, let us restate the fact that "real" cases of brain defect do not lend themselves to such neat discriminations as we have outlined. Moreover, the intrinsic unity of the brain means that injuries invariably disrupt more than one psychological function. In addition to the fact that several specific processes are usually impaired simultaneously, we find that some "reorganization" of general integrative processes is almost always involved, even in minor injuries. These reorganizations are paralleled by a variety of psychological coping adjustments, a topic to which we turn next.

COMPENSATORY COPING EFFORTS

Until now, we have focused our attention on symptoms that represent the direct effects of the biophysical disturbance. The clinical picture we observe, however, is complicated by numerous secondary signs that reflect the damaged individual's attempt to cope with his defects. These measures are employed to enable him to continue to function in his accustomed way, despite his structural limitations. In general, patients exhibit one or more of three types of responses: *catastrophic reactions* as they become aware of their illness and their marked incompetencies; a marked *accentuation of established personality dispositions;* and a *withdrawal* from tasks that tax their limited capacities, and a consequent *rigidity* and *perseveration* in behavior.

Catastrophic Reactions.   The inability to think, feel and act as one could prior to illness poses a serious threat to the impaired individual. Every task which he fails to execute as well as he did in the past is a reminder of his altered state. Each experience of failure carries more meaning to a defective individual than to a normal one since it makes the patient aware of the fundamental change that has taken place. Goldstein illustrates the seriousness of these experiences in the following quote (1942):

Here is a man with a lesion of the frontal lobe, to whom we present a problem in simple arithmetic. He is unable to solve it. But simply noting and recording the fact that he is unable to perform a simple multiplication would be an exceedingly inadequate account of the patient's reaction. Just looking at him, we can see a great deal more than this arithmetical failure. He looks dazed, changes color, becomes agitated, anxious, starts to fumble, his pulse becomes irregular; a moment before amiable, he is now sullen, evasive, exhibits temper, or even becomes aggressive. It takes some time before it is possible to continue the examination. Because the patient is so disturbed in his whole behavior, we call situations of this kind catastrophic situations.

Accentuation of Personality Dispositions.   There are many ways in which individuals may attempt to cope with "catastrophic" anxiety. The symptoms that a patient exhibits will tend to reflect his characteristic way of coping with difficulties. Thus, as a consequence of his physical impairment and the anxieties it evokes, we would expect that a basically dependent person would become notably security oriented as a means of assuring increased support and nurture from others. An independent personality, in contrast, may resist "submitting" to his diminished competence. He may react by becoming more aggressively assertive and domineering than before.

Brain impaired individuals are more likely to exhibit a more marked accentuation of their personality trends in response to stress than normal persons. This stems from the fact that their brain impairments limit their capacity to control their ingrained and "automatic" habits and attitudes. Deprived of normal regulating mechanisms, personality dispositions come to the fore in relatively pure and unmodulated form.

Withdrawal, Rigidity and Perseveration.   The repetition of catastrophic anxiety in chronically impaired individuals and their progressive inability to cope with the affairs of life often "force" them to react by what Goldstein has referred to as a "shrinking of the milieu." In order to preserve the few remnants of their psychological cohesion and to avoid the painful distress of repeated failures, these patients restrict their activities to those which do not tax their limited resources. As a consequence, the organically damaged person narrows his world to activities in which he feels safe, maintains a rigidity in his behavior, perseverates in the few things in which he feels competent and rarely ventures beyond secure boundaries. Goldstein describes the process in the brain-injured as follows (1959):

Observation shows that the patient is withdrawn from the world around him so that a number of stimuli, including dangerous ones, do not arise. He avoids company. He is as much as possible doing something which he is able to do well. What he is doing may not have any particular significance for him, but concentration on activities which are possible for him makes him relatively impervious to dreaded stimulation. Particularly interesting is his excessive orderliness in all respects. Everything in the surrounding world has a definite place. Similarly, he is very meticulous in his behavior as to time, whereby the determination as to when he should do something is related to events and to activities of his which always occur at the same time, or to a definite position of the hands of a clock. This orderliness enables him to prevent too frequent catastrophes.

Let us turn now to the major forms of brain defect.

BRAIN INFECTIONS

Numerous disturbances in behavior may be traced to the invasion of bacteria and viruses within the body. In certain acute infections, such as typhoid and pneumonia, we observe marked disturbances during periods of high fever. Most notable in this regard is delirium. It is the more chronic infections, however, which are of primary interest and concern to the psychopathologist. Among these are *neurosyphilis* and *encephalitis.*

NEUROSYPHILIS (GENERAL PARALYSIS)

The discovery of the role of syphilis as a cause of abnormal behavior was the first tangible source of support for the medical-disease model in psychiatry. Prior to the mid-nineteenth century, no relationship was seen to exist between syphilis, viewed then as a skin disease, and psychological impairments. The sequence of insights and laboratory findings which led to the discovery of its psychiatric significance must be recognized as a major achievement.

The clinical importance of neurosyphilis has decreased in recent years owing to advances in antibiotic therapies. Until the advent of this treatment, over one fourth of all admissions to mental hospitals were ascribed to neurosyphilis. High fever therapy, induced by malarial infection, was employed in the second quarter of this century. This method activated the body's defensive system, which then destroyed the infectious syphilitic spirochete, preventing further brain damage and arresting the deterioration process before it led to complete paralysis and death. Since antibiotic therapy was devised in the 1940's and is prescribed today with the first symptoms of bacterial infection, the progressive effects of the syphilitic infection usually are abruptly terminated. As a result of this early preventive treatment, neurosyphilis accounts now for less than 2 per cent of new hospital admissions.

Etiology and Course.   The syphilitic spirochete enters the body through minute abrasions of the skin or through mucous membranes such as are found in the surface tissue of the mouth and genitals. A directly contagious disease, most commonly transmitted during sexual intercourse, the syphilitic spirochete may also be transferred through kissing, contact with open infected sores and infiltration from mother to fetus during pregnancy.

Once the spirochete enters the body, it spreads with great rapidity, giving evidence of its presence through a sequence of five stages: in the *first* stage a hard chancre or lesion appears at the point of infection ten to 40 days after the contraction of the disease; the *second* stage, appearing one or two months following the chancre, is characterized by a diffuse copper-colored rash over the entire body, and is often accompanied by fever, indigestion and headache; overt symptoms disappear in the *third* stage, although internally the spirochetes continue to destroy bodily tissue and organs, especially blood vessels and nerve cells; the *fourth* stage becomes evident five to 20 years after the initial infection, manifesting itself in a wide variety of symptoms, to be discussed shortly, stemming from the pervasive destruction of vascular and neural tissue; and the *fifth* stage is noted by increasing motor paralysis, confusion and delirium, followed by death.

Clinical Picture.   Among the obvious signs of damage are marked degenerative changes and atrophy of brain tissue. The overall size of the brain is often decreased, shrunken and filled in with cerebrospinal fluid. A common symptom is the *Argyll-Robertson* sign in which the pupil of the eye fails to respond to light, but does accommodate to distance.

Notable impairments to *specific functions* are tremors of fingers, tongue, eyelids and facial muscles. Motor control of speech begins to weaken and falter, resulting in slurring, disarticulation and stuttering. The fine coordination required in writing often gives way. At first, there is an unsteadiness in handwriting; later, writing becomes crude and heavy and finally, there is no more than a few coarse and tremulous lines. Gross motor coordination is gradually eroded, exhibiting itself in the loss of balance and a shuffling unsteady gait, referred to as *locomotor ataxia*. Perceptual-motor dysfunctions are evident in such signs as an inability to button clothes, thread a needle or catch a ball.

Among *general-integrative* impairments are periodic convulsions and loss of consciousness. Less dramatic, but increasingly present, is a decrement in control, at first seen in a general carelessness and slovenliness about personal matters, and later in a gross social tactlessness, hyperdistractibility and emotional impulsivity. Also common are impairments in abstraction, poor retrieval of memories and confusion in thought.

The following case depicts a number of the typical neurosyphilitic features (Kolb, 1968).

CASE 18–1
Marjorie W., Age 26, Married

Marjorie was brought to the hospital because she had become lost when she attempted to return home from a neighborhood grocery store. About seven months before the patient's admission, her husband noticed that she was becoming careless of her personal appearance and neglectful of her household duties. She often forgot to prepare the family meals, or, in an apparent preoccupation, would burn the food. She seemed to have little appreciation of time and would not realize when to get up or go to bed. The patient would sit idly about the house, staring uncomprehendingly into space.

At the hospital Marjorie entered the admission office with an unsteady gait. There, by way of greeting, the physician inquired, "How are you today?" to which she replied in a monotonous, tremulous tone, "N-yes-s, I was-s op-er-a-ted on for 'pen-pendici-ci-tis." She never made any spontaneous remarks and when, a few days after her admission, she was asked if she were sad or happy, she stared vacantly at the physician and, with a fatuous smile, answered, "Yeah." Marjorie sat about the ward for hours, taking no interest in its activities. Sometimes she would hold a book in her lap, aimlessly turning the pages, never reading but often pointing out pictures like a small child and showing satisfaction when she found a new one to demonstrate. Neurological examination showed dilated pupils that reacted but slightly to light and on convergence. There was a tremor of lips and facial muscles on attempting to speak. The protruded tongue showed a coarse temor. All deep tendon reflexes were hyperactive. The Wasserman reaction was strongly positive in both blood serum and cerebrospinal fluid.

Neurosyphilitics often do not give evidence of "catastrophic reactions" since their pathology develops in a rather slow fashion. Because of the gradual and pervasive character of their defect, they often fail to sense the changes that have taken place within them or to grasp its full significance. As their ailment progresses, there is a growing accentuation of their premorbid personality coping styles. This accentuation occurs because of the increased stress they experience as they confront the ordinary tasks of life, and because they have lost the integrative controls with which to adapt to events flexibly.

ENCEPHALITIS

This syndrome, representing the inflammation and frequent destruction of brain tissue, may be traced to a variety of infectious sources, the most probable of which are viruses. On occasion, similar effects are produced by immunization serums and infections such as measles and hepatitis.

Different forms of the disease have been described, the most prominent of which is known as *epidemic encephalitis*. This contagious variety spread throughout Europe and to the United States between 1915 and 1919. Although rarely seen in true epidemic form, another outbreak was reported in India in 1958. Because a marked lethargy is common during the early phase of the disease, it originally was termed encephalitis lethargica. However, these symptoms are not always present.

Most patients react with high fever and drowsiness immediately follow-ing the infection. A few succumb to prolonged sleep for periods of weeks. This sleep is *not* stuporous since they can be roused to take nourishment or converse briefly. Neurological signs are displayed dur-ing this stage, particularly in motor behavior. An irritable hyperactivity often follows the termination of the stuporous period. Patients are rest-less and agitated, cannot sleep, suffer periodic convulsions, become disoriented and delirious and may experience frightening hallucina-tions.

Children often display a postencephalitic impulsiveness and distractibil-ity. They become difficult to discipline, neglectful of personal responsi-bilities and emotionally erratic, agitated and hyperactive — in short, they exhibit a loss of integrative controls. Some find considerable difficulty in monitoring external stimuli and regulating internal impulses. As a result of the disruptive effects of the impairment, their chances for developing a coherent personality are seriously hampered. Thus, many continue into adulthood as undisciplined, erratic and moody persons.

BRAIN TOXINS

In this section we shall review three chemical cripplers of brain tissue: alcohol, drugs and poisons. Before we begin, let us note that alcoholic and drug behavior reactions, discussed in Chapter 10, differ from alco-holic and drug defects, listed in this chapter.

There is little relationship between the chemical make-up of a toxin and the clinical symptoms that a patient exhibits. The specific abnormal be-haviors displayed are determined primarily by the patient's personality and his present environment, *not* by the particular toxin to which he has been subjected. Different toxic agents vary, however, in the potency and duration of their effects. Thus, they may produce different symptoms on these accounts.

All toxins, if ingested in sufficient quantities, cause severe *acute* impair-ments. These are characterized chiefly by a clouding of consciousness and a loss of integrative controls. Concentration is difficult, there may be disorientation as to time and place, recent memory often is impaired, emotions are erratic, a restless hyperactivity may covary with marked fa-tigue, and periods of delirium are not uncommon and are often accom-panied by visual hallucinations and delusions.

Chronic syndromes are characterized by diminished abstraction capaci-ties, motor and language deficits, accentuated premorbid personality traits and, if sufficiently prolonged, social withdrawal, incompetence and behavioral rigidity.

Let us next examine the three major toxic syndromes.

ALCOHOLIC SYNDROMES

Seven subcategories have been distinguished in the DSM-II to represent the disruptive effects of alcohol. Only four will be discussed here: patho-logical intoxication, delirium tremens, alcoholic hallucinosis and alco-holic deterioration. Of these, the first two are acute impairments, the fourth is chronic, and the third may be either. Another defect, known as

Korsakoff's syndrome, is often included among alcoholic impairments; however, alcohol is only one of several different factors which can give rise to this disturbance.

PATHOLOGICAL INTOXICATION

This is an acute disruption of normal brain functioning following immediately after the ingestion of relatively moderate amounts of alcohol. It occurs in individuals whose tolerance is especially low either as a function of neurological disease (e.g., epilepsy), general emotional instability (e.g., paranoid personality) or physical susceptibilities (e.g., states of exhaustion). Disorientation, confusion and delirium are prominent symptoms. During these periods, patients may act out violently, experience intense anxiety, perceive hallucinations or be plunged into a state of depression. The content of these psychological symptoms usually reflects a release and accentuation of the patient's predelirious personality. Delirium typically lasts a few hours, although, on occasion, it may extend to a day or two, following which the patient succumbs to a prolonged and deep sleep. Upon awakening, the patient recalls little or nothing of what happened.

The following case demonstrates the type of behavior that might be observed during these intoxicated states (Kolb, 1968).

CASE 18–2

Nathan W., Age 28, Divorced

Nathan was seen in jail while awaiting trial on a charge of drunkenness and disorderly conduct. The patient's father had committed suicide as he was about to be sent to a hospital for mental diseases. Nathan himself was described as being a friendly but quick-tempered and restless individual whose marriage had terminated in early divorce. He was said never to have been particularly alcoholic, but one July 4 he celebrated the holiday by drinking two bottles of beer and a glass of wine. Soon afterward he attempted to fling himself down an 80-foot embankment and was so greatly excited that he was taken to the police station for the night. The next morning he had no recollection of the affair. Ten months later Nathan called late one afternoon to see friends who invited him to sample what they considered choice varieties of whiskey and gin. He accepted their invitation and drank somewhat more heavily then usual. Soon after leaving the home of his friends he was observed by a police officer to be acting strangely. As the officer spoke to him he attacked him. While the officer was calling for help, Nathan disappeared. About 15 minutes later two women were startled to see a strange man thrust his head through a closed window of their living room and shout, "Help! Murder!" It was Nathan, who then ran on to another house where he rang the doorbell insistently. As the occupant answered the summons he again screamed, "Murder!" and ran to the street once more, where he broke the windshields and headlights of several parked automobiles and tore out the seats and pulled parts from other cars. At this point he was seized and taken to the police station where, on awakening the following morning, he had no recollection of his experience of the previous night.

DELIRIUM TREMENS

This well-publicized and dramatic syndrome is likely to be superimposed upon a pattern of chronic alcoholic addiction. It usually takes the form of a withdrawal symptom following a prolonged binge of heavy drinking (Klett et al., 1971). On occasion, it may appear in an addicted individual in conjunction with a minor head injury or infection.

As the phase of delirium approaches, the patient senses a diffuse apprehensiveness, uncomfortable restlessness and insomnia, and may become distraught over slight noises or sudden movements. Several covarying symptoms appear as the impairment proceeds to its more serious phase.

1. *Physical symptoms:* body temperature rises, perspiration becomes

profuse, there is a rapid heart rate, nausea, unsteady gait, physical weakness and coarse tremors of hands, tongue and lips.

2. *Concentration symptoms:* consciousness becomes clouded, there is disorientation for time and place, and memory for well-known events and people becomes blurred.

3. *Perceptual symptoms:* visual and tactile hallucinations come to the fore; the patient sees strange small objects twisting and running; he feels lice, roaches and spiders crawling all over him.

4. *Anxiety symptoms:* experiences of extreme fear and terror are common, mostly in response to the menacing objects and movements which appear to surround him, but also as a general foreboding that he is doomed to remain forever in his frightening state.

This delirious episode usually lasts for three to six days, and is followed by a deep sleep. Physical symptoms disappear upon awakening, but there is a slight residual of anxiety and a hazy recall of terrifying hallucinations. These tend to deter further drinking for a short period.

The following description illustrates the typical experiences and behaviors of such a patient.

CASE 18–3

James Z., Age 47, Married, No Children

Jim is a moderately successful lawyer, despite his chronic alcoholism. He "goes off on a bender" about once a month, disappearing for several days to a week. In the past ten years, Jim has been briefly hospitalized more than 20 times in conjunction either with delirium tremens or some other alcohol-related difficulty.

In a recent episode, his "girl-friend" called the emergency ward at the local hospital because Jim was jabbing himself with a fork "to get those miserable gnats off" his body. He was screaming and delirious upon admission to the hospital, terrified not only of the hallucinated gnats, but of the "crazy shapes" and "smelly queeries" that were "coming after" him. Nothing could be done to comfort Jim for several hours; he continued to have tremors, sweated profusely, cowered in a corner, drew his blankets over his head, twisted and turned anxiously, vomited several times and kept screaming about hallucinated images which "attacked" him and "ate up his skin."

After three days of delirium, with intermittent periods of fitful sleep, Jim began to regain his normal senses. He was remorseful, apologized to all for his misbehavior and assured them of his "absolute resolution never to hit the bottle again." Unfortunately, as was expected, he again was hospitalized three months later as a consequence of a similar debauche that was followed by delirium tremens.

ALCOHOLIC HALLUCINOSIS

The major symptom in this disturbance is auditory hallucination. In a few cases, this is accompanied by delusions. In contrast to delirium tremens, these patients are not disoriented or confused and are able to carry out their everyday responsibilities, except those involving their particular hallucination. It is highly probable that the syndrome occurs only in individuals already disposed to abnormal tendencies. Alcohol serves merely as a "releaser," a weakener of fragile controls that otherwise barely manage to contain the pathological process.

There is no clear understanding as to why auditory hallucinations in particular come to the fore in these cases. Quite possibly, alcohol may have selective chemical effects upon constitutionally disposed individuals, giving rise to disturbances specifically in the auditory apparatus. Patients will interpret these strange sensations in line with their latent pathological tendencies. Thus, some "hear" threatening voices or pistol shots whereas others recognize comforting sounds or voices, as in the famous play *Harvey,* about a genial drunk and his friendly invisible rabbit.

ALCOHOLIC DETERIORATION

This chronic condition is difficult to separate from prolonged alcoholic addiction since they almost invariably coexist. We attach this label to cases which give evidence both of a progressive destruction of brain cells and an insidious decline of premorbid personality traits. In chronic alcoholic addiction, the habit need not have progressed to the stage of brain atrophy.

The clinical picture seen in these patients is a composite of their various neural and psychological complications. Abstraction capacities are impaired and exhibited in memory defects, poverty of ideas, illogical reasoning and poor judgment (Jones and Parsons, 1971). Controls progressively give way and the patient displays emotional impulsiveness, crudeness and irresponsibility and a growing slovenliness in personal appearance. Depending on premorbid personality traits, he may become irritable and hostile or servile and dependent. A variety of specific functional impairments become evident, notably a loss of fine motor control, speech disarticulation, sluggish reflexes and aphasic symptoms.

DRUG SYNDROMES

Many of these impairments are difficult to differentiate from learned drug reactions (see Chapter 10). Distinctions, although largely academic and impossible to make in acute cases, are justified in chronic drug syndromes in which permanent alterations have occurred in brain tissue.

It should be noted that drugs taken for euphoric and hallucinogenic purposes, e.g., heroin, marijuana and LSD, are not viewed as toxic agents. Three drugs typically are included as toxic agents—morphine, barbiturates and bromides. Moderate levels of these drugs over several months may produce confusion, drowsiness, moodiness, fitful sleep, faulty memory and sluggish reactivity. These are often accompanied by a variety of discomforting physical ailments. Prolonged use of these drugs, even with doses below the level capable of producing acute disturbances, may develop into serious addictions. Withdrawal symptoms as well as possible irreversible changes in neural tissue are inevitable. With the exception of decreased controls, most of the specific and integrative functions of the brain are not severely impaired. There are likely to be a number of personality disturbances, however, usually accentuations of premorbid traits.

POISON SYNDROMES

A variety of both acute and chronic symptoms may occur in response to the ingestion or inhalation of several metals, liquids and gases. Notable among these are lead, mercury, manganese, carbon monoxide and carbon disulfide. Most acute forms of poison intoxication are accidental. Chronic varieties usually arise as a consequence of prolonged occupational exposure. As is typical of most acute syndromes, these patients exhibit confusion, irritability, fatigue, hallucinations, delirium and, where high dosages are involved, severe coma. In chronic cases, the principal symptoms are a progressive deterioration of controls and abstraction capacities. Personality complications, when present, reflect an accentuation of preclinical traits.

BRAIN TRAUMA

Injuries to the head provided ancient man with his first source of data concerning the role of the brain in consciousness and intelligence. Hip-

pocrates identified the connection between these accidents and a variety
of perceptual and motor disabilities. Galen was the first to propose that
head injuries were a primary cause of mental disorders. Today we know
that there are perhaps as many as one million accidents each year in the
United States involving the head region. Many result in severe although
usually temporary mental aberrations. An unknown number of seemingly minor falls and head wounds may cause unrecognized and permanent harm to the developing nervous systems of young children.

TYPES OF INJURY

Trauma to the brain produces several immediate consequences, the nature of which depends on the overall extent and severity of the accident,
and on whether it includes the destruction of brain tissue and its supporting blood vessels. Head injuries have been grouped into four types:
concussions, contusions, lacerations and vascular accidents.

Concussions.   These rather common and temporary impairments stem
from blows to the head which neither penetrate the skull nor damage
brain tissue. There is a brief loss of consciousness followed by a period,
ranging from several minutes to a few days, in which the patient seems
confused, may be nauseated and dizzy and experiences both focal and
diffuse headaches. The knockout blow in boxing typifies this acute
syndrome.

Contusions.   These are abrasions of brain tissue resulting from violent
or jolting head motions, severe cerebral compressions or skull fractures.
Contusions are more serious than concussions since they represent an
actual bruising of neural matter. A period of coma is not uncommon,
lasting from a few hours to several weeks. Upon regaining consciousness, the patient remains somewhat disoriented, may become delirious
and almost invariably experiences both headaches and dizziness. Convulsions are not infrequent, and there may be a temporary loss of
speech, as well as other relatively specific impaired functions.

Lacerations.   The most serious brain traumas are accidents which penetrate the skull and rupture or tear through brain tissue. If the patient
survives his injury, he is likely to remain in a coma for an extended
period. The immediate postcoma symptoms are essentially the same as
were noted for contusions. The nature of specific functional impairments, ranging from total paralysis to aphasia to minor motor deficits,
depends essentially on the locus of injury.

Vascular Accidents.   In this acute impairment, the defect arises either
from a blocking or a bursting of a cerebral blood vessel.

The sudden blocking of circulation, termed *cerebral thrombosis*, prevents
nourishment and the removal of waste products within associated brain
regions. A similar defect, but one that develops much more gradually, is
termed "cerebral arteriosclerosis." This degenerative defect, to be discussed later, occurs as a consequence of the progressive narrowing of the
blood vessels. In both impairments, there may be a paralysis of the
musculature, a variety of sensory anesthesias and cognitive-language
deficits.

The rupture of a circulatory vessel, termed *intracranial hemorrhaging*,
results in a flooding of blood throughout the surrounding brain field. If
the vessel involved is a major one or essential to the neural activation of
vital organs, the result is usually death. In less severe cases, there is a

strong likelihood that the recovery phase will be characterized by paralysis, confusion and other marked functional limitations.

POST-TRAUMATIC SYMPTOMS

Most cases of brain concussion and contusion in adults are followed by a rapid recovery, with no long-term or chronic consequences. Although the evidence is unclear, severe concussions or contusions in childhood, especially during periods of early neurological maturation, may produce developmental retardations. These defects are likely to be limited to spheres of brain capacity that are undergoing rapid neural proliferation at the time of trauma.

Disturbing aftereffects in cases of laceration and vascular accident are rather common but by no means inevitable. The most frequent of the enduring symptoms are headaches and dizziness. Specific defects are determined by the locus of tissue damage. Convulsive seizures persist in about five per cent of these cases. Deterioration of integrative abstraction and control functions is not common in adults unless there has been extensive neural destruction or bilateral (both hemispheres) damage to the frontal lobes.

Changes observed in post-traumatic cases are colored by premorbid traits and attitudes. Some patients exhibit a chronic irritability. Others appear to be in a state of permanent fatigue and invalidism. There is no way to determine the extent to which these changes can be ascribed specifically to neural damage.

The following history is more or less typical of the behavioral consequences of brain trauma (Gregory, 1968).

CASE 18–4

Carl F., Age 69, Married, Three Children

This farmer was admitted to the psychiatric unit of a general hospital with a history of marked personality changes following a serious automobile accident ten months previously. Prior to the accident he had been healthy, hard working, sociable, and easy to get along with. In the automobile accident, he sustained fractures of the arm and skull with severe concussion and brain damage, so that he was unconscious for ten days afterwards.

On awakening from the coma, Carl had no recollection of events that had occurred immediately preceding the accident, and he continued to have difficulty in remembering certain events that happened after he recovered consciousness. What his family noticed most, however, were the marked changes in his behavior that occurred after he left the hospital and returned home to his farm. They found him extremely irritable, easily angered, and unpredictable in his behavior. Carl drove the chickens as though they were cows, and made them so nervous that egg production dropped drastically. He fed the cows just enough for them to stay alive. He carefully locked up empty fuel drums which he had never done previously. He wrecked some of the farm machinery so badly that his son could not repair it. He would not talk to members of his family at all except to berate and swear at them, and he threatened his wife with physical violence many times. He blamed his family for poor crops which were really due to drought, and he frequently got up at night and slammed doors.

Carl's unusual behavior had already improved considerably by the time he was admitted to the psychiatric unit, and throughout the three weeks he remained there, he was pleasant, cooperative, and sociable, with no evidence of depression or paranoid ideation. However, he did show mild disorientation for time and impairment of memory for recent events, which remained fairly constant throughout his hospital stay and did not show the marked changes that sometimes occur in certain types of organic brain syndrome.

Because of the abrupt nature of their impairment, many patients recognize their decreased competence and experience repeated "catastrophic anxieties." As a consequence, they begin to "shrink their milieu," drawing more and more into a narrow world of activities in which they feel secure. It is not uncommon, therefore, that the personality picture in adult patients, once having passed through an initial period in which their preclinical traits were accentuated, begins to be characterized by a pervasive social detachment and rigidity.

BRAIN NEOPLASM

In this classification we include impairments resulting from abnormal growths within the brain or its surrounding tissues. These are found in about two per cent of all autopsied cases and are encountered at all ages, but predominantly in the forties and fifties. *Malignant* growths tend to interfere directly with cellular functioning, result in the paralysis of associated biological processes and almost inevitably result in death. *Benign* tumors, in contrast, usually exert their effects by intracranial pressure. Because the cranium is a rigidly enclosed region, expansion of any part will cause compression of both near and far brain tissue.

The clinical picture associated with neoplasms is extremely varied, reflecting the location, size and rapidity of tumor growth and, as with all brain defects, the preclinical personality of the patient.

Among the more prominent signs of a loss of integrative functions are clouding of consciousness, inability to concentrate, convulsive seizures and memory impairments. Acute symptoms such as delirium may follow a sudden increase in intracranial pressure.

Signs of general impairment are usually intertwined with a number of more specific disturbances. The nature of these circumscribed symptoms depends on the primary locus of tissue damage or pressure. Although tumors in the frontal lobes may result in behaviors that are at variance with a patient's premorbid personality, it is more likely that preclinical traits will simply be accentuated. Temporal and parietal lobe neoplasms are often associated with perceptual motor and cognitive language dysfunctions whereas occipital lobe tumors frequently give rise to visual hallucinations.

Because the brain can accommodate to slowly expanding neoplasms for long periods, no signs of pathology may be evident until the disease process has progressed beyond controllable proportions. In some of these cases, the emergence of symptoms is so closely interwoven with subtle psychological changes as to be overlooked even by a discerning clinical eye.

BRAIN DEGENERATION

Increased longevity is one of the many beneficial consequences of recent advances in medical science. However, this has not been an unmixed blessing since the prolongation of life means that man will be confronted with more of the disabling impairments of old age. Three times as many people survive beyond the age of 65 than they did a century ago, only to suffer now the ravaging effects of physical and mental deterioration. We have seen a sharp upturn in recent years in the total number and percentage of cases admitted to hospitals in conjunction with the degenerative effects of aging. In the past twenty years alone, the proportion of patients over 65 admitted to mental hospitals has increased five times as rapidly as those below that age. At present, almost one fourth of all first admissions are in this age bracket. These figures only touch the surface of the devastating and desolating psychological consequences of growing old. Perhaps as many as a third of a million persons in nursing homes for the aged are there as a result of mental as well as physical deterioration. In addition, there are untold numbers of older persons who are sheltered within their families and communities, despite severe degenerative psychopathology. In short, aging is a major psychological health problem of growing proportions.

Before detailing the subsyndromes of brain degeneration, let us consider some of the determinants which contribute to the aging process.

DEVELOPMENTAL BACKGROUND

Medical science is still unclear as to why men age, and why people differ in both the rapidity and character of the aging process. It was once believed that the progression of bodily deterioration was as intrinsic a biological process in old age as was growth in youth. Recent thought suggests that degeneration, although ultimately inevitable, is fostered by avoidable environmental conditions, such as toxins, faulty nutrition, psychic stress, climate and irradiation, each of which impairs the organism's regenerative powers. We know that the deterioration process is more complicated than once considered. Symptomatology in aged patients is influenced greatly by psychological and social factors. As evidence of this, gerontologists point out that severe psychopathology is often present in old age with but minimal evidence of disease. Conversely, they find cases of pervasive brain degeneration with but few minor psychological disabilities. Clearly then, psychopathology in old age is not simply biogenic or psychogenic. It is a complex interaction of both factors. If we keep this interactive point of view as a framework, we may proceed to the task of separating these two classes of determinants.

BIOLOGICAL INFLUENCES

There are numerous neurological and circulatory changes associated with aging. The total weight of the brain is reduced, with a definite decrease in the number of cells, especially in the cortex. Both large and small blood vessels lose their elasticity and appear convoluted. Fatty deposits proliferate, lining and surrounding both cells and vessels, blocking normal blood flow, retarding the delivery of oxygen and resulting in the reduction of metabolism. Not only do these changes lead to tissue degeneration and decreased efficiency, but they set into motion strains which exhaust the body's energy reserves.

Associated with these internal changes is a general decline in physical energy and an increased vulnerability to illness compounded by slow periods of recuperation. Prominent among changes is a failing memory, with all of its disconcerting effects. Similarly, older persons display an increased intellectual rigidity, a decline in the capacity for new learning or for solving problems that require reflection and imagination. Fortunately, many are still able to draw upon their storehouse of accumulated experience to master the everyday tasks of life.

PSYCHOSOCIAL INFLUENCES

The importance of psychosocial factors is usually secondary in advanced cases of cerebral degeneration. However, the role played by psychological attitudes and social resources is extremely important during the earlier phases of degeneration and may determine the entire course of the aging process. Many an older person remains vigorous, productive and intellectually alert, despite substantial biophysical deterioration. Witness the spirited writings of George Bernard Shaw and Bertrand Russell when they were well into their nineties or the physical stamina and clarity of mind of Amos Alonzo Stagg who continued his football coaching career to the age of 100.

For most individuals, later life is a period of transition that demands adjustments even more challenging than those faced during the turbulent years of adolescence. In contrast to the adolescent, the aging person is not physically robust and pliant, and, more importantly, does not look forward with bright anticipation to his future prospects. Most envision only increasing infirmity and inescapable death. Such cheerfully euphemistic labels as "senior citizen," designed to "soften the blow," only tell him that he is past his peak and is expected to sit on the sidelines while others carry on the game of life. Added on to the realities of failing health and retirement from meaningful work, the realization of a loss of personal status and significance may come as a profound shock (Birren, 1970). As aging persons look about them, they see the values they cherished throughout their lives simply cast aside by "new fangled" ideas and customs. Having little else to hold to than their memories and increasingly distraught by the "arrogance and irreverence" of the young, they begin to exhibit an intolerance and conservatism that irritates others and becomes a source of interpersonal tension that further endangers the affection and respect they so desperately crave. Feelings of alienation and isolation are futher compounded by the death of peer group companions, and the older person suffers increased demoralization and draws ever more into himself. The prospect of loneliness and poverty and of being an unwelcome burden to unreceptive children, adds to their fears and to the indignity of having to depend for survival on the patronizing good will of others. Psychologically isolated, their sense of self-worth destroyed and anticipating a future beset by increased incompetence, infirmity and inescapable death, many older persons "give up" and allow themselves to sink into the "inevitable."

Whether or not the individual's life assumes the bleak sequence of events just outlined depends on his lifelong personality style and outlook and the degree of support and encouragement he finds in his environment (Markson et al., 1971). Possessing an aliveness of spirit, a capacity for self-renewal, an active interest in contemporary affairs and a wholesome family and community environment, the probability is small that the person will succumb readily to the degenerative changes of aging. However, given few inner resources or a discouraging family life, the likelihood of rapid psychological and physical deterioration markedly increases. As we progress in our description of the various clinical subdivisions of degeneration, let us keep in mind this complex background of psychosocial factors which determine the manner and extent to which the individual copes with the inevitable bodily degenerations of aging.

PRESENILE DEMENTIA

For the most part, brain degeneration is a normal process, a sequence of events to which all individuals succumb sooner or later. However, some persons exhibit presenile syndromes, that is, give evidence of biological deterioration earlier in life than usual. Most presenile degenerative syndromes are associated with rare neurological or metabolic defects. In the following sections, we will describe briefly four of these well-delineated disease syndromes. As medical science progresses, the character and details of other presenile groups will no doubt be identified.

HUNTINGTON'S CHOREA

This is a relatively rare chronic disease characterized by progressively severe and uncontrollable jerking movements. First described by the American neurologist George Huntington in 1872, it is transmitted genetically in the form of a Mendelian dominant gene, is found in all races and parts of the world and first occurs in persons between the ages of 30 and 50. Behavioral symptoms frequently precede demonstrable neurological signs. Many patients exhibit increased irritability, defective memory and depression several years prior to the emergence of the choreiform twitching. The first definitive signs are seen in facial grimacing, head nodding and an involuntary smacking of the tongue and lips. As the disease progresses, there is a gradual spreading to the trunk and limbs of irregular and stretching movements. In addition, there are a disjointed walk and explosive speech. The progressive nature of this disease is illustrated in the following case (Kolb, 1968).

CASE 18–5

Rachel A., Age 56, Married, One Child

Rachel was admitted to a mental hospital at the age of 56. The familial incidence of Huntington's chorea was striking. A maternal grandmother, a maternal uncle and his daughter, the patient's mother and four of the patient's siblings exhibited definite symptoms of Huntington's chorea. Two members of the family committed suicide after they had developed the disease. Prior to her illness Rachel was apparently an attractive, well-adjusted person. She was a Girl Scout leader and took part in community affairs. Shortly before she was 35 years of age she began to show an insidious change of personality. She discontinued her church, Girl Scout, card club and other activities; she lost interest in her family and at times wandered away from home, returning at night but giving no information as to where she had been. In this same period she began to drop articles and to show twitching of her hands.

Rachel became neglectful of her personal appearance, refused to comb her hair, bathe, or change her clothes. She refused to launder soiled garments and would hide them in closets or corners. The choreiform movements increased in extent, and she occasionally fell. At times she showed temporary alertness and interest in anticipation of a visit from her daughter, but after one or two days she drifted back into her former seclusiveness and deteriorated habits.

On many occasions Rachel threatened and even attacked her husband, sometimes with a knife, and on one occasion inflicted a four-inch scalp wound. She became profane and her favorite term in addressing her husband was, "You G-d-fool." She was subject to tantrums in which she would threaten to jump from a window. She came to be known to the children in the neighborhood as "the old witch on the third floor." Finally, the choreiform movements became so extreme that it was difficult for her to go up and down stairs and she often fell.

On arrival at the hospital, Rachel's facial expression was vacant and she showed such uncoordinated and choreiform movements of her legs that she had difficulty in walking without assistance. There were gross choreiform movements of the head and all extremities. Her constant grimacing, blinking of her eyes, and twitching of her fingers were quite striking. The coordination of her hands was so poor and the movements of her head were so extreme that she had difficulty in eating. Her speech was explosive and difficult to understand. Although somewhat irritable, demanding, and distrustful, she adjusted to the hospital environments without serious difficulty.

Psychological disturbances are almost inevitable during the mid and later stages of the defect. In some measure, these are a direct product of cerebral changes, especially those associated with the loss of bodily controls. For the greater part, however, they reflect the patient's premorbid personality and the attitude he develops toward his ailment. Some become grossly apathetic, others become severely depressed and still others appear either anxious, delusional, aggressive or hallucinatory. The course of the impairment is irreversible. Hospitalization is inevitable and death usually follows within 15 to 20 years of the onset of symptoms.

ALZHEIMER'S DISEASE

This impairment was first described by the German neurologist Alois Alzheimer in 1906. Although the defect is not clearly a familial disease, research suggests that in some cases a hereditary disposition may be operative. Some investigators believe the defect to be a premature variant of senile dementia which will be described later, but there are several features which tend to differentiate the course and symptomatology of these two syndromes. First, Alzheimer's disease occurs abruptly and at an appreciably earlier age than senility, usually in the 40's or 50's. Second, it is distinguished by marked speech impairments, involuntary movements in the extremities and occasional convulsions, none of which are notably present in senile dementia. Third, degeneration is rapid, with death likely within four or five years after the initial onset of symptoms.

In the early stages, preceding the deterioration in speech and motor functions, patients exhibit impaired reasoning and memory. Both receptive and expressive aphasia are not uncommon as the disease progresses. Accompanying this may be a decrement in control functions, giving rise to disorganized thought, general restlessness, distractibility and emotional lability. In the advanced stage there is an overall deterioration with bodily emaciation, intellectual decline and psychological resignation. The physical exhaustion and distressing awareness of hopelessness and impending death foster a rapid psychic collapse in these patients.

PICK'S DISEASE

The initial description of this extremely rare disease was made by the Czechoslovakian neurologist Arnold Pick in 1892. Neurologically, the degenerative process is limited at first. As the disease advances, atrophy becomes more pervasive, spreading throughout the central nervous system. The age of onset is approximately the same as in Alzheimer's disease; however, in the latter impairment, the degenerative process is pervasive from the beginning. Other distinctions between the two syndromes may be noted. In contrast to Alzheimer's symptom cluster, patients suffering Pick's disease give less evidence of early memory and speech difficulties and tend to be apathetic and indifferent rather than agitated and restless. Also, they are more likely to have ancestors with similar pathological histories. As with Alzheimer's disease, these patients deteriorate rapidly, becoming confused and disorganized in their thinking as degeneration progresses. Death occurs about four years after onset.

PARKINSON'S DISEASE

First described by the English physician James Parkinson in 1817, this defect occurs most often between the ages of 50 and 70, and arises from a circumscribed disease process. In contrast to other presenile impairments, it is not associated with a general deterioration of personality and intellect, nor does it inevitably eventuate in death.

The parkinsonian symptoms of muscular rigidity and tremors, propulsive gait, and indistinct speech have been observed in patients following encephalitis, viral infections and exposure to toxins. In most cases, the symptomatology either disappears in time or fails to be progressive. Despite its basic physical character, the symptoms of the disease are aggravated by emotional stress. Personality changes, such as social withdrawal and apathy, are frequently associated with this syndrome, but do not appear to be an intrinsic part of the disease process. Rather, they seem to reflect the patient's attitude toward his physical disability.

SYNDROMES OF ADVANCED AGE

These impairments stem largely from "normal" processes of brain degeneration and are not viewed as products of disease. Brain changes are highly individual, however, each patient exhibiting a pattern of degeneration that is consonant with his distinctive genetic, nutritional and psychological history. To complicate matters, the final clinical picture is often less a result of this "unique" pattern of neurological deficit than the patient's present coping behaviors and environmental conditions. Two major syndromes are differentiated in conventional practice: *senile dementia* and *cerebral arteriosclerosis.*

SENILE DEMENTIA

These cases comprise about 10 per cent of first admissions to mental hospitals. Although the average age of admission is about 75, the onset of dementia is probably earlier since most patients are cared for by their families prior to hospitalization. No sharp line can be drawn as to when the senile process occurs since degeneration is gradual (Alexander, 1972). Imperceptible changes occur slowly until an inescapable picture exists to justify the syndrome label. Despite the fact that no two patients exhibit the same clinical picture, certain common features are found.

The brains of senile patients are reduced markedly in size as a function of tissue atrophy. Gross neurological examination shows a narrowing of cortical convolutions, a widening of fissures and the presence of numerous scar cells.

Diminished abstraction powers are evident on the psychological level. In less severe cases, there is an ineptness in regulating impulses, an increased carelessness and untidiness in personal habits and a tendency to erratic emotional outbursts. A notable early feature is pronounced forgetfulness, especially for recent events.

As the degenerative process advances, thinking becomes illogical, ideas are fragmented, speech is often rambling and incoherent, and there is a growing disorientation, confusion and loss of identity. Periods of terror, bewilderment and delirium may not be uncommon. Although deficits in general control and abstraction processes characterize the deteriorations of senile dementia, specific disabilities in circumscribed functions may be notable if certain regions of the brain are more severely impaired than others. These may take any number of forms, from a loss of speech to minor paralyses to a total amnesia for a particular life period.

Emotional behavior usually is consistent with premorbid traits. However, since these patients are lacking in normal controls, their feelings are expressed in accentuated form. What often appears as strange and unanticipated behavior on the part of the elderly usually reflects the expression of previously repressed needs which are now manifest since regulating capacities have deteriorated.

As the degenerative process continues its downward trend, the patient slips progressively into a severely deteriorated physical and mental state. He is now totally disoriented, bedridden and reduced to a minimal or vegetable-like existence. With few reserves left to resist disease and with recuperative powers severely weakened, he succumbs readily to some minor infection and dies shortly thereafter.

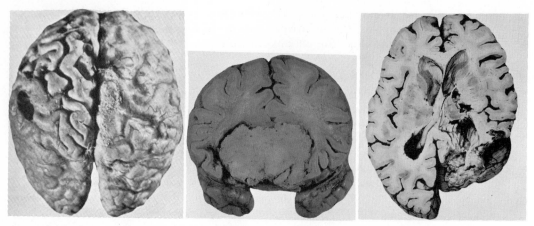

Figure 18-1 Some brain diseases. A, Neurosyphilis. (From Wechsler, I. S.: Clinical Neurology. 9th edition. Philadelphia, W. B. Saunders Co., 1963.) B, Tumor. C, Cerebral arteriosclerosis. (Parts B and C from Bruetsch, W. L.: Mental disorders arising from organic disease. In The Biology of Mental Health and Disease. New York, Hoeber-Harper, 1952.)

CEREBRAL ARTERIOSCLEROSIS

Although this disease is by no means inevitable, most elderly people show signs of a hardening and thickening of the blood vessels, causing a cumulative deprivation of oxygen and nutrients to the brain. Approximately 15 per cent of first admissions to mental hospitals are designated as suffering from this form of arteriosclerotic defect.

The symptom picture and clinical course of these patients are difficult to distinguish from those of senile dementia, especially in cases of slow and progressive development. For the most part, the features noted in the section on senility apply to the arteriosclerotic condition. Several points of distinction may be noted, however. *First,* senile dementia progresses almost invariably in a gradual fashion. Changes in cerebral arteriosclerosis, however, often occur in a rapid and dramatic way, usually as a consequence of a sudden blocking of a major artery. *Second,* the impairments of senile dementia are pervasive in nature and usually affect most prominently integrative capacities such as memory retrieval and abstraction functions. Arteriosclerotics more often give evidence of selective and specific functional impairments, with integrative capacities remaining relatively intact. *Third,* the symptomatology of senile patients is, more or less, even and predictable, evidencing slow, almost imperceptible, changes. The clinical picture of arteriosclerotics tends to fluctuate erratically, flaring up into acute confusional episodes at some times, and then quieting down into equanimity and coherence at others. *Fourth,* few seniles experience pain and discomfort in conjunction with their neurological impairment. In contrast, the arteriosclerotic suffers repeated headaches, dizziness and occasional convulsions.

In the later stages of degeneration, seniles and arteriosclerotics are difficult to distinguish. Both deteriorate to a bedridden state and are confused, emaciated and subject to physical diseases, one of which inevitably proves fatal.

BRAIN EPILEPSY

This syndrome incorporates a variety of clinical states that stem from an excessive discharge of brain cells. It is characterized by periods of unconsciousness, involuntary movements or bizarre sensory hallucinations.

The terms "seizures" and "convulsions" are often used as synonyms for epilepsy. The term *idiopathic* epilepsy has been applied in the past to cases in which the cause of the seizure is unknown. Convulsions are common to many of the syndromes discussed in previous sections. The epileptic classification, to be described here, represents the idiopathic variety.

Epilepsy affects about two million Americans, has its onset at any age (many newborn infants give evidence of the disease) and is found in about the same proportions among various so-called racial groups and among men and women. With minor exceptions, epileptics exhibit the same distribution of intellectual capacities as found in the general population, and do not give evidence of progressive brain or personality deterioration. The proportion of epileptics in mental hospitals is only a shade higher than that of nonepileptics.

CLINICAL VARIETIES

Neurologically, the epileptic process consists of spontaneous and massive discharges of groups of brain cells (Jasper et al., 1969). Whatever its stimulus, the patient experiences in rather intense form the same behaviors, thoughts and feelings that normally are activated by the cerebral tissues involved. Thus, if motor regions are activated, as is often the case, the patient will spontaneously engage in some kind of physical activity. Should the discharge involve visual areas, he may experience visual hallucinations. If regions of the brain that subserve memory are stimulated, then he may suddenly recall some long-forgotten past event.

Before losing consciousness, as is the case in most types of epilepsy, many patients experience what is known as the *aura*, a brief warning of an impending convulsion. This may take different forms depending on the initial site of cellular discharge and the attitudes the patient has acquired toward his convulsive experiences. Some simply feel a diffuse apprehensiveness. Others become dizzy or get an abdominal cramp. Still others sense some unpleasant odor, strange sounds in their ears or an uncontrollable twitching in their legs. These initial signs often provide a useful clue to the primary site of the underlying neural defect. Depending on the locus of the impairment and the extent to which the discharge spreads, the patient may or may not lose consciousness. Periods of unconsciousness are inevitable when brain centers underlying conscious control are overwhelmed. Since neuronal discharges temporarily inactivate the involved cells, the patient remains unconscious for a short period.

The problem of differentiating the various "types" of epilepsy has plagued clinicians ever since its true character was discovered. Attempts to classify the impairment in terms of cause have proven impractical. Not only is there a great divergence of causes, but for the most part origins cannot be identified. Efforts to distinguish epileptic types in accord with the anatomical locus of the initial discharge present similar complications since, in many cases, the area from which the discharge originates cannot be pinpointed.

Despite efforts to develop a classification that coordinates etiology and the primary site of anatomical involvement (Penfield and Jasper, 1954; Symonds, 1955; Goldensohn, 1965), the traditional practice persists of differentiating patients in terms of clinical symptomatology. We shall follow the traditional schema in the following descriptions. Let us be mindful, however, that the categories to be presented do not exhaust the varieties of epilepsy nor are they mutually exclusive; several "types" may be found in the same patient.

GRAND MAL

This dramatic form of epilepsy involves a generalized seizure through-out the brain. Its most prominent psychological correlates are the loss of consciousness and convulsive motor activity. In some cases the patient may undergo vague changes in mood and sensation several hours prior to the seizure. About two thirds experience the aura phenomenon. Just prior to the loss of consciousness, the patient may emit a cry or scream when air is forced from the lungs as a consequence of the involuntary contraction of respiratory muscles. Concurrent with unconsciousness, the patient falls to the ground, displays *tonic* muscular contractions such that the body is rigid with the legs outstretched, arms flexed and fists clenched. This first phase lasts about a minute and is accompanied by respiratory stoppage and marked facial pallor. Immediately thereafter, air is inhaled and the *clonic* phase commences with spasms and rapid jerking movements, during which time the patient thrusts his limbs back and forth and vigorously opens and closes his jaws. Many patients inadvertently harm themselves in this phase, either by biting their tongues or bruising themselves while thrashing about. Following the clonic phase, which also lasts about a minute, convulsive movements gradually ebb and the patient regains consciousness although he usually remains a bit confused, has a headache and feels sleepy. The frequency of these episodes varies from several times a day to as few as once every several years.

JACKSONIAN TYPE

This syndrome is often a prelude to a grand mal seizure. It is characterized by a preliminary motor spasm or sensory disturbance in a circumscribed region of the body which then spreads to encompass a wider sphere of functions. As noted above, it may eventuate in a full-blown or generalized grand mal convulsion. Patients are conscious as the muscular twitching or sensory tingling begins and then "marches" across the body. Although the subsequent loss of consciousness may reflect a spreading of the initial discharge, it is often a product of a psychogenic "blanking out," an anticipatory fainting when the step by step advance of these distressing symptoms is viewed. Of course, in these cases the typical grand mal tonic and clonic symptoms are lacking. These latter features of Jacksonian epilepsy are notable in the following brief sketch.

CASE 18–6

Dora S., Age 27, Two Children

Dora suffered periodic Jacksonian seizures in her left arm since childhood that were not controllable with medication. By the time she was 13 or 14, she "learned" to faint whenever she felt the beginning signs of tremor. At no time did she ever display the traditional grand mal reaction; rather, she would clutch her left hand and quickly sink to the ground in an unconscious state, during which time the arm continued to twitch. Dora would regain consciousness a few minutes following the termination of the tremor, quite aware of what had occurred prior to her faint, and would usually be in good spirits since she had "got away from that crazy feeling that crawled all over me."

PETIT MAL

The term "petit mal" was coined originally to denote a minor or small seizure, but it has come to represent states in which there is a momentary diminution rather than a total loss of consciousness. During these ten to 15 second episodes, occurring as often as 20 or 30 times a day, the patient is completely out of touch with his surroundings, stares vacantly ahead, drops whatever he may be doing or holding and then resumes his activity with no awareness of what has happened.

Traditionally included in the petit mal syndrome are *akinetic* attacks which refer to an abrupt loss of muscle tonus, resulting in such consequences as a sudden falling to the ground, dropping of objects and head nodding. Also included are *myoclonic* spells characterized by brief motor jerking or muscular contractions. Petit mal symptoms rarely appear for the first time after adolescence and usually disappear before the age of 30.

PSYCHOMOTOR TYPES

The principal feature of this condition is a clouding of consciousness during which the patient engages in a rather inappropriate but well organized sequence of activities, following which he returns to full awareness with total amnesia for his intervening behaviors. For example, in the middle of a conversation, the person may suddenly turn from his companion, stroll into a garden and begin weeding the grass. In a few minutes he may return, continue the conversation as if nothing unusual has occurred and have no awareness of his unusual acts. Kolb (1968) reports the following typical case history.

CASE 18–7

Marie, T., Age 20, Unmarried

When 10-years old, Marie was brought to the clinic by her mother after she had suffered a number of episodes of loss of consciousness. These were described by the mother in the following way.

She awakened with a headache, seemed listless, and then was noticed by her mother to develop a twitching movement of the left side of her mouth and eyes. Her arms assumed an "odd," stiff position and became unresponsive. This condition persisted 5 minutes, to be followed by another similar episode 10 minutes later in which she urinated and defecated. These attacks were followed by five others preceded by an aura of "fear"—as the child stated, being "scared." The patient had total amnesia for the attacks.

For years Marie reported only daily brief episodes of "scary feelings." It was necessary to increase the dosage of the anticonvulsant medication, and Mebaral was prescribed as well. At age 14 she was admitted to the hospital with an acute delirious state due to barbiturate overdosage. Following this hospital admission, her mother noticed a character change in that she became resentful and hostile, expressed the attitude that she was disliked, and seemed depressed. Then "slow spike waves" were observed over the left temporal region during periods of sleep.

At this time Marie commenced to have episodes of loss of consciousness, occurring without warning and with subsequent amnesia, in which she suddenly rushed away from her place of work, walking rapidly and aimlessly through the streets, impulsively removing her stockings and placing them in her purse or suddenly staring blankly, smacking her lips, giggling foolishly, and then mumbling incoherently.

It has been reported that psychomotor patients, on occasion, engage in violent or other antisocial acts during their seizures. Such events are extremely rare, and it is not at all unlikely that these seemingly senseless aggressive episodes are more a function of a concurrent psychological disorder than of the basic epileptic defect.

DEVELOPMENTAL BACKGROUND

Epilepsy is a symptom, not a disease, and there are almost as many determinants of this symptom as there are factors which can disturb brain functioning. Among them are birth traumas, infectious diseases, toxins, vascular accidents, neoplasms and tissue degeneration. Hereditary susceptibilities, congenital defects and errors of metabolism and endocrine function are other origins of the seizure symptom. It is general practice to diagnose convulsions which are symptomatic of known etiological agents in the syndrome category associated with that agent, e.g., "defects associated with brain trauma." The so-called idiopathic type, usually of an unknown source, represents the kind of epileptic cases normally · included in the syndrome discussed in this section.

It is not uncommon for seemingly innocuous stimuli to provoke a convulsive episode. Thus, external stimuli may serve to trigger some unusual biophysical sensitivity. For example, certain musical notes or the flickering of lights often activates vulnerable regions and sets off a focal discharge which may then spread into a full-fledged seizure.

Along similar lines, it appears that unusual psychic stress increases the frequency of convulsions among chronic epileptics. It is plausible to speculate in these cases that any situation that taxes the individual's monitoring and control functions will lower the threshold for a seizure. During these periods also, excessive and undischarged tension may cumulate. With lowered controls and a mounting tension, the epileptic's vulnerable region may "give way," resulting in an explosive and convulsive discharge.

There appears to be a more than chance frequency of *mild* personality disturbances among epileptics, especially in the psychomotor type. However, there is no distinctive "epileptic personality" (Tizard, 1962). Although these patients exhibit somewhat more than their share of emotional difficulties and social maladjustments, these traits are likely to be a socially learned correlate of their defect rather than something intrinsic to it. Many epileptics are overprotected by concerned parents. Many experience social stigmatism and humiliation in both their educational and vocational pursuits. It should not be surprising, then, that many develop feelings of inadequacy, self-contempt and interpersonal suspiciousness and hostility.

Many investigators have noted that personality disturbances are especially prominent among patients with temporal lobe epilepsy. It is believed by some clinicians that these persons seem deficient in regulatory control and evidence notable hyperactive, egocentric and aggressive behaviors (Gibbs, 1958; Bingley, 1958). In another study (Small et al., 1962), however, no differences in personality impairment were found between epileptics with temporal lobe lesions and those with lesions localized in other regions.

TREATMENT OF BRAIN DEFECTS

Therapy in most brain defects is principally a matter of medical and surgical responsibility. This is especially true in diseases attributable to infections, toxins, trauma, neoplasms and convulsions.

Disturbances treated principally by medical and surgical procedures are approached in different ways depending on the stage of the impairment. "Active" states, comprising acute disturbances or chronic impairments undergoing a temporary flareup, are handled differently than "static" states, which consist primarily of stabilized chronic conditions.

In *active states*, the two central goals of treatment are the removal of the aggravating agent (e.g., the infectious or toxic invader), and the elimination or diminution of the symptomatology (e.g., delirium, coma or convulsions). As an illustration of the first goal, physicians prescribe a regimen of penicillin for neurosyphilis since this drug effectively destroys the invading spirochete. Similarly, in brain trauma or neoplasm, surgical procedures are employed to remove blood clots, siphon excess fluids and reconstruct circulatory pathways necessary to supply blood to brain tissue. The second or symptomatic goal of treatment is illustrated by the use of medications to curb delirium or to reduce the frequency of convulsions in epilepsy. A quiet and subdued atmosphere may be arranged during periods of confusion and agitation in cases of cerebral degeneration.

In *static* states, in which the disease process has been halted or reversed, the primary focus of treatment is symptomatic relief such as the reduction of pain or the calming of anxiety.

In both active and static states, there may be need to remove the patient to an institutional setting. This should be avoided, when possible, since physically impaired patients tend to recover more rapidly in their home surroundings. However, if the family cannot control a severely disturbed patient, or if they aggravate the problem, the patient is best committed to the care of hospital personnel. In these settings, active cases are treated through direct medical techniques and are usually released after a short stay. Static cases often remain hospitalized in order to undergo programs of long-term milieu therapy.

Degenerative defects of advanced age with few exceptions represent mixtures of both brain impairments and psychosocial deterioration. Until recently, it was believed that the process of decompensation in the elderly was irreversible and that little could or should be done other than to make them comfortable, keep them out of trouble and help them bide their remaining time.

Today, it is recognized that the rapid decline and troublesome behaviors of many elderly patients have little relation to their organic condition. Rather, these problems more often reflect feelings of isolation and hopelessness, a loss of self-worth and usefulness and their realization that no one "really cares" and at best is reluctantly "putting up with them."

The growing awareness that psychosocial factors are more crucial to the continued health and longevity of these patients has led to new therapeutic attitudes, centered largely on social rehabilitation (Blau, 1970; Kahana and Kahana, 1970; Lipscomb, 1971). "Senior citizen" clubs, adult education programs, special homes and hospital wards designed to provide the aging person with helpful counseling, social companionship, worthwhile activities and a sense of purpose and self-worth have begun to "take the edge off" the psychic pain of old age. Feeling accepted and useful and engaging in stimulating and worthwhile activities day after day enable the elderly person to regain his self-respect and to feel that he is of value to others.

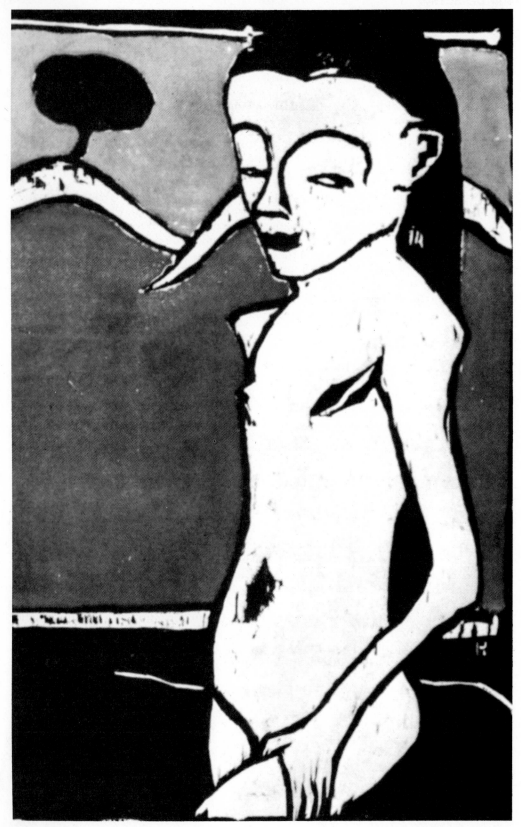

Erich Heckel—*Nude*

19

ABNORMALITIES OF CHILDHOOD AND ADOLESCENCE

INTRODUCTION

Abnormalities of a psychological nature among children have been noted for centuries, but it is only since the turn of this century that clinical practitioners and theorists have explored these difficulties in a systematic manner. Not until Freud's focus on the critical role of childhood experiences in later abnormality, and the emergence of routine psychological testing in American public schools, did professional interest in the emotional problems of children begin to take firm hold. Concern increased substantially in the ensuing years as knowledge about "normal" processes of development advanced and as educators and public health workers recognized the importance of early identification as a major step in the prevention of later serious illness.

Despite these advances, the art and science of abnormal child psychology remains appreciably less well developed than that in the adult field. For example, none of the several classification systems for organizing and labeling child disorders has achieved even a modest degree of acceptance among clinicians (Eisenberg, 1972). The detailed and thoughtful schema prepared by the Committee on Child Psychiatry of the Group for the Advancement of Psychiatry (1966), as well as the well-formulated classification system presented in the DSM-II, has had minimal impact upon practitioners; even child-oriented agencies pay almost no heed to the categories these classifications contain, preferring, when they use diagnostic labels, to employ their own "home-grown" systems. And, much more so than those who work with adults, child practitioners avoid formal diagnoses, tending instead simply to note or describe in summary fashion the essential symptoms of the children they observe. This flexibility and wide divergence in classification procedure presents serious problems for researchers, but until a simple, relevant, and well-validated nosology is published there is little justification for insisting that clinicians adhere to any rigid set of categories.

There is an appreciable overlap in symptomatology among children and adults. For the most part, the syndromes described in previous chapters

415

are to be found among children as well. There are, however, certain abnormalities which occur primarily in youth. It is these to which our attention will turn in this chapter. They will be subsumed under three
broad categories: *learned behavior reactions, severe personality patterns,* and
brain defects. Only as we examine the sub-varieties of these major groupings will we discover such intriguing, and tragic, disturbances as infantile
autism, mental retardation and minimal brain dysfunction.

LEARNED BEHAVIOR REACTIONS

The syndrome labeled *learned behavior reactions* was formulated and discussed in detail in Chapter 10. As noted there, the "reactions" classification consists of a variety of abnormal behaviors associated through learning with specific external events. There are no obscure "causes" or
unconscious processes which underlie them. That is, they are to be understood as relatively straightforward learned responses to realistic circumstances that occurred in the patient's social life history. In this
regard they differ from both abnormal personality patterns and symptom disorders in which complex internal processes play a major role in
shaping the clinical picture. Learned behavior reaction syndromes occur
with significantly greater frequency in childhood than do problems
labeled as personality patterns and symptom disorders. In the first few
years of life, most children have not had ample time to crystallize their
patterns of behavior into an ingrained and stable personality style. With
a few notable exceptions, it is not until certain experiences have recurred
repeatedly and the child has developed a complex "inner world" that his
way of behaving becomes increasingly fixed into a series of enduring and
pervasive traits. What we see then, more often among children than
adults, are learned behavior reactions to specific and circumscribed stimulus situations.

Three groups of syndromes will be distinguished as comprising the
learned behavior reactions of childhood. As will be evident, they parallel
in many respects the reactions described in Chapter 10: *transient situational responses, unextinguished developmental habi s,* and *delinquency behaviors.*

TRANSIENT SITUATIONAL RESPONSES

Transient situational responses are learned reactions to relatively brief
and objectively stressful conditions. In the DSM-II, these disturbances
are characterized as "more or less transient disorders of any severity
(including those of psychotic proportions) that occur in individuals
without any apparent underlying mental disorders." It will be useful to
divide our presentation of the reactions into the same subcategories
formulated in the DSM-II: infancy, childhood and adolescence.

LEARNED RESPONSES OF INFANCY

The symptomatology of learned infantile responses is rather limited.
The infant not only fails to register distinctions among the various difficulties to which he is exposed, but he lacks the means for conveying the
nature of his discomfort with subtlety and precision. We infer the infant's experience of distressful learning through a few gross forms of behavioral and emotional expression.

It is difficult to assert with confidence that infantile reactions result primarily from learning experiences since constitutional dispositions can contribute a major share to their expression. We know that troublesome behaviors are shown in youngsters who have been exposed to genuinely "ideal" rather than adverse environments. This fact should caution us against looking for, and then "uncovering," psychological causes for their presence. In many cases, however, we may rightly ascribe the difficulty, at least in part, to special conditioning or adverse environmental circumstances. These usually stem from the character and style of mother-child interactions or from a lack of caretaker-child contact. Let us briefly review some of the experiences conducive to three typical learned infantile responses that signify a measure of abnormality.

Lack of Responsiveness. Infants deprived of warm body contact, soothing voices, comfort and playful interaction often are flat and apathetic. They frequently seem to be mentally retarded, lack interest in their environment, move about listlessly or are immobile and somnolent. Barring an unusual degree of prior emotional deprivation, these infants can often be rehabilitated with ease. A period of compensatory petting and playful stimulation may ignite the child's social interest.

Fearful Tension. Hypertense, rigid and withdrawn infants may have experienced rather harsh parental treatment, "conditioning" them to anticipate pain and discomfort in association with their environment. In early infancy, these youngsters are most likely to express their discomfort openly, through tears and crying. In time, however, they may acquire an instrumental protective reaction, a "freezing-up," a highstrung avoidance of all sources of potential threat. Quiet, gentle and sincere affection over a brief period may often overcome the infant's anxious withdrawal.

Cranky Irritability. Most common among the infantile reactions is overt irritability and crankiness, especially at night and during feeding. These youngsters are extremely difficult to manage, schedule or placate. They are touchy, fretful, obstinate, moody and exasperating. Whatever the constitutional or social learning cause, once the child proves "difficult," a vicious circle may unfold. Thus, parents may attempt time and again to calm their infant's discontent, but fail repeatedly and finally throw up their hands in disgust and exasperation. Many of these cranky reactions are conditioned and perpetuated by parental vacillation between anxious pampering and angry resentment. Calm and consistent behavioral management efforts often prevent these responses from growing into more permanent abnormal patterns.

Most infantile reactions are not extremely severe. Their importance lies in the fact that they may set the stage for the development of more enduring and serious forms of abnormality. The child's conception of his world, shaped early in life, may often lead to the perpetuation and intensification of his initial problems.

LEARNED CHILDHOOD RESPONSES

As the child advances in maturity and experience, his capacity to perceive and react to the world becomes increasingly differentiated and refined. No longer are we limited to the rather gross behaviors and emotions seen in the infant. The growing child can now discriminate stimuli and discomforts with increasing skill, and can express his feelings and thoughts with a more varied set of reactions than he did in infancy.

"Childhood responses" may best be viewed as classically conditioned learnings or exploratory instrumental efforts to avoid or otherwise deal with environmental experiences. Conceived in this way, they may be seen as *rudimentary forms* of several of the abnormal personality patterns described in earlier chapters. For convenience and consistency, we may organize these learned reactive behaviors into five broad classes:

1. *Withdrawal reactions* (exploratory active-detached strategy), as seen in a fearful mistrustfulness of others, a generalized hesitancy and shyness, a marked introversion and a preference for social isolation.

2. *Overdependency reactions* (exploratory passive-dependent strategy), as shown by an immature clinging to parents and symptoms such as thumb-sucking and school phobias.

3. *Tension reactions* (exploratory passive-ambivalent strategy) noted by a variety of symptoms such as nightmares, nailbiting, eating difficulties, unusual and excessive somatic complaints and phobias.

4. *Oppositional reactions* (exploratory active-ambivalent strategy) characterized by behaviors such as quarrelsomeness, stubbornness, petulance, disobedience and tantrums.

5. *Hostile reactions* (exploratory active-independent strategy), as exhibited in rebellious defiance, school truancy, malicious vandalism, physical cruelty and sadism.

As noted earlier, each of these conditioned responses and exploratory instrumental strategies may generalize, initiate vicious circles of reciprocal reinforcement and stabilize eventually into a more habitual and pervasive personality pattern.

Let us next look at the typical sources which give rise to learned childhood behavior reactions.

First and foremost are conditionings and tensions created within the *family setting.* A sudden awareness of or increment in parental discord may undermine what security the child previously experienced. Struggles over toilet training or other forms of imposed discipline may condition withdrawal, hostile or inadequacy behaviors. Dramatic changes in behavior may follow the birth of a sibling; here, youngsters may be confronted with marked decrements in parental interest and affection, leading to the learning of jealousy, resentment and insecurity.

Difficulties in *school adjustment* are notable sources for learning pathological reactions. Fear of leaving the security of the home, sharing attention and competing with others, submitting to forced discipline and experiencing the humiliation of academic failure may all serve as stimuli for the social learning of behavior pathology.

New tensions are often prompted by difficulties in *peer relationships.* A lack of acceptance by neighborhood age-mates, becoming the butt of jokes and teasings, feeling alone and isolated at school, frequent residential changes and inadequacy in athletic competition may add to sources of stress already present, and result in the acquisition of abnormal learned behaviors.

It is difficult to predict the form of the learned behavioral reaction in children from the source and character of the stimuli to which he was exposed. There are children who withdraw when ostracized by their peers; some, however, will react with hostility, and others may become tense and agitated. Prior learning experiences and instrumental skills serve to shape the form into which the reaction will be cast. Although certain correlations exist between the nature of the stimulus condition and the reaction that is evoked, e.g., depression and clinging behaviors following the death of a parent, the relationship tends to be far from simple and straightforward.

LEARNED ADOLESCENT RESPONSES

Many of the difficulties observed in adolescence are continuations of learned behaviors acquired in childhood. Beyond these, however, are new stimulus events and crises that are especially pronounced in this period of life. We shall concentrate in this section on these unique problems and reactions.

The primary and most troublesome tasks confronting the adolescent are his emancipation from parental control and his need to find a separate identity and an independent course in life. Adolescence is a period of transition and turbulence (Hauser, 1972). The youngster must relinquish childhood standards and behaviors and replace them with something more suitable to his future role as an adult. Innumerable complications arise in this process, and few adolescents pass through this period without at least some degree of discomfort and awkwardness. Surging sexual impulses, heterosexual competition, concerns regarding choice and competence for a vocation and increased self-responsibility, all weigh heavily on the adolescent and make his outlook fraught with anxious anticipation and tension.

We shall focus on two types of learned behavior reaction which are common among the young today and which signify the presence of more than the usual amount of adolescent turbulence. In one way or another, each of these reactions is a response to the problem of parental liberation and growing independence.

Inadequacy Reactions. These are characterized by low self-esteem, an awkward self-consciousness, a hesitant manner in social situations and a tendency to view oneself as incompetent, unattractive, clumsy or stupid. These youngsters feel that they cannot "make the grade," become a part of the peer ingroup or be sought after and valued in the competitive give and take which characterizes adolescent relationships. They dread facing the social responsibilities and expectations that society has established for their age group and are fearful that they will falter in finding a mate, getting a job and so on. In short, they lack the confidence that they can function and be accepted on their own (Gallemore and Wilson, 1972).

These youngsters do not question or reject the established values and goals of the larger society. They very much wish to achieve them and to be considered "regular guys" or attractive girls. However, they experience repeated failures in their quest and slip into increasingly more isolated behaviors, preoccupying themselves with watching TV, daydreams of glory and other forms of fantasy escape. In these, they see themselves as the "football hero" or as the girl with all the boys flocking about her. The more desirous they are of these conventional goals, the more envious they become of those who appear to possess them and the more often they view themselves as inadequate, unattractive and forlorn.

Diffusion Reactions. These are characterized by vague feelings of apathy and boredom, an inability to see any meaning or purpose to life other than momentary gratifications and an aimless and drifting existence without commitment or direction. In contrast to the inadequacy reaction, these youngsters feel estranged from society's traditions and believe them to be false, but are unable or unwilling to find an alternative to replace them. They appear to be suffering from what Erikson (1950) speaks of as an "identity crisis," a sense of uncertainty as to who they are and where they are going.

As the adolescent liberates himself from the traditional roles and customs of his parents' society, he finds himself at loose ends and adrift, questioning whether any system of values can endure or be valid (Shore and Massino, 1969). The "diffused" adolescent's response is not one of hostility and anger, but of passive withdrawal and aimlessness (Myers and Grant, 1972). His dismay over the world of his parents is often mixed with feelings of compassion and concern for their plight. He views them as "fools," trapped in the rut of meaningless work and caught in a web of pretense and unrewarding material success.

As he ponders the grim realities of a society plagued with corrupt politicians and engaged in immoral wars, striving to maintain what he sees as adult hypocrisy and sham, as he senses the futility of long-range plans in a world that soon may be devastated in nuclear war, he convinces himself that nothing really matters, that nothing is worth laboring for or aspiring to. Unable to find a purpose in life, a goal for the future, his behavior becomes aimless, geared only to the pleasures of the moment, with little heed paid to their consequences. Lacking guidelines and goals, he has no reason to act and becomes paralyzed, unable to plan or to commit himself to anything.

Adolescent diffusion often remains latent until the age of 17 or 18, when the youngster goes off to college and is free of parental control and surveillance. Here he often learns "scientific" facts and the skills of critical thinking which enable him to question naive childhood beliefs. He becomes conditioned to think that the world of his parents is phony, stupid, self-defeating and meaningless. Moreover, among his peers, he finds many who share his dismay over the failures and deceptions of the society.

Unable to discipline himself and buckle down to the demands of academic life, lacking a coherent set of values by which he can channel his energies and resistant to the "absurdity" of conventional education, he fails to fulfill even the simplest assignments, and his grades sink precipitously (Hendlin, 1972). This event only "verifies" for him the stupidity and narrow conventions of the adult world. With his former self-image of "intelligence" shattered by poor academic performance, he seeks to reaffirm his status through promiscuous sexual activity, usually with minimal gratification, or by the use of marijuana or LSD, which serves as an emblem of his "copping out" of society. Both of these "prove" his independence of his mortified parents. The following brief case history typifies this reaction.

CASE 19–1

Ted R., Age 18, College Sophomore

Ted entered one of the Ivy League colleges at the age of 16, the valedictorian of his high school class and a two-letter man in swimming and track. For the first time in his life, he found that he was not the center of attention among his peers; furthermore, his first semester final grades ranged between the B and D levels, greatly below those to which he was accustomed. More importantly, he was exposed to "really bright" upper classmen who had "turned against the system," were regularly cutting class, marching in peace and protest demonstrations and "smoking pot." Ted also began to question the values and traditions of his middle-class background. By the midpoint of his sophomore year, he had become a "regular with grass," paid little attention to formal schoolwork, began to read avant-garde poets and philosophers, spent his days idly daydreaming and "sat around nights, just bulling about anything, especially the absurdity of life."

Figure 19–1 Humorous portrayal of adolescent diffusion. (Drawing by Tobey; © 1970 The New Yorker Magazine, Inc.)

"Study hard for what? So I can ride the bar car home every night belting down doubles?"

These youngsters often band together, providing each other with philosophical rationalizations for their shared attitudes and behaviors (Reisman, 1969). Quite often, they assume the garb and s yle of the well-publicized "alienated generation." In this manner they gain not only a measure of notoriety and status, but achieve a measure of support and begin to find a new sys em of values to replace their diffusion and sense of isolation.

UNEXTINGUISHED DEVELOPMENTAL HABITS

Any number and variety of so-called abnormal habits can be acquired by the simple process of direct and indirect learning. These behaviors and attitudes need *not* signify that complex unconscious mechanisms are working to resolve a "disordering" of personality equilibrium. Even compulsions and delusions, which often signify the operation of "underlying" processes, frequently represent the end product of simple conditioning or vicarious learning through observation. *Almost any kind of response can be learned and, if viewed as maladaptive by current societal standards, would be included in this abnormal behavior inventory.*

By what criteria should we narrow the list?

For practical purposes, if for no other, our choice should be based on frequency of occurrence, that is, abnormal habits that are fairly common to large segments of the population. As we begin to uncover these common habits, we find that most of them were "normal" at one stage of development. That is, they were exhibited and considered appropriate by all persons early in their growth process, but were modified or extinguished by most individuals as they matured. Thus, these abnormal developmental habits are acquired in the normal course of human growth and are not a consequence of experiences that are peculiar to just a few. What distinguishes them is *not* that they were learned in the first place, but that they failed to be extinguished or unlearned during maturation.

Three spheres of development display these persistent or unextinguished habits: learning to eat, eliminate and speak. In the following paragraphs we will describe several abnormal habits that were viewed initially as normal developmental behaviors.

EATING HABITS

Several troublesome behaviors may be acquired in conjunction with infantile and childhood feeding experiences. Thumbsucking, excessive eating, perverted appetites (pica), poor appetites (anorexia), gagging and vomiting are among the better known. These may stem from any number of biogenic or psychogenic causes, the latter including sucking indulgence or frustration in infancy, forced feeding, tension at meal times, maternal oversolicitude, nagging or excessive discipline. Many of these habits fade as the child matures, but occasionally they persist into adolescence and adulthood. Behavior modification techniques have been notably successful in treating these habits (Bernal, 1972).

ELIMINATION HABITS

Infancy is a unique period of life in many respects. Not only does the child freely mouth, suck and eject objects with minimal concern for physical consequences or the opinions of others, but he is equally indiscriminate and careless in his practice of wetting and soiling at will. Only gradually are these universal eliminative habits of early life controlled and modulated. Through trial and error and parental conditioning and reinforcement, the child slowly learns to surrender his primitive ways and substitute more sanctioned modes of functioning.

There are two forms of abnormality reflecting the persistence of elimination habits, *enuresis* and *encopresis.* The latter refers to the rare habit of involuntary defecation or "soiling." This response often alternates with prolonged periods of retention and constipation (Edelman, 1971). The former impairment occurs much more frequently and consists of habitual and involuntary urination, most notably at night. Because of its greater prevalence and because more is known about it, we shall limit our discussion to enuresis.

Enuresis.   Failure in bladder control is not considered to be an enuretic habit until the child is at least three years of age. Commonly, bed-wetting occurs from two to five nights a week. Over 80 per cent of reported cases have persisted since infancy. However, most parents do not seek professional assistance until the child is between eight and ten years of age. About 15 per cent of all children referred to mental health clinics have a history of enuresis. The problem occurs with appreciably greater frequency among males (about 2 or 3 to 1). Recent studies indicate the presence of enuretic problems in one fourth of all psychiatric discharges during military recruit training. The reported incidence of the problem declines rapidly with age. With the exception of cases with demonstrated organic pathology it appears to be extremely rare after the age of 30.

The problem of establishing the social learning basis of developmental habits is not that of discovering the conditions which led the child to acquire his habit in the first place. Rather, the task is to determine the factors which *deterred the normal unlearning* of established and previously acceptable habits. Viewed in this way, enuresis reflects the operation of forces which resist or forestall change. With the exception of organically impaired cases, in which the sheer mechanics of sphincter control may be difficult, it appears that most enuretics retain their infantile habit in response to certain conditioning experiences and in order to achieve some instrumental goal. Several such experiences and goals are notable.

Toilet training is often a struggle of power and wit in which coercion and threat are employed both by parents and child to achieve opposing ends. Forced to submit to his parent's wishes as a result of intimidation and harassment, the child may harbor deep resentments and desires for revenge. As a consequence, he may accede to daytime eliminative controls and inhibit any overt expression of his anger. However, at night, when he can deny responsibility for his acts, he may freely "get back" at his parents, discharge his anger and quietly enjoy their futility to exert control over him.

Another instrumental goal associated with enuresis is the desire to prevent an anticipated or real loss of parental interest. The birth of a sibling during toilet training is a common precipitant for a regression to bed-wetting and soiling. Having learned through prior experience that wetting achieves prompt parental attention, these children often revert to their former careless ways of elimination. Whether prompted by a desire to recapture the "bliss" of infancy or merely to extract signs of continued parental solicitude, these youngsters find that enuresis is an effective coping instrument.

Enuretic problems have been approached most successfully through the use of various behavioral techniques. Among the first and best known are the conditioning methods employed by Mowrer and Mowrer (1938). Newer procedures, following an operant or instrumental methodology, have also been especially effective (Kimmel and Kimmel, 1970; Samaan, 1972).

SPEECH HABITS

Learning to speak fluently and to give up the repetitive and stumbling word by word pattern of baby talk, is an achievement of no mean proportions. Some of the innumerable difficulties which may arise during this learning venture are traceable to anatomical defects, but the majority are attributable to parental mismanagement and disruptive emotional experiences. These impairments include delayed speech, phonation and rhythmic difficulties and problems of articulation. The most interesting, from a psychological point of view, is stuttering. We shall confine our discussion of developmental speech reactions to this notoriously troublesome habit because it so often fosters secondary psychological problems that are more serious than the habit itself.

Stuttering.   This impairment, also referred to as stammering, is characterized by spasmodic interruptions in the normal flow of speech. The range of difficulty extends from mild and infrequent blocking of certain syllables at the one extreme to the prolonged failure to produce any words with brief intermittent bursts of unintelligible sounds at the other.

Stuttering symptoms do not appear in all situations calling for speech. For example, it often is not exhibited when the stutterer is relaxed or in the presence of people whom he feels to be his inferiors, or when he is singing, reading or whispering. It is most pronounced in situations that arouse fear or self-consciousness.

About 1 to 2 per cent of the population in the United States exhibit some form of stuttering. It is appreciably more frequent in males than in females, the ratio being roughly of the order of 5 to 1. The fact that the onset in over 90 per cent of the cases takes place before the age of six, with the majority of these between two and four, supports the view that the impairment is in most cases a delay of normal developmental speech fluency.

A review of research and theory on stuttering suggests that most, although by no means all, cases occur among youngsters who evidence a slight maturational lag in speech capacities. This delayed speech development often gives rise to parental anxieties, mismanagement or derogatory comments. Parental attitudes such as these in turn create tensions, self-consciousness and fears of speaking on the part of the child, which in circular fashion feed back to reinforce, intensify and perpetuate the original speech difficulty (Wertheim, 1972).

The primacy of social learning factors in stuttering has been proposed by numerous theorists (e.g., Johnson et al., 1959; Sheehan, 1953, 1970; Barbara, 1962; Glassner, 1970). They point to the fact that normal people often experience speech blocking when they are frightened or self-conscious, e.g., asking an instructor to excuse an absence for an examination or being suddenly faced with the need to introduce a group of people to each other. In these situations, the tension felt in conjunction with the task often decreases the adequacy of its performance. According to social learning theorists, these tension situations parallel those which confront the stutterer as he struggles to coordinate the many complex functions involved in the production of smooth speech. This highly generalized vulnerability was acquired, according to Johnson, when the child first began to speak at about the age of two. At this early stage, the entire complex of speaking was associated with extreme tension and self-consciousness. Complications such as parental derogation were conditioned to the speech learning process, thereby fostering the continuation of the young child's normally hesitant speech. Parents who were unusually critical of the child's speech repetitiveness prevented him from breaking out of the pattern of hesitant speech. By conditioning their anxieties and exasperation to his speech, they caused the child to become unusually self-conscious and tense. As a consequence, he may have been conditioned to a generalized fear of speaking. Once established, these speech behaviors and attitudes may have set into motion a vicious circle. Fear and self-consciousness themselves increased the probability of stammering and speech hesitation. Since fear induced stuttering, the child's expectation that he would stutter was reinforced, and with each reinforcement his dread of speaking was intensified, starting the vicious circle all over again.

Once the process of stuttering becomes an ingrained habit, it tends to spread and create a variety of new psychological complications. We find, for example, that many stutterers are socially shy and hesitant and express the feeling that they are inferior to others. Beneath this overtly awkward and self-conscious style, stutterers frequently harbor deep feelings of resentment and anger toward others for the ridicule and embarrassment to which they have so often been subjected. Thus, stuttering is not only self-perpetuating, but leads frequently to secondary problems such as feelings of inadequacy, frustration and repressed anger. From what little evidence we have, it appears that the few personality traits that correlate with stuttering behavior are more a consequence than a cause of the impairment.

DELINQUENCY BEHAVIORS

The clinical background and features of delinquency behaviors have been reformulated many times over the past century. Throughout its checkered history, this syndrome has served to designate a rather varied collection of behaviors which have little in common other than the fact that they are viewed as contrary or repugnant to the social mores of the time. Essentially, it is found among adolescents seeking liberation from parental control and doing so by a vigorous attack upon established societal norms. This is done by intentional antisocial acts directed at representatives and symbols of the larger society. Thus, theirs is not a passive and semi-intellectual indifference to traditional customs, but a direct and brutal aggression against the powers that be. Their energies are channeled into opposition, toward the end of upsetting or destroying the customs and rules of a society they resent.

There are innumerable ways in which the strain of growing up can be reacted to rebelliously. A common and relatively mild form is running away from home, of simply picking up one day and leaving for a — hopefully — better world (Jenkins, 1971). These youngsters typically are responding to the pressures and expectations of their parents and use the running away mechanism not only as an escape, but as a means of causing their parents public embarrassment and forcing them to lessen their demands. Quite often this behavior arises as a consequence of intolerable parental conflicts that spill over into childhood scapegoating (Anderson, 1968).

More severe rebellious behaviors take the form of persistent truancy, vandalism and sexual misbehavior. These acts signify the youngsters' contempt for what they see as the oppressive rules and customs of a harsh or hypocritical society. Cases like these of so-called juvenile delinquency are found in all families and neighborhoods and are not limited to the slums and the underprivileged (Stojanovich, 1969). Every court is acquainted with privileged adolescents who have reacted to parental indifference, deception and hostility by stealing, drinking and a wide variety of other antisocial acts. Every school, both in "good" and "poor" communities, has its share of truant youngsters.

We will attempt to note a few of the major features which clinicians view to be most characteristic of this syndrome, frequently labeled "juvenile delinquency" and "sociopathy" in the literature. The items to be listed are not mutually exclusive. Neither do they provide a definitive picture of the reaction, since the impairment will take different forms depending on the particular social learning experiences and personality pattern of the patient.

It may be useful to begin with a brief paragraph summarizing the impressions of McCord and McCord (1964) who have undertaken a series of systematic studies of these patients, referred to in their text as "psychopaths":

His conduct often brings him into conflict with society. The psychopath is driven by primitive desires and an exaggerated craving for excitement. In his self-centered search for pleasure, he ignores restrictions of his culture. The psychopath is highly impulsive. He is a man for whom the moment is a segment of time detached from all others. His actions are unplanned and guided by his whims. The psychopath is aggressive. He has learned few socialized ways of coping with frustration. The psychopath feels little, if any, guilt. He can commit the most appalling acts, yet view them without remorse. The psychopath has a warped capacity for love. His emotional relationships, when they exist, are meager, fleeting, and designed to satisfy his own desires. These last two traits, guiltlessness and lovelessness, conspicuously mark the psychopath as different from other men.

If we combine the conclusions of the McCords with those of other researchers in the field, we are led to the following five characteristics as features of delinquent reactions.

Disdain for Social Conventions.   Among the most notable characteristics of these patients is their tendency to flout conventional authority and rules. They act as if the established customs and guidelines for self-discipline and cooperative group behavior do not apply to them. In some, this disdain is evidenced in displays of petty disobedience or in the adoption of unconventional beliefs, values, dress and demeanor. Many, however, express their rebelliousness in minor illegal acts, coming into frequent difficulty with educational and law enforcement authorities. Others are aggressive and hostile, exhibiting a malicious physical brutality as they disrupt the peace, appearing to gain pleasure in intimidating others.

Deceptive Social Facade.   Despite their disrespect for the rights of others, many present a social mask, not only of civility but of sincerity and maturity. Untroubled by feelings of guilt, they often develop a pathological talent for lying. Unconstrained by matters of honesty and truth, they learn with great facility to weave an impressive picture of their superior competencies. Many are disarmingly ingratiating in their initial social encounters. Their alertness to the weaknesses of others may enable them to play their games of deception for long periods. Not uncommonly, however, the pleasure they gain from their ruse begins to flag. Before long their true insincerity may be revealed by their failure to keep "working at" their deceptions or as a consequence of their need to let others know how cleverly deceptive they have been.

Inability or Unwillingness to "Adjust" Following Punishment.   Many delinquents are of better than average intelligence, exhibiting both clarity and logic in their cognitive capacities. Yet they display a marked deficiency in self-insight, and rarely exhibit the foresight which one might expect. In short, despite the fact that they voice a clear grasp of why they should alter their social misconduct, they fail repeatedly to make any modifications.

Punitive measures often reinforce those attitudes which initially gave rise to their misbehavior. To make their socially repugnant behavior more palatable to others, these persons concoct plausible explanations and excuses, usually those of "poor upbringing" and past "misfortunes." Thus, the unfortunate circumstances of their lives operated to lead them astray.

By utilizing their intelligence to fake innocent victimization, they "free" themselves of blame and have a "justification" for continuing their irresponsible behaviors. Should these flippant rationalizations fail to convince others, as when they are caught in obvious lies, they may effect an air of total innocence, claiming without a trace of shame that they have been unfairly accused. Once more, their skills are used to get them out of difficulty and to free them from guilt.

Impulsive Hedonism.   Many delinquents evidence a low tolerance for frustration. They are easily bored and restless and are unable to persist at the day after day responsibilities of marriage or a job. Quite characteristic is a proneness to taking chances and seeking thrills, acting as if they were immune from danger. Others jump from one exciting and momentarily gratifying escapade to another, with little or no care for potentially detrimental consequences.

Insensitivity or Disregard for the Feelings of Others.   Beyond their callous disdain for the social rights of others, delinquents seem deficient in the capacity to share tender feelings and to experience genuine affection for others. Even more, they appear to gain pleasure in the thought and process of hurting others. Thus, not only are they devoid of guilt and remorse, but they seem to obtain a degree of cruel satisfaction thereby. To achieve these ends, they often go out of their way to exploit others, enjoying the distress and pain they leave in their wake.

The following case illustrates a number of these clinical features.

CASE 19–2

James F., Age 22

James was arraigned at a county court for passing a series of forged checks. He was also thought to be the rapist of a 16 year old waitress. His previous record showed a list of minor burglaries, abandonment of a common-law wife and child and acquittal on two charges of passing bad checks.

Jim is a muscular, wiry and "sharply dressed" man who looked even younger than his 22 years. Although he presented an affable veneer when first seen, being both charming and verbally adroit, it was clear that he felt considerable inner tension and suspiciousness of those who sought to question him.

Disentangling Jim's real life from his fabrications was not done easily since he had no compunctions about lying when it suited his purposes. Factually, Jim was the only son of a family of three children. Both girls were younger. His father, a drunkard, abandoned the family when Jim was ten. There is evidence that he mercilessly assaulted both his wife and children. Jim's mother was killed in an auto accident shortly thereafter, and the family unit was separated and placed in different foster homes. When he was 15, Jim was accused of fathering the child of a twelve year old foster sister and was sent to a reformatory school.

In the three years at the reformatory, Jim was one of the "gang leaders," evidencing considerable skill in exploiting the weaknesses of his fellow delinquents. At 18, when he was freed to make his way alone, Jim was a skillful automobile mechanic. He never picked up this trade, however, having lasted but two weeks at a position arranged for him prior to leaving the reformatory.

Jim's whereabouts were not factually recorded for two years. At the age of 20 he was picked up for a minor theft. Despite a number of obscurities, it appeared that he lived with a 15 year old for several months, impregnating and then leaving her. From that point onward he drifted from job to job, lasting little more than a month at each. During that time, he maintained fleeting relationships with prostitutes and drunkards, managing each time to fleece them of their meager belongings, and then moving onward. When brought in for his most recent forgery offense, Jim admitted, confidentially, that he finally "had it good." He was living with and had complete control over three teen-age prostitutes whom he "protected" and solicited for.

SEVERE PERSONALITY PATTERNS

The great majority of seriously disturbed mental patients progress through a gradual and slow course of decompensation, but there is a small number that exhibit markedly severe personality difficulties in early childhood. Four types are well-known in the literature: *infantile autism, childhood schizophrenia, childhood symbiosis* and *childhood hyperkinesis.*

INFANTILE AUTISM

Victims of the first of these impairments, known in the literature as *infantile autism* (Kanner, 1954; Rimland, 1964), are often identifiable within the first 18 months of life, and are usually seen by their parents as "different" or perhaps "feebleminded." Although appearing normal in all other respects, these infants seem totally unresponsive to human stimulation. They demand a consistency and sameness in their physical environment and display an intense preoccupation with inanimate objects. Their impenetrable aloneness and their apparent inner emotional vacuum is summarized well in Bettelheim's phrase "the empty fortress" (1967). Social isolation and a lack of personal identity are two notable features. If they speak at all, they rarely make reference to themselves; the term "I" frequently is lacking in their vocabulary. Presumably, this signifies their marked alienation, not only from others but from themselves.

Another characteristic of these children is their gross insensitivity to pain, further evidence of their lack of affect. Also notable is their tendency to engage in self-mutilating behaviors such as head-knocking and hand-bi ing. This may reflect a desperate need for external stimulation to overcome what may be an extreme deficit in sensory receptivity (Wing, 1966).

Both biological and social learning factors have been proposed as sources for the development of infantile autism (Rutter, 1968, 1970; Ward, 1970).

Rimland (1964), on the basis of a well-reasoned speculation, contends that the impairment derives from a constitutional defect. Bettelheim (1967), based on a series of exhaustively studied case histories, suggests that the aberration stems from a failure on the part of parents to provide stimulation and encouragement in the first two years of life, followed by the child's "disappointment" and subsequent protective withdrawal. Kanner (1954) and Eisenberg and Kanner (1956) waver between the belief that autism has its origin in an inborn affective deficit and the thesis that the child has been exposed to a mother characterized by her "emotional refrigeration." Bender (1959) and Goldstein (1959) view the illness as a psychological defensive maneuver to counter the effects of a basic neurological impairment. In short, a whole range of causal hypotheses has been proposed, despite essential agreement as to the major clinical features.

We shall propose another causal thesis in the hope that it will clarify rather than confuse matters. Specifically, we shall hypothesize that autistic pathology may arise *either* from biological or psychological conditions which may operate independently of each other, and which may be sufficient in themselves to produce the clinical picture. Dividing cases along this line of thinking, we shall propose the concepts of *primary autism* (biological) and *secondary autism* (social learning). Let us note, however, that regardless of which source is most significant in a particular case, the essential element in infantile autism is the failure of the child to learn adequate human attachment behaviors.

In *primary autism*, we suggest that the infant lacks the biological equipment necessary either for experiencing or integrating stimulation during the sensory-attachment s age of neuropsychological development. Such inferences would be appropriate in cases where there is evidence of ample parental warmth and affection. Since we believe that these youngsters possessed deficits in affect reception or integration, they were unable to learn the complex attachments required for establishing human relationships. The child's fate seems to have been sealed since he was constitutionally incapable of sensing or coordinating stimulation for the development of attachment behaviors at its crucial period in infancy. In effect, he now remains locked within himself. The following case depicts this au istic development.

This primary autistic youngster had been raised by highly intelligent parents and older siblings who showed great concern, attention and gentility in their care. Jimmy never evidenced any response to human overtures; he seemed totally oblivious of his parents and sibs, and would content himself in his first three or four years simply by rocking back and forth on his buttocks. At the age of four, he appeared to become fascinated by a number of drawings that an older sister had prepared for him in the hope of "breaking through his blankness." Since then, Jimmy has spent the better part of each day drawing highly complicated and colorful arrangements of squares, circles and triangles, done with extraordinary skill and artistry for his age. Despite this clear-cut sign of abstract intelligence, he still does not talk, smile, cry or otherwise respond to living or mobile objects.

CASE 19-3
Jimmy L., Age 6

Where marked affect deficits are evident in primary autistics, we would expect few or no attachment behaviors to develop. Attachments may be made in less severe cases, but only to simple inanimate objects. Here we assume that sensory functions are intact, but the biological capacity for complex stimulus and emotional integrations is impaired.

The diagnosis of *secondary au ism* assumes that the newborn's biophysical capacities have followed a normal sequence of maturation and are essentially intact. Defects arise as a result of unusual social reinforcement and stimulation deficits. Support for this diagnosis requires clear evidence of parental "coldness" or neglect. In these cases there is a marked retardation in the learning of human attachment behaviors (Freedman, 1971). These youngsters appear similar to those whose difficulties are rooted in biogenic defects. However, since they began life with normal affectivity capacities, these infants frequent.y learn to become attached to inanimate objects that provide them with the sensory stimulation and positive reinforcement they need.

CHILDHOOD SCHIZOPHRENIA

The second of the severe forms of personality abnormality in children is known as *childhood schizophrenia* and is characterized by extraordinary fearfulness, vulnerability to threat, erratic behavior and cognitive confusions (Rutter, 1972).

In a small number of cases, these youngsters display in the first year or two of life an excruciating sensitivity to stimulation, often whimpering or crying at the slightest of disturbances; parents report their children to have had severe and/or persistent colic and to have been difficult to schedule. The greater majority of childhood schizophrenics, however, manifest clinical degrees of abnormality between the ages of 3 and 10, although early trends have often been evident previously. Early tendencies to hyperirritability and fearfulness frequently prove exasperating to parents and often set off a chain of reactions which only intensifies the child's initial disposition.

The following case illustrates several features of an early childhood schizophrenic.

Mary was brought for diagnostic evaluation following withdrawal from nursery school. She was terrified at the prospect of leaving her bedroom each morning and whimpered, but did not otherwise resist being taken to school; she sat in the classroom shivering and in tears.

Her developmental history was presented by an extremely anxious mother whose speech and logic reflected her own apprehensiveness and cognitive disorgan-

CASE 19-4
Mary F., Age 5

ization. The father, an easily irritated and hostile man, came to the diagnostic conference only at the mother's insistence.

Though her parents were with her, Mary sat alone in the waiting room with her head turned downward, fidgeting and whimpering. She evidenced no parental attachment or clinging behaviors. Despite the fact that her mother was not indifferent to her, she made no effort to assuage Mary's apprehension and discomfort, leaving her completely alone in her anguish.

Mary could not be tested by conventional procedures. She failed to respond verbally to questions. According to her mother, Mary had not said a word for several months; she simply whimpered, cried or grunted. After much gentle prodding, it was possible to elicit several nonverbal responses to certain test items; it was evident, even from this limited performance, that Mary was not intellectually deficient.

Mary was the older of two girls by 18 months; rather interestingly, the younger sister displays a similar but less severe clinical picture. According to her mother, Mary was an extremely tense and colicky infant; she stiffened when she was held, cried "constantly" and even whimpered when asleep. The mother was always tired, and the father stayed away from home as much as he could in order to "turn off that screaming brat"; exhaustion and irritability permeated the household.

Mary never smiled; when she learned to recognize people, her face seemed to register "terror" no matter with whom she came into contact. Her days were spent fondling the few toys she had at her disposal; her eyes were always turned from others and focused downward, even when she walked.

Mealtime is a "disaster" period. The mother attempts to feed Mary as well as her younger sister; both children "pick at their food," frequently "spit out" what is given them and often vomit shortly after eating.

Mary began to speak a few words at about the age of two; her earliest verbal communications included such phrases as "I scared" and "no touch me." Fully developed sentences never were achieved, although her single word vocabulary was rather extensive; when she entered nursery school at age four, speech stopped completely.

A sense of inner terror and social aloneness are the most distinctive features of this youngster. She appears neither to seek nor to gain emotional support from her parents. From her viewpoint, the world seems to be a setting of strange and threatening sounds and movements.

The developmental basis of childhood schizophrenia may be viewed as a quantitatively more extreme but qualitatively comparable set of conditions than those which give rise to adult schizophrenia. The parallel lies with the active-detached schizophrenic pattern. As with autism, we shall propose that *either* biogenic *or* psychogenic factors may take precedence.

In *primary childhood schizophrenia* we observe youngsters who evidence extraordinary tension and fearfulness in the first years of life. In these cases, we infer the presence of unusual sensory sensitivities. Such inferences, however, rest on the assumption of a benevolent caretaking environment during infancy. For these youngsters, attachment learning may be disrupted by the intensity or flooding of sensory impressions. Thus, these children must set up a protective barrier against what they sense to be an overwhelming influx of external stimuli. Though complicated by parental mismanagement, the case of Mary F. illustrates the clinical features and development of primary schizophrenic children.

With less severe biological dispositions, the fearful child need not necessarily develop serious pathology. If he possesses parents who are alert to his sensitivities and handle him with care, the child's impairment may be surmounted, enabling him to acquire appropriate human attachments. Despite his disposition, the child's development may take a healthy turn under proper environmental conditions.

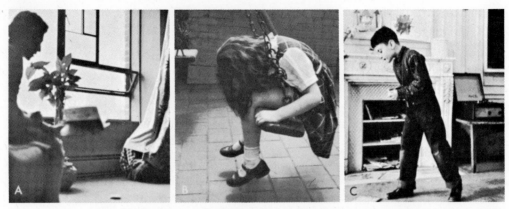

Figure 19-2 Severely withdrawn and psychologically mute children. (Parts A and C, courtesy of the St. Louis Post Dispatch; part B, courtesy of Ken Heyman.)

The developmental background of *secondary childhood schizophrenia* is essentially social learning. These youngsters appear to possess normal sensibilities at birth, but are exposed in their first years to extremely intense and painful sensory stimulation. To handle this stimulation, the child protectively diminishes his contact with the world by reducing his sensory awareness. Diagnosis of these cases should be based on evidence of particularly harsh or chaotic early environments. Many of these children acquire some form of attachment behavior. They discover a small sphere within their environment, usually neutral inanimate objects, which they draw upon repetitively as a "safe" source of positive reinforcement and sensory stimulation.

In general, these youngsters display their pathology at a somewhat later age than primary schizophrenics. However, in cases of extremely harsh early handling, the pathological pattern may already be manifest at the age of one or two. Other less severely treated youngsters may not develop the full-blown disturbance until seven to ten years of age.

Since the advent of behavior modification techniques, both the autistic and the childhood schizophrenic syndromes are no longer as grave a diagnosis as formerly thought (Browning and Stover, 1970; Fischer and Glanville, 1970; Halpern, 1970; Lovaas, 1967).

CHILDHOOD SYMBIOSIS

This impairment parallels the adult passive-dependent (inadequate) personality pattern. In these cases, there is an unusual attachment to the caretaking figure. The child brooks no separation and may be overwhelmed by panic should its mother leave. This contrasts markedly to autistic and schizophrenic children, who seem indifferent to the presence of others or relieved when left alone. Parents describe these youngsters as extremely immature and fearful, as "cry-babies" who cling like appendages, unwilling or unable to stand and do things on their own. (These clinical symptoms do not draw notice usually until the second stage of neuropsychological development, when the child is between the ages of two and four.) Mild cases of overattachment at this age do not signify pathology, since most of these youngsters "grow out of" the habit.

A pattern similar to the moderate form of symbiosis has been described in the 1966 report of the Group for the Advancement of Psychiatry

(GAP) under the label "overly dependent personalities." These cases may be difficult to differentiate from the moderately severe form of "childhood schizophrenia" in that both groups of youngsters exhibit extreme apprehension. The schizophrenic child, however, is pervasively anxious and tense whereas the symbiotic child is so only when parted from the person(s) to whom he is attached.

Excessive dependency may have had its basis in a constitutional vulnerability to threat and anxiety. Parents who responded to their youngsters' pathetic fearfulness by coddling and overprotecting them set the stage for learning intense attachments. Furthermore, the constitutional fearfulness of these children may have disposed them to avoid venturing into unknown situations. At some critical period, such as when the child was enrolled in nursery school or when a new sibling was born, the severe nature of this dependency attachment was brought into sharp relief.

No constitutional disposition need have existed, however, for the development of excessive attachment and dependency. Parental anxieties and an overprotective style of behavior management may have fostered the same condition. Here, too, the problem often first becomes manifest when the youngster panics at periods of separation or forced independence.

CHILDHOOD HYPERKINESIS

Most notable in these children are their behavioral unpredictability and erratic moods. There are prolonged periods of crankiness and testiness. At these times they display a hypermobility and restlessness, a sense of inner conflict and a tendency to severe temper tantrums for no apparent reason. At other times, these same youngsters become extremely attached and cling to their parents in a manner not dissimilar to that typical of the symbiotic child. This attachment seems to be born of fear, however, rather than of affection. Not uncommon are phobias and hypochondriacal traits. The impairment may be displayed as early as the end of the second year, but it is more frequently exhibited between the third and seventh years of life.

Many children display similar immature and negativistic behaviors in mild form. These less severe forms may evolve into a pattern of adolescent or adult active-ambivalence, that is, they may develop into negativistic personalities. The label of hyperkinetic should be reserved, however, for children whose impairment occurs in prepuberty and is so severe as to seriously upset the run of normal home life.

As noted, hyperkinetic children evidence high distractibility, marked negativism, low tolerance for frustration, erratic mood swings and a mixture of demanding and clinging behaviors. Constitutional irregularities in infancy and an uneven sequence of maturation are not uncommon. Central to the impairment, however, is a social learning history of markedly contradictory parental feelings and attitudes. These may have resulted from conflicting behavior styles between parents, as is often the case in schismatic families, or from the ambivalences and cyclical moods of a single parent. Rapid shifting between pampering and hostility, parental signals conducive to the "double-bind," and simultaneous exposure to easily manipulated and hostile caretakers, may have inflicted serious emotional damage and served as models for these children.

The following case depicts a number of the more typical elements found in their background and clinical picture.

Timothy was the older by three years of two boys in a family marked by a deep parental schism. Both parents were strikingly immature, having married at age eighteen when they were freshmen in college. Home life was noted by bitter fights. The father had little to do with his children, and even less, if possible, with his wife. The mother's relationship to her son was distinguished by its high pitch of emotionality and its extreme variability. She would fondle and cling to him one moment and scream and beat him in the next. The character of the relationship can be grasped by the following report of a typical round of feeding. The mother would attempt to coax Timmy to eat, promising candy bribes as a reward; Timmy would balk, and his mother would become exasperated; Timmy then cried; his mother began to "scream and beat him"; contrite almost immediately, his mother would then give Timmy a taste of the candy; Timmy would start to eat his regular food but "choke up" after taking a spoonful or two; his mother would become furious and storm out of the room, leaving Timmy alone. This sequence occurred almost every day; similar sequences characterized many of the other interactions between Timmy and his mother.

Timmy acted in a similar fashion when sent to nursery school; he refused to participate with other children, balked at every request, cried or had temper tantrums when frustrated, sat in a corner fidgeting or restlessly paced back and forth. His speech was grossly immature, monosyllabic and practically incoherent; drawings were very primitive, more like a two year old's; he seemed awkward in his movements and clumsy in balance and coordination. He alternately clung to his teacher, or behaved in an obstinate and demanding manner; if he got his way, he would behave well for a brief period. At no time, however, would he tolerate sharing the attentions of the teacher with other children, constantly trying to draw her interest to him when she was involved elsewhere. After several weeks of this behavior, Timmy had maneuvered the teacher to act in an almost identical manner as his mother. Feeling exasperated, guilty and exhausted, the teacher requested that Timmy be withdrawn from nursery school.

At home, Timmy was "impossible to live with." He became an appendage to his mother and rarely would let her out of his sight, especially if he thought she was attentive to his younger brother. Even when mother gave her full attention to him, he seemed discontent and unsatisfied. Father's presence would send Timmy running to his mother, obviously fearing his father's ire and his demands that Timmy be disciplined firmly and "not be allowed to get away with all the things that mother allows."

Quite obviously, Timmy's inner ambivalence and impulsive and vacillating behaviors reflected the marked schism in the family, and the unfortunate model his mother provided through her own emotional inconsistencies and erratic discipline.

BRAIN DEFECTS

With few exceptions, children are subject to the same brain diseases as are found in adults; hence, most of the syndromes presented in Chapter 18 have their counterparts among children. Two syndromes, not discussed in the previous chapter, have been selected for inclusion here: *mental retardation* and *minimal brain dysfunction*. Although both occur in adults, they begin primarily in early life and have so profound an influence on development that they are best considered as abnormalities of childhood.

MENTAL RETARDATION

Children who lack the intellectual capacity to profit from the teachings of their elders, and adults who seem incapable of grasping many of the basic elements of self and social responsibility have been known to man since earliest history. They are found today in every culture and stratum of society. These unfortunate people are grouped together under the single syndrome label of "mental retardation," despite an immense variety in their clinical characteristics, degrees of deficit and developmental backgrounds. Other labels have been used over the years to describe this syndrome: *feeble-mindedness, mental deficiency, amentia, hypophrenia* and most recently, *mental subnormality*. Each of these descriptive terms has something to commend it, but the label of "mental retardation" appears to be the most common and preferred term in current use.

Although the average incidence of mental retardation is estimated at 3 per cent, there is considerable variation in reported figures depending on the type of population sampled (e.g., urban versus rural, white versus black or northern versus southern), the criteria used for diagnosis (e.g., intelligence-test scores, academic achievement, family history or social competence) and the arbitrary "cut-off" point selected to demarcate "normal" intelligence from retardation. Of the four million children born annually in the United States, approximately 120,000 ultimately will be classed among the mentally retarded, although only 15,000 of these will require complete custodial care. About 200,000 retardates (roughly 4 per cent of the total retarded population) are currently institutionalized (Braginsky and Braginsky, 1971). The others manage to maintain themselves within the community or are cared for by their families.

Much confusion still reigns as to the best means for differentiating and grouping the many varieties of retardation. Classification, although not an end in itself, is an important step in clinical analysis, and is often a useful guide in research, prevention and treatment. Several classification schemas have been proposed with regard to mental retardation (Carter, 1970). We shall outline the three most prominent: gross physical characteristics, measured intellectual ability and social competence.

CLASSIFICATION ACCORDING TO GROSS PHYSICAL CHARACTERISTICS

Man's earliest attempts to group the varieties of mental retardation reflected his crude observation of gross or manifest physical characteristics. It was well known that many who exhibited severe deficits in intellectual and social competence also displayed facial and bodily peculiarities. These varied from minor irregularities in skeletal structure to extremely repulsive distortions of both trunk and head. The following classification schema rests on these identifiable features. As will be evident, similarities in gross physical appearance do not necessarily signify similarities in degree of retardation.

Garden Variety "Familial" Types.   In contrast to the popular image, more than 75 per cent of all mentally retarded individuals display neither overt nor covert physical signs that correlate with their mental defect. In all physical regards they appear "like everyone else," some are attractive, most are "average looking" and some are unattractive. Not only do they fail to exhibit gross structural peculiarities, but their brains give evidence neither of tissue pathology nor abnormal electroencephalographic rhythms. Yet, these "seemingly normal" people, when faced with simple intellectual tasks, become confused and inept and perform in a manner more appropriate to a chronological age much less than theirs.

These "garden variety" retardates do not suffer the more severe types of intellectual deficiency. Many are capable of a basic elementary school education, and often find employment later in life in some routine or unskilled job. For the most part, these milder retardates come from families in which retardation is rather common.

The correspondence among family members of this type of defect suggests two causal hypotheses. *First*, it is quite probable that many of these cases have inherited "normal" genes which endow them with abilities that fall at the lower end of the bell-shaped continuum of intelligence. They do not appear to be suffering the consequences of a disease, but seem merely to *deviate* statistically in accord with natural individual differences from the average. The *second* hypothesis is that children who are reared in families in which parents are intellectually dull and educationally disadvantaged are likely to be deprived of the social learning and stimulation necessary for the full development of their higher mental abilities. These youngsters and their siblings are likely to continue the family pattern *not* for genetic but for environmental reasons.

Since development is a product of a complex and interwoven set of biological and social learning influences, the probabilities are that both the "genetic deviance" and "experiential impoverishment" theses are correct. Parents of limited intellectual endowment pass on their deficit genetic equipment to their children. Also, by virtue of their deficient educational and cultural achievements, they fail to stimulate the limited potentials their children possess (Hurley, 1969). Together, these disadvantages set off a vicious circle that perpetuates the impairment from generation to generation (MacMillan and Keogh, 1971).

Microcephaly.   In this and the following "physical types," the degree of mental subnormality is usually much greater than that found among garden variety retardates. The impairment is likely to stem from a "disease process" and tends to be characterized by gross body deformities.

Microcephaly is a physical descriptive term referring to diseases with different causes and of varying severity. It represents one of the more common types of institutionalized mentally retarded, comprising about 20 per cent of this population. The major distinguishing feature is a cone-shaped cranium with a circumference of less than 17 inches in adulthood, as contrasted to a normal figure of 22 inches. Although variations are present, most possess a sharply receding forehead that is set in contrast to otherwise normally developed facial features. Microcephalics vary intellectually from moderate to profound retardation. All levels are notably deficient in abstract and language functions. In some cases, the impairment may be traced to a genetic disease. Most, however, appear to arise as a consequence of intrauterine complications.

Microcephalics have been characterized as hyperactive but good-natured. However, since the impairment stems from different causes and structural pathologies, and patients have been exposed to different social learning conditions, it is unlikely that this description of temperament could be uniformly applicable. For example, Brandon et al. (1959) found microcephalics to be as varied in their personalities as other retarded types.

Mongolism (Down's Syndrome).   This physical classification represents a distinct disease entity since its characteristic features are found in conjunction with only one causal agent. It was given its popular name in 1866 by a British physician, Langdon Down, who was struck by the similarity in facial characteristics between these children and members of the "mongolian race." The resemblance, however, is limited strictly to the eyes which are almond-shaped and slope upward toward their outer corners.

Estimates suggest that there are over 100,000 cases in the United States alone. Proportionately equal numbers are found throughout the world. The disease appears about once in every 500 births, and comprises between 10 and 15 per cent of institutionalized retardates. The great majority of cases are cared for at home since these patients are usually not severely impaired, are relatively easy to manage and often are of an unobtrusive or pleasant temperament.

In addition to the almond-shaped eyes, the features of these retardates are conspicuous by a flattening of the back of the head, a heavily fissured tongue that tends to protrude through thin, similarly fissured lips and a broad nose that is depressed at the bridge. Hair is sparse and thin, and the skin is delicate and mild-white or rosy. Hands and feet are stubby and clumsy. Overall stature is small. They stand stoop-shouldered, are physically incoordinated and their gait is heavy and shuffling.

Mongoloids tend to be only moderately impaired intellectually. Most can be toilet-trained and are capable of learning simple chores and routine skills. Speech, however, is rather limited, consisting at best of a few meaningful words. Their daily activities often consist of idle TV watching or hours of repetitive play such as putting a set of blocks in a preferred arrangement, destroying the design and commencing again.

The cause of this syndrome is well on the way to being established. About 95 per cent of mongoloids have been found to possess 47 chromosomes instead of the normal complement of 46. Most are trisomic (three rather than two units) for chromosome 21; the remaining 5 per cent exhibit other defects, all of which are related to chromosomal disjunctions. There is minimal evidence of familial correspondence in mongolism. The disease appears to be a mutational aberration occurring during fertilization or shortly thereafter. The well-known fact that mothers beyond the age of 35 are appreciably more likely to give birth to mongoloid children indicates that some anomaly associated with maternal age is centrally involved in many of these cases (Richards, 1973).

Cretinism. As with mongolism, cretinism may properly be classed as a disease entity traceable to a distinct causal background. In contrast with mongolism, however, preventive and remedial measures are known, with strikingly effective results even in severe cases.

These patients appear normal at birth. Toward the end of the first year, there are signs of a general sluggishness and apathy. Normal growth is stunted with the exception of a disproportionately large head. Hands and feet are noticeably stumpy and malformed. The abdomen is swollen and bulgy, legs are bowed and the spine is curved. The face of adult cretins is characterized by a flat nose, widely spaced eyes, large and flabby ears, thick lips and a broad, frequently protruding, tongue. Skin texture is dry and rough and often cold to the touch.

Cretinism is a result of a lack of iodine. This may stem either from an inadequacy in diet or from a congenital defect in the thyroid gland. Cretinism was once common in regions of the world where natural iodine was lacking in the soil, and therefore lacking in the food it supplied. Since this dietary deficiency usually affected several members in a family, it was thought at first to be a hereditary disease. At the turn of the cen-

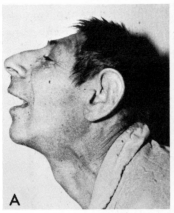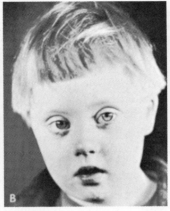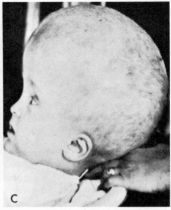

Figure 19-3 Some physical types of mental retardation. A, Microcephaly (Columbus State School, Columbus, Ohio.) B, Mongolism (Courtesy of Dr. Clemens Benda). C, Hydrocephaly (From Wechsler, I. S.: Clinical Neurology. 9th edition. Philadelphia, W. B. Saunders Co., 1963).

tury, however, it was discovered that thyroid extracts countered the deleterious effects seen in cretinism. Shortly thereafter, the crucial role of iodine deficiency was noted. Families that had been subject to the disease as a result of dietary or thyroid deficits were soon rid of its consequences.

Hydrocephalus. Like microcephaly and in distinction to mongolism and cretinism, this physical type is a descriptive category including similar clinical pictures that stem from different origins. Hydrocephalic cases are noted by a globular enlargement of the cranium resulting from the accumulation of abnormal amounts of cerebrospinal fluid. Both face and body remain normal in size, giving the upper part of the head a grotesque appearance. The expansion of the cranial region reduces the pressure exerted upon the brain by the excess fluid. However, any degree of pressure capable of enlarging the cranium must be sufficient also to produce cerebral maldevelopment and tissue atrophy. The extent to which the brain is impaired correlates with age of onset and severity and duration of pressure (Laurence, 1969). Operative procedures in early life, designed to remove accumulated fluid and reestablish normal circulation, may be effective in curtailing the progression of the disease.

CLASSIFICATION ACCORDING TO MEASURED INTELLECTUAL ABILITY

Without elaborating the issue at this point, let us note that most instruments used for intelligence appraisal are weighted heavily in verbal-symbolic materials and tend to tap experiences that are common to the dominant middle-class culture. As such, they may be biased devices for assessing the mental abilities of persons who are not part of the mainstream of American life.

Nevertheless the value of establishing *degrees* of intellectual ability cannot be overlooked as part of the clinical study of retardation. Whatever the cause, whatever physical form in which the patient appears, it is the degree of intellectual impairment which is the relevant factor in determining the diagnosis of retardation. The most frequent basis for making this appraisal is an I.Q. score on an intelligence test. Unfortunately, this single criterion continues to be used despite repeated warnings of its

Approximate IQ Score Range	DSM-11, and AAMD Manual Terminology, 1961 Revision*	Common Former Labels	Educational Terminology
68–85	Borderline	Borderline	Slow learner (sometimes included in educable range)
52–67	Mild	Moron	Educable retarded
36–51	Moderate	Imbecile	Trainable retarded
20–35	Severe	Imbecile	Trainable retarded
Below 20	Profound	Idiot	Total-care group

TABLE 19–1

CORRESPONDENCE OF VARIOUS MENTAL RETARDATION TERMINOLOGIES TO MEASURED INTELLIGENCE

* Heber (1961)

limited and biased utility. Table 19–1 presents a summary of the retardation classification terms that have been applied to I.Q. score categories.

The simplicity of determining retardation by a test procedure and the quantitative precision of degree of retardation implied by a numerical score have given intelligence tests their totally undeserved status as *the* diagnostic criterion. Despite their unquestioned utility as one element in the evaluation of retardation, these instruments are notoriously biased. They overlook cultural differences, are limited in the range of the relevant functions they tap and rest on questionable assumptions regarding the structure and development of intellectual capacities. Moreover, identical I.Q. test scores fail to differentiate individuals in ways relevant to the diagnosis of retardation. Used as the sole criterion, as is so often the case, they neglect causal considerations, intellectual potential and, most important, may mislead us with regard to the individual's capacity for coping with "real life" problems. In short, test scores, when used alone, create a false sense of relevancy and accuracy and often compound the problems of the marginally retarded rather than assist in their solution.

CLASSIFICATION ACCORDING TO SOCIAL COMPETENCE

Discontent with the narrow focus and limited applicability of I.Q. scores has led to a renewed interest in classifying retardates by reference to social competence criteria rather than quantitative test scores. Competence criteria are not new. The eminent English authority A. F. Tredgold wrote in the sixth edition of his text on mental deficiency (1937) that these impairments should be classified in accord with the degree to which the individual can adapt himself to a normal environment, independent of supervision and support. Similarly, a prominent American specialist in the field, Edgar Doll, wrote (1941) that retardation is best viewed in terms of social maturity. More recently, the U. S. Department of Health, Education and Welfare has outlined a chart that coordinates quantitative I.Q. scores with degrees of functional efficiency and social competence (Table 19–2).

To date, however, no completely satisfactory system has been devised to classify retardates in terms of social competence, although the British classification makes an attempt in this direction (Lyons and Heaton-Ward, 1953). Nevertheless, it is mandatory that criteria be included to represent the individual's capacity to learn the fundamentals of self-sufficiency and to acquire attitudes requisite to shared social living.

TABLE 19-2 FUNCTIONAL COMPETENCE OF THE MENTALLY RETARDED*

This table integrates chronological age, degree of retardation, and level of intellectual, vocational, and social functioning.

Degree of Mental Retardation	Preschool Age 0–5 Maturation and Development	School Age 6–20 Training and Education	Adult 21 and Over Social and Vocational Adequacy
Profound (IQ Below 20)	Gross retardation; minimal capacity for functioning in sensorimotor areas; needs nursing care	Some motor development present; may respond to minimal or limited training in self-help	Some motor and speech development; may achieve very limited self-care; needs nursing care
Severe (IQ 20–35)	Poor motor development; speech minimal; generally unable to profit from training in self-help; little or no communication skills	Can talk or learn to communicate; can be trained in elemental health habits; profits from systematic habit training	May contribute partially to self-maintenance under complete supervision; can develop self-protection skills to a minimal useful level in controlled environment
Moderate (IQ 36–51)	Can talk or learn to communicate; poor social awareness; fair motor development; profits from training in self-help; can be managed with moderate supervision	Can profit from training in social and occupational skills; unlikely to progress beyond 2nd grade level in academic subjects; may learn to travel alone in familiar places	May achieve self-maintenance in unskilled or semiskilled work under sheltered conditions; needs supervision and guidance when under mild social or economic stress
Mild (IQ 52–67)	Can develop social and communication skills, minimal retardation in sensorimotor areas; often not distinguished from normal until later age	Can learn academic skills up to approximately 6th grade level by late teens; can be guided toward social conformity	Can usually achieve social and vocational skills adequate to minimum self-support but may need guidance and assistance when under unusual social or economic stress

* Adapted from *Mental Retardation Activities of the U. S. Department of Health, Education, and Welfare*, p. 2. United States Government Printing Office, Washington, 1963

Our discussion of the varied criteria by which retardation may be classified points up again the futility of approaching abnormality from a single frame of reference. As with other abnormalities, retardation is a complex phenomenon that may be viewed and understood from several vantage points. Only when taken together can these seemingly divergent approaches help our complete understanding of the problem, and a better means for its remediation.

TREATMENT APPROACHES

Most *mental retardates* are not benefited by medical or surgical treatment. Among the exceptions are special diets or medications for cases of cretinism and operative procedures for hydrocephalus. There are no known techniques which can "raise" the capacities of retardates. Most treatment methods, then, are designed to help these persons establish a meaningful and gratifying social and vocational life by training and encouraging the maximum development of their given capacities. To achieve this goal, there must be a total commitment involving medical, educational, psychological, community, family and socioeconomic programs (Menolascino, 1968; Sarason and Doris, 1969; Zigler and Harter, 1969). More than the average person, who stands a fair chance of "making a go" of life, the retardate with his intellectual handicaps and social deficits needs the support, guidance and respect of those who raise, educate and socialize with him.

Discouraged, guilt-ridden or overprotective parents will only aggravate the retardate's natural limitations. Thus, parental counseling is often required to assure a maximum of warmth, acceptance and encouragement.

School administrators and teachers must be helped to recognize the many achievements that are possible among these children *if* they are provided with programs geared to their pace and style of development. Given proper training, milder retardates can acquire vocational skills which enable them to become productive, self-respecting and well-adjusted members of the community. More severely retarded youngsters can be educated to perform simple household chores, thereby preparing them to be useful participants within their families.

Community "sheltered workshops" have been developed in many cities, enabling mildly retarded youngsters to find social companionship and to make the transition to an independent adult life. These centers can provide moderately retarded adults with a useful and self-fulfilling vocation, while they still reside at home. Other community, state and federal programs have been established to assess the aptitudes of retardates, train them and then locate employment opportunities in which they may achieve a sense of accomplishment, while they fulfill a useful occupational role.

MINIMAL BRAIN DYSFUNCTIONS

An entirely new cluster of clinical characteristics has been recognized in the last fifteen years, tentatively labeled "minimal brain dysfunctions." While there is much to be learned about this impairment, and much research that still lies before us, there is reason to believe that scientific studies associated with this syndrome will prove to be an important step toward the understanding of many forms of abnormality. Clarification of the subtle elements which comprise this syndrome should provide us with a deeper insight into the complex dimensions of neuropsychological development.

Briefly, these children are characterized by one or more of the following features (Thompson, 1973). They exhibit deficits in integrative and regulatory controls. Thus, for many clinicians, they are best depicted as hyperactive, impulsive, hyperdistractible and behaviorally disorganized. Another significant symptom cluster focuses on specific developmental and learning deficits. Thus, in some quarters, these youngsters are noted by their sensory handicaps, perceptual-motor dysfunctions and speech and reading disabilities.

Youngsters classified in this syndrome display these signs in more subtle forms than are seen in children with gross nervous system defects. Thus, they do not present the severe motor impairments seen in children with cerebral palsy. Also notable is the fact that their learning deficits are often unrelated to general decrements in intelligence. Brain dysfunctions will inevitably disrupt some aspect of intellectual performance, but these need not result in the loss of higher abstraction capacities. Thus, most cases of brain dysfunction evidence specific or circumscribed deficits rather than generalized deficits, as in the case of mentally retarded children.

In the past few years there has been a tremendous rise in the number of children assigned to the brain dysfunction category. In fact, despite the recency of the concept and the difficulty of detection, studies place the incidence of "brain-injured" children at more than 25 per cent of outpatient clinic populations (Paine, 1962; Lezak and Dixon, 1964; Wender, 1971). This striking figure reflects in part a growing awareness of the diagnostic features of this clinical entity and the increased precision of assessment techniques and skills. Moreover, the increased incidence of these cases may be a rather perverse and unintentional product of medical advances; thus, physicians are able to save infants today who would have succumbed to infections and trauma just a few years ago, but many of these youngsters now suffer the residuals of their early ailments. Not to be overlooked as a factor in the increased "identification" of these cases is its appeal to parents who would prefer to think that their children have succumbed to a personally nonimplicating "brain-injury" disease rather than a personally implicating and emotionally threatening "mental illness." Similarly, physicians, inclined by training to look for physical causes or confused by complicated psychological explanations, may readily assign the brain dysfunction label to these difficult to diagnose cases.

CLINICAL PICTURE

As a diagnostic entity, "minimal brain dysfunctions" includes children of near average, average or above average general intelligence who exhibit specific or narrowly delimited developmental, learning or behavioral deficiencies. These deficits may be of mild or moderate but not of marked severity, and be traceable primarily to functional limitations of the central nervous system. Several dysfunctions may coexist in the same child. However, they should not be so pervasive as to decrease markedly the overall level of intellectual functioning (Gunderson, 1971; Weiss et al., 1971).

Despite the value of referring to this syndrome under one label, no uniform pattern is to be observed among these cases. The sheer complexity of the brain itself argues against such simplifications as a *single* clinical prototype of brain dysfunction. In short, the classification comprises many syndromes included under one diagnostic label. The features of each subgroup reflect the particular locus, extent, duration and developmental period in which the nervous system was affected. Complicating the possibilities further, the final clinical picture takes shape not only as a function of neural deficits, but the child's social learning history, compensatory coping responses and the psychosocial environment within which he now lives.

The complex network of influences which often interact is illustrated in the following case.

CASE 19–6

Mark Y., Age 9

Mark was the second of three children in a socioeconomically upper middle-class family with strong intellectual and social aspirations. His father is a successful lawyer and his mother is a former school teacher.

His birth was uneventful and Mark appeared to be a "normal" youngster until, at the age of 18 months, his mother become increasingly concerned that he had walked "late and awkwardly" and that his speech was "rather delayed." She began to "teach him" to speak more articulately, but with little success. At the age of three and a half, when he was first sent to nursery school, Mark spoke in a "babyish manner," slurred words, was still physically awkward and seemed "hypertense and slow" according to his teacher. A "psychological test" was given to Mark when he was four and a half and his parents were told that he might be "slightly retarded." This news "frightened" Mark's mother and she immediately set out to "raise his I.Q."

Over the following two year period, Mark's mother "drilled him" on a variety of verbal and numerical "training programs." The tension that pervaded this teaching process hardly helped Mark's sense of competence and comfort with academic materials. Nevertheless, he progressed quite well in certain spheres, notably in arithmetic where he was able to multiply and divide simple numbers by the time he entered kindergarten.

In first grade, his teacher noted Mark's physical clumsiness and inarticulate speech. More importantly, Mark seemed to have great difficulty in discriminating among many of the letters in the alphabet, and had no facility at all for reading words. He was at a total loss when asked to identify visually the numbers he could readily multiply in his head.

The diagnosis of "minimal brain damage" was given following a detailed neurological and psychological evaluation. Currently, Mark remains tense and self-conscious about his academic impairments, dislikes school, has begun to read haltingly, still confuses letters, has difficulty writing with a pencil and is inept in all sports, but can converse quite intelligently and continues to demonstrate excellent "oral" mathematical ability.

Despite the many varieties of brain dysfunction, certain typical features are seen with sufficient regularity to justify using them as diagnostic criteria. Two broad classes of symptoms may be distinguished: general deficits in integrative and regulatory controls, and specific developmental and learning deficits.

Deficits in Integrative and Regulatory Controls.   There is a complex of behavior symptoms in these children that reflects a general inability to modulate and control both internal and external stimuli. What appears to distinguish brain dysfunction children is the lack of focus and direction to their behavior and their inability to inhibit impulses or restrain themselves from reacting to distractions which other youngsters can do with ease. As in their behavior, these children exhibit an inability to sustain attention for prolonged periods. They are diverted by extraneous stimuli, shuttling back and forth in rapid succession from one trivial distraction to another. This, too, reflects their deficient regulative and integrative controls and their inability to put aside the inconsequential and focus on the relevant.

The consequences of regulatory deficits may extend to the sphere of feelings and impulses, as well. The tendency to be impulsive, to be unable to delay gratification and to act out emotions with little modulation is evident in episodes of unprovoked aggressive outbursts. The character of these emotional expressions depends, of course, on the total life experiences to which these children are exposed. Given support and encouragement in ways that maximize feelings of competence and adequacy, these outbursts are likely to be few and far between. However, should their relationships prove frustrating, feelings of self-deprecation will cumulate and be "touched off" by seemingly trivial events. In general, then, the emotions these youngsters feel will be released with relative ease due to their control deficits. The content and frequency of these expressions, however, depend on the particular character of their environmental relationships.

Specific Developmental and Learning Deficits. The second cluster of symptoms refers to relatively specific impairments, notably deficiencies in the acquisition of certain skills and competencies. Many of these youngsters are characterized as "being slow" at school but only in specific subjects rather than in all areas. They frequently are thought to be lazy because they achieve so much more poorly than they "score" on intelligence tests. Others are spoken of as "immature" since they function both physically and socially at a level appreciably below their age and measured intelligence. They seem clumsy and often behave in an "infantile" manner with their peers.

A careful evaluation of their behaviors indicates a marked unevenness in their functioning, that is, they do not display a uniform or generalized retardation. It is this circumscribed nature of their deficit that distinguishes them from the mentally retarded. The specific impairments they exhibit will depend on the locus, size, duration and developmental age in which the brain was affected. The character of the circumscribed deficit varies from child to child and no two children exhibit the same pattern of maturational lags or learning disabilities.

Many children with brain dysfunctions have difficulty in discriminating visual patterns such as letters or words. Mark Y. obviously suffered from this impairment. Difficulties in coordinating perception and response are notable in many cases. Many seem incapable of reproducing what they see and understand. Others react inconsistently to the same visual configuration. Problems in speech and articulation and difficulties in visual-motor coordination required for legible writing are frequently evident.

Irregularities or developmental lags in communication skills are another sphere in which defects might center. Here we see a variety of spoken and written language confusions, discrepancies between oral reading and comprehension of what has been read and defective memory for symbolic concepts, both mathematical and verbal. In short, many of these children exhibit an inability to grasp and utilize language anywhere near the facility expected, given their overall intellectual level.

DEVELOPMENTAL BACKGROUND

Because of the brief period that has elapsed since this syndrome was described, few, if any, systematic studies have been executed with regard to the role of genetic or constitutional factors. Sources foreign to the organism's natural or endowed neurological make-up may cause either mild or severe damage. Toxic, infectious, traumatic and endocrinological disturbances may affect certain selected regions of the brain more severely than others, thus causing a circumscribed dysfunction rather than a general mental retardation. The maturational stage during which the damage occurred may also be a factor. Thus, the character of the dysfunction may be a matter of *when* the toxic or infectious event assaulted the body (Wender, 1971).

Social learning deprivation may also turn out to be selective in its effects (Silver, 1971). Environmental deficits may slow down developmental progressions, not across the entire brain but only in fairly delimited functional regions, e.g., severely limited verbal experiences, stemming from "cultural deprivation," may result in deficits only in cognitive and language functions.

TREATMENT APPROACHES

Remedial approaches for children with *minimal brain dysfunctions* are designed primarily to establish greater controls and to overcome deficits in development and learning.

Various psychopharmacological agents may be employed to dampen the hyperdistractibility and emotionality of these children, but this medical regimen tends to treat only the surface symptom rather than the basic control deficit. Several educational and behavior modification procedures have been employed to achieve this goal of more effective self-regulation. They seek to minimize disruptive environmental stimulation and to structure the child's activities and daily routine. The normal stimuli of home and classroom usually prove to be excessively distracting to these youngsters. They cannot "get their bearings" in these environments and are flooded with more distractions than they can possibly cope with. As a consequence, efforts to learn the rudiments of regulatory controls are constantly disrupted. To enable such children to acquire these functions, they are provided with settings of minimal stimulation. Step by step, as they learn to respond well to simple stimulus situations, the complexity and variety of the environment are increased. To strengthen this progression toward regulatory controls, the child is exposed to an unvarying daily routine in which the time for awakening, eating and so on is highly systematized. Likewise, the behavioral training programs and materials to which they are exposed are highly organized so as to maximize the development of logical routines, focused perception and structured thinking. Important, also, are parental consistency, firm direction and the establishment of clear limitations in behavior. Not only do these measures aid the youngster directly in controlling his erratic ways, but they serve as models which he may incorporate through imitation.

The specific developmental and learning deficits of these children are attacked best through systematic remediation programs focused on perceptual-motor and speech training. In recent years, numerous procedures have been devised to upgrade these and other circumscribed deficiencies (e.g., Cruickshank, 1965; Kephart, 1960; Frostig, 1964; Edwards et al., 1971).

PART 6

FUTURE DIRECTIONS

Emil Nolde – *The Prophet*

20

FRONTIERS OF ABNORMAL PSYCHOLOGY

INTRODUCTION

Abnormal psychology is not a static science. Given the fact that over 90 per cent of all psychologists who ever lived are professionally active today, we can understand why advances in knowledge continue at a rapid pace. Thus, during the period in which you have read this book, facts and issues presented within it have been reevaluated and are, perhaps, already outdated. New theories of abnormal development and new conceptions of diagnosis and therapy are introduced monthly through dozens of professional journals and books, necessitating a constant reexamination of traditional approaches. Most often, these innovations seek to expand the boundaries of more established ideas. Periodically, however, they take a radical turn, seriously challenging the very foundations of "classical" theories or redefining the scope of the field itself.

Today is a time of such upheaval. Agonizing questions have been raised not only about conventional approaches to diagnosis, but as to whether labeling and classification should be done at all. Modern conceptions of therapy, notably behavior modification and encounter-sensitivity group methods, have not only been proposed as theoretical possibilities, but are being employed so vigorously in some quarters as to totally supplant more traditional procedures. Intense arguments are not only put forth in opposition to classical medical-model treatment techniques, but a whole generation of the best of our younger professionals have turned entirely away from this model and are actively pursuing a social systems approach, devoting their energies to changes in the community life, not of the mentally ill, but of the culturally deprived. Several of these "new frontiers" in abnormal psychology have been woven into the fabric of earlier chapters; this final chapter will bring them into sharper focus, leading the student, thereby, to those advanced regions of ongoing work that intrigue today's scientists and clinicians.

FRONTIERS IN DIAGNOSIS AND CLASSIFICATION

As noted in Chapter 1, there has been an increasing dissatisfaction among clinicians and researchers with the traditional classification system. The lack of a theoretically-based, logical and reliable approach for diagnosing mental disturbances has sharply limited advances in both the science of abnormal psychology and the effective treatment of patients. Despite the continued tendency for most clinicians and researchers to employ traditional psychiatric diagnoses in their work, a growing body of valuable studies in classification methods and theory is accumulating. These strides point to new directions in which progress in the field may be made. In the following sections we will briefly describe a number of these promising developments.

NEW DIAGNOSTIC PROCEDURES

Numerous proposals have been made suggesting alternatives to the traditional way in which clinicians diagnose their patients. Three of these deserve special notation.

FUNCTIONAL BEHAVIORAL ANALYSIS

Kanfer and Saslow (1969, 1973) argue strongly against the use of syndrome groupings and all-inclusive classification systems. They particularly object to methods of diagnostic data-gathering that have little or no relationship to the key purpose of diagnosis, that of planning a course of therapy. Thus, in their alternative to traditional "descriptive" clinical diagnosis, their approach, termed *functional behavioral analysis*, is action-oriented, designed to collect and organize information that will relate directly to specific techniques of treatment intervention. Based largely on learning theory principles and the behavioral approach to therapy, it avoids classifying and assigning patients into broad syndrome categories according to features they possess in common. Rather, each patient is approached as a unique case, and a specific diagnostic assessment is made in terms of those features that distinguish and characterize only him. In addition, current environmental conditions that reinforce and sustain the patient's abnormalities are explicitly identified so that they can be targeted and systematically manipulated to produce changes in problematic behaviors. Kanfer and Saslow have developed a preliminary format of procedures to guide clinicians in probing for and organizing these treatment-oriented data. Their work represents a significant step toward the goal of making diagnosis a more useful clinical procedure.

AUTOMATED CLINICAL PROCEDURES

Toward the end of gathering systematic and quantifiable clinical information, such as would be useful in the diagnostic model proposed above by Kanfer and Saslow, Spitzer and his associates (1966, 1970) have developed a number of automated interview and case record procedures.

The data of most clinical interviews are gathered in a relatively unstandardized and free-flowing manner. In contrast, Spitzer's *Psychiatric Status Schedule* uses a fixed sequence of questions and a matching inventory of 492 typical responses of patients. The clinician's task is to mark these precoded responses as true or false on the basis of each of his patient's replies and behaviors during the interview. By focusing the attention of the clinician on a uniform set of typical patient characteristics, the prospects for gathering comprehensive and comparable data are greatly enhanced.

Along similar lines, Spitzer has devised the *Mental Status Examination Record*, an IBM-scored form for describing clinical features that can be processed and tabulated by automated computer procedures (see Figure 20–1). Not only can the rated information marked on the form be summarized simply for effective case record-keeping, but comparisons for individuals over time or among different patient groups can readily be made because they are assessed on the same items and rated in the same categories. The standardized and quantitative features of these automated schedules are an important step, insuring uniform, comprehensive and reasonably objective methods of clinical analysis.

ACTUARIAL DECISION-MAKING

A number of significant clinical decisions can be made simple by computer analysis when standardized instruments and automated procedures are employed. In a series of important books and papers, Meehl (1954, 1957, 1965) has argued for the use of "cookbook" methods of clinical interpretation and prediction. As briefly noted in Chapter 1, the clinical skills of many diagnosticians are sadly deficient. One solution is the use of actuarial techniques. Actuarial procedures are similar to those employed by insurance companies in their attempt to calculate the longevity prospects of different types of people: evidence is accumulated that people with particular characteristics have varying life expectancies, and on the basis of these past data, predictions are made about the probable longevity of people with similar characteristics. In a parallel fashion, actuarial clinical predictions concerning treatment outcomes would be based on accumulated evidence of correlations between scores obtained on such instruments as Spitzer's Mental Status Examination Record or the Minnesota-Hartford Personality Assay (see Figure 20–2), on the one hand, and responses to different forms of therapy, on the other. For example, instead of "intuitively" deciding what course of therapy a patient should receive, the clinician simply looks into an actuarial cookbook. Here he notes the degree of success found with different treatment techniques for patients who have particular score patterns on Spitzer's, or any other standardized, clinical form or test. With these cookbook data in hand, the task of selecting and predicting patient responses to specific treatment programs cannot only be made simple, but can be achieved with at least a moderate degree of confidence. At this time, unfortunately, few actuarial formulas have been devised that fulfill these decision tasks. Prospects for future developments are good, however.

NEW CLASSIFICATION MODELS

As noted in Chapter 1, numerous criticisms have been made of the traditional system of classification, known in its current form as the DSM-II. Despite important advances in research and theory, the major syndromes of the DSM-II are essentially those formulated by Kraepelin over 70 years ago. As will be described below, new frontiers in classification have been developed recently. One major development is empirical, based on systematic factor analytic research. This frontier proposes numerous modifications in the traditional nosology, particularly with regard to the distinctiveness and homogeneity of syndromes. The other

Form MS 9 (7/69)
MSER

MOTOR BEHAVIOR					
	none	slight	mild	mod	marked
Psychomotor retardation	1	2	3	4	5
catatonic stupor		catatonic rigidity			waxy flexibility
	none	slight	mild	mod	marked
Psychomotor excitement	1	2	3	4	5
		catatonic excitement			
		slight	mild	mod	marked
Tremor		2	3	4	5
Tics		2	3	4	5
Posturing		2	3	4	5
Pacing		2	3	4	5
Fidgeting		2	3	4	5
Gait Unsteadiness		2	3	4	5
Rigidity		2	3	4	5
Slowness		2	3	4	5

Abnormality possibly because of
medication   orthopedic problem   neurological disorder

GENERAL ATTITUDE AND BEHAVIOR

Positive characteristics
helpful   responsible   good sense of humor
cheerful   pleasant   likeable

	none	slight	mild	mod	marked
Uncooperative	1	2	3	4	5
Withdrawn	1	2	3	4	5
Inappropriate	1	2	3	4	5
Impaired functioning in goal directed activities	1	2	3	4	5
Suspicious	1	2	3	4	5
Anger (overt)	1	2	3	4	5

sarcastic   critical   argumentative
sullen   assaultive   physically destructive
irritable   threatens violence

	slight	mild	mod	marked
Provokes anger	2	3	4	5

Suicidal behavior   none   at least threats   at least gesture(s)   attempt(s)

	slight	mild	mod	marked
Self mutilation (degree of disfiguring)	2	3	4	5
Antisocial	2	3	4	5
Impulsive	2	3	4	5
Passive	2	3	4	5
Dependent	2	3	4	5
Domineering	2	3	4	5
Guarded	2	3	4	5
Complaining	2	3	4	5
Ritualistic	2	3	4	5

GENERAL ATTITUDE AND BEHAVIOR (continued)

	slight	mild	mod	mark
Obsequious	2	3	4	5
Despondent	2	3	4	5
Apathetic	2	3	4	5
Fearful	2	3	4	5
Dramatic	2	3	4	5
Sexually seductive	2	3	4	5
Homosexual behavior	2	3	4	5
Alcohol abuse	suspected	2	3	4	5
Drug abuse	suspected	2	3	4	5

hallucinogen   barbiturate   stimulant
narcotic   other

MOOD AND AFFECT

	none	slight	mild	mod	mark
Depression	1	2	3	4	5
Anxiety	1	2	3	4	5
	with episodes of panic				
Anger	1	2	3	4	5
Euphoria		2	3	4	5
Anhedonia		2	3	4	5
Loneliness		2	3	4	5

Quality of mood and affect

	none	slight	mild	mod	mark
Flatness	1	2	3	4	5
Inappropriate	1	2	3	4	5
Lability		2	3	4	5
Diurnal mood variation		2	3	4	5
	worse in morning				worse in evening

QUALITY OF SPEECH AND THOUGHT

Voice   shouts   screams
very loud   monotonous   overly dramatic
whining   very soft

	very slow	slow	average	fast	very fast
Rate					
	markedly reduced	reduced	average	increased	markedly increased
Productivity					

	none	slight	mild	mod	mark
Incoherence	1	2	3	4	5
Irrelevance	1	2	3	4	5
Evasiveness	1	2	3	4	5
Blocking		2	3	4	5

Set no. Mark last 3 digits of Set number from page 1.

0	1	2	3	4		5	6	7	8	9
0	1	2	3	4		5	6	7	8	9
0	1	2	3	4		5	6	7	8	9

IBM M61142

Figure 20–1   Spitzer, R. L., and Endicott, J. Int'l J. Psychiat., 1970, 9, 604–621.

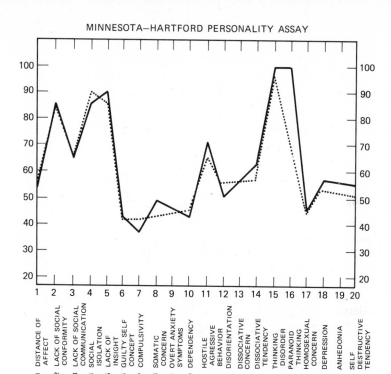

16-5 HAS A WELL FIXED PARANOID SYSTEM WITH DELUSIONS OF REFERENCE AND PERSECUTION. HAS EXPERIENCED HALLUCINATORY EPISODES.

15-5 HIS THOUGHT PROCESSES ARE SERIOUSLY DISTURBED WITH MARKED EVIDENCE OF DEREISTIC THINKING, SEVERE COGNITIVE SLIPPAGE, CONFUSION, AND ASSOCIATIVE DISRUPTION.

04-5 COMPLETELY WITHDRAWN AND ISOLATED FROM OTHERS.

05-5 HAS NO INSIGHT INTO, OR UNDERSTANDING OF THE MOTIVATIONS BEHIND HIS THOUGHTS AND BEHAVIOR.

02-4 HAS CONSIDERABLE DIFFICULTY IN CONFORMING TO SOCIAL EXPECTATIONS, GROOMING, MANNER, AND DRESS FREQUENTLY INAPPROPRIATE OR SOMEWHAT BIZARRE. TENDS TO STAND OUT AS 'DIFFERENT' FROM OTHERS.

19-4 GENERALLY SOMBER, MOROSE, RARELY CAN RESPOND WITH A SMILE, NEVER JESTS OR JOKES, RARELY GETS ANY ENJOYMENT OUT OF LIFE.

09-3 OVERREACTS TO ANXIETY PRODUCING SITUATIONS AND CARRIES A LOW CHRONIC LEVEL OF ANXIETY.

11-3 HAS A QUICK TEMPER. REACTS TO MINOR SLIGHTS WITH HOSTILE, AGGRESSIVE BEHAVIOR THAT AT TIMES IS DIFFICULT TO CONTROL. SOMETIMES PETULANT OR QUERULOUS.

13-3 HAS SOME CONCERN ABOUT HIS MENTAL EQUILIBRIUM AND STABILITY, REQUIRING REASSURANCE FROM OTHERS REGARDING THIS.

01-2 SHOWS ADEQUATE AFFECTIVE CAPACITY, REACTS WELL TO SITUATIONS WITH AFFECT APPROPRIATE IN BOTH QUALITY AND QUANTITY.

14-2 IS WELL INTEGRATED. DOES NOT EXPERIENCE DISTORTION OR DEPERSONALIZATION PHENOMENA EVEN IN PERIODS OF SEVERE STRESS.

12-2 WELL ORIENTED IN ALL SPHERES, WITH CLEAR, INTACT SENSORIUM.

20-2 SHOWS NO EVIDENCE OF SELF-DESTRUCTIVE TENDENCIES.

10-2 MAINTAINS A SATISFACTORY BALANCE BETWEEN INDEPENDENT, SELF-ENERGIZING BEHAVIOR, AND ACCEPTANCE OF HELP WHEN NECESSARY.

08-2 IS ABLE TO RECOGNIZE AND ADMIT PHYSICAL SYMPTOMS WHEN PRESENT.

17-2 SHOWS NO EVIDENCE OF WORRY OR CONCERN ABOUT HIS SEXUAL ADJUSTMENT, ACCEPTS AN ADEQUATE HETEROSEXUAL ADJUSTMENT AS PART OF HIS SELF-CONCEPT.

06-2 IS ABLE TO EXPRESS AND DEMONSTRATE APPROPRIATE FEELINGS OF GUILT AND SHAME WHEN HE HAS BEHAVED IN AN UNACCEPTABLE MANNER.

07-2 HAS REASONABLE CAPACITY TO ORGANIZE HIS DAILY ROUTINE WITHOUT EVIDENCE OF COMPULSIVE CONCERNS.

Figure 20–2 Computer print-out of Minnesota-Hartford Personality Assay may be converted into a graph, as shown above, to demonstrate changes in the behavioral profile. In the case of this patient with paranoid-schizophrenia, the solid line represents the behavioral profile 4 months ago and the dotted line indicates the current profile. The profile is based on an evaluation of 20 factors and the degree to which they are seen in the patient at the time of the rating. These factors are identified at the right of the print-out and by number at the bottom of the graph. Behavior rated above 60 and below 40 is generally abnormal. Narrative statements below the graph identify the factors and describe patient behavior; the first figure (e.g., 16) to the left of the narrative statement identifies the factor while the second figure (e.g., minus 5) indicates the number of standard deviations of the patient from the group norm (Roche Report, 1966).

new frontier is theoretical, the formulation of a system which provides a logical framework for coordinating the various syndromes. Let us turn briefly to these new empirical and theoretical directions in classification.

EMPIRICALLY-BASED CLASSIFICATIONS

Prompted by the low diagnostic reliability of the DSM nosology and the lack of homogeneity of its syndromes, Lorr and his colleagues (1963, 1965, 1966, 1968) embarked on a series of empirical research studies designed to discover new clinical categories that would be based on the statistical methods of factor analysis. In his schema, Lorr sought to extract from a wide range of clinical information those key diagnostic features which cluster together statistically; intercorrelations found among the clinical features of each statistical cluster would serve as the foundation of new or refined diagnostic syndromes. Instead of depending on tradition clinical thinking, Lorr's syndromes were to be based on empirical research and statistically demonstrated covariations among psychologically significant behaviors and traits.

To expedite his research, Lorr developed two diagnostic instruments, the Interpersonal Behavior Inventory (IBI) and the Inpatient Multidimensional Psychiatric Scale (IMPS), the former designed to appraise the interpersonal behavior of both patients and nonpatients, the latter to assess the clinical features of seriously disturbed patients. Using the IBI, Lorr collected information from therapists who rated their patients on between 140 and 171 interpersonal behavior characteristics. Through a factor analysis of data obtained on several hundred patients, Lorr was able to extract 15 categories, comprising sets of highly intercorrelated behaviors, which he termed as follows: Dominance, Exhibition, Sociability, Affiliation, Nurturance, Agreeableness, Deference, Succorance, Submissiveness, Abasement, Inhibition, Detachment, Mistrust, Aggression, and Recognition. Essentially identical factor clusters emerged from an analysis of ratings made on a large group of "normal" persons, supporting the view that similar styles of interpersonal behavior are to be found among nonpatients and patients, a finding consistent with the position that normality-abnormality is a continuum.

In studies utilizing the IMPS with over 500 seriously disturbed patients, Lorr extracted 10 factors, each representing a new major psychotic syndrome. These 10 syndromes correlate with each other in varying degrees, as shown in Figure 20-3. The closer together that two syndromes are on the circle, the greater the probability that a patient will display them together. If the distance between two syndromes is great, there is little or no likelihood that their features will be exhibited in common by a psychotic patient, e.g., excitement would not coexist with retardation and apathy.

Not only has Lorr's research provided a firmer empirical basis for syndrome classification than the traditional nosology, but clinicians show substantially higher reliability in their diagnostic judgments when using the IMPS instrument.

THEORETICALLY-BASED CLASSIFICATIONS

As pointed out in earlier chapters, numerous theories have been proposed to account for the development of virtually every variety of abnormal syndrome. What has been lacking until recent years, however, is a theory from which a logical and coherent system of syndromes could be

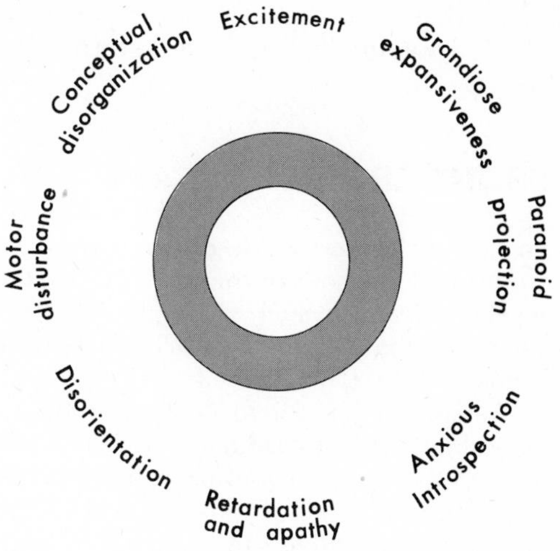

Figure 20–3 Lorr's Factor Syndromes of Psychosis.

derived. Most theories of psychopathology provide hypotheses which "explain" this or that syndrome or offer rather broad statements as to how abnormalities, in general, may develop. What has seemed lacking is a single theory that would coordinate the various syndromes into an integrated classification schema.

The present text borrows heavily from such a classification theory, first formulated in systematic form by one of the authors in another, earlier book (T. Millon, 1969). Thus, the eight mild pathological personality patterns described earlier in Chapters 11 and 12 were derived from a 4×2 matrix combining two basic variables: (a) the primary source from which patients gain positive reinforcements and avoid negative ones (no source, termed "detached" patterns; other persons as source, termed "dependent" patterns; self as source, termed "independent" patterns; and conflict between sources, termed "ambivalent" patterns); and (b) the style of instrumental behavior employed by patients to obtain these reinforcements ("passive" versus "active"). This eightfold breakdown serves as the basis for understanding the major pathological "personality patterns," and accounts for the direction in which patients decompensate and the specific "symptom disorders" they display under stress. Rather than standing on their own as discrete pathological syndromes, each diagnostic class is viewed as an extension or modification of other clinical categories. For example, as illustrated in Chapters 13 through 17, all symptom disorders are considered for purposes of classification to be disruptions of a patient's basic personality, springing forth to dominate his clinical picture under stressful or otherwise unusual circumstances. Viewed this way, categories are not discrete diagnostic entities, but are part of a larger complex of clinical features and developmental histories with which they are often correlated.

As a means of assisting clinicians and researchers who wish to employ the classification model, the same author and his associates have developed a diagnostic instrument (Millon and Diesenhaus, 1972), labeled the Millon-Illinois Self-Report Inventory (MI-SRI). Refined through a series of validation studies, the MI-SRI is currently employed as an operational measure for testing clinical hypotheses and evaluating interrelationships among the theory's syndrome categories. For the first time, a diagnostic instrument has been constructed in line with a comprehensive and systematic theory of psychopathology. As with Lorr's empirical factorial methods, the MI-SRI instrument and its correlated theoretical model opens a potentially important new frontier for research in abnormal psychology.

FRONTIERS IN THERAPY AND BEHAVIOR CHANGE

In earlier chapters we described several modern developments among traditional methods of therapy and behavior change. Each "school" or level of approach, such as psychoanalytic or behavioral, has produced innovations that extend their original boundaries in both technique and focus. Recently, however, a significant shift has taken place among many professionals in the field. No longer is their focus on the rehabilitation of the "abnormal"; it has turned, rather, to the creation of more productive attitudes and a more joyful existence for everyone. The shift is from patients and the relief of "pathological symptoms" toward the "liberation of creative potentials" and the "opening of new horizons" for pleasure and personal growth. This new orientation and its methods are useful also for effecting behavior change among the emotionally disturbed, but the sphere of this "frontier" is with normals who seek a more enriching and psychologically gratifying life. It should be recognized, of course, that those professionals who adhere to more traditional therapies often achieve similar goals. What distinguishes them from the newer procedures is the latter's almost exclusive emphasis on the "normal" person, group interaction and the desire for growth. To illustrate, let us turn next to several of these "frontier" methods.

T-GROUPS

The T-Group method is the forerunner of the newer techniques developed to improve interpersonal effectiveness among normals. It was originated by the National Training Laboratories in the late 1940's as a procedure for increasing the quality of team work in industrial group settings. The principals and methods it promoted have since been employed in diverse settings such as schools, government agencies and community programs. Argyris (1962) summarized the essential features of the T-Group as follows.

Basically, it is a group experience designed to provide maximum possible opportunity for individuals to expose their behavior, give and receive feedback, experiment with new behaviors, and develop everlasting awareness and acceptance of self and others. The T-Group also provides possibilities to learn the nature of effective group functioning. Individuals are able to learn how to develop a group that achieves specific goals with minimal human cost. The T-group becomes a learning experience that most closely approximates the values of the laboratory regarding the use of leadership, rewards, penalties, and information in the development of effective groups. It is in the T-group that one finds the emphasis on the participants creating and diagnosing their own behavior, developing distributive-making norms to protect the deviants, and, finally, showing as much as possible all the information that is created within and as a result of the T-group experience.

T-Group experiences may be arranged in a single intense session of six to ten hours, or may be carried out as part of a larger sequence of planned conference activities, including sessions involving intergroup conflicts, role-playing and case history studies; together, these sessions may continue over a period of several days. The primary focus of T-

Group discussion is on social interaction, role relationships, communication styles, organization patterns and so forth. To convey the open and fluid character desired in the group process, Goldberg (1970) suggests the following introduction by the leader at the first T-Group session.

"This group will meet for many hours and will serve as a kind of laboratory where each individual can increase his understanding of the forces that influence individual behavior and the performance of groups and organizations. The data for learning will be our own behavior, feelings, and reactions. We begin with no definite structure or organization, no agreed-upon procedures, and no specific agenda. It will be up to us to fill the vacuum created by the lack of these familiar elements and to study our group as we evolve. My role will be to help the group to learn from its own experience, but not to act as a traditional chairman nor to suggest how we should organize, what our procedures should be, or exactly what our agenda will include. With these few comments, I think we are ready to begin in whatever way you feel will be most helpful."

T-Group members react in various and highly personal ways to this open-ended introduction. Some seek to structure the group, appoint a chairman, establish an agenda and define clear goals; others "take over," directing activities and mandating topics; others still, sit back and wait for events to unfold. Whatever role a person takes, he quickly learns to observe the reaction of others, his response to them and the effects these interactions produce. Bennis (1962) summarizes the goals of the T-Group experience as follows: They (1) work toward an expanded consciousness and a wider recognition of available choices, (2) embody a spirit of inquiry, (3) stress authenticity in interpersonal relationships and (4) imply a collaborative concept of authority. According to Bennis, these goals become internalized in each member of the group, serving to modify his social role behavior in the direction of a more effective and personally gratifying style.

GROWTH-ENCOUNTER TECHNIQUES

One aspect of the wide-ranging T-Group experience became the primary focus of growth-encounter techniques. Whereas the T-Group orientation remains that of implementing social communication and group effectiveness, growth-encounter methods, although similar in appearance, stress personal expression and self-realization.

The major goals of the encounter technique are enhancement of "creativity" and "authenticity." Through intense, frank and often prolonged social encounters (referred to as marathon groups), previously inhibited feelings and attitudes are aroused, exposed and expressed dramatically. Through the process of honest and shared openness, members are able to release and challenge each other's impulses and to grow and expand awareness of their own and other's feelings. Ultimately, they should become more authentic in their personal expressions, which, in turn, should increase their capacity for genuine and deep intimacy with others. The task of the group is to assist each individual to learn to integrate these deeper feelings into his everyday life, thereby making his future experiences fuller. By drawing upon these deeper inner resources, becoming more committed to express one's authentic self, each person should be able to achieve more creatively and genuinely.

Given the encounter philosophy of openness and creativity, it should not be surprising that a wide variety of styles and goals have developed among its proponents. Some groups are leaderless, depending on the individual members to evolve their own organization; other groups are run as nude marathons where members must shed themselves of all clothing and learn to relate intensely over a continuous 24 hour period; some leaders encourage touching and physical contact while others insist on verbal interactions only. In arranging group composition, some leaders insist that members have no prior outside contact and remain anonymous, whereas others prefer to organize groups composed of close friends or marital pairs.

Groups range in size usually from 6 to 16 members. Sessions are typically carried out in a "bare" physical setting with minimal or no potential distractions from freedom of movement and direct personal interaction. Most leaders become active participants themselves, expressing their feelings and attitudes as fully as they expect group members to do. The leader's task is to assist members to remove their social defenses, to "get in touch" with their real emotions, to express them honestly and openly as they are elicited in the group interaction. Members are encouraged to display their immediate feelings toward one another, that is, to promptly confront others in the group with both the positive and negative emotions they stir up. Reciprocal feedback of counter-feelings is also encouraged so that members can deal openly with the effects their actions produce in others. It is the leader's responsibility to see that constructive resolutions are worked out in these face-to-face confrontations. Most important is his role in providing an atmosphere of security within the group so that confrontations do not prove severely threatening. If effectively executed, within a few hours the group interaction often creates a surprisingly high degree of mutual support and affection among its members.

Numerous special techniques have been devised to break down each participant's constraints against developing open and intimate relationships with others. Among these trusting exercises are methods such as "eyeballing" in which two members are asked to focus on each other's eyes for a minute or two. In another procedure, each member takes a turn falling backward into the arms of another participant or is lifted upward in a prone position and then passed around over the heads of other group members. "Blind mill" is a technique often employed at the early stages of the first encounter session; here, group members move about with their eyes closed, feeling and communicating to others by touch. These warming up and opening up methods are not universally employed; some group leaders believe that techniques such as those described are too contrived and prefer instead that a more natural evolution of feelings take place. Rogers (1970) outlines the usual sequence in which events of the encounter groups unfold as follows:

1. *Milling around.* After the leader indicates that the group has complete freedom, as well as responsibility, for determining the direction of events, there is a period of initial confusion, awkward silence, polite but superficial talk and a minor degree of frustration expressed over the aimlessness and triviality of what has taken place.

2. *Resistance to personal expression or exploration.* At first, some participants are willing to share certain aspects of their more personal lives or feelings. Rather than encouraging similar responses from others, this "private" talk often elicits indifference or defensive disregard on the part of the less-involved group members. On occasion a member may voice

openly his unwillingness to become personally involved on an emotional level.

3. *Description of past feelings.* Despite feelings of ambivalence about the trustworthiness of the group and the dangers of self-exposure, personal reflections and emotions do begin to emerge. These tend, however, to focus on the past or on events outside the group setting. A mother will talk of her disappointments with her children, a husband will express his anger toward his wife, a worker about the frustrations of his job and so forth.

4. *Expression of negative feelings.* Rather interestingly, the first expressions of feeling about events and persons within the group itself take a negative form, usually displayed as anger or disappointment. Rogers illustrates this phase in the following vignette.

In one group in which members introduced themselves at some length, one woman refused, saying that she preferred to be known for what she was in the group and not in terms of her status outside. Very shortly after this, a man in the group attacked her angrily for this stand, accusing her of failing to cooperate, of keeping herself aloof from the group, of being unreasonable. It was the first *current personal feeling* brought into the open in that group.

5. *Expression and exploration of personally meaningful material.* Following the expression of initial negative feelings, the event most likely to occur next is a member's willingness to reveal some genuinely significant aspect of his personal life. Having observed that the prior expression of intense negative attitudes was accepted and integrated within the group without serious repercussions, members become increasingly willing to risk self-disclosure. As this first exposure receives a fair and sympathetic hearing, a climate of trust begins to develop, thereby encouraging others to express their deeper feelings.

6. *Expression of immediate interpersonal feelings.* Once a climate of increasing trust emerges, attitudes and feelings evoked by fellow members are responded to immediately and with minimal reservations about their emotional impact. The atmosphere has "opened up," and hesitations about reacting emotionally to others have been greatly reduced.

7. *Development of a healing capacity.* A striking feature that emerges in these increasingly intense interactions is the spontaneous capacity among the participants for responding to the anguish of others in a supportive and therapeutic way. Persons who have no formal training in helping relationships exhibit a deep sensitivity, a sympathetic grasp of the significance of what others have experienced and are experiencing and a warmth and caring that is truly therapeutic.

8. *Shedding of facades and individual feedback.* Different events and interactions unfold at a rapid pace by this time in the group. Notable is an increasing intolerance of those members who have remained uninvolved. Sometimes gently, but just as often forcefully, each member who has failed to "open up" is made to feel that he must shed the protective mask or facade he employs to hide his personal self. In these confrontations, the formerly uninvolved member is drawn out until he, too, is able to share in the honest and intimate relationships that have evolved within the group.

9. *Expression of positive feelings and behavior change.* As a consequence of

the intense and open interplay of feelings and reactions, a deeper acceptance of one another develops within the group. As Rogers phrases it,

> . . . an inevitable part of the group process seems to be that when feelings are expressed and can be accepted in a relationship, then a great deal of closeness and positive feeling results. Thus as the sessions proceed, an increasing feeling of warmth and group spirit and trust is built up, not out of positive attitudes only but out of a realness which includes both positive and negative feeling.

Following a successful encounter group experience, significant, though gradual, changes often occur on the part of the participant's attitude toward himself and others. There is a tendency to become more spontaneous and honest with members of one's family and associates. Just as significant, the participant frequently senses a liberation from prior feelings of social hesitancy and personal inadequacy, gaining as a consequence a new dimension of freedom and potency.

EVALUATIVE COMMENT

Intensive T-Group and encounter experiences are not always unmixed blessings (Yalom and Liberman, 1971). Several problems often arise, some minor, others serious.

One frequent comment among former participants is that the exhilarating changes that are prompted during the experience simply do not last. More problematic, members may have opened up previously hidden feelings and attitudes which they cannot work through adequately in the encounter sessions; psychotic episodes, even suicides, following encounter experiences are not common but occur with sufficient frequency to be a matter of great concern. As one recent critic put it (English, 1969):

> Today we are witnessing a proliferation of sensitivity training programs aimed at persons in educational, industrial, and community settings. Variations of sensitivity programs have been established that purport to train community development leaders, promote international relations, secure labor-management harmony, increase marital happiness, and resolve other thorny problems via the T-group method of enhancing interpersonal communications. That so much has been promised by sensitivity training and so little delivered by means of evaluation and research findings suggests that psychiatrists should be increasingly aware and distressed about these programs.

> Of primary concern to psychiatrists, many of whom have seen the "casualties" of insensitive sensitivity training programs and "trainers," should be the outright invasion of individual privacy such programs tend to promote. Sensitivity training appears to have been so effectively oversold to an unaware public, clamoring for psychiatric and psychological insights, that it is not uncommon for teachers, business representatives, high government officials, and others to be required, as a function of their jobs, to participate in these sessions . . . .

> For some participants the results have been traumatic indeed!

The long-term effectiveness of T-Group and encounter techniques has not been adequately researched. As these frontiers of abnormal psychology are more thoroughly evaluated, they could either become accepted methods, carried out by responsible mental health workers, or they could be left to cultists and charlatans as another intriguing but deceptive fad. More than likely, something in between will take place, with the field extracting in time the positive features of this movement, incorporating these into established techniques and discarding the rest (Lieberman et al., 1973).

FRONTIERS OF PREVENTION AND HEALTH DELIVERY

There remains much to be learned about the causes and treatment of psychological abnormalities. Despite these deficits in knowledge, sufficient advances have been made in the sciences of psychology and psychiatry to justify developing more effective preventive and health delivery services than in the past. In recent years, mental health professions have acquired enough data to formulate reliable guidelines for preventive action. A major factor in this regard is a growing awareness of the destructive role of poverty and psychosocial deprivation in early life. Similarly, we now know that therapeutic services have been for the most part unavailable to large segments of our populace and that the distribution of these services can be organized more efficiently. In this final section of our final chapter, our attention will turn to these two most important frontiers: mental illness prevention and service delivery.

PREVENTION

Mental illness prevention is a broad and somewhat ambiguous phrase that covers a wide range of activities. Viewed superficially, preventive programs have little in common other than the major objective they share of minimizing the frequency and intensity of psychological disabilities. It would be useful before detailing the specifics of these "frontier" programs to divide them into three broad categories: *primary, secondary* and *tertiary* (Caplan, 1964; Zax and Cowen, 1972).

Primary Prevention. There are two central goals in primary prevention. The first consists of intercepting and blocking the development of emotional disorders, that is, identifying and warding off all influences which can lead to the emergence of psychological problems. The second comprises methods designed to foster positive mental health, that is, to identify and encourage all influences productive of emotional well-being.

As noted earlier, because of the limited nature of our knowledge of the causes of mental disorders, it is difficult to formulate with confidence a systematic program of preventive methods. However imperfect, Caplan (1964) has provided a threefold outline of primary prevention "supplies":

1. *Physical supplies* include a variety of measures designed to maximize physical health, notably the provision of adequate nutrition and shelter. Within this category also would be advice on budgeting family finances, genetic counseling, guidance in child planning, arrangements for proper prenatal and postnatal care and a host of other provisions to encourage healthy functioning and the avoidance of physical disabilities.

2. *Psychosocial supplies* consist of a variety of procedures to maximize "optimal psychological development and functioning." This would include special programs which prepare individuals to deal effectively with the typical stresses that are encountered at different life stages, most particularly adolescence, marriage, the climacteric and old age. Here the focus lies in assisting individuals to develop skills for effective problem solving, for forming gratifying social roles and relationships and for dealing with emotional upsets in constructive ways.

3. *Sociocultural supplies* comprise steps to counter the effects of disabling social conditions such as poverty, ghetto and slum environments, inadequate health services and so forth. Among programs oriented to providing these supplies are low-cost suburban housing projects, Headstart schooling for socially deprived children and legislation of benefits such as Social Security, Medicare, and guaranteed minimum incomes.

Secondary Prevention. The essential goal of secondary prevention is that of stopping a disorder in the early stages from developing into a more serious and prolonged state. This requires the identification and prompt treatment of psychological dysfunctions, hopefully within the community setting.

Caplan (1964) has noted a number of difficulties in achieving secondary prevention tasks. For example, early detection methods are not notably effective since accurate identification often cannot be made until the disturbance has advanced to rather severe proportions. Similarly, those closest to the person in difficulty frequently fail to recognize the developing problem for what it is. Most problematic of all, professional detection programs simply are not available in most communities.

To overcome these deficiencies, epidemiological studies have recently been employed by prevention specialists to identify high-risk communities, that is, those in which psychological disorders have a high incidence: examples are high-turnover neighborhoods and those in which single-person or female-headed households abound (Redick, Goldsmith and Unger, 1971). With the advent of the mental health center programs, an important step has been taken toward early identification and treatment in the community. The recent shift away from large state hospital programs and toward community programs geared to partial hospitalization, crisis intervention and other emergency services, will enable the goals of secondary prevention to be more realistically achieved.

Tertiary Prevention. The aim of tertiary prevention is proper follow-up with individuals who have already succumbed to and been treated for an emotional disorder. The intent is to minimize social and psychological consequences of the patient's disorder and to prevent its recurrence in the future. By helping restore the person to social, familial and occupational functioning, he may be made not only capable of living an adequate life, but able to do so more effectively and in a more satisfying way than before his illness.

In the following sections we will turn to programs that have been designed specifically to achieve the aims of one or more of the goals of prevention.

PREVENTIVE FAMILY PROGRAMS

It is a well accepted thesis that the family provides the crucial environment for molding personality development, either normal or abnormal. Given the primacy, intimacy and continuity of parental and sibling relationships, and the intensity and depth of daily interactions, the family atmosphere is unparalleled as a determinant of attitudes, feelings and behaviors. Although definitive data are lacking to prove the effects of a detrimental family life, there can be little doubt that tense and troubled homes are conducive settings for producing defective reinforcers and models of behavior.

Of recent interest also are concerns about the long-term effects of early psychosocial deprivation, especially in the poorer and underprivileged segments of our society. Special programs have been devised since the mid-60's to educate parents and to actively employ them in compensatory projects to counter these deficiencies. Classes for parents-to-be have become increasingly popular. Designed to involve both parents in the effective rearing of young children, these classes attempt to minimize anxieties about pregnancy and the care of young infants, provide information about typical and expected behaviors at different early stages of development and suggest procedures for proper physical care, nutrition and social stimulation.

Of particular promise in this regard are programs which enlist parents as teachers for the preschool intellectual development of their own children. In one recent study (Karnes et al., 1968), 30 children from underprivileged communities were divided into two groups of 15 each. The mothers of the experimental group attended 11 weekly two-hour sessions directed by three experienced preschool teachers; the mothers of the control group children received no special training. The experimental mothers prepared materials under supervision for use with their youngsters each week. A discussion of appropriate ways to use these materials at home composed a major portion of each session. Using a standard intelligence scale as a gauge, the experimental group children exhibited an average increase during the training period of approximately 8 IQ points, whereas the control group showed no increase.

In other programs, parents and siblings are employed actively as therapists for youngsters with various psychological disorders. Guerney (1969) has collected a wide range of case studies and research reports demonstrating the use of mothers as behavior-modifiers, of special family play techniques which he terms "filial" therapy, as well as a whole host of other specifically tailored home "treatment" methods. Although nonprofessional parents and siblings lack formal advanced training in psychotherapy, these reports show that a short period of training can produce skills that are useful in generating important behavior changes. The ability to apply their knowledge and techniques within the natural context of the home, and at times when the need and the effect can be greatest, gives family members a special power and effectiveness often lacking in the professional.

PREVENTIVE SCHOOL PROGRAMS

In many ways schools can and do play a major role in achieving a variety of preventive goals. Long-standing problems that are generated initially in the home frequently are not brought to professional attention until the child enters school. Many parents simply refuse to act on, or even acknowledge, the presence of family and child difficulties. Others are inclined to admit problems, and even wish assistance, but lack the knowledge and means to implement these desires until their children begin school; it is their hope that professional guidance will be made available to them at that time. In many communities, schools do provide such services, some efficiently and well, others in only a skimpy and scattered fashion.

Because of their central administration of funds and personnel, schools possess the necessary organizational means to mount a unified and systematic program for identifying and treating childhood disorders.

Moreover, the school is the only formal institution that has a mandated and continuous relationship with a geographical community, particularly during the important formative years. For these reasons, then, the school can serve as a major entry point and continuing resource for large-scale and significant preventive programs. In the following sections we will briefly describe several of the more promising projects devised for use in this setting.

Compensatory Programs.   A free public education through high school is available for all children in this country. Nevertheless, it has become increasingly evident that youngsters who are deprived of adequate intellectual stimulation prior to formal schooling suffer marked disadvantages in their cognitive abilities. As a consequence, many fail to catch up, lagging further and further behind their peers as they progress through the school years. In other words, initial differences widen over time, separating these socially and intellectually deprived youngsters increasingly from their more fortunate classmates.

Several novel programs have been developed in the past decade to prevent or compensate for these early psychosocial disadvantages; the best known of these is the national project labeled *Headstart*. Included in Headstart, which has recently suffered a cutback of funds at the federal level as a consequence of hastily reached evaluations of its effectiveness, were programs to provide basic health services, nutrition and dental care as well as a wide-ranging social-educational curriculum. Engaging mothers, community workers and numerous volunteers, Headstart stimulated a marked increase in concern and sophistication among a segment of our population that had not previously acquired a deep interest and involvement in early education. Although preliminary evaluative evidence failed to show significant and sustained gains among youngsters in the program, these evaluations have been based on short-term effects, thereby overlooking the slow and cumulative gains that are necessary to overcome generations of poverty, deprivation and poor education.

Often overlapping with Headstart, but having a more specific focus, are programs designed to overcome the low self-image that our society has created among members of various minority groups — in particular, blacks and chicanos. The depreciation of the potentials of these minority group children, not only by the majority whites but also by themselves, has been a serious deterrent to their achievement strivings and school performance. In a special compensatory program to counter these self-devaluations, Shore et al. (1971) organized an academic sequence which sought to reinforce curiosity and provide opportunities for independence and successful functioning. The nine-month plan was implemented and resulted in significant changes when compared to a control group in self-confidence, self-worth and feelings of competence in controlling events and directing one's life.

Problem Identification Programs.   It is not unusual for youngsters to begin to display a variety of academic or behavior difficulties in the first grade. Labeled "problem children" by their teachers, these first graders often continue to exhibit deficiencies in performance throughout their school career. Zax and Cowen (1972) summarize a study they carried out to verify these consequences as follows:

Investigators identified, at first grade, children with manifest or incipient problems of ineffective school function. The early detection procedure was based on an amalgam of social-work interview with the mothers of all first grade children, group screening using psychological assessment procedures, direct classroom observation, and teacher reports. Evaluation of the early detected sample at the end of the third school year indicated that they were doing significantly more poorly than their normal functioning peers in school achievement, on self, peer, and teacher ratings and on a variety of everyday school behavioral measures such as attendance and frequency of illness. Follow-up four years later, at seventh grade level, yielded data indicating that children with early detected dysfunction continued, through their elementary school careers, to do more poorly than peers in salient areas of educational and personal function.

As a follow-up project, Zax and Cowen, using similar identification procedures, divided first grade children into two groups: a "Red-Tag" group judged as likely to develop continuing problems and a "Non-Red-Tag" group judged likely to make an adequate to good future school adjustment. They introduced a series of preventive programs on the Red-Tag group with the intent of reducing the frequency and intensity of later difficulties. Conferences were held with teachers, principals, school psychologists, social workers, nurses and other personnel. The special problems of each of these children were discussed and collaborative programing was fostered among participating professional staff. Moreover, the parents of these youngsters were asked to attend regular evening meetings to educate them on matters such as child development and discipline. Teachers also attended special seminars on topics designed to increase their awareness of individual differences in ability and temperament. And finally, the children themselves were engaged in after-school activities planned to enhance their interpersonal skills and feelings of competence.

The results of the the program were most encouraging. Compared to a control group of Red-Tag children who were not participants in the project, the experimental group had better attendance records, fewer cases of underachievement, and higher grades, and they were judged, in general, to be more competent and adjusted by their teachers. Although more confirmatory research is needed to prove the efficacy of this and similar projects, the evidence from the Zax and Cowen study strongly supports the utility of such programs in achieving preventive goals. Unfortunately, most school districts lack the funds and resources to undertake projects of this scope and caliber.

Behavior Science Education Programs. Despite the novelty of the idea, and perhaps the resistance to it by more rigid and traditional educators, there appears to be no reason why "behavior science" or "psychology of human relations" courses could not profitably be included in the elementary school curriculum. In fact, Roen (1967) has devised and instituted such a course for fourth-graders with rather impressive effects. Guiding youngsters to learn about themselves and to cope wisely with their social and personal problems should be no less important a part of a well-planned educational curriculum than the learning of facts about 17th century British history or the metamorphosis of queen bees.

Along similar lines, many high schools in recent years have developed practicum programs in which students actively participate in helping services to the aged and mentally ill (Guerney, 1969). Learning such prosocial behaviors is not only of value in instilling useful and altruistic attitudes, but often produces significant mental health gains for the participants themselves.

HEALTH DELIVERY

The Mental Health Study Act of 1955 was passed by the United States Congress because prior research suggested that the health professions had failed to meet the needs of the country's mentally ill. A nongovernmental group, named the Joint Commission on Mental Illness and Health, was formed by members from every discipline in the mental health field and was given the responsibility of evaluating the status of the nation's psychiatric and psychosocial services. Numerous studies were carried out by subcommittees of the Joint Commission; they focused on several major topics, such as manpower trends, community needs and the distribution and effectiveness of delivery of mental health services. Among their major findings were the following rather dismaying facts: the professional manpower pool in the foreseeable future could not possibly meet the needs of the nation without a dramatic increase in training programs; less than 20 per cent of Americans with psychological problems turn to mental health professionals for assistance (most go to their clergyman or their family physician); not only does the demand far outstrip the supply, but the distribution of mental health resources is markedly skewed, with most services available only to those in the upper and middle classes located in seven or eight major metropolitan and suburban areas.

The Joint Commission's findings spurred a dramatic effort in the 1960's to train more and better qualified mental health workers. Thus, Arnhoff et al. (1969) calculated that between 1950 and 1966 the number of psychiatrists in the country was increased by 350 per cent; similarly, there was a 500 per cent increase in psychologists, 400 per cent in psychiatric social workers and 250 per cent in psychiatric nurses. Despite this remarkable growth in trained personnel, Arnhoff went on to observe, "Our society has changed drastically in the last two decades; the increased demand and expectation for services in all segments of health, education, and welfare have been phenomenal, and the competition for educated and trained persons grows more acute." It would appear, then, that the manpower expansion of the late 50's and 60's still lags behind the need. That the deficiencies continue to be compounded by a persistent maldistribution of services is powerfully illustrated in the following quote from Albee (1970):

In the final report of the Joint Commission on Mental Illness and Health we suggested that the ideal goal to strive for was one mental hygiene clinician for every fifty thousand people. It happens that there is one city in the United States today that exceeds this idealized goal! Boston is Psychiatryland. Boston exceeds in its psychiatric manpower all of the states of Appalachia. Yet a recent survey of the unmet mental health needs of Boston spells out in clear and unambiguous detail the fact that the people most in need of intervention for their emotional problems are not getting any significant amount of help. These five groups . . . include seriously-disturbed children, disturbed adolescents, multi-problem families, the aged, and discharged state mental hospitals survivors. So . . . just what difference really does it make whether we do or do not reach the goal of one center for every hundred thousand people, when twice as many Boston centers do not deal with the people most in need of help. In Boston the typical "psychiatric patient" is a white upper-middle class, nonCatholic, college-educated female between the ages of 30 and 40, in private psychotherapy.

. . . half of the country's total psychiatrists are to be found in five favored states: Massachusetts, New York, Pennsylvania, Illinois, and California. And within these states there is still maldistribution. A recent survey found that most psychiatric practice is private office suburban practice with relatively affluent "patients" seeking talking psychotherapy.

Confronted with these distressing realities, the mental health profession has sought to remedy the problem through a number of strategies. First and foremost are efforts to produce significant breakthroughs in our knowledge of the causes and treatment of mental disorders. Advances in these areas might markedly reduce the "need" for time-consuming services; unfortunately, with the exception of psychopharmacologic agents, progress has been slow. Two additional programs to help resolve deficits in health service delivery have made a modicum of progress, and it is to these that we will turn our attention next: inner-city programs and New Career paraprofessionals.

INNER-CITY PROGRAMS

America's major cities have changed radically in the past two decades. In the first half of this century, they were not only centers of bustling activity and growth, but attracted the successful and upwardly mobile of our populace. Since the late 1940's, however, the character of these large metropolitan areas has been altered drastically. Now the fortunate and affluent are moving to thriving suburbs while the less fortunate and poor remain behind. Additionally, the cities of the North have attracted a mass exodus of underprivileged minority groups from other regions, particularly the Southern black and Spanish-speaking populations. As Pfautz (1969) has noted, "In less than a generation, Negro Americans have been transformed from a regional, rural, and agricultural population to an essentially national, urban and industrial population."

The shift to the Northern cities of underprivileged minority groups was prompted by their desire to free themselves from prejudice, physical destitution and poverty, hopefully for better conditions and opportunities. Not only have most failed to achieve their aspirations, but many have found greater degradation and squalor than they left behind.

The persistence of poverty and neglect in the Northern cities is fundamentally an economic and social issue, but it has significant psychological consequences, as well. As noted in preceding chapters of the text, the incidence of severe psychological disorders is highest in low-income groups and, most particularly among underprivileged minority groups who live in the inner cities (Wittman, 1972). Although the central task in overcoming these problems will require changes in the socioeconomic status of these minority groups, there is a pressing need also to furnish them with effective health services. Without such assistance, these groups may suffer so great a degree of physical and psychological damage that they will be unable to take advantage of the economic opportunities which may be available to them. The special programs described in preceding sections concerning efforts to encourage cognitive growth, intellectual curiosity and feelings of self esteem among underprivileged children become especially critical in this regard. Since we have previously discussed these youth-oriented enrichment programs, albeit briefly, the following paragraphs will focus, again in summary fashion, on other mental health projects designed to counteract these adverse conditions.

Catchment Areas and Citizen Control. The term catchment area has come to mean a specified neighborhood or geographic region whose entire population will be treated on an equal basis by a local and centrally coordinated body of health personnel. Kunnes (1970) states the rationale of these programs as follows:

The purpose of catchment areas was to prevent the arbitrary exclusion of patients from treatment centers and to insure that all patients within a catchment area received the same care from publicly funded institutions—in other words, to protect the community . . . . Publicly and politically defined, catchment areas divide the community along lines of rational needs as opposed to lines of empire and exploitation . . . . Perhaps the most threatening aspect of catchment areas is that they *define institutional responsibility*. Given a catchment area, an elite private institution . . . is assigned a community which it must relate to, a public that it must account to. Geographical assignments ultimately threaten the institution's "right" to select its patients (an extrapolation of the psychiatrist's "right" to select interesting, wealthy patients).

As can be seen from the above quote, the primary intent of the catchment area concept is that of guaranteeing comparable health service delivery to diverse economic populations who are typically not served either on an equitable basis or in terms of need. Moreover, as a check to insure that these services are provided without bias, substantial control over funding and program evaluation is placed, not in the hands of potentially elitist medical specialists or boards, but in the lay citizenry of the catchment area. Although such lay boards and citizens' councils often lack the technical sophistication to appraise the quality of the services provided, they do have the know-how to judge whether the needs of the poor and less fortunate within their neighborhoods are being met on a fair and impartial basis.

Skid Row Projects.   There is no inner-city group that exhibits greater extremes of human devastation and degradation than that found among the inhabitants of "skid row." These drop-outs from life come together in the peripheral wastelands of major cities to teeter only on the edge of life. Most are psychologically and physically shattered men whose aspirations have been crushed. Increasingly, these settings have begun to attract, in addition to their typical perennial middle-age male alcoholic inhabitants, former mental patients and, most recently, small groups of younger drug addicts and derelicts. In the impersonal environment of cheap and transient hotels, without meaningful family and friendship ties, these unanchored and lost persons drift deeper into their isolation and deterioration.

The skid row community epitomizes the "end of the line" of social disintegration and hence serves as a true test of the seriousness and effectiveness of inner-city programs. To date, however, minimal efforts have been made to rehabilitate this population. What little has been tried has proved to be essentially a failure (Bloomberg et al., 1966). Most of these homeless men oppose programs of relocation; the "hard-core," long-term residents typically are unskilled and incapable of filling jobs which would provide them with a sense of worth and self-esteem. To complicate matters, many suffer debilitating physical illnesses. Comprehensive programs of health services and rehabilitation are needed to overcome the complex of physical, psychological and social damage involved in their disintegration (Plaut, 1972). Unless inner-city projects are geared to provide this most deteriorated group with medical care, sheltered workshops, vocational training and placement, proper lodging in foster family settings or in supervised half-way houses where adequate psychological counseling is available, the prospects will indeed be poor that these most unfortunate beings will ever be rehabilitated.

NEW CAREER PARAPROFESSIONALS

We have stated repeatedly that the need for effective health service delivery continues, particularly in those regions and with those populations where the toll of human misery and poverty has been most serious. Although the number of available positions for mental health workers has increased in these communities, most are unfilled because of the all-too-common unwillingness on the part of well-trained professionals to locate in underprivileged areas. How can society attract mental health workers to these neighborhoods? A most promising answer in response to this question will be the topic of the following paragraphs.

Although there are those within the mental health profession who believe that extensive graduate-level training is a prerequisite for work in the field, an increasing number of equally respected professionals contend that such advanced training is not necessary. For example, Halleck (1971) states, "There are many relatively uneducated but otherwise intelligent and sensitive persons in all strata of our society who could and would make excellent therapists if they were properly trained."

Numerous programs have been devised to implement the training of what are called "paraprofessionals" (Guerney, 1969). In an early novel project, Rioch (1963) developed a special two year training program for married women in their forties, demonstrating at the end of this period their excellence as therapists. Similar programs for college students (Matarazzo, 1971), lay volunteers (Katkin et al., 1971) and former mental patients have been designed with equally fruitful results.

The most significant and relevant innovation, however, has been the emergence of the New Career paraprofessional, that is, indigenous laymen and women recruited from the inner city to work in human service functions with the ill and poor of their own neighborhoods. The several values derived by drawing upon the community itself for paraprofessional trainees are summarized well in the following statement (Zax and Cowen, 1972):

The indigenous nonprofessional *is* an inner-city person. He has been there. His language, his way of operating, his life style are all very much the same as those whom he serves. He is capable of fielding problems in the concrete form in which they typically arise. He can communicate readily with constituents seeking help and can gain their trust. He is thus an ideal bridge between the mental health professional and the community. He is neither limited to, nor encumbered by, professional ways of doing things. He can provide individual services or promote community action, and a sense of having a determining stake or power among the disenfranchised . . . . Two points bear emphasis here. First, the use of indigenous inner-city nonprofessionals promises to extend vastly the reach of helping services where they are sorely needed and, second, it is a mechanism for engaging problems in the concrete and realistic ways they occur and in which need is experienced in this setting. These ends go far beyond mere help for the beleaguered professional; they represent innovative, preventively oriented modes of manpower utilization.

The idea for the New Career program was proposed in the early 1960's with pilot projects begun in several major cities of the northeast; in a brief period, the program was expanded and is currently in operation in more than 200 community centers. Several important advantages are achieved in the New Career training model. First, it provides meaningful employment for the able poor who have little opportunity for educational growth and vocational advancement. Second, it extends the scope of health delivery to those among the poor who previously could not or did not utilize these services.

The major features of a well-organized New Careers program were outlined by two of its active proponents, Pearl and Reissman (1965). They state that these projects must be organized to insure permanent career jobs for their participants; further, advancement must be a built-in feature so that talented "New Careerists" can progress to higher positions on the job ladder; and, most central, vocations must be oriented toward providing human services in the community from which the workers were drawn. In following these guidelines, the New Career program will create a beneficent circle, one in which the occupational gains achieved by the New Careerists will feed-back in a positive fashion and enhance the community, its future and growth.

FINAL THOUGHTS ON THE FUTURE

Can mental health be achieved in isolation? Are not the complexities of technological society so vast and intertwined as to undermine the meagre efforts of a single discipline searching to find for man a more harmonious and humanistic way of life? Racism, sexism, war, pollution, international strife, poverty, government corruption, "future shock" and a host of other tensions which impinge upon our daily existence seem so overwhelming as to negate the feeble steps we may make. Not only are vast sums of our nation's wealth expended to combat illusory enemies or to achieve illusory material goals, but these funds and energies are thereby drained from the possibilities of increasing the nation's health, education and general welfare.

To withdraw or become apathetic and cynical is not the choice. Students must draw upon their youthful zest for life, for meeting and overcoming challenges so that their futures and those of their children will approach the possibilities of utopian thinkers. And it is the special province of psychology as a profession, we believe, to furnish the vehicle by which such aims may be achieved. For as Maslow (1957) has said:

I believe that psychologists occupy the most centrally important position in the world today. I say this because all the important problems of mankind — war and peace, exploitation and brotherhood, hatred and love, sickness and health, misunderstanding and understanding, happiness and unhappiness — will yield only to a better understanding of human nature, and to this psychology alone wholly applies itself.

GLOSSARY

This glossary is included with two purposes in mind: (1) to define terms that may not be found in standard and more complete psychological and psychiatric dictionaries, and (2) to provide a quick reference for terms that occur repeatedly in sections of the text other than those in which they are fully discussed.

Ablation: Surgical removal of body tissue.

Abnormal: Deviating from the norm or average; extraordinary or unusual; often but not necessarily maladaptive.

Abreaction: Discharge of emotions when consciously recalling previously repressed unpleasant experiences.

Abstract thinking: Capacity to generalize, to transcend immediate experiences and to reflect and plan logically.

Acetylcholine: Chemical neurohormone associated with synaptic transmission.

Acrophobia: Neurotic fear of heights.

Acting-out: Direct and overt expression of unconscious emotions and conflicts that normally are controlled or moderated by intrapsychic mechanisms.

Activation: Energy arousal and mobilization associated with increased alertness and physical vigor.

Active: Engaging in overt instrumental behaviors.

Active-ambivalence: A basic instrumental strategy characterized by erratic and negativistic behaviors, and by the vacillation of attitudes and moods.

Active-dependence: A basic instrumental strategy characterized by gregarious and seductive behaviors, and by the pursuit of interpersonal attention and approval.

Active-detachment: A basic instrumental strategy characterized by the avoidance of social relationships, and by feelings of self-alienation.

Active-independence: A basic instrumental strategy characterized by domineering, aggressive and vindictive social behaviors.

Addiction: Psychological or physiological dependence on drugs or alcohol.

Adient: Pertaining to a drive that orients the person positively or toward some object or activity.

Adrenal glands: Endocrine glands located adjacent to the kidneys; the inner portion is termed the adrenal medulla and the outer portion is termed the adrenal cortex.

Adrenaline: See *Epinephrine.* The principal hormone secreted by the adrenal medulla; it stimulates energy mobilization and body alertness. Also known as epinephrine.

Adrenergic: Tending to activate the sympathetic nervous system.

Affect: Feeling tone or mood.

Affective disorders: A group of clinical syndromes characterized by intense emotional moods, such as depressions or manias.

Aggressive personality: Mildly severe or basic pathological pattern characterized by assertive and intimidating behaviors and associated with an active-independent instrumental strategy.

Agitated depression disorder: Psychotic disorder characterized by apprehensiveness, restlessness, verbalized guilt, controlled hostility and depressed mood.

Agnosia: Impaired ability to recognize familiar objects or persons.

Agraphia: Impaired ability to express language in writing.

Alexia: Impaired ability to understand written language.

Allergy: Hypersensitivity of body tissue to physical or chemical stimuli.

Ambivalence: Coexistence of conflicting feelings or attitudes toward the same object or person.

Amnesia: Partial or total loss of memory.

Amphetamines: Stimulants composed of synthetic chemicals that activate the brain, increasing temporarily both activity and mood.

Analytic psychology: Theory of abnormality and therapy formulated by Jung.

Anesthesia: Impaired sensitivity to stimuli.

Anhedonia: Dimension of temperament signifying a marked and chronic inability to experience pleasure; also, a general although less severe inability to experience most emotions.

Anoxia: Insufficiency of oxygen.

Anterograde amnesia: Memory loss following psychic trauma or physical shock.

Anti-depressant drugs: Pharmaceuticals designed to relieve dejection and depressive moods.

Anxiety: Psychogenic apprehension and tension, the source of which is usually unknown or unrecognized.

Anxiety disorder: A clinical syndrome characterized either by a state of chronic and moderately severe apprehension or by acute and intense anxiety and panic attacks.

Aphasia: Impaired ability to speak and communicate language (expressive or motor aphasia), or to comprehend language (receptive or sensory aphasia), attributable usually to brain defects.

Aplasia: Deficient development of body tissue.

Apraxia: Impaired ability to carry out purposeful movements, usually without demonstrable organic defects.

Arteriosclerosis: Loss of elasticity and hardening of the arteries, usually associated with aging.

Asthenic personality: Mildly severe or basic pathological pattern characterized by social indifference and emotional apathy and associated with a passive-detached instrumental strategy.

Atrophy: Shrinking and weakening of a body organ.

Attachment: The state of being bound to and dependent on another.

Attitude: A learned readiness to perceive and react in a particular way to a person, object or situation.

Aura: Sensations signifying an impending convulsion.

Autistic thinking: Grossly unrealistic fantasies consonant with pathological needs.

Automatism: Mechanical and repetitious actions, usually of a symbolic nature, carried out without conscious intent or control.

Autonomic nervous system: The portion of the nervous system not subject to voluntary control, serving to regulate major internal organs such as the viscera, glands and smooth muscles. It consists of sympathetic and parasympathetic divisions.

Autonomy: Capacity for self-reliance and independent functioning.

Avoidant personality: Mildly severe or basic pathological pattern characterized by social aversiveness and self-alienation and associated with an active-detached instrumental strategy.

Barbiturates: Brain depressants typically used as sedatives; use frequently results in addiction.

Basic personality patterns: The mild level of pathological severity in personality functioning. There are eight subtypes, each characterized by the presence of pervasive, ingrained and self-perpetuating maladaptive attitudes and instrumental strategies. Patterns develop gradually as a function of the interaction of both constitutional and experiential differences.

Behavioral level: Data and concepts reflecting the observable responses or actions of patients.

Behavior control: Actions taken by others designed to shape the content of what people learn and the style in which these learnings will be expressed.

Behavior modification: Therapies based largely on the application of "learning" principles, and focusing on the alteration of overt actions rather than on subjective feelings or unconscious processes.

Behaviorism: A theoretical approach to psychological issues stressing overt and observable data.

Belle indifférence: A lack of concern for the implications of one's own disabilities, occasionally seen in patients with conversion disorders.

Biogenic: Traceable to physical and biological sources.

Biophysical level: Data and concepts representing the biological substrate of psychological functioning.

Biophysical treatment: Pharmaceutical, electrical and surgical therapeutic methods employed to alter the biological substrates of behavior, emotion and thought.

Blocking: Emotionally based and involuntary interruption of a train of thought or speech.

Borderline personality patterns: The moderate level of pathological severity in personality functioning; there are three major subtypes—schizoid, cycloid and paranoid—each characterized in part by deficits in social competence and by periodic but reversible psychotic episodes.

Brain defects: A group of syndromes in which there is a clear-cut impairment of the biological substrate of the central nervous system.

Bronchi: Lung vessels that permit the passage of air.

Cardiovascular: Pertaining to the circulatory system (heart and blood vessels).

Case history: All available biographical data that facilitate the understanding of a patient's current state.

Catastrophic anxiety: A term coined by Goldstein to signify the frightening awareness of one's incompetence. It is experienced by patients following severe brain injury.

Catatonia: Acute disorder of schizophrenia characterized chiefly by motor rigidity and withdrawal; often punctuated periodically with brief periods of excitement.

Catalepsy: Lack of motor responsiveness; patients are characterized by their resistance to change from an assumed semirigid and trance-like position.

Catharsis: Recalling and describing painful experiences and attitudes, and venting their associated emotions.

Cathexis: A psychoanalytic term signifying the attachment of intense emotions to a particular object or person.

Cerebral cortex: The surface layer of gray matter of the brain associated with higher mental processes.

Childhood hyperkinesis: Moderately and markedly severe personality patterns evidenced in childhood, and characterized by crankiness, pouting, behavioral unpredictability and erratic moods.

Childhood symbiosis: Moderate and markedly severe passive-dependent personality patterns evidenced in childhood, and characterized by a gross immaturity and a pathological attachment to caretakers.

Chemotherapy: Pharmaceutical treatment.

Choleria: Dimension of temperament signifying a disposition to irritability and hostility.

Cholinergic: Tending to activate the parasympathetic nervous system.

Chorea: Involuntary spasmodic movements of head and extremities.

Chronic disorders: Longstanding impairments that are likely to be permanent.

Chromosomes: Separable rod-like bodies found in the nucleus of cells. They contain the genes.

Circumstantiality: Intruding and elaborating irrelevant or trivial details in conversation.

Claustrophobia: Anxiety displaced symbolically in a fear of closed places.

Clinical picture: Current status of patient based on a cross-sectional analysis of behavioral, phenomenological, intrapsychic and biophysical data.

Cognitive processes: Modes of thought, knowing and symbolic representation, including comprehension, judgment, memory, imagining and reasoning.

Coma: Stupor and unconsciousness.

Commitment: Legal procedure for mandatory hospitalization of persons suffering severe mental impairments.

Compensation: Intrapsychic mechanism by which undesirable traits are cloaked and overcome by accentuating or strengthening a more desirable one.

Competence: Capacity to function in one's environment independent of assistance and supervision.

Compulsion: Irresistible and repetitive urge to engage in an act that is recognized as irrational.

Compulsive personality: Mild pathological pattern characterized by rigid and conforming behaviors and associated with passive-ambivalent coping strategy.

Concepts: Symbols or labels employed to represent phenomena relevant to a theory.

Concordance: Presence of a trait in both members of a twin pair.

Concrete thinking: Impaired ability to reflect and generalize; thinking limited to the world of immediate stimuli.

Conditioning: A process of learning in which a response comes to be elicited by a stimulus that formerly did not elicit that response.

Conflict: Presence of opposing or incompatible desires or demands.

Confusion: Disturbed orientation, clouded consciousness and muddled thinking.

Congenital: Present from birth.

Consciousness: State of awareness.

Consonance: Attitudes, emotions or events that are compatible.

Constitution: Intrinsic and relatively enduring biological characteristics.

Contiguity: A principle that claims that the essential feature of learning is the closeness of association in space or time between two events.

Contingent: Signifying dependence on special associated circumstances.

Continuum: A continuous dimension or scale such that additional points may always be found between any two points.

Control group: Subjects used for comparison purposes in research to insure that incidental variables do not account for the study's results.

Control level: Capacity to cope effectively under conditions of stress.

Conversion disorder: Neurotic syndrome in which anxiety is converted, unconsciously and symbolically, into a loss or alteration of a sensory or motor function.

Correlates: Characteristics or scores that are related or vary such that changes in one are accompanied by predictable changes in the others.

Criterion: A measure or event that serves as a standard for judging other measures or events.

Critical period: A stage in neuropsychological maturation when certain forms of experience have notably pronounced effects; also known as "sensitive periods."

Cycloid personality: Moderately severe or borderline pathological patterns associated with various dependent and ambivalent instrumental strategies.

Cyclophrenic personality: Markedly severe or decompensated pathological pattern associated with various dependent and ambivalent instrumental strategies.

Decompensated personality patterns: A marked level of pathological severity in personality functioning; there are three major subtypes—schizophrenia, cyclophrenia and paraphrenia—each characterized in part by social invalidism, cognitive disorganization and feelings of estrangement.

Decompensation: Progressive personality disintegration evidenced in the loss of cognitive and emotional controls and in decreased reality awareness.

Defense mechanism: An unconscious process in which unpleasant or anxiety-producing events are denied or distorted; also known as "intrapsychic mechanism."

Dejection disorder: A neurotic syndrome characterized by worrisomeness, guilt feelings and mild depression.

Delirium: A markedly confused state characterized by excitement, incoherence and disorientation; illusions and hallucinations are often present.

Delusion: A false belief maintained despite objective evidence to the contrary.

Delusion disorder: A psychotic syndrome characterized chiefly by the presence of delusions.

Dementia praecox: Obsolescent term for schizophrenia.

Demonology: Early belief that evil spirits determine the behavior of man.

Denial mechanisms: A group of intrapsychic processes that enable the individual to keep from consciousness intolerable thoughts, perceptions or feelings, e.g., repression, isolation or projection.

Dependence: Reliance on others for support and the satisfaction of needs.

Depersonalization: Feeling of self-estrangement and unreality.

Detachment: Social disaffiliation or self-alienation.

Deviancy: Traits at the quantitative extremes of the normal curve.

Diagnosis: Description, identification and labeling of a pathological condition.

Discordance: Presence of a trait in only one member of a twin pair.

Discrimination: In perception, the ability to detect or react differently to objectively dissimilar stimuli.

Diseases: Pathological conditions traceable primarily to impairments in the biological substrate.

Displacement: Intrapsychic mechanism by which emotions are transferred from their original object to a more acceptable substitute.

Dissociation disorder: A neurotic syndrome in which normally associated segments of memory and thought are split off from each other, e.g., amnesia or somnambulism.

Dissonance: Attitudes, emotions or events that are incompatible.

Distortion mechanisms: A group of intrapsychic processes that enable the person to transform and disguise intolerable thoughts, feelings and memories so as to make them personally and socially more acceptable, e.g., fantasy, rationalization and sublimation.

Dizygotic twins: Twins from separate ova; fraternal twins.

Double bind: Communications containing intrinsically contradictory requests that "trap" the recipient since he cannot provide a satisfactory response.

Drives: Innate or learned forces that prompt certain forms of behavior and sensitize the organism to respond to relevant associated stimuli.

DSM-II: The official classification of psychopathological conditions published in 1968 under the title "Diagnostic and Statistical Manual of Mental Disorders" by the American Psychiatric Association.

Dysfunction: Impaired or disturbed functioning.

Echolalia: Automatic and meaningless repetition by a patient of what is said to him.

Echopraxia: Repetitive and automatic imitation by a patient of another person's movements.

Ectomorphy: Term employed by Sheldon to represent the body dimension of thinness, linearity and fragility.

Ego: Term employed by intrapsychic theorists to represent that division of the personality structure associated with mediating and resolving conflicts between the instinctual drives of the "id," the prohibitions and ideals of the "super-ego" and the reality conditions of the environment.

Egocentric: Preoccupied with self needs, and lacking interest and concern for those of others; in contrast to narcissism, egocentricity does not necessarily signify a high opinion of self.

Ego-dystonia: Feelings and behaviors exhibited by the patient which are experienced as alien or repugnant to his conception of himself.

Ego strength: The capacity of the patient to cope with the stresses of life.

Ego-syntonia: Feelings and behaviors exhibited by the patient which are experienced as consonant with his conception of himself.

Electroconvulsive therapy (ECT): A form of biological treatment in which an electric current is passed through the brain to produce a convulsion.

Electroencephalograph (EEG): Graphic recording of brain potentials.

Empathy: Insightful awareness of and ability to share the emotions, thoughts and behaviors of another person.

Empirical: Pertaining to observable and tangible events.

Encounter group: A therapeutic group technique designed to focus on personal growth through the direct expression of feelings among participating members.

Endocrine glands: Ductless glands that secrete hormones into the lymph or blood stream.

Endogenous: Pertaining to causal influences that originate from sources within the patient.

Endomorphy: Term employed by Sheldon to represent the body dimension of fat, softness and rotundity.

Environment: External conditions capable of influencing an organism.

Environmental management: A general category of therapy referring to methods that exploit the patient's family, social and work surroundings for purposes of treatment and rehabilitation, e.g., casework or milieu therapy.

Enzyme: Organic catalysts that modify other organic substances.

Epidemiology: Study of the statistical location and distribution of pathological conditions.

Epilepsy: A brain disorder characterized by convulsions and a loss of consciousness.

Epinephrine: The principal hormone secreted by the adrenal medulla; it stimulates energy mobilization and body alertness.

Erotic: Pertaining to sexual impulses.

Estrangement: A variant of the dissociative disorder signifying a feeling that ordinarily well-known objects, persons and events seem different, unreal or distant.

Etiology: Study of the causation of pathological conditions.

Existential anxiety: An intense state of personal discomfort deriving from an inability to find a meaningful identity and satisfying goal in life.

Exogenous: Pertaining to causal influences that originate from sources other than from within the patient himself.

Exorcism: An ancient practice of incantation designed to purge demonic spirits from the minds of men.

Extinction: In learning, the elimination of an acquired response.

Extravert: A personality type formulated by Jung to represent highly sociable, impulsive and emotionally expressive persons.

Factor: (a) A generic term for a distinctive psychological function, trait or influence; (b) In statistics, an independent psychological attribute derived from commonalities exhibited in behavior or test performance.

Familial: Pertaining to the family or to characteristics that tend to occur frequently in particular families.

Family therapy: A form of treatment in which the entire family, rather than any single member, is the prime focus of therapy.

Fantasy: Daydreaming; an intrapsychic mechanism in which unconscious conflicts are resolved and unconscious desires are gratified through fanciful imagination.

Fixation: An intrapsychic mechanism in which the normal developmental progression is arrested and the patient persists in behaving at an immature level in order to avoid the conflicts and challenges typical of his chronological age.

Flexibility: Capacity or inclination to change habitual behaviors in accord with changing circumstances.

Flight of ideas: Fragmentary skipping from one verbalized but unfinished idea to another with no logical progression.

Focal lesion: A defect that is localized in a circumscribed brain area.

Fragmentation disorder: A psychotic syndrome, more commonly known as hebephrenia, characterized by marked cognitive, emotional and behavioral disorganization.

Free association: An intrapsychic technique of therapy in which the patient is asked to relax his usual controls and to verbalize every passing thought and emotion.

Frontal lobe: The most anterior region of the cerebral cortex, serving as the primary substrate for higher thought processes.

Frustration: Experiencing the thwarting of a desire or need.

Gene: A submicroscopic unit of inheritance arranged within the chromosomes.

General paresis: Synonym for chronic neurosyphilis.

Generalization: Transfer of learnings acquired in one situation to another situation that is somewhat similar to the first.

Genetic factors: Inherited influences or dispositions.

Genital: Pertaining to the sexual organs.

Gerontology: Study of old age.

Guilt: Feelings of self-depreciation and apprehension stemming from engaging in thoughts or behaviors that are forbidden or run contrary to one's conscience.

Habit: A repetitive mode of response.

Hallucination: A perception that has no basis in external reality.

Hallucinogen: Chemical agent that produces hallucinations; also known as psychotomimetic drug.

Hebephrenia: An acute schizophrenic disorder characterized by cognitive fragmenting and emotional disorganization.

Heredity: Genetic transmission of traits from parent to child.

Heterogeneous: Composed of dissimilar characteristics throughout.

Heterozygous: Carrying both a dominant and recessive gene for a particular trait.

Homeostasis: Maintaining optimal constancy and balance among physiological processes.

Homogeneous: Composed of similar characteristics throughout.

Hormone: Chemical substance secreted by endocrine glands to stimulate and regulate physiological processes.

Hostile excitement disorder: A psychotic syndrome, more commonly known as manic excitement, characterized by irrational anger and uninhibited aggressiveness.

Humanistic theory: A group of theories, largely stimulated by A. H. Maslow, designed to focus on the worth of each individual and his efforts at self-actualization.

Hyperkinesia: Excessive motor activity.

Hypermnesia: Unusually retentive memory.

Hypnosis: Trance-like state of high suggestibility induced artificially by another person.

Hypochondriacal disorder: A neurotic syndrome in which there is a persistent and exaggerated concern about diminished health and energy in the absence of demonstrable organic pathology.

Hypothalamus: Complex of neural cells at the base of the brain involved in the regulation and expression of emotion and motivation.

Hypothesis: A provisional explanation set forth for purposes of empirical confirmation or disconfirmation.

Hysteria: Traditional diagnostic label for conversion and dissociative neurotic disorders.

Hysterical personality: Mildly severe or basic pathological pattern, characterized by a superficial gregariousness and associated with an active-dependent instrumental strategy.

Id: Term employed by intrapsychic theorists to represent that division of the personality structure associated with primitive instinctual impulses.

Identification: An intrapsychic mechanism in which the individual associates himself with another person, group or movement, usually as a means of enhancing his feelings of self-worth.

Idiopathic: Of unknown causation, and presumed to be inherent in the individual's constitutional make-up.

Illusion: Misinterpretation or false perception of a real sensory experience.

Impassive disorder: A psychotic syndrome, more commonly known as catatonic withdrawal, characterized by mutism, emotional apathy and social withdrawal.

Implicit learning: Acquiring new ideas and behaviors through reflective thought and imaginative self-reinforcement.

Imprinting: Learning to associate a biologically disposed response to a specific stimulus pattern in early maturation.

Impulse: With reference to behavior, the urge to act.

Impulsive: Pertaining to the tendency to act out desires without reflecting on their consequences.

Inadequate personality: Mildly severe or basic pathological pattern, characterized by a lack of assertiveness and self-confidence and associated with a passive-dependent instrumental strategy.

Incidence: Frequency or rate of occurrence of new cases in a specified time period.

Incoherence: Disconnected and difficult to understand communications.

Incontinence: Loss of bladder or bowel control.

Independence: Capacity or disposition for self-reliance.

Infantile autism: A markedly severe passive-detached personality pattern evidenced in early childhood, and characterized by mutism, interpersonal indifference and repetitive meaningless acts.

Inferred concepts: Terms representing deductions or generalizations based on observable clinical signs.

Inhibition: The restraint of urges, usually those considered to be socially disapproved.

Innate: Inborn.

Inpatient: Institutionalized patient.

Insanity: A legal term for severe mental impairments in which the person is judged incapable of assuming responsibility for his actions.

Insight: Seeing meaningful relationships and understanding their psychological significance.

Instinct: Inherited disposition to behavior that is characteristic of all members of a species.

Instrumental behavior: Activities that are executed to effect changes in the environment.

Instrumental learning: Acquiring new responses on the basis of their capacity to produce reinforcements.

Instrumental strategy: A person's basic and characteristic pattern of approaching his environment so as to maximize achieving positive reinforcements and minimize experiencing negative reinforcements.

Intracortical-initiative stage: Third stage of neuropsychological development beginning at about four years of age and extending through adolescence; characterized by the rapid proliferation of higher cortical connections, and enabling the growing child to reflect, plan and act in novel ways independent of parental supervision.

Intrapsychic level: Data and concepts representing processes that take place beneath the level of awareness, i.e., in the unconscious.

Intrapsychic reconstruction: Therapies designed to make the patient aware of his unconscious drives and conflicts, and to rework them for purposes of reorganizing the patient's personality.

Introjection: An intrapsychic mechanism in which the attributes of other persons are internalized and assumed to be true of oneself.

Introvert: A personality type formulated by Jung to represent socially awkward, emotionally reserved and self-absorbed persons.

Isolation: An intrapsychic mechanism in which the association between a thought and its accompanying emotion is separated.

Labile: Pertaining to instability or changeability, especially with regard to emotions.

Latent: Pertaining to a disposition that is dormant or inactive.

Learned behavior reactions: A group of behaviors, judged abnormal but acquired in the same manner in which most learnings are acquired; they tend to be stimulus-specific and circumscribed behaviors, rather than pervasive styles of functioning.

Lesion: Neural tissue damage due to injury or disease.

Life style: Roughly, personality pattern.

Limbic system: Neural structures located at the base of the cerebral hemispheres (notably the amygdala, septal nuclei and hypothalamus) involved in the activation and expression of emotions.

Linkage: Connection between two or more genes that increases the probability that they will be inherited together.

Logorrhea: Excessive and often incoherent speech.

Maladaptive: Pertaining to deficient or inappropriate responses to environmental circumstances.

Mania: A suffix denoting extreme preoccupation with a specific idea or activity, e.g., kleptomania (inclinations to steal) or nymphomania (excessive desire of females for intercourse).

Manic-depressive illness: Markedly severe psychopathological conditions characterized by intense and often alternating moods.

Mannerism: A repeated, peculiar and stereotyped gesture or posture.

Masochism: Obtaining gratification, usually sexual, through the experience of pain.

Masturbation: Genital self-stimulation for sexual pleasure.

Maturation: Sequence of development in which initially diffuse structures of the body progressively unfold into specific functional units.

Mechanism: Intrapsychic (unconscious) processes employed to deny or distort discomforting thoughts or emotions, e.g., repression, rationalization and sublimation.

Mecholyl: A chemical agent that leads to a brief drop in blood pressure.

Medical model: An approach to psychological abnormalities that suggests that these abnormalities are akin to physical diseases.

Melancholia: Dimension of temperament signifying a tendency to experience sadness and pain; also used as a synonym for depression.

Menopause: Period in middle life when menstruation stops.

Mental illness: General term to signify the presence of a psychological disorder. The implication of an underlying physical disease suggested by the word "illness" has led many professionals to drop the term.

Mesomorphy: Term employed by Sheldon to represent the body dimension of skeletal breadth and muscularity.

Milieu therapy: Environmental management within a hospital setting to promote the patient's social rehabilitation.

MMPI (Minnesota Multiphasic Personality Inventory):   An empirically designed self-report personality questionnaire designed to facilitate psychopathological diagnosis.

Model: (a) A person whose behavior and attitudes are imitated. (b) A schema or system that provides a suggestive framework for a theory.

Monozygotic twins: Twins developed from a single ovum; identical twins.

Mood: Prevailing or characteristic emotional state.

Morbid: Pathological.

Morphology: The study of body structures; also employed to represent the manifestations of body forms.

Motivation: A state characterized by increased activation and drive-fulfillment. See *Drives*.

Motor rigidity disorder: A psychotic syndrome, more commonly known as catatonic rigidity, characterized by mutism, the assumption of inflexible postures and resistance to social suggestions.

Multidimensional approach: An orientation that takes into consideration several variables and theoretical schemas in the analysis of a problem.

Mutism: Inability or refusal to speak.

Narcissistic personality: Mildly severe or basic pathological pattern characterized by high self-regard and exploitive behaviors and associated with passive-independent instrumental strategy.

Negative reinforcement: Any condition that weakens the strength of a response with which it is associated, leading usually to the acquisition of alternative responses.

Negativistic personality: Mildly severe or basic pathological pattern characterized by the rapid vacillation of moods and behaviors and associated with active-ambivalent instrumental strategy.

Neologism: A new word, usually condensed from several conventional words, and having special meaning to the patient who coined it.

Neurohormone: Chemical substance involved in neural impulse transmission; also known as neurohumor.

Neuron: Individual nerve cell.

Neuropsychological stages: Broad periods of development during which stimulus experiences have particularly pronounced effects on the maturation of neural structures and their associated psychological functions.

Neurotic disorders: A group of syndromes often seen in patients with only mild degrees of personality decompensation; characterized by dramatic symptoms (e.g., phobias or conversions) that reflect attempts to solicit social support while discharging unconscious anxieties and hostilities in disguised form. Also referred to as neurosis and psychoneurosis.

Normal: Typical of a particular social group; in the central region of a bell-shaped curve; nonclinical or lacking in pathology.

Nosology: Systematic classification of pathological conditions.

Obsession: Repetitive idea that is recognized as irrational, but cannot be dismissed from thought.

Obsession-compulsion disorder: A neurotic syndrome characterized by the persistence of unwanted thoughts or impulses which cannot be terminated by reason or without a consequent feeling of anxiety.

Organic impairments: Psychopathology due primarily to tissue damage or physiological dysfunction.

Outcome research: Studies concerned with the overall efficacy or success of treatment techniques.

Outpatient: A noninstitutionalized patient receiving treatment.

Overdetermination: A term signifying the confluence of several influences in shaping a single symptom.

Overt signs: Observable clinical indices.

Paranoid personality: Moderately severe or borderline pathological pattern associated with various independent and ambivalent instrumental strategies.

Paraphrenic personality: Markedly severe or decompensated pathological pattern associated with various independent and ambivalent instrumental strategies.

Parasympathetic nervous system: Division of the autonomic nervous system that is generally inhibitory in function.

Parmia: Dimension of temperament signifying a disposition to fearlessness and venturesomeness.

Passive: Pertaining to indirect and minimally displayed instrumental behaviors.

Passive-ambivalence: A basic instrumental strategy characterized by rigid behavior, social conformity and the repression of all contrary thoughts and feelings.

Passive-dependence: A basic instrumental strategy characterized by socially submissive and clinging behaviors, and by a self-image of inadequacy and incompetence.

Passive-detachment: A basic instrumental strategy characterized by emotional apathy and social indifference.

Passive-independence: A basic instrumental strategy characterized by narcissistic attitudes, self-confidence and interpersonal exploitation.

Pathogenic: Conducive to pathology.

Pathognomonic: Characteristic of symptoms that are typical and somewhat distinctive to a particular diagnostic syndrome.

Pathological personality pattern: A broad class of syndromes characterized by deeply ingrained and pervasively maladaptive styles of life.

Pathology: The study of impaired mental or physical functions. Also employed as a general synonym for the manifestations of these conditions.

Perseveration: Involuntary continuation and repetition of a behavioral response once it has been initiated.

Phases of epigenesis: Erikson's formulation of the stages of psychosocial and ego development; these parallel but extend the range of Freud's psychosexual stages.

Phenomenological level: Data and concepts representing subjective states or reports of conscious experience.

Phenomenological reorientation: Therapies that focus on redirecting the patient's self-defeating attitudes toward life.

Phenylketonuria (PKU): A congenital defect of protein metabolism resulting in profound mental retardation.

Phobic disorder: A neurotic syndrome in which unconscious anxiety is kept from awareness by displacing it onto a symbolic substitute in the environment that can be actively avoided.

Placebo: A procedure or inactive substance that simulates a form of treatment; although possessing no intrinsic therapeutic merit, it is often associated with beneficial results.

Polygenic: Signifying the influence of several simultaneously operating genes in the expression of a manifest trait.

Positive reinforcement: Any condition that strengthens the learning of a response with which it is associated.

Posturing: Unusual positions maintained for long periods.

Precipitating cause: A stressful event occurring shortly before the overt manifestation of psychopathology.

Predisposing cause: A source of influence in the patient's past, or a latent disposition within his personality make-up, that inclines him to succumb to psychopathology under conditions of stress.

Premorbid: Existing prior to manifest pathology.

Prenatal: Pertaining to development before birth.

Prepotent: Dominant or ascendant.

Prevalence: Total number of cases currently existing in a given population at any particular time.

Process research: Studies concerned with unraveling those ingredients of a therapeutic technique associated with its efficacy or success.

Prodromal: Pertaining to an early sign of pathology.

Prognosis: Prediction of the course and outcome of a pathological condition.

Projection: An intrapsychic mechanism in which the person denies his own unacceptable traits and impulses and ascribes them to others.

Projective technique: A personality test consisting of partially unstructured stimuli designed to reveal the subject's unexpressed attitudes, conflicts and coping strategies.

Psychiatric social work: Field of social work concerned with the environmental management and counseling of psychiatric patients.

Psychiatry: Field of medicine concerned with the diagnosis and treatment of psychopathological conditions.

Psychoanalysis: A school of psychopathology founded by Sigmund Freud oriented to the understanding of intrapsychic processes and their development, and to the treatment of psychiatric conditions by methods that expose the unconscious elements of personality functioning.

Psychogenic: Traceable to psychological experiences and learning.

Psychopathology: Field of medicine and psychology concerned with the study of maladaptive behavior, its etiology, development, diagnosis and therapy. Also employed as a general synonym for the manifestations of these conditions.

Psychopharmacology: The study of the effects of biochemicals upon the brain; also, the process of treating abnormal psychological conditions through the use of drugs.

Psychophysiologic disorders: A group of syndromes signifying the presence of structural organic impairments attributable to psychogenic influences and their accompanying persistent physiological tensions. Also known as psychosomatic disorders.

Psychotherapy: A general term for treatment by psychological procedures.

Psychotic disorders: A group of syndromes signifying a transient episode of markedly severe psychopathology, and characterized by bizarre coping efforts or the disintegration of such efforts (e.g., agitated depression, catatonic rigidity or hebephrenic fragmentation).

Puberty: Period during early adolescence when secondary sex characteristics appear.

Randomization: Method of selecting research samples and assigning subjects to them that assures that each member of the population has an equal chance of being chosen and assigned to the various groups, thereby minimizing the possibility of bias in the results.

Rapport: Reciprocal feelings of comfort, acceptance and confidence between therapist and patient.

Rationalization: An intrapsychic mechanism in which consciously logical explanations and justifications are provided to account for unconsciously unacceptable feelings, thoughts and actions.

Reaction formation: An intrapsychic mechanism in which intolerable feelings or thoughts are repressed and their converse are expressed.

Regression: An intrapsychic mechanism in which the patient retreats to an earlier and less mature style of functioning in response to current stress.

Reinforcement: Any condition that alters the strength of a response with which it is associated. See *Positive reinforcement* and *Negative reinforcement.*

Reliability: The degree to which a measuring device produces the same results with the same subjects from one time to another.

Remedial approach: A general term for methods of management and treatment of pathological conditions.

Remission: A period of significant improvement following a pathological condition.

Repetition compulsion: An unconscious tendency to recreate earlier experiences and to engage again in the maladaptive responses with which they were formerly approached.

Repression: An intrapsychic mechanism in which painful memories and impulses are expunged and kept from consciousness.

Resistance: Opposition to therapeutic efforts, especially a defensive reluctance to explore repressed material.

Retarded depression disorder: A psychotic syndrome characterized by a sad and woeful look, a stooped posture and gloomy disconsolate verbalizations.

Reticular formation: Neural fibers that sweep between the brain and spinal cord and are known to be involved in maintaining and controlling alertness and arousal; they are believed by some theorists to serve as a relay station for coordinating impulses among lower and upper brain centers.

Retrograde amnesia: Loss of memory for experiences that occurred shortly prior to a trauma or shock.

Rigidity: Inability or resistance to change habitual behaviors in accord with changing circumstances.

Rorschach test: A projective technique consisting of ten standard inkblots.

Sadism: Obtaining gratification, usually sexual, by inflicting pain upon others.

Sample: A group of subjects selected for research purposes; preferably, they should be representative of the population to which the results will be generalized.

Schizoid personality: Moderately severe or borderline pathological pattern associated with detached instrumental strategies.

Schizophrenia: A group of syndromes including both acute psychotic disorders and severe personality decompensation characterized by withdrawal behaviors and emotional and cognitive disorganization.

Schizophrenic personality: Markedly severe or decompensated pathological pattern associated with detached instrumental strategies.

Secondary gain: Advantages gained through a neurotic symptom other than the reduction of anxiety.

Self-actualization: The drive to realize one's inherent potentials.

Self-image: The person's conception of his own traits and their worth.

Self-perpetuation: Tendency to create conditions that accentuate and intensify traits already present within oneself.

Sensitive developmental period: See *Critical period.*

Sensorimotor-autonomy stage: Second stage of neuropsychological development, extending in its peak development roughly between 12 months and six years of age; noted by the rapid differentiation of motor capacities and their integration with established sensory functions, enabling the young child to assume a measure of independence through increasingly skillful locomotion, manipulation and verbalization.

Sensory-attachment stage: First stage of neuropsychological development, generally from birth to 18 months, evidencing rapid maturation of sensory receptors and characterized by dependency of the infant upon others.

Sequelae: Residual symptoms following an acute pathological condition.

Serendipity: The art of accidental discovery.

Shaping: An instrumental learning procedure in which a series of small steps toward an ultimate larger set of behaviors are specified, stimulated and reinforced.

Sibling: Offspring of the same parents.

Social competence: Range of skills for living effectively in normal community life.

Sociopathic disorders: A group of syndromes characterized by a disdain for social responsibilities and conventions, and a lack of interpersonal loyalty.

Somatotype: Physique or body build.

Stereotype: A prejudiced and difficult to alter conception of the traits of others.

Stimuli: Events that impinge upon the organism.

Stimulus nutriment: Concept formulated by Rapaport to signify the periodic stimulation needed to facilitate the development of ego capacities.

Stress: Any condition — biological or psychological — that taxes the coping capacities of a person.

Stupor: State of lethargy or unresponsiveness.

Sublimation: An intrapsychic mechanism in which unacceptable or thwarted impulses are channeled into socially approved substitute activities.

Superego: Term employed by intrapsychic theorists to represent that division of personality structure associated with social prohibitions and morality.

Supportive therapy: Methods designed to re-establish the patient's normal equilibrium or mode of functioning, usually during periods of stress.

Symbolization: An unconscious process by which one idea or object comes to represent another.

Sympathetic nervous system: That division of the autonomic nervous system active in preparing the individual for emergency situations.

Symptom: A clinically significant sign.

Symptom disorders: A broad group of syndromes characterized by the emergence of distinctive and often dramatic clinical signs; these disorders occur in pathological personality patterns under conditions of special stress; the symptoms exhibited stand out in sharp relief against the patients' more prosaic symptomatology.

Synapse: Junction where impulses from one neuron pass to another.

Syndrome: A constellation of symptoms that covary and are more or less distinctive of a particular pathological condition.

Systematic desensitization: A form of behavior modification designed to replace maladaptive responses by interposing a competing adaptive behavior.

Systemic: Pertaining to or affecting the body as a whole.

T-group: Training group. A variant of the newer group methods for educating or treating difficulties in interpersonal behavior.

Temperament: Constitutional disposition to react emotionally.

Theory: A framework of concepts and hypothesized propositions from which empirical events can be explained and predicted.

Therapy: Generic term for treatment of pathological conditions.

Threctia: Dimension of temperament signifying a disposition to fearfulness.

Token economy: A method of behavior modification based on selective positive reinforcement; characterized by disbursing valuable tokens for the performance of adaptive behaviors.

Toxic: Poisonous.

Trait: A more or less enduring characteristic of a person.

Tranquilizer: A psychopharmacologic drug designed to sedate the patient by blocking the biochemical basis of anxiety and tension.

Transference: In therapy, an unconscious tendency to generalize to the therapist attitudes and feelings learned in relation to one's parents.

Transient situational reactions: A group of syndromes, found in basically nonpathological personalities, characterized by pathological responses, usually of relatively brief duration, to objectively stressful stimulus conditions.

Trauma: Severe physical or psychological injury.

Tremor: Continuous and involuntary spasms involving a small group of muscles.

Typology: A system for grouping persons into relatively distinctive classes on the basis of a single dominant characteristic.

Unconscious: Out of awareness; in intrapsychic theory, the portion of the psyche containing repressed memories and emotions that cannot be brought to awareness except through special techniques such as hypnosis and free-association.

Undoing: An intrapsychic mechanism in which guilt for past misdeeds is atoned for through symbolic acts of expiation.

Vacillation: Fluctuating between two or more choices.

Validity: In general, the extent to which a hypothesis is empirically verified, or a test measures what it purports to measure.

Variable: A trait or characteristic in which events or people differ.

Verbigeration: Meaningless repetition of words or sentences.

Vicarious learning: Acquisition of behaviors or attitudes without direct experience, usually through incidental observation or imitation.

Vicious circle: Sequences in which certain attempts to solve problems tend to perpetuate these problems and create new ones.

Waxy flexibility: A willingness to assume any physical position molded by others.

Withdrawal symptoms: Clinical signs which appear upon the termination of drug use among those who have been physiologically addicted to it.

Word salad: Incoherent jumble of meaningful words and neologisms.

BIBLIOGRAPHY

Abel, G. G., Levis, D. J., and Clancy, J. Aversion therapy applied to taped sequences of deviant behavior in exhibitionism and other sexual deviations: A preliminary report. *J. Behav. Res. Exp. Psychiat.*, *1*(1), 59–66, 1970.

Abraham, K. *Selected Papers.* London: Hogarth Press, 1927.

Ackerman, N. W. *The Psychodynamics of Family Life.* New York: Basic Books, 1958.

Agras, W. S. An investigation of the decrement of anxiety responses during systematic desensitization therapy. *Beh. Res. Ther.*, *2*, 267–270, 1965.

Ainsworth, M. D. S. Attachment and dependency: A comparison. In J. Gewirtz (ed.), *Attachment and Dependency.* Washington: Winston, 1972.

Alanen, Y. O. The families of schizophrenic patients. *Proc. Roy. Soc. Med.*, *63*, 227–230, 1970.

Albee, G. W. Through the looking glass. *Int'l. J. Psychiat.*, *9*, 293–298, 1970.

Alexander, D. A. Senile dementia: A changing perspective. *Brit. J. Psychiat.*, *121*, 207–214, 1972.

Alexander, F. *Psychosomatic Medicine.* New York: Norton, 1950.

Alexander, F. *Psychoanalysis of the Total Personality.* New York: Nervous and Mental Disease Publications, 1930.

Alexander, F., French, T. M., and Pollock, G. H. *Psychosomatic Specificity.* Vol. 1. *Experimental Study and Results.* Chicago: University of Chicago Press, 1968.

Alexander, L. *Treatment of Mental Disorder.* Philadelphia: Saunders, 1953.

Allen, F. The psychopathic delinquent child: Round table. *Amer. J. Orthopsychiat.*, *20*, 223–265, 1950.

Allen, F. *Psychotherapy with Children.* New York: Norton, 1942.

Altschule, M. *Bodily Physiology in Mental and Emotional Disorders.* New York: Grune and Stratton, 1953.

Amante, D., Margules, P. H., Hartmann, D. M., Storey, D. B., and Weeber, L. J. The epidemiological distribution of CNS dysfunction. *J. Social Issues*, *26*, 105–136, 1970.

American Psychiatric Association, *Diagnostic and Statistical Manual of Mental Disorders.* Washington, D.C.: Mental Hospitals Service, 1952, 1968.

Anastasi, A. Heredity, environment, and the question "how"? *Psychol. Rev.*, *65*, 197–208, 1958.

Anderson, R. E. Where's Dad? Paternal deprivation and delinquency. *Arch. Gen. Psychiat.*, *18*(6), 641–649, 1968.

Apfelberg, B., Sugar, C., and Pfeffer, A. Z. A psychiatric study of 250 sex offenders. *Amer. J. Psychiat.*, *100*, 762–800, 1944.

Apperson, L. D., and McAdoo, W. G., Jr. Parental factors in the childhood of homosexuals. *J. Abn. Psychol.*, *73*, 201–206, 1968.

Argyris, C. *Interpersonal Competence and Organizational Effectiveness.* Homewood, Ill.: Dorsey Press, 1962.

Arnhoff, F. N., et al. *Manpower for Mental Health.* Chicago: Aldine, 1969.

Aronfreed, J. The concept of internalization. In D. Goslin (ed.), *Handbook of Socialization Theory and Research.* Chicago: R. McNally, 1969.

Aronfreed, J. *Conduct and Conscience: The Socialization of Internalized Control over Behavior.* New York: Academic Press, 1968.

Ash, P. The reliability of psychiatric diagnosis. *J. Abnorm. Soc. Psychol.*, *44*, 272–277, 1949.

Ax, A. F. Emotional learning deficits common to schizophrenias and other motivational disorders. *Biol. Psychiat.*, *2*, 251–260, 1970.

Axline, V. M. *Play Therapy.* Boston: Houghton Mifflin, 1947.

Ayllon, T., and Azrin, N. H. *The Token Economy: A Motivational System for Therapy and Reha-bilitation.* New York: Appleton-Century-Crofts, 1968.

Ayllon, T., and Azrin, N. H. The measurement and reinforcement of behavior in psychot-ics. *J. Exp. Anal. Beh., 8,* 357–383, 1965.

Ayllon, T., and Michael, J. L. The psychiatric nurse as a behavioral engineer. *J. Exp. Anal. Beh., 2,* 323–334, 1959.

Azima, H. Prolonged sleep treatment in mental disorders. *J. Ment. Sci., 101,* 593–599, 1955.

Bachrach, A. J., Erwin, W. J., and Mohr, J. P. The control of eating behavior in an anorexic by operant conditioning techniques. In Ullmann, L., and Krasner, L. (eds.), *Case Studies of Behavior Modification.* New York: Holt, Rinehart and Winston, 1965.

Bagby, E. The etiology of phobias. *J. Abnorm. Soc. Psychol., 17,* 16–18, 1922.

Baldwin, A. L. A cognitive theory of socialization. In D. Goslin (ed.), *Handbook of Socializa-tion Theory and Research.* Chicago: R. McNally, 1969.

Bandura, A. *Principles of Behavior Modification.* New York: Holt, Rinehart and Winston, 1969.

Bandura, A. Social-learning theory of the identificatory process. In D. Goslin (ed.), *Hand-book of Socialization Theory and Research.* Chicago: R. McNally, 1969.

Bandura, A. A social learning interpretation of psychological dysfunctions. In London, P., and Rosenhan, D. (eds.), *Foundations of Abnormal Psychology.* New York: Holt, Rinehart and Winston, 1968.

Bandura, A. Behavioral modification through modeling procedures. In Krasner, L., and Ullmann, L. (eds.), *Research in Behavior Modification.* New York: Holt, Rinehart and Winston, 1965.

Bandura, A. Social learning through imitation. In Jones, M. R. (ed.), *Nebraska Symposium on Motivation.* Lincoln: Univ. of Nebraska Press, 1962.

Bandura, A. Psychotherapy as a learning process. *Psychol. Bull., 58,* 143–159, 1961.

Bandura, A., Grusec, J. E. and Menlove, F. L. Vicarious extinction of avoidance behavior. *J. Pers. Soc. Psychol., 5,* 16–23, 1967.

Bandura, A., and Huston, A. C. Identification as a process of incidental learning. *J. Ab-norm. Soc. Psychol., 63,* 311–318, 1961.

Bandura, A., and Walters, R. H. *Social Learning and Personality Development.* New York: Holt, Rinehart and Winston, 1963.

Bandura, A., and Walters, R. H. *Adolescent Aggression.* New York: Ronald, 1959.

Barbara, D. (ed.) *The Psychotherapy of Stuttering.* Springfield, Ill.: Thomas, 1962.

Barrett, C. L. Systematic desensitization versus implosive therapy. *J. Abn. Psychol., 74,* 587–592, 1969.

Barthell, C. N. and Holmes, D. S. High school yearbooks: A nonreactive measure of social isolation in graduates who later became schizophrenics. *J. Abn. Psychol., 73,* 313–316, 1968.

Bateson, G., Jackson, D. D., Haley, J., and Weakland, J. H. Toward a theory of schi-zophrenia. *Beh. Sci., 1,* 251–264, 1956.

Bateson, G., and Ruesch, J. *Communication, the Social Matrix of Psychiatry.* New York: Nor-ton, 1951.

Baumrind, D., and Black, A. E. Socialization practices associated with dimensions of com-petence in preschool boys and girls. *Child Development, 38,* 291–327, 1967.

Bayley, N. Development of mental abilities. In P. H. Mussen (ed.), *Carmichael's Manual of Child Psychology.* New York: Wiley, 1970.

Beach, F., and Jaynes, J. Effects of early experience upon the behavior of animals. *Psychol. Bull., 51,* 239–262, 1954.

Beck, A. T. Cognition, affect and psychopathology. *Arch. Gen. Psychiat., 24,* 495–500, 1971.

Beck, A. T. Thinking and depression: Idiosyncratic content and cognitive distortions. *A.M.A. Arch. Gen. Psychiat., 9,* 324–333, 1963.

Becker, W. C. Consequences of different kinds of parental discipline. In Hoffman, M., and Hoffman, L. (eds.), *Review of Child Development Research.* Vol. I. New York: Russell Sage, 1964.

Becker, W. C. The process-reactive distinction: A key to the problem of schizophrenia. *J. Nerv. Ment. Dis., 129,* 442–449, 1959.

Bell, R. Q. A reinterpretation of the direction of effects in studies of socialization. *Psychol. Rev., 75,* 81–95, 1968.

Bellack, A. Reciprocal inhibition of a laboratory conditioned fear. *Beh. Res. Ther., 11,* 11–18, 1973.

Bender, L. Autism in children with mental deficiency. *Amer. J. Ment. Defic., 63,* 81–86, 1959.

Bender, L. Art and therapy in the mental disturbances of children. *J. Nerv. Ment. Dis., 86,* 249–263, 1937.

Bender, L., and Paster, S. Homosexual trends in children. *Amer. J. Orthopsychiat., 11,* 730–744, 1941.

Benedict, R. Anthropology and the abnormal. *J. Gen. Psychol., 10,* 59–82, 1934.

Bennis, W. G. Goals and meta-goals of laboratory training. *NTL Hum. Rel. Tr. News, 6,* 1–4, 1962.

Bentler, P. M., Sherman, R. W., and Prince, C. Personality characteristics of male transvestites. *J. Clin. Psychol., 126*(3), 287–291, 1970.

Bergin, A. E. An empirical analysis of therapeutic issues. In Arbuckle, D. S. (ed.), *Counseling and Psychotherapy.* New York: McGraw-Hill, 1967.

Bergin, A. E. Some implications of psychotherapy research for therapeutic practice. *J. Abnorm. Soc. Psychol., 71,* 235–246, 1966.

Bergin, A. E. The effects of psychotherapy: Negative results revisited. *J. Counsel. Psychol., 10,* 244–250, 1963.

Bergin, A. E., and Garfield, S. L. *Handbook of Psychotherapy and Behavior Change.* New York: Wiley, 1971.

Bergin, A. E., and Strupp, H. H. *Changing Frontiers in the Science of Psychotherapy.* Chicago: Aldine, 1972.

Bergman, P., and Escalona, S. Unusual sensitivities in very young children. In *Psychoanalytic Study of the Child.* Vols. 3–4. New York: Int'l. Univ. Press, 1949.

Berlyne, D. E. Children's reasoning and thinking. In P. H. Mussen (ed.), *Carmichael's Manual of Child Psychology.* New York: Wiley, 1970.

Bernal, M. E. Behavioral treatment of a child's dating problem. *J. Beh. Ther. Exp. Psychiat., 3,* 43–50, 1972.

Berne, E. *Games People Play.* New York: Grove, 1964.

Berne, E. *Transactional Analysis in Psychotherapy.* New York: Grove, 1961.

Bernstein, D. A. Situational factors in behavioral fear assessment: A progress report. *Beh. Ther., 4,* 41–48, 1973.

Berrien, F. K. *General and Social Systems.* New Brunswick, N. J.: Rutgers University Press, 1968.

Bettelheim, B. *The Empty Fortress.* New York: Free Press, 1967.

Bibace, R., Kaplan, B., and Wapner, S. *Developmental Approaches to Psychopathology.* New York: McGraw-Hill (in press).

Bieber, I., et al. *Homosexuality: A Psychoanalytic Study.* New York: Basic Books, 1962.

Bierer, J. *Therapeutic Social Clubs.* London: Lewis, 1948.

Bijou, S. W. Reinforcement history and socialization. In R. A. Hoppe, et al. (eds.), *Early Experiences and the Processes of Socialization.* New York: Academic Press, 1970.

Biller, H. B. Father absence and the personality development of the male child. *Devel. Psychol., 2,* 134–156, 1970.

Binet, A. *Etudes de psychologie expérimentale: le fétichisme dans l'amour.* Paris: Doin, 1888.

Bingley, T. Mental symptoms in temporal lobe gliomas. *Acta Psychiat. Neurol. Scand. Suppl., 33,* 1–151, 1958.

Binswanger, L. Existential analysis and psychotherapy. *Psychoanal. and Psychoanal. Rev., 45,* 79–83, 1958.

Binswanger, L. Existential analysis and psychotherapy. In Fromm-Reichmann, F., and Moreno, J. L. (eds.), *Progress in Psychotherapy.* Vol. 1. New York: Grune and Stratton, 1956.

Binswanger, L. *Ausgewählte Vorträge und Aufsätze.* Berne: Francke, 1947.

Binswanger, L. *Grundformen und Erkenntnis menschlichen Daseins.* Zurich: Niehaus, 1942.

Binswanger, L., and Boss, M. Existential analysis and daseinsanalysis. In T. Millon (ed.), *Theories of Psychopathology and Personality.* Philadelphia: Saunders, 1973.

Birch, H. G. (ed.) *Brain Damage in Children: The Biological and Social Aspects.* Baltimore: Williams and Wilkins, 1964.

Birley, J. L. T., and Brown, G. W. Crises and life changes preceding the onset and relapse of acute schizophrenia. *Brit. J. Psychiat., 116,* 327–333, 1970.

Birren, J. E. The abuse of the urban aged. *Psych. Today, 3*(10), 37–38, 1970.

Blacker, K. H., Jones, R. T., Stone, G. C., and Pfefferbaum, D. Chronic users of LSD: The "acidheads." *Amer. J. Psychiat., 125*(3), 97–107, 1968.

Blau, D. The course of psychiatric hospitalization in the aged. *J. Geriat. Psychol., 3*(2), 210–223, 1970.

Bleuler, E. P. The Physiogenic and psychogenic in schizophrenia. In T. Millon (ed.), *Theories of Psychopathology and Personality.* Philadelphia: Saunders, 1973.

Bleuler, E. P. *Dementia Praecox, or the Group of Schizophrenias.* New York: International Universities Press, 1950.

Bloodstein, O. *A Handbook on Stuttering for Professional Workers.* Chicago: National Society for Crippled Children and Adults, 1959.

Bloomberg, L., et al. The development, major goals and strategies of a skid row program: Philadelphia. *Quart. J. Studies Alcoh. 27,* 242–258, 1966.

Blumer, H. *The World of Youthful Drug Use.* Berkeley: School of Criminology, University of California, 1967.

Böök, J. A. Genetical aspects of schizophrenic psychoses. In Jackson, D. (ed.), *The Etiology of Schizophrenia.* New York: Basic Books, 1960.

Böök, J. A. Schizophrenia as a gene mutation. *Acta Genetica, 4,* 133–139, 1953.

Boss, M. *Psychoanalysis and Daseinsanalysis.* New York: Basic Books, 1963.

Boss, M. *Psychoanalyse und Daseinsanalytik.* Berne: Hans Huber, 1957.

Boszormenyi-Nagy, I., and Framo, J. L. *Intensive Family Therapy*. New York: Harper and Row, 1965.

Bowden, C. L., and Maddux, J. F. Methadone maintenance: Myth and reality. *Amer. J. Psychiat.*, *129*, 435–446, 1972.

Bowlby, J. *Attachment and Loss. Vol. 1, Attachment*. London: Hogarth, 1969.

Bowlby, J. *Maternal Care and Mental Health*. Geneva: World Health Organization, 1952.

Bowman, K. M., and Simon, A. Studies in electronarcosis therapy. *Amer. J. Psychiat.*, *105*, 15–21, 1948.

Brady, J. V. Ulcers in "executive" monkeys. *Sci. Amer.*, *199*, 95–100, 1958.

Braginsky, B. M., et al. *Methods of Madness: The Mental Hospital as a Last Resort*. New York: Holt, Rinehart and Winston, 1969.

Braginsky, D. D., and Braginsky, B. M. *Hansels and Gretels: Studies of Children in Institutions for the Mentally Retarded*. New York: Holt, Rinehart and Winston, 1971.

Brandon, M. W. G., Kirman, B. H., and Williams, C. E. Microcephaly. *J. Ment. Sci.*, *105*, 721–747, 1959.

Brannon, E. P., and Graham, W. L. Intensive insulin shock therapy: A five year survey. *Amer. J. Psychiat.*, *11*, 659–663, 1955.

Breger, L., and McGaugh, J. L. Critique and reformulation of "learning-theory" approaches to psychotherapy and neurosis. *Psychol. Bull.*, *63*, 338–358, 1965.

Brickner, R. M. *The Intellectual Functions of the Frontal Lobes*. New York: Macmillan, 1936.

Brill, N. Q., Crumpton, E., and Grayson, H. M. Personality factors in marihuana use. *Arch. Gen. Psychiat.*, *24*, 163–165, 1971.

Broen, W. E., and Nakamura, C. Y. Reduced range of sensory sensitivity in chronic non-paranoid schizophrenics. *J. Abn. Soc. Psychol.*, *79*, 106–111, 1972.

Brown, G. W., Birley, J. L. T., and Wing, J. K. Influence of family life on the course of schizophrenic disorders. *Brit. J. Psychiat.*, *121*, 241–258, 1972.

Browning, R. M., and Stover, D. O. *Behavior Modification and Child Treatment*. Chicago: Aldine, 1970.

Buckner, H. T. The transvestic career path. *Psychiatry*, *33*(3), 381–389, 1970.

Bunney, W. E., et al. The "switch process" in manic-depressive illness. *Arch. Gen. Psychiat.*, *27*, 293–317, 1972.

Burgess, E. P. The modification of depressive behaviors. In R. Rubin and C. M. Franks (eds.), *Advances in Behavior Therapy*. New York: Academic Press, 1969.

Burnham, W. H. *The Normal Mind*. New York: Appleton, 1924.

Buss, A. H., and Lang, P. J. Psychological deficit in schizophrenia, I: Affect, reinforcement, and concept attainment. *J. Abnorm. Soc. Psychol.*, *70*, 2–24, 1965.

Butler, J. M., and Rice, L. N. Adience, self-actualization and drive theory. In Wepman, J., and Heine, R. (eds.), *Concepts of Personality*. Chicago: Aldine, 1963.

Cade, J. F. J. Lithium salts in the treatment of psychotic excitement. *Med. J. Austral.*, *2*, 349–352, 1949.

Cahoon, D. D. Symptom substitution and the behavior therapies: A reappraisal. *Psychol. Bull.*, *69*, 149–156, 1968.

Cairns, R. B. Attachment and dependency: A psychobiological and social-learning synthesis. In J. Gewirtz (ed.), *Attachment and Dependency*. Washington: Winston, 1972.

Cairns, R. B. Attachment behavior in mammals. *Psychol. Rev.*, *73*, 409–426, 1966.

Caldwell, B. M. The effects of psychosocial deprivation on human development in infancy. *Merrill-Palmer Quarterly 16*, 146–154, 1970.

Caldwell, B. M. The effect of infant care. In Hoffman, M., and Hoffman, L. (eds.), *Review of Child Development Research*. Vol. I. New York: Russell Sage, 1964.

Callahan, E. J., and Leitenberg, H. Aversion therapy for sexual deviation: Contingent shock and covert sensitization. *J. Abn. Psychol.*, *81*, 60–73, 1973.

Cameron, N. *Personality Development and Psychopathology*. New York: Houghton Mifflin, 1963.

Cameron, N. Paranoid conditions and paranoia. In S. Arieti (ed.), *American Handbook of Psychiatry*. New York: Basic Books, pp. 508–539, 1959.

Cameron, N. *The Psychology of Behavior Disorders*. New York: Houghton Mifflin, 1947.

Cameron, N., and Magaret, A. *Behavior Pathology*. New York: Houghton Mifflin, 1951.

Campbell, J. D. *Manic-Depressive Disease*. Philadelphia: Lippincott, 1953.

Caplan, G. *Principles of Preventive Psychology*. New York: Basic Books, 1964.

Carlson, C., Hersen, M., and Eisler, R. M. Token economy programs in the treatment of hospitalized adult psychiatric patients. *J. Nerv. Ment. Dis.*, *155*, 192–204, 1972.

Carothers, J. C. The African mind in health and disease. *World Health Organization Monograph, 17*, Geneva: World Health Organization, 1953.

Carter, C. H. *Handbook of Mental Retardation Syndromes*. 2nd ed. Springfield, Ill.: Charles C Thomas, 1970.

Cartwright, R. D., and Vogel, J. L. A comparison of changes in psychoneurotic patients during matched periods of therapy and nontherapy. *J. Consult. Psychol.*, *24*, 121–127, 1960.

Cattell, R. B. *The Scientific Analysis of Personality*. Baltimore: Penguin Books, 1965.

Cattell, R. B., and Scheier, I. H. *The Meaning and Measurement of Neuroticism and Anxiety.* New York: Ronald, 1961.

Cerletti, U., and Bini, L. Electric shock treatment. *Boll. Accad. Med. Roma, 64,* 36, 1938.

Cheek, F. E. Parental social control mechanisms in the family of the schizophrenic—A new look at the family environment in schizophrenia. *J. Schizophrenia, 1,* 18–53, 1967.

Chess, S., Thomas, A., Birch, H. G., and Hertzig, M. Implications of a longitudinal study of child development for child psychiatry. *Amer. J. Psychiat., 117,* 434–441, 1960.

Child, C. M. *Patterns and Problems of Development.* Chicago: U. of Chicago Press, 1941.

Chittendon, G. E. An experimental study in measuring and modifying assertive behavior in young children. *Monogr. Soc. Res. Child Develop., 31,* 1942.

Chodoff, P. The depressive personality. *Arch. Gen. Psychiat., 27,* 666–673, 1972.

Cholden, L. (ed.) *Lysergic Acid Diethylamide and Mescaline in Experimental Psychiatry.* New York: Grune and Stratton, 1956.

Clark, R. E. Psychoses, income and occupational prestige. *Amer. J. Sociol., 54,* 433–440, 1949.

Clausen, J. A. Family structure, socialization, and personality. In Hoffman, L., and Hoffman, M. (eds.), *Review of Child Development Research.* Vol. II. New York: Russell Sage, 1966.

Clausen, J. A., and Kohn, M. L. Relation of schizophrenia to the social structure of a small city. In Pasamanick, B. (ed.), *Epidemiology of Mental Disorders.* Washington, D.C.: American Association for the Advancement of Science, 1959.

Cleckley, H. *The Mask of Sanity.* St. Louis: Mosby, 1950.

Cobb, S. *Borderlands of Psychiatry.* Cambridge: Harvard U. Press, 1943.

Colby, K. M. Psychotherapeutic processes. In Farnsworth, P., et al. (eds.), *Annual Review of Psychology.* Vol. 15. Palo Alto, Calif.: Annual Reviews, 1964.

Cole, J. O., et al. Phenothiazine treatment in acute schizophrenia: Effectiveness. *A.M.A. Arch. Gen. Psychiat., 10,* 246–261, 1964.

Cole, J. O., and Davis, J. M. Antidepressant drugs. In Freedman, A. M., and Kaplan, H. I. (eds.), *Comprehensive Textbook of Psychiatry.* Baltimore: Williams and Wilkins, 1967.

Coleman, J. C. *Abnormal Psychology and Modern Life.* 3rd edition. Chicago: Scott, Foresman, 1964.

Conel, J. L. *The Postnatal Development of the Human Cerebral Cortex.* Five Volumes. Cambridge, Mass.: Harvard U. Press, 1939–1955.

Cooper, J. E. A study of behavior therapy in thirty psychiatric patients. *Lancet, 1,* 411–415, 1963.

Coppen, A. J. Body-build of male homosexuals. *Brit. Med. J., 2,* 1443–1445, 1959.

Corsini, R. J. *Role-playing in Psychotherapy: A Manual.* Chicago: Aldine, 1966.

Cortes, C. S., and Fleming, E. S. The effect of father absence on the adjustment of culturally deprived boys. *J. of Special Education, 2,* 413–420, 1970.

Cortis, J. B., and Gatti, F. M. Physique and propensity. *Psychol. Today, 4*(5), 42–44, 82, 84, 1970.

Cross, A. J. The outcome of psychotherapy: A selected analysis of research findings. *J. Consult. Psychol., 28,* 413–417, 1964.

Cruickshank, W. M. (ed.) *The Teacher of Brain-Injured Children: A Discussion of the Bases for Competency.* Syracuse: Syracuse Univ. Press, 1966.

David, P. R., and Snyder, L. H. Some interrelations between psychology and genetics. In Koch, S. (ed.), *Psychology: A Study of a Science.* Vol. 4. New York: McGraw-Hill, 1962.

Davidson, M. A., et al. The distribution of personality traits in seven-year-old children: A combined psychological, psychiatric, and somatotype study. *Brit. J. Educ. Psychol., 27,* 48–61, 1957.

Davies, M. Blood pressure and personality. *J. Psychosom. Res., 14*(1), 89–104, 1970.

Davis, J. M. Efficacy of tranquilizing and antidepressant drugs. *A.M.A. Arch. Gen. Psychiat., 13,* 552–572, 1965.

Davison, G. C. Systematic desensitization as a counterconditioning process. *J. Abnorm. Soc. Psychol., 73,* 91–99, 1968.

Davison, G. C. The influence of systematic desensitization, relaxation, and graded exposure to imaginal stimuli in the modification of phobic behavior. Unpublished doctoral dissertations, Stanford University, 1965.

Dejerine, J., and Gaukler, E. *Psychoneurosis and Psychotherapy.* Philadelphia: Lippincott, 1913.

Delafresnaye, J. F. (ed.) *Brain Mechanisms and Learning.* Springfield, Ill.: Thomas, 1961.

Delgado, J. M. R. Emotional behavior in animals and humans. *Psychiat. Res. Repts., 12,* 259–266, 1960.

Delgado, J. M. R., Roberts, W. W., and Miller, N. Learning motivated by electrical stimulation of subcortical structures in the monkey brain. *J. Comp. Physiol. Psychol., 49,* 373–380, 1954.

Denber, H. C. B. (ed.) *Research Conference on the Therapeutic Community.* Springfield, Ill: Thomas, 1960.

Denker, P. G. Results of treatment of psychoneurosis by the general practitioner: A follow-up study of 500 cases. *N.Y.S.J. Med., 46,* 2164–2166, 1946.

Denner, B., and Price, R. H. (eds.) *Community mental health: Social action and Reaction.* New York: Holt, Rinehart and Winston, 1973.

Derogatis, L. R., et al. Factorial invariance of symptom dimensions in anxious and depressive neuroses. *Arch. Gen. Psychiat., 27,* 659–665, 1972.

Deur, J. I., and Parke, R. D. Effects of inconsistent punishment on aggression in children. *Develop. Psych., 2,* 403–411, 1970.

Deutsch, A. *The Shame of the States.* New York: Harcourt, Brace and Co., 1948.

Deyken, E. Y., and DiMascio, A. Relationship of patient background characteristics to efficacy of pharmacotherapy in depression. *J. Nerv. Ment. Dis., 155,* 209–215, 1972.

DiCara, L. V. Learning in the autonomic nervous system. *Scientif. Amer., 222*(1), 30–39, 1970.

Dittmann, A. T. Psychotherapeutic Processes. In Farnsworth, P. R., et al. (eds.), *Annual Review of Psychology.* Vol. 16. Palo Alto: Annual Reviews, 1966.

Dixon, J. J., et al. Patterns of anxiety: The phobias. *Brit. J. Med. Psychol., 30,* 34–40, 1957.

Dohrenwend, B. P., and Dohrenwend, B. S. *Social Status and Psychological Disorder.* New York: Wiley, 1969.

Dohrenwald, B. S., and Dohrenwald, B. P. Stress situations, birth order, and psychological symptoms. *J. Abnorm. Soc. Psychol., 71,* 215–223, 1966.

Doll, E. A. The essentials of an inclusive concept of mental deficiency. *Amer. J. Ment. Def., 46,* 214–221, 1941.

Dollard, J., and Miller, N. E. How symptoms are learned. In T. Millon (ed.), *Theories of Psychopathology and Personality.* Philadelphia: Saunders, 1973.

Dollard, J., and Miller, N. E. *Personality and Psychotherapy.* New York: McGraw-Hill, 1950.

Dorzab, J., Baker, M., Cadoret, R., and Winokur, G. Depressive disease: Familial psychiatric illness. *Amer. J. Psychiat., 127*(9), 48–60, 1971.

DuBois, P. *The Psychic Treatment of Mental Disorders.* New York: Funk and Wagnall, 1909.

Dunbar, H. F. *Emotions and Bodily Changes.* New York: Columbia U. Press, 1935.

Dunham, H. W. Epidemiology of psychiatric disorders as a contribution to medical ecology. *A.M.A. Arch. Gen. Psychiat., 14,* 1–19, 1966.

Dunlap, K. *Habits: Their Making and Unmaking.* New York: Liveright, 1932.

Dupont, R. L., Jr., and Gruenbaum, H. Willing victims: The husbands of paranoid women. *Amer. J. Psychiat., 125*(2), 151–159, 1968.

Edelman, R. I. Operant conditioning treatment of encopresis. *J. Behav. Ther. Exp. Psychiat., 2,* 71–73, 1971.

Edwards, R. P., Alley, G. R., and Snider, W. Academic achievement and minimal brain dysfunction. *J. Learn. Dis., 3*(4), 134–138, 1970.

Einstein, G., and Moss, M. Some thoughts on sibling relationships. *Social Casework, 48,* 549–555, 1967.

Eisenberg, L. The classification of childhood psychosis reconsidered. *J. Autism Childhood Schiz., 2,* 338–342, 1972.

Eisenberg, L. Normal child development. In Freedman, A., and Kaplan, H. (eds.), *Comprehensive Textbook of Psychiatry.* Baltimore: Williams and Wilkins, 1967.

Eisenberg, L., and Kanner, L. Early infantile autism. 1943–1955. *Amer. J. Orthopsychiat., 26,* 556–566, 1956.

Eisler, R. M., et al. Effects of modeling on components of assertive behavior. *J. Beh. Ther. Exp. Psychiat., 4,* 1–6, 1973.

Ellinwood, E. H. Assault and homicide associated with amphetamine abuse. *Amer. J. Psychiat., 127*(9), 90–95, 1971.

Ellis, A. Rational psychotherapy. In T. Millon (ed.), *Theories of Psychopathology and Personality.* Philadelphia: Saunders, 1973.

Ellis, A. Goals of psychotherapy. In Mahrer, A. R. (ed.), *The Goals of Psychotherapy.* New York: Appleton-Century-Crofts, 1967.

Ellis, A. *Reason and Emotion in Psychotherapy.* New York: Lyle Stuart, 1962.

Ellis, A. Rational psychotherapy. *J. Gen. Psychol., 59,* 35–49, 1958.

Ellis, A. Outcome of employing three techniques of psychotherapy. *J. Clin. Psychol., 13,* 344–350, 1957.

English, J. T. Sensitivity training: promise and performance. *Amer. J. Psychiat., 126,* 142–147, 1969.

Epstein, S. and Coleman, M. Drive theory and schizophrenia. *Psychosomatic Med., 32,* 113–140, 1970.

Erikson, E. H. Growth and crises. In T. Millon (ed.), *Theories of Psychopathology and Personality.* Philadelphia: Saunders, 1973.

Erikson, E. H. Growth and crises of the healthy personality. In Klein, G. S. (ed.), *Psychological Issues.* New York: Int'l. Univ. Press, 1959.

Erikson, E. H. Identity and the life cycle. In Klein, G. S. (ed.), *Psychological Issues.* New York: Int'l. Univ. Press, 1959.

Erikson, E. H. *Childhood and Society.* New York: Norton, 1950.

Escalona, S. *Roots of Individuality.* Chicago: Aldine, 1968.

Escalona, S., and Heider, G. *Prediction and Outcome.* New York: Basic Books, 1959.

Escalona, S., and Leitch, M. *Early Phases of Personality Development: A Non-normative Study of Infancy Behavior.* Evanston, Ill: Child Development Publications, 1953.

Essen-Moller, E. *Psychiatrische Geisteskranken Elternpaare.* Stuttgart: G. Thieme, 1952.

Essen-Moller, E. Psychiatrische Untersuchungen an einer Serie von Zwillingen. *Acta Psychiat. Neurol. Suppl., 23,* 1941.

Evans, R. B. Childhood parental relationships of homosexual men. *J. Consult. Clin. Psychol., 33*(2), 129–135, 1969.

Eysenck, H. J. Learning therapy and behavior therapy. In T. Millon (ed.), *Theories of Psychopathology and Personality.* Philadelphia: Saunders, 1973.

Eysenck, H. J. The classification of depressive illness. *Brit. J. Psychiat., 117,* 241–250, 1970.

Eysenck, H. J. *The Effects of Psychotherapy.* New York: Int'l. Science Press, 1966.

Eysenck, H. J. The effects of psychotherapy. *Int'l. J. Psychiat., 1,* 99–142, 1965.

Eysenck, H. J. The outcome problem in psychotherapy: A reply. *Psychotherapy, 1,* 97–100, 1964.

Eysenck, H. J. The effects of psychotherapy. In Eysenck, H. J. (ed.), *Handbook of Abnormal Psychology.* New York: Basic Books, 1961.

Eysenck, H. J. (ed.) *Behavior Therapy and the Neuroses.* London: Pergamon Press, 1960.

Eysenck, H. J. Learning theory and behavior therapy. *J. Ment. Sci., 105,* 61–75, 1959.

Eysenck, H. J. *The Structure of Personality.* London: Methuen, 1957.

Eysenck, H. J. *Dimensions of Personality.* London: Routledge and Kegan Paul, 1953.

Eysenck, H. J. The effects of psychotherapy: An evaluation. *J. Consult. Psychol., 16,* 319–324, 1952.

Eysenck, H. J., and Rachman, S. *The Causes and Cures of Neurosis.* London: Routledge and Kegan Paul, 1965.

Fabing, H. Trends in biological research in schizophrenia. *J. Nerv. Ment. Dis., 124,* 1–7, 1956.

Fairweather, G. W., et al. Relative effectiveness of psychotherapeutic programs: A multicriteria comparison of four programs for three different patient groups. *Psychol. Monogr.,* Whole #492, 1960.

Faris, R. E. L., and Dunham, H. W. *Mental Disorders in Urban Areas.* Chicago: U. of Chicago Press, 1939.

Feinsilver, D. Communication in families of schizophrenic patients. *A.M.A. Arch. Gen. Psychiat., 22,* 143–148, 1970.

Feldman, M. P. Aversion therapy for sexual deviations: A critical review. *Psychol. Bull., 65,* 65–79, 1966.

Feldstein, A., Hoagland, H., and Freeman, H. Blood and urinary serotonin and 5-hydroxyindoleacetic acid levels in schizophrenic patients and normal subjects. *J. Nerv. Ment. Dis., 129,* 62–68, 1959.

Fenichel, O. *The Psychoanalytic Theory of Neuroses.* New York: Norton, 1945.

Ferguson, L. R. Dependency motivation in socialization. In R. A. Hoppe, et al. (eds.), *Early Experiences and the Processes of Socialization.* New York: Academic Press, 1970.

Ferster, C. B. Positive reinforcement and behavior deficits in autistic children. In Franks, C. M. (ed.), *Conditioning Techniques in Clinical Practice and Research.* New York: Springer, 1964.

Ferster, C. B. Reinforcement and punishment in the control of human behavior by social agencies. *Psychiat. Res. Repts., 10,* 101–118, 1958.

Feshbach, S. Aggression. In P. H. Mussen (ed.), *Carmichael's Manual of Child Psychology.* New York: Wiley, 1970.

Fiedler, F. E. Factor analyses of psychoanalytic, nondirective, and Adlerian therapeutic relationships. *J. Consult. Psychol., 15,* 32–38, 1951.

Fiedler, F. E. A comparison of therapeutic relationships in psychoanalytic, nondirective, and Adlerian therapy. *J. Consult. Psychol., 14,* 436–445, 1950.

Fischer, I., and Glanville, B. W. K. Programmed teaching of autistic children. *Arch. Gen. Psychiat., 23*(1), 90–94, 1970.

Flaherty, J. A. The psychiatric use of isonicotinic acid hydrazine: A case report. *Del. Med. J., 24,* 198–201, 1952.

Fleming, T. C. An inquiry into the mechanism of action of electric shock treatments. *J. Nerv. Ment. Dis., 124,* 440–450, 1956.

Fookes, B. H. Some experiences in the use of aversion therapy in male homosexuality, exhibitionism and fetishism-transvestism. *Brit. J. Psychiat., 115,* 339–341, 1969.

Ford, D. H., and Urban, H. B. *Systems of Psychotherapy.* New York: Wiley, 1963.

Fowler, W. The problems of deprivation and developmental learning. *Merrill-Palmer Quart., 16*(2), 141–162, 1970.

Frank, G. A. The role of the family in the development of psychopathology. *Psychol. Bull., 64,* 191–208, 1965.

Frank, J. D. *Persuasion and Healing: A Comparative Study of Psychotherapy.* Baltimore: Johns Hopkins Press, 1961.

Frank, L. K. Society as the patient. *Amer. J. Sociology, 42,* 335–344, 1936.

Frankl, V. E. Meaninglessness: A challenge to psychologists. In T. Millon (ed.), *Theories of Psychopathology and Personality.* Philadelphia: Saunders, 1973.

Frankl, V. E. Logotherapy and existential analysis: A review. *Amer. J. Psychother., 20,* 252–260, 1966.

Frankl, V. E. *Man's Search for Meaning.* Boston: Beacon, 1962.

Frankl, V. E. *The Doctor and the Soul: An Introduction to Logotherapy.* New York: Knopf, 1955.

Franks, C. M. (ed.) *Conditioning Techniques in Clinical Practice and Research.* New York: Springer, 1964.

Franks, C. M. Conditioning and abnormal behavior. In Eysenck, H. J. (ed.), *Handbook of Abnormal Psychology.* New York: Basic Books, 1961.

Freedman, D. A. Congenital and perinatal sensory deprivation: some studies in early development. *Amer. J. Psychiat., 127*(11), 1539–1545, 1971.

Freeman, E. H., et al. Psychological variables in allergic disorders: A review. *Psychosom. Med., 26,* 543–576, 1964.

Freeman, W., and Watts, J. *Psychosurgery in the Treatment of Mental Disorders and Pain.* Springfield, Ill.: Thomas, 1950.

Freeman, W., and Watts, J. *Psychosurgery.* Springfield, Ill.: Thomas, 1942.

Freud, A. *Introduction to the Technique of Child Analysis.* Washington, D.C.: Nerv. Ment. Dis. Publ., 1928.

Freud, K., et al. Heterosexual aversion in homosexual males. *Brit. J. Psychiat., 122,* 163–170, 1973.

Freud, S. *Collected Papers.* Vol. IV. New York: Basic Books, 1959.

Freyhan, F. A. Clinical and investigative aspects. In Kline, N. S. (ed.), *Psychopharmacology Frontiers.* Boston: Little, Brown, 1959.

Friedman, A. S., Cowitz, B., Cohen, H. W., and Granick, S. Syndromes and themes of psychotic depression. *A.M.A. Arch. Gen. Psychiat., 9,* 504–512, 1963.

Fromm, E. Non-productive character orientations. In T. Millon (ed.), *Theories of Psychopathology and Personality.* Philadelphia: Saunders, 1973.

Fromm, E. *The Sane Society.* New York: Rinehart, 1955.

Fromm, E. *Man for Himself.* New York: Rinehart, 1947.

Frostig, J. P., et al. Electronarcosis in animals and in man. *A.M.A. Arch. Neurol. Psychiat., 51,* 232–237, 1944.

Frostig, M., and Horne, D. *The Frostig Program for the Development of Visual Perception: Teacher's Guide.* Chicago: Follett, 1964.

Frumkin, R. M. Occupation and mental disorder. In Rose, A. M. (ed.), *Mental Health and Mental Disorder.* New York: Norton, 1955.

Fuller, J. L. Genetic influences on socialization. In R. A. Hoppe, et al. (eds.), *Early Experiences and the Processes of Socialization.* New York: Academic Press, 1970.

Fuller, J. L., and Thompson, W. R. *Behavior Genetics.* New York: Wiley, 1960.

Fulton, J. F. *Physiology of the Nervous System.* New York: Oxford, 1943.

Fulton, J. F., and Jacobsen, C. F. The functions of the frontal lobes: A comparative study in monkeys, chimpanzee and man. *Abstr. 2nd Int'l. Neurol. Cong.,* London, 1935.

Gallemore, J. L., and Wilson, W. P. Adolescent maladjustment or affective disorder? *Amer. J. Psychiat., 129,* 608–612, 1972.

Gardner, G. G., The psychotherapeutic relationship. *Psychol. Bull., 61,* 426–437, 1964.

Garma, A. Gastric neurosis. *Int'l. J. Psychoanal., 31,* 53–61, 1950.

Garmezy, N. Process and reactive schizophrenia: Some conceptions and issues. In Katz, M., et al. (eds.), *The Role and Methodology of Classification in Psychiatry and Psychopathology.* Washington, D.C.: Public Health Service, 1968.

Gattozzi, A. Lithium in the treatment of mood disorders. *Nat'l. Clearinghouse for Mental Health Information.* Washington, D.C.: Government Printing Office, Publication No. 5033, 1970.

Gelfand, D. M., and Hartmann, D. P. Behavior therapy with children: A review and evaluation of research methodology. *Psychol. Bull., 69,* 204–215, 1968.

Gellhorn, E. *Autonomic Imbalance and the Hypothalamus: Implications for Physiology, Medicine, Psychology, and Neuropsychiatry.* Minneapolis: U. of Minnesota Press, 1957.

Gellhorn, E. *Autonomic Regulations: Their Significance for Physiology, Psychology and Neuropsychiatry.* New York: Interscience, 1943.

Gesell, A., et al. *The First Five Years of Life.* New York: Harper, 1940.

Gewirtz, J. L. (ed.). *Attachment and Dependency.* Washington: Winston, 1972.

Gewirtz, J. L. A learning analysis of the effects of normal stimulation upon social and exploratory behavior in the human infant. In Foss, B. M. (ed.), *Determinants of Infant Behavior II.* New York: Wiley, 1963.

Gibbs, F. A. Abnormal electrical activity in the temporal regions and its relationship to abnormalities in behavior. *Res. Publ. Assn. Res. Nerv. Ment. Dis., 36,* 278–294, 1958.

Gill, M., and Brenman, M. Research in psychotherapy. *Amer. J. Orthopsychiat., 18,* 100–110, 1948.

Giora, Z. Psychosomatics: promise and fulfillment. *Brit. J. Med. Psychol., 45,* 203–208, 1972.

Glasner, P. J. Developmental view. In J. Sheehan (ed.), *Stuttering: Research and Therapy.* New York: Harper and Row, 1970.

Glasser, W. *Reality Therapy.* New York: Harper and Row, 1965.

Glasser, W. *Mental Health or Mental Illness.* New York: Harper and Row, 1961.

Glidewell, J. C. (ed.) *Parental Attitudes and Child Behavior.* Springfield, Ill.: Thomas, 1961.

Glueck, B. Personal communication. 1968.

Glueck, B. C., et al. The quantitative assessment of personality. *Comp. Psychiat., 5,* 15–23, 1964.

Glueck, S., and Glueck, E. *Family Environment and Delinquency.* Boston: Houghton Mifflin, 1962.

Goffman, E. The Inmate World. In T. Millon (ed.), *Theories of Psychopathology and Personality.* Philadelphia: Saunders, 1973.

Goldberg, C. Group sensitivity training. *Int'l. J. Psychiat., 9,* 165–192, 1970.

Goldberg, E. M., and Morrison, S. L. Schizophrenia and social class. *Brit. J. Psychiat., 109,* 785–802, 1963.

Goldensohn, E. Seizures and convulsive disorders. In Wolman, B. (ed.), *Handbook of Clinical Psychology.* New York: McGraw-Hill, 1965.

Goldfarb, W. Emotional and intellectual consequences of psychologic deprivation in infancy: A reevaluation. In Hoch, P., and Zubin, J. (eds.), *Psychopathology of Childhood.* New York: Grune and Stratton, 1955.

Goldhamer, H., and Marshall, A. W. *Psychosis and Civilization.* Glencoe, Ill.: Free Press, 1953.

Goldman, A. E. A comparative-developmental approach to schizophrenia. *Psychol. Bull., 59,* 57–69, 1962.

Goldstein, A. P., et al. The use of modeling to increase independent behavior. *Behav. Res. Ther., 11,* 31–42, 1973.

Goldstein, A. P., and Dean, S. J. (eds.) *The Investigation of Psychotherapy.* New York: Wiley, 1966.

Goldstein, K. The organismic approach. In Arieti, S. (ed.), *American Handbook of Psychiatry.* New York: Basic Books, 1959.

Goldstein, K. *Aftereffects of Brain Injuries in War.* New York: Grune and Stratton, 1942.

Goldstein, K. *The Organism.* New York: American Book Co., 1939.

Goodman, P. *Growing Up Absurd.* New York: Random House, 1960.

Goodwin, D. W., Guge, S. B., and Robbins, E. Follow-up studies in obsessional neurosis. *Arch. Gen. Psychiat., 20,* 182–187, 1969.

Goodwin, F. K., et al. Lithium response in unipolar versus bipolar depression. *Amer. J. Psychiat., 129,* 44–47, 1972.

Gordon, A. M. Patterns of delinquency in drug addiction. *Brit. J. Psychiat., 122,* 205–210, 1973.

Gordon, H. L. Fifty shock therapy theories. *The Military Surgeon, 3,* 397–401, 1948.

Gordon, J. S. Who is mad? Who is sane? The radical psychiatry of R. D. Laing. *Atlantic, 227(1),* 50–66, 1971.

Gottesman, I. I., and Shields, J. Genetic theorizing and schizophrenia. *Brit. J. Psychiat., 122,* 15–30, 1973.

Gottesman, I. I., and Shields, J. *Schizophrenia and Genetics—From the Vantage Point of a Twin Study.* New York: Academic Press, 1972.

Gottesman, I. I., and Shields, J. Cross-national diagnosis and the heritability of schizophrenia. Symposium: *The Transmission of Schizophrenia.* Fifth World Congress of Psychiatry, 1971.

Gottesman, I. I., and Shields, J. A polygenic theory of schizophrenia. *Proc. Nat'l. Acad. Sci., 58,* 199–205, 1967.

Gottesman, I. I., and Shields, J. Schizophrenia in twins: 16 years' consecutive admissions to a psychiatric clinic. *Brit. J. Psychiat., 112,* 809–818, 1966.

Gottschalk, L. A., and Auerbach, A. H. (eds.) *Methods of Research in Psychotherapy.* New York: Appleton-Century-Crofts, 1966.

Grace, W. J., and Graham, D. T. Relationship of specific attitudes and emotions to certain bodily diseases. *Psychosom. Med., 14,* 242–251, 1952.

Greco, M. C., and Wright, J. C. The correctional institution in the etiology of chronic homosexuality. *Amer. J. Orthopsychiat., 14,* 295–308, 1944.

Greenacre, P. Conscience in the psychopath. *Amer. J. Orthopsychiat., 15,* 495–509, 1945.

Greenblatt, M., Arnot, A., and Solomon, H. C. *Studies in Lobotomy.* New York: Grune and Stratton, 1950.

Greenblatt, M., Levinson, D. J., and Williams, R. H. (eds.) *The Patient and the Mental Hospital.* Glencoe, Ill.: Free Press, 1957.

Greenblatt, M., and Solomon, H. C. *Frontal Lobes and Schizophrenia.* New York: Springer, 1953.

Gregory, I. *Fundamentals of Psychiatry.* Philadelphia: Saunders, 1968.

Gregory, I. Genetic factors in schizophrenia. *Amer. J. Psychiat., 116,* 961–972, 1960.

Gregory, I. An analysis of familial data on psychiatric patients: Parental age, family size, birth order and ordinal position. *Brit. J. Prev. Soc. Med., 12,* 42–59, 1958.

Grinker, R. R., Sr. An essay on schizophrenia and science. *Arch. Gen. Psychiat., 20,* 1–24, 1969.

Grinker, R. R., Sr., Werble, B., and Drye, R. C. *The Borderline Syndrome.* New York: Basic Books, 1968.

Grinker, R. R., Sr. A demonstration of the transactional model. In Stein, M. I. (ed.), *Contemporary Psychotherapies.* Glencoe, Ill.: Free Press, 1961.

Grinker, R. R., Sr., Miller, J., Sabshin, M., Nunn, R., and Nunnally, J. C. *The Phenomena of Depressions.* New York: Hoeber, 1961.

Grossberg, J. M. Behavior therapy: A review. *Psychol. Bull., 62,* 73–88, 1964.

Group for the Advancement of Psychiatry. *Psychopathological Disorders in Childhood: Theoretical Considerations and a Proposed Classification.* New York: Group for the Advancement of Psychiatry, 1966.

Grunbaum, A. Causality and the science of human behavior. *Amer. Scientist,* 665–676, 1952.

Guerney, B. G. (ed.) *Psychotherapeutic Agents.* New York: Holt, Rinehart and Winston, 1969.

Gunderson, B. F. Diagnosis of learning disabilities: the team approach. *J. Learn. Dis., 4*(2), 107–113, 1971.

Guze, S. B. The diagnosis of hysteria: What are we trying to do? *Amer. J. Psychiat., 124*(4), 491–498, 1967.

Guze, S. B., and Perley, M. J. Observations on the natural history of hysteria. *Am. J. Psychiat., 119,* 960–965, 1963.

Halevy, A., Moss, R. H., and Solomon, G. F. A relationship between blood serotonin concentrations and behavior of psychiatric patients. *J. Psychiat. Res., 3,* 1–10, 1965.

Haley, J. *Strategies of Psychotherapy.* New York: Grune and Stratton, 1963.

Haley, J. An interactional description of schizophrenia. *Psychiatry, 22,* 321–332, 1959.

Halikas, J. A., et al. Marihuana use and psychiatric illness. *Arch. Gen. Psychiat., 27,* 162–165, 1972.

Halleck, S. L. Therapy is the hand maiden of the status quo. *Psychol. Today, 4,* 30–32, 98–100, 1971.

Halleck, S. L. The goal of protection. *Int'l. J. Psychiat., 9,* 552–557, 1970.

Halleck, S. L. Hysterical personality traits. *Arch. Gen. Psychiat., 16,* 750–757, 1967.

Halpern, W. The schooling of autistic children: Preliminary findings. *Amer. J. Orthopsychiat., 40*(4), 665–671, 1970.

Hardt, R. H., and Feinhandler, S. J. Social class and mental hospital prognosis. *Amer. Sociol. Rev., 24,* 815–821, 1959.

Hargrove, E. A., Bennett, A. E., and Steele, M. An investigational study using carbon dioxide as an adjunct to psychotherapy in neuroses. American Psychiatric Association Meetings, May 7, 1953.

Harlow, H. F. The maternal affectional system. In Foss, B. M. (ed.), *Determinants of Infant Behavior II.* New York: Wiley, 1963.

Harlow, H. F. Primary affectional patterns in primates. *Amer. J. Orthopsychiat., 30,* 67–84, 1960.

Harlow, H. F., and Harlow, M. K. The affectional systems. In Schrier, A., et al. (eds.), *Behavior of Non-Human Primates.* Vol. 2. New York: Academic Press, 1965.

Harlow, H. F., and Suomi, S. J. Nature of love—simplified. *Amer. Psychologist, 25*(1), 161–168, 1970.

Harper, L. V. The young as a source of stimuli controlling caretaker behavior. *Devel. Psychol., 4,* 73–88, 1971.

Harris, A. Day hospitals and night hospitals in psychiatry. *Lancet,* Vol. 1, 729, 1951.

Hartmann, H. *Ego Psychology and the Problem of Adaptation.* New York: Int'l. Univ. Press, 1958.

Hartup, W. H. Peer interaction and social organization. In P. H. Mussen (ed.), *Carmichael's Manual of Child Psychology.* New York: Wiley, 1970.

Hartup, W. H., and Coates, B. The role of imitation in childhood socialization. In R. A. Hoppe, et al. (eds.), *Early Experiences and the Processes of Socialization.* New York: Academic Press, 1970.

Hauser, S. T. Adolescent self-image development. *Arch. Gen. Psychiat., 27,* 537–541, 1972.

Hay, A. J., and Forrest, A. D. The diagnosis of schizophrenia and paranoid psychosis: An attempt at clarification. *Brit. J. Med. Psychol., 45,* 233–242, 1972.

Heath, R. G. Schizophrenia: Biochemical and physiologic aberrations. *Int'l. J. Neuropsychiat., 2,* 597–610, 1966.

Heath, R. G. Brain centers and control of behavior—man. In Nodine, J., and Moyer, J. H. (eds.), *Psychosomatic Medicine.* Philadelphia: Lea and Febiger, 1962.

Heath, R. G. A biochemical hypothesis on the etiology of schizophrenia. In Jackson, D. D. (ed.), *The Etiology of Schizophrenia.* New York: Basic Books, 1960.

Heath, R. G. *Studies of Schizophrenia.* Cambridge: Harvard U. Press, 1954.

Heath, R. G., et al. Effect on behavior in humans with the administration of taraxein. *Amer. J. Psychiat., 114,* 14–24, 1957.

Hebb, D. O. *The Organization of Behavior.* New York: Wiley, 1949.

Heber, R. A manual on terminology and classification in mental retardation. *Amer. J. Ment. Def., 64,* Monogr. Suppl. 2, 1959.

Heilbrun, A. B. Styles of adaptation to experienced aversive maternal control and interpersonal distancing following failure. *J. Nerv. Ment. Dis., 155,* 177–183, 1972.

Helson, H. Adaptation-level as a basis for a quantitative theory of frames of reference. *Psychol. Rev., 55,* 297–313, 1948.

Henderson, D. K. *Psychopathic States.* New York: Norton, 1939.

Hendlin, H. The psychodynamics of flunking out. *J. Nerv. Ment. Dis., 155,* 131–143, 1972.

Henry, G. W. *All the Sexes: A Study of Masculinity and Femininity.* New York: Holt, Rinehart and Winston, 1955.

Hess, E. H. Ethology and developmental psychology. In P. H. Mussen (ed.), *Carmichael's Manual of Child Psychology.* New York: Wiley, 1970.

Hess, E. H. Imprinting. *Sci., 130,* 133–141, 1959.

Higgins, J. Process-reactive schizophrenia: Recent developments. *J. Nerv. Ment. Dis., 149,* 450–472, 1969.

Higgins, J. The concept of process-reactive schizophrenia: Criteria and related research. *J. Nerv. Ment. Dis., 138,* 9–25, 1964.

Hill, D. EEG in episodic psychotic and psychopathic behavior. *EEG Clin. Neurophysiol., 4,* 419–422, 1952.

Himmelbach, J. M., et al. Treatment of previously intractable depressions with tranyl-cypromine and lithium. *J. Nerv. Ment. Dis., 155,* 216–220, 1972.

Hinckley, R. G., and Hermann, L. *Group Treatment in Psychotherapy.* Minneapolis: Univ. of Minnesota Press, 1951.

Hirsch, S. R., and Leff, J. P. Parental abnormalities of verbal communication in the transmission of schizophrenia. *Psychol. Med., 1,* 118–127, 1971.

Hirschfeld, G. Observations with non-convulsive electric-stimulation. *Psychiat. Quart. Suppl.,* part 2, 1950.

Hoagland, H. Metabolic and physiologic disturbances in the psychoses. In *Biology of Mental Health and Disease.* New York: Hoeber, 1952.

Hoch, P. H., and Zubin, J. (eds.) *The Evaluation of Psychiatric Treatment.* New York: Grune and Stratton, 1964.

Hoffer, A., and Osmond, H. The adrenochrome model and schizophrenia. *J. Nerv. Ment. Dis., 128,* 18–35, 1959.

Hoffman, M. I. Moral development. In P. H. Mussen (ed.), *Carmichael's Manual of Child Psychology.* New York: Wiley, 1970.

Hogan, R. A., and Kirchner, J. H. Preliminary report of the extinction of learned fears via short-term implosive therapy. *J. Abnorm. Soc. Psychol., 72,* 106–109, 1967.

Hollingshead, A. B., and Redlich, F. C. *Social Class and Mental Illness.* New York: Wiley, 1958.

Hooker, E. The homosexual community. In *Proceedings of the XIV International Congress of Applied Psychology. Vol. II: Personality Research.* Copenhagen: Munksgaard, 1962.

Hooker, E. The adjustment of the male overt homosexual. *J. Proj. Tech. 21,* 18–31, 1957.

Horney, K. *Neurosis and Human Growth.* New York: Norton, 1950.

Horney, K. *Our Inner Conflicts.* New York: Norton, 1945.

Horney, K. *The Neurotic Personality of Our Time.* New York: Norton, 1937.

Hoskins, R. G. *The Biology of Schizophrenia.* New York: Norton, 1946.

Hunt, H. F., and Brady, J. W. Some effects of electroconvulsive shock on a conditioned response ("anxiety"). *J. Comp. Physiol. Psychol., 44,* 88–98, 1951.

Hunt, J. McV. Toward an integrated program of research on psychotherapy. *J. Consult. Psychol., 16,* 237–246, 1952.

Hurley, R. *Poverty and Mental Retardation: A Causal Relationship.* New York: Random, 1969.

Hussain, A.: Behavior therapy in 105 cases. In Wolpe, J., et al. (ed.), *Conditioning Therapies.* New York: Holt, Rinehart and Winston, 1964.

Huston, P. E., and Locher, L. M. Manic-depressive psychosis: Course when treated and untreated with electric shock. *A.M.A. Arch. Neurol. Psychiat., 60,* 37–48, 1948.

Itard, J. M. G. *The Wild Boy of Aveyron.* (Translation.) New York: Appleton-Century, 1932.

Jackson, D. D., and Weakland, J. H. Conjoint family therapy: Some considerations on theory, technique and results. *Psychiat., 24,* 30–45, 1961.

Jacobson, E. *Progressive Relaxation.* Chicago: U. of Chicago Press, 1938.

Janis, I. L. Psychological effects of electric convulsive treatments. *J. Nerv. Ment. Dis., 3,* 359–397, 469–489, 1950.

Janowsky, D. S., Leff, M., and Epstein, R. Playing the manic game. *Arch. Gen. Psychiat., 22,* 252–261, 1970.

Jasper, H. H., Ward, A. A., and Pope, A. (eds.) *Basic Mechanisms of the Epilepsies.* Boston: Little, Brown, 1969.

Jaspers, K. *Allegemaine Psychopathologie.* Berlin: Springer, 1913.

Jellinek, E. M. *The Disease Concept of Alcoholism.* New Haven: Hillside Press, 1960.

Jellinek, E. M. Phases of alcohol addiction. *Quart. J. Stud. Alcohol, 13,* 673–678, 1952.

Jenkins, R. I. The runaway reaction. *Amer. J. Psychiat., 128*(2), 168–173, 1971.

Jervis, G. A. The mental deficiencies. In Arieti, S. (ed.) *American Handbook of Psychiatry.* New York: Basic Books, 1959.

Johnson, W. *Stuttering and What You Can Do About It.* Minneapolis: U. of Minn. Press, 1961.

Johnson, W., et al. *The Onset of Stuttering.* Minneapolis: U. of Minnesota Press, 1959.

Jones, B., and Parsons, O. A. Impaired abstracting ability in chronic alcoholics. *Arch. Gen. Psychiat., 24*(1), 71–75, 1971.

Jones, C, H., et al. Peripheral electrical stimulation: A new form of psychiatric treatment. *Dis. Nerv. Syst., 16,* 323–332, 1955.

Jones, E. *Life and Works of Sigmund Freud.* Vol. 1. New York: Basic Books, 1953.

Jones, M. The therapeutic community: Milieu therapy. In T. Millon (ed.), *Theories of Psychopathology and Personality.* Philadelphia: Saunders, 1973.

Jones, M. Personality correlates and antecedents of drinking patterns in adult males. *J. Consult. Clin. Psychol., 32*(1), 2–12, 1968.

Jones, M. *The Therapeutic Community: A New Treatment Method in Psychiatry.* New York: Basic Books, 1953.

Jones, M. C. Personality antecedents and correlates of drinking patterns in women. *J. Consult. Clin. Psychol., 36*(1), 61–69, 1971.

Jones, M. C. The elimination of children's fears. *J. Exper. Psychol., 7,* 383–390, 1924.

Jordan, B., and Kempler, B. Hysterical personality: An experimental investigation of sex-role conflict. *J. Abn. Psychol., 75,* 172–176, 1970.

Jung, C. G. *Psychological Types or the Psychology of Individuation.* New York: Harcourt, Brace, 1923.

Jung, C. G. *Psychology of the Unconscious.* New York: Moffat, Yard, 1916.

Kahana, B., and Kahana, E. Charges in mental status of elderly patients in age-integrated and age-segregated hospital milieus. *J. Abnorm. Psychol., 75,* 177–181, 1970.

Kalinowsky, L. B. The convulsive therapies. In Freedman, A. M., and Kaplan, H. I. (eds.), *Comprehensive Textbook of Psychiatry.* Baltimore: Williams and Wilkins, 1967.

Kalinowsky, L. B. *Shock Treatments, Psychosurgery and other Somatic Treatments.* New York: Grune and Stratton, 1946.

Kalinowsky, L. B., and Hoch, P. *Somatic Treatments in Psychiatry.* New York: Grune and Stratton, 1961.

Kallmann, F. J. The genetics of human behavior. In T. Millon (ed.), *Theories of Psychopathology and Personality.* Philadelphia: Saunders, 1973.

Kallmann, F. J. *Heredity in Mental Health and Disorder.* New York: Norton, 1953.

Kallmann, F. J. *The Genetics of Schizophrenia.* New York: J. J. Augustin, 1938.

Kanfer, F. H., and Phillips, J. S. *Learning foundations of behavior therapy.* New York: Wiley, 1970.

Kanfer, F. H., and Phillips, J. S. Behavior therapy. *A.M.A. Arch. Gen. Psychiat., 15,* 114–127, 1966.

Kanfer, F. H., and Saslow, G. Behavioral analysis: An alternative to diagnostic classification. In T. Millon (ed.), *Theories of Psychopathology and Personality.* Philadelphia: Saunders, 1973.

Kanfer, F. H., and Saslow, G. Behavioral diagnosis. In C. M. Franks (ed.), *Behavior Therapy: Appraisal and Status.* New York: McGraw-Hill, 1969.

Kanfer, F. H., and Saslow, G. Behavioral analysis: An alternative to diagnostic classification. *A.M.A. Arch. Gen. Psychiat., 12,* 529–538, 1965.

Kanner, L. To what extent is early infantile autism determined by constitutional inadequacy? *Proc. Assoc. Res. Nerv. Mental Dis., 33,* 378–385, 1954.

Kanner, L. Problems of nosology and psychodynamics of early infantile autism. *Amer. J. Orthopsychiat., 19,* 416–426, 1949.

Kantor, R. E., and Herron, W. G. *Reactive and Process Schizophrenia.* Palo Alto: Science and Behavior Books, 1966.

Kantor, R. E., Wallner, J., and Winder, C. Process and reactive schizophrenia. *J. Consult. Psychol., 17,* 157–162, 1953.

Kaplan, H. I., and Kaplan, H. S. Current theoretical concepts in psychosomatic medicine. *Amer. J. Psychiat., 115,* 1091–1096, 1959.

Karner, M. B., Studley, W. M., Wright, W. R., and Hidgins, A. S. An approach for working with mothers of disadvantaged pre-school children. *Merrill-Palmer Quart. 14,* 174–184, 1968.

Karpman, B. On the need for separating psychopathy into two distinct clinical types: Symptomatic and idiopathic. *J. Crim. Psychopath., 3,* 112–137, 1941.

Kasius, C. (ed.) *A Comparison of Diagnostic and Functional Casework Concepts.* New York: Family Service Association of America, 1950.

Katkin, S., et al. Effectiveness of female volunteers in the treatment of outpatients. *J. Counsel. Psychol., 18,* 97–100, 1971.

Katkovsky, W. Social-learning theory and maladjustment. In Gorlow, L., and Katkovsky, W. (eds.), *Readings in the Psychology of Adjustment.* Second edition. New York: McGraw-Hill, 1968.

Katz, M. M., and Cole, J. O. Research conference in drugs and community care: A review and analysis. *Psychopharm. Serv. Cent. Bull.,* 1–13, December 1961.

Katz, M. M., Cole, J. O., and Barton, W. E. (eds.) *Role and Methodology of Classification in Psychiatry and Psychopathology.* Washington, D.C.: Public Health Service, 1968.

Katz, M. M., Waskow, E. E., and Olsson, J. Characteristics of the psychological state produced by LSD. *J. Abnorm. Psychol., 73*(1), 1–14, 1968.

Kaufman, J., Allen, J. R., and West, L. J. Runaways, hippies and marijuana. *Amer. J. Psychiat., 126*(5), 163–166, 1969.

Kazdin, A. E. Covert modeling and the reduction of avoidance behavior. *J. Abnorm. Psychol., 81,* 87–95, 1973.

Keisler, D. J. Some myths of psychotherapy research and the search for a paradigm. *Psychol. Bull., 65,* 110–136, 1966.

Kelly, G. A. Personal construct theory. In T. Millon (ed.), *Theories of Psychopathology and Personality.* Philadelphia: Saunders, 1973.

Kelly, G. A. *The Psychology of Personal Constructs.* New York: Norton, 1955.

Kelly, J. G. The quest for valid preventive interventions. In C. D. Spielberger (ed.), *Current Topics in Clinical and Community Psychology.* New York: Academic Press, 1971.

Kelly, J. G. Towards an ecological conception of preventive interventions. In J. W. Carter (ed.), *Research Contributions from Psychology to Community Mental Health.* New York: Behavioral Publications, pp. 75–97, 1968.

Kelly, J. G. Ecological constraints on mental health services. *Amer. Psychol., 21,* 535–539, 1966.

Kendell, R. E. Relationship between aggression and depression. *Arch. Gen. Psychiat., 22,* 308–318, 1970.

Kendell, R. E. *The Classification of Depressive Illnesses.* New York: Oxford University Press, 1968.

Kenyon, F. E. Hypochondriasis: A survey of some historical, clinical and social aspects. *Int'l. J. Psychiat., 2,* 308–325, 1966.

Kephart, N. C., *The Slow Learner in the Classroom.* Columbus: Merrill, 1960.

Kernberg, O. Borderline personality organization. *J. Amer. Psychoanal. Assoc., 15,* 641–685, 1967.

Kety, S. S. Biochemical hypotheses of schizophrenia. In T. Millon (ed.), *Theories of Psychopathology and Personality.* Philadelphia: Saunders, 1973.

Kety, S. S. The relevance of biochemical studies to the etiology of schizophrenia. In Romano, J. (ed.), *Origins of Schizophrenia.* Amsterdam: Excerpta Medica Foundation, 1968.

Kimmel, H. D., and Kimmel, E. An instrumental conditioning method for treatment of enuresis. *J. Behav. Ther. Exp. Psychiat., 1,* 121–123, 1970.

King, G. F., Armitage, S. G., and Tilton, J. R. A therapeutic approach to schizophrenics of extreme pathology. *J. Abnorm. Soc. Psychol., 61,* 276–286, 1960.

Kinsey, A. C., Pomeroy, W. B., and Martin, C. E. *Sexual Behavior in the Human Female.* Philadelphia: Saunders, 1953.

Kinsey, A. C., Pomeroy, W. B., and Martin, C. E. *Sexual Behavior in the Human Male.* Philadelphia: Saunders, 1948.

Kish, G. B. Reduced cognitive innovation and stimulus-seeking in chronic schizophrenia. *J. Clin. Psychol., 26,* 170–174, 1970.

Klein, D. C., and Lindemann, E. Preventive intervention in individual and family crisis situations. In T. Millon (ed.), *Theories of Psychopathology and Personality.* Philadelphia: Saunders, 1973.

Klett, C. J., Point, P., Hollister, L., Caffey, E., and Kaim, S. Evaluating changes in symptoms during acute alcohol withdrawal. *Arch. Gen. Psychiat., 24*(2), 174–178, 1971.

Knapp, P. H. The asthmatic and his environment. *J. Nerv. Ment. Dis., 149*(2), 133–151, 1969.

Kohlberg, L. Stage and sequence: The cognitive-developmental approach to socialization. In D. Goslin (ed.), *Handbook of Socialization Theory and Research.* Chicago: R. McNally, 1969.

Kohut, H. *The Analysis of Self.* New York: Wiley, 1970.

Kolansky, H., and Moore, W. T. Clinical effects of marijuana on the young. *Int'l. J. Psychiat., 10,* 134–145, 1972.

Kolb, L. *Noyes' Modern Clinical Psychiatry.* 8th ed. Philadelphia: Saunders, 1973.

Kopp, S. B. The character structure of sex offenders. *Amer. J. Psychother., 16,* 64–70, 1962.

Koran, L. M., and Maxim, P. E. Field dependence in manic-depressive patients. *J. Nerv. Ment. Dis., 155,* 205–208, 1972.

Korner, I. Hope as a method of coping. *J. Clin. Consult. Psychol., 34*(2), 134–139, 1970.

Kovach, J. K. Critical period or optimal arousal? *Develop. Psychol., 3,* 88–97, 1970.

Kraepelin, E. Clinical psychiatry. In T. Millon (ed.), *Theories of Psychopathology and Personality.* Philadelphia: Saunders, 1973.

Kraepelin, E. *Psychiatrie: ein Lehrbuch für Studierende und Ärtze.* (various editions) Leipzig: Barth, 1888–1927.

Kraepelin, E. *Lectures on Clinical Psychiatry.* New York: William Wood, 1904.

Krech, D., and Crutchfield, R. S. *Theory and Problems of Social Psychology.* New York: McGraw-Hill, 1948.

Kretschmer, E. *Physique and Character.* New York: Macmillan, 1936.

Kretschmer, E. *Physique and Character.* New York: Harcourt Brace, 1925.

Kringlen, E. Schizophrenia in twins: An epidemiological-clinical study. *Psychiatry, 29,* 172–184, 1966.

Kringlen, E. Discordance with respect to schizophrenia in monozygotic male twins: Some genetic aspects. *J. Nerv. Ment. Dis., 138,* 26–31, 1964.

Kroeber, A. L. Cultural anthropology. In I. M. Bentley and E. V. Cowdrey (eds.), *The Problems of Mental Disorder.* New York: McGraw-Hill, pp. 346–353, 1934.

Kuhn, D. Mechanisms of change in the development of cognitive structures. *Child Devel., 43,* 833–844, 1972.

Kunnes, R. Will the real community psychiatry please stand up. *Int'l. J. Psychiat., 9,* 302–311, 1970.

L'Abate, L. *Principles of Clinical Psychology.* New York: Grune and Stratton, 1964.

Lacey, J. I. The evaluation of autonomic responses: Toward a general solution. *Annals N.Y. Acad. Sci., 67,* 123–164, 1956.

Lacey, J. I., and Lacey, B. C. Verification and extension of the principle of autonomic response stereotype. *Amer. J. Psychol., 71,* 50–73, 1958.

Lachman, S. *Psychosomatic Disorders.* New York: Wiley, 1971.

Laing, R. D. Ontological insecurity. In T. Millon (ed.), *Theories of Psychopathology and Personality.* Philadelphia: Saunders, 1973.

Laing, R. D., and Esterson, A. *Sanity, Madness and the Family: Families of Schizophrenics.* 2nd ed. London: Tavistock, 1970.

Lang, P. J., and Buss, A. H. Psychological deficit in schizophrenia, II: Interference and activation. *J. Abnorm. Soc. Psychol., 70,* 77–106, 1965.

Lang, P. J., and Lazovik, A. D. Experimental desensitization of a phobia. *J. Abnorm. Soc. Psychol., 67,* 519–525, 1963.

Lang, P. J., Lazovik, A. D., and Reynolds, D. J. Desensitization, suggestibility, and pseudotherapy. *J. Abnorm. Soc. Psychol., 70,* 395–402, 1965.

Langner, T. S., and Michael, S. T. *Life Stress and Mental Health.* Glencoe, Ill.: Free Press, 1963.

Laurence, K. M. Neurological and intellectual sequelae of hydrocephalus. *Arch. Neurol., 20*(1), 73–81, 1969.

Lazarus, A. A. Learning theory in the treatment of depression. *Beh. Res. Ther., 8,* 83–89, 1968.

Lazarus, A. A. The results of behavior therapy in 126 cases of severe neurosis. *Beh. Res. Ther., 1,* 69–79, 1963.

Lazarus, A. A. Group therapy of phobic disorders by systematic desensitization. *J. Abnorm. Soc. Psychol., 63,* 504–510, 1961.

Leary, T., *Interpersonal Diagnosis of Personality.* New York: Ronald, 1957.

Leary, T., and Coffey, H. S. Interpersonal diagnosis: Some problems of methodology and validation. *J. Abnorm. Soc. Psychol., 50,* 110–124, 1955.

Lefcourt, H. M. Internal versus external control of reinforcement: A review. *Psychol. Bull., 65,* 206–220, 1966.

Lehmann, H. E. Concepts, rationale, and research. In Kline, N. S. (ed.), *Psychopharmacology Frontiers.* Boston: Little, Brown, 1959.

Lemere, F., and Voegtlin, W. L. An evaluation of the aversion treatment of alcoholism. *Quart. J. Stud. Alc., 11,* 199–204, 1950.

Leonhard, K. Cycloid psychoses—endogenous psychoses which are neither schizophrenic nor manic-depressive. *J. Ment. Sci., 107,* 633–648, 1961.

Lerner, R. C. The therapeutic social club: Social rehabilitation for mental patients. *Int'l. J. Soc. Psychiat., 6,* Nos. 1 and 2, 1960.

Lerner, R. M. The development of stereotyped expectancies of body build-behavior relations. *Child Devel., 40,* 137–141, 1969.

Lerner, R. M., and Korn, S. J. The development of body build stereotypes in males. *Child Devel., 43,* 908–920, 1972.

Levis, D. J., and Carrera, R. Effects of ten hours of implosive therapy in the treatment of outpatients. *J. Abnorm. Soc. Psychol., 72,* 504–508, 1967.

Levitt, E. E. The results of psychotherapy with children: An evaluation. *J. Consult. Psychol., 21,* 189–196, 1957.

Levy, D. M. Psychopathic behavior in infants and children: Round table. *Amer. J. Orthopsychiat., 21,* 223–272, 1951.

Levy, D. M. Maternal overprotection. In N. D. C. Lewis and B. L. Pacella (eds.), *Modern Trends in Child Psychiatry.* New York: International Univ. Press, 1945.

Levy, R. I. The psychodynamic functions of alcohol. *Quart. J. Stud. Alc., 19,* 649–659, 1958.

Lewis, N. D. C. *A Short History of Psychiatric Treatment.* New York: Norton, 1941.

Lewis, N. D. C., Landis, C., and King, H. E. *Studies in Topectomy.* New York: Grune and Stratton, 1956.

Lezak, M. D., and Dixon, H. H. The brain-injured child in a clinic population: A statistical description. *Except. Children, 30,* 237–240, 1964.

Lidz, T., Cornelison, A., Terry, D., and Fleck, S. The intrafamilial environment of the schizophrenic patient: VI. The transmission of irrationality. *A.M.A. Arch. Neur. Psychiat., 79,* 305–316, 1958.

Lieberman, M. A., et al. Encounter: The leader makes the difference. *Psychol. Today, 6*(10), 69–77, 1973.

Liebson, I. Conversion reaction: A learning theory approach. *Beh. Res. Ther.*, 7, 217–218, 1969.

Lindegard, B. Variations in human body-build. *Acta Psychiat. Neurolog.*, 86, 1–163, 1953.

Lindegard, B., and Nyman, G. E. Interrelations between psychologic, somatologic, and endocrine dimensions. *Lunds Universitets Arsskrift*, 52, 1–54, 1956.

Lindemann, E. Symptomatology and management in acute grief. *Amer. J. Psychiat.*, 101, 141–148, 1944.

Linton, R. *Culture and Mental Disorders.* Springfield, Ill.: Thomas, 1956.

Lipscomb, C. F. The care of psychiatrically disturbed elderly patients in the community. *Amer. J. Psychiat.*, 127(8), 107–114, 1971.

Lipton, E. L., Steinschneider, A., and Richmond, J. B. Autonomic function in the neonate. *Psychosom. Med.*, 23, 472–479, 1961.

Loeb, A., Beck, A. T., and Diggory, J. Differential effects of success and failure of depressed and nondepressed patients. *J. Nerv. Ment. Dis.*, 152, 106–114, 1971.

Lombroso, C. *Crime: Its Causes and Remedies.* Boston: Little, Brown, 1911.

Lombroso, C. *L'Uomo Delinquente.* Bocca: Torina, 1889.

London, P. *The Modes and Morals of Psychotherapy.* New York: Holt, Rinehart and Winston, 1964.

Lorenz, K. Der Kumpan in der Umwelt des Vogels. Der Artgenosse als auslösendes Moment Socialzer Verhaltungsweissen. *J. orn. Ipz.*, 83, 137–213; 289–413, 1935.

Lorr, M. A typology for functional psychotics. In M. M. Katz, J. O. Cole, and W. E. Barton (eds.), *The Role and Methodology of Classification in Psychiatry and Psychopathology.* Chevy Chase, Md.: Nat'l. Inst. of Mental Health, 1968.

Lorr, M. (ed.) *Explorations in Typing Psychotics.* New York: Pergamon, 1966.

Lorr, M., Klett, C. J., and McNair, D. M. *Syndromes of Psychosis.* New York: Macmillan, 1963.

Lovaas, O. I. Some studies on the treatment of childhood schizophrenia. In Shlien, J. (ed.), *Research in Psychotherapy.* Vol. III. Washington, D.C.: American Psychological Association, 1968.

Lovaas, O. I. Behavior therapy approach to treating childhood schizophrenia. In J. Hill (ed.), *Minnesota Symposium on Child Development.* Minneapolis: Univ. of Minn. Press, 1967.

Lovaas, O. I., et al. Acquisition of imitative speech by schizophrenic children. *Sci.*, 151, 705–707, 1966.

Lu, Y. C. Contradictory parental expectations in schizophrenia. *Psychiat.*, 19, 231–236, 1956.

Luxenburger H. Die Schizophrenie and ihr Erbkreis. In Just, G. (ed.), *Hdbh. d. Erbbiologie.* Vol. 5. Berlin: Springer, 1939.

Lynn, R. Russian theory and research on schizophrenia. *Psychol. Bull.*, 60, 486–498, 1963.

Lyons, J. F., and Heaton-Ward, W. A. *Notes on Mental Deficiency.* Bristol: Wright, 1953.

Lystad, M. H. Social mobility among selected groups of schizophrenic patients. *Amer. Sociol. Rev.*, 22, 282–292, 1957.

Maccoby, E. E., and Masters, J. C. Attachment and dependency. In P. H. Mussen (ed.), *Carmichael's Manual of Child Psychology.* New York: Wiley, 1970.

MacMahon, B., and Sowa, J. M. Physical damage to the fetus. In *Causes of Mental Disorder: A Review of Epidemiological Knowledge.* New York: Milbank Memorial Fund, 1961.

MacMillan, D. L., and Koegh, B. K. Normal and retarded children's expectancy for failure. *Develop. Psychol.*, 4(3), 343–348, 1971.

Maddi, S. R. The existential neurosis. *J. Abnorm. Psychol.*, 72, 311–325, 1967.

Maher, B. A. *Principles of Psychopathology.* New York: McGraw-Hill, 1966.

Mahl, G. F. Physiological changes during chronic fear. *Annals N.Y. Acad. Sci.*, 56, 240–249, 1953.

Mahler, M. S. On child psychosis and schizophrenia: Autistic and symbiotic infantile psychosis. In *Psychoanalytic Study of the Child.* Vol. 7. New York: Int'l. Univ. Press, 1952.

Maier, N. R. F. *Frustration: A Study of Behavior Without a Goal.* New York: McGraw-Hill, 1949.

Malmo, R. B. Activation. In Bachrach, A. J. (ed.), *Experimental Foundations of Clinical Psychology.* New York: Basic Books, 1962.

Malmo, R. B., and Shagass, C. Physiological studies of reaction to stress in anxiety states and early schizophrenia. *Psychosom. Med.*, 11, 9–24, 1949.

Malmo, R. B., Shagass, C., and Davis, F. H. Electromyographic studies of muscular tension in psychiatric patients under stress. *J. Clin. Exper. Psychopath.*, 12, 45–66, 1951.

Malzberg, B. Important statistical data about mental illness. In Arieti, S. (ed.), *American Handbook of Psychiatry.* New York: Basic Books, 1959.

Malzberg, B. *Social and Biological Aspects of Disease.* Utica: State Hospitals Press, 1940.

Manosevitz, M. Early sexual behavior in adult homosexual and heterosexual males. *J. Abnorm. Psychol.*, 76(3), 396–402, 1970.

Margolin, S. G. Genetic and dynamic psychophysiological determinants of pathophysiological process. In Deutsch, F. (ed.), *The Psychosomatic Concept in Psychoanalysis.* New York: Int'l. Univ. Press, 1953.

Marks, I., and Gelder, M. A controlled retrospective study of behavior therapy in phobic patients. *Brit. J. Psychiat., 111*, 561–573, 1966.

Markson, E., Kowh, A., Cumming, J., and Crummin, E. Alternatives to hospitalization for psychiatrically ill geriatric patients. *Amer. J. Psychiat., 128*(8), 95–102, 1971.

Maslow, A. H. *The Farther Reaches of Human Nature.* New York: Wiley, 1971.

Maslow, A. H. *Toward a Psychology of Being.* Princeton: Van Nostrand, 1962.

Masserman, J. H. *Behavior and Neurosis.* Chicago: U. of Chicago Press, 1943.

Masters, J. C. Effects of success, failure and reward outcome on contingent and non-contingent self-reinforcement. *Devel. Psychol., 7*, 110–118, 1972.

Matarazzo, J. D. Some national developments in the utilization of non-traditional mental health manpower. *Amer. Psychol., 26*, 363–372,

Mather, M. D. The treatment of an obsessive-compulsive patient by discrimination learning and reinforcement of decision-making. *Behav. Res. Ther., 8*(3), 315–318, 1970.

Max, L. W. Breaking up a homosexual fixation by the conditioned reaction technique: A case study. *Psychol. Bull., 32*, 734, 1935.

May, R. Existential psychology. In T. Millon (ed.), *Theories of Psychopathology and Personality.* Philadelphia: Saunders, 1973.

May, R. Love and will. *Psych. Today, 3*(3), 17–64, 1969.

May, R., et al. (eds.) *Existence.* New York: Basic Books, 1958.

May, R., Angel, E., and Ellenberger, H. F. (eds.) *Existence: A New Dimension in Psychiatry and Psychology.* New York: Basic Books, 1958.

May, R., and Van Kaam, A. Existential theory and therapy. In Masserman, J. H. (ed.), *Current Psychiatric Therapies.* Vol. 3. New York: Grune and Stratton, 1963.

McClelland, D. C. *Personality.* New York: Dryden, 1951.

McClelland, D. C., et al. *The Achievement Motive.* New York: Appleton-Century-Crofts, 1953.

McConagy, N. Aversive therapy of homosexuality: Measures of efficacy. *Amer. J. Psychiat., 127*(9), 141–144, 1971.

McCord, W., and McCord, J. *The Psychopath: An Essay on the Criminal Mind.* Princeton: Van Nostrand, 1964.

McGlothin, W. H., and Arnold, D. O. LSD revisited. *Arch. Gen. Psychiat., 24*(1), 35–49, 1971.

McGraw, M. B. The Neuromuscular Maturation of the *Human Infant.* New York: Columbia U. Press, 1943.

McNair, D. M., and Lorr, M. Differential typing of psychiatric outpatients. *Psychol. Rec., 15*, 33–41, 1965.

Mead, G. H. *Mind, Self, and Society.* Chicago: U. of Chicago Press, 1934.

Meehl, P. E. Schizotaxia, schizotypy, schizophrenia. In T. Millon (ed.), *Theories of Psychopathology and Personality.* Philadelphia: Saunders, 1973.

Meehl, P. E. Seer over sign: The first good example. *J. Exp. Res. Personality, 1*, 27–32, 1965.

Meehl, P. E. Schizotozia, schizotypy, schizophrenia. *Amer. Psychol., 17*, 827–838, 1962.

Meehl, P. E. Some ruminations on the validation of clinical procedures. *Canad. J. Psychol., 13*, 102–128, 1959.

Meehl, P. E. When shall we use our heads instead of the formula? *J. Counsel. Psychol., 4*, 268–273, 1957.

Meehl, P. E. *Clinical Versus Statistical Prediction.* Minneapolis: U. of Minnesota Press, 1954.

Mehlman, B. The reliability of psychiatric diagnoses. *J. Abn. Soc. Psychol., 47*, 577–578, 1952.

Meili, R. A longitudinal study of personality development. In Jessner, L., and Pavenstedt, E. (eds.), *Dynamic Psychopathology of Childhood.* New York: Grune and Stratton, 1959.

Meissner, W. W. Sibling relations in the schizophrenic family. *Family Process, 9*, 1–25, 1970.

Melzack, R. Effects of early experience on behavior: Experimental and conceptual considerations. In Hoch, P., and Zubin, J. (eds.), *Psychopathology of Perception.* New York: Grune and Stratton, 1965.

Mendels, J. *Concepts of Depression.* New York: Wiley, 1970.

Mendels, J., Weinstein, N., and Cochrane, C. The relationship between depression and anxiety. *Arch. Gen. Psychiat., 27*, 649–653, 1972.

Menninger, K. Psychiatric diagnosis. *Bull. Menninger Clin., 23*, 226–240, 1959.

Menninger, K., Pruyser, P., and Mayman, M. *The Vital Balance.* New York: Viking Press, 1963.

Menninger, K. *Man Against Himself.* New York: Basic Books, 1938.

Menninger, W. C. *Psychiatry in a Troubled World.* New York: Macmillan, 1948.

Menolascino, F. J. Emotional disturbances in mentally retarded children. *Arch. Gen. Psychiat., 19*, 456–464, 1968.

Miller, G. A., Galanter, E., and Pribam, K. H. *Plans and the Structure of Behavior.* New York: Holt, Rinehart and Winston, 1960.

Miller, N. E. Learning of visceral and glandular responses. *Science, 163*(3866), 434–445, 1969.

Miller, N. E. Experiments relating Freudian displacement to generalization of conditioning. *Psychol. Bull., 36*, 516–517, 1939.

Millon, T. *Modern Psychopathology.* Philadelphia: Saunders, 1969.

Millon, T. A biosocial-learning approach. In T. Millon (ed.), *Theories of Psychopathology and Personality.* Philadelphia: Saunders, 1973.

Millon, T., and Diesenhaus, H. I. *Research Methods in Psychopathology.* New York: Wiley, 1972.

Milner, E. *Human Neural and Behavioral Development.* Springfield, Ill.: Thomas, 1967.

Milton, G. A. The socialization of cognition. In R. A. Hoppe, et al. (eds.), *Early Experiences and the Processes of Socialization.* New York: Academic Press, 1970.

Mirin, S. M., Shapiro, L. M., Meyer, R. E., Pillard, R. G., and Fisher, S. Casual versus heavy use of marijuana: A redefinition of the marijuana problem. *Amer. J. Psychiat., 127*(9), 1134–1141, 1971.

Mirsky, I. A. Physiologic, psychologic, and social determinants in the etiology of duodenal ulcer. *Amer. J. Digest. Dis., 3,* 285–314, 1958.

Mischel, W. *Personality and Assessment.* New York: Wiley, 1968.

Mitchell, K. R., and Mitchell, D. M. Migraine: An exploratory treatment application of programmed behavior therapy techniques. *J. Psychosom. Res., 15*(2), 137–157, 1971.

Moltz, H. Some effects of previous breeding experience on the maternal behavior in the rat. In L. Aronson (ed.), *Development and Evolution of Behavior.* San Francisco: Freeman, 1970.

Moltz, H. An epigenetic interpretation of the imprinting phenomenon. In Newton, G., and Levine, S. (eds.) *Early Experience and Behavior.* Springfield, Ill.: Thomas, 1968.

Moniz, E. How I succeeded in performing the prefrontal leukotomy. *J. Clin. Exp. Psychopath., 15,* 373–379, 1954.

Moniz, E. Prefrontal leucotomy in the treatment of mental disorder. *Amer. J. Psychiat., 93,* 1379–1385, 1936.

Moreno, J. L. *Psychodrama.* Vol. 1. Beacon, N.Y.: Beacon House, 1946.

Moreno, J. L. *Who Shall Survive?* Washington, D.C.: Nerv. Ment. Dis. Publ., 1934.

Morrison, J. R. Catatonia. *Arch. Gen. Psychiat., 28,* 39–43, 1973.

Moruzzi, R. S., and Magoun, H. W. Brain stem reticular formation and activation of the EEG. *EEG Clin. Neurophysiol., 1,* 455–473, 1949.

Mowrer, O. H. The behavior therapies, with special reference to modeling and imitation. *Amer. J. Psychother., 20,* 439–461, 1966.

Mowrer, O. H. Integrity therapy: A self-help approach. *Psychother., 3,* 14–19, 1965.

Mowrer, O. H. Learning theory and behavior therapy. In Wolman, B. (ed.), *Handbook of Clinical Psychology.* New York: McGraw-Hill, 1965.

Mowrer, O. H. *The Crisis in Psychiatry and Religion.* Princeton: Van Nostrand, 1961.

Mowrer, O. H. *Learning Theory and Personality Dynamics.* New York: Ronald, 1950.

Mowrer, O. H., and Mowrer, W. M. Enuresis: A method for its study and treatment. *Amer. J. Orthopsychiat., 8,* 436–459, 1938.

Murphy, G. *Personality: A Biosocial Approach to Origins and Structures.* New York: Harper, 1947.

Murphy, L. B. Discussion of papers in the light of research in human development. In Katz, M., et al. (eds.), *The Role and Methodology of Classification in Psychiatry and Psychopathology.* Washington, D.C.: Public Health Service, 1968.

Murphy, L. B., et al. *The Widening World of Childhood.* New York: Basic Books, 1962.

Musaph, H. Aggression and symptom formation in dermatology. *J. Psychosom. Res., 13*(3), 257–264, 1969.

Myers, D. H., and Grant, G. A study of depersonalization in students. *Brit. J. Psychiat., 121,* 59–65, 1972.

Myers, J. K., and Roberts, B. H. *Family and Class Dynamics in Mental Illness.* New York: Wiley, 1959.

National Commission on Community Health Services. *Health Is a Community Affair.* Boston: Harvard U. Press, 1967.

Naumberg, M. *Dynamically Oriented Art Therapy: Its Principles and Practice.* New York: Grune and Stratton, 1966.

Newbrough, J. R. Community mental health: "A movement in search of a theory." In *Community Mental Health: Individual Adjustment or Social Planning?* Bethesda, Md.: Nat'l. Inst. Mental Health, pp. 1–18, 1964.

Newman, N. N., Freeman, F. N., and Holzinger, K. J. *Twins: A Study of Heredity and Environment.* Chicago: U. of Chicago Press, 1937.

Newton, G., and Levine, S. (eds.) *Early Experience and Behavior.* Springfield, Ill.: Thomas, 1968.

Nowlis, H. H. *Drugs on the College Campus.* Garden City, N.Y.: Anchor-Doubleday, 1968.

Noyes, A. P., and Kolb, L. *Modern Clinical Psychiatry.* 7th ed. Philadelphia: Saunders, 1968.

O'Brien, C. P., et al. Group vs. individual psychotherapy with schizophrenics. *Arch. Gen. Psychiat., 27,* 474–483, 1972.

O'Connor, N. Children in restricted environments. In Newton, G., and Levine, S. (eds.), *Early Experience and Behavior.* Springfield, Ill.: Thomas, 1968.

Odegaard, O. Polygenic theory of schizophrenia etiology. In A. R. Kaplan (ed.), *Genetic Factors in Schizophrenia.* Springfield, Ill.: Thomas, 1971.

Odegaard, O. New data on marriage and mental disease: The incidence of psychosis in the widowed and the divorced. *J. Ment. Sci., 99,* 778–785, 1953.

Odenheimer, J. F. Day hospital as an alternative to the psychiatric ward. *A.M.A. Arch Gen. Psychiat., 13,* 46–53, 1965.

Offord, D. R., and Cross, L. A. Behavioral antecedents of adult schizophrenia: A review. *Arch. Gen. Psychiat., 21,* 267–283, 1969.

Olds, J. Hypothalamic substrates of reward. *Physiol. Rev., 42,* 554–604, 1962.

Olds, J. Pleasure centers of the brain. *Sci. Amer., 195,* 104–116, 1956.

Olshansky, S. The transitional sheltered workshop: A survey. *J. Soc. Issues, 16,* 33–39, 1960.

Orlansky, H. Infant care and personality. *Psychol. Bull., 46,* 1–48, 1949.

Osborne, R. H., and DeGeorge, F. V. *Genetic Bases of Morphological Variation.* Cambridge: Harvard U. Press, 1959.

Osmond, H., and Smythies, J. Schizophrenia: A new approach. *J. Ment. Sci., 98,* 309–315, 1952.

Osofsky, J. D. Children's influences upon parental behavior. *Genetic Psychol. Monogr., 83,* 147–169, 1971.

Osofsky, J. D., and O'Connell, E. J. Parent-child interaction: Daughters' effects upon mothers' and fathers' behaviors. *Devel. Psychol., 7,* 157–168, 1972.

Ottoson, J. O. Experimental studies of the mode of action of electroconvulsive therapy. *Acta Psychiat. Neurolog. Scand., 35,* Supplement 145, 1960.

Overall, J. E., and Henry, B. W. Decisions about drug therapy. *Arch. Gen. Psychiat., 28,* 81–91, 1973.

Paine, R. S. Minimal chronic brain syndromes in children. *Devel. Med. Child Neurolog., 4,* 21–27, 1962.

Palmer, F. H. Inferences to the socialization of the child from animal studies. In D. Goslin (ed.), *Handbook of Socialization Theory and Research.* Chicago: R. McNally, 1969.

Parke, R. D. The role of punishment in the socialization process. In R. A. Hoppe, et al. (eds.), *Early Experiences and the Processes of Socialization.* New York: Academic Press, 1970.

Parker, J. B., et al. Factors in manic-depressive reactions. *Dis. Nerv. Syst., 20,* 1–7, 1959.

Parry-Jones, W., Santer-Weststrate, H. G., and Crawley, R. C. Behavior therapy in a case of hysterical blindness. *Behav. Res. Ther., 8*(1), 79–85, 1970.

Pasamanick, B., et al. Socioeconomic status: Some precursors of neuropsychiatric disorders. *Amer. J. Orthopsychiat., 26,* 594–601, 1956.

Pasamanick, B., Dinitz, S., and Lefton, M. Psychiatric orientation and its relation to diagnosis and treatment in a mental hospital. *Amer. J. Psychiat., 116,* 127–132, 1959.

Patrick, H. T., and Bassoe, P. *Nervous and Mental Diseases.* Chicago: Year Book Publishers, 1910.

Patterson, C. H. *Theories of Counseling and Psychotherapy.* New York: Harper and Row, 1966.

Paul, G. L. Two-year follow-up of systematic desensitization in therapy groups. *J. Abn. Psychol., 73,* 119–130, 1968.

Paul, G. L. Insight versus desensitization in psychotherapy two years after termination. *J. Consult. Psychol., 31,* 333–348, 1967.

Paul, G. L. *Effects of Insight, Desensitization, and Attention Placebo Treatment of Anxiety.* Stanford: Stanford Univ. Press, 1966.

Paul, G. L., and Shannon, D. T. Treatment of anxiety through systematic desensitization in therapy groups. *J. Abnorm. Psychol., 71,* 124–135, 1966.

Paul, N. L., Fitzgerald, E., and Greenblatt, M. The long-term comparative results of three different lobotomy procedures. *Amer. J. Psychiat., 113,* 808–814, 1957.

Pavlov, I. P. *Lectures on Conditioned Reflexes.* Vol. 1. New York: International Publishers, 1928.

Pavlov, I. P. *Lectures on Conditioned Reflexes.* New York: Int'l. Univ. Press, 1941.

Pavlov, I. P. *Conditioned reflexes: An Investigation of the Physiological Activity of the Cerebral Cortex.* London: Oxford Univ. Press, 1927.

Paykel, E. S. Correlates of a depressive typology. *Arch. Gen. Psychiat., 27,* 203–210, 1972.

Pearl, A., and Reissman, F. *New careers for the poor.* New York: Free Press, 1965.

Penfield, W., and Jasper, H. *Epilepsy and the Functional Anatomy of the Human Brain.* Boston: Little, Brown, 1954.

Penfield, W., and Roberts, L. *Speech and Brain-mechanisms.* Princeton: Princeton U. Press, 1959.

Penrose, L. S. *The Biology of Mental Defect.* 2nd ed. New York: Grune and Stratton, 1964.

Penrose, L. S. The genetical background of common diseases. *Acta Genetica, 4,* 257–265, 1953.

Penrose, L. S. Research methods in human genetics. In *Congrés International de Psychiatrie VI. Psychiatrie Sociale.* Paris: Hermann et Cie, 1950.

Peterson, D. R., et al. Parental attitudes and child adjustment. *Child Devel., 30,* 119–130, 1959.

Pfantz, H. W. The American dilemma: Perspectives and proposals for white Americans. In C. V. Daley (ed.), *Urban Violence.* Chicago: University of Chicago Press, 1969.

Phillips, E. L. *Psychotherapy: A Modern Theory and Practice.* Englewood Cliffs, N.J.: Prentice-Hall, 1956.

Phillips, L. *Human Adaptation and its Failures.* New York: Academic Press, 1968.

Phillips, L. Social competence, the process-reactive distinction, and the nature of mental disorder. In Hoch, P., and Zubin, J. (eds.), *Psychopathology of Schizophrenia.* New York: Grune and Stratton, 1966.

Phillips, L., and Rabinovitch, M. Social role and patterns of symptomatic behaviors. *J. Abnorm. Soc. Psychol.,* 57, 181–186, 1958.

Piaget, J. *The Origins of Intelligence in Children.* New York: Int'l. Univ. Press, 1952.

Pincus, G., and Hoagland, H. Adrenal cortical responses to stress in normal men and in those with personality disorders. *Amer. J. Psychiat.,* 106, 641–650, 1950.

Plaut, T. F. A. Prevention of alcoholism. In S. E. Golann and C. Eisdorfer (eds.), *Handbook of Community Mental Health.* New York: Appleton-Century-Crofts, 1972.

Pollin, W. The pathogenesis of schizophrenia. *Arch. Gen. Psychiat.,* 27, 29–37, 1972.

Powdermaker, F. B., and Frank, J. D. *Group Psychotherapy.* Cambridge, Mass.: Harvard Univ. Press, 1953.

President's Panel on Mental Retardation. *A Proposed Program for National Action to Combat Mental Retardation.* Washington, D.C.: U.S. Government Printing Office, 1963.

Price, R. H., and Denner, B. (eds.) *The Making of a Mental Patient.* New York: Holt, Rinehart and Winston, 1973.

Priest, P. N. The destiny of psychological therapies. *Brit. J. Med. Psychol.,* 45, 209–220, 1972.

Pritchard, M. Homosexuality and genetic sex. *J. Ment. Sci.,* 108, 616–623, 1962.

Rachman, S. Systematic desensitization. *Psychol. Bull.,* 67, 93–103, 1967.

Rachman, S. Studies in desensitization: III. The speed of generalization. *Beh. Res. Ther.,* 4, 205–208, 1966.

Rachman, S. Studies in desensitization: I. The separate effects of relaxation and desensitization. *Beh. Res. Ther.,* 3, 245–252, 1965.

Rachman, S. Introduction to behavior therapy. *Beh. Res. Ther.,* 1, 3–15, 1963.

Rachman, S., and Eysenck, H. J. Reply to a "critique and reformulation" of behavior therapy. *Psychol. Bull.,* 65, 165–169, 1966.

Rachman, S. J., and Teasdale, J. Aversion therapy: An appraisal. In C. M. Franks (ed.), *Behavior Therapy: Appraisal and Status.* New York: McGraw-Hill, 1969.

Rado, S. *Psychoanalysis of Behavior.* New York: Grune and Stratton, 1962.

Raines, G. N., and Rohrer, J. H. The operational matrix of psychiatric practice. I: Consistency and variability in interview impressions of different psychiatrists. *Amer. J. Psychiat.,* 111, 721–733, 1955.

Ramer, B. S., Zaslove, M., and Langan, J. Is methadone enough? The use of ancillary treatment during methadone maintenance. *Amer. J. Psychiat.,* 127(8), 80–84, 1971.

Rank, O. *Will Therapy: An Analysis of the Therapeutic Process in Terms of Relationship.* New York: Knopf, 1936.

Rank, O. *The Trauma of Birth.* New York: Harcourt, Brace, 1929.

Rapaport, D. The Structure of psychoanalytic theory: A systematizing attempt. In Koch, S. (ed.), *Psychology: A Study of a Science.* Vol. 3. New York: McGraw-Hill, 1959.

Rapaport, D. The theory of ego autonomy: A generalization. *Bull. Menninger Clin.,* 22, 13–35, 1958.

Rapaport, D. The autonomy of the ego. *Bull. Meninger Clin.,* 15, 113–123, 1951.

Rapaport, R. N. Principles for developing a therapuetic community. In Masserman, J. (ed.), *Current Psychiatric Therapies.* Vol. 3. New York: Grune and Stratton, 1963.

Rappaport, S. R. (ed.) *Childhood Aphasia and Brain Damage.* Narberth, Pa.: Livingston, 1965.

Redick, R. W., Goldsmith, H. F., and Unger, E. L. *1970 Census Data Used to Indicate Areas with Different Potentials for Mental Health and Related Problems.* Chevy Chase, Md.: NIMH, Mental Health Statistics Series C, 1971.

Rees, L. Constitutional factors and abnormal behavior. In Eysenck, H. J. (ed.), *Handbook of Abnormal Psychology.* New York: Basic Books, 1961.

Rees, L. Physical characteristics of the schizophrenic patient. In Richter, D. (ed.), *Somatic Aspects of Schizophrenia.* London: Pergamon, 1957.

Rees, L., and Eysenck, H. J. A factorial study of some morphological and psychological aspects of human constitution. *J. Ment. Sci.,* 91, 8, 1945.

Reich, C. *The Greening of America.* New York: Random House, 1970.

Reil, J. C. *Rhapsodies in the Application of Psychie Methods in the Treatment of Mental Disturbances.* 1803.

Reisman, D. The young are captives of each other. *Psych. Today,* 3(5), 28–31, 1969.

Reisman, D. *The Lonely Crowd.* New Haven: Yale U. Press, 1950.

Reitz, W. E., and Keil, W. E. Behavioral treatment of an exhibitionist. *J. Behav. Ther. Exp. Psychiat.,* 2, 67–69, 1971.

Renaud, H., and Estess, F. Life history interviews with one hundred normal American males: Pathogenicity in childhood. *Amer. J. Orthopsychiat.,* 31, 786–802, 1961.

Renne, K. S. Correlates of dissatisfaction in marriage. *J. Marr. Fam.,* 54–67, Feb. 1970.

Revitch, E., and Weiss, R. G. The pedophiliac offender. *Dis. Nerv. Syst.,* 23, 73–78, 1962.

Rheingold, H. L. The effect of environmental stimulation upon social and exploratory behavior in the human infant. In Foss, B. M. (ed.), *Determinants of Infant Behavior II*. New York: Wiley, 1963.

Rheingold, H. L., and Eckerman, C. O. The infant separates himself from his mother. *Science, 168*, 78–83, 1970.

Ribble, M. A. *The Rights of Infants*. New York: Columbia U. Press, 1943.

Richards, B. W. Mongols and their mothers. *Brit. J. Psychiat., 122*, 1–14, 1973.

Riesen, A. H. Stimulation as a requirement for growth and function in behavioral development. In Fiske, D., and Maddi, S. (eds.), *Functions of Varied Experience*. Homewood, Ill.: Dorsey, 1961.

Rimland, B. *Infantile Autism*. New York: Appleton-Century-Crofts, 1964.

Rinkel, M., and Himwich, H. (eds.) *Insulin Treatment in Psychiatry*. New York: Philosophical Library, 1959.

Robbin, A. A. The value of leucotomy in relation to diagnosis. *J. Neurol. Neurosurg. Psychiat., 22*, 132–136, 1959.

Robbin, A. A. A controlled study of the effects of leucotomy. *J. Neurol. Neurosurg. Psychiat., 21*, 262–269, 1958.

Roberts, J. A. F. The genetics of mental deficiency. *Eug. Rev., 44*, 71–83, 1952.

Rodnick, E. H. The psychopathology of development: Investigating the etiology of schizophrenia. *Amer. J. Orthopsychiat., 38*, 784–798, 1968.

Roe, A. Community resources centers. *Amer. Psychologist, 25*, 1033–1040, 1970.

Roe, A. Integration of personality theory and clinical practice. *J. Abnorm. Soc. Psychol., 44*, 36–41, 1949.

Roe, A., Burks, B., and Mittleman, B. Adult adjustment of foster children of alcoholic and psychotic parentage and the influence of the foster home. *Memoirs of the Section on Alcohol*. Yale Univ., 1945.

Roen, S. R. Primary prevention in the classroom through a teaching program in behavioral sciences. In E. L. Cowen, et al. (eds.), *Emergent Approaches to Mental Health Problems*. New York: Appleton-Century-Crofts, 1967.

Roff, M. Some problems in life history research. In M. Roff and D. F. Ricks (eds.), *Life History Research in Psychopathology*. Minneapolis: Minnesota Press, 1970.

Roff, M., and Ricks, D. F. (eds.) *Life History Research in Psychopathology*. Minneapolis: Minnesota Press, 1970.

Rogers, C. R. A theory of personality. In T. Millon (ed.), *Theories of Psychopathology and Personality*. Philadelphia: Saunders, 1973.

Rogers, C. R. *Carl Rogers on Encounter Groups*. New York: Harper and Row, 1970.

Rogers, C. R. Psychotherapy today or where do we go from here? *Amer. J. Psychother., 17*, 5–16, 1963.

Rogers, C. R. *On Becoming a Person*. Boston: Houghton Mifflin, 1961.

Rogers, C. R. A theory of therapy, personality, and interpersonal relationships, as developed in the client-centered framework. In Koch, S. (ed.), *Psychology, a Study of a Science*. Vol. 3. New York: McGraw-Hill, 1959.

Rogers, C. R. *Client-Centered Therapy*. Boston: Houghton Mifflin, 1951.

Rogers, C. R. *Counseling and Psychotherapy*. Boston: Houghton Mifflin, 1942.

Rogers, C. R., and Dymond, R. F. (eds.) *Psychotherapy and Personality Change*. Chicago: U. of Chicago Press, 1954.

Rogers, C. R., et al. *The Therapeutic Relationship and Its Impact*. Madison: U. of Wisconsin Press, 1967.

Rosanoff, A. J., et al. The etiology of so-called schizophrenic psychoses. *Amer. J. Psychiat., 91*, 247–286, 1934.

Rose, A. M., and Stub, H. R. Summary of studies on the incidence of mental disorders. In Rose, A. M. (ed.), *Mental Health and Mental Disorder*. New York: Norton, 1955.

Rosen, E., and Gregory, I. *Abnormal Psychology*. Philadelphia: Saunders, 1965.

Rosen, E., and Rizzo, G. Preliminary standardization of the MMPI for use in Italy: A case study of inter-cultural and intracultural differences. *Educ. Psychol. Measmt., 21*, 629–636, 1961.

Rosenthal, D. *Genetic Theory and Abnormal Behavior*. New York: McGraw-Hill, 1971.

Rosenthal, D. An historical and methodological review of genetic studies in schizophrenia. In Romano, J. (ed.), *Origins of Schizophrenia*. Amsterdam: Excerpta Medica Foundation, 1968.

Rosenthal, D. Some factors associated with concordance and discordance with respect to schizophrenia in monozygotic twins. *J. Nerv. Ment. Dis., 129*, 1–10, 1959.

Rosenthal, R. Experimenter outcome-orientation and the results of the psychological experiment. *Psychol. Bull., 61*, 405–412, 1964.

Rosenthal, R., and Jacobson, L. *Pygmalion in the Classroom: Teacher Expectations and Pupil's Intellectual Development*. New York: Holt, Rinehart and Winston, 1968.

Rosenwald, G. C. Effectiveness of defenses against anal impulse arousal. *J. Consult. Clin. Psychol., 39*, 292–298, 1972.

Rosenzweig, M. R., et al. Effect of environmental complexity and training on brain chemistry and anatomy: A replication and extension. *J. Comp. Physiol. Psychol., 55*, 429–437, 1962.

Rosenzweig, S. A transvaluation of psychotherapy: A reply to Hans Eysenck. *J. Abnorm. Soc. Psychol.*, *49*, 298–304, 1954.

Rostan, L. *Cours élémentaire d'hygiéne.* Paris, 1828.

Roth, M., et al. Studies in the classification of affective disorders. *Brit. J. Psychiat.*, *121*, 147–161, 1972.

Rotter, J. B. Generalized expectancies for internal versus external control of reinforcements. *Psychol. Monogr.*, *80*, 1–28, 1966.

Rotter, J. B. Some implications of a social learning theory for the practice of psychotherapy. Mimeographed paper, 1962.

Rotter, J. B. *Social Learning and Clinical Psychology.* Englewood Cliffs, N.J.: Prentice-Hall, 1954.

Rotter, J. B., Chance, J. E., and Phares, E. J. *Applications of a Social Learning Theory of Personality.* New York: Holt, 1972.

Rubenstein, E. A., and Parloff, M. B. (eds.) *Research in Psychotherapy.* Washington, D.C.: American Psychological Association, 1959.

Rubin, L. S. Patterns of adrenergic-cholinergic imbalance in the functional psychoses. *Psychol. Rev.*, *69*, 501–519, 1962.

Ruesch, J., et al. Chronic disease and psychosomatic invalidism. *Psychosom. Med. Monogr.*, Whole #9, 1946.

Rutter, M. Childhood schizophrenia reconsidered. *J. Autism Childhood Schiz.*, *2*, 315–337, 1972.

Rutter, M. Autistic children. *Seminars in Psychiatry*, *2*, 435–449, 1970.

Rutter, M. Concepts of autism: A review of research. *J. Child. Psychol. Psychiat.*, *9*, 1–25, 1968.

Sabshin, M. Theoretical models in community and social psychiatry. In T. Millon (ed.), *Theories of Psychopathology and Personality.* Philadelphia: Saunders, 1973.

Salzman, L. Obsessions and phobias. *Inter. J. Psychiat.*, *6*, 451–468, 1968.

Salzman, L. Paranoid state—theory and therapy. *Arch. Gen. Psychiat.*, *2*, 679–693, 1960.

Samaan, M. The control of nocturnal enuresis by operant conditioning. *J. Behav. Ther. Exp. Psychiat.*, *3*, 103–105, 1972.

Sanford, N. Personality and patterns of alcohol consumption. *J. Consult. Clin. Psychol.*, *32*, 13–17, 1968.

Sarason, S. B., and Doris, J. *Psychological Problems in Mental Deficiency.* 4th ed. New York: Harper and Row, 1969.

Sarbin, T. R. A contribution to the study of actuarial and statistical methods of prediction. *Amer. J. Sociol.*, *48*, 593–602, 1943.

Sarbin, T. R., and Mancuso, J. C. Failure of a moral enterprise: Attitudes of the public toward mental illness. *J. Consult. Clin. Psychol.*, *35*, 159–173, 1970.

Sarbin, T. R., Taft, R., and Bailey, D. E. *Clinical Inference and Cognitive Theory.* New York: Holt, Rinehart and Winston, 1960.

Sarvis, M. A. Paranoid reactions: Perceptual distortion as an etiological agent. *Arch. Gen. Psychiat.*, *6*, 157–162, 1962.

Sarwer-Foner, G. J. Theoretical aspects of the modes of action. In Kline, N. S. (ed.), *Psychopharmacology Frontiers.* Boston: Little, Brown, 1959.

Satir, V. M. *Conjoint Family Therapy.* (Rev. Ed.). Palo Alto, Calif.: Science and Behavior Books, 1967.

Schan, M. New evidence of the prophylactic value of lithium carbonate. *Highlights of the 15th Annual Conference.* Houston: Veterans Administration Cooperative Studies in Psychiatry, pp. 116–126, April 2–4, 1970.

Scheff, T. J. The role of the mentally ill and the dynamics of mental disorder. In T. Millon (ed.), *Theories of Psychopathology and Personality.* Philadelphia: Saunders, 1973.

Scheibel, A. B., and Scheibel, M. E. Substrates for integrative action in the brain stem reticular formation. In *International Symposium on Reticular Formation*, Ford Foundation. Boston: Little, Brown, 1958.

Scheibel, M. E., and Scheibel, A. B. Some neural substrates of postnatal development. In Hoffman, M., and Hoffman, L (eds.), *Review of Child Development Research.* Vol. I. New York: Russell Sage, 1964.

Schilder, P. Results and problems of group psychotherapy in severe neuroses. *Ment. Hyg.*, *23*, 87–98, 1939.

Schmideberg, M. The borderline patient. In Arieti, S. (ed.), *American Handbook of Psychiatry.* Vol. 1. New York: Basic Books, 1959.

Schmidt, H. O., and Fonda, C. P. The reliability of psychiatric diagnosis: A new look. *J. Abnorm. Soc. Psychol.*, *52*, 262–267, 1956.

Schmneige, G. R. The current status of LSD as a therapeutic tool: A summary of the clinical literature. *J. Med. Soc. N.J.*, *60*, 203–207, 1963.

Schorer, C. E., et al. Improvement without treatment. Paper presented at *American Psychiatric Association Meetings.* May, 1966.

Schulz, B. Kinder manisch-depressiven und anderer Affektiv psychotischer Elternpaare. *Zeitschr. Neurol.*, *169*, 311–328, 1940.

Schwartz, G. E., Shapiro, D., and Tursky, B. Learned control of cardio-vascular integration in man through operant conditioning. *Psychosom. Med., 33*(1), 57–62, 1971.

Scott, J. P. *Early Experience and the Organization of Behavior.* Belmont, Calif.: Brooks-Cole, 1968.

Scott, J. P. Comparative social psychology. In Waters, R. H. (ed.), *Principles of Comparative Psychology.* New York: McGraw-Hill, 1960.

Scott, W. A. Social psychological correlates of mental illness and mental health. *Psychol. Bull., 55,* 65–87, 1958.

Sears, R. R. Attachment dependency and frustration. In J. Gewirtz (ed.), *Attachment and Dependency.* Washington: Winston, 1972.

Sears, R. R., Maccoby, E. E., and Levin, H. *Patterns of Child Rearing.* Evanston, Ill.: Row, Peterson, 1957.

Seidman, G. Theories of depersonalization: A reappraisal. *Brit. J. Psychiat., 117,* 1–14, 1970.

Seligman, M. E., and Hager, J. L. (eds.) *The Biological Boundaries of Learning.* New York: Appleton, 1972.

Selyé, H. *The Stress of Life.* New York: McGraw-Hill, 1956.

Shakow, D., and Huston, P. E. Studies of motor function in schizophrenia. *J. Gen. Psychol., 15,* 63–106, 1936.

Shapiro, D. A. Symbiosis in adulthood. *Amer. J. Psychiat., 129,* 289–292, 1972.

Shaw, C. R. *The Jack-Roller.* Chicago: U. of Chicago Press, 1930.

Shaw, E., and Woolley, D. W. Some serotonin-like activities in lysergic acid diethylamide. *Sci., 124,* 121–122, 1956.

Shaw, F. J. A stimulus-response analysis of repression and insight in psychotherapy. *Psychol. Rev., 53,* 36–42, 1946.

Sheehan, J. G. (ed.). *Stuttering: Research and Therapy.* New York: Harper and Row, 1970.

Sheehan, J. G. Theory and treatment of stuttering as an approach-avoidance conflict. *J. Psychol., 36,* 27–49, 1953.

Sheer, D. (ed.) *Electrical Stimulation of the Brain.* Houston: U. of Texas Press, 1961.

Sheldon, W. H. Constitutional psychiatry. In T. Millon (ed.), *Theories of Psychopathology and Personality.* Philadelphia: Saunders, 1973.

Sheldon, W. H., et al. *Atlas of Men: A Guide for Somatotyping the Male at All Ages.* New York: Harper, 1954.

Sheldon, W. H., et al. *Varieties of Delinquent Youth: An Introduction to Constitutional Psychiatry.* New York: Harper, 1949.

Sheldon, W. H., and Stevens, S. S. *The Varieties of Temperament: A Psychology of Constitutional Differences.* New York: Harper, 1942.

Sheldon, W. H., et al. *The Varieties of Human Physique: An Introduction to Constitutional Psychology.* New York: Harper, 1940.

Sherif, M., and Sherif, C. (eds.) *Problems of Youth: Transition to Adulthood in a Changing World.* Chicago: Aldine, 1965.

Shields, J., and Slater, E. Heredity and psychological abnormality. In Eysenck, H. J. (ed.), *Handbook of Abnormal Psychology.* New York: Basic Books, 1961.

Shlien, J. M., et al. (eds.) *Research in Psychotherapy.* Vol. III. Washington, D.C.: American Psychological Association, 1968.

Shoben, E. J. A learning-theory interpretation of psychotherapy. *Harvard Educ. Rev., 18,* 129–145, 1948.

Shore, M. F., Milgram, N. A., and Malasky, C. The effectiveness of an enrichment program for disadvantaged young children. *Amer. J. Orthopsychiat., 41,* 442–449, 1971.

Shore, M. F., and Massino, J. L. The alienated adolescent: A challenge to the mental health profession. *Adolescence, 4*(13), 19–34, 1969.

Short, J. F. Juvenile delinquency: The sociocultural content. In Hoffman, L., and Hoffman, M. (eds.), *Review of Child Development Research.* Vol. II. New York: Russell Sage, 1966.

Silver, L. B. A proposed view on the etiology of the neurological learning disability system. *J. Learn. Dis., 4*(3), 123–133, 1971.

Silverman, D. Clinical and electroencephalographic studies of criminal psychopaths. *A.M.A. Arch. Neurol. Psychiat., 50,* 18–33, 1943.

Silverman, J. Scanning-control mechanism and "cognitive filtering" in paranoid and non-paranoid schizophrenia. *J. Consult. Psychol., 28,* 385–393, 1964a.

Silverman, J. The problem of attention in research and theory in schizophrenia. *Psychol. Rev., 71,* 352–379, 1964b.

Simmel, E. C. The biology of socialization. In R. A. Hoppe, et al. (eds.), *Early Experiences and the Processes of Socialization.* New York: Academic Press, 1970.

Simpson, G. M., et al. Role of antidepressants and neuroleptics in the treatment of depression. *Arch. Gen. Psychiat., 27,* 337–345, 1972.

Singer, M. T., and Wynne, L. C. Thought disorder and family relations of schizophrenics,

III: Methodology using projective techniques. *A.M.A. Arch. Gen. Psychiat., 12,* 187–212, 1965.

Skinner, B. F. *Beyond Freedom and Dignity.* New York: Knopf, 1971.

Skinner, B. F. *Cumulative Record.* New York: Appleton-Century-Crofts, 1959.

Skinner, B. F. What is psychotic behavior? In *Theory and Treatment of the Psychoses.* St. Louis: Washington University Press, 1956.

Skinner, B. F. *Science and Human Behavior.* New York: Macmillan, 1953.

Slater, E., and Shields, J. *Psychotic and Neurotic Illnesses in Twins.* London: H. M. Stationery Office, 1953.

Slavson, S. R. *A Textbook in Analytic Group Psychotherapy.* New York: Int'l. Univ. Press, 1964.

Slavson, S. R. *An Introduction to Group Therapy.* New York: The Commonwealth Fund, 1943.

Small, J. G., Milstein, V., and Stephens, J. R. Are psychomotor epileptics different? A controlled study. *A.M.A. Arch. Neurol., 7,* 17–194, 1962.

Small, I., Small, J., Alig, V., and Moore, S. Passive-aggressive personality disorder: A search for a syndrome. *Amer. J. Psychiat., 126,* 97–107, 1970.

Smart, R., and Jones, D. Illicit LSD users: Their personality characteristics and psychopathology. *J. Abnorm. Psychol., 75,* 286–292, 1970.

Smith, R. C., and Carlen, J. Behavior modification using interlocking reinforcement on a short term psychiatric ward. *Arch. Gen. Psychiat., 27,* 386–389, 1972.

Smith, R. P. A clinical investigation of phobias. *Brit. J. Psychiat., 114,* 673–697, 1968.

Smith, S., and Guthrie, E. R. Exhibitionism. *J. Abnorm. Soc. Psychol., 17,* 206–209, 1922.

Snortum, J. R., Marshall, J. E., Gillespie, J. E., McLaughlin, J. P., and Mosberg, L. Family dynamics and homosexuality. *Psychol Rep., 24*(3), 763–770, 1969.

Sobell, M. B., and Sobell, L. C. Individualized behavior therapy for alcoholics. *Behav. Ther., 4,* 49–72, 1973.

Socarides, C. W. Homosexuality: Basic concepts and psychodynamics. *Int'l. J. Psychiat., 10,* 118–125, 1972.

Solomon, R. L., and Wynne, L. C. Traumatic avoidance learning: The principles of anxiety conservation and partial irreversibility. *Psychol. Rev., 61,* 353–385, 1954.

Spitz, R. A. *The First Year of Life.* New York: Int'l. Univ. Press, 1965.

Spitzer, R. L., and Endicott, J. Automation of psychiatric case records. *Int'l. J. Psychiat., 9,* 604–621, 1970.

Spitzer, R. L. The mental status schedule: Potential use as a criterion measure in psychotherapy research. *Amer. J. Psychother., 20,* 156–167, 1966.

Srole, L., et al. *Mental Health in the Metropolis; the Midtown Manhattan Study.* Vol. I. New York: McGraw-Hill, 1962.

Stainbrook, E. Some characteristics of the psychopathology of schizophrenic behavior in Bahian society. *Amer. J. Psychiat., 109,* 330–335, 1952.

Stampfl, T. G., and Levis, D. J. Essentials of implosive therapy: A learning-theory-based psychodynamic behavioral therapy. *J. Abnorm. Soc. Psychol., 72,* 496–503, 1967.

Staudt, V., and Zubin, J. A biometric evaluation of the somatotherapies in schizophrenia. *Psychol. Bull., 56,* 171–196, 1957.

Stein, L. Neurochemistry of reward and punishment: Some implications for the etiology of schizophrenia. *J. Psychiat. Res., 8,* 345–361, 1971.

Stephens, J. H., and Kamp, M. On some aspects of hysteria: A clinical study. *J. Nerv. Ment. Dis., 134,* 305–315, 1962.

Stern, J. A., and McDonald, D. G. Physiological correlates of mental disease. *Ann. Rev. Psychol., 16,* 225–264, 1965.

Stevenson, I. Is the human personality more plastic in infancy and childhood? *Amer. J. Psychiat., 114,* 152–161, 1957.

Stojanovich, K. Antisocial and dyssocial. *Arch. Gen. Psychiat., 21*(5), 561–567, 1969.

Stollak, G. E., Guerney, B. G., and Rothberg, M. (eds.) *Psychotherapy Research.* Chicago: Rand McNally, 1966.

Stone, L., et al. (eds.) *The Competent Infant.* New York: Basic Books, 1973.

Strauss, A. A., and Kephart, N. *Psychopathology and Education of the Brain Injured Child.* Vol. II. New York: Grune and Stratton, 1955.

Strauss, A. A., and Lehtinen, L. *Psychopathology and Education of the Brain Injured Child.* Vol. I. New York: Grune and Stratton, 1947.

Strupp, H. H. The outcome problem in psychotherapy revisited. *Psychother., 1,* 1–13, 1963.

Strupp, H. H., and Luborsky, L. (eds.) *Research in Psychotherapy.* Vol. II. Washington, D.C.: American Psychological Association, 1962.

Stuart, R. B. *Trick or Treatment: How and When Psychotherapy Fails.* Champaign, Ill.: Research Press, 1970.

Sullivan, H. S. *The Psychiatric Interview.* New York: Norton, 1954.

Sullivan, H. S. *The Interpersonal Theory of Psychiatry.* New York: Norton, 1953.

Sundberg, N. D., and Tyler, L. E. *Clinical Psychology.* New York: Appleton-Century-Crofts, 1962.

Swanson, B. W., Bohmert, T. J., and Smith, J. A. *The Paranoid.* Boston: Little, Brown, 1970.

Symonds, C. Classification of epilepsies. *Brit. Med. J., 1*, 1235–1238, 1955.

Szasz, T. S. The myth of mental illness. In T. Millon (ed.), *Theories of Psychopathology and Personality*. Philadelphia: Saunders, 1973.

Szasz, T. S. The ethics of addiction. *Int'l. J. Psychiat., 10*, 51–61, 1972.

Szasz, T. S. *Law, Liberty and Psychiatry*. New York: Macmillan, 1963.

Szasz, T. S. The problem of psychiatric nosology. *Amer. J. Psychiat., 114*, 405–413, 1957.

Taft, J. *The Dynamics of Therapy in a Controlled Relationship*. New York: Macmillan, 1933.

Tennenbaum, G. The walk-in clinic. In S. Arieti (ed.), *American Handbook of Psychiatry*. Vol. III. New York: Basic Books, pp. 576–587, 1966.

Terr, L. A family study of child abuse. *Amer. J. Psychiat., 127*, 665–671, 1970.

Thomas, E. J. Selected sociobehavioral techniques and principles: An approach to interpersonal helping. *Social Work, 13*, 12–26, 1968.

Thomas, A., Chess, S., and Birch, H. G. *Temperament and Behavior Disorders in Children*. New York: New York Univ. Press, 1968.

Thomas, A., et al. *Behavioral Individuality in Early Childhood*. New York: New York University Press, 1963.

Thompson, E. T., and Hayden, A. C. (eds.) *A.M.A. Handbook on Standard Nomenclature of Diseases and Operations*. 5th ed. New York: McGraw-Hill, 1961.

Thompson, L. J. Learning disabilities: an overview. *Amer. J. Psychiat., 130*, 393–399, 1973.

Thompson, W. R. Influence of prenatal and maternal anxiety on emotionality in young rats. *Sci., 125*, 698–699, 1957.

Thompson, W. R., and Grusec, J. Studies on early experience. In P. H. Mussen (ed.), *Carmichael's Manual of Child Psychology*. New York: Wiley, 1970.

Thompson, W. R., and Schaefer, T. Early environmental stimulation. In Fiske, D., and Maddi, S. (eds.), *Functions of Varied Experience*. Homewood, Ill.: Dorsey, 1961.

Thorndike, E. L. *The Elements of Psychology*. New York: A. G. Seiler, 1905.

Thorne, F. C. Principles of directive counseling and psychotherapy. *Amer. Psychol., 3*, 160–165, 1948.

Thorne, F. C. Etiological studies of the psychopathic personality: The ego-inflated, defectively conditioned type. *J. Consult. Psychol., 11*, 299–310, 1947.

Thorne, F. C. A critique of nondirective methods of psychotherapy. *J. Abnorm. Soc. Psychol., 39*, 459–470, 1944.

Thorpe, J. G. The current status of prognostic test indicators for electroconvulsive therapy. *Psychosom. Med., 24*, 554–567, 1962.

Tienari, P. Psychiatric illnesses in identical twins. *Acta Psychiat. Scand., 39*, Suppl. 171, 1–195, 1963.

Tizard, B. The personality of epileptics: A discussion of the evidence. *Psychol. Bull., 59*, 196–210, 1962.

Toderick, A., Tait, A. C., and Marshall, E. F. Blood platelet 5-hydroxytryptamine levels in psychiatric patients. *J. Ment. Sci., 106*, 884–890, 1960.

Toffler, A. *Future Shock*. New York: Random House, 1970.

Toman, W. Birth order rules all. *Psychol. Today, 4*(7), 45–49, 1970.

Tredgold, A. F. *A Textbook of Mental Deficiency*. 6th ed. Baltimore: Williams and Wilkins, 1937.

Turner, R., Dopkeen, L., and Labreche, G. Marital status and schizophrenia: A study of incidence and outcome. *J. Abnorm. Psychol., 73*(1), 1–14, 1968.

Ullmann, L. P., and Krasner, L. (eds.), *Case Studies in Behavior Modification*. New York: Holt, Rinehart and Winston, 1965.

Ungersma, A. J. *The Search for Meaning*. Philadelphia: Westminster, 1961.

Vandenberg, S. G. Contributions of twin research to psychology. *Psychol. Bull., 66*, 327–352, 1966.

Venables, P. H. Experimental psychological studies of chronic schizophrenia. In M. Shepard and D. L. Davies (eds.), *Studies in Psychiatry*. London: Oxford, 1968.

Venables, P. H. Input dysfunction in schizophrenia. In Maher, B. A. (ed.), *Progress in Experimental Personality Research*. Vol. I. New York: Academic Press, 1964.

Viola, G. *La Constituzione Individuale*. Bologna: Capelli, 1932.

Vogler, R. E., Lunde, S. E., Johnson, G. R., and Martin, P. L. Aversion conditioning with chronic alcoholics. *J. Consult. Clin. Psychol., 34*(3), 302–307, 1970.

Von Mering, O., and King, S. H. *Remotivating the Mental Patient*. New York: Russell Sage Foundation, 1957.

Von Neumann, J., and Morgenstern, O. *The Theory of Games and Economic Behavior*. New York: Princeton, 1944.

Walter, G. Electroencephalographic development of children. In Tanner, J. M., and Inhelder, B. (eds.), *Discussions on Child Development*. New York: Int'l. Univ. Press, 1953.

Walton, D. The application of learning theory to the treatment of a case of neurodermatitis. In Eysenck, H. J. (ed.), *Behavior Therapy and the Neuroses*. New York: Pergamon, 1960.

Ward, A. J. Early infantile autism: Diagnosis, etiology, and treatment. *Psych. Bull., 73*, 350–362, 1970.

Ward, C. H., Beck, A. T., Mendelson, M., Mock, J. R., and Erbaugh, J. K. The psychiatric nomenclature: Reasons for diagnostic disagreement. *Arch. Gen. Psychiat., 7,* 198–205, 1967.

Watson, J. B., and Rayner, R. Conditioned emotional reaction. *J. Exper. Psychol., 3,* 1–4, 1920.

Wechsler, H. Half-way houses for former mental patients: A survey. *J. Soc. Issues, 16,* 20–26, 1960.

Weigert, E. V. Psychoanalytic notes on sleep and convulsion treatment in functional psychoses. *Psychiat., 3,* 189–194, 1940.

Weinberg, I., and Lobstein, J. Inheritance in schizophrenia. *Acta Psychiat. Neurolog., 18,* 93–140, 1943.

Weinberg, S. K. *Society and Personality Disorders.* New York: Prentice-Hall, 1952.

Weiss, G., Minde, K., Werry, J. S., Douglas, J., and Nemeth, E. Studies on the hyperactive child. VIII. *Arch. Gen. Psychiat., 24*(5), 409–421, 1971.

Wender, P. H. The minimal brain dysfunction syndrome in children. *J. Nerv. Ment. Dis., 155,* 55–71, 1972.

Wender, P. H. *Minimal Brain Dysfunction in Children.* New York: Wiley, 1971.

Wener, C., and Coulter, J. B. A reliability study of developmental histories. *Child Development, 33,* 453–462, 1962.

Wertheim, E. S. A bio-adaptive theory of stuttering. *Brit. J. Med. Psychol., 45,* 283–296, 1972.

West, F. H., et al. Insulin coma therapy in schizophrenia: A fourteen-year follow-up study. *Amer. J. Psychiat., 11,* 583–589, 1955.

White, R. W. *The Abnormal Personality.* 3rd ed. New York: Ronald, 1964.

White, R. W. Competence and the psychosexual stages of development. In Jones, M. R. (ed.), *Nebraska Symposium on Motivation.* Lincoln: U. of Nebraska Press, 1960.

Whorf, B. *Language, Thought and Reality.* New York: Wiley, 1956.

Willett, R. The effects of psychosurgical procedures on behavior. In Eysenck, H. J. (ed.), *Handbook of Abnormal Psychology.* New York: Basic Books, 1961.

Williams, C. D. The elimination of tantrum behavior by extinction procedures. *J. Abnorm. Soc. Psychol., 59,* 269, 1959.

Williams, G. J. The effect of electroconvulsive shock on an instrumental conditioned emotional response ("conflict"). *J. Comp. Physiol. Psychol., 54,* 633–637, 1961.

Williams, R. J. The biological approach to the study of personality. In T. Millon (ed.), *Theories of Psychopathology and Personality.* Philadelphia: Saunders, 1973.

Williams, R. J. The biological approach to the study of personality. *Berkeley Conference on Personality Development,* 1960.

Williams, R. J. *Biochemical Individuality.* New York: Wiley, 1956.

Windle, C. Psychological tests in psychopathological prognosis. *Psychol. Bull., 49,* 451–482, 1952.

Wing, J. K. *Early Childhood Autism.* London: Pergamon, 1966.

Winokur, G., Clayton, P. J., and Reich, T. *Manic-Depressive Illness.* St. Louis: Mosby, 1967.

Wittenborn, J. R. The dimensions of psychosis. *J. Nerv. Ment. Dis., 134,* 117–128, 1967.

Wittenborn, J. R., Holzberg, J., and Simon, B. Symptom correlates for descriptive diagnosis. *Genet. Psychol. Monogr., 47,* 237–301, 1953.

Wittenborn, J. R., and May, P. R. A. (eds.) *Prediction of Response to Pharmacotherapy.* Springfield, Ill.: Thomas, 1966.

Wittman, M. The social welfare system: Its relation to community mental health. In S. E. Golann and C. Eisdorfer (eds.) *Handbook of Community Mental Health.* New York: Appleton-Century-Crofts, 1972.

Wittman, P., Sheldon, W. H., and Katz, C. J. A study of the relationship between constitutional variations and fundamental psychotic behavior reaction. *J. Nerv. Ment. Dis., 108,* 470–476, 1948.

Wolberg, A. The "borderline patient." *Amer. J. Psychother., 6,* 694–701, 1952.

Wolberg, L. R.: *The Technique of Psychotherapy.* 2nd ed. New York: Grune and Stratton, 1967.

Wolf, A. The psychoanalysis of groups. *Amer. J. Psychother., 3,* 525–558, 1949; *4,* 16–50, 1950.

Wolf, A., and Schwartz, E. K. *Psychoanalysis in Groups.* New York: Grune and Stratton, 1962.

Wolman, B. (ed.) *Handbook of Clinical Psychology.* New York: McGraw-Hill, 1965.

Wolpe, J. *The Practice of Behavior Therapy.* New York: Pergamon Press, 1969.

Wolpe, J. Behavior therapy in complex neurotic states. In Shlien, J. (ed.), *Research in Psychotherapy.* Vol. III. Washington, D.C.: American Psychological Association, 1968.

Wolpe, J. Behavior therapy in complex neurotic states. *Brit. J. Psychiat., 110,* 28–34, 1964.

Wolpe, J. The prognosis in unpsychoanalyzed recovery from neuroses. *Amer. J. Psychiat., 117,* 35–39, 1961.

Wolpe, J. *Psychotherapy by Reciprocal Inhibition.* Stanford, Calif.: Stanford U. Press, 1958.

Woltman, A. G. Play therapy and related techniques. In Brower, D., and Abt, L. (eds.), *Progress in Clinical Psychology.* Vol. 3. New York: Grune and Stratton, 1959.

Woolley, D. W. *The Biochemical Bases of Psychoses.* New York: Wiley, 1962.

Woolley, D. W., and Shaw, E. A biochemical and pharmacological suggestion about certain mental disorders. *Sci., 119,* 587–588, 1954.

Wortis, S. B., et al. Brain metabolism: The effects of electric shock and some newer drugs. *Amer. J. Psychiat., 98,* 354–361, 1941.

Wynne, L. C. Methodological and conceptual issues in the study of schizophrenics and their families. In D. Rosenthal and S. Kety (eds.), *The Transmission of Schizophrenia.* New York: Pergamon, 1968.

Yalom, I. D. *The Theory and Practice of Group Psychotherapy.* New York: Basic Books, 1970.

Yalom, I. D., and Lieberman, M. A. A study of encounter group casualties. *Arch. Gen. Psychiat., 25,* 16–30, 1971.

Yarrow, L. J. Maternal deprivation: Toward an empirical and conceptual reevaluation. *Psychol. Bull., 58,* 459–490, 1961.

Yarrow, L. J., and Goodwin, M. S. The immediate impact of separation. In L. Stone, et al. (eds.), *The Competent Infant.* New York: Basic Books, 1973.

Yarrow, L. J., and Goodwin, M. S. Some conceptual issues in the study of mother-child interactions. *Amer. J. Orthopsychiat., 35,* 473–481, 1965.

Yarrow, M. R., et al. Child effects on adult behavior. *Devel. Psychol., 5,* 300–311, 1971.

Yarrow, M. R. Problems of methods in parent-child research. *Child Development, 34,* 215–216, 1963.

Zax, M., and Cowen, E. L. *Abnormal Psychology: Changing Conceptions.* New York: Holt, Rinehart and Winston, 1972.

Zigler, E. Social class and the socialization process. *Rev. Educ. Res., 40,* 1970.

Zigler, E., and Harter, S. Socialization of the mentally retarded. In D. Goslin (ed.), *Handbook of Socialization Theory and Research.* New York: Rand McNally, 1969.

Zigler, E., and Phillips, L. Psychiatric diagnosis. *J. Abnorm. Soc. Psychol., 63,* 607–618, 1961a.

Zigler, E., and Phillips, L. Psychiatric diagnosis and symptomatology. *J. Abnorm. Soc. Psychol., 63,* 69–75, 1961b.

Zigler, E., and Phillips, L. Social effectiveness and symptomatic behaviors. *J. Abnorm. Soc. Psychol., 61,* 231–238, 1960.

Zubin, J. Evaluation of therapeutic outcome in mental disorders. *J. Nerv. Ment. Dis., 117,* 95–111, 1953.

Zuckerman, M., et al. What is the sensation seeker? Personality trait and experience correlates of the sensation seeking scales. *J. Consult. Clin. Psychol., 39,* 308–321, 1972.

Zwerling, I., and Rosenbaum, M. Alcoholic addiction and personality. In Arieti, S. (ed.), *American Handbook of Psychiatry.* New York: Basic Books, 1959.

INDEX OF NAMES

INDEX OF SUBJECTS

Page numbers in *italic* type refer to tables or illustrations.